MICROECONOMICS

CANADA IN THE GLOBAL ENVIRONMENT

FIFTH EDITION

MICHAEL PARKIN

University of Western Ontario

ROBIN BADE

PEARSON

Addison
Wesley

Toronto

Vice President, Editorial Director:	Michael J. Young
Acquisitions Editor:	Gary Bennett
Marketing Manager:	Deborah Meredith
Senior Developmental Editor:	Suzanne Schaan
Senior Production Editor:	Marisa D'Andrea
Copy Editor:	Laurel Sparrow
Production Coordinator:	Deborah Starks
Permissions and Photo Research:	Lisa Brant
Page Layout:	Bill Renaud
Illustrator:	Richard Parkin
Art Director:	Mary Opper
Interior and Cover Design:	Anthony Leung
Cover Image (background):	Gary Holscher/Gettyimages
Cover Image (spot image):	Michael Pohuski/Gettyimages

National Library of Canada Cataloguing in Publication

Parkin, Michael, 1939–
    Microeconomics : Canada in the global environment / Michael Parkin,
    Robin Bade — 5th ed.

Includes index.
ISBN 0-321-15413-4

1. Microeconomics.   2. Canada—Economic conditions—1991–
I. Bade, Robin   II. Title.

HB172.P37 2003   338.5   C2002-902846-9

Statistics Canada information is used with the permission of the Minister of
Industry, as Minister responsible for Statistics Canada. Information on the
availability of the wide range of data from Statistics Canada can be obtained
from Statistics Canada's Regional Offices, its World Wide Web site at
http://www.statcan.ca, and its toll-free access number 1-800-263-1136.

ABOUT THE AUTHORS

MICHAEL PARKIN received his training as an economist at the Universities of Leicester and Essex in England. Currently in the Department of Economics at the University of Western Ontario, Canada, Professor Parkin has held faculty appointments at Brown University, the University of Manchester, the University of Essex, and Bond University. He is a past president of the Canadian Economics Association and has served on the editorial boards of the *American Economic Review* and the *Journal of Monetary Economics* and as managing editor of the *Canadian Journal of Economics*. Professor Parkin's research on macroeconomics, monetary economics, and international economics has resulted in over 160 publications in journals and edited volumes, including the *American Economic Review*, the *Journal of Political Economy*, the *Review of Economic Studies*, the *Journal of Monetary Economics*, and the *Journal of Money, Credit and Banking*. He became most visible to the public with his work on inflation that discredited the use of wage and price controls. Michael Parkin also spearheaded the movement toward European monetary union.

ROBIN BADE earned degrees in mathematics and economics at the University of Queensland and her Ph.D. at the Australian National University. She has held faculty appointments in the business schools at the University of Edinburgh and Bond University and in the economics departments at the University of Manitoba, the University of Toronto, and the University of Western Ontario. Her research on international capital flows appears in the *International Economic Review* and the *Economic Record*.

Professor Parkin and Dr. Bade are the joint authors of *Modern Macroeconomics* (Pearson Education Canada), an intermediate text, and *Foundations of Economics* (Pearson Education Canada), and have collaborated on many research and textbook writing projects. They are both experienced and dedicated teachers of introductory economics.

PREFACE

This book presents economics as a serious, lively, and evolving science. Its goal is to open students' eyes to the "economic way of thinking" and to help them gain insights into how the economy works and how it might be made to work better. ◆ We provide a thorough and complete coverage of the subject, using a straightforward, precise, and clear writing style. ◆ We are conscious that many students find economics hard, so we place the student at centre stage and write for the student. We use language that doesn't intimidate and that allows the student to concentrate on the substance. ◆ We open each chapter with a clear statement of learning objectives, a real-world student-friendly vignette to grab attention, and a brief preview. We illustrate principles with examples that are selected to hold the student's interest and to make the subject lively. And we put principles to work by using them to illuminate current real-world problems and issues. ◆ We present some new ideas, such as dynamic comparative advantage, game theory, the modern theory of the firm, public choice theory, rational expectations, new growth theory, and real business cycle theory. But we explain these topics with familiar core ideas and tools. ◆ Today's course springs from today's issues—the information revolution, the impending global slowdown of 2003, the Kyoto debate, and the expansion of international trade and investment. But the principles that we use to understand these issues remain the core principles of our science. ◆ Governments and international agencies place renewed emphasis on long-term fundamentals as they seek to sustain economic growth. This book reflects this emphasis. ◆ To help promote a rich, active learning experience, we have developed a comprehensive online learning environment featuring diagnostic quizzes, a dynamic eText, eStudy Guide, interactive tutorials, practice exams, frequent news updates, and more.

The Fifth Edition Revision

ECONOMICS: CANADA IN THE GLOBAL ENVIRONMENT, Fifth Edition, retains all of the improvements achieved in its predecessor with its thorough and detailed presentation of modern economics, emphasis on real-world examples and critical thinking skills, diagrams renowned for pedagogy and precision, and path-breaking technology.

New to this edition are

- New introductory chapter
- All new chapter on global stock markets
- Revised and updated microeconomics content
- Revised and updated macroeconomics content
- Vastly expanded Web site

New Introductory Chapter

Chapter 1 has been completely rewritten to emphasize the central role of tradeoffs in economics, setting the tone for the rest of the book.

All-New Chapter 35 on Global Stock Markets

This exciting addition provides a valuable framework for addressing students' questions about how the stock market works. *What is a stock? What determines stock prices? Why are stock prices volatile? Why is it rational to diversify? How does the stock market influence the economy, and vice versa?*

Revised and Updated Microeconomics Content

The four major revisions in the microeconomics chapters are

1. The Economic Problem (Chapter 2): A revised and more carefully paced explanation of the gains from specialization and exchange.
2. Monopolistic Competition and Oligopoly (Chapter 13): An expanded explanation of repeated games and sequential games. These traditionally advanced topics are explained with examples and illustrations that bring the ideas within the grasp of beginning students.
3. Economic Inequality (Chapter 15): Two chapters from the Fourth Edition have been combined, streamlined, and given a new focus to explain the sources of the trend in the distribution of income—the widening gap between the highest- and lowest-income households.

4. Externalities (Chapter 18): Reorganized to explain the full range of positive and negative production and consumption externalities.

Revised and Updated Macroeconomics Content

The five major revisions in the macroeconomics chapters are

1. Measuring GDP and Economic Growth (Chapter 20): A reorganized and more focused explanation of GDP and its measurement, along with a new and simplified explanation of the chain-weighted method of calculating real GDP.
2. Monitoring Cycles, Jobs, and the Price Level (Chapter 21): A much reorganized chapter that describes how we identify a recession and how Statistics Canada measures the labour market and the CPI. The chapter also explains the significance and interpretation of data on the labour market and price level.
3. Economic Growth (Chapter 30): A simplified and mainstreamed explanation and illustration of the classical, neoclassical, and new theories of economic growth.
4. Macroeconomic Policy Challenges (Chapter 32): Explanation of the Taylor rule and comparison of Bank of Canada interest rate decisions with such a rule.
5. Thorough and extensive updating to reflect the Canadian economy and the global economy of 2001 and 2002 and prospects for 2003 and beyond, as well as the response to the heightened security situation following the September 11 attacks on the United States.

Vastly Expanded Web Site

Our new Web site is the centrepiece of this Fifth Edition revision. The site is organized around "8 steps to success in economics." The 8 steps are

1. Diagnostic quizzes that provide feedback with hyperlinks to all the Web-based learning tools.
2. Online glossary with definitions, examples, and links to related terms.
3. Online eText—the entire textbook in electronic form with hyperlinks to all other components of the Web site and with Flash animations of every figure in the textbook.
4. Online eStudy Guide—the entire study guide in electronic form.

5. *Economics in Action*—our market-leading interactive tutorial software program now accessed on the Web. This Java-based learning tool has been expanded to cover each and every chapter in the textbook. Students manipulate figures from the textbook by changing the conditions that lie behind them and observing how the economy responds to events.

6. PowerPoint lecture notes for students to review.

7. Web-based exercises with links to data and other online sources.

8. Practice exams—students can select from five question types (fill-in-the-blank, true-or-false, multiple-choice, complete-the-graph, and numeric) to be worked with or without detailed feedback.

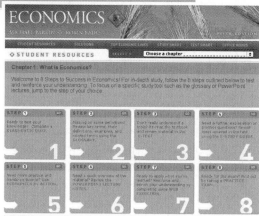

Features to Enhance Teaching and Learning

HERE, WE DESCRIBE THE CHAPTER FEATURES that are designed to enhance the learning process. Each chapter contains the following learning aids.

Chapter Opener

Each chapter opens with a one-page student-friendly, attention-grabbing vignette. The vignette raises questions that both motivate the student and focus the chapter. The Fifth Edition now carries this story into the main body of the chapter, and relates it to the chapter-ending *Reading Between the Lines* feature.

Chapter Objectives

A list of learning objectives enables students to see exactly where the chapter is going and to set their goals before they begin the chapter. We link these goals directly to the chapter's major headings.

After studying this chapter, you will be able to

■ Describe a market and explain the link between price as an opportunity cost

■ Explain the influences on demand

■ Explain the influences on supply

■ Explain how demand and supply determine prices and quantities bought and sold

■ Use demand and supply to make predictions about changes in prices and quantities

In-Text Review Quizzes

A review quiz at the end of most major sections enables students to determine whether a topic needs further study before moving on.

> ### REVIEW QUIZ
>
> 1 What is scarcity?
> 2 Give some examples of scarcity in today's world.
> 3 Define economics.
> 4 Use the headlines in today's news to illustrate the distinction between microeconomics and macroeconomics.

Key Terms

Highlighted terms within the text simplify the student's task of learning the vocabulary of economics. Each highlighted term appears in an end-of-chapter list with page numbers, in an end-of-book glossary, boldfaced in the index, and on the Parkin–Bade Web site.

rve. The **marginal benefit** of a good or service is the nefit received from consuming one more unit of it.
We measure the marginal benefit of rvice by what a person is *willing to pay* onal unit of it. The idea is that you are .y what the good is worth to you. It is v arginal benefit, and you're willing to pa nount up to the marginal benefit. So w .y measures marginal benefit.
The **marginal benefit curve** shows the tween marginal benefit of a good and that g doing, 45 e mor efit 39

KEY TERMS

Absolute advantage, 45
Allocative efficiency, 39
Capital accumulation, 40
Comparative advantage, 42
Dynamic comparative advantage, 45
Economic growth, 40

Above full-employment equilibrium A macroeconomic equilibrium in which real GDP exceeds potential GDP. (p. 510)

Absolute advantage A person has an absolute advantage if that person can produce more goods with amount of resources than son can; a country has an advantage if its output pe inputs of all goods is large of another country. (p. 45

After-tax income Total in tax pa ments b househol

Diagrams That Show the Action

This book has set new standards of clarity in its diagrams. Our goal has always been to show "where the economic action is." The diagrams in this book continue to generate an enormously positive response, which confirms our view that graphical analysis is the most powerful tool available for teaching and learning economics. But many students find graphs hard to work with. For this reason, we have developed the entire art program with the study and review needs of the student in mind. The diagrams feature

- Shifted curves, equilibrium points, and other important features highlighted in red
- Colour-blended arrows to suggest movement
- Graphs paired with data tables
- Diagrams labelled with boxed notes
- Extended captions that make each diagram and its caption a self-contained object for study and review

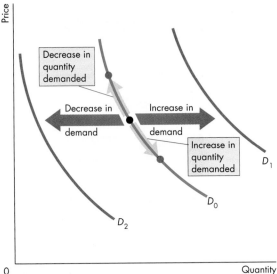

Reading Between the Lines

Each chapter ends with an economic analysis of a significant news article from the popular press together with a thorough economic analysis of the issues raised in the article. The Fifth Edition features all new *Reading Between the Lines* articles. We have chosen each article so that it sheds additional light on the questions first raised in the chapter opener.

Special "You're the Voter" sections in selected chapters invite students to analyze typical campaign topics and to probe their own stances on key public policy issues. Critical thinking questions about the article appear with the end-of-chapter questions and problems.

End-of-Chapter Study Material

Each chapter closes with a concise summary organized by major topics, lists of key terms (all with page references), problems, critical thinking questions, and Web exercises. The problems are arranged in parallel pairs with solutions to the odd-numbered problems provided on the Web site. Most of the even-numbered problems and the Web exercises are new for the Fifth Edition. We provide the links needed for the Web exercises on our Web site.

For the Instructor

THIS BOOK ENABLES YOU TO ACHIEVE THREE objectives in your principles course:

- Focus on the economic way of thinking
- Explain the issues and problems of our time
- Choose your own course structure

Focus on the Economic Way of Thinking

You know how hard it is to encourage a student to think like an economist. But that is your goal. Consistent with this goal, the text focuses on and repeatedly uses the central ideas: choice; tradeoff; opportunity cost; the margin; incentives; the gains from voluntary exchange; the forces of demand, supply, and equilibrium; the pursuit of economic rent; and the effects of government actions on the economy.

Explain the Issues and Problems of Our Time

Students must use the central ideas and tools if they are to begin to understand them. There is no better way to motivate students than by using the tools of economics to explain the issues that confront students in today's world. These issues include the anticipated 2003 global slowdown, environment, widening income gaps, energy deregulation, budget deficits or surpluses, restraining inflation, understanding the stock market, avoiding protectionism, and the long-term growth of output and incomes.

Choose Your Own Course Structure

You want to teach your own course. We have organized this book to enable you to do so. We demonstrate the book's flexibility in the flexibility chart and alternative sequences table that appear on pp. xvi–xvii. You can use this book to teach a traditional course that blends theory and policy or a current policy issues course. Your micro course can emphasize theory or policy. You can structure your macro course to emphasize long-term growth and supply-side fundamentals. Or you can follow a traditional macro sequence and emphasize short-term fluctuations. The choices are yours.

Instructor's Manual

The Instructor's Manual, written by Torben Drewes of Trent University, integrates the teaching and learning package and is a guide to all the supplements. Each chapter contains a chapter outline, what's new in the Fifth Edition, teaching suggestions, a look at where we have been and where we are going, lists of available overhead transparencies, descriptions of the electronic supplements, additional discussion questions, answers to the Review Quizzes, solutions to end-of-chapter problems, additional problems, and solutions to the additional problems. The chapter outline and teaching suggestions sections are keyed to the PowerPoint lecture notes.

Two Test Banks

To provide even greater choice when preparing tests and exams, we now offer two Test Banks with a total of more than 9,000 questions. Test Bank 1, prepared by Jane Waples and Saeed Moshiri of Memorial University, contains over 4,500 multiple-choice questions and is a thoroughly revised, upgraded, and improved version of our previous Test Bank. Test Bank 2, prepared by Glen Stirling of the University of Western Ontario and Ather Akbari of Saint Mary's University, contains about 4,300 *all new* multiple-choice, true-false, and short-answer questions.

PowerPoint Resources

We have developed a full-colour Microsoft PowerPoint Lecture Presentation for each chapter that includes all the figures from the text, animated graphs, and speaking notes. The slide outlines are based on the chapter outlines in the Instructor's Manual, and the speaking notes are based on the Instructor's Manual teaching suggestions. The presentations can be used electronically in the classroom or can be printed to create hard-copy transparency masters, and they can be accessed using Windows or Macintosh.

Overhead Transparencies

Full-colour transparencies of key figures from the text will improve the clarity of your lectures. They are available to qualified adopters of the text (contact your Pearson Education Canada sales representative).

Instructor's Resource CD with Computerized Test Banks

This CD contains Computerized Test Bank files, Instructor's Manual files in Microsoft Word, and PowerPoint files. Both test banks are available in Test Generator Software (TestGen-EQ with QuizMaster-EQ). Fully networkable, it is available for Windows and Macintosh. TestGen-EQ's new graphical interface enables instructors to view, edit, and add questions; transfer questions to tests; and print different forms of tests. Tests can be formatted with varying fonts and styles, margins, and headers and footers, as in any word-processing document. Search and sort features let the instructor quickly locate questions and arrange them in a preferred order. QuizMaster-EQ, working with your school's computer network, automatically grades the exams, stores the results on disk, and allows the instructor to view or print a variety of reports.

Course Management Systems

We offer three alternative course management systems—CourseCompass, Blackboard, and WebCT. Each system provides a dynamic, interactive, content-rich, and flexible online course management tool that enables instructors to easily and effectively customize online course materials to suit their needs. Instructors can track and analyze student performance on an array of Internet activities. Please contact your Pearson Education Canada representative for more details.

Economics in Action Software

Instructors can use *Economics in Action* interactive software in the classroom. Its many analytical graphs can be used as "electronic transparencies" for live graph manipulation in lectures. Its real-world data sets and graphing utility bring animated time-series graphs and scatter diagrams to the classroom.

The Parkin–Bade Web Site

The Fifth Edition of the textbook continues the tradition of path-breaking technology with *Parkin Online* at www.pearsoned.ca/parkin. The instructor side of *Parkin Online* includes all of the same resources as the student's side, but with the addition of speaking notes in the PowerPoint lecture notes, easy access to Instructor's Manual files, and an online "Consult the Authors" feature: Ask your questions or make your suggestions via e-mail, and we will answer you within 24 hours.

For the Student

Study Guide

The Fifth Edition Study Guide by Avi Cohen of York University and Harvey King of the University of Regina is carefully coordinated with the main text. For the first time, the Study Guide is available online. Print copies are also available.

Each chapter of the Study Guide contains

- Key concepts
- Helpful hints
- True/false questions that ask students to explain their answers
- Multiple-choice questions
- Short-answer questions

Each part allows students to test their cumulative understanding with questions that go across chapters and work a sample midterm examination.

Economics in Action Interactive Software

With *Economics in Action* now available on the Web, students will have fun working the tutorials, answering questions that give instant explanations, and testing themselves ahead of their midterm tests. One of our students told us that using *Economics in Action* is like having a private professor in your dorm room! New modules now cover each and every chapter in the text.

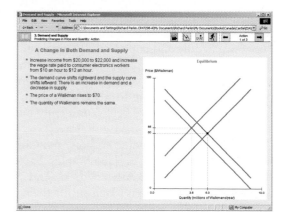

The Parkin–Bade Web Site

Parkin Online is the market-leading Web site for the principles of economics course. No other Web site comes close to matching the material offered on this site, on which students will find

■ Diagnostic quizzes with feedback hyperlinked to all the Web-based learning tools

■ The textbook—the *entire textbook in PDF format* with hyperlinks and Flash animated figures

■ *Economics in Action*—tutorials, quizzes, and graphing tools that make curves shift and graphs come to life with a click of the mouse

■ Study Guide—*the entire Study Guide, online*—with online quizzes

■ PowerPoint lecture notes

■ "Economics in the News" updated several times a week during the school year

■ Online "Office Hours": Ask your question via e-mail, and we will answer within 24 hours!

■ Economic links—links to Web sites that keep you up to date with what's going on in the economy and that enable you to work end-of-chapter Web exercises

■ Solutions to odd-numbered end-of-chapter problems

The power of *Parkin Online* lies not only in the breadth and depth of the learning tools available, but also in the way that we have linked the tools together and provided a mind map to show you these links. When a student submits a diagnostic quiz, he or she receives a report card with an explanation of why answers are correct or incorrect *and hyperlinks* to the part of the e-text that the student needs to read to better understand the concept, to the tutorial in *Economics in Action* that the student needs to work, and to related questions in the eStudy Guide and *Economics in Action*. The student is thus able to navigate easily through the site and to maximize the payoff from her or his study efforts.

Acknowledgments

WE THANK OUR CURRENT AND FORMER colleagues and friends at the University of Western Ontario who have taught us so much. They are Jim Davies, Jeremy Greenwood, Ig Horstmann, Peter Howitt, Greg Huffman, David Laidler, Phil Reny, Chris Robinson, John Whalley, and Ron Wonnacott. We also thank Doug McTaggart and Christopher Findlay, co-authors of the Australian edition, and Melanie Powell and Kent Matthews, co-authors of the European edition. Suggestions arising from their adaptations of earlier editions have been helpful to us in preparing this edition.

We thank the several thousand students whom we have been privileged to teach. The instant response that comes from the look of puzzlement or enlightenment has taught us how to teach economics.

It is an especial joy to thank the many outstanding managers, editors, and others at Pearson Education Canada who have contributed to the concerted publishing effort that brought this edition to completion. Tony Vander Woude, Chairman, and Allan Reynolds, President and CEO, have once again provided outstanding corporate direction. They have worked hard to ensure that Pearson evolves a culture that builds on the best of Addison Wesley and Prentice Hall, from which the new company has grown. Michael Young, Vice President and Editorial Director for Higher Education, has been a devoted contributor through his appointment and management of the outstanding editors with whom we've worked. When we began the revision, Dave Ward was our Acquisitions Editor. Dave has moved on to a new range of duties, but we want to place on the record the valuable contribution that he made to this revision in its early stages. Dave was succeeded by Gary Bennett as Acquisitions Editor. Gary played a major role in bringing this revision to completion and in finding and managing a team of outstanding supplements authors.

Suzanne Schaan brought her experience and dedicated professionalism to the development effort.

Toni Chahley, New Media Developmental Editor, provided direction and leadership in designing our new *Parkin Online* Web site. Deborah Meredith, Marketing Manager, provided inspired marketing direction. Her brochures and, more important, her timely questions and prodding for material had a significant impact on the shape of the text. Anthony Leung, Designer, designed the cover, text, and package and surpassed the challenge of ensuring that we meet the highest design standards. Marisa D'Andrea, our Production Editor, worked miracles on a tight production schedule and coped calmly with late-changing content. Laurel Sparrow copyedited the text manuscript. We thank all of these wonderful people. It has been inspiring to work with them and to share in creating what we believe is a truly outstanding educational tool.

We thank our supplements authors, Avi Cohen, Harvey King, Torben Drewes, Jane Waples, Saeed Moshiri, Glen Stirling, and Ather Akbari. And we thank Kit Pasula and Rosilyn Coulson for their extraordinarily careful accuracy review of near-final pages.

We thank the people who work directly with us. Jeannie Gillmore provided outstanding research assistance on many topics, including all the *Reading Between the Lines* news articles. Jane McAndrew provided excellent library help. Richard Parkin created the electronic art files and offered many ideas that improved the figures in this book. And Laurel Davies managed an ever-growing and more complex *Economics in Action* database.

As with the previous editions, this one owes an enormous debt to our students. We dedicate this book to them and again thank them for their careful reading and critical comments on the previous edition. We especially thank Chang Song and Johnathan Raiken, students at the University of Western Ontario in 2002, for finding errors and less-than-clear passages in the Fourth Edition.

Classroom experience will continue to test the value of this book. We would appreciate hearing from instructors and students about how we can continue to improve it in future editions.

Michael Parkin
Robin Bade
London, Ontario, Canada
michael.parkin@uwo.ca
robin@econ100.com

Reviewers

Ather H. Akbari, Saint Mary's University
Aurelia Best, Centennial College
Caroline Boivin, Université de Sherbrooke
Beverly Cameron, University of Manitoba
Scott Cawfield, Centennial College
Brian Coulter, University College of the Fraser Valley
Torben Drewes, Trent University
C.M. Fellows, Mount Royal College
Brian Ferguson, University of Guelph
Oliver Franke, Athabasca University
David Gray, University of Ottawa
Eric Kam, University of Western Ontario
Gordon Lee, University of Alberta
David Murrell, University of New Brunswick
Steve Rakoczy, Humber College
Kenneth Rea, University of Toronto
Jim Sentance, University of Prince Edward Island
Lance Shandler, Kwantlen University College
Lewis Soroka, Brock University
Glen Stirling, University of Western Ontario
Brian VanBlarcom, Acadia University
Joe Vieira, Confederation College
Graham Voss, University of Victoria
Baotai Wang, University of Northern British Columbia
Richard Watuwa, Saint Mary's University
Christopher Worswick, Carleton University
Emmanuel Yiridoe, Nova Scotia Agricultural College
Ayoub Yousefi, University of Western Ontario

Microeconomics Flexibility Chart

Core	Policy	Optional

Core

1. What Is Economics?

2. The Economic Problem

3. Demand and Supply

4. Elasticity

5. Efficiency and Equity
   A chapter that provides a non-technical explanation of efficiency and equity that unifies the micro coverage and permits early coverage of policy issues.

10. Output and Costs

11. Perfect Competition

12. Monopoly

13. Monopolistic Competition and Oligopoly

14. Demand and Supply in Factor Markets
    Enables you to cover all the factor market issues in a single chapter. Includes an explanation of present value.

Policy

6. Markets in Action
   A unique chapter that gives extensive applications of demand and supply.

15. Economic Inequality

16. Public Goods and Taxes
    Introduces the role of government in the economy and explains the positive theory of government.

17. Competition Policy

18. Externalities

Optional

1. Appendix: Graphs in Economics
   A good appendix to assign to the student with a fear of graphs.

7. Utility and Demand
   Although this chapter is optional, it may be covered if desired *before* demand in Chapter 3.

8. Possibilities, Preferences, and Choices
   A full chapter on this strictly optional topic to ensure that it is covered clearly with intuitive explanations and illustrations. The standard short appendix treatment of this topic makes it indigestible.

9. Organizing Production
   This chapter may be skipped or assigned as a reading.

14. Appendix: Labour Markets

33. Trading with the World

35. Global Stock Markets

Four Alternative Micro Sequences

Traditional Theory and Policy Mix	Challenging Theory Emphasis	Public Choice Emphasis	Policy Emphasis (shorter)
1. What Is Economics?	1. What Is Economics?	1. What Is Economics?	1. What Is Economics?
2. The Economic Problem	2. The Economic Problem	2. The Economic Problem	2. The Economic Problem
3. Demand and Supply	3. Demand and Supply	3. Demand and Supply	3. Demand and Supply
4. Elasticity	4. Elasticity	4. Elasticity	4. Elasticity
5. Efficiency and Equity	5. Efficiency and Equity	5. Efficiency and Equity	5. Efficiency and Equity
6. Markets in Action	6. Markets in Action	6. Markets in Action	6. Markets in Action
7. Utility and Demand or	8. Possibilities, Preferences, and Choices	7. Utility and Demand	14. Demand and Supply in Factor Markets
8. Possibilities, Preferences, and Choices	9. Organizing Production	9. Organizing Production	15. Economic Inequality
9. Organizing Production	10. Output and Costs	10. Output and Costs	16. Public Goods and Taxes
10. Output and Costs	11. Perfect Competition	11. Perfect Competition	18. Externalities
11. Perfect Competition	12. Monopoly	12. Monopoly	33. Trading with the World
12. Monopoly	13. Monopolistic Competition and Oligopoly	13. Monopolistic Competition and Oligopoly	
13. Monopolistic Competition and Oligopoly	14. Demand and Supply in Factor Markets	16. Public Goods and Taxes	
17. Competition Policy	17. Competition Policy	17. Competition Policy	
14. Demand and Supply in Factor Markets	33. Trading with the World	18. Externalities	
15. Economic Inequality	35. Global Stock Markets		
33. Trading with the World			
35. Global Stock Markets			

CREDITS

Photo Credits

Part 1: p. 54, Corbis-Bettman; p. 55 (left), Culver Pictures, p. 55 (right), Bruce Ando/Tony Stone Images.

Part 2: p. 148, Stock Montage; p. 149 (left), National Archives; p. 149 (right), PhotoDisc, Inc.

Part 3: p. 190, Corbis-Bettman; p. 191 (left), Keystone-Mast Collection (V22542) UCR/California Museum of Photography, University of California, Riverside; p. 191 (right), China Tourism Press/Getty Images; p. 192, Loren Santow.

Part 4: p. 205 (left), PhotoDisc, Inc.; p. 205 (left, inset), Dick Morton; p. 205 (right), Dick Morton; p. 205 (right, inset), © Reuters NewMedia Inc./CORBIS/MAGMA; p. 213, Jonathan Hayward/CP Photo Archive; p. 310, Stock Montage; p. 311 (left), Culver Pictures; p. 311 (right), Don Wilson/West Stock.

Part 5: p. 368, Corbis-Bettman; p. 369 (left), courtesy of The Bostonian Society/Old State House; p. 369 (right), Mark E. Gibson.

Part 6: p. 432, David Joel/David Joel Photography, Inc.; p. 433 (left), Jim Baron/The Image Finders; p. 433 (right), Patrick Mullen.

Figure and Table Credits

The sources below were extracted from the Statistics Canada CANSIM II database <http://cansim2.statcan.ca/cgi-win/CNSMCGI.EXE>.

Figure 33.5: "Canadian Tariffs: 1867–2001," adapted from the Statistics Canada CANSIM II database, tables 380-0002 and 380-0007, and from the Statistics Canada publication *Historical Statistics of Canada,* catalogue 11-516, series G485, 1983.

Figure 35.8: "Two Views of the Personal Saving Rate," adapted from the Statistics Canada CANSIM II database, tables 378-0004 and 380-0031.

BRIEF CONTENTS

PART 1   INTRODUCTION

Chapter 1   **What Is Economics?**

Chapter 2   **The Economic Problem**

PART 2   HOW MARKETS WORK

Chapter 3   **Demand and Supply**

Chapter 4   **Elasticity**

Chapter 5   **Efficiency and Equity**

Chapter 6   **Markets in Action**

PART 3   HOUSEHOLDS' CHOICES

Chapter 7   **Utility and Demand**

Chapter 8   **Possibilities, Preferences, and Choices**

PART 4   FIRMS AND MARKETS

Chapter 9   **Organizing Production**

Chapter 10   **Output and Costs**

Chapter 11   **Perfect Competition**

Chapter 12   **Monopoly**

Chapter 13   **Monopolistic Competition and Oligopoly**

PART 5   FACTOR MARKETS

Chapter 14   **Demand and Supply in Factor Markets**

Chapter 15   **Economic Inequality**

PART 6   MARKET FAILURE AND GOVERNMENT

Chapter 16   **Public Goods and Taxes**

Chapter 17   **Competition Policy**

Chapter 18   **Externalities**

PART 10   THE GLOBAL ECONOMY

Chapter 33   **Trading with the World**

Chapter 35   **Global Stock Markets**

CONTENTS

PART 1   INTRODUCTION

Chapter I   **What Is Economics?**   I

Choice, Change, Challenge, and Opportunity   I

Definition of Economics   **2**
  Scarcity   **2**
  Microeconomics   **2**
  Macroeconomics   **2**

Three Big Microeconomic Questions   **3**
  What Goods and Services Are Produced?   **3**
  How Are Goods and Services Produced?   **4**
  For Whom Are Goods and Services Produced?   **5**

Three Big Macroeconomic Questions   **6**
  What Determines the Standard of Living?   **6**
  What Determines the Cost of Living?   **7**
  Why Does Our Economy Fluctuate?   **8**

The Economic Way of Thinking   **9**
  Choices and Tradeoffs   **9**
  Microeconomic Tradeoffs   **9**
  Macroeconomic Tradeoffs   **10**
  Opportunity Cost   **11**
  Margins and Incentives   **11**

Economics: A Social Science   **12**
  Observation and Measurement   **12**
  Model Building   **12**
  Testing Models   **12**
  Obstacles and Pitfalls in Economics   **13**
  Agreement and Disagreement   **14**

Chapter 1 Appendix   Graphs in Economics   17

Graphing Data   **17**
   Time-Series Graphs   **18**
   Cross-Section Graphs   **18**
   Scatter Diagrams   **19**

Graphs Used in Economic Models   **20**
   Variables That Move in the Same Direction   **20**
   Variables That Move in Opposite Directions   **21**
   Variables That Have a Maximum or a Minimum   **22**
   Variables That Are Unrelated   **23**

The Slope of a Relationship   **24**
   The Slope of a Straight Line   **24**
   The Slope of a Curved Line   **25**

Graphing Relationships Among More Than Two
   Variables   **26**

MATHEMATICAL NOTE
Equations to Straight Lines   **28**

*Summary (Key Points, Key Figures and Tables, and
Key Terms), Problems, Critical Thinking, and Web
Exercises appear at the end of each chapter.*

Chapter 2   The Economic Problem   33

Good, Better, Best!   **33**

Production Possibilities and Opportunity Cost   **34**
   Production Possibilities Frontier   **34**
   Production Efficiency   **35**
   Tradeoff Along the *PPF*   **35**
   Opportunity Cost   **35**

Using Resources Efficiently   **37**
   The *PPF* and Marginal Cost   **37**
   Preferences and Marginal Benefit   **38**
   Efficient Use of Resources   **39**

Economic Growth   **40**
   The Cost of Economic Growth   **40**
   Economic Growth in Canada and Hong Kong   **41**

Gains from Trade   **42**
   Comparative Advantage   **42**
   Achieving the Gains from Trade   **43**
   Absolute Advantage   **45**
   Dynamic Comparative Advantage   **45**

The Market Economy   **46**
   Property Rights   **46**
   Markets   **46**
   Circular Flows in the Market Economy   **46**
   Coordinating Decisions   **47**

READING BETWEEN THE LINES
POLICY WATCH
The Cost and Benefit of Education   **48**

PART 1   WRAP UP
Understanding the Scope of Economics   53
   Probing the Ideas: The Sources of Economic Wealth
      54
   Talking with Lawrence H. Summers   **56**

PART 2   HOW MARKETS WORK

Chapter 3   Demand and Supply   59

Slide, Rocket, and Roller Coaster   59

Markets and Prices   60

Demand   61
    What Determines Buying Plans?   61
    The Law of Demand   61
    Demand Curve and Demand Schedule   62
    A Change in Demand   63
    A Change in the Quantity Demanded Versus a Change
       in Demand   64

Supply   66
    What Determines Selling Plans?   66
    The Law of Supply   66
    Supply Curve and Supply Schedule   66
    A Change in Supply   67
    A Change in the Quantity Supplied Versus a Change
       in Supply   68

Market Equilibrium   70
    Price as a Regulator   70
    Price Adjustments   71

Predicting Changes in Price and Quantity   72
    A Change in Demand   72
    A Change in Supply   73
    A Change in Both Demand and Supply   74

READING BETWEEN THE LINES
Demand and Supply: The Price of Computers   76

MATHEMATICAL NOTE
Demand, Supply, and Equilibrium   78

Chapter 4   Elasticity   83

Predicting Prices   83

Price Elasticity of Demand   84
    Calculating Elasticity   85
    Inelastic and Elastic Demand   86
    Elasticity Along a Straight-Line Demand Curve   87
    Total Revenue and Elasticity   88
    Your Expenditure and Your Elasticity   89
    The Factors That Influence the Elasticity of Demand
       89

More Elasticities of Demand   91
    Cross Elasticity of Demand   91
    Income Elasticity of Demand   92
    Real-World Income Elasticities of Demand   93

Elasticity of Supply   94
    Calculating the Elasticity of Supply   94
    The Factors That Influence the Elasticity of Supply
       95

READING BETWEEN THE LINES
Elasticities of Demand and Supply in the Global Oil
    Market   98

Chapter 5   Efficiency and Equity   103

More for Less   103

Efficiency: A Refresher   104
  Marginal Benefit   104
  Marginal Cost   104
  Efficiency and Inefficiency   105

Value, Price, and Consumer Surplus   106
  Value, Willingness to Pay, and Demand   106
  Consumer Surplus   107

Cost, Price, and Producer Surplus   108
  Cost, Minimum Supply-Price, and Supply   108
  Producer Surplus   109

Is the Competitive Market Efficient?   110
  Efficiency of Competitive Equilibrium   110
  The Invisible Hand   111
  The Invisible Hand at Work Today   111
  Obstacles to Efficiency   111
  Underproduction   112
  Overproduction   113

Is the Competitive Market Fair?   114
  It's Not Fair If the *Result* Isn't Fair   114
  It's Not Fair If the *Rules* Aren't Fair   116

READING BETWEEN THE LINES
POLICY WATCH
  Efficiency and Equity in the Market for Drugs   118

Chapter 6   Markets in Action   123

Turbulent Times   123

Housing Markets and Rent Ceilings   124
  The Market Response to a Decrease in Supply   124
  Long-Run Adjustments   125
  A Regulated Housing Market   125
  Search Activity   126
  Black Markets   126
  Inefficiency of Rent Ceilings   127

The Labour Market and the Minimum Wage   128
  The Minimum Wage   129
  The Minimum Wage in Practice   130
  Inefficiency of the Minimum Wage   130

Taxes   131
  Who Pays a Sales Tax?   131
  Tax Division and Elasticity of Demand   132
  Tax Division and Elasticity of Supply   133
  Sales Taxes in Practice   134
  Taxes and Efficiency   134

Markets for Illegal Goods   135
  A Free Market for Drugs   135
  A Market for Illegal Drugs   135
  Legalizing and Taxing Drugs   136

Stabilizing Farm Revenues   137
  An Unregulated Agricultural Market   137
  Speculative Markets in Inventories   138
  Farm Marketing Boards   139
  Efficiency and Equity in Farm Markets   141

READING BETWEEN THE LINES
POLICY WATCH
  Who Pays the Airport Security Tax?   142

PART 2   WRAP UP
Understanding How Markets Work   147
  Probing the Ideas: Discovering the Laws of Demand
    and Supply   148
  Talking with John McMillan   150

PART 3 HOUSEHOLDS' CHOICES

Chapter 7 Utility and Demand 153

Water, Water, Everywhere 153

Household Consumption Choices 154
  Consumption Possibilities 154
  Preferences 154
  Total Utility 154
  Marginal Utility 155
  Temperature: An Analogy 155

Maximizing Utility 157
  The Utility-Maximizing Choice 157
  Equalizing Marginal Utility per Dollar Spent 157

Predictions of Marginal Utility Theory 159
  A Fall in the Price of a Movie 159
  A Rise in the Price of Pop 160
  A Rise in Income 162
  Individual Demand and Market Demand 163
  Marginal Utility and Elasticity 164

Efficiency, Price, and Value 164
  Consumer Efficiency and Consumer Surplus 164
  The Paradox of Value 164

READING BETWEEN THE LINES
What's the Marginal Utility of a Boat Ride? 166

Chapter 8 Possibilities, Preferences, and Choices 171

Subterranean Movements 171

Consumption Possibilities 172
  The Budget Equation 173

Preferences and Indifference Curves 175
  Marginal Rate of Substitution 176
  Degree of Substitutability 177

Predicting Consumer Behaviour 178
  A Change in Price 179
  A Change in Income 180
  Substitution Effect and Income Effect 181
  Back to the Facts 182

Work–Leisure Choices 182
  Labour Supply 182
  The Labour Supply Curve 183

READING BETWEEN THE LINES
Regular Books versus Print-on-Demand Books 184

PART 3 WRAP UP
Understanding Households' Choices 189
  Probing the Ideas: People as Rational Decision Makers 190
  Talking with Gary S. Becker 192

PART 4   FIRMS AND MARKETS

Chapter 9   **Organizing Production**   195

Spinning a Web   195

The Firm and Its Economic Problem   196
    The Firm's Goal   196
    Measuring a Firm's Profit   196
    Opportunity Cost   196
    Economic Profit   197
    Economic Accounting: A Summary   197
    The Firm's Constraints   198

Technological and Economic Efficiency   199
    Technological Efficiency   199
    Economic Efficiency   199

Information and Organization   201
    Command Systems   201
    Incentive Systems   201
    Mixing the Systems   201
    The Principal–Agent Problem   202
    Coping with the Principal–Agent Problem   202
    Types of Business Organization   202
    Pros and Cons of Different Types of Firms   203
    The Relative Importance of Different Types of Firms   204

Markets and the Competitive Environment   205
    Measures of Concentration   206
    Concentration Measures for the Canadian Economy   207
    Limitations of Concentration Measures   207
    Market Structures in the North American Economy   209

Markets and Firms   210
    Market Coordination   210
    Why Firms?   210

READING BETWEEN THE LINES
Nortel's Problem   212

Chapter 10   **Output and Costs**   217

What Does a Doughnut Cost?   217

Decision Time Frames   218
    The Short Run   218
    The Long Run   218

Short-Run Technology Constraint   219
    Product Schedules   219
    Product Curves   219
    Total Product Curve   220
    Marginal Product Curve   220
    Average Product Curve   222
    Marginal Grade and Grade Point Average   222

Short-Run Cost   223
    Total Cost   223
    Marginal Cost   224
    Average Cost   224
    Why the Average Total Cost Curve Is U-Shaped   224
    Cost Curves and Product Curves   226
    Shifts in the Cost Curves   226

Long-Run Cost   228
    The Production Function   228
    Short-Run Cost and Long-Run Cost   228
    The Long-Run Average Cost Curve   230
    Economies and Diseconomies of Scale   230

READING BETWEEN THE LINES
The Cost of a Doughnut   232

Chapter 11   **Perfect Competition   237**

Sweet Competition   237

Competition   238
How Perfect Competition Arises   238
Price Takers   238
Economic Profit and Revenue   238

The Firm's Decisions in Perfect Competition   240
Profit-Maximizing Output   240
Marginal Analysis   242
Profits and Losses in the Short Run   243
The Firm's Short-Run Supply Curve   244
Short-Run Industry Supply Curve   245

Output, Price, and Profit in Perfect Competition   246
Short-Run Equilibrium   246
A Change in Demand   246
Long-Run Adjustments   247
Entry and Exit   247
Changes in Plant Size   248
Long-Run Equilibrium   249

Changing Tastes and Advancing Technology   250
A Permanent Change in Demand   250
External Economies and Diseconomies   251
Technological Change   253

Competition and Efficiency   254
Efficient Use of Resources   254
Choices, Equilibrium, and Efficiency   254
Efficiency of Perfect Competition   255

READING BETWEEN THE LINES
Perfect Competition in Maple Syrup   256

Chapter 12   **Monopoly   261**

The Profits of Generosity   261

Market Power   262
How Monopoly Arises   262
Monopoly Price-Setting Strategies   263

A Single-Price Monopoly's Output and Price Decision   264
Price and Marginal Revenue   264
Marginal Revenue and Elasticity   265
Output and Price Decision   266

Single-Price Monopoly and Competition Compared   268
Comparing Output and Price   268
Efficiency Comparison   269
Redistribution of Surpluses   270
Rent Seeking   270
Rent-Seeking Equilibrium   270

Price Discrimination   271
Price Discrimination and Consumer Surplus   271
Profiting by Price Discriminating   272
Perfect Price Discrimination   273
Efficiency and Rent Seeking with Price Discrimination   274

Monopoly Policy Issues   275
Gains from Monopoly   275
Regulating Natural Monopoly   276

READING BETWEEN THE LINES
POLICY WATCH
Domestic Airline Monopoly   278

Chapter 13   **Monopolistic Competition and Oligopoly   283**

PC War Games   283

Monopolistic Competition   284
 Large Number of Firms   284
 Product Differentiation   284
 Competing on Quality, Price, and Marketing   284
 Entry and Exit   285
 Examples of Monopolistic Competition   285

Output and Price in Monopolistic Competition   286
 Short Run: Economic Profit   286
 Long Run: Zero Economic Profit   287
 Monopolistic Competition and Efficiency   287

Product Development and Marketing   288
 Innovation and Product Development   288
 Marketing   289

Oligopoly   291
 The Kinked Demand Curve Model   291
 Dominant Firm Oligopoly   292

Oligopoly Games   293
 What Is a Game?   293
 The Prisoners' Dilemma   293
 An Oligopoly Price-Fixing Game   295
 Other Oligopoly Games   299
 An R&D Game   299

Repeated Games and Sequential Games   301
 A Repeated Duopoly Game   301
 A Sequential Entry Game in a Contestable Market   302

READING BETWEEN THE LINES
POLICY WATCH
 Oligopoly in Action: A Book Seller's War   304

PART 4 WRAP UP
Understanding Firms and Markets   309
 Probing the Ideas: Market Power   310
 Talking with Bengt Holmstrom   312

PART 5   FACTOR MARKETS

Chapter 14   **Demand and Supply in Factor Markets   315**

Many Happy Returns   315

Prices and Incomes in Competitive Factor Markets   316

Labour Markets   317
 The Demand for Labour   317
 Marginal Revenue Product   318
 The Labour Demand Curve   319
 Equivalence of Two Conditions for Profit Maximization   320
 Changes in the Demand for Labour   321
 Market Demand   322
 Elasticity of Demand for Labour   322
 The Supply of Labour   322
 Labour Market Equilibrium   324

Capital Markets   325
 The Demand for Capital   325
 Discounting and Present Value   326
 The Present Value of a Computer   327
 Demand Curve for Capital   329
 The Supply of Capital   329
 Supply Curve of Capital   330
 The Interest Rate   330

Natural Resource Markets   331
 The Supply of a Renewable Natural Resource   331
 The Supply of a Nonrenewable Natural Resource   332
 Price and the Hotelling Principle   332

Income, Economic Rent, and Opportunity Cost   334
 Large and Small Incomes   334
 Economic Rent and Opportunity Cost   334

READING BETWEEN THE LINES
 Rents and Opportunity Costs on the Ice   336

Chapter 14 Appendix   Labour Unions   341

Market Power in the Labour Market   **341**
    Union Objectives and Constraints   **341**
    A Union in a Competitive Labour Market   **342**
    How Unions Try to Change the Demand for Labour
        343
    The Scale of Union–Nonunion Wage Differentials
        343

Monopsony   **344**
    Monopsony Tendencies   **345**
    Monopsony and a Union   **345**
    Monopsony and the Minimum Wage   **345**

Chapter 15   Economic Inequality   347

Rags and Riches   **347**

Measuring Economic Inequality   **348**
    The Distribution of After-Tax Income   **348**
    The Income Lorenz Curve   **349**
    The Distribution of Wealth   **350**
    Wealth Versus Income   **350**
    Annual or Lifetime Income and Wealth?   **351**
    Trends in Inequality   **351**
    Poverty   **352**
    Who Are the Rich and the Poor?   **352**

The Sources of Economic Inequality   **354**
    Human Capital   **354**
    Discrimination   **357**
    Unequal Ownership of Capital   **358**

Income Redistribution   **359**
    Income Taxes   **359**
    Income Maintenance Programs   **359**
    Subsidized Services   **359**
    The Scale of Income Redistribution   **360**
    The Big Tradeoff   **361**

READING BETWEEN THE LINES
Trends in Inequality   **362**

PART 5   **WRAP UP**
Understanding Factor Markets   367
    Probing the Ideas: Running Out of Resources   **368**
    Talking with Janet Currie   **370**

PART 6   MARKET FAILURE AND GOVERNMENT

Chapter 16   Public Goods and Taxes   373

Government: The Solution or the Problem? 373

The Economic Theory of Government   374
  Public Goods   374
  Taxes and Redistribution   374
  Monopoly   374
  Externalities   374
  Public Choice and the Political Marketplace   375
  Political Equilibrium   375

Public Goods and the Free-Rider Problem   376
  Public Goods   376
  The Free-Rider Problem   376
  The Benefit of a Public Good   377
  The Efficient Quantity of a Public Good   378
  Private Provision   378
  Public Provision   378
  The Role of Bureaucrats   380
  Rational Ignorance   380
  Two Types of Political Equilibrium   381
  Why Government Is Large and Grows   381
  Voters Strike Back   381

Taxes   382
  Income Taxes   382
  Employment, Health, and Social Insurance Taxes   384
  Provincial Sales Taxes and the GST   385
  Property Taxes   385
  Excise Taxes   386

READING BETWEEN THE LINES
POLICY WATCH
An Increase in Demand for a Public Good   388

Chapter 17   Competition Policy   393

Public Interest or Special Interests?   393

Market Intervention   394
  Regulation   394
  Public Ownership   394
  Anti-Combine Law   394

Economic Theory of Regulation   394
  Demand for Regulation   394
  Supply of Regulation   395
  Political Equilibrium   395

Regulation and Deregulation   396
  The Scope of Regulation   396
  The Regulatory Process   396
  Natural Monopoly   397
  Public Interest or Capture?   400
  Cartel Regulation   401
  Making Predictions   402

Public Ownership   403
  Efficient Crown Corporation   403
  A Bureaucracy Model of Public Enterprise   404
  Crown Corporations in Reality   405
  Privatization   405

Anti-Combine Law   406
  Canada's Anti-Combine Law   406
  Some Recent Anti-Combine Cases   406
  Public or Special Interest?   407

READING BETWEEN THE LINES
Fixing Vitamin Prices   408

Chapter 18   **Externalities   413**

Greener and Smarter   **413**

Externalities in Our Lives   **414**
    Negative Production Externalities   **414**
    Positive Production Externalities   **414**
    Negative Consumption Externalities   **414**
    Positive Consumption Externalities   **414**

Negative Externalities: Pollution   **415**
    The Demand for a Pollution-Free Environment   **415**
    The Sources of Pollution   **415**
    Private Costs and Social Costs   **417**
    Production and Pollution: How Much?   **418**
    Property Rights   **418**
    The Coase Theorem   **419**
    Government Actions in the Face of External Costs
    420

Positive Externalities: Knowledge   **421**
    Private Benefits and Social Benefits   **421**
    Government Actions in the Face of External Benefits
    423

READING BETWEEN THE LINES
The Air Pollution Debate   **426**

PART 6   WRAP UP
Understanding Market Failure and Government
431
    Probing the Ideas: Externalities and Property Rights
    432
    Talking with John McCallum   **434**

PART 10   THE GLOBAL ECONOMY

Chapter 33   **Trading with the World   785**

Silk Routes and Sucking Sounds   **785**

Patterns and Trends in International Trade   **786**
    Trade in Goods   **786**
    Trade in Services   **786**
    Geographical Patterns of International Trade   **786**
    Trends in the Volume of Trade   **786**
    Net Exports and International Borrowing   **786**

The Gains from International Trade   **787**
    Opportunity Cost in Farmland   **787**
    Opportunity Cost in Mobilia   **788**
    Comparative Advantage   **788**
    The Gains from Trade: Cheaper to Buy Than to
        Produce   **788**
    The Terms of Trade   **788**
    Balanced Trade   **789**
    Changes in Production and Consumption   **789**
    Calculating the Gains from Trade   **791**
    Gains for All   **791**
    Gains from Trade in Reality   **791**

International Trade Restrictions   **793**
    The History of Tariffs   **793**
    How Tariffs Work   **794**
    Nontariff Barriers   **796**
    How Quotas and VERs Work   **796**

The Case Against Protection   **797**
    The Employment Argument   **797**
    The Infant-Industry Argument   **797**
    The Dumping Argument   **798**
    Maintains National Security   **798**
    Allows Us to Compete with Cheap Foreign Labour
    798
    Brings Diversity and Stability   **799**
    Penalizes Lax Environmental Standards   **799**
    Protects National Culture   **799**
    Prevents Rich Countries from Exploiting Developing
        Countries   **800**

Why Is International Trade Restricted?   **800**
  Tariff Revenue   **800**
  Rent Seeking   **800**
  Compensating Losers   **801**
  Compensating Losers from Protection   **801**

The North American Free Trade Agreement   **802**
  The Terms of the Canada–United States Agreement
  802
  The Extension of the Agreement: NAFTA   **803**
  Effects of the Free Trade Agreement   **803**

READING BETWEEN THE LINES
Tariffs in Action: Lumber   **804**

Chapter 35   **Global Stock Markets   829**

Irrational Exuberance?   **829**

Stock Market Basics   **830**
  What Is Stock?   **830**
  What Is a Stock Exchange?   **830**
  Stock Prices and Returns   **831**
  Earnings and the Price-Earnings Ratio   **831**
  Reading the Stock Market Report   **832**
  Stock Price Indexes   **832**
  Stock Price Performance   **834**
  Stock Prices   **834**
  Earnings Per Share   **835**

How Are Stock Prices Determined?   **836**
  Market Fundamentals   **836**
  Speculative Bubbles   **838**
  The Booming Nineties: A Bubble?   **839**

Risk and Return   **840**
  Risk Premium   **840**
  Portfolio Diversification   **840**

The Stock Market and the Economy   **841**
  Trends and Cycles in Earnings Growth   **841**
  Central Bank Monetary Policy   **842**
  Taxes   **843**
  Wealth, Consumption Expenditure, and Saving   **843**
  The Distribution of Wealth   **845**

READING BETWEEN THE LINES
Stock Price Uncertainties   **846**

Glossary   **G-1**

Index   **I-1**

MICROECONOMICS

WHAT IS ECONOMICS? — CHAPTER 1

Choice, Change, Challenge, and Opportunity

You are studying economics, the science of choice, at a time of enormous change, challenge, and opportunity. Economics studies the choices that we make as we cope with the hard fact of life: we can't have everything we want. ◆ The engine of change is information technology, which has created the Internet and transformed our lives at both work and play. This transformation will continue, but in 2001 it was challenged by a U.S. recession and by the terrorist attacks of September 11. The events of September 11 have brought long-lasting changes to the political and security landscape and to the economic landscape. People now face choices not previously imagined. Some people are avoiding air travel, a choice that is sending shock waves through travel agencies, airports, airlines, airplane builders, and hotels and restaurants. Security at the Canada–U.S. border and at our airports and seaports is stepped up. Governments, airlines, and airport operators are buying more video and electronic surveillance equipment, which is creating new business and job opportunities. ◆ As 2003 began, people were wondering whether economic recovery and renewed expansion was just around the corner or whether there would be a second U.S. recession—a "double dip"—and worrying about how such a development might influence the Canadian economy.

◆ You've just glimpsed some of the economic issues in today's world. Your course in economics will help you to understand the powerful forces that are shaping this world. This chapter takes the first step. It describes the questions that economists try to answer, the way they think about choices, and the methods they use. An appendix provides a guide to the graphical methods that are widely used in economics.

After studying this chapter, you will be able to

- **Define economics and distinguish between microeconomics and macroeconomics**
- **Explain the three big questions of microeconomics**
- **Explain the three big questions of macroeconomics**
- **Explain the ideas that define the economic way of thinking**
- **Explain how economists go about their work as social scientists**

Definition of Economics

ALL ECONOMIC QUESTIONS ARISE BECAUSE WE want more than we can get. We want a peaceful and secure world. We want clean air, lakes, and rivers. We want long and healthy lives. We want good schools, colleges, and universities. We want spacious and comfortable homes. We want an enormous range of sports and recreational gear, from running shoes to jet skis. We want the time to enjoy sports, games, novels, movies, music, travel, and hanging out with our friends.

Scarcity

What each one of us can get is limited by time, by the income we earn, and by the prices we must pay. Everyone ends up with some unsatisfied wants. What we can get as a society is limited by our productive resources. These resources include the gifts of nature, human labour and ingenuity, and tools and equipment that we have produced.

Our inability to satisfy all our wants is called **scarcity.** The poor and the rich alike face scarcity. A child wants a $1.00 can of pop and two 50¢ packs of gum but has only $1.00 in his pocket. He faces scarcity. A millionaire wants to spend the weekend playing golf *and* spend the same weekend at the office attending a business strategy meeting. She faces scarcity. A society wants to provide improved health care, install a computer in every classroom, explore space, clean polluted lakes and rivers, and so on. Even parrots face scarcity!

Faced with scarcity, we must make choices. We must *choose* among the available alternatives. The child must *choose* the pop *or* the gum. The millionaire must *choose* the golf game *or* the meeting. As a society, we must *choose* among health care, highways, peacekeeping, the environment, and so on.

Economics is the social science that studies the choices that we make as we cope with scarcity and the institutions that have evolved to influence and reconcile our choices. The subject divides into

- Microeconomics
- Macroeconomics

Microeconomics

Microeconomics is the study of the choices that individuals and businesses make, the way these choices interact, and the influence that governments exert on them. Some examples of microeconomic questions are: Why are more people buying SUVs and fewer people buying minivans? How will a decline in air travel affect the producers of airplanes? How would a tax on e-commerce affect the growth of the Internet? Who benefits from minimum wage laws?

Macroeconomics

Macroeconomics is the study of the effects on the national economy and the global economy of the choices that individuals, businesses, and governments make. Some examples of macroeconomic questions are: Why did production and jobs shrink in 2001? Why has Japan been in a long period of economic stagnation? Can the government bring prosperity by cutting interest rates? Will a tax cut increase the number of jobs and total production?

Not only do I want a cracker—we all want a cracker!

REVIEW QUIZ

1 What is scarcity?
2 Give some examples of scarcity in today's world.
3 Define economics.
4 Use the headlines in today's news to illustrate the distinction between microeconomics and macroeconomics.

Three Big Microeconomic Questions

LOOK AT THE WORLD AROUND YOU. YOU SEE AN enormous range of things that you might buy and jobs that you might do. You also see a huge range of incomes and wealth. Microeconomics explains much of what you see by addressing three big questions:

- What goods and services are produced?
- How are goods and services produced?
- For whom are goods and services produced?

What Goods and Services Are Produced?

The objects that people value and produce to satisfy wants are called **goods and services.** Goods are physical objects such as golf balls. Services are tasks performed for people such as haircuts.

What *are* the goods and services that we produce in Canada today? Figure 1.1 shows the surprising answer. Canada is a service economy. Wholesale trade and retail trade are two of the three largest services. Between them, they represent nearly 12 percent of the value of total production. Health care, education, and financial services, such as banking and stock brokering, complete the five largest services. Among goods, only construction matches the size of the larger service items. Each of the other largest categories of goods—motor vehicles, crude oil and natural gas, food, and electrical and electronic products—accounts for less than 3 percent of the value of total production.

Figure 1.2 shows the trends in what we produce. Fifty years ago, almost 20 percent of Canadians worked on farms, 60 percent in mining, construction, and manufacturing, and 20 percent produced services. Today, more than 70 percent of working Canadians have service jobs. Mining, construction, and manufacturing jobs have shrunk to 25 percent, and farm jobs have almost disappeared.

You've reviewed some of the facts about *what* we produce. These facts raise the deeper question: What determines the quantities of retail services, new homes, DVD players, and wheat that we produce? Microeconomics provides some answers to these questions.

FIGURE 1.1   What We Produce

The production of wholesale trade and retail trade greatly exceeds the production of goods such as motor vehicles.

Source: Statistics Canada.

FIGURE 1.2   Trends in What We Produce

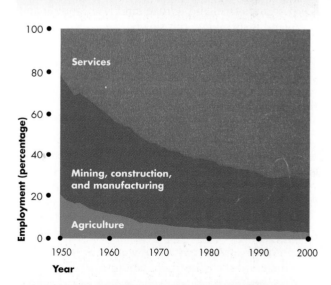

Services have expanded, and agriculture, mining, construction, and manufacturing have shrunk.

Source: Statistics Canada.

How Are Goods and Services Produced?

The range of jobs that you might do keeps changing. When Henry Ford built the world's first auto assembly line, he destroyed the jobs of the skilled craft workers who built cars using hand tools and created jobs for a new type of auto assembly worker. Every year, as businesses adopt new production technologies, similar changes occur. Today, it is information technology businesses that are producing new products, creating new jobs, and destroying old ones.

We call the resources that businesses use to produce goods and services **factors of production**. Factors of production are grouped into four categories:

- Land
- Labour
- Capital
- Entrepreneurship

Land The "gifts of nature" that we use to produce goods and services are called **land.** In economics, land is what in everyday language we call natural resources. It includes land in the everyday sense, minerals, energy, water, and air.

Canada covers 9.9 billion square kilometres and we live on about 3.5 percent of this land. Almost 10 percent of Canada's land surface is water, about 30 percent is forest land, 50 percent is wild land, and 6.5 percent is farmland. Urban land is expanding and rural land is shrinking, but slowly.

Our land surface and water resources are renewable, and some of our mineral resources can be recycled. But many mineral resources, and all those that we use to create energy, are nonrenewable resources— they can be used only once.

Labour The work time and work effort that people devote to producing goods and services is called **labour.** Labour includes the physical and mental efforts of all the people who work on farms and construction sites and in factories, shops, and offices.

In Canada in 2002, 16 million people had jobs or were available for work. An increasing population and an increasing percentage of women with jobs have increased the quantity of labour available.

The *quality* of labour depends on **human capital,** which is the knowledge and skill that people obtain from education, on-the-job training, and work experience. You are building your own human capital right now as you work on your economics course,

and your human capital will continue to grow as you become better at your job. Today, more than 80 percent of the Canadian population has completed high school and more than 40 percent has post-secondary certificates, diplomas, or university degrees. Figure 1.3 shows a measure of the growth of human capital in Canada over the past few decades.

Capital The tools, instruments, machines, buildings, and other constructions that businesses now use to produce goods and services are called **capital.** The quantity of capital grows steadily over time.

Entrepreneurship The human resource that organizes labour, land, and capital is called **entrepreneurship.** Entrepreneurs come up with new ideas about what and how to produce, make business decisions, and bear the risks that arise from these decisions.

You've reviewed some of the facts about *how* we produce in Canada. These facts raise deeper questions such as: What determines the quantities of labour and capital that get used? Microeconomics provides some answers to these questions.

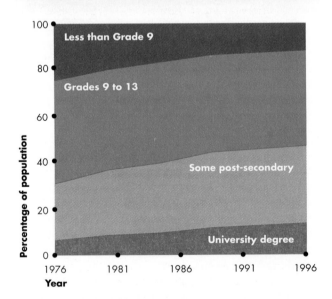

FIGURE 1.3   A Measure of Human Capital

Today, more than 40 percent of the Canadian population has post-secondary certificates, diplomas, or university degrees. A further 41 percent has completed high school.

Source: Statistics Canada.

For Whom Are Goods and Services Produced?

Who gets the goods and services that are produced depends on the incomes that people earn. The movie star who earns a few million dollars a year buys a large quantity of goods and services. A homeless unemployed person has few options and a small quantity of goods and services.

To earn an income, people sell the services of the factors of production they own:

- Land earns **rent**.
- Labour earns **wages**.
- Capital earns **interest**.
- Entrepreneurship earns **profit**.

Which factor of production earns the most income? The answer is labour. Total wages (including fringe benefits) were 69 percent of total income in 2000. Land, capital, and entrepreneurship share the remaining 31 percent. And over time, these percentages have been remarkably constant.

Knowing how income is shared among the factors of production doesn't tell us how it is shared among individuals. You know of lots of people who earn very large incomes. The average NHL player's salary in 2000 was about $3 million, and some stars, such as Mats Sundin of the Toronto Maple Leafs, earn almost $12 million a year. You know of even more people who earn very small incomes. Servers at McDonald's average around $7 an hour; checkout clerks, gas station attendants, and textile and leather workers earn less than $10 an hour.

You probably know about other persistent differences in incomes. Men, on the average, earn more than women. University and college graduates, on the average, earn more than high-school graduates. Canadians and Americans, on the average, earn more than Europeans, who in turn earn more, on the average, than Asians and Africans.

Figure 1.4 shows the incomes for five groups, each of which represents 20 percent of the population. If incomes were equal, each 20 percent group would earn 20 percent of total income. You know that incomes are unequal, and the figure provides a measure of just how unequal they are.

The 20 percent of individuals with the lowest incomes earn only 4 percent of total income. The 20 percent with the second lowest incomes earn 10 percent of total income. The next 20 percent—the middle 20 percent—earn 16 percent of total income.

FIGURE 1.4   The Distribution of Income in Canada

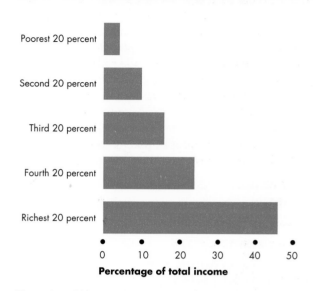

The richest 20 percent of the population earn 46 percent of total income. The poorest 20 percent earn only 4 percent of total income. (The data are for 1998.)

Source: Statistics Canada.

The 20 percent with the second highest incomes earn 24 percent of total income. And the 20 percent of individuals with the highest incomes earn 46 percent of total income.

You've reviewed some of the facts about *for whom* we produce in Canada. These facts raise deeper questions such as: Why do women earn less than men?

The three big microeconomic questions give you a sense of the *scope of microeconomics*. Next, we'll look at the big questions of macroeconomics.

REVIEW QUIZ

1 Does Canada produce more goods than services? What item accounts for the largest percent of the value of what we produce?
2 What are the trends in what we produce?
3 What are the factors of production and what are some of the changes in the way we produce goods and services?
4 Describe the distribution of income that shows for whom goods and services are produced.

Three Big Macroeconomic Questions

YOU'VE LIVED THROUGH A PERIOD OF DRAMATIC change in the way we work and play. The information age has created what has been called a "new economy" with rising living standards and new job opportunities. At the same time, prices have been remarkably stable. But you've also seen that our economy does not always expand. In 2001, economic slowdown brought job losses for millions of people. Macroeconomics explains these events by focusing on three big questions:

- What determines the standard of living?
- What determines the cost of living?
- Why does our economy fluctuate?

What Determines the Standard of Living?

What is the standard of living? How do we measure it? How do we compare the standard of living in Africa with that in Canada and the United States?

The **standard of living** is the level of consumption that people enjoy, on the average, and is measured by average income per person. The greater the income per person, the higher is the standard of living, other things remaining the same.

Figure 1.5 shows the number of Canadian dollars per day earned on the average in different places. You can see that in the United States, the average is $148 a day. This number tells you that an average person in the United States can buy goods and services that cost $148—about five times the world average. Living standards fall off as we move down the figure, with average incomes in India and Africa of only $8 a day.

Most people live in the countries that have incomes below the world average. You can see this fact by looking at the population numbers shown in the figure. The poorest five countries or regions—China, Central Asia, Other Asia, India, and Africa—have a total population of 4 billion, which is two-thirds of the world's population.

What makes the standard of living rise? What can Indians and Africans do to increase their standard of living? Your study of macroeconomics will help you to understand some answers to questions like these.

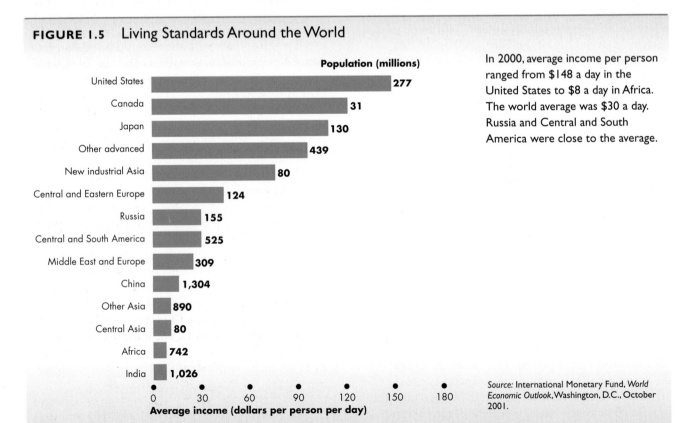

FIGURE 1.5   Living Standards Around the World

In 2000, average income per person ranged from $148 a day in the United States to $8 a day in Africa. The world average was $30 a day. Russia and Central and South America were close to the average.

Source: International Monetary Fund, *World Economic Outlook*, Washington, D.C., October 2001.

What Determines the Cost of Living?

In your great-grandparents' youth, when the electric light bulb was the latest big thing, the average Canadian earned $1 a day. But your great-grandparents' five cents would buy what you need a dollar to buy. The dollar of 2003 is worth only one-twentieth of the dollar of 1903. If the dollar continues to shrink in value at its average rate of loss, by the time you retire (sure, that's a long time in the future), you'll need almost $5 to buy what $1 buys today. The cost of living is rising.

The **cost of living** is the amount of money it takes to buy the goods and services that the average family consumes. In Canada, we measure money in dollars. So the cost of living in Canada is the number of dollars it takes to buy the goods and services that the average family buys. In the United Kingdom, it is the number of pounds; in Japan, it is the number of yen; and in Russia, it is the number of rubles.

Prices in Different Currencies   To make this idea concrete, think about what a Big Mac costs. Table 1.1 shows some prices in 10 countries. The average price of a Big Mac in Canada is $3.00. In the United Kingdom, it is £2.00, and in Japan, it is ¥294. So in the United Kingdom, it costs a smaller number of money units to buy a Big Mac than it does in Canada, and in Japan, it costs a larger number of money units. But a Big Mac costs more in the United Kingdom than in either Canada or Japan. The reason is that a pound is worth 2.40 Canadian dollars, so £2.00 is equivalent to $4.80. And a pound is worth 182 yen, so £2.00 is equivalent to ¥364.

The number of money units that something costs is not so important. But the rate at which the number is changing is very important. A rising cost of living is called **inflation** and a falling cost of living is called **deflation**. Inflation brings a shrinking value of the dollar and deflation brings a rising value of the dollar.

Inflation and Deflation   Have we experienced inflation and a rising cost of living or deflation and a falling cost of living? If we look back over the past 100 years, we see that the cost of living has increased and the value of the dollar has shrunk.

In Canada, on the average between 1902 and 2002, the cost of living increased by 3 percent a year. Most people do not regard inflation at this rate as a big problem. But to place this inflation in perspective, it means that the dollar of 1902 was worth just 5 cents in 2002. At this inflation rate, a dollar earned in 2002 will be worth about 25 cents in 2052, a year in which you will probably be living on your pension!

Most of the advanced economies have low inflation. But the developing economies have higher inflation rates, some of them spectacularly so. In Central and South America, the average inflation rate during the 1980s and 1990s was 107 percent a year. A 100 percent change means a doubling. At this inflation rate, prices are rising by 6 percent a *month*. Inflation this rapid poses huge problems as people struggle to cope with an ever-falling value of money.

During the past few years, the cost of living has increased slowly. Can we count on it rising slowly in the future? What will the dollar buy next year? What will it buy in 10 years when you are paying off your student loan? And what will it buy in 50 years when you are spending your life's savings in retirement?

You've seen that over the years, our standard of living has increased. Why doesn't a rising *cost* of living mean that people must constantly cut back on their spending and endure a falling *standard* of living? Although the cost of living has increased steadily, incomes have increased more quickly. And because incomes have increased faster than the cost of living, the standard of living has increased.

What causes inflation? What can we do to avoid it? Your study of macroeconomics will help you to understand some answers to these questions.

TABLE 1.1	The Cost of a Big Mac in 10 Countries	
Country	Name of currency	Price of a Big Mac
United Kingdom	Pound	2.00
United States	U.S. Dollar	2.50
Canada	Canadian Dollar	3.00
Brazil	Real	3.60
South Africa	Rand	9.70
Israel	Shekel	13.90
Russia	Ruble	35.00
Japan	Yen	294
South Korea	Won	3,000
Indonesia	Rupiah	14,700

Source: Economist.com

FIGURE 1.6   Business Cycle Phases and Turning Points

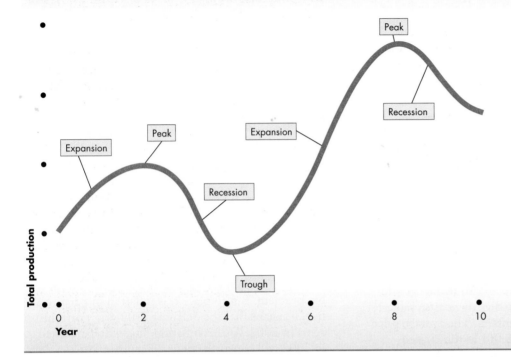

In a business cycle expansion, production and jobs increase more rapidly than normal. In a recession, production and jobs shrink. An expansion ends at a peak, and a recession ends at a trough.

Why Does Our Economy Fluctuate?

Over long periods, both the standard of living and the cost of living increase. But these increases are not smooth and continuous. During 2001, the number of Canadians who wanted a job increased by 330,000. But the Canadian economy created only 103,000 additional jobs. Our economy slowed. We call the periodic but irregular up-and-down movement in production and jobs the **business cycle.**

When production and jobs are increasing more rapidly than normal, the economy is in a business cycle expansion. When production and jobs are shrinking, the economy is in a recession.

Figure 1.6 illustrates the phases and turning points of a business cycle. A *recession* runs from year 2 to year 4, followed by an *expansion* from year 4 through year 8. Another recession runs from year 8 through year 10. A recession ends at a *trough,* and an expansion ends at a *peak.*

The most recent expansion in Canada began in 1991. The deepest recession of the 1990s was in Russia, where production fell by almost 30 percent between 1990 and 1994. The most persistent recession of recent years has been in Japan. The worst recession ever experienced occurred during the 1930s

in an episode called the Great Depression. During this period, production in Canada shrank by 28 percent.

When a recession occurs, unemployment increases. During the Great Depression, almost 20 percent of the labour force in Canada was unable to find jobs. During the recession of the early 1990s, the unemployment rate climbed to 12 percent of the labour force.

What causes the business cycle? What can we do to smooth out the business cycle? Economists remain unsure about the answers to these questions. But in your study of macroeconomics, you will learn what economists have discovered about economic fluctuations.

REVIEW QUIZ

1 What are the three big issues that macroeconomics addresses?
2 What do we mean by the standard of living and what is its range from the richest to the poorest countries?
3 What do we mean by the cost of living? If the cost of living keeps rising, does the standard of living keep falling?
4 What are the phases of the business cycle?

The Economic Way of Thinking

THE DEFINITION OF ECONOMICS AND THE questions of microeconomics and macroeconomics tell you about the *scope of economics.* But they don't tell you how economists *think* about these questions and go about seeking answers to them.

You're now going to begin to see how economists approach economic questions. First, in this section, we'll look at the ideas that define the *economic way of thinking.* This way of thinking needs practice, but it is a powerful way of thinking and as you become more familiar with it, you'll begin to see the world around you with a new and sharp focus.

Choices and Tradeoffs

Because we face scarcity, we must make choices. And when we make a choice, we select from the available alternatives. For example, you can spend the weekend studying for your next economics test and having fun with your friends, but you can't do both of these activities at the same time. You must choose how much time to devote to each. Whatever choice you make, you could have chosen something else instead.

You can think about your choice as a tradeoff. A **tradeoff** is an exchange—giving up one thing to get something else. When you choose how to spend your weekend, you trade off between studying and hanging out with your friends.

Guns Versus Butter The classic tradeoff is guns versus butter. "Guns" and "butter" stand for any pair of goods and services. They might actually be guns and butter. Or they might be broader categories such as peacekeeping and food. Or they might be any pair of specific goods or services such as cola and bottled water, baseball bats and tennis racquets, colleges and hospitals, realty services and career counselling.

Regardless of the specific objects that guns and butter represent, the guns-versus-butter tradeoff captures a hard fact of life: If we want more of one thing, we must trade something else in exchange for it.

The idea of a tradeoff is central to the whole of economics. We can pose all the questions of microeconomics and macroeconomics in terms of tradeoffs. Let's return to these questions and view them in terms of tradeoffs.

Microeconomic Tradeoffs

The questions of what, how, and for whom goods and services are produced all involve tradeoffs that are similar to that of guns versus butter.

"What" Tradeoffs What goods and services get produced depends on choices made by each one of us, by our government, and by the businesses that produce the things we buy. Each of these choices involves a tradeoff.

Each one of us faces a tradeoff when we choose how to spend our income. You go to the movies this week, but you forgo a few cups of coffee to buy the ticket—you trade off coffee for a movie.

The federal government faces a tradeoff when it chooses how to spend our tax dollars. Parliament votes for more hospitals but cuts back on educational programs—Parliament trades off education for hospitals.

Businesses face a tradeoff when they decide what to produce. Nike hires Tiger Woods and allocates resources to designing and marketing a new golf ball but cuts back on its development of a new running shoe—Nike trades off running shoes for golf balls.

"How" Tradeoffs How goods and services get produced depends on choices made by the businesses that produce the things we buy. These choices involve a tradeoff. For example, Tim Hortons opens a new doughnut store with an automated production line and closes an older store with a traditional kitchen. Tim Hortons trades off labour for capital.

"For Whom" Tradeoffs For whom goods and services are produced depends on the distribution of buying power. Buying power can be redistributed—transferred from one person to another—in three ways: by voluntary payments, by theft, or through taxes and benefits organized by government. Redistribution brings tradeoffs.

Each of us faces a tradeoff when, for example, we choose how much to contribute to the United Nations famine relief fund. You donate $50 and cut your spending on other items by that amount. You trade off your own level of spending for a small increase in economic equality.

We make choices that influence redistribution by theft when we vote to make theft illegal and to devote resources to law enforcement. We trade off goods and services for an increase in the security of our property.

We also vote for taxes and social programs that redistribute buying power from the rich to the poor. Government redistribution confronts society with what has been called the **big tradeoff**—the tradeoff between equality and efficiency. Taxing the rich and making transfers to the poor bring greater economic equality. But taxing productive activities such as running a business, working hard, saving, and investing in capital discourages these activities. So taxing productive activities means producing less—it creates inefficiency.

You can think of the big tradeoff as being the problem of how to share a pie that everyone contributes to baking. If each person receives a share of the pie that reflects the size of her or his effort, everyone will work hard and the pie will be as large as possible. But if the pie is shared equally, regardless of contribution, some talented bakers will slacken off and the pie will shrink. The big tradeoff is one between the size of the pie and how equally it is shared. We trade off some efficiency for increased equality.

We've reviewed some microeconomic tradeoffs. Let's now look at some macroeconomic tradeoffs.

Macroeconomic Tradeoffs

The three macroeconomic questions about the standard of living, the cost of living, and the business cycle involve tradeoffs that are similar to that of guns versus butter.

Standard of Living Tradeoffs   The standard of living is higher in Canada than in Africa. And the standard of living improves over time, so today it is higher than it was a generation ago. Our standard of living and its rate of improvement depend on the many choices made by each one of us, by governments, and by businesses. And these choices involve tradeoffs.

One choice is that of how much of our income to consume and how much to save. Our saving can be channelled through the financial system to finance businesses and to pay for new capital that increases productivity. The more we save and invest, the faster our productivity and our standard of living increase. When you decide to save an extra $1,000 and forgo a vacation, you trade off the vacation for a higher future income. If everyone saves an extra $1,000 and businesses invest in more equipment that increases productivity, the average income per person rises and the standard of living improves. As a society, we trade off current consumption for increased productivity and a higher future standard of living.

A second choice is how much effort to devote to education and training. By becoming better educated and more highly skilled, we become more productive and our standard of living rises. When you decide to remain in school for another two years to complete a professional degree and forgo a huge chunk of leisure time, you trade off leisure for a higher future income. If everyone becomes better educated, productivity increases, income per person rises, and the standard of living improves. As a society, we trade off current consumption and leisure time for increased productivity and a higher future standard of living.

A third choice, usually made by businesses, is how much effort to devote to research and the development of new products and production methods. Ford Motor Company can hire engineers to do research on a new robot assembly line or to operate the existing plant and produce cars. More research brings greater productivity in the future but means smaller current production—a tradeoff of current production for greater future production.

Output-Inflation Tradeoff   When policy actions lower the interest rate and speed the pace at which money is created, spending, output, and employment increase. Higher spending brings rising inflation—the cost of living rises more rapidly. Eventually, output returns to its previous level. But the higher inflation rate has been accompanied by a temporary increase in output.

Similarly, when policy actions raise the interest rate and slow the pace at which money is created, spending, output, and employment decrease. Lower spending brings falling inflation—the cost of living rises more slowly. Again, output eventually returns to its previous level and the lower inflation rate has been accompanied by a temporary decrease in output.

When the inflation rate is too high, policy makers would like to lower inflation without lowering output. But they face an **output-inflation tradeoff** because the policy action that lowers inflation also lowers output and a policy action that boosts output increases inflation.

Seeing choices as tradeoffs emphasizes the idea that to get something, we must give up something. What we give up is the *cost* of what we get. Economists call this cost the *opportunity cost*.

Opportunity Cost

The highest-valued alternative that we give up to get something is the **opportunity cost** of the activity chosen. "There's no such thing as a free lunch" is not just a clever throwaway line. It expresses the central idea of economics: that every choice involves a cost.

You can quit school right now, or you can remain in school. If you quit school and take a job at Tim Hortons, you might earn enough to buy some CDs, go to the movies, and spend lots of free time with your friends. If you remain in school, you can't afford these things. You will be able to buy these things later, and that is one of the payoffs from being in school. But for now, when you've bought your books, you might have nothing left for CDs and movies. And doing assignments means that you've got less time for hanging around with your friends. The opportunity cost of being in school is the highest-valued alternative that you would have chosen if you had quit school.

All of the tradeoffs that we've just considered involve opportunity cost. The opportunity cost of some guns is the butter forgone; the opportunity cost of a movie ticket is the number of cups of coffee forgone; the opportunity cost of lower inflation is the output temporarily forgone.

Margins and Incentives

You can allocate the next hour between studying and e-mailing your friends. But the choice is not all or nothing. You must decide how many minutes to allocate to each activity. To make this decision, you compare the benefit of a little bit more study time with its cost—you make your choice at the **margin**.

The benefit that arises from an increase in an activity is called **marginal benefit**. For example, suppose that you're working four nights a week at your courses and your grade point average is 3.0. You decide that you want a higher grade and decide to study an extra night each week. Your grade now rises to 3.5. The marginal benefit from studying for one additional night a week is the 0.5 increase in your grade. It is *not* the 3.5 grade. The reason is that you already have the benefit from studying for four nights a week, so we don't count this benefit as resulting from the decision you are now making.

The cost of an increase in an activity is called **marginal cost**. For you, the marginal cost of increasing your study time by one night a week is the cost of

the additional night not spent with your friends (if that is your best alternative use of the time). It does not include the cost of the four nights you are already studying.

To make your decision, you compare the marginal benefit from an extra night of study with its marginal cost. If the marginal benefit exceeds the marginal cost, you study the extra night. If the marginal cost exceeds the marginal benefit, you do not study the extra night.

By evaluating marginal benefits and marginal costs and choosing only those actions that bring greater benefit than cost, we use our scarce resources in the way that makes us as well off as possible.

Our choices respond to incentives. An **incentive** is an inducement to take a particular action. The inducement can be a benefit—a carrot—or a cost—a stick. A change in marginal cost and a change in marginal benefit change the incentives that we face and lead us to change our choices.

For example, suppose your economics instructor gives you some problem sets and tells you that all the problems will be on the next test. The marginal benefit from working these problems is large, so you diligently work them all. Suppose, in contrast, that your math instructor gives you some problem sets and tells you that none of the problems will be on the next test. The marginal benefit from working these problems is lower, so you skip most of them.

The central idea of economics is that we can predict the way choices will change by looking at changes in incentives. More of an activity is undertaken when its marginal cost falls or its marginal benefit rises; less of an activity is undertaken when its marginal cost rises or its marginal benefit falls.

REVIEW QUIZ

1 What is a tradeoff?
2 Provide three examples of microeconomic tradeoffs.
3 What is the big tradeoff and how does it arise?
4 Provide two examples of macroeconomic tradeoffs.
5 What is the short-run tradeoff of macroeconomics?
6 What is opportunity cost?
7 How do economists predict changes in choices?

Economics: A Social Science

ECONOMICS IS A SOCIAL SCIENCE (ALONG WITH political science, psychology, and sociology). Economists try to discover how the economic world works, and in pursuit of this goal (like all scientists), they distinguish between two types of statements:

- What *is*
- What *ought to be*

Statements about what *is* are called *positive* statements and they might be right or wrong. We can test a positive statement by checking it against the facts. When a chemist does an experiment in a laboratory, she is attempting to check a positive statement against the facts.

Statements about what *ought to be* are called *normative* statements. These statements depend on values and cannot be tested. When Parliament debates a motion, it is ultimately trying to decide what ought to be. It is making a normative statement.

To see the distinction between positive and normative statements, consider the controversy over global warming. Some scientists believe that centuries of the burning of coal and oil are increasing the carbon dioxide content of the earth's atmosphere and leading to higher temperatures that eventually will have devastating consequences for life on this planet. "Our planet is warming because of an increased carbon dioxide buildup in the atmosphere" is a positive statement. It can (in principle and with sufficient data) be tested. "We ought to cut back on our use of carbon-based fuels such as coal and oil" is a normative statement. You can agree or disagree with this statement, but you can't test it. It is based on values. Health-care reform provides an economic example of the distinction. "Universal health care cuts the amount of work time lost to illness" is a positive statement. "All Canadians should have equal access to health care" is a normative statement.

The task of economic science is to discover positive statements that are consistent with what we observe and that help us to understand the economic world. This task can be broken into three steps:

- Observation and measurement
- Model building
- Testing models

Observation and Measurement

Economists observe and measure data on such things as natural and human resources, wages and work hours, the prices and quantities of the different goods and services produced, taxes and government spending, and the quantities of goods and services bought from and sold to other countries.

Model Building

The second step towards understanding how the economic world works is to build a model. An **economic model** is a description of some aspect of the economic world that includes only those features of the world that are needed for the purpose at hand. A model is simpler than the reality it describes. What a model includes and what it leaves out result from assumptions about what is essential and what are inessential details.

You can see how ignoring details is useful—even essential—to our understanding by thinking about a model that you see every day: the TV weather map. The weather map is a model that helps to predict the temperature, wind speed and direction, and precipitation over a future period. The weather map shows lines called isobars—lines of equal barometric pressure. It doesn't show the highways. The reason is that our theory of the weather tells us that the pattern of air pressure, not the location of the highways, determines the weather.

An economic model is similar to a weather map. It tells us how a number of variables are determined by a number of other variables. For example, an economic model of Vancouver's bid for the 2010 Winter Olympic Games might tell us the effects of the games on the number of houses and apartments, rents and prices, jobs, transportation facilities, and the outputs and profits of the businesses in the region.

Testing Models

The third step is testing the model. A model's predictions might correspond to the facts or be in conflict with them. By comparing the model's predictions with the facts, we can test a model and develop an economic theory. An **economic theory** is a generalization that summarizes what we think we understand about the economic choices that people make and the performance of industries and entire economies. It is a bridge between an economic model and the real economy.

The process of building and testing models creates theories. For example, meteorologists have a theory that if the isobars form a particular pattern at a particular time of the year (a model), then it will snow (reality). They have developed this theory by repeated observation and by carefully recording the weather that follows specific pressure patterns.

Economics is a young science. It was born in 1776 with the publication of Adam Smith's *Wealth of Nations* (see p. 54). Over the years since then, economists have discovered many useful theories. But in many areas, economists are still looking for answers. The gradual accumulation of economic knowledge gives most economists some faith that their methods will, eventually, provide usable answers to the big economic questions.

But progress in economics comes slowly. Let's look at some of the obstacles to progress in economics.

Obstacles and Pitfalls in Economics

We cannot easily do economic experiments. And most economic behaviour has many simultaneous causes. For these two reasons, it is difficult in economics to unscramble cause and effect.

Unscrambling Cause and Effect By changing one factor at a time and holding all the other relevant factors constant, we isolate the factor of interest and are able to investigate its effects in the clearest possible way. This logical device, which all scientists use to identify cause and effect, is called *ceteris paribus*. **Ceteris paribus** is a Latin term that means "other things being equal" or "if all other relevant things remain the same." Ensuring that other things are equal is crucial in many activities, and all successful attempts to make scientific progress use this device.

Economic models (like the models in all other sciences) enable the influence of one factor at a time to be isolated in the imaginary world of the model. When we use a model, we are able to imagine what would happen if only one factor changed. But *ceteris paribus* can be a problem in economics when we try to test a model.

Laboratory scientists, such as chemists and physicists, perform experiments by actually holding all the relevant factors constant except for the one under investigation. In non-experimental sciences such as economics (and astronomy), we usually observe the outcomes of the simultaneous operation

of many factors. Consequently, it is hard to sort out the effects of each individual factor and to compare them with what a model predicts. To cope with this problem, economists take three complementary approaches.

First, they look for pairs of events in which other things were equal (or similar). An example might be to study the effects of unemployment benefits on the unemployment rate by comparing the United States with Canada on the presumption that the people in the two economies are sufficiently similar. Second, economists use statistical tools—called econometrics. Third, when they can, they perform experiments. This relatively new approach puts real subjects (usually students) in a decision-making situation and varies their incentives in some way to discover how they respond to a change in one factor at a time.

Economists try to avoid fallacies—errors of reasoning that lead to a wrong conclusion. But two fallacies are common, and you need to be on your guard to avoid them. They are the

- Fallacy of composition
- *Post hoc* fallacy

Fallacy of Composition The fallacy of composition is the (false) statement that what is true of the parts is true of the whole or that what is true of the whole is true of the parts. Think of the true statement "Speed kills" and its implication: Going more slowly saves lives. If an entire highway moves at a lower speed, everyone on the highway has a safer ride.

But suppose that only one driver slows down and all the other drivers try to maintain their original speed. In this situation, there will probably be more accidents because more cars will change lanes to overtake the slower vehicle. So in this example, what is true for the whole is not true for a part.

The fallacy of composition arises mainly in macroeconomics, and it stems from the fact that the parts interact with each other to produce an outcome for the whole that might differ from the intent of the parts. For example, a firm lays off some workers to cut costs and improve its profits. If all firms take similar actions, income falls and so does spending. The firm sells less, and its profits don't improve.

Post Hoc Fallacy Another Latin phrase—*post hoc, ergo propter hoc*—means "after this, therefore because of this." The *post hoc* fallacy is the error of reasoning that a first event *causes* a second event because the first occurred before the second. Suppose you are a visitor from a far-off world. You observe lots of people shopping in early December, and then you see them opening gifts and partying in the holiday season. You wonder, "Does the shopping cause the holiday season?" After a deeper study, you discover that the holiday season causes the shopping. A later event causes an earlier event.

Unravelling cause and effect is difficult in economics. And just looking at the timing of events often doesn't help. For example, the stock market booms, and some months later the economy expands—jobs and incomes grow. Did the stock market boom cause the economy to expand? Possibly, but perhaps businesses started to plan the expansion of production because a new technology that lowered costs had become available. As knowledge of the plans spread, the stock market reacted to *anticipate* the economic expansion. To disentangle cause and effect, economists use economic models and data and, to the extent that they can, perform experiments.

Economics is a challenging science. Does the difficulty of getting answers in economics mean that anything goes and that economists disagree on most questions? Perhaps you've heard the joke "If you laid all the economists in the world end to end, they still wouldn't reach agreement." Surprisingly, perhaps, the joke does not describe reality.

Agreement and Disagreement

Economists agree on a remarkably wide range of questions. And often the agreed-upon view of economists disagrees with the popular and sometimes politically correct view. When Bank of Canada Governor David Dodge testifies before Parliament, his words are rarely controversial among economists, even when they generate endless debate in the press and Parliament.

Here are 12 propositions with which at least 7 out of every 10 economists broadly agree:

- Tariffs and import restrictions make most people worse off.
- A large budget deficit has an adverse effect on the economy.
- A minimum wage increases unemployment among young workers and low-skilled workers.

- Cash payments to welfare recipients make them better off than do transfers-in-kind of equal cash value.
- A tax cut can help to lower unemployment when the unemployment rate is high.
- The distribution of income should be more equal.
- Inflation is primarily caused by a rapid rate of money creation.
- The government should restructure welfare along the lines of a "negative income tax."
- Rent ceilings cut the availability of housing.
- Pollution taxes are more effective than pollution limits.
- The redistribution of income is a legitimate role for the government.
- The federal budget should be balanced on the average over the business cycle but not every year.

Which of these propositions are positive and which are normative? Notice that economists are willing to offer their opinions on normative issues as well as their professional views on positive questions. Be on the lookout for normative propositions dressed up as positive propositions.

REVIEW QUIZ

1 What is the distinction between a positive statement and a normative statement? Provide an example (different from those in the chapter) of each type of statement.
2 What is a model? Can you think of a model that you might use (probably without thinking of it as a model) in your everyday life?
3 What is a theory? Why is the statement "It might work in theory, but it doesn't work in practice" a silly statement?
4 What is the *ceteris paribus* assumption and how is it used?
5 Try to think of some everyday examples of the fallacy of composition and the *post hoc* fallacy.

SUMMARY

KEY POINTS

Definition of Economics (p. 2)

- All economic questions arise from scarcity—from the fact that wants exceed the resources available to satisfy them.
- Economics is the social science that studies the choices that people make as they cope with scarcity.
- The subject divides into microeconomics and macroeconomics.

Three Big Microeconomic Questions (pp. 3–5)

- Three big questions that summarize the scope of microeconomics are
  1. What goods and services are produced?
  2. How are goods and services produced?
  3. For whom are goods and services produced?

Three Big Macroeconomic Questions (pp. 6–8)

- Three big questions that summarize the scope of macroeconomics are
  1. What determines the standard of living?
  2. What determines the cost of living?
  3. Why does our economy fluctuate?

The Economic Way of Thinking (pp. 9–11)

- Every choice is a tradeoff—exchanging more of something for less of something else.
- The classic guns-versus-butter tradeoff represents all tradeoffs.
- All economic questions involve tradeoffs.
- The big social tradeoff is that between equality and efficiency.
- A macroeconomic tradeoff is the short-run tradeoff between output and inflation.
- The highest-valued alternative forgone is the opportunity cost of what is chosen.
- Choices are made at the margin and respond to incentives.

Economics: A Social Science (pp. 12–14)

- Economists distinguish between positive statements—what *is*—and normative statements—what *ought* to be.
- To explain the economic world, economists develop theories by building and testing economic models.
- Economists use the *ceteris paribus* assumption to try to disentangle cause and effect and are careful to avoid the fallacy of composition and the *post hoc* fallacy.
- Economists agree on a wide range of questions about how the economy works.

KEY TERMS

Big tradeoff, 10
Business cycle, 8
Capital, 4
Ceteris paribus, 13
Cost of living, 7
Deflation, 7
Economic model, 12
Economics, 2
Economic theory, 12
Entrepreneurship, 4
Factors of production, 4
Goods and services, 3
Human capital, 4
Incentive, 11
Inflation, 7
Interest, 5
Labour, 4
Land, 4
Macroeconomics, 2
Margin, 11
Marginal benefit, 11
Marginal cost, 11
Microeconomics,2
Opportunity cost, 11
Output-inflation tradeoff, 10
Profit, 5
Rent, 5
Scarcity, 2
Standard of living, 6
Tradeoff, 9
Wages, 5

PROBLEMS

*1. Your friends go the movies one evening and you decide to stay home and do your economics assignment and practice test. You get 80 percent on your next economics exam compared with the 70 percent that you normally score. What is the opportunity cost of your extra points?

2. You go to the movies one evening instead of doing your economics assignment and practice test. You get 50 percent on your next economics exam compared with the 70 percent that you normally score. What is the opportunity cost of going to the movies?

*3. You plan to go to school this summer. If you do, you won't be able to take your usual job that pays $6,000 for the summer, and you won't be able to live at home for free. The cost of tuition is $2,000 and the cost of textbooks is $200, and living expenses are $1,400. What is the opportunity cost of going to summer school?

4. You plan to go skiing next weekend. If you do, you'll have to miss doing your usual weekend job that pays $100, you won't be able to study for 8 hours, and you won't be able to use your prepaid college meal plan. The cost of travel and accommodation will be $350, the cost of renting skis is $60, and your food will cost $40. What is the opportunity cost of the weekend ski trip?

*5. The local mall has free parking, but the mall is always very busy, and it usually takes 30 minutes to find a parking space. Today when you found a vacant spot, Harry also wanted it. Is parking really free at this mall? If not, what did it cost you to park today? When you parked your car today, did you impose any costs on Harry? Explain your answers.

6. The university has built a new movie theatre. Admission for students is free and there are always plenty of empty seats. But when the theatre screened *The Lord of the Rings*, the lines were long. So the theatre decided to charge $4 per student. Cadbury Schweppes offered students a free soft drink. Compare a student's opportunity cost of seeing the movie *The Lord of the Rings* with that of any other movie screened this year. Which is less costly and by how much?

*You can obtain the solutions to the odd-numbered problems on the Parkin–Bade Web site.

CRITICAL THINKING

1. Use the three big questions of microeconomics, the three big questions of macroeconomics, and the economic way of thinking to organize a short essay about the economic life of a homeless man. Does he face scarcity? Does he make choices? Can you interpret his choices as being in his own best interest? Can either his own choices or the choices of others make him better off? If so, how?

WEB EXERCISES

1. Use the link on the Parkin–Bade Web site to visit the CBC.
   a. What is the top economic news story today?
   b. With which of the big questions does it deal? (It must deal with at least one of them and might deal with more than one.)
   c. What tradeoffs does the news item discuss?
   d. Write a brief summary of the news item in a few bulleted points using as much as possible of the economic vocabulary that you have learned in this chapter and that is in the key terms list on p. 15.

2. Use the link on the Parkin–Bade Web site to visit *Resources For Economists on the Internet*. This site is a good place from which to search for economic information on the Internet.
   a. Scroll down the page and click on General Interest.
   b. Visit the "general interest" sites and become familiar with the types of information they contain.

3. Use the link on the Parkin–Bade Web site to visit Statistics Canada.
   a. What is the number of people employed (non-farm employment) in your area?
   b. Has employment increased or decreased?
   c. What is income per person (per capita income) in your area?

APPENDIX

Graphs in Economics

After studying this appendix, you will be able to

- ■ Make and interpret a time-series graph, a cross-section graph, and a scatter diagram
- ■ Distinguish between linear and nonlinear relationships and between relationships that have a maximum and a minimum
- ■ Define and calculate the slope of a line
- ■ Graph relationships among more than two variables

Graphing Data

A GRAPH REPRESENTS A QUANTITY AS A DISTANCE on a line. Figure A1.1 shows two examples. Here, a distance on the horizontal line represents temperature, measured in degrees Celsius. A movement from left to right shows an increase in temperature. The point marked 0 represents zero degrees Celsius. To the right of 0, the temperature is positive. To the left of 0 (as indicated by the minus sign), the temperature is negative. A distance on the vertical line represents altitude or height, measured in thousands of metres above sea level. The point marked 0 represents sea level. Points above 0 represent metres above sea level. Points below 0 (indicated by a minus sign) represent metres below sea level.

By setting two scales perpendicular to each other, as in Fig. A1.1, we can visualize the relationship between two variables. The scale lines are called *axes*. The vertical line is the *y-axis*, and the horizontal line is the *x-axis*. Each axis has a zero point, which is shared by the two axes. This zero point, common to both axes, is called the *origin*.

To show something in a two-variable graph, we need two pieces of information: the value of the *x*-variable and the value of the *y*-variable. For example, off the coast of British Columbia on a winter's day, the temperature is 10 degrees—the value of *x*. A fishing boat is located at 0 metres above sea level—the value of *y*. These two bits of information appear as point *A* in Fig. A1.1. A climber at the top of Mt. McKinley on a cold day is 6,194 metres above sea level in a zero-degree gale. These two pieces of information appear as point *B*. The position of the

FIGURE A1.1 Making a Graph

Graphs have axes that measure quantities as distances. Here, the horizontal axis (*x*-axis) measures temperature, and the vertical axis (*y*-axis) measures height. Point *A* represents a fishing boat at sea level (0 on the *y*-axis) on a day when the temperature is 10°C. Point *B* represents a climber on Mt. McKinley, 6,194 metres above sea level, at a temperature of 0°C. Point *C* represents a climber on Mt. McKinley, 6,194 metres above sea level, at a temperature of 10°C.

climber on a warmer day might be at the point marked *C*. This point represents the peak of Mt. McKinley at a temperature of 10 degrees.

We can draw two lines, called *coordinates*, from point *C*. One, called the *y*-coordinate, runs from *C* to the horizontal axis. Its length is the same as the value marked off on the *y*-axis. The other, called the *x*-coordinate, runs from *C* to the vertical axis. Its length is the same as the value marked off on the *x*-axis. We describe a point in a graph by the values of its *x*-coordinate and its *y*-coordinate.

Graphs like that in Fig. A1.1 can show any type of quantitative data on two variables. Economists use three types of graphs based on the principles in Fig. A1.1 to reveal and describe the relationships among variables. They are

- ■ Time-series graphs
- ■ Cross-section graphs
- ■ Scatter diagrams

17

Time-Series Graphs

A **time-series graph** measures time (for example, months or years) on the x-axis and the variable or variables in which we are interested on the y-axis. Figures 1.2 and 1.3 on pp. 3 and 4 are examples of time-series graphs. So is Fig. A1.2, which provides some information about the price of coffee.

In Fig. A1.2, we measure time in years running from 1971 to 2001. We measure the price of coffee (the variable that we are interested in) on the y-axis.

The point of a time-series graph is to enable us to visualize how a variable has changed over time and how its value in one period relates to its value in another period.

A time-series graph conveys an enormous amount of information quickly and easily, as this example illustrates. It shows

- The *level* of the price of coffee—when it is *high* and *low*. When the line is a long way from the x-axis, the price is high. When the line is close to the x-axis, the price is low.

- How the price *changes*—whether it *rises* or *falls*. When the line slopes upward, as in 1976, the price is rising. When the line slopes downward, as in 1978, the price is falling.

- The *speed* with which the price changes—whether it rises or falls *quickly* or *slowly*. If the line is very steep, then the price rises or falls quickly. If the line is not steep, the price rises or falls slowly. For example, the price rose quickly in 1976 and 1977 and slowly in 1983. The price fell quickly in 1978 and slowly in 1984.

A time-series graph also reveals whether there is a trend. A **trend** is a general tendency for a variable to move in one direction. A trend might be upward or downward. In Fig. A1.2, you can see that the price of coffee had a general tendency to fall from the late 1970s to the early 1990s. That is, although the price rose and fell, the general tendency was for it to fall—the price had a downward trend.

A time-series graph also helps us detect cycles in variables. You can see some peaks and troughs in the price of coffee in Fig. A1.2. Figure 1.6 on p. 8 illustrates the business cycle. We rarely see a cycle as clear as the one shown in that figure.

Finally, a time-series graph also lets us compare the variable in different periods quickly. Figure A1.2 shows that the 1980s were different from the

FIGURE A1.2   A Time-Series Graph

A time-series graph plots the level of a variable on the y-axis against time (day, week, month, or year) on the x-axis. This graph shows the price of coffee (in 1996 dollars per kilogram) each year from 1971 to 2001. It shows us when the price of coffee was *high* and when it was *low*, when the price *increased* and when it *decreased*, and when it changed *quickly* and when it changed *slowly*.

1970s. The price of coffee fluctuated more violently in the 1970s than it did in the 1980s.

You can see that a time-series graph conveys a wealth of information. And it does so in much less space than we have used to describe only some of its features. But you do have to "read" the graph to obtain all this information.

Cross-Section Graphs

A **cross-section graph** shows the values of an economic variable for different groups in a population at a point in time. Figure 1.4 on p. 5, called a *bar chart*, is an example of a cross-section graph. Figure A1.3 shows another example.

The bar chart in Fig. A1.3 shows the number of visitors to each province in 1999. The length of each bar indicates the number of visitors. This figure enables you to compare the number of visitors across the provinces. And you can do so much more quickly and clearly than you could by looking at a list of numbers.

FIGURE A1.3   A Cross-Section Graph

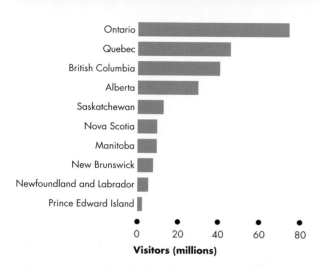

A cross-section graph shows the level of a variable across the members of a population. This bar chart shows the number of visitors to each province in 1999.

Scatter Diagrams

A **scatter diagram** plots the value of one variable against the value of another variable. Such a graph reveals whether a relationship exists between two variables and describes their relationship. Figure A1.4(a) shows the relationship between expenditure and income. Each point shows expenditure per person and income per person in a given year from 1984 to 2001. The points are "scattered" within the graph. The point labelled *A* tells us that in 1996, income per person was $18,095 and expenditure per person was $16,450. The dots in this graph form a pattern, which reveals that as income increases, expenditure increases.

Figure A1.4(b) shows the relationship between the number of international phone calls and the price of a call. This graph show that as the price per minute falls, the number of calls increases.

Figure A1.4(c) shows a scatter diagram of inflation and unemployment in Canada. Here, the dots show no clear relationship between these two variables. The dots in this graph reveal that there is no simple relationship between these variables.

FIGURE A1.4   Scatter Diagrams

(a) Expenditure and income

(b) International phone calls and prices

(c) Unemployment and inflation

A scatter diagram reveals the relationship between two variables. Part (a) shows the relationship between expenditure and income. Each point shows the values of the two variables in a specific year. For example, point A shows that in 1996, average income was $18,095 and average expenditure was $16,450. The pattern formed by the points shows that as income increases, expenditure increases.

Part (b) shows the relationship between the price of an international phone call and the number of calls made. This graph shows that as the price of a phone call falls, the number of calls made increases. Part (c) shows a scatter diagram of the inflation rate and unemployment rate in Canada. This graph shows that the inflation rate and the unemployment rate are not closely related.

Breaks in the Axes Two of the graphs you've just looked at, Fig. A1.4(a) and Fig. A1.4(c), have breaks in their axes, as shown by the small gaps. The breaks indicate that there are jumps from the origin, 0, to the first values recorded.

In Fig. A1.4(a), the breaks are used because the lowest value of expenditure exceeds $13,000 and the lowest value of income exceeds $17,000. With no breaks in the axes of this graph, there would be a lot of empty space, all the points would be crowded into the top right corner, and we would not be able to see whether a relationship exists between these two variables. By breaking the axes, we are able to bring the relationship into view.

Putting a break in the axes is like using a zoom lens to bring the relationship into the centre of the graph and magnify it so that it fills the graph.

Misleading Graphs Breaks can be used to highlight a relationship. But they can also be used to mislead—to make a graph that lies. The most common way of making a graph lie is to use axis breaks and either to stretch or to compress a scale. For example, suppose that in Fig. A1.4(a), the *y*-axis ran from zero to $45,000 while the *x*-axis was the same as the one shown. The graph would now create the impression that despite a huge increase in income, expenditure had barely changed.

To avoid being misled, it is a good idea to get into the habit of always looking closely at the values and the labels on the axes of a graph before you start to interpret it.

Correlation and Causation A scatter diagram that shows a clear relationship between two variables, such as Fig. A1.4(a) or Fig. A1.4(b), tells us that the two variables have a high correlation. When a high correlation is present, we can predict the value of one variable from the value of the other variable. But correlation does not imply causation.

Sometimes a high correlation is a coincidence, but sometimes it does arise from a causal relationship. It is likely, for example, that rising income causes rising expenditure (Fig. A1.4a) and that the falling price of a phone call causes more calls to be made (Fig. A1.4b).

You've now seen how we can use graphs in economics to show economic data and to reveal relationships between variables. Next, we'll learn how economists use graphs to construct and display economic models.

Graphs Used in Economic Models

THE GRAPHS USED IN ECONOMICS ARE NOT always designed to show real-world data. Often they are used to show general relationships among the variables in an economic model.

An *economic model* is a stripped down, simplified description of an economy or of a component of an economy, such as a business or a household. It consists of statements about economic behaviour that can be expressed as equations or as curves in a graph. Economists use models to explore the effects of different policies or other influences on the economy in ways that are similar to the use of model airplanes in wind tunnels and models of the climate.

You will encounter many different kinds of graphs in economic models, but there are some repeating patterns. Once you've learned to recognize these patterns, you will instantly understand the meaning of a graph. Here, we'll look at the different types of curves that are used in economic models, and we'll see some everyday examples of each type of curve. The patterns to look for in graphs are the four cases:

- Variables that move in the same direction
- Variables that move in opposite directions
- Variables that have a maximum or a minimum
- Variables that are unrelated

Let's look at these four cases.

Variables That Move in the Same Direction

Figure A1.5 shows graphs of the relationships between two variables that move up and down together. A relationship between two variables that move in the same direction is called a **positive relationship** or a **direct relationship.** A line that slopes upward shows such a relationship.

Figure A1.5 shows three types of relationships: one that has a straight line and two that have curved lines. But all the lines in these three graphs are called curves. Any line on a graph—no matter whether it is straight or curved—is called a *curve*.

A relationship shown by a straight line is called a **linear relationship**. Figure A1.5(a) shows a linear rela-

FIGURE A1.5   Positive (Direct) Relationships

(a) Positive, linear relationship

(b) Positive, becoming steeper

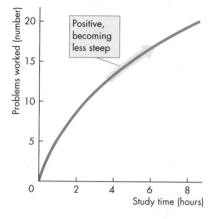

(c) Positive, becoming less steep

Each part of this figure shows a positive (direct) relationship between two variables. That is, as the value of the variable measured on the *x*-axis increases, so does the value of the variable measured on the *y*-axis. Part (a) shows a linear relationship—as the two variables increase together, we move along a straight line. Part (b) shows a positive relationship such that as the two variables increase together, we move along a curve that becomes steeper. Part (c) shows a positive relationship such that as the two variables increase together, we move along a curve that becomes less steep.

tionship between the number of kilometres travelled in 5 hours and speed. For example, point *A* shows that we will travel 200 kilometres in 5 hours if our speed is 40 kilometres an hour. If we double our speed to 80 kilometres an hour, we will travel 400 kilometres in 5 hours.

Figure A1.5(b) shows the relationship between distance sprinted and recovery time (the time it takes the heart rate to return to its normal resting value). This relationship is an upward-sloping one that starts out quite flat but then becomes steeper as we move along the curve away from the origin. The reason this curve slopes upward and becomes steeper is because the additional recovery time needed from sprinting an additional 100 metres increases. It takes less than 5 minutes to recover from the first 100 metres, but it takes more than 10 minutes to recover from the second 100 metres.

Figure A1.5(c) shows the relationship between the number of problems worked by a student and the amount of study time. This relationship is an upward-sloping one that starts out quite steep and becomes flatter as we move away from the origin. Study time becomes less productive as the student spends more hours studying and become more tired.

Variables That Move in Opposite Directions

Figure A1.6 shows relationships between things that move in opposite directions. A relationship between variables that move in opposite directions is called a **negative relationship** or an **inverse relationship**.

Figure A1.6(a) shows the relationship between the number of hours available for playing squash and the number of hours for playing tennis when the total is 5 hours. One extra hour spent playing tennis means one hour less playing squash and vice versa. This relationship is negative and linear.

Figure A1.6(b) shows the relationship between the cost per kilometre travelled and the length of a journey. The longer the journey, the lower is the cost per kilometre. But as the journey length increases, the cost per kilometre decreases, and the fall in the cost is smaller, the longer the journey. This feature of the relationship is shown by the fact that the curve slopes downward, starting out steep at a short journey length and then becoming flatter as the journey length increases. This relationship arises because some of the costs are fixed (such as auto insurance), and the fixed cost is spread over a longer journey.

FIGURE A1.6   Negative (Inverse) Relationships

(a) Negative, linear relationship

(b) Negative, becoming less steep

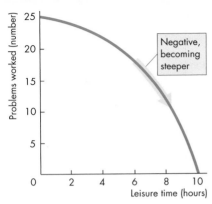

(c) Negative, becoming steeper

Each part of this figure shows a negative (inverse) relationship between two variables. That is, as the value of the variable measured on the *x*-axis increases, the value of the variable measured on the *y*-axis decreases. Part (a) shows a linear relationship. The total time spent playing tennis and squash is 5 hours. As the time spent playing tennis increases, the time spent playing squash decreases, and we move along a straight line. Part (b) shows a negative relationship such that as the journey length increases, the curve becomes less steep. Part (c) shows a negative relationship such that as leisure time increases, the curve becomes steeper.

Figure A1.6(c) shows the relationship between the amount of leisure time and the number of problems worked by a student. Increasing leisure time produces an increasingly large reduction in the number of problems worked. This relationship is a negative one that starts out with a gentle slope at a small number of leisure hours and becomes steeper as the number of leisure hours increases. This relationship is a different view of the idea shown in Fig. A1.5(c).

Variables That Have a Maximum or a Minimum

Many relationships in economic models have a maximum or a minimum. For example, firms try to make the maximum possible profit and to produce at the lowest possible cost. Figure A1.7 shows relationships that have a maximum or a minimum.

Figure A1.7(a) shows the relationship between rainfall and wheat yield. When there is no rainfall, wheat will not grow, so the yield is zero. As the rainfall increases up to 10 days a month, the wheat yield increases. With 10 rainy days each month, the wheat yield reaches its maximum at 2 tonnes per hectare (point *A*). Rain in excess of 10 days a month starts to lower the yield of wheat. If every day is rainy, the wheat suffers from a lack of sunshine and the yield decreases to zero. This relationship is one that starts out sloping upward, reaches a maximum, and then slopes downward.

Figure A1.7(b) shows the reverse case—a relationship that begins sloping downward, falls to a minimum, and then slopes upward. Most economic costs are like this relationship. An example is the relationship between the cost per kilometre and speed for a car trip. At low speeds, the car is creeping in a traffic jam. The number of kilometres per litre is low, so the cost per kilometre is high. At high speeds, the car is travelling faster than its efficient speed, using a large quantity of gasoline, and again the number of kilometres per litre is low and the cost per kilometre is high. At a speed of 100 kilometres an hour, the cost per kilometre is at its minimum (point *B*). This relationship is one that starts out sloping downward, reaches a minimum, and then slopes upward.

FIGURE A1.7   Maximum and Minimum Points

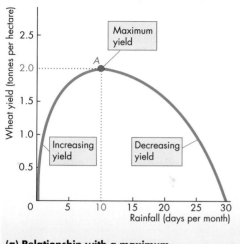

(a) Relationship with a maximum

(b) Relationship with a minimum

Part (a) shows a relationship that has a maximum point, A. The curve slopes upward as it rises to its maximum point, is flat at its maximum, and then slopes downward.

Part (b) shows a relationship with a minimum point, B. The curve slopes downward as it falls to its minimum, is flat at its minimum, and then slopes upward.

Variables That Are Unrelated

There are many situations in which no matter what happens to the value of one variable, the other variable remains constant. Sometimes we want to show the independence between two variables in a graph, and Fig. A1.8 shows two ways of achieving this.

In describing the graphs in Fig. A1.5 through A1.7, we have talked about curves that slope upward and downward, and curves that become less steep or steeper. Let's spend a little time discussing exactly what we mean by slope and how we measure the slope of a curve.

FIGURE A1.8   Variables That Are Unrelated

(a) Unrelated: y constant

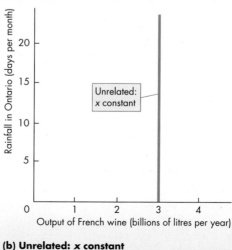

(b) Unrelated: x constant

This figure shows how we can graph two variables that are unrelated. In part (a), a student's grade in economics is plotted at 75 percent on the y-axis regardless of the price of bananas on the x-axis. The curve is horizontal.

In part (b), the output of the vineyards of France on the x-axis does not vary with the rainfall in Ontario on the y-axis. The curve is vertical.

The Slope of a Relationship

WE CAN MEASURE THE INFLUENCE OF ONE variable on another by the slope of the relationship. The **slope** of a relationship is the change in the value of the variable measured on the y-axis divided by the change in the value of the variable measured on the x-axis. We use the Greek letter Δ (*delta*) to represent "change in." Thus Δy means the change in the value of the variable measured on the y-axis, and Δx means the change in the value of the variable measured on the x-axis. Therefore the slope of the relationship is

$$\Delta y / \Delta x$$

If a large change in the variable measured on the y-axis (Δy) is associated with a small change in the variable measured on the x-axis (Δx), the slope is large and the curve is steep. If a small change in the variable measured on the y-axis (Δy) is associated with a large change in the variable measured on the x-axis (Δx), the slope is small and the curve is flat.

We can make the idea of slope sharper by doing some calculations.

The Slope of a Straight Line

The slope of a straight line is the same regardless of where on the line you calculate it. The slope of a straight line is constant. Let's calculate the slopes of the lines in Fig. A1.9. In part (a), when x increases from 2 to 6, y increases from 3 to 6. The change in x

---

FIGURE A1.9   The Slope of a Straight Line

(a) Positive slope

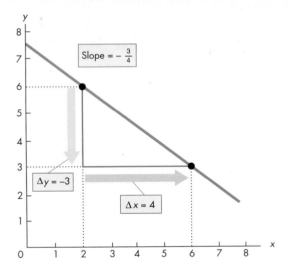

(b) Negative slope

To calculate the slope of a straight line, we divide the change in the value of the variable measured on the y-axis (Δy) by the change in the value of the variable measured on the x-axis (Δx), as we move along the curve. Part (a) shows the calculation of a positive slope. When x increases from 2 to 6, Δx equals 4. That change in x brings about an increase in y from 3 to 6, so Δy equals 3. The slope ($\Delta y/\Delta x$) equals 3/4. Part (b) shows the calculation of a negative slope. When x increases from 2 to 6, Δx equals 4. That increase in x brings about a decrease in y from 6 to 3, so Δy equals −3. The slope ($\Delta y/\Delta x$) equals −3/4.

is +4—that is, Δx is 4. The change in y is +3—that is, Δy is 3. The slope of that line is

$$\frac{\Delta y}{\Delta x} = \frac{3}{4}.$$

In part (b), when x increases from 2 to 6, y decreases from 6 to 3. The change in y is *minus* 3—that is, Δy is –3. The change in x is *plus* 4—that is, Δx is 4. The slope of the curve is

$$\frac{\Delta y}{\Delta x} = \frac{-3}{4}.$$

Notice that the two slopes have the same magnitude (3/4) but the slope of the line in part (a) is positive (+3/+4 = 3/4), while that in part (b) is negative (–3/+4 = –3/4). The slope of a positive relationship is positive; the slope of a negative relationship is negative.

The Slope of a Curved Line

The slope of a curved line is trickier. The slope of a curved line is not constant. Its slope depends on where on the line we calculate it. There are two ways to calculate the slope of a curved line: You can calculate the slope at a point, or you can calculate the slope across an arc of the curve. Let's look at the two alternatives.

Slope at a Point   To calculate the slope at a point on a curve, you need to construct a straight line that has the same slope as the curve at the point in question. Figure A1.10 shows how this is done. Suppose you want to calculate the slope of the curve at point A. Place a ruler on the graph so that it touches point A and no other point on the curve, then draw a straight line along the edge of the ruler. The straight red line is this line, and it is the tangent to the curve at point A. If the ruler touches the curve only at point A, then the slope of the curve at point A must be the same as the slope of the edge of the ruler. If the curve and the ruler do not have the same slope, the line along the edge of the ruler will cut the curve instead of just touching it.

Now that you have found a straight line with the same slope as the curve at point A, you can calculate the slope of the curve at point A by calculating the slope of the straight line. Along the straight line, as x

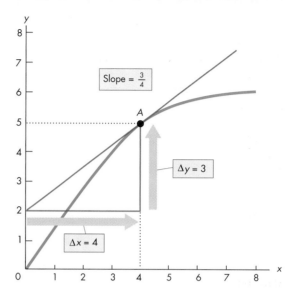

FIGURE A1.10   Slope at a Point

Slope = $\frac{3}{4}$

A

$\Delta y = 3$

$\Delta x = 4$

To calculate the slope of the curve at point A, draw the red line that just touches the curve at A—the tangent. The slope of this straight line is calculated by dividing the change in y by the change in x along the red line. When x increases from 0 to 4, Δx equals 4. That change in x is associated with an increase in y from 2 to 5, so Δy equals 3. The slope of the red line is 3/4. So the slope of the curve at point A is 3/4.

increases from 0 to 4 ($\Delta x = 4$) y increases from 2 to 5 ($\Delta y = 3$). Therefore the slope of the line is

$$\frac{\Delta y}{\Delta x} = \frac{3}{4}.$$

Thus the slope of the curve at point A is 3/4.

Slope Across an Arc   An arc of a curve is a piece of a curve. In Fig. A1.11, you are looking at the same curve as in Fig. A1.10. But instead of calculating the slope at point A, we are going to calculate the slope across the arc from B to C. You can see that the slope at B is greater than at C. When we calculate the slope across an arc, we are calculating the average slope between two points. As we move along the arc from B to C, x increases from 3 to 5 and y increases from 4 to 5.5. The change in x is 2 ($\Delta x = 2$), and the change

FIGURE A1.11   Slope Across an Arc

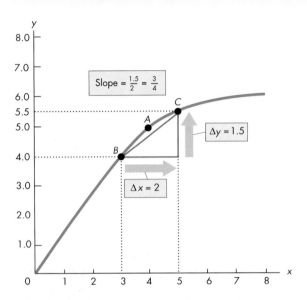

To calculate the average slope of the curve along the arc BC, draw a straight line from B to C. The slope of the line BC is calculated by dividing the change in y by the change in x. In moving from B to C, Δx equals 2 and Δy equals 1.5. The slope of the line BC is 1.5 divided by 2, or 3/4. So the slope of the curve across the arc BC is 3/4.

in y is 1.5 ($\Delta y = 1.5$). Therefore the slope of the line is

$$\frac{\Delta y}{\Delta x} = \frac{1.5}{2} = \frac{3}{4}.$$

Thus the slope of the curve across the arc BC is 3/4.

This calculation gives us the slope of the curve between points B and C. The actual slope calculated is the slope of the straight line from B to C. This slope approximates the average slope of the curve along the arc BC. In this particular example, the slope across the arc BC is identical to the slope of the curve at point A. But the calculation of the slope of a curve does not always work out so neatly. You might have some fun constructing some more examples and some counterexamples.

You now know how to make and interpret a graph. But so far, we've limited our attention to graphs of two variables. We're now going to learn how to graph more than two variables.

Graphing Relationships Among More Than Two Variables

WE HAVE SEEN THAT WE CAN GRAPH THE relationship between two variables as a point formed by the x- and y-coordinates in a two-dimensional graph. You may be thinking that although a two-dimensional graph is informative, most of the things in which you are likely to be interested involve relationships among many variables, not just two. For example, the amount of ice cream consumed depends on the price of ice cream and the temperature. If ice cream is expensive and the temperature is low, people eat much less ice cream than when ice cream is inexpensive and the temperature is high. For any given price of ice cream, the quantity consumed varies with the temperature; and for any given temperature, the quantity of ice cream consumed varies with its price.

Figure A1.12 shows a relationship among three variables. The table shows the number of litres of ice cream consumed each day at various temperatures and ice cream prices. How can we graph these numbers?

To graph a relationship that involves more than two variables, we use the *ceteris paribus* assumption.

Ceteris Paribus   We noted in the chapter (see p. 13) that every laboratory experiment is an attempt to create *ceteris paribus* and isolate the relationship of interest. We use the same method to make a graph when more than two variables are involved.

Figure A1.12(a) shows an example. There, you can see what happens to the quantity of ice cream consumed when the price of ice cream varies and the temperature is held constant. The line labelled 21°C shows the relationship between ice cream consumption and the price of ice cream if the temperature remains at 21°C. The numbers used to plot that line are those in the third column of the table in Fig. A1.12. For example, if the temperature is 21°C, 10 litres are consumed when the price is 60¢ a scoop and 18 litres are consumed when the price is 30¢ a scoop. The curve labelled 32°C shows consumption as the price varies if the temperature remains 32°C.

We can also show the relationship between ice cream consumption and temperature when the price of ice cream remains constant, as shown in

FIGURE A1.12   Graphing a Relationship Among Three Variables

(a) Price and consumption at a given temperature

(b) Temperature and consumption at a given price

(c) Temperature and price at a given consumption

Price	Ice cream consumption			
	(litres per day)			
(cents per scoop)	−10°C	10°C	21°C	32°C
15	12	18	25	50
30	10	12	18	37
45	7	10	13	27
60	5	7	10	20
75	3	5	7	14
90	2	3	5	10
105	1	2	3	6

The quantity of ice cream consumed depends on its price and the temperature. The table gives some hypothetical numbers that tell us how many litres of ice cream are consumed each day at different prices and different temperatures. For example, if the price is 60¢ a scoop and the temperature is 21°C, 10 litres of ice cream are consumed. This set of values is highlighted in the table and each part of the figure.

To graph a relationship among three variables, the value of one variable is held constant. Part (a) shows the relationship between price and consumption when temperature is held constant. One curve holds temperature at 32°C and the other at 21°C. Part (b) shows the relationship between temperature and consumption when price is held constant. One curve holds the price at 60¢ a scoop and the other at 15¢ a scoop. Part (c) shows the relationship between temperature and price when consumption is held constant. One curve holds consumption at 10 litres and the other at 7 litres.

Fig. A1.12(b). The curve labelled 60¢ shows how the consumption of ice cream varies with the temperature when ice cream costs 60¢ a scoop, and a second curve shows the relationship when ice cream costs 15¢ a scoop. For example, at 60¢ a scoop, 10 litres are consumed when the temperature is 21°C and 20 litres when the temperature is 32°C.

Figure A1.12(c) shows the combinations of temperature and price that result in a constant consumption of ice cream. One curve shows the combination that results in 10 litres a day being consumed, and the other shows the combination that results in 7 litres a day being consumed. A high price and a high temperature lead to the same consumption as a lower price and a lower temperature. For example, 10 litres of ice cream are consumed at 21°C and 60¢ a scoop, 32°C and 90¢ a scoop, and at 10°C and 45¢ a scoop.

◆ With what you have learned about graphs, you can move forward with your study of economics. There are no graphs in this book that are more complicated than those that have been explained in this appendix.

Mathematical Note:
Equations To Straight Lines

IF A STRAIGHT LINE IN A GRAPH DESCRIBES THE relationship between two variables, we call it a **linear relationship**. Figure 1 shows the linear relationship between a person's expenditure and income. This person spends $100 a week (by borrowing or spending previous savings) when income is zero. And out of each dollar earned, this person spends 50 cents (and saves 50 cents).

All linear relationships are described by the same general equation. We call the quantity that is measured on the horizontal (or x-axis) x and we call the quantity that is measured on the vertical (or y-axis) y. In the case of Fig. 1, x is income and y is expenditure.

A Linear Equation

The equation that describes a straight-line relationship between x and y is

$$y = a + bx.$$

In this equation, a and b are fixed numbers and they are called constants. The values of x and y vary so these numbers are called variables. Because the equation describes a straight line, it is called a **linear equation.**

The equation tells us that when the value of x is zero, the value of y is a. We call the constant a the y-axis intercept. The reason is that on the graph the straight line hits the y-axis at a value equal to a. Figure 1 illustrates the y-axis intercept.

For positive values of x, the value of y exceeds a. The constant b tells us by how much y increases above a as x increases. The constant b is the slope of the line.

Slope of Line

As we explain in the chapter, the **slope** of a relationship is the change in the value of y divided by the change in the value of x. We use the Greek letter Δ (delta) to represent "change in." Thus Δy means the change in the value of the variable measured on the y-axis, and Δx means the change in the value of the variable measured on the x-axis. Therefore the slope of the relationship is

$$\Delta y/\Delta x.$$

To see why the slope is b, suppose that initially the value of x is x_1, or $200 in Fig. 2. The corresponding value of y is y_1, also $200 in Fig. 2. The equation to the line tells us that

$$y_1 = a + bx_1. \tag{1}$$

Now the value of x increases by Δx to $x_1 + \Delta x$ (or $400 in Fig. 2). And the value of y increases by Δy to $y_1 + \Delta y$ (or $300 in Fig. 2).

Figure 1 Linear relationship

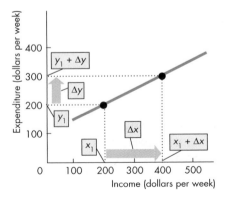

Figure 2 Calculating slope

The equation to the line now tells us that

$$y_1 + \Delta y = a + b(x_1 + \Delta x) \qquad (2)$$

To calculate the slope of the line, subtract equation (1) from equation (2) to obtain

$$\Delta y = b\Delta x \qquad (3)$$

and now divide equation (3) by Δx to obtain

$$\frac{\Delta y}{\Delta x} = b.$$

So, the slope of the line is b.

Position of Line

The y-axis intercept determines the position of the line on the graph. Figure 3 illustrates the relationship between the y-axis intercept and the position of the line on the graph. The y-axis measures saving and the x-axis measures income. When the y-axis intercept, a, is positive, the line hits the y-axis at a positive value of y—as the blue line does. When the y-axis intercept, a, is zero, the line hits the y-axis at the origin—as the purple line does. When the y-axis intercept, a, is negative, the line hits the y-axis at a negative value of y—as the red line does. As the equations to the three lines show, the value of the y-axis intercept does not influence the slope of the line.

Positive Relationships

Figure 1 shows a positive relationship—the two variables x and y move in the same direction. All positive relationships have a slope that is positive. In the equation to the line, the constant b is positive. In this example, the y-axis intercept, a, is 100. The slope b equals $\Delta y/\Delta x$, which is 100/200 or 0.5. The equation to the line is

$$y = 100 + 0.5x.$$

Negative Relationships

Figure 4 shows a negative relationship—the two variables x and y move in the opposite direction. All negative relationships have a slope that is negative. In the equation to the line, the constant b is negative. In the example in Fig. 4, the y-axis intercept, a, is 30. The slope, b, equals $\Delta y/\Delta x$, which is −20/2 or −10. The equation to the line is

$$y = 30 + (-10)x$$

or,

$$y = 30 - 10x.$$

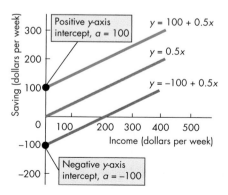

Figure 3 The y-axis intercept

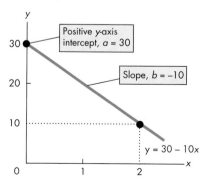

Figure 4 Negative relationship

KEY POINTS

Graphing Data (pp. 17–20)

- A time-series graph shows the trend and fluctuations in a variable over time.
- A cross-section graph shows how variables change across the members of a population.
- A scatter diagram shows the relationship between two variables. It shows whether two variables are positively related, negatively related, or unrelated.

Graphs Used in Economic Models (pp. 20–23)

- Graphs are used to show relationships among variables in economic models.
- Relationships can be positive (an upward-sloping curve), negative (a downward-sloping curve), positive and then negative (have a maximum point), negative and then positive (have a minimum point), or unrelated (a horizontal or vertical curve).

The Slope of a Relationship (pp. 24–26)

- The slope of a relationship is calculated as the change in the value of the variable measured on the y-axis divided by the change in the value of the variable measured on the x-axis—that is, $\Delta y/\Delta x$.
- A straight line has a constant slope.
- A curved line has a varying slope. To calculate the slope of a curved line, we calculate the slope at a point or across an arc.

Graphing Relationships Among More Than Two Variables (pp. 26–27)

- To graph a relationship among more than two variables, we hold constant the values of all the variables except two.
- We then plot the value of one of the variables against the value of another.

KEY FIGURES

Figure A1.1   Making a Graph, 17
Figure A1.5   Positive (Direct) Relationships, 21
Figure A1.6   Negative (Inverse) Relationships, 22
Figure A1.7   Maximum and Minimum Points, 23
Figure A1.9   The Slope of a Straight Line, 24
Figure A1.10 Slope at a Point, 25
Figure A1.11 Slope Across an Arc, 26

KEY TERMS

Cross-section graph, 18
Direct relationship, 20
Inverse relationship, 21
Linear relationship, 20
Negative relationship, 21
Positive relationship, 20
Scatter diagram, 19
Slope, 24
Time-series graph, 18
Trend, 18

REVIEW QUIZ

1. What are the three types of graphs used to show economic data?
2. Give an example of a time-series graph.
3. List three things that a time-series graph shows quickly and easily.
4. Give three examples, different from those in the chapter, of scatter diagrams that show a positive relationship, a negative relationship, and no relationship.
5. Draw some graphs to show the relationships between two variables that
   a. Move in the same direction.
   b. Move in opposite directions.
   c. Have a maximum.
   d. Have a minimum.
6. Which of the relationships in question 5 is a positive relationship and which is a negative relationship?
7. What are the two ways of calculating the slope of a curved line?
8. How do we graph a relationship among more than two variables?

PROBLEMS

The spreadsheet provides data on the Canadian economy: Column A is the year, column B is the inflation rate, column C is the interest rate, column D is the growth rate, and column E is the unemployment rate. Use this spreadsheet to answer problems 1, 2, 3, and 4.

	A	B	C	D	E
1	1991	2.8	9.8	−2.1	10.3
2	1992	1.2	8.8	0.9	11.2
3	1993	1.5	7.8	2.3	11.4
4	1994	1.1	8.6	4.8	10.4
5	1995	2.3	8.3	2.8	9.4
6	1996	1.7	7.5	1.6	9.6
7	1997	0.9	6.4	4.2	9.1
8	1998	−0.5	5.5	4.1	8.3
9	1999	1.3	5.7	5.4	7.6
10	2000	3.6	5.9	4.5	6.8
11	2001	1.4	5.8	1.5	7.2

*1. a. Draw a time-series graph of the inflation rate.
   b. In which year(s) (i) was inflation highest, (ii) was inflation lowest, (iii) did it increase, (iv) did it decrease, (v) did it increase most, and (vi) did it decrease most?
   c. What was the main trend in inflation?

2. a. Draw a time-series graph of the interest rate.
   b. In which year(s) was the interest rate highest, (ii) was the interest rate lowest, (iii) did it increase, (iv) did it decrease, (v) did it increase most, and (vi) did it decrease most?
   c. What was the main trend in the interest rate?

*3. Draw a scatter diagram to show the relationship between the inflation rate and the interest rate. Describe the relationship.

4. Draw a scatter diagram to show the relationship between the growth rate and the unemployment rate. Describe the relationship.

*5. Draw a graph to show the relationship between the two variables x and y:

x	0	1	2	3	4	5	6	7	8
y	0	1	4	9	16	25	36	49	64

   a. Is the relationship positive or negative?
   b. Does the slope of the relationship increase or decrease as the value of x increases?
   c. Think of some economic relationships that might be similar to this one.

6. Draw a graph that shows the relationship between the two variables x and y:

x	0	1	2	3	4	5
y	25	24	22	16	8	0

   a. Is the relationship positive or negative?
   b. Does the slope of the relationship increase or decrease as the value of x increases?
   c. Think of some economic relationships that might be similar to this one.

*7. In problem 5, calculate the slope of the relationship between x and y when x equals 4.

8. In problem 6, calculate the slope of the relationship between x and y when x equals 3.

*9. In problem 5, calculate the slope of the relationship across the arc when x increases from 3 to 4.

10. In problem 6, calculate the slope of the relationship across the arc when x increases from 4 to 5.

*11. Calculate the slope of the relationship shown at point A in the following figure.

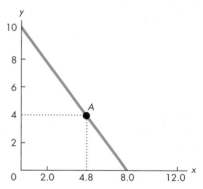

12. Calculate the slope of the relationship shown at point A in the following figure.

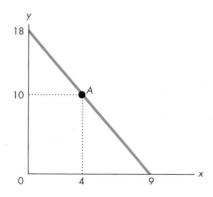

*13. Use the following figure to calculate the slope of the relationship:

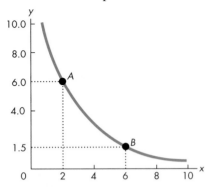

a. At points *A* and *B*.
b. Across the arc *AB*.

14. Use the following figure to calculate the slope of the relationship:

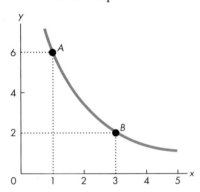

a. At points *A* and *B*.
b. Across the arc *AB*.

*15. The table gives the price of a balloon ride, the temperature, and the number of rides a day.

| Price | Balloon rides (number per day) | | |
(dollars per ride)	10°C	20°C	30°C
5.00	32	40	50
10.00	27	32	40
15.00	18	27	32
20.00	10	18	27

Draw graphs to show the relationship between
a. The price and the number of rides, holding the temperature constant.
b. The number of rides and temperature, holding the price constant.
c. The temperature and price, holding the number of rides constant.

16. The table gives the price of an umbrella, the amount of rainfall, and the number of umbrellas purchased.

| Price | Umbrellas (number per day) | | |
| (dollars per umbrella) | 0 | 2 | 10 |
	(mm of rainfall)		
10	7	8	12
20	4	7	8
30	2	4	7
40	1	2	4

Draw graphs to show the relationship between
a. The price and the number of umbrellas purchased, holding the amount of rainfall constant.
b. The number of umbrellas purchased and the amount of rainfall, holding the price constant.
c. The amount of rainfall and the price, holding the number of umbrellas purchased constant.

WEB EXERCISES

1. Use the link on the Parkin–Bade Web site and find the Consumer Price Index (CPI) for the latest 12 months. Make a graph of the CPI. During the most recent month, was the CPI rising or falling? Was the rate of rise or fall increasing or decreasing?

2. Use the link on the Parkin–Bade Web site and find the unemployment rate for the latest 12 months. Graph the unemployment rate. During the most recent month, was it rising or falling? Was the rate of rise or fall increasing or decreasing?

3. Use the data that you obtained in Web Exercises 1 and 2. Make a graph to show whether the CPI and the unemployment rate are related to each other.

4. Use the data that you obtained in Web Exercises 1 and 2. Calculate the percentage change in the CPI each month. Make a graph to show whether the percentage change in the CPI and the unemployment rate are related to each other.

CHAPTER 2

THE ECONOMIC PROBLEM

Good, Better, Best!

We live in a style that surprises our grandparents and would have astonished our great-grandparents. MP3s, video games, cell phones, gene splicing, and personal computers, which didn't exist even 25 years ago, have transformed our daily lives. For most of us, life is good, and getting better. But we still make choices and face costs. We still choose what we think is best for us. ◆ Perhaps the biggest choice that you will make is when to quit school and begin full-time work. When you've completed your current program, will you remain in school and work towards a postgraduate degree or a professional degree? What are the costs and consequences of this choice? We'll return to this question in *Reading Between the Lines* at the end of this chapter. ◆ We see an incredible amount of specialization and trade in the world. Each one of us specializes in a particular job—as a lawyer, a journalist, a home-maker. Why? How do we benefit from specialization and trade? ◆ Over many centuries, social institutions have evolved that we take for granted. One of them is property rights and a political and legal system that protects them. Another is markets. Why have these institutions evolved?

◆ These are the questions that we study in this chapter. We begin with the core economic problem—scarcity and choice—and the concept of the production possibilities frontier. We then learn about the central idea of economics: efficiency. We also discover how we can expand production by accumulating capital and by specializing and trading with each other. What you will learn in this chapter is the foundation on which all economics is built.

After studying this chapter, you will be able to

- **Define the production possibilities frontier and calculate opportunity cost**

- **Distinguish between production possibilities and preferences and describe an efficient allocation of resources**

- **Explain how current production choices expand future production possibilities**

- **Explain how specialization and trade expand our production possibilities**

- **Explain why property rights and markets have evolved**

Production Possibilities and Opportunity Cost

EVERY WORKING DAY, IN MINES, FACTORIES, shops, and offices and on farms and construction sites across Canada, 27 million people produce a vast variety of goods and services valued at more than $3 billion. But the quantities of goods and services that we can produce are limited by our available resources and by technology. And if we want to increase our production of one good, we must decrease our production of something else—we face tradeoffs. You are going to learn about the production possibilities frontier, which describes the limit to what we can produce and provides a neat way of thinking about and illustrating the idea of a tradeoff.

The **production possibilities frontier** (*PPF*) is the boundary between those combinations of goods and services that can be produced and those that cannot. To illustrate the *PPF*, we focus on two goods at a time and hold constant the quantities produced of all the other goods and services. That is, we look at a *model* economy in which everything remains the same (*ceteris paribus*) except for the production of the two goods we are considering.

Let's look at the production possibilities frontier for the classic general example of "guns" and "butter," which stand for *any* pair of goods or services.

Production Possibilities Frontier

The *production possibilities frontier* for guns and butter shows the limits to the production of these two goods, given the total resources available to produce them. Figure 2.1 shows this production possibilities frontier. The table lists some combinations of the quantities of butter and guns that can be produced in a month given the resources available. The figure graphs these combinations. The *x*-axis shows the quantity of butter produced, and the *y*-axis shows the quantity of guns produced.

Because the *PPF* shows the *limits* to production, we cannot attain the points outside the frontier. They are points that describe wants that can't be satisfied. We can produce at all the points *inside* the *PPF* and *on* the *PPF*. They are attainable points. Suppose that in a typical month, we produce 4 tonnes of butter and 5 guns. Figure 2.1 shows this combination as point *E* and as possibility *E* in the table. The figure also shows

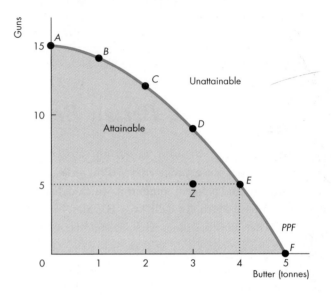

FIGURE 2.1   Production Possibilities Frontier

Possibility	Butter (tonnes)		Guns (units)
A	0	and	15
B	1	and	14
C	2	and	12
D	3	and	9
E	4	and	5
F	5	and	0

The table lists six points on the production possibilities frontier for guns and butter. Row *A* tells us that if we produce no butter, the maximum quantity of guns we can produce is 15. Points *A*, *B*, *C*, *D*, *E*, and *F* in the figure represent the rows of the table. The line passing through these points is the production possibilities frontier (*PPF*). It separates the attainable from the unattainable. Production is possible at any point inside the orange area or on the frontier. Points outside the frontier are unattainable. Points inside the frontier, such as point *Z*, are inefficient because resources are wasted or misallocated. At such points, it is possible to use the available resources to produce more of either or both goods.

other production possibilities. For example, we might stop producing butter and move all the people who produce it into producing guns. Point *A* in the figure and possibility *A* in the table show this case. The quantity of guns produced increases to 15, and butter production dries up. Alternatively, we might close the gun factories and switch all the resources into producing butter. In this situation, we produce 5 tonnes of butter. Point *F* in the figure and possibility *F* in the table show this case.

Production Efficiency

We achieve **production efficiency** if we cannot produce more of one good without producing less of some other good. When production is efficient, we are at a point *on* the *PPF*. If we are at a point *inside* the *PPF*, such as point *Z*, production is *inefficient* because we have some *unused* resources or we have some *misallocated* resources or both.

Resources are unused when they are idle but could be working. For example, we might leave some of the gun factories idle or some workers unemployed.

Resources are *misallocated* when they are assigned to tasks for which they are not the best match. For example, we might assign skilled butter-making machine operators to work in a gun factory and skilled gun makers to work in a dairy. We could get more butter *and* more guns from these same workers if we reassigned them to the tasks that more closely match their skills.

If we produce at a point inside the *PPF* such as *Z*, we can use our resources more efficiently to produce more butter, more guns, or more of *both* butter and guns. But if we produce at a point *on* the *PPF*, we are using our resources efficiently and we can produce more of one good only if we produce less of the other. That is, along the *PPF*, we face a *tradeoff*.

Tradeoff Along the *PPF*

Every choice *along* the *PPF* involves a *tradeoff*—we must give up something to get something else. On the *PPF* in Fig. 2.1, we must give up some guns to get more butter or give up some butter to get more guns.

Tradeoffs arise in every imaginable real-world situation, and you reviewed several of them in Chapter 1. At any given point in time, we have a fixed amount of labour, land, capital, and entrepreneurship. By using our available technologies, we can employ these resources to produce goods and services. But we are limited in what we can produce. This limit defines a boundary between what we can attain and what we cannot attain. This boundary is the real world's production possibilities frontier, and it defines the tradeoffs that we must make. On our real-world *PPF*, we can produce more of any one good or service only if we produce less of some other goods or services.

When doctors say that we must spend more on AIDS and cancer research, they are suggesting a tradeoff: more medical research for less of some other things. When the prime minister says that he wants to spend more on education and health care, he is suggesting a tradeoff: more education and health care for less peacekeeping and national security or less private spending (because of higher taxes). When an environmental group argues for less logging, it is suggesting a tradeoff: greater conservation of endangered wildlife for less paper. When your parents say that you should study more, they are suggesting a tradeoff: more study time for less leisure or sleep.

All tradeoffs involve a cost—an opportunity cost.

Opportunity Cost

The *opportunity cost* of an action is the highest-valued alternative forgone. The *PPF* helps us to make the concept of opportunity cost precise and enables us to calculate it. Along the *PPF*, there are only two goods, so there is only one alternative forgone: some quantity of the other good. Given our current resources and technology, we can produce more butter only if we produce fewer guns. The opportunity cost of producing an additional tonne of butter is the number of guns we must forgo. Similarly, the opportunity cost of producing an additional gun is the quantity of butter we must forgo.

For example, at point *C* in Fig. 2.1, we produce less butter and more guns than at point *D*. If we choose point *D* over point *C*, the additional tonne of butter *costs* 3 guns. One tonne of butter costs 3 guns.

We can also work out the opportunity cost of choosing point *C* over point *D* in Fig. 2.1. If we move from point *D* to point *C*, the quantity of guns produced increases by 3 and the quantity of butter produced decreases by 1 tonne. So if we choose point *C* over point *D*, the additional 3 guns *cost* 1 tonne of butter. One gun costs 1/3 of a tonne of butter.

Opportunity Cost Is a Ratio Opportunity cost is a ratio. It is the decrease in the quantity produced of one good divided by the increase in the quantity produced of another good as we move along the production possibilities frontier.

Because opportunity cost is a ratio, the opportunity cost of producing an additional gun is equal to the *inverse* of the opportunity cost of producing an additional tonne of butter. Check this proposition by returning to the calculations we've just worked through. When we move along the *PPF* from *C* to *D*, the opportunity cost of a tonne of butter is 3 guns. The inverse of 3 is 1/3, so if we decrease the production of butter and increase the production of guns by moving from *D* to *C*, the opportunity cost of a gun must be 1/3 of a tonne of butter. You can check that this number is correct. If we move from *D* to *C*, we produce 3 more guns and 1 tonne less of butter. Because 3 guns cost 1 tonne of butter, the opportunity cost of 1 gun is 1/3 of a tonne of butter.

Increasing Opportunity Cost The opportunity cost of a tonne of butter increases as the quantity of butter produced increases. Also, the opportunity cost of a gun increases as the quantity of guns produced increases. This phenomenon of increasing opportunity cost is reflected in the shape of the *PPF*—it is bowed outward.

When a large quantity of guns and a small quantity of butter are produced—between points *A* and *B* in Fig. 2.1—the frontier has a gentle slope. A given increase in the quantity of butter *costs* a small decrease in the quantity of guns, so the opportunity cost of a tonne of butter is a small quantity of guns.

When a large quantity of butter and a small quantity of guns are produced—between points *E* and *F* in Fig. 2.1—the frontier is steep. A given increase in the quantity of butter *costs* a large decrease in the quantity of guns, so the opportunity cost of a tonne of butter is a large quantity of guns.

The *PPF* is bowed outward because resources are not all equally productive in all activities. People with many years of experience working for Smith & Wesson are very good at producing guns but not very good at making butter. So if we move some of these people from Smith & Wesson to Sealtest Dairies, we get a small increase in the quantity of butter but a large decrease in the quantity of guns.

Similarly, people who have spent years working at Sealtest Dairies are good at producing butter but not so good at producing guns. So if we move some of these people from Sealtest Dairies to Smith & Wesson, we get a small increase in the quantity of guns but a large decrease in the quantity of butter.

The more we try to produce of either good, the less productive are the additional resources we use to produce that good and the larger is the opportunity cost of a unit of that good.

Increasing Opportunity Costs Are Everywhere
Just about every activity that you can think of is one with an increasing opportunity cost. The most skilful farmers use the most fertile land to produce food. The best doctors use the least fertile land to produce health-care services. If hospitals buy fertile land, convert tractors into ambulances, and hire farmers as hospital porters, food production drops drastically and the production of health-care services increases by a tiny amount. The opportunity cost of a unit of health-care services rises. Similarly, if a farmer buys a hospital, converts it to a hydroponic tomato factory, and hires people who were previously doctors and nurses as farm workers, the decrease in the production of health-care services is large, but the increase in food production is small. The opportunity cost of a unit of food rises.

This example is extreme and unlikely, but these same considerations apply to any pair of goods that you can imagine.

REVIEW QUIZ
1 How does the production possibilities frontier illustrate scarcity?
2 How does the production possibilities frontier illustrate production efficiency?
3 How does the production possibilities frontier show that every choice involves a tradeoff?
4 How does the production possibilities frontier illustrate opportunity cost?
5 Why is opportunity cost a ratio?
6 Why does the *PPF* for most goods bow outward so that opportunity cost increases as the quantity produced of a good increases?

We've seen that what we can produce is limited by the production possibilities frontier. We've also seen that production on the *PPF* is efficient. But we can produce many different quantities on the *PPF*. How do we choose among them? How do we know which point on the *PPF* is the best one?

Using Resources Efficiently

YOU'VE SEEN THAT POINTS INSIDE THE *PPF* waste resources or leave them unused and are inefficient. You've also seen that points *on* the *PPF* are efficient—we can't produce more of one good unless we forgo some units of another good. But there are many such points on the *PPF*. Each point on the *PPF* achieves production efficiency. Which point is the best? How can we choose among them? What are the efficient quantities of butter and guns to produce?

These questions are examples of real-world questions of enormous consequence such as: How much should we spend on treating AIDS and how much on cancer research? Should we expand education and health-care programs or cut taxes? Should we spend more on the environment and the conservation of endangered wildlife?

To determine the efficient quantities to produce, we must compare costs and benefits.

The *PPF* and Marginal Cost

The limits to production, which are summarized by the *PPF*, determine the marginal cost of each good or service. **Marginal cost** is the opportunity cost of producing *one more unit.* We can calculate marginal cost in a way that is similar to the way we calculate opportunity cost. *Marginal cost* is the opportunity cost of *one* additional tonne of butter—the quantity of guns that must be given up to get one more tonne of butter—as we move along the *PPF*.

Figure 2.2 illustrates the marginal cost of butter. If butter production increases from zero to 1 tonne—a move from *A* to *B*—the quantity of guns decreases from 15 to 14. So the opportunity cost of the first tonne of butter is 1 gun. If butter production increases from 1 tonne to 2 tonnes—a move from *B* to *C*—the quantity of guns decreases by 2. So the second tonne of butter costs 2 guns.

You can repeat this calculation for an increase in butter production from 2 to 3 tonnes, from 3 to 4 tonnes, and from 4 to 5 tonnes. Figure 2.2 shows the opportunity costs as a series of steps. Each extra tonne of butter costs more guns than the preceding tonne.

We've just calculated the opportunity cost of a tonne of butter and generated the steps in Fig. 2.2(a). The opportunity cost of a tonne of butter is also the *marginal cost* of producing a tonne of butter. In Fig. 2.2(b), the line labelled *MC* shows the marginal cost.

FIGURE 2.2 The *PPF* and Marginal Cost

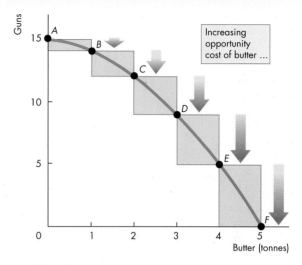

(a) *PPF* and opportunity cost

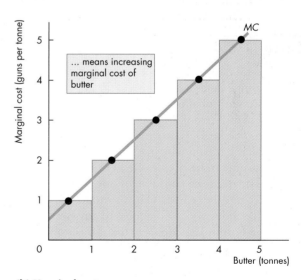

(b) Marginal cost

Opportunity cost is measured along the *PPF* in part (a). If the production of butter increases from zero to 1 tonne, the opportunity cost of a tonne of butter is 1 gun. If the production of butter increases from 1 to 2 tonnes, the opportunity cost of a tonne of butter is 2 guns. The opportunity cost of butter increases as the production of butter increases. Part (b) shows the marginal cost of a tonne of butter as the *MC* curve.

Preferences and Marginal Benefit

Look around your classroom and notice the wide variety of shirts, caps, pants, and shoes that you and your fellow students are wearing today. Why is there such a huge variety? Why don't you all wear the same styles and colours? The answer lies in what economists call preferences. **Preferences** are a description of a person's likes and dislikes.

You've seen that we have a concrete way of describing the limits to production: the *PPF*. We need a similarly concrete way of describing preferences. To describe preferences, economists use the concepts of marginal benefit and the marginal benefit curve. The **marginal benefit** of a good or service is the benefit received from consuming one more unit of it.

We measure the marginal benefit of a good or service by what a person is *willing to pay* for an additional unit of it. The idea is that you are willing to pay what the good is worth to you. It is worth its marginal benefit, and you're willing to pay an amount up to the marginal benefit. So willingness to pay measures marginal benefit.

The **marginal benefit curve** shows the relationship between marginal benefit of a good and the quantity of that good consumed. It is a general principle that the more we have of any good or service, the smaller is its marginal benefit and the less we are willing to pay for an additional unit of it. This tendency is so widespread and strong that we call it a principle—the *principle of decreasing marginal benefit.*

The basic reason why marginal benefit decreases as we consume more of any one item is that we like variety. The more we consume of one item, the more we can see of other things that we would like better.

Think about your willingness to pay for a coffee. You buy a bottomless cup. The first fill is important to you. You'd pay a lot more for it than what it costs. You can refill your cup as often as you wish. But you go back for only one more fill. You enjoy your second cup, but not as much as the first one. And you don't want a third cup, even though it is free.

In everyday life, we think of what we pay for something as the money that we give up—dollars. But you've learned to think about cost as opportunity cost, which is a cost in terms of other goods or services forgone, not a dollar cost. You can think about willingness to pay in the same terms. The price you are willing to pay for something is the quantity of other goods and services that you are willing to forgo. Let's illustrate preferences this way.

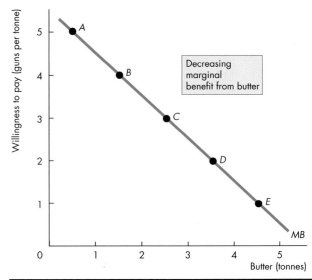

FIGURE 2.3   Preferences and the Marginal Benefit Curve

Possibility	Butter (tonnes)	Willingness to pay (guns per tonne)
A	0.5	5
B	1.5	4
C	2.5	3
D	3.5	2
E	4.5	1

The smaller the quantity of butter produced, the more guns people are willing to give up for an additional tonne of butter. If butter production is 0.5 tonnes, people are willing to pay 5 guns per tonne. But if butter production is 4.5 tonnes, people are willing to pay only 1 gun per tonne. Willingness to pay measures marginal benefit. And decreasing marginal benefit is a universal feature of people's preferences.

Figure 2.3 illustrates preferences in this way. In row *A*, butter production is 0.5 tonnes, and at that quantity, people are willing to pay 5 guns per tonne. As the quantity of butter produced increases, the amount that people are willing to pay for it falls. When butter production is 4.5 tonnes, people are willing to pay only 1 gun per tonne.

Let's now use the concepts of marginal cost and marginal benefit to describe the efficient quantity of butter to produce.

Efficient Use of Resources

When we cannot produce more of any one good without giving up some other good, we have achieved *production efficiency*, and we're producing at a point on the *PPF*. When we cannot produce more of any good without giving up some other good that we *value more highly*, we have achieved **allocative efficiency**, and we are producing at the point on the *PPF* that we prefer above all other points.

Suppose in Fig. 2.4, we produce 1.5 tonnes of butter. The marginal cost of butter is 2 guns per tonne, but the marginal benefit from butter is 4 guns per tonne. Because someone values an additional tonne of butter more highly than it costs to produce, resources get used more efficiently if butter production increases and gun production decreases.

Now suppose we produce 3.5 tonnes of butter. The marginal cost of butter is now 4 guns per tonne, but the marginal benefit from butter is only 2 guns per tonne. Because the additional butter costs more to produce than anyone thinks it is worth, we can get more value from our resources by moving some of them away from producing butter and into producing guns.

But suppose we produce 2.5 tonnes of butter. Marginal cost and marginal benefit are now equal at 3 guns per tonne. This allocation of resources between butter and guns is efficient. If more butter is produced, the forgone guns are worth more than the additional butter. If less butter is produced, the forgone butter is worth more than the additional guns.

REVIEW QUIZ

1 What is marginal cost and how is it measured?
2 What is marginal benefit and how is it measured?
3 How does the marginal benefit from a good change as the quantity produced of that good increases?
4 What is production efficiency and how does it relate to the production possibilities frontier?
5 What conditions must be satisfied if resources are used efficiently?

You now understand the limits to production and the conditions under which resources are used efficiently. Your next task is to study the expansion of production possibilities.

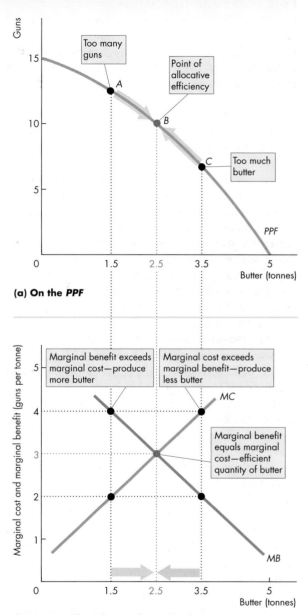

FIGURE 2.4   The Efficient Use of Resources

(a) On the PPF

(b) Marginal benefit equals marginal cost

The greater the quantity of butter produced, the smaller is the marginal benefit (*MB*) from it—the fewer guns people are willing to give up to get an additional tonne of butter. But the greater the quantity of butter produced, the greater is the marginal cost (*MC*) of butter—the more guns people must give up to get an additional tonne of butter. When marginal benefit equals marginal cost, resources are being used efficiently.

Economic Growth

DURING THE PAST 30 YEARS, PRODUCTION PER person in Canada has doubled. Such an expansion of production is called **economic growth**. Economic growth increases our standard of living, but it doesn't overcome scarcity and avoid opportunity cost. To make our economy grow, we face a tradeoff—the standard of living tradeoff (p. 10)—and the faster we make production grow, the greater is the opportunity cost of economic growth.

The Cost of Economic Growth

Two key factors influence economic growth: technological change and capital accumulation. **Technological change** is the development of new goods and of better ways of producing goods and services. **Capital accumulation** is the growth of capital resources, which include *human capital*.

As a consequence of technological change and capital accumulation, we have an enormous quantity of cars that enable us to produce more transportation than was available when we had only horses and carriages; we have satellites that make global communications possible on a scale that is much larger than that produced by the earlier cable technology. But new technologies and new capital have an opportunity cost. To use resources in research and development and to produce new capital, we must decrease our production of consumption goods and services. Let's look at this opportunity cost.

Instead of studying the *PPF* of butter and guns, we'll hold the quantity of guns produced constant and examine the *PPF* for butter and butter-making machines. Figure 2.5 shows this *PPF* as the blue curve *ABC*. If we devote no resources to producing butter-making machines, we produce at point *A*. If we produce 3 tonnes of butter, we can produce 6 butter-making machines at point *B*. If we produce no butter, we can produce 10 machines at point *C*.

The amount by which our production possibilities expand depends on the resources we devote to technological change and capital accumulation. If we devote no resources to this activity (point *A*), our *PPF* remains at *ABC*—the blue curve in Fig. 2.5. If we cut the current production of butter and produce 6 machines (point *B*), then in the future, we'll have more capital and our *PPF* will rotate outward to the position shown by the red curve. The fewer resources

FIGURE 2.5 Economic Growth

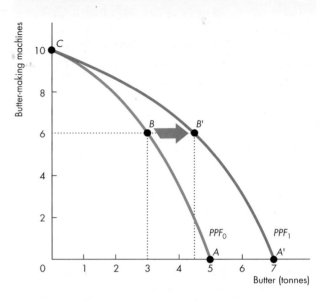

PPF_0 shows the limits to the production of butter and butter-making machines, with the production of all other goods and services remaining the same. If we devote no resources to producing butter-making machines and produce 5 tonnes of butter, we remain at point *A*. But if we decrease butter production to 3 tonnes and produce 6 machines, at point *B*, our production possibilities expand. After one period, the *PPF* rotates outward to PPF_1 and we can produce at point *B'*, a point outside the original *PPF*. We can rotate the *PPF* outward, but we cannot avoid opportunity cost. The opportunity cost of producing more butter in the future is less butter today.

we devote to producing butter and the more resources we devote to producing machines, the greater is the expansion of our production possibilities.

Economic growth is not free. To make it happen, we devote resources to producing new machines and less to producing butter. In Fig. 2.5, we move from *A* to *B*. There is no free lunch. The opportunity cost of more butter in the future is less butter today. Also, economic growth is no magic formula for abolishing scarcity. On the new production possibilities frontier, we continue to face a tradeoff and opportunity cost.

The ideas about economic growth that we have explored in the setting of the dairy industry also apply to nations. Let's look at two examples.

Economic Growth in Canada and Hong Kong

If as a nation we devote all our resources to producing consumer goods and none to research and capital accumulation, production possibilities per person will be the same in the future as they are today. To expand our production possibilities in the future, we must devote fewer resources to producing consumption goods and some resources to accumulating capital and developing technologies so that we can produce more consumption goods in the future. The decrease in today's consumption is the opportunity cost of an increase in future consumption.

The experiences of Canada and Hong Kong make a striking example of the effects of our choices on the rate of economic growth. In 1960, the production possibilities per person in Canada were three times those in Hong Kong (see Fig. 2.6). Canada devoted one-fifth of its resources to accumulating capital and the other four-fifths to consumption. In 1960, Canada was at point *A* on its *PPF*. Hong Kong devoted one-third of its resources to accumulating capital and two-thirds to consumption. In 1960, Hong Kong was at point *A* on its *PPF*.

Since 1960, both countries have experienced economic growth, but growth in Hong Kong has been more rapid than that in Canada. Because Hong Kong devoted a bigger fraction of its resources to accumulating capital, its production possibilities have expanded more quickly.

By 2000, the production possibilities per person in Hong Kong and Canada were similar. If Hong Kong continues to devote more resources to accumulating capital than we do (at point *B* on its 2000 *PPF*), it will continue to grow more rapidly than Canada. But if Hong Kong increases consumption and decreases capital accumulation (moving to point *D* on its 2000 *PPF*), then its rate of economic growth will slow.

Canada is typical of the rich industrial countries, which include the United States, Western Europe, and Japan. Hong Kong is typical of the fast-growing Asian economies, which include Taiwan, Thailand, South Korea, and China. Growth in these countries slowed during the Asia Crisis of 1998 but quickly rebounded. Production possibilities expand in these countries by between 5 percent a year and almost 10 percent a year. If these high growth rates are maintained, these other Asian countries will eventually close the gap on Canada as Hong Kong has done.

FIGURE 2.6   Economic Growth in Canada and Hong Kong

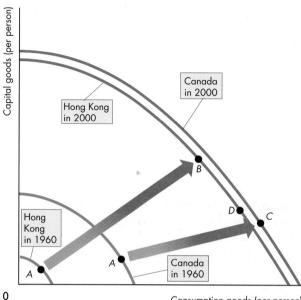

In 1960, the production possibilities per person in Canada were much larger than those in Hong Kong. But Hong Kong devoted more of its resources to accumulating capital than did Canada, so its production possibilities frontier has shifted outward more quickly than has that of Canada. In 2000, Hong Kong's production possibilities per person were similar to those in Canada.

REVIEW QUIZ

1   What are the two key factors that generate economic growth?
2   How does economic growth influence the production possibilities frontier?
3   What is the opportunity cost of economic growth?
4   Why has Hong Kong experienced faster economic growth than Canada has?

Next, we're going to study another way in which we expand our production possibilities—the amazing fact that *both* buyers and sellers gain from specialization and trade.

Gains from Trade

PEOPLE CAN PRODUCE FOR THEMSELVES ALL THE goods that they consume, or they can concentrate on producing one good (or perhaps a few goods) and then trade with others—exchange some of their own goods for those of others. Concentrating on the production of only one good or a few goods is called *specialization*. We are going to discover how people gain by specializing in the production of the good in which they have a *comparative advantage* and trading with each other.

Comparative Advantage

A person has a **comparative advantage** in an activity if that person can perform the activity at a lower opportunity cost than anyone else. Differences in opportunity costs arise from differences in individual abilities and from differences in the characteristics of other resources.

No one excels at everything. One person is an outstanding pitcher but a poor catcher; another person is a brilliant lawyer but a poor teacher. In almost all human endeavours, what one person does easily, someone else finds difficult. The same applies to land and capital. One plot of land is fertile but has no mineral deposits; another plot of land has outstanding views but is infertile. One machine has great precision but is difficult to operate; another is fast but often breaks down.

Although no one excels at everything, some people excel and can outperform others in many activities. But such a person does not have a *comparative* advantage in each of those activities. For example, Robertson Davies was a better actor than most people. But he was an even better writer. So his *comparative* advantage was in writing.

Because people's abilities and the quality of their resources differ, they have different opportunity costs of producing various goods. Such differences give rise to comparative advantage. Let's explore the idea of comparative advantage by looking at two CD factories: one operated by Tom and the other operated by Nancy.

Tom's Factory To simplify the story quite a lot, suppose that CDs have just two components: a disc and a plastic case. Tom has two production lines: one for discs and one for cases. Figure 2.7 shows Tom's

FIGURE 2.7 Production Possibilities in Tom's Factory

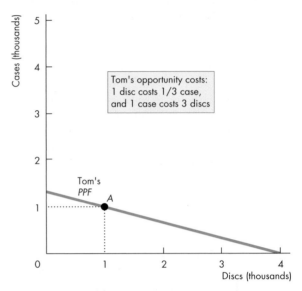

Tom can produce discs and cases along the production possibilities frontier *PPF*. For Tom, the opportunity cost of 1 disc is 1/3 of a case and the opportunity cost of 1 case is 3 discs. If Tom produces at point A, he can produce 1,000 cases and 1,000 discs an hour.

production possibilities frontier for discs and cases. It tells us that if Tom uses all his resources to make discs, he can produce 4,000 discs an hour. The *PPF* in Fig. 2.7 also tells us that if Tom uses all his resources to make cases, he can produce 1,333 cases an hour. But to produce cases, Tom must decrease his production of discs. For each case produced, he must decrease his production of discs by 3. So

Tom's opportunity cost of producing 1 case is 3 discs.

Similarly, if Tom wants to increase his production of discs, he must decrease his production of cases. And for each 1,000 discs produced, he must decrease his production of cases by 333. So

Tom's opportunity cost of producing 1 disc is 0.333 of a case.

Tom's *PPF* is linear because his workers have similar skills so if he reallocates them from one activity to another, he faces a constant opportunity cost.

Nancy's Factory   The other factory, operated by Nancy, also produces cases and discs. But Nancy's factory has machines that are custom made for case production, so they are more suitable for producing cases than discs. Also, Nancy's work force is more skilled in making cases.

These differences between the two factories mean that Nancy's production possibilities frontier—shown along with Tom's *PPF* in Fig. 2.8—is different from Tom's. If Nancy uses all her resources to make discs, she can produce 1,333 an hour. If she uses all her resources to make cases, she can produce 4,000 an hour. To produce discs, Nancy must decrease her production of cases. For each 1,000 additional discs produced, she must decrease her production of cases by 3,000. So

Nancy's opportunity cost of producing 1 disc is 3 cases.

Similarly, if Nancy wants to increase her production of cases, she must decrease her production of discs. For each 1,000 additional cases produced, she must decrease her production of discs by 333. So

Nancy's opportunity cost of producing 1 case is 0.333 of a disc.

Suppose that Tom and Nancy produce both discs and cases and that each produces 1,000 discs and 1,000 cases—1,000 CDs—an hour. That is, each produces at point *A* on his or her *PPF*. Total production is 2,000 CDs an hour.

In which of the two goods does Nancy have a comparative advantage? Recall that comparative advantage is a situation in which one person's opportunity cost of producing a good is lower than another person's opportunity cost of producing that same good. Nancy has a comparative advantage in producing cases. Nancy's opportunity cost of producing a case is 0.333 of a disc, whereas Tom's is 3 discs.

You can see Nancy's comparative advantage by looking at the production possibilities frontiers for Nancy and Tom in Fig. 2.8. Nancy's production possibilities frontier is steeper than Tom's. To produce one more case, Nancy must give up fewer discs than Tom has to. Hence Nancy's opportunity cost of producing a case is less than Tom's. Nancy has a comparative advantage in producing cases.

Tom's comparative advantage is in producing discs. His production possibilities frontier is less steep than Nancy's. This means that to produce one more disc, Tom must give up fewer cases than Nancy has to.

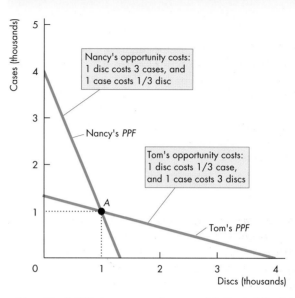

FIGURE 2.8   Comparative Advantage

Along Tom's *PPF*, the opportunity cost of 1 disc is 1/3 of a case and the opportunity cost of 1 case is 3 discs. Along Nancy's *PPF*, the opportunity cost of 1 disc is 3 cases and the opportunity cost of 1 case is 1/3 of a disc. Like Tom, Nancy produces 1,000 cases and 1,000 discs an hour at point *A*. Nancy's opportunity cost of a case is less than Tom's, so Nancy has a comparative advantage in cases. Tom's opportunity cost of a disc is less than Nancy's, so Tom has a comparative advantage in discs.

Tom's opportunity cost of producing a disc is 0.333 of a case, which is less than Nancy's 3 cases per disc. So Tom has a comparative advantage in producing discs.

Because Nancy has a comparative advantage in producing cases and Tom has a comparative advantage in producing discs, they can both gain from specialization and exchange.

Achieving the Gains from Trade

If Tom, who has a comparative advantage in producing discs, puts all his resources into that activity, he can produce 4,000 discs an hour—point *B* on his *PPF*. If Nancy, who has a comparative advantage in producing cases, puts all her resources into that activity, she can produce 4,000 cases an hour—point *B'* on her *PPF*. By specializing, Tom and Nancy together can produce 4,000 cases and 4,000 discs an hour, double the total production they can achieve without specialization.

By specialization and exchange, Tom and Nancy can get *outside* their individual production possibilities frontiers. To achieve the gains from specialization, Tom and Nancy must trade with each other.

Figure 2.9 shows how Tom and Nancy gain from trade. They make the following deal: Tom agrees to increase his production of discs from 1,000 an hour to 4,000 an hour—a move along his *PPF* from point *A* to point *B* in Fig. 2.9(a). Nancy agrees to increase her production of cases from 1,000 an hour to 4,000 an hour—a move along her *PPF* from point *A* to point *B'* in Fig. 2.9(b).

They also agree to exchange cases and discs at a "price" of one case for one disc. So Tom sells discs to Nancy for one case per disc, and Nancy sells cases to Tom for one disc per case.

With this deal in place, Tom and Nancy exchange along the red "Trade line." They exchange 2,000 cases and 2,000 discs, and each moves to point *C* (in both parts of the figure). At point *C*, each has 2,000 discs and 2,000 cases, or 2,000 CDs. So each

now produces 2,000 CDs an hour—double the previous output. This increase in production of 2,000 CDs an hour is the gain from specialization and trade.

Both parties to the trade share the gains. Nancy, who can produce discs at an opportunity cost of 3 cases per disc, can buy discs from Tom at a cost of 1 case per disc. Tom, who can produce cases at an opportunity cost of 3 discs per case, can buy cases from Nancy at a cost of 1 disc per case.

For Nancy, the cost of a disc falls from 3 cases to 1 case. So she gets her discs more cheaply than she can produce them herself. For Tom, the cost of a case falls from 3 discs to 1 disc. So he gets his cases more cheaply than he can produce them himself.

Because both Tom and Nancy obtain the items they buy from the other at a lower cost than that at which they can produce the items themselves, they both gain from specialization and trade.

The gains that Canada achieves from international trade are similar to those achieved by Tom and Nancy in this example. When Canadians buy T-shirts

FIGURE 2.9   The Gains from Trade

(a) Tom

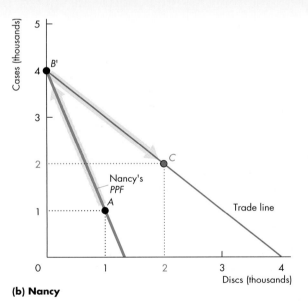

(b) Nancy

Tom and Nancy initially produce at point *A* on their respective *PPFs*. Tom has a comparative advantage in discs, and Nancy has a comparative advantage in cases. If Tom specializes in discs, he produces at point *B* on his *PPF*. If Nancy specializes in cases, she produces at point *B'* on her *PPF*. They exchange cases for discs along the red "Trade

line." Nancy buys discs from Tom for less than her opportunity cost of producing them, and Tom buys cases from Nancy for less than his opportunity cost of producing them. Each goes to point *C*—a point outside his or her *PPF*—where each produces 2,000 CDs an hour. Tom and Nancy increase production with no change in resources.

from China and when China buys regional jets from Canada, both countries gain. We get our shirts at a lower cost than that at which we can produce them, and China gets its regional jets at a lower cost than that at which it can produce them.

Tom and Nancy are equally productive. Tom can produce the same quantities of discs as Nancy can produce cases. But this equal productivity is not the source of the gains from specialization and trade. The gains arise from comparative advantage and would be available even if one of the trading partners was much more productive than the other. To see that comparative advantage is the source of the gains, let's look at Tom and Nancy when Nancy is much more productive than Tom.

Absolute Advantage

A person has an **absolute advantage** if that person can produce more goods with a given amount of resources than another person can. Absolute advantage arises from differences in productivity. A person who has a better technology or more capital or is more skilled than another person has an absolute advantage. (Absolute advantage also applies to nations.)

The gains from trade arise from *comparative* advantage, so people can gain from trade in the presence of *absolute* advantage. To see how, suppose that Nancy invents and patents a new production process that makes her *four* times as productive as she was before in the production of both cases and discs. With her new technology, Nancy can produce 16,000 cases an hour (4 times the original 4,000) if she puts all her resources into making cases. Alternatively, she can produce 5,332 discs (4 times the original 1,333) if she puts all her resources into making discs. Nancy now has an absolute advantage.

But Nancy's *opportunity cost* of 1 disc is still 3 cases. And this opportunity cost is higher than Tom's. So Nancy can still get discs at a lower cost by exchanging cases for discs with Tom.

In this example, Nancy will no longer produce only cases. With no trade, she would produce 4,000 discs and 4,000 cases. With trade, she will increase her production of cases to 7,000 and decrease her production of discs to 3,000. Tom will produce 4,000 discs and no cases. Tom will provide Nancy with 2,000 discs in exchange for 2,000 cases. So Tom's CD production will increase from 1,000 to 2,000 as before. Nancy's CD production will increase from 4,000 to 5,000.

Both Tom and Nancy have gained 1,000 CDs by taking advantage of comparative advantage, the same gains as before.

The key point to recognize is that even though someone (or some nation) has an absolute advantage, this fact does not destroy comparative advantage.

Dynamic Comparative Advantage

At any given point in time, the resources and technologies available determine the comparative advantages that individuals and nations have. But just by repeatedly producing a particular good or service, people become more productive in that activity, a phenomenon called **learning-by-doing**. Learning-by-doing is the basis of *dynamic* comparative advantage. **Dynamic comparative advantage** is a comparative advantage that a person (or country) possesses as a result of having specialized in a particular activity and, as a result of learning-by-doing, having become the producer with the lowest opportunity cost.

Hong Kong and Singapore are examples of countries that have pursued dynamic comparative advantage vigorously. They have developed industries in which initially they did not have a comparative advantage but, through learning-by-doing, became low opportunity cost producers in those industries. A specific example is the decision to develop a genetic engineering industry in Singapore. Singapore probably did not have a comparative advantage in genetic engineering initially. But it might develop one as its scientists and production workers become more skilled in this activity.

REVIEW QUIZ

1 What gives a person a comparative advantage?
2 Is production still efficient when people specialize?
3 Why do people specialize and trade?
4 What are the gains from specialization and trade?
5 What is the source of the gains from trade?
6 Distinguish between comparative advantage and absolute advantage.
7 How does dynamic comparative advantage arise?

The Market Economy

INDIVIDUALS AND COUNTRIES GAIN BY specializing in the production of those goods and services in which they have a comparative advantage and then trading with each other. Adam Smith identified this source of economic wealth in his *Wealth of Nations,* published in 1776—see p. 54.

To enable billions of people who specialize in producing millions of different goods and services to reap these gains, trade must be organized. But trade need not be *planned* or *managed* by a central authority. In fact, when such an arrangement has been tried, as it was for 60 years in Russia, the result has been less than dazzling.

Trade is organized by using social institutions. Two key social institutions are

■ Property rights
■ Markets

Property Rights

Property rights are social arrangements that govern the ownership, use, and disposal of resources, goods, and services. *Real property* includes land and buildings—the things we call property in ordinary speech—and durable goods such as factories and equipment. *Financial property* includes stocks and bonds and money in the bank. *Intellectual property* is the intangible product of creative effort. This type of property includes books, music, computer programs, and inventions of all kinds and is protected by copyrights and patents.

If property rights are not enforced, the incentive to specialize and produce the goods in which each person has a comparative advantage is weakened, and some of the potential gains from specialization and trade are lost. If people can easily steal the production of others, then time, energy, and resources are devoted not to production but to protecting possessions.

Property rights evolved because they enable societies to reap the gains from trade. If we had not developed property rights, we would still be hunting and gathering like our Stone Age ancestors.

Even in countries where property rights are well established, such as Canada, protecting intellectual property is proving to be a challenge in the face of modern technologies that make it relatively easy to copy audio and video material, computer programs, and books.

Markets

In ordinary speech, the word *market* means a place where people buy and sell goods such as fish, meat, fruits, and vegetables. In economics, a *market* has a more general meaning. A **market** is any arrangement that enables buyers and sellers to get information and to do business with each other. An example is the market in which oil is bought and sold—the world oil market. The world oil market is not a place. It is the network of oil producers, users, wholesalers, and brokers who buy and sell oil. In the world oil market, decision makers do not meet physically. They make deals throughout the world by telephone, fax, and direct computer link.

Nancy and Tom can get together and do a deal without markets. But for billions of individuals to specialize and trade millions of goods and services, markets are essential. Like property rights, markets have evolved because they facilitate trade. Without organized markets, we would miss out on a substantial part of the potential gains from trade. Enterprising individuals, each one pursuing his or her own goals, have profited from making markets, standing ready to buy or sell the items in which they specialize.

Circular Flows in the Market Economy

Figure 2.10 identifies two types of markets: goods markets and factor markets. *Goods markets* are those in which goods and services are bought and sold. *Factor markets* are those in which factors of production are bought and sold.

Households decide how much of their labour, land, capital, and entrepreneurship to sell or rent in factor markets. Households receive incomes in the form of wages, rent, interest, and profit. Households also decide how to spend their incomes on goods and services produced by firms. Firms decide the quantities of factors of production to hire, how to use them to produce goods and services, what goods and services to produce, and in what quantities to produce them.

Figure 2.10 shows the flows that result from these decisions by households and firms. The red flows are the factors that go from households through factor markets to firms and the goods and services that go from firms through goods markets to households. The green flows in the opposite direction are the payments made in exchange for these items.

How do markets coordinate all these decisions?

FIGURE 2.10   Circular Flows in the Market Economy

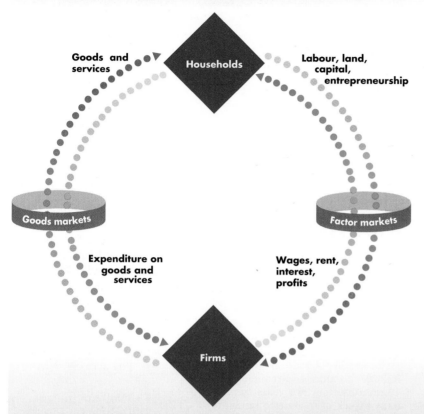

Goods and services

Households

Labour, land, capital, entrepreneurship

Goods markets

Factor markets

Expenditure on goods and services

Wages, rent, interest, profits

Firms

Households and firms make economic choices. Households choose the quantities of labour, land, capital, and entrepreneurship to sell or rent to firms in exchange for wages, rent, interest, and profit. Households also choose how to spend their incomes on the various types of goods and services available. Firms choose the quantities of factors of production to hire and the quantities of the various goods and services to produce. Goods markets and factor markets coordinate these choices of households and firms. Factors of production and goods flow clockwise (red), and money payments flow counterclockwise (green).

Coordinating Decisions

Markets coordinate individual decisions through price adjustments. To see how, think about your local market for hamburgers. Suppose that some people who want to buy hamburgers are not able to do so. To make the choices of buyers and sellers compatible, buyers must scale down their appetites or more hamburgers must be offered for sale (or both must happen). A rise in the price of a hamburger produces this outcome. A higher price encourages producers to offer more hamburgers for sale. It also encourages some people to change their lunch plans. Fewer people buy hamburgers, and more buy hot dogs. More hamburgers (and more hot dogs) are offered for sale.

Alternatively, suppose that more hamburgers are available than people want to buy. In this case, to make the choices of buyers and sellers compatible, more hamburgers must be bought or fewer hamburgers must be offered for sale (or both). A fall in the price of a hamburger achieves this outcome. A lower price encourages firms to produce a smaller quantity of hamburgers. It also encourages people to buy more hamburgers.

REVIEW QUIZ

1 Why are social arrangements such as markets and property rights necessary?
2 What are the main functions of markets?

◆ You have now begun to see how economists approach economic questions. Scarcity, choice, and divergent opportunity costs explain why we specialize and trade and why property rights and markets have developed. You can see all around you the lessons you've learned in this chapter. *Reading Between the Lines* on pp. 48–49 gives an example. It explores the *PPF* of a student like you and the choices that students must make that influence their own economic growth—the growth of their incomes.

The Cost and Benefit of Education

Essence of the Story

■ Jeffrey Pfeffer and Christina Fong of the Stanford Graduate School of Business say that MBA programs teach little of use in the business world.

■ The salaries earned by MBA graduates tell a different story.

■ The average starting salary for an MBA is $95,000, up from $59,750 before the MBA.

■ At the Rotman School of Management at the University of Toronto, students entering the two-year program have an average salary of $50,000 and an average starting salary of $89,000 after graduation.

■ Brian Bemmels said the UBC business school had over 700 applicants for 100 places and most were graduates of medicine, engineering, and general arts.

THE GLOBE AND MAIL, AUGUST 28, 2002

Academics leap to defence of the MBA

They don't come with a guarantee, but business degrees offer students well-paying jobs with reputable companies, say many of Canada's top business schools, throwing cold water on a new study questioning the value of an MBA. ...

After surveying decades of research, Jeffrey Pfeffer and Christina Fong of Stanford's graduate school of business have concluded that, with the possible exception of the most elite programs, master's degrees in business administration teach little that would be of real use in the business world. ...

The salaries for these graduates are a telling story. At Queen's University's School of Business, for example, the average starting salary is $95,000. Before joining the program, the average salary of students is $59,750. And at the Rotman School of Management at the University of Toronto, students entering the two-year program have salaries in the $50,000 on average. But the average starting salary for this year's graduate was $89,000. ...

Brian Bemmels, associate dean for academic programs at the University of British Columbia's faculty of commerce, said the research article forces schools to evaluate their programs. He added that the article is based on a lot of opinion.

UBC's business school made a major change in 1995, restructuring its MBA program and reducing it to 15 months from two years to minimize losses of income to students. The average age of students in the program is 31.

Mr. Bemmels said the demand for an MBA degree speaks for itself. UBC had well over 700 applicants for 100 seats this year. Only 17 per cent of the incoming class has a business degree, he said. The rest are graduates of medicine, engineering and general arts.

"All these people wouldn't be doing it if they didn't think it was valuable," Mr. Bemmels said.

"I don't believe the notion that they have been fooled and tricked into something that's no good to them," he added.

Reprinted with permission from *The Globe and Mail.*

Economic Analysis

■ Education increases human capital and expands production possibilities.

■ The opportunity cost of a degree is forgone consumption. The payoff is an increase in lifetime production possibilities.

■ Figure 1 shows the choices facing a high school graduate who can consume education goods and services and consumption goods and services on the blue *PPF*.

■ Working full time, this person can consume at point *A* on the blue *PPF* in Fig. 1.

■ By attending university, the student moves from point *A* to point *B* along her *PPF*, forgoes current consumption (the opportunity cost of education), and increases the use of educational goods and services.

■ On graduating from university, earnings jump so production possibilities expand to the red *PPF* in Fig. 1.

■ Figure 2 shows a university graduate's choices. The blue curve is the same *PPF* as the red *PPF* in Fig. 1.

■ Working full time, this person earns enough to consume at point *C* on the blue *PPF* in Fig. 2.

■ By pursuing an MBA, the student moves from point *C* to point *D* along her *PPF*, forgoes current consumption (the opportunity cost of an MBA), and increases the use of educational goods and services.

■ With an MBA, a person's earnings jump again, so production possibilities expand to the red *PPF* in Fig. 2.

■ For people who have the required ability, the benefits of post-secondary and post-graduate education exceed the costs.

You're The Voter

■ The Canada Millennium Scholarship Foundation, funded by the federal government, provides $4,000 a year to 900 young Canadians.

■ Do you think the Canada Millennium Scholarship Foundation should be expanded so that more students can benefit from it?

■ With the huge return from post-secondary and post-graduate education, why don't more people remain in school for longer?

■ Would you vote for or against a tax increase to provide greater funding for the Canada Millennium Scholarship Foundation? Why?

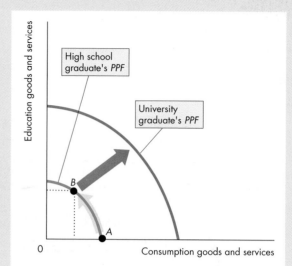

Figure 1 High school graduate's choices

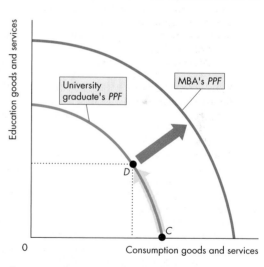

Figure 2 University graduate's choices

49

SUMMARY

KEY POINTS

Production Possibilities and Opportunity Cost (pp. 34–36)

- The production possibilities frontier, *PPF*, is the boundary between production levels that are attainable and those that are not attainable when all the available resources are used to their limit.
- Production efficiency occurs at points on the *PPF*.
- Along the *PPF*, the opportunity cost of producing more of one good is the amount of the other good that must be given up.
- The opportunity cost of all goods increases as the production of the good increases.

Using Resources Efficiently (pp. 37–39)

- The marginal cost of a good is the opportunity cost of producing one more unit.
- The marginal benefit from a good is the maximum amount of another good that a person is willing to forgo to obtain more of the first good.
- The marginal benefit of a good decreases as the amount available increases.
- Resources are used efficiently when the marginal cost of each good is equal to its marginal benefit.

Economic Growth (pp. 40–41)

- Economic growth, which is the expansion of production possibilities, results from capital accumulation and technological change.
- The opportunity cost of economic growth is forgone current consumption.

Gains from Trade (pp. 42–45)

- A person has a comparative advantage in producing a good if that person can produce the good at a lower opportunity cost than everyone else.
- People gain by specializing in the activity in which they have a comparative advantage and trading with others.
- Dynamic comparative advantage arises from learning-by-doing.

The Market Economy (pp. 46–47)

- Property rights and markets enable people to gain from specialization and trade.
- Markets coordinate decisions and help to allocate resources to *higher* valued uses.

KEY FIGURES

Figure 2.1   Production Possibilities Frontier, 34
Figure 2.4   The Efficient Use of Resources, 39
Figure 2.9   The Gains from Trade, 44
Figure 2.10   Circular Flows in the Market Economy, 47

KEY TERMS

Absolute advantage, 45
Allocative efficiency, 39
Capital accumulation, 40
Comparative advantage, 42
Dynamic comparative advantage, 45
Economic growth, 40
Learning-by-doing, 45
Marginal benefit, 38
Marginal benefit curve, 38
Marginal cost, 37
Market, 46
Preferences, 38
Production efficiency, 35
Production possibilities frontier, 34
Property rights, 46
Technological change, 40

PROBLEMS

*1. Use the figure to calculate Wendell's opportunity cost of one hour of tennis when he increases the time he plays tennis from
a. 4 to 6 hours a week. 2.5 % /hrs
b. 6 to 8 hours a week. 5% /hr.

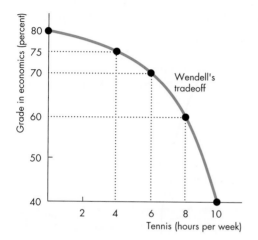

2. Use the figure to calculate Tina's opportunity cost of a day of skiing when she increases her time spent skiing from
a. 2 to 4 days a month.
b. 4 to 6 days a month.

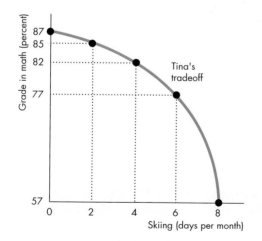

*3. In problem 1, describe the relationship between the time Wendell spends playing tennis and the opportunity cost of an hour of tennis.

4. In problem 2, describe the relationship between the time Tina spends skiing and the opportunity cost of a day of skiing.

*5. Wendell, in problem 1, has the following marginal benefit curve:

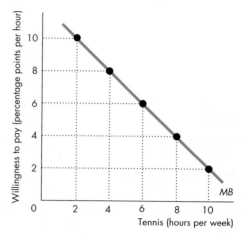

a. If Wendell is efficient, what is his grade? 65%
b. Why would Wendell be worse off getting a higher grade?

6. Tina, in problem 2, has the following marginal benefit curve:

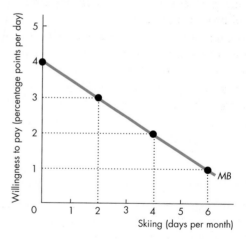

a. If Tina is efficient, how much does she ski?
b. Why would Tina be worse off spending more days a month skiing?

*7. Sunland's production possibilities are

Food		Sunscreen
(kilograms per month)		(litres per month)
300	and	0
200	and	50
100	and	100
0	and	150

a. Draw a graph of Sunland's production possibilities frontier.

b. What are Sunland's opportunity costs of producing food and sunscreen at each output?

8. Jane's Island's production possibilities are

Corn (kilograms per month)		Cloth (metres per month)
6	and	0
4	and	2
2	and	4
0	and	6

a. Draw a graph of the *PPF* on Jane's Island.
b. What are Jane's opportunity costs of producing corn and cloth at each output in the table?

*9. In problem 7, to get a litre of sunscreen, the people of Sunland are willing to give up: 5 kilograms of food if they have 25 litres of sunscreen; 2 kilograms of food if they have 75 litres of sunscreen; and 1 kilogram of food if they have 125 litres of sunscreen.
a. Draw a graph of Sunland's marginal benefit from sunscreen.
b. What is the efficient quantity of sunscreen?

10. In problem 8, to get a metre of cloth, Jane is willing to give up: 1.5 kilograms of corn if she has 2 metres of cloth; 1.0 kilogram of corn if she has 4 metres of cloth; and 0.5 kilograms of corn if she has 6 metres of cloth.
a. Draw a graph of Jane's marginal benefit from cloth.
b. What is Jane's efficient quantity of cloth?

*11. Busyland's production possibilities are

Food (kilograms per month)		Sunscreen (litres per month)
150	and	0
100	and	100
50	and	200
0	and	300

Calculate Busyland's opportunity costs of food and sunscreen at each output in the table.

12. Joe's Island's production possibilities are

Corn (kilograms per month)		Cloth (metres per month)
12	and	0
8	and	1
4	and	2
0	and	3

What are Joe's opportunity costs of producing corn and cloth at each output in the table?

*13. In problems 7 and 11, Sunland and Busyland each produce and consume 100 kilograms of food and 100 litres of sunscreen per month, and they do not trade. Now the countries begin to trade with each other.
a. What good does Sunland sell to Busyland, and what good does it buy from Busyland?
b. If Sunland and Busyland divide the total output of food and sunscreen equally, what are the gains from trade?

14. In problems 8 and 12, Jane's Island and Joe's Island each produce and consume 4 kilograms of corn and 2 metres of cloth and they do not trade. Now the islands begin to trade.
a. What good does Jane sell to Joe and what good does Jane buy from Joe?
b. If Jane and Joe divide the total output of corn and cloth equally, what are the gains from trade?

CRITICAL THINKING

1. After you have studied *Reading Between the Lines* on pp. 48–49, answer the following questions:
a. At what point on the blue *PPF* in Fig. 1 on p. 49 is the combination of education goods and services and consumption goods and services efficient? Explain your answer.
b. Students are facing rising tuition. How does higher tuition change the opportunity cost of education and how does it change the *PPF*s in Fig. 1 and Fig. 2?
c. Who receives the benefits from education? Is the marginal cost of education equal to the marginal benefit of education? Is resource use in the market for education efficient?

WEB EXERCISES

1. Use the links on the Parkin–Bade Web site and obtain data on the tuition and other costs of enrolling in the MBA program of a school that interests you. If an MBA graduate can earn as much as the amounts reported in the news article in *Reading Between the Lines* on pp. 48–49, does the marginal benefit of an MBA exceed its marginal cost? Why doesn't everyone get an MBA?

Your Economic Revolution

You are making progress in your study of economics. You've already encountered the big questions and big ideas of economics. And you've learned about the key insight of Adam Smith, the founder of economics: specialization and exchange create economic wealth. ◆ You are studying economics at a time that future historians will call the *Information Revolution*. We reserve the word "Revolution" for big events that influence all future generations. ◆ During the *Agricultural Revolution*, which occurred 10,000 years ago, people learned to domesticate animals and plant crops. They stopped roaming in search of food and settled in villages and eventually towns and cities, where they developed markets in which to exchange their products. ◆ During the *Industrial Revolution*, which began 240 years ago, people used science to create new technologies. This revolution brought extraordinary wealth for some but created conditions in which others were left behind. It brought social and political tensions that we still face today. ◆ During today's *Information Revolution*, people who embraced the new technologies prospered on an unimagined scale. But the incomes and living standards of the less educated are falling behind, and social and political tensions are increasing. Today's revolution has a global dimension. Some of the winners live in previously poor countries in Asia, and some of the losers live here in North America. ◆ So you are studying economics at an interesting time. Whatever *your* motivation is for studying economics, *our* objective is to help you do well in your course, to enjoy it, and to develop a deeper understanding of the economic world around you. ◆ There are three reasons why we hope that we both succeed: First, a decent understanding of economics will help you to become a full participant in the Information Revolution. Second, an understanding of economics will help you play a more effective role as a citizen and voter and enable you to add your voice to those who are looking for solutions to our social and political problems. Third, you will enjoy the sheer fun of *understanding* the forces at play and how they are shaping our world. ◆ If you are finding economics interesting, think seriously about majoring in the subject. A degree in economics gives the best training available in problem solving, offers lots of opportunities to develop conceptual skills, and opens doors to a wide range of graduate courses, including the MBA, and to a wide range of jobs. You can read more about the benefits of an economics degree in the essay by Robert Whaples and Harvey King in the *Study Guide*. ◆ Economics was born during the Industrial Revolution. We'll look at its birth and meet its founder, Adam Smith. Then we'll talk about the progress that economists have made and some of the outstanding policy problems of today with one of today's most distinguished economists, Lawrence H. Summers, President of Harvard University.

PROBING THE IDEAS
The Sources of Economic Wealth

ADAM SMITH *was a giant of a scholar who contributed to ethics and jurisprudence as well as economics. Born in 1723 in Kirkcaldy, a small fishing town near Edinburgh, Scotland, Smith was the only child of the town's customs officer (who died before Adam was born).*

His first academic appointment, at age 28, was as Professor of Logic at the University of Glasgow. He subsequently became tutor to a wealthy Scottish duke, whom he accompanied on a two-year grand European tour, following which he received a pension of £300 a year—ten times the average income at that time.

With the financial security of his pension, Smith devoted ten years to writing An Inquiry into the Nature and Causes of The Wealth of Nations, *which was published in 1776. Many people had written on economic issues before Adam Smith, but he made economics a science. Smith's account was so broad and authoritative that no subsequent writer on economics could advance ideas without tracing their connections to those of Adam Smith.*

"It is not from the benevolence of the butcher, the brewer, or the baker that we expect our dinner, but from their regard to their own interests."

ADAM SMITH
The Wealth of Nations

Why are some nations wealthy while others are poor? This question lies at the heart of economics. And it leads directly to a second question: What can poor nations do to become wealthy?

Adam Smith, who is regarded by many scholars as the founder of economics, attempted to answer these questions in his book *The Wealth of Nations*, published in 1776. Smith was pondering these questions at the height of the Industrial Revolution. During these years, new technologies were invented and applied to the manufacture of cotton and wool cloth, iron, transportation, and agriculture.

Smith wanted to understand the sources of economic wealth, and he brought his acute powers of observation and abstraction to bear on the question. His answer:

- The division of labour
- Free markets

The division of labour—breaking tasks down into simple tasks and becoming skilled in those tasks—is the source of "the greatest improvement in the productive powers of labour," said Smith. The division of labour became even more productive when it was applied to creating new technologies. Scientists and engineers, trained in extremely narrow fields, became specialists at inventing. Their powerful skills accelerated the advance of technology, so by the 1820s, machines could make consumer goods faster and more accurately than any craftsman could. And by the 1850s, machines could make other machines that labour alone could never have made.

But, said Smith, the fruits of the division of labour are limited by the extent of the market. To make the market as large as possible, there must be no impediments to free

54

trade both within a country and among countries. Smith argued that when each person makes the best possible economic choice, that choice leads as if by "an invisible hand" to the best outcome for society as a whole. The butcher, the brewer, and the baker each pursue their own interests but, in doing so, also serve the interests of everyone else.

Adam Smith speculated that one person, working hard, using the hand tools available in the 1770s, might possibly make 20 pins a day. Yet, he observed, by using those same hand tools but breaking the process into a number of individually small operations in which people specialize—by the **division of labour**—ten people could make a staggering 48,000 pins a day. One draws out the wire, another straightens it, a third cuts it, a fourth points it, a fifth grinds it. Three specialists make the head, and a fourth attaches it. Finally, the pin is polished and packaged. But a large market is needed to support the division of labour: One factory employing ten workers would need to sell more that 15 million pins a year to stay in business.

If Adam Smith were here today, the computer chip would fascinate him. He would see it as an extraordinary example of the productivity of the division of labour and of the use of machines to make machines that make other machines. From a design of a chip's intricate circuits, cameras transfer an image to glass plates that work like stencils. Workers prepare silicon wafers on which the circuits are printed. Some slice the wafers, others polish them, others bake them, and yet others coat them with a light-sensitive chemical. Machines transfer a copy of the circuit onto the wafer. Chemicals then etch the design onto the wafer. Further processes deposit atom-sized transistors and aluminum connectors. Finally, a laser separates the hundreds of chips on the wafers. Every stage in the process of creating a computer chip uses other computer chips. And like the pin of the 1770s, the computer chip of today benefits from the large market—a global market—to buy chips in the huge quantities in which they are produced efficiently.

Many economists have worked on the big themes that Adam Smith began. One of these is Lawrence H. Summers, President of Harvard University and distinguished economist.

TALKING WITH

LAWRENCE H. SUMMERS

is President of Harvard University. Born in 1954 in New Haven, Connecticut, into a family of distinguished economists, he was an undergraduate at the Massachusetts Institute of Technology and a graduate student at Harvard University. While still in his 20s, he became one of the youngest tenured economics professors at Harvard University. In Washington, he has held a succession of public service jobs at the World Bank and in the U.S. government, culminating in 1999 with his appointment as Secretary of the Treasury—the chief financial officer of the United States and the president's highest-ranking adviser.

Dr. Summers's research has covered an enormous range of macroeconomic and public policy issues that include capital taxation, unemployment, global financial crises, the transition to a market economy in Eastern Europe, and the problem of speeding progress in the developing countries.

Michael Parkin and Robin Bade talked with Lawrence Summers about his career and the progress that economists have made since the pioneering days of Adam Smith.

Lawrence H. Summers

How does Adam Smith's assessment of the "nature and causes of the wealth of nations" look today in light of the lessons that economists have learned over the past two centuries?

Adam Smith is looking very good today. I think one of the most important insights of the social sciences of the last several centuries is Smith's idea that good things can come from the invisible hand—from decentralization rather than from central planning and direction. But Smith is also prescient in recognizing the various qualifications to the argument for the invisible hand, whether involving fairness, externalities, or monopoly.

What do we know today that Adam Smith didn't know?

We know today much more than Smith did about economic fluctuations and about the role of money—about what we today call macroeconomics. We know more today about economic situations that involve bargaining, whether between two individuals or between small numbers of firms in an industry, or between a buyer and a seller. We know much more today about markets without perfect information. I know how good my used car is when I sell it—you don't when you buy it. I know whether I'm sick when I buy medical insurance, but you the insurance company have to try to figure it out. The role of information in markets, which turns out to be quite profound, is something we understand much better today. And we also understand much better today the role of politics and governments in shaping the economy, which is far larger than it was in Smith's day.

Coincidentally, a few weeks before we're holding this conversation, a new nation was born—East Timor. What advice can economists offer a new and extremely poor nation as it takes its first steps?

Much of economic success involves strong rights to property. Has anyone ever washed a rented car or taken as good care of their hotel room as their home? When people own their farmlands, they're much more likely to farm them sustainably. When businesses own their machinery, they're much more likely to take care of it. When individuals own what they produce, they're much more likely to work hard.

Strong property rights and the framework of laws that support them are profoundly important to the market-based exchanges that are essential to economic success. So also is stable money that can be a basis for exchange. So also is an educated and capable population. But if there is a single lesson that is important for a starting economy, it is that strong property rights can motivate individuals.

One lesson that we've learned from your work at the World Bank is that the return to educating girls in developing countries is very high. What did you discover in that work?

Primary education, and especially for girls, may be the highest return investment available in the developing world. Those who read produce more and therefore earn more. Girls who are educated grow up to be better mothers who have smaller, happier, healthier families. Women who are educated are empowered with greater career options. They are less likely to fall into prostitution, and that reduces the spread of AIDS. Women who are educated are much more likely to take care of the environment. So it is in many respects that primary education, and especially that of girls, generates very large returns.

Are there any other activities that yield comparable returns for developing countries?

Maybe some investments in health care that generate very large returns—it's a difficult evaluation to make. The really crucial lesson is that a country's most pre-

> "The really crucial lesson is that a country's most precious assets are its people, and investments in people are likely to be the most important investments of all."

cious assets are its people, and investments in people are likely to be the most important investments of all.

Some of your earliest research was on taxing the income from capital. Why isn't the income from capital just like the income from labour?

Think about it this way: two individuals both earn a hundred dollars. One spends it all this year; the other saves half of it and earns 10 percent interest next year. Who should pay more total taxes? Plausibly, for fairness, both should pay the same tax. A tax on income will lead to the same taxes in the first year for the two individuals; and higher taxes in the second year for the individual who saved.

In effect, taxes on capital income are taxes on future consumption, and it is far from clear why a society should want to tax future consumption more highly than present consumption.

On the other hand, very large fortunes often show up as capital income, and so designing a workable and fair tax system that doesn't tax investment income is something that is very difficult to do.

Would you say that we have not yet managed to figure this one out?

We'll all be working on finding the best tax systems for a long time to come. And it may mean that the income tax is, as Churchill said of democracy, terrible but the best alternative.

The United States has a large and persistent current account deficit, a low personal saving rate, and a projected deficit in the Social Security and Medicare trust funds. Are you concerned about these problems?

Herb Stein, who was a leading American policy economist, once said that the unsustainable cannot be sustained and must surely end!

This is a concern, given that U.S. national debt to foreigners is rising faster than U.S. income. And it's a concern in terms of the financing of Social Security and Medicare as our population ages. In a way, the solution to both these problems is more American saving, because that will put us in a stronger position as our population ages, and will allow us to have investments in the United States without incurring debts to foreigners.

Probably the most potent way of increasing a country's national savings is to improve the position of its budget. Whether to increase taxes or cut expenditures is a judgment for the congress to debate. My guess is that some combination would be appropriate. There are aspects of expenditures that are going to be hard to control. On the other hand, there are other aspects in terms of transfer payments and in terms of various subsidies where economies probably are possible. And one virtue of a strong fiscal position is that it reduces interest expense down the road.

Did you always want to be an economist? How did you choose economics?

I thought I would be a mathematician or a physicist, but found myself very interested in questions of public policy. I was very involved in debate when I was in college. So I found myself wanting very much to combine an interest in public policy issues with an analytical approach, and economics gave me a way to do that. I also found that I had some aptitude, relative to my aptitude for pure mathematics or physics, so I gravitated to economics.

What led a brilliant academic economist to Washington? What did you want to achieve?

I hoped to put to use some of what I had learned in my studies in a direct way and to enhance my understanding of the way actual economies work by seeing how the policy process operated. I had a great time in Washington and feel that my economics training made a huge difference in everything I did. Whether it was thinking about how to respond to the Mexican and Asian financial crises or working on financial deregulation. Whether it was choosing optimal investments for the Customs Department in protecting our borders or designing tax incentives to promote saving. Whether it was supporting the protection of the Social Security trust fund or thinking about enforcement policies against corporate tax shelters. Principles of economics—in terms of maximizing benefits relative to costs, in terms of always thinking of the margin, in terms of always recognizing the opportunity cost of choices taken, in terms of always needing to see things add up—was quite valuable.

And what insights does economics bring to the task of running a major university?

I came to Harvard because I thought after my time in government the two most important resources that were going to shape the economies of the future were leaders and new ideas, and those are the two things that a university produces.

Successful leadership in a university is all about what economists think about all the time—incentives—whether it's for professors to do a good job teaching, attracting the best scholars in a particular area, or motivating concern and research about the most important problems.

Leadership and management for the university are very much about economics because they're very much about incentives. Some of them are pecuniary and involve money, but other incentives come from people's feelings of being appreciated; they come from the teams in which people have an opportunity to work; they come from the way in which the university is organized. If working at the treasury was heavily about applied macroeconomics, leadership in the university is heavily about applied microeconomics.

What is your advice to a student who is just setting out to become an economist? What other subjects work well with economics?

The best advice to students is, don't be a commodity that's available in a perfectly competitive market. Stand out by developing your own distinctive expertise in something you care deeply about. It matters much less what it is and much more that it be yours and it not be a hundred other people's.

I think there is enormous potential in almost every area of economics, but I think that the people who will contribute the most to economics over the next quarter century will be those who have some keen understanding of the context in which economics is playing out—the international context, the technological context, and the political context. So my hope would be that those interested in economics would understand that economics is very different from physics in that it is tracking a changing reality and that in order to do the best economics in a given period, you have to be able to track that changing reality, and that means understanding international, technological, and political contexts.

DEMAND AND SUPPLY — CHAPTER 3

Slide, Rocket, and Roller Coaster

Slide, rocket, and roller coaster—Canada's Wonderland rides? No, they are commonly used descriptions of price changes. ◆ The price of a personal computer took a dramatic slide from around $3,000 in 2000 to around $700 in 2001. What caused this price slide? We'll answer this question in *Reading Between the Lines*. ◆ Occasionally, a price will rocket. But a price rocket, like a satellite-launching rocket, has a limited life. It eventually runs out of fuel. One spectacular price rocket occurred when the price of coffee shot skyward from $1.32 a kilogram in 1993 to $4.95 a kilogram in 1994. Why did the price of coffee rise so spectacularly? ◆ Over longer periods, the price of coffee, along with the prices of bananas and other agricultural commodities, rises and falls like a roller coaster ride. ◆ Economics is about the choices people make to cope with scarcity. These choices are guided by costs and benefits and are coordinated through markets. ◆ Demand and supply is the tool that explains how markets work. It is the main tool of economics. It is used to study the price of a CD, wage rates and jobs, rents and housing, pollution, crime, consumer protection, education, welfare, the value of money, and interest rates.

◆ Your careful study of this topic will bring big rewards both in your further study of economics and in your everyday life. When you have completed your study of demand and supply, you will be able to explain how prices are determined and make predictions about price slides, rockets, and roller coasters. Once you understand demand and supply, you will view the world through new eyes.

After studying this chapter, you will be able to

- Describe a market and explain the link between price and opportunity cost
- Explain the influences on demand
- Explain the influences on supply
- Explain how demand and supply determine prices and quantities bought and sold
- Use demand and supply to make predictions about changes in prices and quantities

Markets and Prices

WHEN YOU NEED A NEW PAIR OF RUNNING shoes, want a bagel and a latte, plan to upgrade your stereo system, or fly to Florida for the winter break, you must find someone who is selling these items or offering these services. You will find them in a *market*. You learned in Chapter 2 (p. 46) that a market is any arrangement that enables buyers and sellers to get information and to do business with each other.

A market has two sides: buyers and sellers. There are markets for *goods* such as apples and hiking boots, for *services* such as haircuts and tennis lessons, for *factors of production* such as computer programmers and earthmovers, and for other manufactured *inputs* such as memory chips and auto parts. There are also markets for money such as Japanese yen and for financial securities such as Yahoo! stock. Only our imagination limits what can be traded in markets.

Some markets are physical places where buyers and sellers meet and where an auctioneer or a broker helps to determine the prices. Examples of this type of market are the New York Stock Exchange and the wholesale fish, meat, and produce markets.

Some markets are groups of people spread around the world who never meet and know little about each other but are connected through the Internet or by telephone and fax. Examples of this type of market are the e-commerce markets and currency markets.

But most markets are unorganized collections of buyers and sellers. You do most of your trading in this type of market. An example is the market for running shoes. The buyers in this vast international market are the millions of joggers (or those who want to make a fashion statement) who are looking for a new pair of shoes. The sellers are the tens of thousands of retail sports equipment and footwear stores. Each buyer can visit several different stores, and each seller knows that the buyer has a choice of stores.

Markets vary in the intensity of competition that buyers and sellers face. In this chapter, we're going to study a **competitive market**—a market that has many buyers and many sellers, so that no single buyer or seller can influence the price.

Producers offer items for sale only if the price is high enough to cover their opportunity cost. And consumers respond to changing opportunity cost by seeking cheaper alternatives to expensive items.

We are going to study the way people respond to *prices* and the forces that determine prices. But to pursue these tasks, we need to understand the relationship between a price and an opportunity cost.

In everyday life, the *price* of an object is the number of dollars that must be given up in exchange for it. Economists refer to this price as the *money price*.

The *opportunity cost* of an action is the highest-valued alternative forgone. If, when you buy a coffee, the highest-valued thing you forgo is some gum, then the opportunity cost of the coffee is the *quantity* of gum forgone. We can calculate the quantity of gum forgone from the money prices of coffee and gum.

If the money price of coffee is $1 a cup and the money price of gum is 50¢ a pack, then the opportunity cost of one cup of coffee is two packs of gum. To calculate this opportunity cost, we divide the price of a cup of coffee by the price of a pack of gum and find the *ratio* of one price to the other. The ratio of one price to another is called a **relative price**, and a *relative price is an opportunity cost*.

We can express the relative price of coffee in terms of gum or any other good. The normal way of expressing a relative price is in terms of a "basket" of all goods and services. To calculate this relative price, we divide the money price of a good by the money price of a "basket" of all goods (called a *price index*). The resulting relative price tells us the opportunity cost of an item in terms of how much of the "basket" we must give up to buy it.

The theory of demand and supply that we are about to study determines *relative prices,* and the word "price" means *relative* price. When we predict that a price will fall, we do not mean that its *money* price will fall—although it might. We mean that its *relative* price will fall. That is, its price will fall *relative* to the average price of other goods and services.

REVIEW QUIZ

1 What is the distinction between a money price and a relative price?
2 Why is a relative price an opportunity cost?
3 Can you think of an example of a good whose money price and relative price have risen?
4 Can you think of an example of a good whose money price and relative price have fallen?

Let's begin our study of demand and supply, starting with demand.

Demand

└ IF YOU DEMAND SOMETHING, THEN YOU

1. Want it,
2. Can afford it, and
3. Have made a definite plan to buy it.

Wants are the unlimited desires or wishes that people have for goods and services. How many times have you thought that you would like something "if only you could afford it" or "if it weren't so expensive"? Scarcity guarantees that many—perhaps most—of our wants will never be satisfied. Demand reflects a decision about which wants to satisfy.

The **quantity demanded** of a good or service is the amount that consumers plan to buy during a given time period at a particular price. The quantity demanded is not necessarily the same as the quantity actually bought. Sometimes the quantity demanded exceeds the amount of goods available, so the quantity bought is less than the quantity demanded.

The quantity demanded is measured as an amount per unit of time. For example, suppose that you buy one cup of coffee a day. The quantity of coffee that you demand can be expressed as 1 cup per day, 7 cups per week, or 365 cups per year. Without a time dimension, we cannot tell whether the quantity demanded is large or small.

What Determines Buying Plans?

The amount of any particular good or service that consumers plan to buy depends on many factors. The main ones are

1. The price of the good
2. The prices of related goods
3. Expected future prices
4. Income
5. Population
6. Preferences

We first look at the relationship between the quantity demanded and the price of a good. To study this relationship, we keep all other influences on consumers' planned purchases the same and ask: How does the quantity demanded of the good vary as its price varies, other things remaining the same?

The Law of Demand

The **law of demand** states

Other things remaining the same, the higher the price of a good, the smaller is the quantity demanded.

Why does a higher price reduce the quantity demanded? For two reasons:

■ Substitution effect
■ Income effect

Substitution Effect   When the price of a good rises, other things remaining the same, its *relative* price—its opportunity cost—rises. Although each good is unique, it has *substitutes*—other goods that can be used in its place. As the opportunity cost of a good rises, people buy less of that good and more of its substitutes.

Income Effect   When a price rises and all other influences on buying plans remain unchanged, the price rises *relative* to people's incomes. So faced with a higher price and an unchanged income, people cannot afford to buy all the things they previously bought. They must decrease the quantities demanded of at least some goods and services, and normally, the good whose price has increased will be one of the goods that people buy less of.

To see the substitution effect and the income effect at work, think about the effects of a change in the price of a recordable compact disc—a CD-R. Several different goods are substitutes for a CD-R. For example, an audiotape and prerecorded CD provide services similar to those of a CD-R.

Suppose that a CD-R initially sells for $3 and then its price falls to $1.50. People now substitute CD-Rs for audiotapes and prerecorded CDs—the substitution effect. And with a budget that now has some slack from the lower price of a CD-R, people buy more CD-Rs—the income effect. The quantity of CD-Rs demanded increases for these two reasons.

Now suppose that a CD-R initially sells for $3 and then the price doubles to $6. People now substitute prerecorded CDs and audiotapes for CD-Rs—the substitution effect. And faced with a tighter budget, people buy fewer CD-Rs—the income effect. The quantity of CD-Rs demanded decreases for these two reasons.

Demand Curve and Demand Schedule

You are now about to study one of the two most used curves in economics: the demand curve. And you are going to encounter one of the most critical distinctions: the distinction between *demand* and *quantity demanded*.

The term **demand** refers to the entire relationship between the price of the good and the quantity demanded of the good. Demand is illustrated by the demand curve and the demand schedule. The term *quantity demanded* refers to a point on a demand curve—the quantity demanded at a particular price.

Figure 3.1 shows the demand curve for CD-Rs. A **demand curve** shows the relationship between the quantity demanded of a good and its price when all other influences on consumers' planned purchases remain the same.

The table in Fig. 3.1 is the demand schedule for CD-Rs. A *demand schedule* lists the quantities demanded at each price when all other influences on consumers' planned purchases—prices of related goods, expected future prices, income, population, and preferences—remain the same. For example, if the price of a CD-R is 50¢, the quantity demanded is 9 million a week. If the price is $2.50, the quantity demanded is 2 million a week. The other rows of the table show the quantities demanded at prices of $1.00, $1.50, and $2.00.

We graph the demand schedule as a demand curve with the quantity demanded of CD-Rs on the *x*-axis and the price of a CD-R on the *y*-axis. The points on the demand curve labelled *A* through *E* represent the rows of the demand schedule. For example, point *A* represents a quantity demanded of 9 million CD-Rs a week at a price of 50¢ a disc.

Willingness and Ability to Pay   Another way of looking at the demand curve is as a willingness-and-ability-to-pay curve. And the willingness-and-ability-to-pay is a measure of *marginal benefit.*

If a small quantity is available, the highest price that someone is willing and able to pay for one more unit is high. But as the quantity available increases, the marginal benefit of each additional unit falls and the highest price that someone is willing and able to pay also falls along the demand curve.

In Fig. 3.1, if only 2 million CD-Rs are available each week, the highest price that someone is willing to pay for the 2 millionth CD-R is $2.50. But if 9 million CD-Rs are available each week, someone is willing to pay 50¢ for the last CD-R bought.

FIGURE 3.1   The Demand Curve

	Price (dollars per disc)	Quantity demanded (millions of discs per week)
A	0.50	9
B	1.00	6
C	1.50	4
D	2.00	3
E	2.50	2

The table shows a demand schedule for CD-Rs. At a price of 50¢ a disc, 9 million a week are demanded; at a price of $1.50 a disc, 4 million a week are demanded. The demand curve shows the relationship between quantity demanded and price, everything else remaining the same. The demand curve slopes downward: As price decreases, the quantity demanded increases.

The demand curve can be read in two ways. For a given price, the demand curve tells us the quantity that people plan to buy. For example, at a price of $1.50 a disc, the quantity demanded is 4 million discs a week. For a given quantity, the demand curve tells us the maximum price that consumers are willing and able to pay for the last disc available. For example, the maximum price that consumers will pay for the 6 millionth disc is $1.00.

A Change in Demand

When any factor that influences buying plans other than the price of the good changes, there is a **change in demand.** Figure 3.2 illustrates an increase in demand. When demand increases, the demand curve shifts rightward and the quantity demanded is greater at each and every price. For example, at $2.50 a disc, the quantity demanded on the original (blue) demand curve is 2 million discs a week. On the new (red) demand curve, the quantity demanded is 6 million discs a week. Look at the numbers in the table and check that the quantity demanded is greater at each price.

Let's look at the factors that bring a change in demand. There are five key factors to consider.

1. Prices of Related Goods The quantity of CD-Rs that consumers plan to buy depends in part on the prices of substitutes for CD-Rs. A **substitute** is a good that can be used in place of another good. For example, a bus ride is a substitute for a train ride; a hamburger is a substitute for a hot dog; and a prerecorded CD is a substitute for a CD-R. If the price of a substitute for a CD-R rises, people buy less of the substitute and more CD-Rs. For example, if the price of a prerecorded CD rises, people buy fewer CDs and more CD-Rs. The demand for CD-Rs increases.

The quantity of CD-Rs that people plan to buy also depends on the prices of complements with CD-Rs. A **complement** is a good that is used in conjunction with another good. Hamburgers and fries are complements. So are spaghetti and meat sauce, and so are CD-Rs and CD burners. If the price of a CD burner falls, people buy more CD burners *and more* CD-Rs. A fall in the price of a CD burner increases the demand for CD-Rs in Fig. 3.2.

2. Expected Future Prices If the price of a good is expected to rise in the future and if the good can be stored, the opportunity cost of obtaining the good for future use is lower today than it will be when the price has increased. So people retime their purchases—they substitute over time. They buy more of the good today before its price is expected to rise (and less after), so the current demand for the good increases.

For example, suppose that Florida is hit by a frost that damages the season's orange crop. You expect the price of orange juice to rise in the future. So you fill your freezer with enough frozen juice to get you through the next six months. Your current demand for frozen orange juice has increased and your future demand has decreased.

FIGURE 3.2   An Increase in Demand

A change in any influence on buyers' plans other than the price of the good itself results in a new demand schedule and a shift of the demand curve. A change in the price of a CD burner changes the demand for CD-Rs. At a price of $1.50 a disc, 4 million discs a week are demanded when the price of a CD burner is $300 (row C of the table) and 8 million CD-Rs a week are demanded when the price of a CD burner is $100. A *fall* in the price of a CD burner *increases* the demand for CD-Rs. The demand curve shifts *rightward*, as shown by the shift arrow and the resulting red curve.

Original demand schedule CD burner $300			New demand schedule CD burner $100		
	Price (dollars per disc)	**Quantity demanded** (millions of discs per week)		**Price** (dollars per disc)	**Quantity demanded** (millions of discs per week)
A	0.50	9	A'	0.50	13
B	1.00	6	B'	1.00	10
C	1.50	4	C'	1.50	8
D	2.00	3	D'	2.00	7
E	2.50	2	E'	2.50	6

Similarly, if the price of a good is expected to fall in the future, the opportunity cost of buying the good today is high relative to what it is expected to be in the future. So again, people retime their purchases. They buy less of the good now before its price falls, so the demand for the good decreases today and increases in the future.

Computer prices are constantly falling, and this fact poses a dilemma. Will you buy a new computer now, in time for the start of the school year, or will you wait until the price has fallen some more? Because people expect computer prices to keep falling, the current demand for computers is less (the future demand is greater) than it otherwise would be.

3. Income Consumers' income influences demand. When income increases, consumers buy more of most goods, and when income decreases, consumers buy less of most goods. Although an increase in income leads to an increase in the demand for *most* goods, it does not lead to an increase in the demand for *all* goods. A **normal good** is one for which demand increases as income increases. An **inferior good** is one for which demand decreases as income increases. Long-distance transportation has examples of both normal goods and inferior goods. As incomes increase, the demand for air travel (a normal good) increases and the demand for long-distance bus trips (an inferior good) decreases.

4. Population Demand also depends on the size and the age structure of the population. The larger the population, the greater is the demand for all goods and services; the smaller the population, the smaller is the demand for all goods and services.

For example, the demand for parking spaces or movies or CD-Rs or just about anything that you can imagine is much greater in Ottawa than it is in North Bay.

Also, the larger the proportion of the population in a given age group, the greater is the demand for the types of goods and services used by that age group.

For example, in 2001, there were 2.1 million 20-24-year-olds in Canada compared with 2.5 million in 1981. As a result, the demand for college places decreased between 1981 and 2001. During those same years, the number of Canadians aged 85 years and over increased from 195,000 to 430,000. As a result, the demand for nursing home services increased.

TABLE 3.1 The Demand for CD-Rs

The Law of Demand

The quantity of CD-Rs demanded

Decreases if:	Increases if:
■ The price of a CD-R rises	■ The price of a CD-R falls

Changes in Demand

The demand for CD-Rs

Decreases if:	Increases if:
■ The price of a substitute falls	■ The price of a substitute rises
■ The price of a complement rises	■ The price of a complement falls
■ The price of a CD-R is expected to fall in the future	■ The price of a CD-R is expected to rise in the future
■ Income falls*	■ Income rises*
■ The population decreases	■ The population increases

*A CD-R is a normal good.

---

5. Preferences Demand depends on preferences. *Preferences* are an individual's attitudes towards goods and services. For example, a rock music fanatic has a much greater preference for CD-Rs than does a tone-deaf technophobe. As a consequence, even if they have the same incomes, their demands for CD-Rs will be very different.

Table 3.1 summarizes the influences on demand and the direction of those influences.

A Change in the Quantity Demanded Versus a Change in Demand

Changes in the factors that influence buyers' plans cause either a change in the quantity demanded or a change in demand. Equivalently, they cause either a movement along the demand curve or a shift of the demand curve.

The distinction between a change in the quantity demanded and a change in demand is the same as that between a movement along the demand curve and a shift of the demand curve.

A point on the demand curve shows the quantity demanded at a given price. So a movement along the demand curve shows a **change in the quantity demanded.** The entire demand curve shows demand. So a shift of the demand curve shows a *change in demand.* Figure 3.3 illustrates and summarizes these distinctions.

Movement Along the Demand Curve If the price of a good changes but everything else remains the same, there is a movement along the demand curve. Because the demand curve slopes downward, a fall in the price of a good or service increases the quantity demanded of it and a rise in the price of the good or service decreases the quantity demanded of it—the law of demand.

In Fig. 3.3, if the price of a good falls when everything else remains the same, the quantity demanded of that good increases and there is a movement down along the demand curve D_0. If the price rises when everything else remains the same, the quantity demanded of that good decreases and there is a movement up along the demand curve D_0.

A Shift of the Demand Curve If the price of a good remains constant but some other influence on buyers' plans changes, there is a change in the demand for that good. We illustrate a change in demand as a shift of the demand curve. For example, if the price of a CD burner falls, consumers buy more CD-Rs regardless of whether the price of a CD-R is high or low. That is what a rightward shift of the demand curve shows—more CD-Rs are bought at each and every price.

In Fig. 3.3, when any influence on buyers' planned purchases changes, other than the price of the good, there is a *change in demand* and the demand curve shifts. Demand *increases* and the demand curve *shifts rightward* (to the red demand curve D_1) if the price of a substitute rises, the price of a complement falls, the expected future price of the good rises, income increases (for a normal good), or the population increases. Demand *decreases* and the demand curve *shifts leftward* (to the red demand curve D_2) if the price of a substitute falls, the price of a complement rises, the expected future price of the good falls, income decreases (for a normal good), or the population decreases. (For an inferior good, the effects of changes in income are in the direction opposite to those described above.)

FIGURE 3.3 A Change in the Quantity Demanded Versus a Change in Demand

When the price of the good changes, there is a movement along the demand curve and *a change in the quantity demanded,* shown by the blue arrows on demand curve D_0. When any other influence on buyers' plans changes, there is a shift of the demand curve and a *change in demand.* An increase in demand shifts the demand curve rightward (from D_0 to D_1). A decrease in demand shifts the demand curve leftward (from D_0 to D_2).

REVIEW QUIZ

1 Define the quantity demanded of a good or service.
2 What is the law of demand and how do we illustrate it?
3 If a fixed amount of a good is available, what does the demand curve tell us about the price that consumers are willing to pay for that fixed quantity?
4 List all the influences on buying plans that change demand, and for each influence say whether it increases or decreases demand.
5 What happens to the quantity of Palm Pilots demanded and the demand for Palm Pilots if the price of a Palm Pilot falls and all other influences on buying plans remain the same?

Supply

IF A FIRM SUPPLIES A GOOD OR SERVICE, THE FIRM

1. Has the resources and technology to produce it,
2. Can profit from producing it, and
3. Has made a definite plan to produce it and sell it.

A supply is more that just having the *resources* and the *technology* to produce something. *Resources and technology* are the constraints that limit what is possible.

Many useful things can be produced, but they are not produced unless it is profitable to do so. Supply reflects a decision about which technologically feasible items to produce.

The **quantity supplied** of a good or service is the amount that producers plan to sell during a given time period at a particular price. The quantity supplied is not necessarily the same amount as the quantity actually sold. Sometimes the quantity supplied is greater than the quantity demanded, so the quantity bought is less than the quantity supplied.

Like the quantity demanded, the quantity supplied is measured as an amount per unit of time. For example, suppose that GM produces 1,000 cars a day. The quantity of cars supplied by GM can be expressed as 1,000 a day, 7,000 a week, or 365,000 a year. Without the time dimension, we cannot tell whether a particular number is large or small.

What Determines Selling Plans?

The amount of any particular good or service that producers plan to sell depends on many factors. The main ones are

1. The price of the good
2. The prices of resources used to produce the good
3. The prices of related goods produced
4. Expected future prices
5. The number of suppliers
6. Technology

Let's first look at the relationship between the price of a good and the quantity supplied. To study this relationship, we keep all other influences on the quantity supplied the same. We ask: How does the quantity supplied of a good vary as its price varies?

The Law of Supply

The **law of supply** states

Other things remaining the same, the higher the price of a good, the greater is the quantity supplied.

Why does a higher price increase the quantity supplied? It is because *marginal cost increases.* As the quantity produced of any good increases, the marginal cost of producing the good increases. (You can refresh your memory of increasing marginal cost in Chapter 2, p. 37.)

It is never worth producing a good if the price received for it does not at least cover the marginal cost of producing it. So when the price of a good rises, other things remaining the same, producers are willing to incur the higher marginal cost and increase production. The higher price brings forth an increase in the quantity supplied.

Let's now illustrate the law of supply with a supply curve and a supply schedule.

Supply Curve and Supply Schedule

You are now going to study the second of the two most used curves in economics: the supply curve. And you're going to learn about the critical distinction between *supply* and *quantity supplied.*

The term **supply** refers to the entire relationship between the quantity supplied and the price of a good. Supply is illustrated by the supply curve and the supply schedule. The term *quantity supplied* refers to a point on a supply curve—the quantity supplied at a particular price.

Figure 3.4 shows the supply curve of CD-Rs. A **supply curve** shows the relationship between the quantity supplied of a good and its price when all other influences on producers' planned sales remain the same. The supply curve is a graph of a supply schedule.

The table in Fig. 3.4 sets out the supply schedule for CD-Rs. A *supply schedule* lists the quantities supplied at each price when all the other influences on producers' planned sales remain the same. For example, if the price of a CD-R is 50¢, the quantity supplied is zero—in row *A* of the table. If the price of a CD-R is $1.00, the quantity supplied is 3 million CD-Rs a week—in row *B*. The other rows of the table show the quantities supplied at prices of $1.50, $2.00, and $2.50.

FIGURE 3.4   The Supply Curve

The table shows the supply schedule of CD-Rs. For example, at a price of $1.00, 3 million discs a week are supplied; at a price of $2.50, 6 million discs a week are supplied. The supply curve shows the relationship between the quantity supplied and price, everything else remaining the same. The supply curve usually slopes upward: As the price of a good increases, so does the quantity supplied.

A supply curve can be read in two ways. For a given price, it tells us the quantity that producers plan to sell. And for a given quantity, it tells us the minimum price that producers are willing to accept for that quantity.

	Price (dollars per disc)	Quantity supplied (millions of discs per week)
A	0.50	0
B	1.00	3
C	1.50	4
D	2.00	5
E	2.50	6

To make a supply curve, we graph the quantity supplied on the x-axis and the price on the y-axis, just as in the case of the demand curve. The points on the supply curve labelled A through E represent the rows of the supply schedule. For example, point A on the graph represents a quantity supplied of zero at a price of 50¢ a CD-R.

Minimum Supply Price Just as the demand curve has two interpretations, so too does the supply curve. The demand curve can be interpreted as a willingness-and-ability-to-pay curve. The supply curve can be interpreted as a minimum-supply-price curve. It tells us the lowest price at which someone is willing to sell another unit.

If a small quantity is produced, the lowest price at which someone is willing to produce one more unit is low. But if a large quantity is produced, the lowest price at which someone is willing to sell one more unit is high.

In Fig. 3.4, if 6 million CD-Rs a week are produced, the lowest price that a producer is willing to accept for the 6 millionth disc is $2.50. But if only 4 million CD-Rs are produced each week, the lowest price that a producer is willing to accept for the 4 millionth disc is $1.50.

A Change in Supply

When any factor that influences selling plans other than the price of the good changes, there is a **change in supply**. Let's look at the five key factors that change supply.

1. Prices of Productive Resources The prices of productive resources influence supply. The easiest way to see this influence is to think about the supply curve as a minimum-supply-price curve. If the price of a productive resource rises, the lowest price a producer is willing to accept rises, so supply decreases. For example, during 2001, the price of jet fuel increased and the supply of air transportation decreased. Similarly, a rise in the minimum wage decreases the supply of hamburgers. If the wages of disc producers rise, the supply of CD-Rs decreases.

2. Prices of Related Goods Produced The prices of related goods and services that firms produce influence supply. For example, if the price of a prerecorded CD rises, the supply of CD-Rs decreases. CD-Rs and prerecorded CDs are *substitutes in production*—goods that can be produced by using the same resources.

If the price of beef rises, the supply of cowhide increases. Beef and cowhide are *complements in production*—goods that must be produced together.

3. Expected Future Prices If the price of a good is expected to rise, the return from selling the good in the future will be higher than it is today. So supply decreases today and increases in the future.

4. The Number of Suppliers The larger the number of firms that produce a good, the greater is the supply of the good. And as firms enter an industry, the supply in that industry increases. As firms leave an industry, the supply in that industry decreases. For example, over the past two years, there has been a huge increase in the number of firms that design and manage Web sites. As a result of this increase, the supply of Internet and World Wide Web services has increased enormously.

5. Technology New technologies create new products and lower the costs of producing existing products. As a result, they change supply. For example, the use of new technologies in the Taiwan factories that make CD-Rs for Imation Enterprises Corporation, a Minnesota based firm, have lowered the cost of producing a CD-R and increased its supply.

   Figure 3.5 illustrates an increase in supply. When supply increases, the supply curve shifts rightward and the quantity supplied is larger at each and every price. For example, at a price of $1.00, on the original (blue) supply curve, the quantity supplied is 3 million discs a week. On the new (red) supply curve, the quantity supplied is 6 million discs a week. Look closely at the numbers in the table in Fig. 3.5 and check that the quantity supplied is larger at each price.

   Table 3.2 summarizes the influences on supply and the directions of those influences.

A Change in the Quantity Supplied Versus a Change in Supply

Changes in the factors that influence producers' planned sales cause either a change in the quantity supplied or a change in supply. Equivalently, they cause either a movement along the supply curve or a shift of the supply curve.

   A point on the supply curve shows the quantity supplied at a given price. A movement along the supply curve shows a **change in the quantity supplied.** The entire supply curve shows supply. A shift of the supply curve shows a *change in supply.*

FIGURE 3.5   An Increase in Supply

Original supply schedule			New supply schedule		
Old technology			New technology		
	Price (dollars per disc)	Quantity supplied (millions of discs per week)		Price (dollars per disc)	Quantity supplied (millions of discs per week)
A	0.50	0	A'	0.50	3
B	1.00	3	B'	1.00	6
C	1.50	4	C'	1.50	8
D	2.00	5	D'	2.00	10
E	2.50	6	E'	2.50	12

A change in any influence on sellers' plans other than the price of the good itself results in a new supply schedule and a shift of the supply curve. For example, if Imation invents a new, cost-saving technology for producing CD-Rs, the supply of CD-Rs changes.

   At a price of $1.50 a disc, 4 million discs a week are supplied when producers use the old technology (row *C* of the table) and 8 million CD-Rs a week are supplied when producers use the new technology. An advance in technology *increases* the supply of CD-Rs. The supply curve shifts *rightward*, as shown by the shift arrow and the resulting red curve.

Figure 3.6 illustrates and summarizes these distinctions. If the price of a good falls and everything else remains the same, the quantity supplied of that good decreases and there is a movement down along the supply curve S_0. If the price of a good rises and everything else remains the same, the quantity supplied increases and there is a movement up along the supply curve S_0. When any other influence on selling plans changes, the supply curve shifts and there is a *change in supply*. If the supply curve is S_0 and if production costs fall, supply increases and the supply curve shifts to the red supply curve S_1. If production costs rise, supply decreases and the supply curve shifts to the red supply curve S_2.

FIGURE 3.6 A Change in the Quantity Supplied Versus a Change in Supply

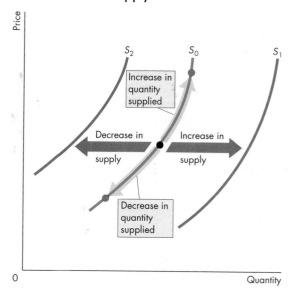

When the price of the good changes, there is a movement along the supply curve and *a change in the quantity supplied*, shown by the blue arrows on supply curve S_0. When any other influence on selling plans changes, there is a shift of the supply curve and a *change in supply*. An increase in supply shifts the supply curve rightward (from S_0 to S_1), and a decrease in supply shifts the supply curve leftward (from S_0 to S_2).

TABLE 3.2 The Supply of CD-Rs

The Law of Supply

The quantity of CD-Rs supplied

Decreases if:	Increases if:
■ The price of a CD-R falls	■ The price of a CD-R rises

Changes in Supply

The supply of CD-Rs

Decreases if:	Increases if:
■ The price of a resource used to produce CD-Rs rises	■ The price of a resource used to produce CD-Rs falls
■ The price of a substitute in production rises	■ The price of a substitute in production falls
■ The price of a complement in production falls	■ The price of a complement in production rises
■ The price of a CD-R is expected to rise in the future	■ The price of a CD-R is expected to fall in the future
■ The number of CD-R producers decreases	■ The number of CD-R producers increases
	■ More efficient technologies for producing CD-Rs are discovered

---

REVIEW QUIZ

1 Define the quantity supplied of a good or service.
2 What is the law of supply and how do we illustrate it?
3 What does the supply curve tell us about the price at which firms will supply a given quantity of a good?
4 List all the influences on selling plans, and for each influence say whether it changes supply.
5 What happens to the quantity of Palm Pilots supplied and the supply of Palm Pilots if the price of a Palm Pilot falls?

Your next task is to use what you've learned about demand and supply and learn how prices and quantities are determined.

Market Equilibrium

WE HAVE SEEN THAT WHEN THE PRICE OF A good rises, the quantity demanded *decreases* and the quantity supplied *increases*. We are now going to see how prices coordinate the plans of buyers and sellers and achieve an equilibrium.

An *equilibrium* is a situation in which opposing forces balance each other. Equilibrium in a market occurs when the price balances the plans of buyers and sellers. The **equilibrium price** is the price at which the quantity demanded equals the quantity supplied. The **equilibrium quantity** is the quantity bought and sold at the equilibrium price. A market moves towards its equilibrium because

- Price regulates buying and selling plans.
- Price adjusts when plans don't match.

Price as a Regulator

The price of a good regulates the quantities demanded and supplied. If the price is too high, the quantity supplied exceeds the quantity demanded. If the price is too low, the quantity demanded exceeds the quantity supplied. There is one price at which the quantity demanded equals the quantity supplied. Let's work out what that price is.

Figure 3.7 shows the market for CD-Rs. The table shows the demand schedule (from Fig. 3.1) and the supply schedule (from Fig. 3.4). If the price of a disc is 50¢, the quantity demanded is 9 million discs a week, but no discs are supplied. There is a shortage of 9 million discs a week. This shortage is shown in the final column of the table. At a price of $1.00 a disc, there is still a shortage, but only of 3 million discs a week. If the price of a disc is $2.50, the quantity supplied is 6 million discs a week, but the quantity demanded is only 2 million. There is a surplus of 4 million discs a week. The one price at which there is neither a shortage nor a surplus is $1.50 a disc. At that price, the quantity demanded is equal to the quantity supplied: 4 million discs a week. The equilibrium price is $1.50 a disc, and the equilibrium quantity is 4 million discs a week.

Figure 3.7 shows that the demand curve and the supply curve intersect at the equilibrium price of $1.50 a disc. At each price *above* $1.50 a disc, there is a surplus of discs. For example, at $2.00 a disc, the

FIGURE 3.7   Equilibrium

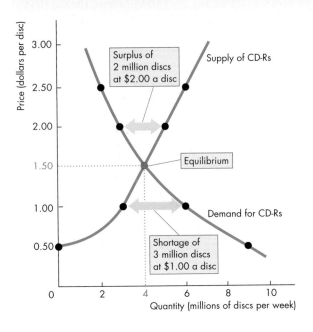

Price (dollars per disc)	Quantity demanded	Quantity supplied	Shortage (–) or surplus (+)
	(millions of discs per week)		
0.50	9	0	–9
1.00	6	3	–3
1.50	4	4	0
2.00	3	5	+2
2.50	2	6	+4

The table lists the quantities demanded and quantities supplied as well as the shortage or surplus of discs at each price. If the price is $1.00 a disc, 6 million discs a week are demanded and 3 million are supplied. There is a shortage of 3 million discs a week, and the price rises. If the price is $2.00 a disc, 3 million discs a week are demanded and 5 million are supplied. There is a surplus of 2 million discs a week, and the price falls. If the price is $1.50 a disc, 4 million discs a week are demanded and 4 million are supplied. There is neither a shortage nor a surplus. Neither buyers nor sellers have any incentive to change the price. The price at which the quantity demanded equals the quantity supplied is the equilibrium price.

surplus is 2 million discs a week, as shown by the blue arrow. At each price *below* $1.50 a disc, there is a shortage of discs. For example, at $1.00 a disc, the shortage is 3 million discs a week, as shown by the red arrow.

Price Adjustments

You've seen that if the price is below equilibrium, there is a shortage, and that if the price is above equilibrium, there is a surplus. But can we count on the price to change and eliminate a shortage or a surplus? We can, because such price changes are beneficial to both buyers and sellers. Let's see why the price changes when there is a shortage or a surplus.

A Shortage Forces the Price Up   Suppose the price of a CD-R is $1. Consumers plan to buy 6 million discs a week, and producers plan to sell 3 million discs a week. Consumers can't force producers to sell more than they plan, so the quantity that is actually offered for sale is 3 million discs a week. In this situation, powerful forces operate to increase the price and move it towards the equilibrium price. Some producers, noticing lines of unsatisfied consumers, raise the price. Some producers increase their output. As producers push the price up, the price rises towards its equilibrium. The rising price reduces the shortage because it decreases the quantity demanded and increases the quantity supplied. When the price has increased to the point at which there is no longer a shortage, the forces moving the price stop operating and the price comes to rest at its equilibrium.

A Surplus Forces the Price Down   Suppose the price of a CD-R is $2. Producers plan to sell 5 million discs a week, and consumers plan to buy 3 million discs a week. Producers cannot force consumers to buy more than they plan, so the quantity that is actually bought is 3 million discs a week. In this situation, powerful forces operate to lower the price and move it towards the equilibrium price. Some producers, unable to sell the quantities of CD-Rs they planned to sell, cut their prices. In addition, some producers scale back production. As producers cut prices, the price falls towards its equilibrium. The falling price decreases the surplus because it increases the quantity demanded and decreases the quantity supplied. When the price has fallen to the point at which there is no longer a surplus, the forces moving the price stop operating and the price comes to rest at its equilibrium.

The Best Deal Available for Buyers and Sellers
When the price is below equilibrium, it is forced up towards the equilibrium. Why don't buyers resist the increase and refuse to buy at the higher price? Because they value the good more highly than the current price and they cannot satisfy all their demands at the current price. In some markets—an example is the market for houses in Canada during 2001 and 2002—the buyers might even be the ones who force the price up by offering higher prices to divert the limited quantities away from other buyers.

When the price is above equilibrium, it is bid down towards the equilibrium. Why don't sellers resist this decrease and refuse to sell at the lower price? Because their minimum supply price is below the current price and they cannot sell all they would like to at the current price. Normally, it is the sellers who force the price down by offering lower prices to gain market share from their competitors.

At the price at which the quantity demanded and the quantity supplied are equal, neither buyers nor sellers can do business at a better price. Buyers pay the highest price they are willing to pay for the last unit bought, and sellers receive the lowest price at which they are willing to supply the last unit sold.

When people freely make offers to buy and sell and when demanders try to buy at the lowest possible price and suppliers try to sell at the highest possible price, the price at which trade takes place is the equilibrium price—the price at which the quantity demanded equals the quantity supplied. The price coordinates the plans of buyers and sellers.

REVIEW QUIZ

1 What is the equilibrium price of a good or service?
2 Over what range of prices does a shortage arise?
3 Over what range of prices does a surplus arise?
4 What happens to the price when there is a shortage?
5 What happens to the price when there is a surplus?
6 Why is the price at which the quantity demanded equals the quantity supplied the equilibrium price?
7 Why is the equilibrium price the best deal available for both buyers and sellers?

Predicting Changes in Price and Quantity

THE DEMAND AND SUPPLY THEORY THAT WE HAVE just studied provides us with a powerful way of analyzing influences on prices and the quantities bought and sold. According to the theory, a change in price stems from a change in demand, a change in supply, or a change in both demand and supply. Let's look first at the effects of a change in demand.

A Change in Demand

What happens to the price and quantity of CD-Rs if the demand for CD-Rs increases? We can answer this question with a specific example. Between 1998 and 2001, the price of a CD burner fell from $300 to $100. Because the CD burner and CD-R discs are complements, the demand for discs increased, as is shown in the table in Fig. 3.8. The original demand schedule and the new one are set out in the first three columns of the table. The table also shows the supply schedule for CD-Rs.

The original equilibrium price is $1.50 a disc. At that price, 4 million discs a week are demanded and supplied. When demand increases, the price that makes the quantity demanded equal the quantity supplied is $2.50 a disc. At this price, 6 million discs are bought and sold each week. When demand increases, both the price and the quantity increase.

Figure 3.8 shows these changes. The figure shows the original demand for and supply of CD-Rs. The original equilibrium price is $1.50 a CD-R, and the quantity is 4 million CD-Rs a week. When demand increases, the demand curve shifts rightward. The equilibrium price rises to $2.50 a CD-R, and the quantity supplied increases to 6 million CD-Rs a week, as highlighted in the figure. There is an *increase in the quantity supplied* but *no change in supply*—a movement along, but no shift of, the supply curve.

We can reverse this change in demand. Start at a price of $2.50 a disc with 6 million CD-Rs a week being bought and sold, and then work out what happens if demand decreases to its original level. Such a decrease in demand might arise from a fall in the price of an MP3 player (a substitute for CD-R technology). The decrease in demand shifts the demand curve leftward. The equilibrium price falls to $1.50 a disc, and the equilibrium quantity decreases to 4 million discs a week.

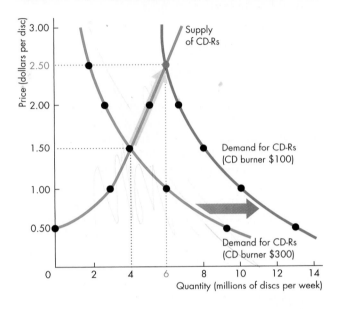

FIGURE 3.8   The Effects of a Change in Demand

Price	Quantity demanded (millions of discs per week)		Quantity supplied
(dollars per disc)	CD burner $300	CD burner $100	(millions of discs per week)
0.50	9	13	0
1.00	6	10	3
1.50	**4**	**8**	**4**
2.00	3	7	5
2.50	**2**	**6**	**6**

With the price of a CD burner at $300, the demand for CD-Rs is shown by the blue demand curve. The equilibrium price is $1.50 a disc, and the equilibrium quantity is 4 million discs a week. When the price of a CD burner falls from $300 to $100, the demand for CD-Rs increases and the demand curve shifts rightward to become the red curve.

At $1.50 a disc, there is now a shortage of 4 million discs a week. The price of a disc rises to a new equilibrium of $2.50. As the price rises to $2.50, the quantity supplied increases—shown by the blue arrow on the supply curve—to the new equilibrium quantity of 6 million discs a week. Following an increase in demand, the quantity supplied increases but supply does not change—the supply curve does not shift.

We can now make our first two predictions:

1. When demand increases, both the price and the quantity increase.

2. When demand decreases, both the price and the quantity decrease.

A Change in Supply

When Imation and other producers introduce new cost-saving technologies in their CD-R production plants, the supply of CD-Rs increases. The new supply schedule (the same one that was shown in Fig. 3.5) is presented in the table in Fig. 3.9. What are the new equilibrium price and quantity? The answer is highlighted in the table: The price falls to $1.00 a disc, and the quantity increases to 6 million a week. You can see why by looking at the quantities demanded and supplied at the old price of $1.50 a disc. The quantity supplied at that price is 8 million discs a week, and there is a surplus of discs. The price falls. Only when the price is $1.00 a disc does the quantity supplied equal the quantity demanded.

Figure 3.9 illustrates the effect of an increase in supply. It shows the demand curve for CD-Rs and the original and new supply curves. The initial equilibrium price is $1.50 a disc, and the quantity is 4 million discs a week. When the supply increases, the supply curve shifts rightward. The equilibrium price falls to $1.00 a disc, and the quantity demanded increases to 6 million discs a week, highlighted in the figure. There is an *increase in the quantity demanded* but *no change in demand*—a movement along, but no shift of, the demand curve.

We can reverse this change in supply. If we start out at a price of $1.00 a disc with 6 million discs a week being bought and sold, we can work out what happens if supply decreases to its original level. Such a decrease in supply might arise from an increase in the cost of labour or raw materials. The decrease in supply shifts the supply curve leftward. The equilibrium price rises to $1.50 a disc, and the equilibrium quantity decreases to 4 million discs a week.

We can now make two more predictions:

1. When supply increases, the quantity increases and the price falls.

2. When supply decreases, the quantity decreases and the price rises.

FIGURE 3.9   The Effects of a Change in Supply

Price (dollars per disc)	Quantity demanded (millions of discs per week)	Quantity supplied (millions of discs per week)	
		Old technology	New technology
0.50	9	0	3
1.00	6	3	6
1.50	4	4	8
2.00	3	5	10
2.50	2	6	12

With the old technology, the supply of CD-Rs is shown by the blue supply curve. The equilibrium price is $1.50 a disc, and the equilibrium quantity is 4 million discs a week. When the new technology is adopted, the supply of CD-Rs increases and the supply curve shifts rightward to become the red curve.

At $1.50 a disc, there is now a surplus of 4 million discs a week. The price of a CD-R falls to a new equilibrium of $1.00 a disc. As the price falls to $1.00, the quantity demanded increases—shown by the blue arrow on the demand curve—to the new equilibrium quantity of 6 million discs a week. Following an increase in supply, the quantity demanded increases but demand does not change—the demand curve does not shift.

A Change in Both Demand and Supply

You can now predict the effects of a change in either demand or supply on the price and the quantity. But what happens if *both* demand and supply change together? To answer this question, we look first at the case in which demand and supply move in the same direction—either both increase or both decrease. Then we look at the case in which they move in opposite directions—demand decreases and supply increases or demand increases and supply decreases.

Demand and Supply Change in the Same Direction We've seen that an increase in the demand for CD-Rs raises the price and increases the quantity bought and sold. And we've seen that an increase in the supply of CD-Rs lowers the price and increases the quantity bought and sold. Let's now examine what happens when both of these changes occur together.

The table in Fig. 3.10 brings together the numbers that describe the original quantities demanded and supplied and the new quantities demanded and supplied after the fall in the price of the CD burner and the improved CD-R production technology. These same numbers are illustrated in the graph. The original (blue) demand and supply curves intersect at a price of $1.50 a disc and a quantity of 4 million discs a week. The new (red) supply and demand curves also intersect at a price of $1.50 a disc but at a quantity of 8 million discs a week.

An increase in either demand or supply increases the quantity. So when both demand and supply increase, so does the quantity.

An increase in demand raises the price, and an increase in supply lowers the price, so we can't say whether the price will rise or fall when demand and supply increase together. In this example, the price does not change. But notice that if demand increases by slightly more than the amount shown in the figure, the price will rise. And if supply increases by slightly more than the amount shown in the figure, the price will fall.

We can now make two more predictions:

1. When *both* demand and supply increase, the quantity increases and the price might increase, decrease, or remain the same.
2. When *both* demand and supply decrease, the quantity decreases and the price might increase, decrease, or remain the same.

FIGURE 3.10 The Effects of an Increase in Both Demand and Supply

	Original quantities (millions of discs per week)		New quantities (millions of discs per week)	
Price (dollars per disc)	**Quantity demanded** CD burner $300	**Quantity supplied** old technology	**Quantity demanded** CD burner $100	**Quantity supplied** new technology
0.50	9	0	13	3
1.00	6	3	10	6
1.50	4	4	8	8
2.00	3	5	7	10
2.50	2	6	6	12

When a CD burner costs $300 and firms use the old technology to produce discs, the price of a disc is $1.50 and the quantity is 4 million discs a week. A fall in the price of the CD burner increases the demand for CD-Rs, and improved technology increases the supply of CD-Rs. The new supply curve intersects the new demand curve at $1.50 a disc, the same price as before, but the quantity increases to 8 million discs a week. These increases in demand and supply increase the quantity but leave the price unchanged.

Demand and Supply Change in Opposite Directions Let's now see what happens when demand and supply change together in *opposite* directions. A new production technology increases the supply of CD-Rs as before. But now the price of an MP3 download rises. An MP3 download is a *complement* of a CD-R. With more costly MP3 downloads, some people switch from buying CD-Rs to buying prerecorded CDs. The demand for CD-Rs decreases.

Figure 3.11 illustrates the original (blue) and new (red) demand and supply curves. The original equilibrium price is $2.50 a disc, and the quantity is 6 million discs a week. The new supply and demand curves intersect at a price of $1.00 a disc and at the original quantity of 6 million discs a week.

A decrease in demand or an increase in supply lowers the price. So when a decrease in demand and an increase in supply occur together, the price falls.

A decrease in demand decreases the quantity, and an increase in supply increases the quantity, so we can't say for sure which way the quantity will change when demand decreases and supply increases at the same time. In this example, the quantity doesn't change. But notice that if demand had decreased by slightly more than is shown in the figure, the quantity would have decreased. And if supply had increased by slightly more than is shown in the figure, the quantity would have increased.

We can now make two more predictions:

1. When demand decreases and supply increases, the price falls and the quantity might increase, decrease, or remain the same.
2. When demand increases and supply decreases, the price rises and the quantity might increase, decrease, or remain the same.

REVIEW QUIZ

1 What is the effect on the price of a CD-R and the quantity of CD-Rs if (a) the price of a PC falls or (b) the price of an MP3 download rises or (c) more firms produce CD-Rs or (d) CD-R producers' wages rise or (e) any two of these events occur at the same time? (Draw the diagrams!)

◆ To complete your study of demand and supply, take a look at *Reading Between the Lines* on pp. 76–77, which answers the question that we posed at the start of the chapter about falling prices.

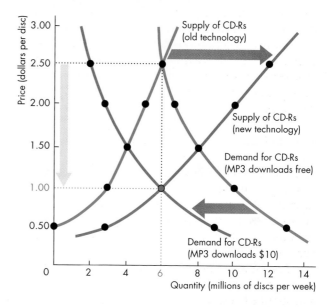

FIGURE 3.11   The Effects of a Decrease in Demand and an Increase in Supply

Price	Original quantities (millions of discs per week)		New quantities (millions of discs per week)	
(dollars per disc)	Quantity demanded MP3 download free	Quantity supplied old technology	Quantity demanded MP3 download $10	Quantity supplied new technology
0.50	13	0	9	3
1.00	10	3	6	6
1.50	8	4	4	8
2.00	7	5	3	10
2.50	6	6	2	12

When MP3 downloads are free and firms use the old technology to produce discs, the price of a CD-R is $2.50 and the quantity is 6 million discs a week. A rise in the price of an MP3 download decreases the demand for CD-Rs, and improved technology increases the supply of CD-Rs. The new equilibrium price is $1.00 a disc, a lower price, but in this case the quantity remains constant at 6 million discs a week. This decrease in demand and increase in supply lower the price but leave the quantity unchanged.

Demand and Supply: The Price of Computers

THE GLOBE AND MAIL, December 31, 2001

Analysts see tough year ahead for PC industry

...
"It's going to be a tough year," said George Shiffler, a principal analyst at Gartner Dataquest ...

Worldwide shipments of PCs are projected to reach 129.3 million units in 2002, up 4 per cent from 124.3 million in 2001, but down slightly from 130.5 million in 2000 according to Gartner.

In Canada, PC shipments, which are expected to fall 6.6 per cent this year from 2000, are forecast to increase 3.8 per cent to 3.8 million units in 2002.
...

Analysts are counting on falling PC prices, increased demand for wireless networking and mobile computing, and Microsoft Corp.'s latest operating systems to help stimulate PC sales. But experts say the most important factor that will drive the market will be a turnaround in the sagging U.S. economy, which has hurt consumer confidence.

This was a particularly good year to buy a computer, and consumers and companies can also expect good bargains in 2002. Chip maker Intel Corp. has been dropping the prices of its components throughout this year, partly in response to competition from rival Advanced Micro Devices Inc. That means computer manufacturers can source cheaper parts and pass the savings on to buyers.
...

Reprinted with permission from *The Globe and Mail.*

Essence of the Story

■ Worldwide shipments of PCs are projected to reach 129.3 million units in 2002, up 4 percent from 124.3 million in 2001, but down from 130.5 million in 2000.

■ In Canada, PC shipments are expected to fall 6.6 percent in 2001 and to increase 3.8 percent to 3.8 million units in 2002.

■ Falling PC prices, increased demand for wireless networking and mobile computing, and Microsoft Corp.'s WindowsXP might help stimulate PC sales.

■ But only a turnaround in the sagging U.S. economy will restore the industry.

■ Computer buyers can expect bargains in 2002.

■ Intel Corp. and Advanced Micro Devices Inc. have cut the prices of chips, which has lowered the costs of PC makers.

76

Economic Analysis

■ Figure 1 shows the global market for personal computers in 2000. The demand curve is D_{00} and the supply curve is S_{00}. The equilibrium quantity is 130.5 million (as in the news article) and the equilibrium price is \$3,500.

■ Figure 2 shows what happened during 2001. A recession in the United States lowered incomes, both in the United States and in many other countries. With a fall in average incomes, the demand for PCs decreased and the demand curve shifted leftward from D_{00} to D_{01}.

■ Falling chip prices lowered the cost of producing a PC and the supply of PCs increased. The supply curve shifted rightward from S_{00} to S_{01}.

■ With a decrease in demand and an increase in supply, the price of a PC fell. But because the decrease in demand was greater than the increase in supply, the quantity of PCs decreased.

■ Figure 3 shows the market for PCs in 2002. Factors such as the increased demand for wireless technology and the introduction of WindowsXP increased demand. But these forces were not strong enough to offset the depressing effects on demand of the continued global economic slowdown. So the demand for PCs didn't change in 2002.

■ But the supply of PCs increased again as the prices of chips continued to tumble. The supply curve shifted rightward from S_{01} to S_{02}.

■ With an increase in supply and no change in demand, the price of a PC fell further and the quantity of PCs increased.

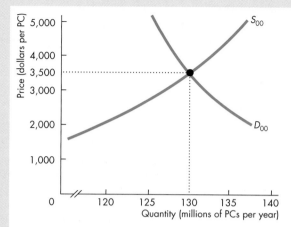

Figure 1 The PC market in 2000

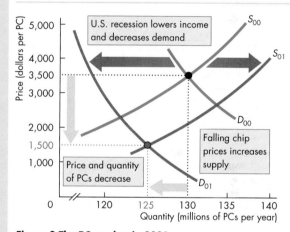

Figure 2 The PC market in 2001

Figure 3 The PC market in 2002

Mathematical Note
Demand, Supply, and Equilibrium

Demand Curve

The law of demand says that as the price of a good or service falls, the quantity demanded of that good or service increases. We illustrate the law of demand by setting out a demand schedule, by drawing a graph of the demand curve, or by writing down an equation. When the demand curve is a straight line, the following linear equation describes it

$$P = a - bQ_D,$$

where P is the price and Q_D is the quantity demanded. The a and b are positive constants.

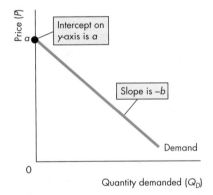

This equation tells us three things:

1. The price at which no one is willing to buy the good (Q_D is zero). That is, if the price is a, then the quantity demanded is zero. You can see the price a on the graph. It is the price at which the demand curve hits the y-axis—what we call the demand curve's "intercept on the y-axis."

2. As the price falls, the quantity demanded increases. If Q_D is a positive number, then the price P must be less than a. And as Q_D gets larger, the price P becomes smaller. That is, as the quantity increases, the maximum price that buyers are willing to pay for the good falls.

3. The constant b tells us how fast the maximum price that someone is willing to pay for the good falls as the quantity increases. That is, the constant b tells us about the steepness of the demand curve. The equation tells us that the slope of the demand curve is $-b$.

Supply Curve

The law of supply says that as the price of a good or service rises, the quantity supplied of that good increases. We illustrate the law of supply by setting out a supply schedule, by drawing a graph of the supply curve, or by writing down an equation. When the supply curve is a straight line, the following linear equation describes it

$$P = c + dQ_S,$$

where P is the price and Q_S is the quantity supplied. The c and d are positive constants.

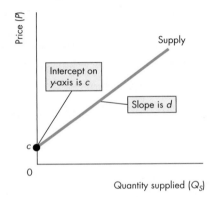

This equation tells us three things:

1. The price at which sellers are not willing to supply the good (Q_S is zero). That is, if the price is c, then no one is willing to sell the good. You can see the price c on the graph. It is the price at which the supply curve hits the y-axis—what we call the supply curve's "intercept on the y-axis."

2. As the price rises, the quantity supplied increases. If Q_S is a positive number, then the price P must be greater than c. And as Q_S increases, the price P gets larger. That is, as the quantity increases, the minimum price that sellers are willing to accept rises.

3. The constant d tells us how fast the minimum price at which someone is willing to sell the good rises as the quantity increases. That is, the constant d tells us about the steepness of the supply curve. The equation tells us that the slope of the supply curve is d.

Market Equilibrium

Demand and supply determine market equilibrium. The figure shows the equilibrium price (P^*) and equilibrium quantity (Q^*) at the intersection of the demand curve and the supply curve.

We can use the equations to find the equilibrium price and equilibrium quantity. The price of a good adjusts until the quantity demanded equals the quantity supplied. That is,

$$Q_D = Q_S.$$

So at the equilibrium price (P^*) and equilibrium quantity (Q^*),

$$Q_D = Q_S = Q^*.$$

To find the equilibrium price and equilibrium quantity, substitute Q^* for Q_D in the demand equation and Q^* for Q_S in the supply equation. Then the price is the equilibrium price (P^*), which gives

$$P^* = a - bQ^*$$

$$P^* = c + dQ^*.$$

Notice that

$$a - bQ^* = c + dQ^*.$$

Now solve for Q^*:

$$a - c = bQ^* + dQ^*$$

$$a - c = (b + d)Q^*$$

$$Q^* = \frac{a - c}{b + d}.$$

To find the equilibrium price, (P^*), substitute for Q^* in either the demand equation or the supply equation.

Using the demand equation, we have

$$P^* = a - b\left(\frac{a - c}{b + d}\right)$$

$$P^* = \frac{a(b + d) - b(a - c)}{b + d}$$

$$P^* = \frac{ad + bc}{b + d}.$$

Alternatively, using the supply equation, we have

$$P^* = c + d\left(\frac{a - c}{b + d}\right)$$

$$P^* = \frac{c(b + d) + d(a - c)}{b + d}$$

$$P^* = \frac{ad + bc}{b + d}.$$

An Example

The demand for ice-cream cones is

$$P = 800 - 2Q_D.$$

The supply of ice-cream cones is

$$P = 200 + 1Q_S.$$

The price of a cone is expressed in cents, and the quantities are expressed in cones per day.

To find the equilibrium price (P^*) and equilibrium quantity (Q^*), substitute Q^* for Q_D and Q_S and P^* for P in the demand and supply equations. That is,

$$P^* = 800 - 2Q^*$$

$$P^* = 200 + 1Q^*.$$

Now solve for Q^*:

$$800 - 2Q^* = 200 + 1Q^*$$

$$600 = 3Q^*$$

$$Q^* = 200.$$

And

$$P^* = 800 - 2(200)$$

$$= 400.$$

The equilibrium price is $4 a cone, and the equilibrium quantity is 200 cones per day.

KEY POINTS

Markets and Prices (p. 60)

- A competitive market is one that has so many buyers and sellers that no one can influence the price.
- Opportunity cost is a relative price.
- Demand and supply determine relative prices.

Demand (pp. 61–65)

- Demand is the relationship between the quantity demanded of a good and its price when all other influences on buying plans remain the same.
- The higher the price of a good, other things remaining the same, the smaller is the quantity demanded—the law of demand.
- Demand depends on the prices of substitutes and complements, expected future prices, income, population, and preferences.

Supply (pp. 66–69)

- Supply is the relationship between the quantity supplied of a good and its price when all other influences on selling plans remain the same.
- The higher the price of a good, other things remaining the same, the greater is the quantity supplied—the law of supply.
- Supply depends on the prices of resources used to produce a good, the prices of related goods produced, expected future prices, the number of suppliers, and technology.

Market Equilibrium (pp. 70–71)

- At the equilibrium price, the quantity demanded equals the quantity supplied.
- At prices above equilibrium, there is a surplus and the price falls.
- At prices below equilibrium, there is a shortage and the price rises.

Predicting Changes in Price and Quantity (pp. 72–75)

- An increase in demand brings a rise in price and an increase in the quantity supplied. (A decrease in demand brings a fall in price and a decrease in the quantity supplied.)
- An increase in supply brings a fall in price and an increase in the quantity demanded. (A decrease in supply brings a rise in price and a decrease in the quantity demanded.)
- An increase in demand and an increase in supply bring an increased quantity, but the price might rise, fall, or remain the same. An increase in demand and a decrease in supply bring a higher price, but the quantity might increase, decrease, or remain the same.

KEY FIGURES

Figure 3.1   The Demand Curve, 62
Figure 3.3   A Change in the Quantity Demanded Versus a Change in Demand, 65
Figure 3.4   The Supply Curve, 67
Figure 3.6   A Change in the Quantity Supplied Versus a Change in Supply, 69
Figure 3.7   Equilibrium, 70
Figure 3.8   The Effects of a Change in Demand, 72
Figure 3.9   The Effects of a Change in Supply, 73

KEY TERMS

Change in demand, 63
Change in supply, 67
Change in the quantity demanded, 65
Change in the quantity supplied, 68
Competitive market, 60
Complement, 63
Demand, 62
Demand curve, 62
Equilibrium price, 70
Equilibrium quantity, 70
Inferior good, 64
Law of demand, 61
Law of supply, 66
Normal good, 64
Quantity demanded, 61
Quantity supplied, 66
Relative price, 60
Substitute, 63
Supply, 66
Supply curve, 66

PROBLEMS

*1. What is the effect on the price of an audiotape and the quantity of audiotapes sold if
 a. The price of a CD rises?
 b. The price of a Walkman rises?
 c. The supply of CD players increases?
 d. Consumers' incomes increase?
 e. Workers who make audiotapes get a pay raise?
 f. The price of a Walkman rises at the same time as the workers who make audiotapes get a pay raise?

2. What is the effect on the price of a DVD player and the quantity of DVD players sold if
 a. The price of a DVD rises?
 b. The price of a DVD falls?
 c. The supply of DVD players increases?
 d. Consumers' incomes decrease?
 e. The wage rate of workers who produce DVD players increases?
 f. The wage rate of workers who produce DVD players rises and at the same time the price of a DVD falls?

*3. Suppose that the following events occur one at a time:
 (i) The price of crude oil rises.
 (ii) The price of a car rises.
 (iii) All speed limits on highways are abolished.
 (iv) Robot technology cuts car production costs.
 Which of these events increases or decreases (state which):
 a. The demand for gasoline?
 b. The supply of gasoline?
 c. The quantity of gasoline demanded?
 d. The quantity of gasoline supplied?

4. Suppose that the following events occur one at a time:
 (i) The price of airfares halves.
 (ii) The price of beef falls.
 (iii) A cheap new strong cloth, a close substitute for leather, is invented.
 (iv) A new high-speed technology for cutting leather is invented.
 Which of these events will increase or decrease (state which):
 a. The demand for leather bags?
 b. The supply of leather bags?
 c. The quantity of leather bags demanded?
 d. The quantity of leather bags supplied?

*5. The figure illustrates the market for pizza.
 a. Label the curves in the figure.
 b. What are the equilibrium price of a pizza and the equilibrium quantity of pizza?

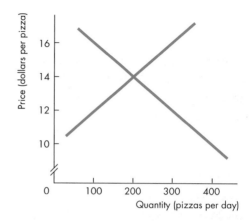

6. The figure illustrates the market for fish.
 a. Label the curves in the figure.
 b. What are the equilibrium price of a fish and the equilibrium quantity of fish?

 *7. The demand and supply schedules for gum are

Price (cents per pack)	Quantity demanded	Quantity supplied
	(millions of packs per week)	
20	180	60
30	160	80
40	140	100
50	120	120
60	100	140
70	80	160
80	60	180

a. Draw a graph of the gum market and mark in the equilibrium price and quantity.

b. Suppose that gum is 70 cents a pack. Describe the situation in the gum market and explain how the price of gum adjusts.

8. The demand and supply schedules for potato chips are

Price (cents per bag)	Quantity demanded	Quantity supplied
	(millions of bag per week)	
50	160	130
60	150	140
70	140	150
80	130	160
90	120	170
100	110	180

a. Draw a graph of the potato chip market and mark in the equilibrium price and quantity.

b. Suppose that chips are 60 cents a bag. Describe the situation in the market for chips and explain how the price adjusts.

*9. In problem 7, suppose that a fire destroys some gum-producing factories and the supply of gum decreases by 40 million packs a week.

a. Has there been a shift of or a movement along the supply curve of gum?

b. Has there been a shift of or a movement along the demand curve for gum?

c. What are the new equilibrium price and equilibrium quantity of gum?

10. In problem 8, suppose a new dip comes onto the market and the demand for potato chips increases by 30 million bags per week.

a. Has there been a shift of or a movement along the supply curve of potato chips?

b. Has there been a shift of or a movement along the demand curve for potato chips?

c. What are the new equilibrium price and equilibrium quantity of potato chips?

*11. In problem 9, suppose an increase in the teenage population increases the demand for gum by 40 million packs per week at the same time as the fire occurs. What are the new equilibrium price and quantity of gum?

12. In problem 10, suppose that a virus destroys several potato farms with the result that the supply of potato chips decreases by 40 million bags a week at the same time as the dip comes onto the market. What are the new equilibrium price and quantity of potato chips?

CRITICAL THINKING

1. After you have studied *Reading Between the Lines* on pp. 76–77, answer the following questions:

a. What were the factors that changed the demand for and supply of PCs during 2001 and 2002?

b. How did competition between Intel and AMD influence the market for PCs?

c. How do you think the development of CD-R technology has changed the demand for PCs and the equilibrium price of a PC?

WEB EXERCISES

1. Use the links on the Parkin–Bade Web site and obtain data on the prices and quantities of wheat.

a. Make a figure similar to Fig. 3.7 on p. 70 to illustrate the market for wheat in 1999 and 2000.

b. Show the changes in demand and supply and the changes in the quantity demanded and the quantity supplied that are consistent with the price and quantity data.

2. Use the link on the Parkin–Bade Web site and obtain data on the price of oil.

a. Describe how the price of oil has changed over the past five years.

b. Draw a demand-supply diagram to explain what happens to the price when there is an increase or a decrease in supply and no change in demand.

c. What do you predict would happen to the price of oil if a new drilling technology permitted deeper ocean sources to be used?

d. What do you predict would happen to the price of oil if a clean and safe nuclear technology were developed?

e. What do you predict would happen to the price of oil if automobiles were powered by batteries instead of by internal combustion engines?

4

Predicting Prices

The Organization of Oil Exporting Countries (OPEC) is a big enough player in the global oil market to influence the price of oil. To raise the price, OPEC must cut production. If it does so, by how much will the price rise? Will non-OPEC producers also cut production? Or will they produce more to take advantage of the higher price achieved by OPEC's actions? To answer questions like these, we need to know the quantitative relationship between price and the quantities demanded and supplied. ◆ All firms are interested in the factors that influence prices and in predicting prices. A pizza producer wants to know if the arrival of a new competitor will lower the price of pizza and whether as people's incomes rise they will spend more or less on pizza. A labour union wants to know whether, if it goes for a large wage rise, the number of people employed will fall by a lot or by a little.

◆ In this chapter, you will learn about a tool that helps us to answer questions like the ones we've just considered. You will learn about the elasticity of demand and supply. We'll return to the questions that OPEC needs to answer in *Reading Between the Lines* and see how the concept of elasticity helps us to understand the effects of OPEC's actions on the price of crude oil, a price that has a big impact on the price that you end up paying for gasoline.

After studying this chapter, you will be able to

- ◾ **Define, calculate, and explain the factors that influence the price elasticity of demand**

- ◾ **Define, calculate, and explain the factors that influence the cross elasticity of demand and the income elasticity of demand**

- ◾ **Define, calculate, and explain the factors that influence the elasticity of supply**

84   CHAPTER 4   ELASTICITY

Price Elasticity of Demand

YOU KNOW THAT WHEN SUPPLY INCREASES, THE equilibrium price falls and the equilibrium quantity increases. But does the price fall by a large amount and the quantity increase by a little? Or does the price barely fall and the quantity increase by a large amount?

The answer depends on the responsiveness of the quantity demanded to a change in price. You can see why by studying Fig. 4.1, which shows two possible scenarios in a local pizza market. Figure 4.1(a) shows one scenario, and Fig. 4.1(b) shows the other.

In both cases, supply is initially S_0. In part (a), the demand for pizza is shown by the demand curve D_A. In part (b), the demand for pizza is shown by the demand curve D_B. Initially, in both cases, the price is $20 a pizza and the quantity of pizza produced and consumed is 10 pizzas an hour.

Now a large pizza franchise opens up, and the supply of pizza increases. The supply curve shifts rightward to S_1. In case (a), the price falls by an enormous $15 to $5 a pizza, and the quantity increases by only 3 to 13 pizzas an hour. In contrast, in case (b), the price falls by only $5 to $15 a pizza and the quantity increases by 7 to 17 pizzas an hour.

The different outcomes arise from differing degrees of responsiveness of the quantity demanded to a change in price. But what do we mean by responsiveness? One possible answer is slope. The slope of demand curve D_A is steeper than the slope of demand curve D_B.

In this example, we can compare the slopes of the two demand curves. But we can't always do so. The reason is that the slope of a demand curve depends on the units in which we measure the price and quantity. And we often must compare the demand curves for different goods and services that are measured in unrelated units. For example, a pizza producer might want to compare the demand for pizza with the demand for soft drinks. Which quantity demanded is more responsive to a price change? This question can't be answered by comparing the slopes of two demand curves. The units of measurement of pizza and soft drinks are unrelated. The question can be answered with a measure of responsiveness that is independent of units of measurement. Elasticity is such a measure.

The **price elasticity of demand** is a units-free measure of the responsiveness of the quantity demanded of a good to a change in its price when all other influences on buyers' plans remain the same.

FIGURE 4.1   How a Change in Supply Changes Price and Quantity

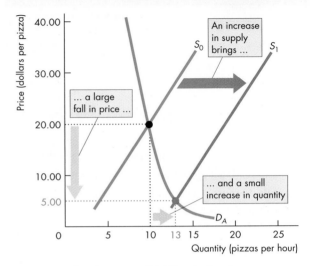

(a) Large price change and small quantity change

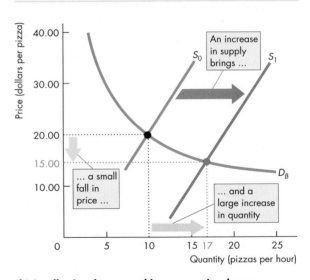

(b) Small price change and large quantity change

Initially the price is $20 a pizza and the quantity sold is 10 pizzas an hour. Then supply increases from S_0 to S_1. In part (a), the price falls by $15 to $5 a pizza, and the quantity increases by only 3, to 13 pizzas an hour. In part (b), the price falls by only $5 to $15 a pizza, and the quantity increases by 7, to 17 pizzas an hour. This price change is smaller and the quantity change is larger than in case (a). The quantity demanded is more responsive to price in case (b) than in case (a).

Calculating Elasticity

We calculate the *price elasticity of demand* by using the formula:

$$\text{Price elasticity of demand} = \frac{\text{Percentage change in quantity demanded}}{\text{Percentage change in price}}.$$

To use this formula, we need to know the quantities demanded at different prices when all other influences on buyers' plans remain the same. Suppose we have the data on prices and quantities demanded of pizza and we calculate the price elasticity of demand for pizza.

Figure 4.2 zooms in on the demand curve for pizza and shows how the quantity demanded responds to a small change in price. Initially, the price is $20.50 a pizza and 9 pizzas an hour are sold—the original point in the figure. The price then falls to $19.50 a pizza, and the quantity demanded increases to 11 pizzas an hour—the new point in the figure. When the price falls by $1 a pizza, the quantity demanded increases by 2 pizzas an hour.

To calculate the price elasticity of demand, we express the changes in price and quantity demanded as percentages of the *average price* and the *average quantity*. By using the average price and average quantity, we calculate the elasticity at a point on the demand curve midway between the original point and the new point. The original price is $20.50 and the new price is $19.50, so the average price is $20. The $1 price decrease is 5 percent of the average price. That is,

$$\Delta P/P_{ave} = (\$1/\$20) \times 100 = 5\%.$$

The original quantity demanded is 9 pizzas and the new quantity demanded is 11 pizzas, so the average quantity demanded is 10 pizzas. The 2 pizza increase in the quantity demanded is 20 percent of the average quantity. That is,

$$\Delta Q/Q_{ave} = (2/10) \times 100 = 20\%.$$

So the price elasticity of demand, which is the percentage change in the quantity demanded (20 percent) divided by the percentage change in price (5 percent) is 4. That is,

$$\text{Price elasticity of demand} = \frac{\%\Delta Q}{\%\Delta P}$$
$$= \frac{20\%}{5\%} = 4.$$

FIGURE 4.2   Calculating the Elasticity of Demand

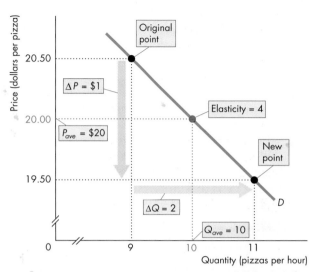

The elasticity of demand is calculated by using the formula:*

$$\text{Price elasticity of demand} = \frac{\text{Percentage change in quantity demanded}}{\text{Percentage change in price}}$$
$$= \frac{\%\Delta Q}{\%\Delta P}$$
$$= \frac{\Delta Q/Q_{ave}}{\Delta P/P_{ave}}$$
$$= \frac{2/10}{1/20}$$
$$= 4.$$

This calculation measures the elasticity at an average price of $20 a pizza and an average quantity of 10 pizzas an hour.

*In the formula, the Greek letter delta (Δ) stands for "change in" and %Δ stands for "percentage change in."

Average Price and Quantity   Notice that we use the *average* price and *average* quantity. We do this because it gives the most precise measurement of elasticity—at the midpoint between the original price and the new price. If the price falls from $20.50 to $19.50, the $1 price change is 4.9 percent of $20.50. The 2 pizza change in quantity is 22.2 percent of 9, the original quantity. So if we use these numbers, the elasticity of demand is 22.2 divided by 4.9, which equals 4.5. If the price rises from $19.50 to $20.50, the $1 price

change is 5.1 percent of $19.50. The 2 pizza change in quantity is 18.2 percent of 11, the original quantity. So if we use these numbers, the elasticity of demand is 18.2 divided by 5.1, which equals 3.6.

By using percentages of the *average* price and *average* quantity, we get the same value for the elasticity regardless of whether the price falls from $20.50 to $19.50 or rises from $19.50 to $20.50.

Percentages and Proportions Elasticity is the ratio of two percentage changes. So when we divide one percentage change by another, the 100s cancel. A percentage change is a *proportionate* change multiplied by 100. The proportionate change in price is $\Delta P/P_{ave}$, and the proportionate change in quantity demanded is $\Delta Q/Q_{ave}$. So if we divide $\Delta Q/Q_{ave}$ by $\Delta P/P_{ave}$ we get the same answer as we get by using percentage changes.

A Units-Free Measure Now that you've calculated a price elasticity of demand, you can see why it is a *units-free measure*. Elasticity is a units-free measure because the percentage change in each variable is independent of the units in which the variable is measured. And the ratio of the two percentages is a number without units.

Minus Sign and Elasticity When the price of a good *rises*, the quantity demanded *decreases* along the demand curve. Because a *positive* change in price brings a *negative* change in the quantity demanded, the price elasticity of demand is a negative number. But it is the magnitude, or absolute value, of the price elasticity of demand that tells us how responsive—how elastic—demand is. To compare elasticities, we use the magnitude of the price elasticity of demand and ignore the minus sign.

Inelastic and Elastic Demand

Figure 4.3 shows three demand curves that cover the entire range of possible elasticities of demand. In Fig. 4.3(a), the quantity demanded is constant regardless of the price. If the quantity demanded remains constant when the price changes, then the price elasticity of demand is zero and the good is said to have **perfectly inelastic demand.** One good that has a very low price elasticity of demand (perhaps zero over some price range) is insulin. Insulin is of such importance to some diabetics that if the price rises or falls, they do not change the quantity they buy.

If the percentage change in the quantity demanded equals the percentage change in price, then the price elasticity equals 1 and the good is said to have **unit elastic demand.** The demand in Fig. 4.3(b) is an example of unit elastic demand.

Between the cases shown in Fig. 4.3(a) and Fig. 4.3(b) is the general case in which the percentage

---

FIGURE 4.3 Inelastic and Elastic Demand

(a) Perfectly inelastic demand **(b) Unit elastic demand** **(c) Perfectly elastic demand**

Each demand illustrated here has a constant elasticity. The demand curve in part (a) illustrates the demand for a good that has a zero elasticity of demand. The demand curve in part (b) illustrates the demand for a good with a unit elasticity of demand. And the demand curve in part (c) illustrates the demand for a good with an infinite elasticity of demand.

change in the quantity demanded is less than the percentage change in price. In this case, the price elasticity of demand is between zero and 1 and the good is said to have **inelastic demand.** Food and housing are examples of goods with inelastic demand.

If the quantity demanded changes by an infinitely large percentage in response to a tiny price change, then the price elasticity of demand is infinity and the good is said to have **perfectly elastic demand.** Figure 4.3(c) shows perfectly elastic demand. An example of a good that has a very high elasticity of demand (almost infinite) is a soft drink from two campus machines located side by side. If the two machines offer the same soft drinks for the same price, some people buy from one machine and some from the other. But if one machine's price is higher than the other's, by even a small amount, no one will buy from the machine with the higher price. Soft drinks from the two machines are perfect substitutes.

Between the cases in Fig. 4.3(b) and Fig. 4.3(c) is the general case in which the percentage change in the quantity demanded exceeds the percentage change in price. In this case, the price elasticity is greater than 1 and the good is said to have **elastic demand.** Automobiles and furniture are examples of goods that have elastic demand.

Elasticity Along a Straight-Line Demand Curve

Along a straight-line demand curve, such as the one in Fig. 4.4, the elasticity varies. At high prices and small quantities, the elasticity is large; at low prices and large quantities, the elasticity is small. To convince yourself of this fact, calculate the elasticity at three average prices.

First, suppose the price falls from $25 to $15 a pizza. The quantity demanded increases from zero to 20 pizzas an hour. The average price is $20, so the percentage change in price is $10 divided by $20 multiplied by 100, which equals 50. The average quantity is 10 pizzas, so the percentage change in quantity is 20 pizzas divided by 10 pizzas, multiplied by 100, which equals 200. So dividing the percentage change in the quantity demanded (200) by the percentage change in price (50), you see that the elasticity of demand at an average price of $20 is 4.

Next, suppose that the price falls from $15 to $10 a pizza. The quantity demanded increases from 20 to 30 pizzas an hour. The average price is now $12.50, so the percentage change in price is $5

divided by $12.50 multiplied by 100, which equals 40 percent. The average quantity is 25 pizzas an hour, so the percentage change in the quantity demanded is 10 pizzas divided by 25 pizzas multiplied by 100, which also equals 40 percent. So dividing the percentage change in the quantity demanded (40) by the percentage change in price (40), you see that the elasticity of demand at an average price of $12.50 is 1. The elasticity of demand is always equal to 1 at the midpoint of a straight-line demand curve.

Finally, suppose that the price falls from $10 to zero. The quantity demanded increases from 30 to 50 pizzas an hour. The average price is now $5, so the percentage change in price is $10 divided by $5 multiplied by 100, which equals 200 percent. The average quantity is 40 pizzas an hour, so the percentage change in the quantity demanded is 20 pizzas divided by 40 pizzas multiplied by 100, which also equals 50 percent. So dividing the percentage change in the quantity demanded (50) by the percentage change in price (200), you see that the elasticity of demand at an average price of $5 is 1/4.

FIGURE 4.4   Elasticity Along a Straight-Line Demand Curve

On a straight-line demand curve, elasticity decreases as the price falls and the quantity demanded increases. Demand is unit elastic at the midpoint of the demand curve (elasticity is 1). Above the midpoint, demand is elastic; below the midpoint, demand is inelastic.

Total Revenue and Elasticity

The **total revenue** from the sale of a good equals the price of the good multiplied by the quantity sold. When a price changes, total revenue also changes. But a rise in price does not always increase total revenue. The change in total revenue depends on the elasticity of demand in the following way:

- If demand is elastic, a 1 percent price cut increases the quantity sold by more than 1 percent and total revenue increases.

- If demand is inelastic, a 1 percent price cut increases the quantity sold by less than 1 percent and total revenue decreases.

- If demand is unit elastic, a 1 percent price cut increases the quantity sold by 1 percent and so total revenue does not change.

Figure 4.5 shows how we can use this relationship between elasticity and total revenue to estimate elasticity using the total revenue test. The **total revenue test** is a method of estimating the price elasticity of demand by observing the change in total revenue that results from a change in the price (when all other influences on the quantity sold remain the same).

- If a price cut increases total revenue, demand is elastic.

- If a price cut decreases total revenue, demand is inelastic.

- If a price cut leaves total revenue unchanged, demand is unit elastic.

In Fig. 4.5(a), over the price range from $25 to $12.50, demand is elastic. Over the price range from $12.50 to zero, demand is inelastic. At a price of $12.50, demand is unit elastic.

Figure 4.5(b) shows total revenue. At a price of $25, the quantity sold is zero, so total revenue is also zero. At a price of zero, the quantity demanded is 50 pizzas an hour but total revenue is again zero. A price cut in the elastic range brings an increase in total revenue—the percentage increase in the quantity demanded is greater than the percentage decrease in price. A price cut in the inelastic range brings a decrease in total revenue—the percentage increase in the quantity demanded is less than the percentage decrease in price. At unit elasticity, total revenue is at a maximum.

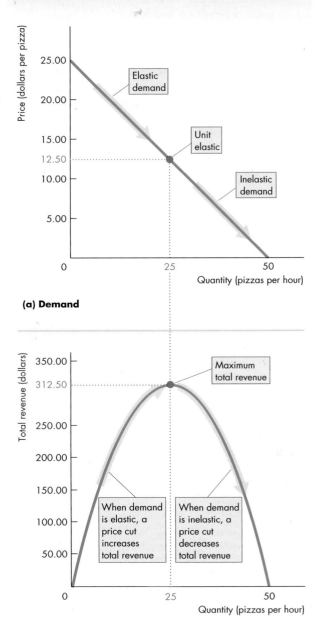

FIGURE 4.5   Elasticity and Total Revenue

(a) Demand

(b) Total revenue

When demand is elastic, in the price range from $25 to $12.50, a decrease in price (part a) brings an increase in total revenue (part b). When demand is inelastic, in the price range from $12.50 to zero, a decrease in price (part a) brings a decrease in total revenue (part b). When demand is unit elastic, at a price of $12.50 (part a), total revenue is at a maximum (part b).

Your Expenditure and Your Elasticity

When a price changes, the change in your expenditure on the good depends on *your* elasticity of demand.

- If your demand is elastic, a 1 percent price cut increases the quantity you buy by more than 1 percent and your expenditure on the item increases.
- If your demand is inelastic, a 1 percent price cut increases the quantity you buy by less than 1 percent and your expenditure on the item decreases.
- If your demand is unit elastic, a 1 percent price cut increases the quantity you buy by 1 percent and your expenditure on the item does not change.

So if when the price of an item falls, you spend more on it, your demand for that item is elastic; if you spend the same amount, your demand is unit elastic; and if you spend less, your demand is inelastic.

The Factors That Influence the Elasticity of Demand

Table 4.1 lists some estimates of actual elasticities in the real world. You can see that these real-world elasticities of demand range from 1.52 for metals, the item with the most elastic demand in the table, to 0.05 for oil, the item with the most inelastic demand in the table. What makes the demand for some goods elastic and the demand for others inelastic?

Elasticity depends on three main factors:

- The closeness of substitutes
- The proportion of income spent on the good
- The time elapsed since the price change

Closeness of Substitutes The closer the substitutes for a good or service, the more elastic is the demand for it. For example, oil from which we make gasoline has substitutes but none that are currently very close (imagine a steam-driven, coal-fueled car). So the demand for oil is inelastic. Plastics are close substitutes for metals, so the demand for metals is elastic.

The degree of substitutability between two goods also depends on how narrowly (or broadly) we define them. For example, the elasticity of demand for meat is low, but the elasticity of demand for beef or pork is high. The elasticity of demand for personal computers is low, but the elasticity of demand for a Compaq, Dell, or IBM is high.

In everyday language we call some goods (such as food and housing) *necessities* and other goods (such as exotic vacations) *luxuries*. A necessity is a good that

---

TABLE 4.1   Some Real-World Price Elasticities of Demand

Good or Service	Elasticity
Elastic Demand	
Metals	1.52
Electrical engineering products	1.39
Mechanical engineering products	1.30
Furniture	1.26
Motor vehicles	1.14
Instrument engineering products	1.10
Professional services	1.09
Transportation services	1.03
Inelastic Demand	
Gas, electricity, and water	0.92
Chemicals	0.89
Drinks (all types)	0.78
Clothing	0.64
Tobacco	0.61
Banking and insurance services	0.56
Housing services	0.55
Agricultural and fish products	0.42
Books, magazines, and newspapers	0.34
Food	0.12
Oil	0.05

Sources: Ahsan Mansur and John Whalley, "Numerical Specification of Applied General Equilibrium Models: Estimation, Calibration, and Data," in *Applied General Equilibrium Analysis*, eds. Herbert E. Scarf and John B. Shoven (New York: Cambridge University Press, 1984), 109, and Henri Theil, Ching-Fan Chung, and James L. Seale, Jr., *Advances in Econometrics, Supplement I, 1989, International Evidence on Consumption Patterns* (Greenwich, Conn.: JAI Press Inc., 1989), and Geoffrey Heal, Columbia University, Web site.

---

has poor substitutes and that is crucial for our well-being. So generally, a necessity has an inelastic demand. In Table 4.1, food and oil might be classified as necessities that have inelastic demand.

A luxury is a good that usually has many substitutes, one of which is not buying it. So a luxury generally has an elastic demand. In Table 4.1, furniture and motor vehicles might be classified as luxuries that have elastic demand.

Proportion of Income Spent on the Good Other things remaining the same, the greater the proportion of income spent on a good, the more elastic is the demand for it.

Think about your own elasticity of demand for chewing gum and housing. If the price of chewing gum doubles, you consume almost as much gum as before. Your demand for gum is inelastic. If apartment rents double, you shriek and look for more students to share accommodation with you. Your demand for housing is more elastic than your demand for gum. Why the difference? Housing takes a large proportion of your budget, and gum takes only a tiny proportion. You don't like either price increase, but you hardly notice the higher price of gum, while the higher rent puts your budget under severe strain.

Figure 4.6 shows the proportion of income spent on food and the price elasticity of demand for food in 10 countries. This figure confirms the general tendency we have just described. The larger the proportion of income spent on food, the larger is the price elasticity of demand for food. For example, in Tanzania, a nation where 62 percent of income is spent on food, the price elasticity of demand for food is 0.77. In contrast, in Canada, where 14 percent of income is spent on food, the price elasticity of demand for food is 0.13.

Time Elapsed Since the Price Change The longer the time that has elapsed since the price change, the more elastic is demand. When the price of oil increased by 400 percent during the 1970s, people barely changed the quantity of oil and gasoline they consumed. But gradually, as more efficient auto and airplane engines were developed, the quantity consumed decreased. The demand for oil has become more elastic as more time has elapsed since the huge price hike. Similarly, when the price of a PC fell, the quantity of PCs demanded increased only slightly at first. But as more people have become better informed about the variety of ways of using a PC, the quantity of PCs bought has increased sharply. The demand for PCs has become more elastic.

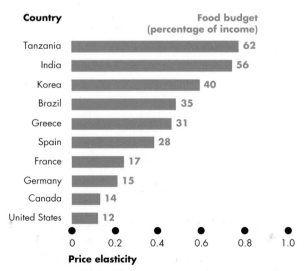

FIGURE 4.6 Price Elasticities in 10 Countries

As income increases and the proportion of income spent on food decreases, the demand for food becomes less elastic.

Source: Henri Theil, Ching-Fan Chung, and James L. Seale, Jr., *Advances in Econometrics, Supplement 1, 1989, International Evidence on Consumption Patterns* (Greenwich, Conn.: JAI Press, Inc., 1989).

REVIEW QUIZ

1 Why do we need a units-free measure of the responsiveness of the quantity demanded of a good or service to a change in its price?
2 Can you define and calculate the price elasticity of demand?
3 Why, when we calculate the price elasticity of demand, do we express the change in price as a percentage of the *average* price and the change in quantity as a percentage of the *average* quantity?
4 What is the total revenue test and why does it work?
5 What are the main influences on the elasticity of demand that make the demand for some goods elastic and the demand for other goods inelastic?
6 Why is the demand for a luxury generally more elastic than the demand for a necessity?

You've now completed your study of the *price* elasticity of demand. Two other elasticity concepts tell us about the effects of other influences on demand. Let's look at these other elasticities of demand.

More Elasticities of Demand

BACK AT THE PIZZERIA, YOU ARE TRYING TO WORK out how a price cut by the burger shop next door will affect the demand for your pizza. You know that pizzas and burgers are substitutes. And you know that when the price of a substitute for pizza falls, the demand for pizza decreases. But by how much?

You also know that pizza and soft drinks are complements. And you know that if the price of a complement of pizza falls, the demand for pizza increases. So you wonder whether you might keep your customers by cutting the price you charge for soft drinks. But again by how much? To answer these questions, you need to calculate the cross elasticity of demand. Let's examine this elasticity measure.

Cross Elasticity of Demand

We measure the influence of a change in the price of a substitute or complement by using the concept of the cross elasticity of demand. The **cross elasticity of demand** is a measure of the responsiveness of the demand for a good to a change in the price of a substitute or complement, other things remaining the same. We calculate the *cross elasticity of demand* by using the formula:

$$\text{Cross elasticity of demand} = \frac{\text{Percentage change in quantity demanded}}{\text{Percentage change in price of a substitute or complement}}.$$

The cross elasticity of demand can be positive or negative. It is *positive* for a *substitute* and it is *negative* for a *complement.*

Substitutes Suppose that the price of pizza is constant and 9 pizzas an hour are sold. The price of a burger then rises from $1.50 to $2.50. No other influence on buying plans changes, and the quantity of pizzas sold increases to 11 an hour.

The change in the quantity demanded is the new quantity, 11 pizzas, minus the original quantity, 9 pizzas, which is +2 pizzas. The average quantity is 10 pizzas. So the quantity of pizzas demanded increases by 20 percent (+20). That is,

$$\Delta Q/Q_{ave} = (+2/10) \times 100 = +20\%.$$

The change in the price of a burger, a substitute for pizza, is the new price, $2.50, minus the original price, $1.50, which is +$1. The average price is $2. So the price of a burger rises by 50 percent (+50). That is,

$$\Delta P/P_{ave} = (+1/2) \times 100 = +50\%.$$

So the cross elasticity of demand for pizza with respect to the price of a burger is

$$\frac{+20\%}{+50\%} = 0.4.$$

Figure 4.7 illustrates the cross elasticity of demand. Pizza and burgers are substitutes. Because they are substitutes, when the price of a burger rises, the demand for pizza increases. The demand curve for pizza shifts rightward from D_0 to D_1. Because a *rise* in the price of a burger brings an *increase* in the demand for pizza, the cross elasticity of demand for pizza with respect to the price of a burger is *positive.* Both the price and the quantity change in the same direction.

FIGURE 4.7 Cross Elasticity of Demand

A burger is a *substitute* for pizza. When the price of a burger rises, the demand for pizza increases and the demand curve for pizza shifts rightward from D_0 to D_1. The cross elasticity of the demand for pizza is *positive.*

Soft drinks are a *complement* of pizza. When the price of a soft drink rises, the demand for pizza decreases and the demand curve for pizza shifts leftward from D_0 to D_2. The cross elasticity of the demand for pizza is *negative.*

Complements Now suppose that the price of a pizza is constant and 11 pizzas an hour are sold. The price of a soft drink rises from $1.50 to $2.50. No other influence on buying plans changes, and the quantity of pizzas sold falls to 9 an hour.

The change in the quantity demanded is the opposite of what we've just calculated: The quantity of pizzas demanded decreases by 20 percent (−20).

The change in the price of a soft drink, a complement of pizza, is the same as the percentage change in the price of a burger that we've just calculated: The price rises by 50 percent (+50). So the cross elasticity of demand of pizza with respect to the price of a soft drink is

$$\frac{-20\%}{+50\%} = -0.4.$$

Because pizza and soft drinks are complements, when the price of a soft drink rises, the demand for pizza decreases. In Fig. 4.7, the demand curve for pizza shifts leftward from D_0 to D_2. Because a *rise* in the price of soft drinks brings a *decrease* in the demand for pizza, the cross elasticity of demand for pizza with respect to the price of soft drinks is *negative*. The price and quantity change in *opposite* directions.

The magnitude of the cross elasticity of demand determines how far the demand curve shifts. The larger the cross elasticity (absolute value), the greater is the change in demand and the larger is the shift in the demand curve.

If two items are very close substitutes, such as two brands of spring water, the cross elasticity is large. If two items are close complements, such as movies and popcorn, the cross elasticity is large.

If two items are somewhat unrelated to each other, such as newspapers and orange juice, the cross elasticity is small—perhaps even zero.

Income Elasticity of Demand

Suppose the economy is expanding and people are enjoying rising incomes. This prosperity is bringing an increase in the demand for most types of goods and services. But by how much will the demand for pizza increase? The answer depends on the **income elasticity of demand,** which is a measure of the responsiveness of the demand for a good or service to a change in income, other things remaining the same.

The income elasticity of demand is calculated by using the formula:

$$\text{Income elasticity of demand} = \frac{\text{Percentage change in quantity demanded}}{\text{Percentage change in income}}.$$

Income elasticities of demand can be positive or negative and fall into three interesting ranges:

- Greater than 1 (*normal* good, income elastic)
- Positive and less than 1 (*normal* good, income inelastic)
- Negative (*inferior* good)

Income Elastic Demand Suppose that the price of pizza is constant and 9 pizzas an hour are sold. Then income rises from $975 to $1,025 a week. No other influence on buying plans changes, and the quantity of pizzas sold increases to 11 an hour.

The change in the quantity demanded is +2 pizzas. The average quantity is 10, so the quantity demanded increases by 20 percent. The change in income is +$50 and the average income is $1,000, so the income increases by 5 percent. The income elasticity of demand for pizza is

$$\frac{20\%}{5\%} = 4.$$

As income increases, the quantity of pizza demanded increases faster than does income. The demand for pizza is income elastic. Other goods in this category include ocean cruises, international travel, jewellery, and works of art.

Income Inelastic Demand If the percentage increase in the quantity demanded is less than the percentage increase in income, the income elasticity of demand is positive and less than 1. In this case, the quantity demanded increases as income increases, but income increases faster than does the quantity demanded. The demand for the good is income inelastic. Goods in this category include food, clothing, newspapers, and magazines.

Inferior Goods If when income increases, the quantity demanded of a good decreases, the income elasticity of demand is negative. Goods in this category include small motorcycles, potatoes, and rice. Low-income consumers buy most of these goods.

Real-World Income Elasticities of Demand

Table 4.2 shows estimates of some real-world income elasticities of demand. The demand for a necessity, such as food or gasoline, is income inelastic, while the demand for a luxury, such as transportation, which includes airline and foreign travel, is income elastic.

But what is a necessity and what is a luxury depends on the level of income. For people with a low income, food and clothing can be luxuries. So the *level* of income has a big effect on income elasticities of demand. Figure 4.8 shows this effect on the income elasticity of demand for food in 10 countries. In countries with low incomes, such as Tanzania and India, the income elasticity of demand for food is high. In countries with high incomes, such as Canada, the income elasticity of demand for food is low.

TABLE 4.2   Some Real-World Income Elasticities of Demand

Elastic Demand

Airline travel	5.82
Movies	3.41
Foreign travel	3.08
Electricity	1.94
Restaurant meals	1.61
Local buses and trains	1.38
Haircuts	1.36
Automobiles	1.07

Inelastic Demand

Tobacco	0.86
Alcoholic drinks	0.62
Furniture	0.53
Clothing	0.51
Newspapers and magazines	0.38
Telephone	0.32
Food	0.14

Sources: H.S. Houthakker and Lester D. Taylor, *Consumer Demand in the United States* (Cambridge, Mass.: Harvard University Press, 1970), and Henri Theil, Ching-Fan Chung, and James L. Seale, Jr., *Advances in Econometrics, Supplement 1, 1989, International Evidence on Consumption Patterns* (Greenwich, Conn.: JAI Press, Inc., 1989).

FIGURE 4.8   Income Elasticities in 10 Countries

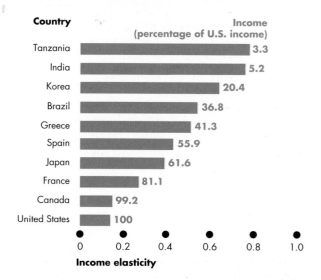

As income increases, the income elasticity of demand for food decreases. The percentage of any increase in income that is spent on food is larger for low-income consumers than for high-income consumers.

Source: Henri Theil, Ching-Fan Chung, and James L. Seale, Jr., *Advances in Econometrics, Supplement 1, 1989, International Evidence on Consumption Patterns* (Greenwich, Conn.: JAI Press, Inc., 1989).

REVIEW QUIZ

1   What does the cross elasticity of demand measure?
2   What does the sign (positive versus negative) of the cross elasticity of demand tell us about the relationship between two goods?
3   What does the income elasticity of demand measure?
4   What does the sign (positive versus negative) of the income elasticity of demand tell us about a good?
5   Why does the level of income influence the magnitude of the income elasticity of demand?

You've now completed your study of the *cross elasticity* of demand and the *income elasticity* of demand. Let's look at the other side of a market and examine the elasticity of supply.

Elasticity of Supply

You know that when demand increases, the price rises and the quantity increases. But does the price rise by a large amount and the quantity increase by a little? Or does the price barely rise and the quantity increase by a large amount?

The answer depends on the responsiveness of the quantity supplied to a change in price. You can see why by studying Fig. 4.9, which shows two possible scenarios in a local pizza market. Figure 4.9(a) shows one scenario, and Fig. 4.9(b) shows the other.

In both cases, demand is initially D_0. In part (a), the supply of pizza is shown by the supply curve S_A. In part (b), the supply of pizza is shown by the supply curve S_B. Initially, in both cases, the price is $20 a pizza and the quantity produced and consumed is 10 pizzas an hour.

Now increases in income and population increase the demand for pizza. The demand curve shifts rightward to D_1. In case (a), the price rises by $10 to $30 a pizza, and the quantity increases by only 3 to 13 an hour. In contrast, in case (b), the price rises by only $1 to $21 a pizza, and the quantity increases by 10 to 20 pizzas an hour.

The different outcomes arise from differing degrees of responsiveness of the quantity supplied to a change in price. We measure the degree of responsiveness by using the concept of the elasticity of supply.

Calculating the Elasticity of Supply

The **elasticity of supply** measures the responsiveness of the quantity supplied to a change in the price of a good when all other influences on selling plans remain the same. It is calculated by using the formula:

$$\text{Elasticity of supply} = \frac{\text{Percentage change in quantity supplied}}{\text{Percentage change in price}}.$$

We use the same method that you learned when you studied the elasticity of demand. Let's calculate the elasticity of supply for the supplies illustrated in Fig. 4.9.

In Fig. 4.9(a), when the price rises from $20 to $30, the price rise is $10 and the average price is $25, so the price rises by 40 percent of the average price. The quantity increases from 10 to 13, so the increase

FIGURE 4.9   How a Change in Demand Changes Price and Quantity

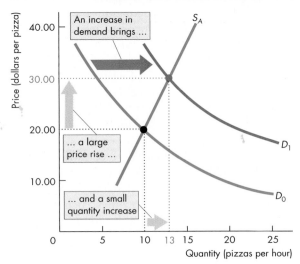

(a) Large price change and small quantity change

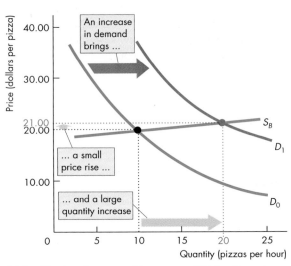

(b) Small price change and large quantity change

Initially, the price is $20 a pizza, and the quantity sold is 10 pizzas an hour. Then increases in income and population increase the demand for pizza. The demand curve shifts rightward to D_1. In part (a) the price rises by $10, to $30 a pizza, and the quantity increases by only 3, to 13 pizzas an hour. In part (b), the price rises by only $1, to $21 a pizza, and the quantity increases by 10, to 20 pizzas an hour. The price change is smaller and the quantity change is larger in case (b) than in case (a). The quantity supplied is more responsive to price in case (b) than in case (a).

is 3, the average quantity is 11.5, and the quantity increases by 26 percent. The elasticity of supply is equal to 26 percent divided by 40 percent, which equals 0.65.

In Fig. 4.9(b), when the price rises from $20 to $21, the price rise is $1 and the average price is $20.50, so the price rises by 4.9 percent of the average price. The quantity increases from 10 to 20, so the increase is 10, the average quantity is 15, and the quantity increases by 67 percent. The elasticity of supply is equal to 67 percent divided by 4.9 percent, which equals 13.67.

Figure 4.10 shows the range of supply elasticities. If the quantity supplied is fixed regardless of the price, the supply curve is vertical and the elasticity of supply is zero. Supply is perfectly inelastic. This case is shown in Fig. 4.10(a). A special intermediate case is when the percentage change in price equals the percentage change in quantity. Supply is then unit elastic. This case is shown in Fig. 4.10(b). No matter how steep the supply curve is, if it is linear and passes through the origin, supply is unit elastic. If there is a price at which sellers are willing to offer any quantity for sale, the supply curve is horizontal and the elasticity of supply is infinite. Supply is perfectly elastic. This case is shown in Fig. 4.10(c).

The Factors That Influence the Elasticity of Supply

The magnitude of the elasticity of supply depends on

- Resource substitution possibilities
- Time frame for the supply decision

Resource Substitution Possibilities Some goods and services can be produced only by using unique or rare productive resources. These items have a low, even perhaps a zero, elasticity of supply. Other goods and services can be produced by using commonly available resources that could be allocated to a wide variety of alternative tasks. Such items have a high elasticity of supply.

A Van Gogh painting is an example of a good with a vertical supply curve and a zero elasticity of supply. At the other extreme, wheat can be grown on land that is almost equally good for growing corn. So it is just as easy to grow wheat as corn, and the opportunity cost of wheat in terms of forgone corn is almost constant. As a result, the supply curve of wheat is almost horizontal and its elasticity of supply is very large. Similarly, when a good is produced in many different countries (for example, sugar and beef), the supply of the good is highly elastic.

FIGURE 4.10   Inelastic and Elastic Supply

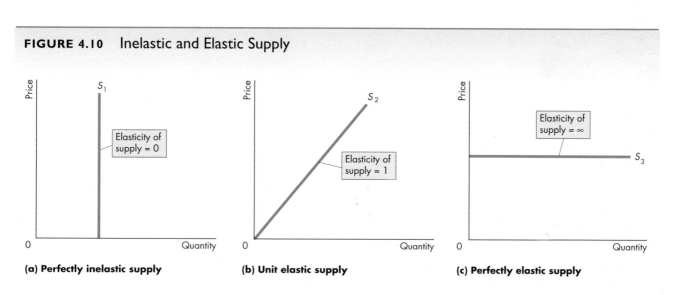

(a) Perfectly inelastic supply (b) Unit elastic supply (c) Perfectly elastic supply

Each supply illustrated here has a constant elasticity. The supply curve in part (a) illustrates the supply of a good that has a zero elasticity of supply. The supply curve in part (b) illustrates the supply for a good with a unit elas-ticity of supply. All linear supply curves that pass through the origin illustrate supplies that are unit elastic. The supply curve in part (c) illustrates the supply for a good with an infinite elasticity of supply.

The supply of most goods and services lies between the two extremes. The quantity produced can be increased but only by incurring a higher cost. If a higher price is offered, the quantity supplied increases. Such goods and services have an elasticity of supply between zero and infinity.

Time Frame for the Supply Decision To study the influence of the length of time elapsed since a price change, we distinguish three time frames of supply:

1. Momentary supply
2. Long-run supply
3. Short-run supply

When the price of a good rises or falls, the *momentary supply curve* shows the response of the quantity supplied immediately following a price change.

Some goods, such as fruits and vegetables, have a perfectly inelastic momentary supply—a vertical supply curve. The quantities supplied depend on crop-planting decisions made earlier. In the case of oranges, for example, planting decisions have to be made many years in advance of the crop being available. The momentary supply curve is vertical because, on a given day, no matter what the price of oranges, producers cannot change their output. They have picked, packed, and shipped their crop to market, and the quantity available for that day is fixed.

In contrast, some goods have a perfectly elastic momentary supply. Long-distance phone calls are an example. When many people simultaneously make calls, there is a big surge in the demand for telephone cables, computer switching, and satellite time and the quantity bought increases. But the price remains constant. Long-distance carriers monitor fluctuations in demand and reroute calls to ensure that the quantity supplied equals the quantity demanded without changing the price.

The *long-run supply curve* shows the response of the quantity supplied to a change in price after all the technologically possible ways of adjusting supply have been exploited. In the case of oranges, the long run is the time it takes new plantings to grow to full maturity—about 15 years. In some cases, the long-run adjustment occurs only after a completely new production plant has been built and workers have been trained to operate it—typically a process that might take several years.

The *short-run supply curve* shows how the quantity supplied responds to a price change when only *some* of the technologically possible adjustments to production have been made. The short-run response to a price change is a sequence of adjustments. The first adjustment that is usually made is in the amount of labour employed. To increase output in the short run, firms work their labour force overtime and perhaps hire additional workers. To decrease their output in the short run, firms either lay off workers or reduce their hours of work. With the passage of time, firms can make additional adjustments, perhaps training additional workers or buying additional tools and other equipment. The short-run supply curve slopes upward because producers can take action quite quickly to change the quantity supplied in response to a price change. For example, if the price of oranges falls, growers can stop picking and leave oranges to rot on the trees. Or if the price rises, they can use more fertilizer and improved irrigation to increase the yields of their existing trees. In the long run, they can plant more trees and increase the quantity supplied even more in response to a given price rise.

R E V I E W   Q U I Z

1 Why do we need to measure the responsiveness of the quantity supplied of a good or service to a change in its price?
2 Can you define and calculate the elasticity of supply?
3 What are the main influences on the elasticity of supply that make the supply of some goods elastic and the supply of other goods inelastic?
4 Can you provide examples of goods or services whose elasticity of supply are (a) zero, (b) greater than zero but less than infinity, and (c) infinity?
5 How does the time frame over which a supply decision is made influence the elasticity of supply?

◆ You have now studied the theory of demand and supply, and you have learned how to measure the elasticities of demand and supply. All the elasticities that you've met in this chapter are summarized in Table 4.3. In the next chapter, we are going to study the efficiency of competitive markets. But before doing that, take a look at *Reading Between the Lines* on pp. 98–99 to see elasticity in action.

TABLE 4.3   A Compact Glossary of Elasticities

Price Elasticities of Demand

A relationship is described as	When its magnitude is	Which means that
Perfectly elastic or infinitely elastic	Infinity	The smallest possible increase in price causes an infinitely large decrease in the quantity demanded*
Elastic	Less than infinity but greater than 1	The percentage decrease in the quantity demanded exceeds the percentage increase in price
Unit elastic	1	The percentage decrease in the quantity demanded equals the percentage increase in price
Inelastic	Greater than zero but less than 1	The percentage decrease in the quantity demanded is less than the percentage increase in price
Perfectly inelastic or completely inelastic	Zero	The quantity demanded is the same at all prices

Cross Elasticities of Demand

A relationship is described as	When its value is	Which means that
Perfect substitutes	Infinity	The smallest possible increase in the price of one good causes an infinitely large increase in the quantity demanded of the other good
Substitutes	Positive, less than infinity	If the price of one good increases, the quantity demanded of the other good also increases
Independent	Zero	If the price of one good increases, the quantity demanded of the other good remains the same
Complements	Less than zero	If the price of one good increases, the quantity demanded of the other good decreases

Income Elasticities of Demand

A relationship is described as	When its value is	Which means that
Income elastic (normal good)	Greater than 1	The percentage increase in the quantity demanded is greater than the percentage increase in income
Income inelastic (normal good)	Less than 1 but greater than zero	The percentage increase in the quantity demanded is less than the percentage increase in income
Negative income elastic (inferior good)	Less than zero	When income increases, quantity demanded decreases

Elasticities of Supply

A relationship is described as	When its magnitude is	Which means that
Perfectly elastic	Infinity	The smallest possible increase in price causes an infinitely large increase in the quantity supplied
Elastic	Less than infinity but greater than 1	The percentage increase in the quantity supplied exceeds the percentage increase in the price
Inelastic	Greater than zero but less than 1	The percentage increase in the quantity supplied is less than the percentage increase in the price
Perfectly inelastic	Zero	The quantity supplied is the same at all prices

*In each description, the directions of change may be reversed. For example, in this case, the smallest possible *decrease* in price causes an infinitely large *increase* in the quantity demanded.

*Elasticities of Demand and Supply
in the Global Oil Market*

CALGARY HERALD, AUGUST 10, 2002

Growth in demand for oil weaker than agency expected

The International Energy Agency, an adviser to 26 nations on oil policy, reduced its forecast for growth in world oil demand this year, citing a "moderate" rate of economic recovery in the U.S. and Europe. ...

The forecast comes six weeks before the Organization of Petroleum Exporting Countries, which has reduced output quotas to the lowest since 1991, meets to discuss whether to raise members' production ceiling. Algeria and Nigeria have asked OPEC for an increase in their quota. ...

The U.S. economy, the world's largest, grew at a 1.1 per cent annual rate in the second quarter after expanding at a five per cent rate in the first quarter. The European Commission trimmed its economic growth forecast after plunging stock prices threatened the region's recovery.

OPEC reduced production quotas three times last year and again on Jan. 1 to support prices as demand declined. The group maintained those quotas in June and will discuss whether to increase supply at a meeting in Osaka, Japan on Sept. 19.

World oil production is rising, in part because OPEC members are pumping more than their official limits, the IEA report shows. In July, supply averaged 76.5 million barrels a day, up 780,000 barrels from June, led by Iran and other members of OPEC.

The 10 OPEC members who agree to limit supply, all except Iraq, produced 23.2 million barrels a day in July, up 360,000 barrels from June and 1.5 million barrels more than their collective target. ...

Calgary Herald, 10 August 2002, page D2.
Reprinted with permission of the *Calgary Herald*.

Essence of the Story

■ The U.S. economy grew at a 1.1 percent annual rate in the second quarter and the European Commission trimmed its economic growth forecast.

■ The International Energy Agency forecasts that slow economic growth in the United States and Europe will keep the demand for oil low.

■ The Organization of Petroleum Exporting Countries (OPEC) cut production quotas three times in 2001 and again on Jan. 1 2002 to the lowest since 1991, but quotas have been exceeded by 1.5 million barrels a day.

■ Total oil production in July 2002 was 76.5 million barrels a day.

■ OPEC will decide in September 2002 whether to change its production quotas.

Economic Analysis

■ Demand and supply in a global market determine the price of crude oil.

■ OPEC is the largest supplier of oil (with a 36 percent market share), and it tries to limit production to raise the price. But the actions of individual OPEC members and of non-OPEC producers make it impossible for OPEC to control the price of crude oil.

■ Figure 1 shows how the price of crude oil has fluctuated since 1997 (an example of a price roller coaster).

■ Figure 2 shows demand and supply in the market for crude oil in 2000 and 2001.

■ The elasticity of demand is 0.05 and the elasticity of supply is 0.1. These elasticity values are suggested by Geoffrey Heal of Columbia University, a leading natural resource economist.

■ In 2000 and 2001, the supply curve was S_{2001}. In 2001, demand decreased from D_{2000} to D_{2001}. The decrease in demand brought a fall in the price and a decrease in the quantity.

■ Figure 3 shows the market in 2002. OPEC cut its production quotas by 5 million barrels a day. But OPEC members violated the quotas and supply decreased by less

than this amount. In 2002, the supply of oil had decreased to S_{2002}.

■ The U.S. and European recessions decreased the demand for oil and, if no other influences had been at work, the demand for oil would have been similar in 2002 to its 2001 level.

■ But another influence was at work. People expected a further decrease in supply to arise from political instability and possibly war in Iraq.

■ Because the demand for oil is inelastic, a small decrease in supply would generate a large rise in the price.

■ With the demand curve D_{2001}, a decrease in supply of just a few million barrels a day would send the price up to $30 a barrel or more.

■ Expecting such a price rise led firms and governments to decide to buy more oil in 2002 and increase their inventories. So the demand for oil increased to D_{2002}.

■ This increase in demand combined with OPEC's cut in its production quotas brought a sharp rise in price.

■ But because the increase in demand exceeded the decrease in supply, the quantity of oil produced actually increased.

Figure 1 The price of crude oil

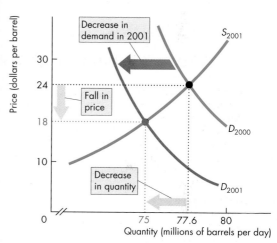

Figure 2 The oil market in 2001

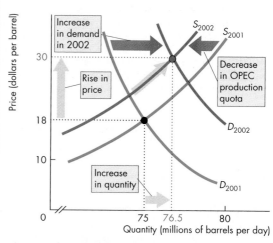

Figure 3 The oil market in 2002

99

SUMMARY

KEY POINTS

Price Elasticity of Demand (pp. 84–90)

- Elasticity is a measure of the responsiveness of the quantity demanded of a good to a change in its price.
- Price elasticity of demand equals the percentage change in the quantity demanded divided by the percentage change in price.
- The larger the magnitude of the elasticity of demand, the greater is the responsiveness of the quantity demanded to a given change in price.
- Price elasticity of demand depends on how easily one good serves as a substitute for another, the proportion of income spent on the good, and the length of time elapsed since the price change.
- If demand is elastic, a decrease in price leads to an increase in total revenue. If demand is unit elastic, a decrease in price leaves total revenue unchanged. And if demand is inelastic, a decrease in price leads to a decrease in total revenue.

More Elasticities of Demand (pp. 91–93)

- Cross elasticity of demand measures the responsiveness of demand for one good to a change in the price of a substitute or a complement.
- The cross elasticity of demand with respect to the price of a substitute is positive. The cross elasticity of demand with respect to the price of a complement is negative.
- Income elasticity of demand measures the responsiveness of demand to a change in income. For a normal good, the income elasticity of demand is positive. For an inferior good, the income elasticity of demand is negative.
- When the income elasticity is greater than 1, as income increases, the percentage of income spent on the good increases.
- When the income elasticity is less than 1 but greater than zero, as income increases, the percentage of income spent on the good decreases.

Elasticity of Supply (pp. 94–96)

- Elasticity of supply measures the responsiveness of the quantity supplied of a good to a change in its price.
- The elasticity of supply is usually positive and ranges between zero (vertical supply curve) and infinity (horizontal supply curve).
- Supply decisions have three time frames: momentary, long run, and short run.
- Momentary supply refers to the response of sellers to a price change at the instant that the price changes.
- Long-run supply refers to the response of sellers to a price change when all the technologically feasible adjustments in production have been made.
- Short-run supply refers to the response of sellers to a price change after some technologically feasible adjustments in production have been made.

KEY FIGURES AND TABLE

Figure 4.2   Calculating the Elasticity of Demand, 85
Figure 4.3   Inelastic and Elastic Demand, 86
Figure 4.4   Elasticity Along a Straight-Line Demand Curve, 87
Figure 4.5   Elasticity and Total Revenue, 88
Figure 4.7   Cross Elasticity of Demand, 91
Figure 4.10 Inelastic and Elastic Supply, 95
Table 4.3   A Compact Glossary of Elasticities, 97

KEY TERMS

Cross elasticity of demand, 91
Elastic demand, 87
Elasticity of supply, 94
Income elasticity of demand, 92
Inelastic demand, 87
Perfectly elastic demand, 87
Perfectly inelastic demand, 86
Price elasticity of demand, 84
Total revenue, 88
Total revenue test, 88
Unit elastic demand, 86

PROBLEMS

*1. Heavy rain spoils the strawberry crop. As a result, the price of strawberries rises from $4 to $6 a box and the quantity demanded decreases from 1,000 to 600 boxes a week. Over this price range,
a. What is the price elasticity of demand?
b. Describe the demand for strawberries.

2. Good weather brings a bumper tomato crop. The price falls from $7 to $5 a basket, and the quantity demanded increases from 300 to 500 baskets a day. Over this price range,
a. What is the price elasticity of demand?
b. Describe the demand for tomatoes.

*3. The figure shows the demand for videotape rentals.

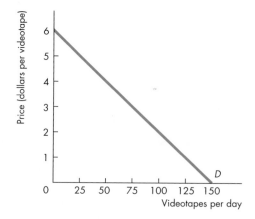

a. Calculate the elasticity of demand for a rise in rental price from $3 to $5.
b. At what price is the elasticity of demand equal to 1?

4. The figure shows the demand for pens.

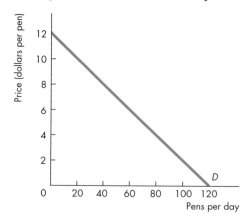

a. Calculate the elasticity of demand for a rise in price from $6 to $10.

b. At what prices is the elasticity of demand equal to 1, greater than 1, and less than 1?

*5. If the quantity of dental services demanded increases by 10 percent when the price of dental services falls by 10 percent, is the demand for dental service inelastic, elastic, or unit elastic?

6. If the quantity of haircuts demanded decreases by 10 percent when the price of a haircut rises by 5 percent, is the demand for haircuts elastic, inelastic, or unit elastic?

*7. The demand schedule for computer chips is

Price (dollars per chip)	Quantity demanded (millions of chips per year)
200	50
250	45
300	40
350	35
400	30

a. What happens to total revenue if the price of a chip falls from $400 to $350?
b. What happens to total revenue if the price of a chip falls from $350 to $300?
c. At what price is total revenue at a maximum? Use the total revenue test to answer this question.
d. At an average price of $350, is the demand for chips elastic or inelastic? Use the total revenue test to answer this question.

8. The demand schedule for sugar is

Price (dollars per kilogram)	Quantity demanded (millions of kilograms per year)
5	25
10	20
15	15
20	10
25	5

a. What happens to total revenue if the price of sugar rises from $5 to $15 per kilogram?
b. What happens to total revenue if the price rises from $15 to $25 per kilogram?
c. At what price is total revenue a maximum? Use the total revenue test to answer this question.
d. At an average price of $20 a kilogram, is the demand for sugar elastic or inelastic? Use the total revenue test to answer this question.

*9. In problem 7, at $250 a chip, is the demand for chips elastic or inelastic? Use the total revenue test to answer this question.

10. In problem 8, at $10 a kilogram, is the demand for sugar elastic or inelastic? Use the total revenue test to answer this question.

*11. If a 12 percent rise in the price of orange juice decreases the quantity of orange juice demanded by 22 percent and increases the quantity of apple juice demanded by 14 percent, calculate the cross elasticity of demand between orange juice and apple juice.

12. If a 5 percent fall in the price of chicken decreases the quantity of beef demanded by 20 percent and increases the quantity of chicken demanded by 15 percent, calculate the cross elasticity of demand between chicken and beef.

*13. Alex's income has increased from $3,000 to $5,000. Alex increased his consumption of bagels from 4 to 8 a month and decreased his consumption of doughnuts from 12 to 6 a month. Calculate Alex's income elasticity of demand for (a) bagels and (b) doughnuts.

14. Judy's income has increased from $13,000 to $17,000. Judy increased her demand for concert tickets by 15 percent and decreased her demand for bus rides by 10 percent. Calculate Judy's income elasticity of demand for (a) concert tickets and (b) bus rides.

*15. The table gives the supply schedule for long-distance phone calls.

Price (cents per minute)	Quantity supplied (millions of minutes per day)
10	200
20	400
30	600
40	800

Calculate the elasticity of supply when
a. The price falls from 40 cents to 30 cents a minute.
b. The price is 20 cents a minute.

16. The table gives the supply schedule for jeans.

Price (dollars per pair)	Quantity supplied (millions of pairs per year)
120	2,400
125	2,800
130	3,200
135	3,600

Calculate the elasticity of supply when
a. The price rises from $125 to $135 a pair.
b. The price is $125 a pair.

CRITICAL THINKING

1. Study *Reading Between the Lines* (pp. 98–99) on the market for crude oil and then answer the following questions:
   a. Why did the price of oil fall during 2001?
   b. What is the elasticity that tells us the effect of a change in supply on the price and quantity of crude oil?
   c. What is the elasticity that tells us the effect of a change in demand on the price and quantity of crude oil?
   d. Why did OPEC want to cut production during 2002?
   e. Calculate the elasticity of supply in Fig. 2 on page 99 when demand decreases and confirm that it is (approximately) 0.1.
   f. If the decrease in supply in Fig. 3 on page 99 was sufficient to increase the price to $30 a barrel along D_{2001}, what would have been the change in the quantity, given the elasticity of demand of 0.05?

WEB EXERCISES

1. Use the link on the Parkin–Bade Web site and
   a. Find the price of gasoline in the summer of 2002.
   b. Use the concepts of demand, supply, and elasticity to explain recent changes in the price of gasoline.
   c. Find the price of crude oil.
   d. Use the concepts of demand, supply, and elasticity to explain recent changes in the price of crude oil.

2. Use the link on the Parkin–Bade Web site and
   a. Find the number of gallons in a barrel and the cost of crude oil in a gallon of gasoline.
   b. What are the other costs that make up the total cost of a gallon of gasoline?
   c. If the price of crude oil falls by 10 percent, by what percentage would you expect the price of gasoline to change, other things remaining the same?
   d. Which demand do you think is more elastic: that for crude oil, or that for gasoline? Why?

3. Use the link on the Parkin–Bade Web site to review and write a brief report on *Geoffrey Heal's* lecture on the oil market during the 1990s.

EFFICIENCY AND EQUITY

CHAPTER 5

More for Less

People constantly strive to get more for less. The government of South Africa was pleased when it found a source of supply of AZT, a drug used to treat AIDS, for $275 per person per year instead of the $23,000 charged by GlaxoSmithKline, the British company that developed the drug. Every time we buy something or decide *not* to buy something, we express our view about how scarce resources should be used. We try to spend our incomes in ways that get the most out of our scarce resources. ◆ Is the allocation of our resources between leisure and education, pizza and sandwiches, inline skates and squash balls, AIDS treatments and other drugs the right one? ◆ Some firms make huge profits year after year. Microsoft, for example, has generated enough profit over the past ten years to rocket Bill Gates, one of its founders, into the position of being one of the richest people in the world. Is that kind of business success a sign of efficiency? ◆ And is it fair that Bill Gates is so incredibly rich while others live in miserable poverty?

◆ These are the issues you'll explore in this chapter. You will discover that competitive markets can be efficient. But you will also discover some sources of inefficiency. You will discover that firms that make huge profits, while efficient in one sense, might be inefficient in a broader sense. And you'll return to the controversial issue of whether South Africa should be able to buy AIDS treatments in a cut-price market in *Reading Between the Lines* at the end of the chapter.

After studying this chapter, you will be able to

- **Define efficiency**
- **Distinguish between value and price and define consumer surplus**
- **Distinguish between cost and price and define producer surplus**
- **Explain the conditions under which markets move resources to their highest-valued uses and the sources of inefficiency in our economy**
- **Explain the main ideas about fairness and evaluate claims that markets result in unfair outcomes**

Efficiency: A Refresher

IT IS HARD TO TALK ABOUT EFFICIENCY IN ordinary conversation without generating disagreement. To an engineer, an entrepreneur, a politician, a working mother, or an economist, getting more for less seems like a sensible thing to aim for. But some people think that the pursuit of efficiency conflicts with other, worthier goals. Environmentalists worry about contamination from "efficient" nuclear power plants. And car producers worry about competition from "efficient" foreign producers.

Economists use the idea of efficiency in a special way that avoids these disagreements. An **efficient allocation** of resources occurs when we produce the goods and services that people value most highly (see Chapter 2, pp. 37–39). Equivalently, resource use is efficient when we cannot produce more of a good or service without giving up some other good or service that we value more highly.

If people value a nuclear-free environment more highly than they value cheap electric power, it is efficient to use higher-cost, nonnuclear technologies to produce electricity. Efficiency is not a cold, mechanical concept. It is a concept based on value, and value is based on people's feelings.

Think about the efficient quantity of pizza. To produce more pizza, we must give up some other goods and services. For example, we might give up some sandwiches. So to produce more pizzas, we forgo sandwiches. If we have fewer pizzas, we can have more sandwiches. What is the efficient quantity of pizza to produce? The answer depends on marginal benefit and marginal cost.

Marginal Benefit   — chapter 2

If we consume one more pizza, we receive a marginal benefit. **Marginal benefit** is the benefit that a person receives from consuming *one more unit* of a good or service. The marginal benefit from a good or service is measured as the maximum amount that a person is willing to pay for one more unit of it. So the marginal benefit from a pizza is the maximum amount of other goods and services that people are willing to give up to get one more pizza. The marginal benefit from pizza decreases as the quantity of pizza consumed increases —the principle of *decreasing marginal benefit.*

We can express the marginal benefit from a pizza as the number of sandwiches that people are willing to forgo to get one more pizza. But we can also express marginal benefit as the dollar value of other goods and services that people are willing to forgo. Figure 5.1 shows the marginal benefit from pizza expressed in this way. As the quantity of pizza increases, the value of other items that people are willing to forgo to get yet one more pizza decreases.

Marginal Cost

If we produce one more pizza, we incur a marginal cost. **Marginal cost** is the opportunity cost of producing *one more unit* of a good or service. The marginal cost of a good or service is measured as the value of the best alternative forgone. So the marginal cost of a pizza is the value of the best alternative forgone to get one more pizza. The marginal cost of a pizza increases as the quantity of pizza produced increases—the principle of *increasing marginal cost.*

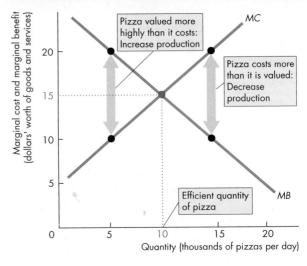

FIGURE 5.1   The Efficient Quantity of Pizza

The marginal benefit curve (MB) shows what people *are willing to* forgo to get one more pizza. The marginal cost curve (MC) shows what people *must* forgo to get one more pizza. If fewer than 10,000 pizzas a day are produced, marginal benefit exceeds marginal cost. Greater value can be obtained by producing more pizzas. If more than 10,000 pizzas a day are produced, marginal cost exceeds marginal benefit. Greater value can be obtained by producing fewer pizzas. If 10,000 pizzas a day are produced, marginal benefit equals marginal cost and the efficient quantity of pizza is available.

We can express marginal cost as the number of sandwiches we must forgo to produce one more pizza. But we can also express marginal cost as the dollar value of other goods and services we must forgo. Figure 5.1 shows the marginal cost of pizza expressed in this way. As the quantity of pizza produced increases, the value of other items we must forgo to produce yet one more pizza increases.

Efficiency and Inefficiency

To determine the efficient quantity of pizza, we compare the marginal cost of a pizza with the marginal benefit from a pizza. There are three possible cases:

- Marginal benefit exceeds marginal cost.
- Marginal cost exceeds marginal benefit.
- Marginal benefit equals marginal cost.

Marginal Benefit Exceeds Marginal Cost

Suppose the quantity of pizza produced is 5,000 a day. Figure 5.1 shows that at this quantity, the marginal benefit of a pizza is $20. That is, when the quantity of pizza available is 5,000 a day, people are willing to pay $20 for the 5,000th pizza. The figure also shows that the marginal cost of the 5,000th pizza is $10. That is, to produce one more pizza, the value of other goods and services that we must forgo is $10.

If pizza production increases from 4,999 to 5,000, the value of the additional pizza is $20 and its marginal cost is $10. If this pizza is produced, the value of the pizza produced exceeds the value of the goods and services we must forgo by $10. Resources will be used more efficiently—they will create more value—if we produce an extra pizza and fewer other goods and services. This same reasoning applies all the way up to the 9,999th pizza. Only when we get to the 10,000th pizza does marginal benefit not exceed marginal cost.

Marginal Cost Exceeds Marginal Benefit

Suppose the quantity of pizza produced is 15,000 a day. Figure 5.1 shows that at this quantity, the marginal benefit of a pizza is $10. That is, when the quantity of pizza available is 15,000 a day, people are willing to pay $10 for the 15,000th pizza. The figure also shows that the marginal cost of the 15,000th pizza is $20. That is, to produce one more pizza, the value of the other goods and services that we must forgo is $20.

If pizza production decreases from 15,000 to 14,999, the value of the one pizza forgone is $10 and its marginal cost is $20. So if this pizza is not produced, the value of the other goods and services produced exceeds the value of the pizza forgone by $10. Resources will be used more efficiently—they will create more value—if we produce one fewer pizza and more other goods and services. This same reasoning applies all the way down to the 10,001st pizza. Only when we get to the 10,000th pizza does marginal cost not exceed marginal benefit.

Marginal Benefit Equals Marginal Cost

Suppose the quantity of pizza produced is 10,000 a day. Figure 5.1 shows that at this quantity, the marginal benefit of a pizza is $15. That is, when the quantity of pizza available is 10,000 a day, people are willing to pay $15 for the 10,000th pizza. The figure also shows that the marginal cost of the 10,000th pizza is $15. That is, to produce one more pizza, the value of other goods and services that we must forgo is $15.

In this situation, we cannot increase the value of the goods and services produced by either increasing or decreasing the quantity of pizza. If we increase the quantity of pizza, the 10,001st pizza costs more to produce than it is worth. If we decrease the quantity of pizza produced, the 9,999th pizza is worth more than it costs to produce. So when marginal benefit equals marginal cost, resource use is efficient.

REVIEW QUIZ

1 If the marginal benefit of pizza exceeds the marginal cost of pizza, are we producing too much pizza and too little of other goods, or are we producing too little pizza and too much of other goods?
2 If the marginal cost of pizza exceeds the marginal benefit of pizza, are we producing too much pizza and too little of other goods, or are we producing too little pizza and too much of other goods?
3 What is the relationship between the marginal benefit of pizza and the marginal cost of pizza when we are producing the efficient quantity of pizza?

Does a competitive market in pizza produce the efficient quantity of pizza? Let's answer this question.

Value, Price, and Consumer Surplus

To INVESTIGATE WHETHER A COMPETITIVE market is efficient, we need to learn about the connection between demand and marginal benefit and the connection between supply and marginal cost.

Value, Willingness to Pay, and Demand

In everyday life, we talk about "getting value for money." When we use this expression, we are distinguishing between *value* and *price*. Value is what we get, and the price is what we pay.

The **value** of one more unit of a good or service is its *marginal benefit*. Marginal benefit can be expressed as the maximum price that people are willing to pay for another unit of the good or service. The willingness to pay for a good or service determines the demand for it.

In Fig. 5.2(a) the demand curve *D* shows the quantity demanded at each price. For example, when the price of a pizza is $15, the quantity demanded is

10,000 pizzas a day. In Fig. 5.2(b), the demand curve *D* shows the maximum price that people are willing to pay when there is a given quantity. For example, when 10,000 pizzas a day are available, the most that people are willing to pay for the 10,000th pizza is $15. This second interpretation of the demand curve means that the marginal benefit from the 10,000th pizza is $15. The demand curve is also the marginal benefit curve *MB*.

When we draw a demand curve, we use a *relative price*, not a *money* price. We express the relative price in dollars, but the relative price measures the number of dollars' worth of other goods and services forgone to obtain one more unit of the good in question (see Chapter 3, p. 60). So a demand curve tells us the value of other goods and services that people are willing to forgo to get an additional unit of a good. But this is what a marginal benefit curve tells us too. So

A demand curve is a marginal benefit curve.

We don't always have to pay the maximum price that we are willing to pay. When we buy something, we often get a bargain. Let's see how.

FIGURE 5.2   Demand, Willingness to Pay, and Marginal Benefit

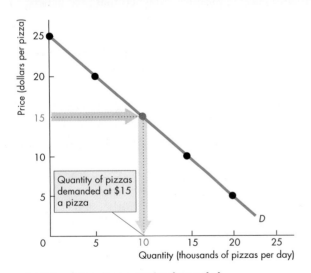

(a) Price determines quantity demanded

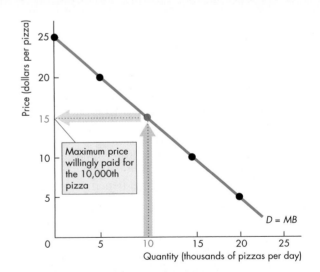

(b) Quantity determines willingness to pay

The demand curve for pizza, *D*, shows the quantity of pizza demanded at each price, other things remaining the same. It also shows the maximum price that consumers are willing to pay if a given quantity of pizza is available. At a price of $15 a pizza, the quantity demanded is 10,000 pizzas a day (part a). If 10,000 pizzas a day are available, the maximum price that consumers are willing to pay for the 10,000th pizza is $15 (part b).

Consumer Surplus

When people buy something for less than it is worth to them, they receive a consumer surplus. A **consumer surplus** is the value of a good minus the price paid for it, summed over the quantity bought.

To understand consumer surplus, let's look at Lisa's demand for pizza in Fig. 5.3. Lisa likes pizza, but the marginal benefit she gets from it decreases quickly as her consumption increases.

To keep things simple, suppose Lisa can buy pizza by the slice and that there are 10 slices in a pizza. If a pizza costs $2.50 a slice (or $25 a pizza), Lisa spends her fast-food budget on items that she values more highly than pizza. At $2 a slice (or $20 a pizza), she buys 10 slices (1 pizza) a week. At $1.50 a slice, she buys 20 slices a week; at $1 a slice, she buys 30 slices a week; and at 50 cents a slice ($5 a pizza), she eats nothing but pizza and buys 40 slices a week.

Lisa's demand curve for pizza in Fig. 5.3 is also her *willingness-to-pay* or marginal benefit curve. It tells us that if Lisa can have only 10 slices (1 pizza) a week, she is willing to pay $2 a slice. Her marginal benefit from the 10th slice is $2. If she can have 20 slices (2 pizzas) a week, she is willing to pay $1.50 for the 20th slice. Her marginal benefit from the 20th slice is $1.50.

Figure 5.3 also shows Lisa's consumer surplus from pizza when the price is $1.50 a slice. At this price, she buys 20 slices a week. The most that Lisa is willing to pay for the 20th slice is $1.50 a slice, so its marginal benefit equals the price she pays for it.

But Lisa is willing to pay almost $2.50 for the first slice. So the marginal benefit from this slice is close to $1 more than she pays for it. So on her first slice of pizza, she receives a *consumer surplus* of almost $1. At a quantity of 10 slices of pizza a week, Lisa's marginal benefit is $2 a slice. So on the 10th slice, she receives a consumer surplus of 50 cents.

To calculate Lisa's consumer surplus, we find the consumer surplus on each slice she buys and add them together. This sum is the area of the green triangle—the area below the demand curve and above the market price line. This area is equal to the base of the triangle (20 slices) multiplied by the height of the triangle ($1) divided by 2, which is $10.

The area of the blue rectangle in Fig. 5.3 shows what Lisa pays for pizza, which is $30. This area is equal to 20 slices a week multiplied by $1.50 a slice.

All goods and services are like the pizza example you've just studied. Because of decreasing marginal

benefit, people receive more benefit from their consumption than the amount they pay.

FIGURE 5.3   A Consumer's Demand and Consumer Surplus

Lisa's demand curve for pizza tells us that at $2.50 a slice, she does not buy pizza. At $2 a slice, she buys 10 slices a week; at $1.50 a slice, she buys 20 slices a week. Lisa's demand curve also tells us that she is willing to pay $2 for the 10th slice and $1.50 for the 20th. She actually pays $1.50 a slice—the market price—and buys 20 slices a week. Her consumer surplus from pizza is $10—the area of the green triangle.

REVIEW QUIZ

1 How do we measure the value or marginal benefit of a good or service?
2 What is the relationship between marginal benefit and the demand curve?
3 What is consumer surplus? How do we measure it?

You've seen how we distinguish between value—marginal benefit—and price. And you've seen that buyers receive a consumer surplus because marginal benefit exceeds price. Next, we're going to study the connection between supply and marginal cost and learn about producer surplus.

Cost, Price, and Producer Surplus

WHAT YOU ARE NOW GOING TO LEARN ABOUT cost, price, and producer surplus parallels the related ideas about value, price, and consumer surplus that you've just studied.

Firms are in business to make a profit. To do so, they must sell their output for a price that exceeds the cost of production. Let's investigate the relationship between cost and price.

Cost, Minimum Supply-Price, and Supply

Earning a profit means receiving more (or at least receiving no less) for the sale of a good or service than the cost of producing it. Just as consumers distinguish between *value* and *price*, so producers distinguish between *cost* and *price*. Cost is what a producer gives up, and price is what a producer receives.

The cost of producing one more unit of a good or service is its *marginal cost*. And marginal cost is the minimum price that producers must receive to induce them to produce another unit of the good or service. This minimum acceptable price determines supply.

In Fig. 5.4(a), the supply curve *S* shows the quantity supplied at each price. For example, when the price of a pizza is $15, the quantity supplied is 10,000 pizzas a day. In Fig. 5.4(b), the supply curve shows the minimum price that producers must be offered to produce a given quantity of pizza. For example, the minimum price, which producers must be offered to get them to produce 10,000 pizzas a day is $15 a pizza. This second view of the supply curve means that the marginal cost of the 10,000th pizza is $15. The supply curve is also the marginal cost curve *MC*.

Because the price is a relative price, a supply curve tells us the quantity of other goods and services that *sellers must forgo* to produce one more unit of the good. But a marginal cost curve also tells us the quantity of other goods and services that we must

FIGURE 5.4   Supply, Minimum Supply-Price, and Marginal Cost

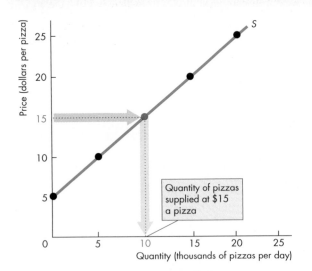

(a) Price determines quantity supplied

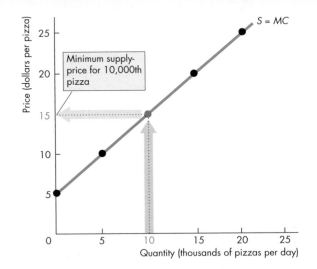

(b) Quantity determines minimum supply-price

The supply curve of pizza, *S*, shows the quantity of pizza supplied at each price, other things remaining the same. It also shows the minimum price that producers must be offered to get them to produce a given quantity of pizza.

At a price of $15 a pizza, the quantity supplied is 10,000 pizzas a day (part a). To get firms to produce 10,000 pizzas a day, the minimum price they must be offered for the 10,000th pizza is $15 (part b).

forgo to get one more unit of the good. So

A supply curve is a marginal cost curve.

If the price producers receive exceeds the cost they incur, they earn a producer surplus. This producer surplus is analogous to consumer surplus.

Producer Surplus

When price exceeds marginal cost, the firm obtains a producer surplus. A **producer surplus** is the price of a good minus the opportunity cost of producing it, summed over the quantity sold. To understand producer surplus, let's look at Max's supply of pizza in Fig. 5.5.

Max can produce pizza or bake bread that people like a lot. The more pizza he makes, the less bread he can bake. His opportunity cost of a pizza is the value of the bread he must forgo. This opportunity cost increases as Max increases his production of pizza. If a pizza sells for only $5, Max produces no pizza. He uses his kitchen to bake bread. Pizza just isn't worth producing. But at $10 a pizza, Max produces 50 pizzas a day, and at $15 a pizza, he produces 100 a day.

Max's supply curve is also his *minimum supply-price* curve. It tells us that if Max can sell only one pizza a day, the minimum that he must be paid for it is a little more than $5. If he can sell 50 pizzas a day, the minimum that he must be paid for the 50th pizza is $10, and so on.

Figure 5.5 also shows Max's producer surplus. If the price of a pizza is $15, Max plans to sell 100 pizzas a day. The minimum that he must be paid for the 100th pizza is $15. So its opportunity cost is exactly the price he receives for it. But the opportunity cost of the first pizza is just a bit more than $5. So this first pizza costs $10 less to produce than Max receives for it. He receives a *producer surplus* from his first pizza of almost $10. He receives a slightly smaller producer surplus on the second pizza, less on the third, and so on until he receives no producer surplus on the 100th pizza.

Figure 5.5 shows Max's producer surplus as the blue triangle—the area above the supply curve and below the market price line. This area is equal to the base of the triangle (100 pizzas a week) multiplied by the height ($10 a pizza) divided by 2, which equals $500 a day. Figure 5.5 also shows Max's opportunity costs as the red area below the supply curve.

FIGURE 5.5   A Producer's Supply and Producer Surplus

Max's supply curve of pizza tells us that at a price of $5, Max plans to sell no pizza. At a price of $10, he plans to sell 50 pizzas a day; and at a price of $15, he plans to sell 100 pizzas a day. Max's supply curve also tells us that the minimum he must be offered is $10 for the 50th pizza a day and $15 for the 100th pizza a day. If the market price is $15 a pizza, he sells 100 pizzas a day and receives $1,500. The red area shows Max's cost of producing pizza, which is $1,000 a day, and the blue area shows his producer surplus, which is $500 a day.

REVIEW QUIZ

1 What is the relationship between the marginal cost or opportunity cost of producing a good or service and the minimum supply-price—the minimum price that producers must be offered?
2 What is the relationship between marginal cost and the supply curve?
3 What is producer surplus? How do we measure it?

Consumer surplus and producer surplus can be used to measure the efficiency of a market. Let's see how we can use these concepts to study the efficiency of a competitive market.

Is the Competitive Market Efficient?

FIGURE 5.6 SHOWS THE MARKET FOR PIZZA. The demand curve D shows the demand for pizza. The supply curve S shows the supply of pizza. The equilibrium price is $15 a pizza, and the equilibrium quantity is 10,000 pizzas a day.

The market forces that you studied in Chapter 3 (pp. 70–71) will pull the pizza market to this equilibrium. If the price is greater than $15 a pizza, a surplus will force the price down. If the price is less than $15 a pizza, a shortage will force the price up. Only if the price is $15 a pizza is there neither a surplus nor a shortage and no forces operate to change the price.

So the market price and quantity are pulled towards their equilibrium values. But is this competitive equilibrium efficient? Does a competitive pizza market produce the efficient quantity of pizza?

Efficiency of Competitive Equilibrium

The equilibrium in Fig. 5.6 is efficient. Resources are being used to produce the quantity of pizza that people value most highly. It is not possible to produce more pizza without giving up some other good or service that is valued more highly. And if a smaller quantity of pizza is produced, resources are used to produce some other good that is not valued as highly as the pizza forgone.

To see why the equilibrium in Fig. 5.6 is efficient, think about the interpretation of the demand curve as the marginal benefit curve and the supply curve as the marginal cost curve. The demand curve tells us the marginal benefit from pizza. The supply curve tells us the marginal cost of pizza. So where the demand curve and the supply curve intersect, marginal benefit equals marginal cost.

But this condition—marginal benefit equals marginal cost—is the condition that delivers an efficient use of resources. A competitive market puts resources to work in the activities that create the greatest possible value. So a competitive equilibrium is efficient.

If production is less than 10,000 pizzas a day, the marginal pizza is valued more highly than its opportunity cost. If production exceeds 10,000 pizzas a day, the marginal pizza costs more to produce than the value that consumers place on it.

FIGURE 5.6 An Efficient Market for Pizza

Resources are used efficiently when the sum of consumer surplus and producer surplus is maximized. Consumer surplus is the area below the demand curve and above the market price—the green triangle. Producer surplus is the area below the market price and above the supply curve—the blue triangle. Here, consumer surplus is $50,000, producer surplus is $50,000, and the sum is $100,000. This sum of consumer surplus and producer surplus is maximized when the willingness to pay equals the opportunity cost. The efficient quantity of pizza is 10,000 pizzas per day.

Only when 10,000 pizzas a day are produced is the marginal pizza worth exactly what it costs. The competitive market pushes the quantity of pizza produced to its efficient level of 10,000 a day. If production is less than 10,000 a day, a shortage raises the price, which increases production. If production exceeds 10,000 a day, a surplus lowers the price, which decreases production.

In a competitive equilibrium, resources are used efficiently to produce the goods and services that people value most highly. And when the competitive market uses resources efficiently, the sum of consumer surplus and producer surplus is maximized.

Buyers and sellers each attempt to do the best they can for themselves, and no one plans for an efficient outcome for society as a whole. Buyers seek the lowest possible price, and sellers seek the highest possible price. And the market comes to an equilibrium in which resources are allocated efficiently.

The Invisible Hand

Writing in his *Wealth of Nations* in 1776, Adam Smith was the first to suggest that competitive markets send resources to the uses in which they have the highest value (see pp. 54–55). Smith believed that each participant in a competitive market is "led by an invisible hand to promote an end [the efficient use of resources] which was no part of his intention."

You can see the invisible hand at work in the cartoon. The cold drinks vendor has both cold drinks and shade. He has an opportunity cost of each and a minimum supply-price of each. The park-bench reader has a marginal benefit from a cold drink and from shade. You can see that the marginal benefit from shade exceeds the marginal cost, but the marginal cost of a cold drink exceeds its marginal benefit. The transaction that occurs creates producer surplus and consumer surplus. The vendor obtains a producer surplus from selling the shade for more than its opportunity cost, and the reader obtains a consumer surplus from buying the shade for less than its marginal benefit. In the third frame of the cartoon, both the consumer and the producer are better off than they were in the first frame. The umbrella has moved to its highest-valued use.

The Invisible Hand at Work Today

The market economy relentlessly performs the activity illustrated in the cartoon and in Fig. 5.6 to achieve an efficient allocation of resources. And rarely has the market been working as hard as it is today. Think about a few of the changes taking place in our economy that the market is guiding towards an efficient use of resources.

New technologies have cut the cost of producing computers. As these advances have occurred, supply has increased and the price has fallen. Lower prices have encouraged an increase in the quantity demanded of this now less costly tool. The marginal benefit from computers is brought to equality with their marginal cost.

A Florida frost cuts the supply of oranges. With fewer oranges available, the marginal benefit from oranges increases. A shortage of oranges raises their price, so the market allocates the smaller quantity available to the people who value them most highly.

Market forces persistently bring marginal cost and marginal benefit to equality and maximize the sum of consumer surplus and producer surplus.

Obstacles to Efficiency

Although markets generally do a good job of sending resources to where they are most highly valued, markets do not always get the correct answer. Sometimes they overproduce a good or service, and sometimes they underproduce. The most significant obstacles to achieving an efficient allocation of resources in the market economy are

- Price ceilings and price floors
- Taxes, subsidies, and quotas
- Monopoly
- Public goods
- External costs and external benefits

Price Ceilings and Price Floors A *price ceiling* is a regulation that makes it illegal to charge a price higher than a specified level. An example is a price ceiling on apartment rents, which some cities impose. A *price floor* is a regulation that makes it illegal to pay a lower price than a specified level. An example is the minimum wage. (We study both of these restrictions on buyers and sellers in Chapter 6.)

The presence of a price ceiling or a price floor blocks the forces of demand and supply and might result in a quantity produced that differs from the quantity determined in an unregulated market.

Taxes, Subsidies, and Quotas *Taxes* increase the prices paid by buyers and lower the prices received by sellers. Taxes decrease the quantity produced (for reasons that are explained in Chapter 6, on pp. 131–134). All kinds of goods and services are taxed, but the highest taxes are on gasoline, alcohol, and tobacco.

Subsidies, which are payments by the government to producers, decrease the prices paid by buyers and increase the prices received by sellers. Subsidies increase the quantity produced.

Quotas, which are limits to the quantity that a firm is permitted to produce, restrict output below the quantity that a competitive market produces. Farms are sometimes subject to quotas.

Monopoly A *monopoly* is a firm that has sole control of a market. For example, Microsoft has a near monopoly on operating systems for personal computers. Although a monopoly can earn a large profit, it prevents the market from achieving an efficient use of resources. The goal of a monopoly is to maximize profit. To achieve this goal, it restricts production and raises price. (We study monopoly in Chapter 12.)

Public Goods A *public good* is a good or service that is consumed simultaneously by everyone, even if they don't pay for it. Examples are national security and the enforcement of law and order. Competitive markets would produce too small a quantity of public goods because of a *free-rider problem*. It is not in each person's interest to buy her or his share of a public good. So a competitive market produces less than the efficient quantity. (We study public goods and the free-rider problem in Chapter 16.)

External Costs and External Benefits An *external cost* is a cost that is borne not by the producer but by other people. The cost of pollution is an example of an external cost. When an electric power utility burns coal to generate electricity, it puts sulfur dioxide into the atmosphere. This pollutant falls as acid rain and damages vegetation and crops. The utility does not consider the cost of pollution when it decides the quantity of electric power to supply. Its supply curve is based on its own costs, not on the costs that it inflicts on others. As a result, the utility produces more power than the efficient quantity.

An *external benefit* is a benefit that accrues to people other than the buyer of a good. An example is when someone in a neighbourhood paints her home or landscapes her yard. The homeowner does not consider her neighbour's marginal benefit when she decides whether to do this type of work. So the demand curve for house painting and yard improvement does not include all the benefits that accrue. In this case, the quantity falls short of the efficient quantity. (We study externalities in Chapter 18.)

The impediments to efficiency that we've just reviewed and that you will study in greater detail in later chapters result in two possible outcomes:

- Underproduction
- Overproduction

Underproduction

Suppose that one firm owns all the pizza outlets in a city and that it produces only 5,000 pizzas a day. Figure 5.7(a) shows that at this quantity, consumers are willing to pay $20 for the marginal pizza—marginal benefit is $20. The marginal cost of a pizza is only $10. So there is a gap between what people are willing to pay and what producers must be offered—a gap between marginal benefit and marginal cost.

The sum of consumer surplus and producer surplus is decreased by the amount of the grey triangle in Fig. 5.7(a). This triangle is called deadweight loss. **Deadweight loss** is the decrease in consumer surplus and producer surplus that results from an inefficient level of production.

The 5,000th pizza brings a benefit of $20 and costs only $10 to produce. If we don't produce this pizza, we are wasting $10. Similar reasoning applies all the way up to the 9,999th pizza. By producing more pizza and less of other goods and services, we get more value from our resources.

The deadweight loss is borne by the entire society. It is not a loss for the consumers and a gain for the producer. It is a *social* loss.

FIGURE 5.7 Underproduction and Overproduction

(a) Underproduction

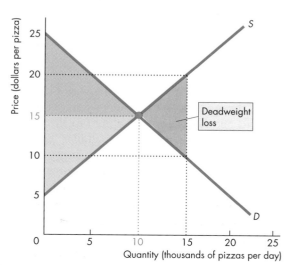

(b) Overproduction

If pizza production is cut to only 5,000 a day, a deadweight loss (the grey triangle) arises (part a). Consumer surplus and producer surplus (the green and blue areas) are reduced. At 5,000 pizzas, the benefit of one more pizza exceeds its cost. The same is true for all levels of production up to 10,000 pizzas a day. If production increases to 15,000, a deadweight loss arises (part b). At 15,000 pizzas a day, the cost of the 15,000th pizza exceeds its benefit. The cost of each pizza above 10,000 exceeds its benefit. Consumer surplus plus producer surplus equals the sum of the green and blue areas minus the grey deadweight loss triangle.

Overproduction

Suppose the pizza lobby gets the government to pay the pizza producers a fat subsidy and that production increases to 15,000 a day. Figure 5.7(b) shows that at this quantity, consumers are willing to pay only $10 for that marginal pizza but the opportunity cost of that pizza is $20. It now costs more to produce the marginal pizza than consumers are willing to pay for it. The gap gets smaller as production approaches 10,000 pizzas a day, but it is present at all quantities greater than 10,000 a day.

Again, deadweight loss is shown by the grey triangle. The sum of consumer surplus and producer surplus is smaller than its maximum by the amount of deadweight loss. The 15,000th pizza brings a benefit of only $10 but costs $20 to produce. If we produce this pizza, we are wasting $10. Similar reasoning applies all the way down to the 10,001st pizza. By producing fewer pizzas and more of other goods and services, we get more value from our resources.

REVIEW QUIZ

1 What is a competitive market? Do competitive markets use resources efficiently? Explain why or why not.

2 Do markets with a price ceiling or price floor, taxes, subsidies, or quotas, monopoly, public goods, or externalities result in the quantity produced being the efficient quantity?

3 What is deadweight loss and under what conditions does it occur?

4 Does a deadweight loss occur in a competitive market when the quantity produced equals the competitive equilibrium quantity and the resource allocation is efficient?

You now know the conditions under which the resource allocation is efficient. You've seen how a competitive market can be efficient, and you've seen some impediments to efficiency.

But is an efficient allocation of resources fair? Does the competitive market provide people with fair incomes for their work? And do people always pay a fair price for the things they buy? Don't we need the government to step into some competitive markets to prevent the price from rising too high or falling too low? Let's now study these questions.

Is the Competitive Market Fair?

WHEN A NATURAL DISASTER STRIKES, SUCH AS A severe winter storm or a hurricane, the prices of many essential items jump. The reason the prices jump is that some people have a greater demand and greater willingness to pay when the items are in limited supply. So the higher prices achieve an efficient allocation of scarce resources. News reports of these price hikes almost never talk about efficiency. Instead, they talk about equity or fairness. The claim often made is that it is unfair for profit-seeking dealers to cheat the victims of natural disaster.

Similarly, when low-skilled people work for a wage that is below what most would regard as a "living wage," the media and politicians talk of employers taking unfair advantage of their workers.

How do we decide whether something is fair or unfair? You know when *you* think something is unfair. But how do you know? What are the *principles* of fairness?

Philosophers have tried for centuries to answer this question. Economists have offered their answers too. But before we look at the proposed answers, you should know that there is no universally agreed-upon answer.

Economists agree about efficiency. That is, they agree that it makes sense to make the economic pie as large as possible and to bake it at the lowest possible cost. But they do not agree about equity. That is, they do not agree about what are fair shares of the economic pie for all the people who make it. The reason is that ideas about fairness are not exclusively economic ideas. They touch on politics, ethics, and religion. Nevertheless, economists have thought about these issues and have a contribution to make. So let's examine the views of economists on this topic.

To think about fairness, think of economic life as a game—a serious game. All ideas about fairness can be divided into two broad groups. They are

- It's not fair if the *result* isn't fair.
- It's not fair if the *rules* aren't fair.

It's Not Fair If the *Result* Isn't Fair

The earliest efforts to establish a principle of fairness were based on the view that the result is what matters. And the general idea was that it is unfair if people's incomes are too unequal. It is unfair that

bank presidents earn millions of dollars a year while bank tellers earn only thousands of dollars a year. It is unfair that a store owner enjoys a larger profit and her customers pay higher prices in the aftermath of a winter storm.

There was a lot of excitement during the nineteenth century when economists thought they had made the incredible discovery that efficiency requires equality of incomes. To make the economic pie as large as possible, it must be cut into equal pieces, one for each person. This idea turns out to be wrong, but there is a lesson in the reason that it is wrong. So this nineteenth century idea is worth a closer look.

Utilitarianism The nineteenth century idea that only equality brings efficiency is called *utilitarianism*. **Utilitarianism** is a principle that states that we should strive to achieve "the greatest happiness for the greatest number." The people who developed this idea were known as utilitarians. They included the most eminent thinkers, such as Jeremy Bentham and John Stuart Mill.

Utilitarians argued that to achieve "the greatest happiness for the greatest number," income must be transferred from the rich to the poor up to the point of complete equality—to the point at which there are no rich and no poor.

They reasoned in the following way: First, everyone has the same basic wants and a similar capacity to enjoy life. Second, the greater a person's income, the smaller is the marginal benefit of a dollar. The millionth dollar spent by a rich person brings a smaller marginal benefit to that person than the marginal benefit of the thousandth dollar spent by a poorer person. So by transferring a dollar from the millionaire to the poorer person, more is gained than is lost and the two people added together are better off.

Figure 5.8 illustrates this utilitarian idea. Tom and Jerry have the same marginal benefit curve, *MB*. (Marginal benefit is measured on the same scale of 1 to 3 for both Tom and Jerry.) Tom is at point *A*. He earns $5,000 a year, and his marginal benefit of a dollar of income is 3. Jerry is at point *B*. He earns $45,000 a year, and his marginal benefit of a dollar of income is 1. If a dollar is transferred from Jerry to Tom, Jerry loses 1 unit of marginal benefit and Tom gains 3 units. So together, Tom and Jerry are better off. They are sharing the economic pie more efficiently. If a second dollar is transferred, the same thing happens: Tom gains more than Jerry loses. And the same is true for every dollar transferred until they both reach point *C*. At point *C*, Tom and Jerry have

FIGURE 5.8   Utilitarian Fairness

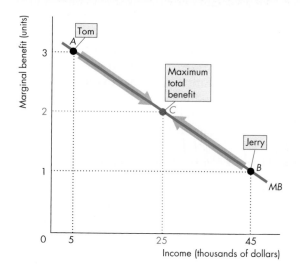

Tom earns $5,000 and has 3 units of marginal benefit at point A. Jerry earns $45,000 and has 1 unit of marginal benefit at point B. If income is transferred from Jerry to Tom, Jerry's loss is less than Tom's gain. Only when each of them has $25,000 and 2 units of marginal benefit (at point C) can the sum of their total benefit increase no further.

$25,000 each, and each has a marginal benefit of 2 units. Now they are sharing the economic pie in the most efficient way. It is bringing the greatest attainable happiness to Tom and Jerry.

The Big Tradeoff One big problem with the utilitarian ideal of complete equality is that it ignores the costs of making income transfers. Recognizing the cost of making income transfers leads to what is called the **big tradeoff,** which is a tradeoff between efficiency and fairness.

The big tradeoff is based on the following facts. Income can be transferred from people with high incomes to people with low incomes only by taxing incomes. Taxing people's income from employment makes them work less. It results in the quantity of labour being less than the efficient quantity. Taxing people's income from capital makes them save less. It results in the quantity of capital being less than the efficient quantity. With smaller quantities of both labour and capital, the quantity of goods and services produced is less than the efficient quantity. The economic pie shrinks.

The tradeoff is between the size of the economic pie and the degree of equality with which it is shared. The greater the amount of income redistribution through income taxes, the greater is the inefficiency— the smaller is the economic pie.

A second source of inefficiency arises because a dollar taken from a rich person does not end up as a dollar in the hands of a poorer person. Some of it is spent on administration of the tax and transfer system. The cost of tax-collecting agencies, such as Canada Customs and Revenue Agency, and welfare-administering agencies, such as Health Canada, must be paid with some of the taxes collected. Also, taxpayers hire accountants, auditors, and lawyers to help them ensure that they pay the correct amount of taxes. These activities use skilled labour and capital resources that could otherwise be used to produce goods and services that people value.

You can see that when all these costs are taken into account, transferring a dollar from a rich person does not give a dollar to a poor person. It is even possible that with high taxes, those with low incomes end up being worse off. Suppose, for example, that highly taxed entrepreneurs decide to work less hard and shut down some of their businesses. Low-income workers get fired and must seek other, perhaps even lower-paid work.

Because of the big tradeoff, those who say that fairness is equality propose a modified version of utilitarianism.

Make the Poorest as Well Off as Possible A Harvard philosopher, John Rawls, proposed a modified version of utilitarianism in a classic book entitled *A Theory of Justice,* published in 1971. Rawls says that, taking all the costs of income transfers into account, the fair distribution of the economic pie is the one that makes the poorest person as well off as possible. The incomes of rich people should be taxed, and after paying the costs of administering the tax and transfer system, what is left should be transferred to the poor. But the taxes must not be so high that they make the economic pie shrink to the point at which the poorest person ends up with a smaller piece. A bigger share of a smaller pie can be less than a smaller share of a bigger pie. The goal is to make the piece enjoyed by the poorest person as big as possible. Most likely, this piece will not be an equal share.

The "fair results" ideas require a change in the results after the game is over. Some economists say that these changes are themselves unfair and propose a different way of thinking about fairness.

It's Not Fair If the *Rules* Aren't Fair

The idea that it's not fair if the rules aren't fair is based on a fundamental principle that seems to be hardwired into the human brain: the symmetry principle. The **symmetry principle** is the requirement that people in similar situations be treated similarly. It is the moral principle that lies at the centre of all the big religions and that says, in some form or other, "behave towards other people in the way you expect them to behave towards you."

In economic life, this principle translates into *equality of opportunity*. But equality of opportunity to do what? This question is answered by the late Harvard philosopher, Robert Nozick, in a book entitled *Anarchy, State, and Utopia*, published in 1974.

Nozick argues that the idea of fairness as an outcome or result cannot work and that fairness must be based on the fairness of the rules. He suggests that fairness obeys two rules:

1. The state must enforce laws that establish and protect private property.
2. Private property may be transferred from one person to another only by voluntary exchange.

The first rule says that everything that is valuable must be owned by individuals and that the state must ensure that theft is prevented. The second rule says that the only legitimate way a person can acquire property is to buy it in exchange for something else that the person owns. If these rules, which are the only fair rules, are followed, then the result is fair. It doesn't matter how unequally the economic pie is shared, provided that it is baked by people each one of whom voluntarily provides services in exchange for the share of the pie offered in compensation.

These rules satisfy the symmetry principle. If these rules are not followed, the symmetry principle is broken. You can see these facts by imagining a world in which the laws are not followed.

First, suppose that some resources or goods are not owned. They are common property. Then everyone is free to participate in a grab to use these resources or goods. The strongest will prevail. But when the strongest prevails, the strongest effectively *owns* the resources or goods in question and prevents others from enjoying them.

Second, suppose that we do not insist on voluntary exchange for transferring ownership of resources from one person to another. The alternative is *involuntary* transfer. In simple language, the alternative is theft.

Both of these situations violate the symmetry principle. Only the strong get to acquire what they want. The weak end up with only the resources and goods that the strong don't want.

In contrast, if the two rules of fairness are followed, everyone, strong and weak, is treated in a similar way. Everyone is free to use their resources and human skills to create things that are valued by themselves and others and to exchange the fruits of their efforts with each other. This is the only set of arrangements that obeys the symmetry principle.

Fairness and Efficiency If private property rights are enforced and if voluntary exchange takes place in a competitive market, resources will be allocated efficiently if there are no

1. Price ceilings and price floors
2. Taxes, subsidies, and quotas
3. Monopolies
4. Public goods
5. External costs and external benefits

And according to the Nozick rules, the resulting distribution of income and wealth will be fair. Let's study a concrete example to examine the claim that if resources are allocated efficiently, they are also allocated fairly.

A Price Hike in a Natural Disaster An earthquake has broken the pipes that deliver drinking water to a city. The price of bottled water jumps from $1 a bottle to $8 a bottle in the 30 or so shops that have water for sale.

First, let's agree that the water is being used *efficiently*. There is a fixed amount of bottled water in the city, and given the quantity available, some people are willing to pay $8 to get a bottle. The water goes to the people who value it most highly. Consumer surplus and producer surplus are maximized.

So the water resources are being used efficiently. But are they being used fairly? Shouldn't people who can't afford to pay $8 a bottle get some of the available water for a lower price that they can afford? Isn't the fair solution for the shops to sell water for a lower price that people can afford? Or perhaps it might be fairer if the government bought the water and then made it available through a government store at a "reasonable" price? Let's think about these alternative solutions to the water problem of this city. Should water somehow be made available at a more reasonable price?

Shop Offers Water for $5 Suppose that Kris, a shop owner, offers water at $5 a bottle. Who will buy it? There are two types of buyers. Chuck is an example of one type. He values water at $8—is willing to pay $8 a bottle. Recall that given the quantity of water available, the equilibrium price is $8 a bottle. If Chuck buys the water, he consumes it. Chuck ends up with a consumer surplus of $3 on the bottle, and Kris receives $3 less of producer surplus.

Mitch is an example of the second type of buyer. Mitch would not pay $8 for a bottle. In fact, he wouldn't even pay $5 to consume a bottle of water. But he buys a bottle for $5. Why? Because he plans to sell the water to someone who is willing to pay $8 to consume it. When Mitch buys the water, Kris again receives a producer surplus of $3 *less* than she would receive if she charged the going market price. Mitch now becomes a water dealer. He sells the water for $8 and earns a producer surplus of $3.

So by being public-spirited and offering water for less than the market price, Kris ends up $3 a bottle worse off and the buyers end up $3 a bottle better off. The same people consume the water in both situations. They are the people who value the water at $8 a bottle. But the distribution of consumer surplus and producer surplus is different in the two cases. When Kris offers the water for $5 a bottle, she ends up with a smaller producer surplus and Chuck and Mitch with a larger consumer surplus and producer surplus.

So which is the fair arrangement? The one that favours Kris or the one that favours Chuck and Mitch? The fair-rules view is that both arrangements are fair. Kris voluntarily sells the water for $5, so in effect, she is helping the community to cope with its water problem. It is fair that she should help, but the choice is hers. She owns the water. It is not fair that she should be compelled to help.

Government Buys Water Now suppose instead that the government buys all the water. The going price is $8 a bottle, so that's what the government pays. Now the government offers the water for sale for $1 a bottle, its "normal" price.

The quantity of water supplied is exactly the same as before. But now, at $1 a bottle, the quantity demanded is much larger than the quantity supplied. There is a shortage of water.

Because there is a large water shortage, the government decides to ration the amount that anyone may buy. Everyone is allocated one bottle. So everyone lines up to collect his or her bottle. Two of these people are Chuck and Mitch. Chuck, you'll recall, is willing to pay $8 a bottle. Mitch is willing to pay less than $5. But they both get a bargain. Chuck drinks his $1 bottle and enjoys a $7 consumer surplus. What does Mitch do? Does he drink his bottle? He does not. He sells it to another person who values the water at $8. And he enjoys a $7 producer surplus from his temporary water-trading business.

So the people who value the water most highly consume it. But the consumer and producer surpluses are distributed in a different way from what the free market would have delivered. Again the question arises, which arrangement is fair?

The main difference between the government scheme and Kris's private charitable contributions lies in the fact that to buy the water for $8 and sell it for $1, the government must tax someone $7 for each bottle sold. So whether this arrangement is fair depends on whether the taxes are fair.

Taxes are an involuntary transfer of private property, so according to the fair-rules view, they are unfair. But most economists, and most people, think that there is such a thing as a fair tax. So it seems that the fair-rules view needs to be weakened a bit. Agreeing that there is such a thing as a fair tax is the easy part. Deciding what is a fair tax brings endless disagreement and debate.

REVIEW QUIZ

1 What are the two big approaches to thinking about fairness?
2 What is the utilitarian idea of fairness and what is wrong with it?
3 Explain the big tradeoff. What idea of fairness has been developed to deal with it?
4 What is the main idea of fairness based on fair rules?

◆ You've now studied the two biggest issues that run right through the whole of economics: efficiency and equity, or fairness. In the next chapter, we study some sources of inefficiency and unfairness. And at many points throughout this book—and in your life—you will return to and use the ideas about efficiency and fairness that you've learned in this chapter. *Reading Between the Lines* on pp. 118–119 looks at an example of an inefficiency and, some would argue, an unfairness in our economy today.

READING BETWEEN THE LINES

POLICY WATCH

Efficiency and Equity in the Market for Drugs

MONTREAL GAZETTE, FEBRUARY 20, 2001

Drug firms take on South Africa

A critical battle is about to begin in the Pretoria High Court, where 42 pharmaceutical companies, including the British giant GlaxoSmithKline, are attempting to block the South African government from importing the cheap medicines to treat people suffering from such diseases as diarrhea, meningitis, AIDS and tuberculosis. ...

The rest of Africa will be closely watching. So will developing countries on other continents.

With the death toll from infectious diseases inexorably rising, especially in Africa, a tide of outrage is swelling among local activists and international-aid organizations, which see medicines denied to the sick in the name of commerce.

There are more than 32 million men, women and children infected by HIV in developing countries. AZT and 3TC, the basic anti-retroviral drugs in

the West, would keep them alive and well, but the price tag is R79,000 (about $15,000 Canadian) to R120,000 (about $23,300 Canadian) per patient per year.

The majority of employed people in South Africa, with families to support, earn less than R20000 ($4,000 Canadian) a year, and by comparison with most of the rest of the continent they are rich.

But there are now alternatives— cheap copies of life-saving medicines called generics, made mainly in Brazil, India and Thailand.

Thailand believes it could reduce the cost to R 1,400 (about $275 Canadian) per patient per year.

It is a price the South African government might be able to pay for the life of its people, but the drug companies, fearing potential worldwide consequences if their prices are undercut, have said no.

Originally appeared as "At the Mercy of the Drug Giants" by Sarah Bosley, February 12, 2001 in *The Guardian*.

Essence of the Story

■ Pharmaceutical companies are attempting to block the South African government from importing the cheap medicines to treat diarrhea, meningitis, AIDS, and tuberculosis.

■ More than 32 million people are infected by HIV in developing countries.

■ The drugs that treat AIDS (such as AZT and 3TC) cost from $15,000 to $23,000 per patient per year.

■ The majority of employed people in South Africa earn less than $4,000 a year, and by comparison with the rest of Africa, they are rich.

■ Cheap generic copies of AIDS medicines made in Brazil, India, and Thailand cost $275 per patient per year.

118

Economic Analysis

■ The efficient quantity of AZT is that at which its marginal benefit equals its marginal cost.

■ We can measure the marginal benefit of AZT by the amount that people are willing to pay for it.

■ The marginal benefit to people who buy AZT at its retail price in North America is between $15,000 and $23,000 a year.

■ The marginal benefit to the government of South Africa is $275 per person per year.

■ We do not know the marginal cost of producing AZT. But we know that producers in Brazil, India, and Thailand are willing to sell AZT for $275 per person per year. So we can be sure that the marginal cost of a year of AZT treatment is not greater than $275 and most likely it is less than this amount.

■ Because most AZT sells for a price that exceeds $275, the quantity of AZT produced is less than the efficient quantity.

■ Figure 1 illustrates the market for AZT. The demand curve is *D*, and the marginal cost curve is *MC*. (It is an assumption that *MC* is constant at $275 per person per year.)

■ The price of a year's treatment per person is $23,000. At this price, the producer earns a large producer surplus shown by the blue rectangle.

■ Some consumers would be willing to pay even more than $23,000 for a year's treatment, so there is a consumer surplus shown by the green triangle.

■ Because price (marginal benefit) exceeds marginal cost, there is a deadweight loss shown by the grey triangle.

■ Figure 2 illustrates the market for AZT if cheap generic versions are available at $275 per person per year.

■ The quantity consumed increases, producer surplus and deadweight loss disappear, and consumer surplus expands.

■ The market for an existing drug is different from that for a new drug that is still being developed. The development cost of an existing drug is a sunk cost.

■ The cost of developing a new drug is part of the opportunity cost that the producer must take into account when deciding whether to continue the development process.

■ If a drug developer cannot recover the opportunity cost of development, new drugs might not be developed.

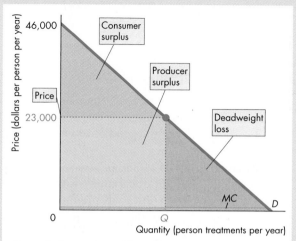

Figure 1 The market without cheap copies

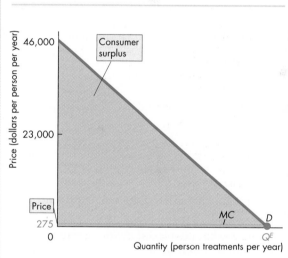

Figure 2 The market with cheap copies

You're The Voter

■ Do you support the production of cheap generic drugs to treat AIDS and other diseases that afflict people in poor developing countries? Explain why or why not.

119

SUMMARY

KEY POINTS

Efficiency: A Refresher (pp. 104–105)

- The marginal benefit received from a good or service—the benefit of consuming one additional unit—is the *value* of the good or service to its consumers.
- The marginal cost of a good or service—the cost of producing one additional unit—is the *opportunity cost* of one more unit to its producers.
- Resource allocation is efficient when marginal benefit equals marginal cost.
- If marginal benefit exceeds marginal cost, an increase in production uses resources more efficiently.
- If marginal cost exceeds marginal benefit, a decrease in production uses resources more efficiently.

Value, Price, and Consumer Surplus (pp. 106–107)

- Marginal benefit is measured by the maximum price that consumers are willing to pay for a good or service.
- Marginal benefit determines demand, and a demand curve is a marginal benefit curve.
- Value is what people are *willing to* pay; price is what people *must* pay.
- Consumer surplus equals value minus price, summed over the quantity consumed.

Cost, Price, and Producer Surplus (pp. 108–109)

- Marginal cost is measured by the minimum price producers must be offered to increase production by one unit.
- Marginal cost determines supply, and a supply curve is a marginal cost curve.
- Opportunity cost is what producers pay; price is what producers receive.
- Producer surplus equals price minus opportunity cost, summed over the quantity produced.

Is the Competitive Market Efficient? (pp. 110–113)

- In a competitive equilibrium, marginal benefit equals marginal cost and resource allocation is efficient.
- Monopoly restricts production and creates deadweight loss.
- A competitive market provides too small a quantity of public goods because of the free-rider problem.
- A competitive market provides too large a quantity of goods and services that have external costs and too small a quantity of goods and services that have external benefits.

Is the Competitive Market Fair? (pp. 114–117)

- Ideas about fairness can be divided into two groups: fair *results* and fair *rules*.
- Fair-results ideas require income transfers from the rich to the poor.
- Fair-rules ideas require property rights and voluntary exchange.

KEY FIGURES

Figure 5.1   The Efficient Quantity of Pizza, 104
Figure 5.3   A Consumer's Demand and Consumer Surplus, 107
Figure 5.5   A Producer's Supply and Producer Surplus, 109
Figure 5.6   An Efficient Market for Pizza, 110
Figure 5.7   Underproduction and Overproduction, 113

KEY TERMS

Big tradeoff, 115
Consumer surplus, 107
Deadweight loss, 112
Efficient allocation, 104
Marginal benefit, 104
Marginal cost, 104
Producer surplus, 109
Symmetry principle, 116
Utilitarianism, 114
Value, 106

PROBLEMS

*1. The figure illustrates the market for floppy discs.

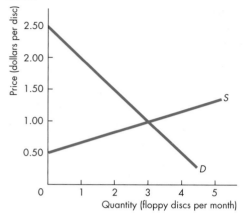

a. What are the equilibrium price and equilibrium quantity of floppy discs?
b. Calculate the amount consumers paid for floppy discs.
c. Calculate the consumer surplus.
d. Calculate the producer surplus.
e. Calculate the cost of producing the floppy discs sold.
f. What is the efficient quantity?

2. The figure illustrates the market for CDs.

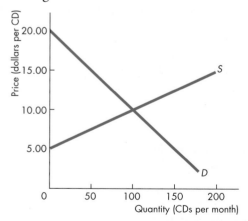

a. What are the equilibrium price and equilibrium quantity of CDs?
b. Calculate the amount consumers paid for CDs.
c. Calculate the consumer surplus.
d. Calculate the producer surplus.
e. Calculate the cost of producing the CDs sold.
f. What is the efficient quantity of CDs?

*3. The table gives the demand and supply schedules for sandwiches.

Price (dollars per sandwich)	Quantity demanded (sandwiches per hour)	Quantity supplied
0	400	0
1	350	50
2	300	100
3	250	150
4	200	200
5	150	250
6	100	300
7	50	350
8	0	400

a. What is the maximum price that consumers are willing to pay for the 250th sandwich?
b. What is the minimum price that producers are willing to accept for the 250th sandwich?
c. Are 250 sandwiches a day less than or greater than the efficient quantity?
d. If the sandwich market is efficient, what is the consumer surplus? (Draw the graph.)
e. If the sandwich market is efficient, what is the producer surplus? (Draw the graph.)
f. If sandwich makers produce 250 a day, what is the deadweight loss? (Draw the graph.)

4. The table gives the demand and supply schedules for sunscreen.

Price (dollars per bottle)	Quantity demanded (bottles per day)	Quantity supplied
0	900	0
1	800	100
2	700	200
3	600	300
4	500	400
5	400	500
6	300	600
7	200	700
8	100	800
9	0	900

a. What is the maximum price that consumers are willing to pay for the 300th bottle?
b. What is the minimum price that producers are willing to accept for the 300th bottle?
c. Are 300 bottles a day less than or greater than the efficient quantity? (Draw the graph.)
d. If the market for sunscreen is efficient, what is the consumer surplus? (Draw the graph.)

e. If the market for sunscreen is efficient, what is the producer surplus? (Draw the graph.)

f. If sunscreen bottlers produce 300 bottles a day, what is the deadweight loss?

*5. The table gives the demand schedules for train travel for Ben, Beth, and Bo.

Price	Quantity demanded (passenger kilometres)		
(cents per passenger kilometre)	Ben	Beth	Bo
10	500	300	60
20	450	250	50
30	400	200	40
40	350	150	30
50	300	100	20
60	250	50	10
70	200	0	0

a. If the price of train travel is 40 cents a passenger kilometre, what is the consumer surplus of each traveller?

b. Which traveller has the largest consumer surplus? Explain why.

c. If the price rises to 50 cents a passenger kilometre, what is the change in consumer surplus of each traveller?

6. The table gives the demand schedules for air travel for Ann, Arthur, and Abby.

Price	Quantity demanded (passenger kilometres)		
(dollars per passenger kilometre)	Ann	Arthur	Abby
10.00	500	600	300
12.50	450	500	250
15.00	400	400	200
17.50	350	300	150
20.00	300	200	100
22.50	250	100	50
25.00	200	0	0

a. If the price is $20 a passenger kilometre, what is the consumer surplus of each traveller?

b. Which consumer has the largest consumer surplus? Explain why.

c. If the price falls to $15 a passenger kilometre, what is the change in consumer surplus of each traveller?

CRITICAL THINKING

1. Study *Reading Between the Lines* on pp. 118–119 about AZT and then answer the following questions:

a. Is the quantity of AZT produced greater than, less than, or equal to the efficient quantity? Explain your answer by using the concepts of marginal benefit, marginal cost, price, consumer surplus, and producer surplus.

b. If GlaxoSmithKline agreed to sell some AZT for $275 to the government of South Africa, would this deal increase or decrease consumer surplus? Would it increase or decrease GlaxoSmithKline's producer surplus? Would it bring the quantity of AZT closer to the efficient quantity? Explain your answer by using the concepts of marginal benefit, marginal cost, price, consumer surplus, and producer surplus.

c. Drug producers in Brazil, India, and Thailand make a generic AZT and sell it at a much lower price than GlaxoSmithKline's price. Do generic drugs increase or decrease consumer surplus? Does a generic AZT increase or decrease GlaxoSmithKline's producer surplus? Does it bring the quantity of AZT closer to the efficient quantity? Explain your answer by using the concepts of marginal benefit, marginal cost, price, consumer surplus, and producer surplus.

WEB EXERCISES

1. Use the links on the Parkin-Bade Web site and read the article by Augustine Faucher entitled "Cipro and the Free Riders." Then answer the following questions:

a. What does the author claim is the problem in the market for antibiotics that can treat anthrax?

b. What does the author claim is the solution to the problem in this market?

c. Explain why you agree or disagree with the author.

MARKETS IN ACTION

CHAPTER

Turbulent Times

Apartment rents are rising in Toronto, and people are screaming for help. Can the government limit rent increases to help renters live in affordable housing? ◆ Almost every day, a new machine is invented that saves labour and increases productivity. Take a look at the machines in McDonald's that have replaced some low-skilled workers. Can we protect low-skilled workers with minimum wage laws that enable people to earn a living wage? ◆ Almost everything we buy is taxed. And a new tax on air travel has been introduced to pay the cost of increased airport security. How much of the airport security tax gets paid by the traveller and how much by the airlines? We explore this question in *Reading Between the Lines* at the end of the chapter. Do taxes help or hinder the market in its attempt to move resources to where they are valued most highly? ◆ Trade in items such as drugs, automatic firearms, and enriched uranium is illegal. How do laws that make trading in a good or service illegal affect its price and the quantity bought and sold? ◆ In 1996, ideal conditions brought record yields and global grain production increased. But in 2001, yields were low and global grain production decreased. How do farm prices and revenues react to such output fluctuations?

◆ In this chapter, we use the theory of demand and supply (Chapter 3) and the concepts of elasticity (Chapter 4) and efficiency (Chapter 5) to answer questions like those that we've just posed.

After studying this chapter, you will able to

- Explain how housing markets work and how price ceilings create housing shortages and inefficiency

- Explain how labour markets work and how minimum wage laws create unemployment and inefficiency

- Explain the effects of the sales tax

- Explain how markets for illegal goods work

- Explain why farm prices and revenues fluctuate and how speculation and farm marketing boards influence farm prices and farm revenues

123

Housing Markets and Rent Ceilings

To SEE HOW A HOUSING MARKET WORKS, LET'S transport ourselves to San Francisco in April 1906, as the city is suffering from a massive earthquake and fire. You can sense the enormity of San Francisco's problems by reading a headline from the April 19, 1906, *New York Times* about the first days of the crisis:

> Over 500 Dead, $200,000,000 Lost in San Francisco Earthquake
>
> Nearly Half the City Is in Ruins and 50,000 Are Homeless

The commander of federal troops in charge of the emergency described the magnitude of the problem:

> Not a hotel of note or importance was left standing. The great apartment houses had vanished ... two hundred-and-twenty-five thousand people were ... homeless.[1]

Almost overnight, more than half the people in a city of 400,000 had lost their homes. Temporary shelters and camps alleviated some of the problem, but it was also necessary to utilize the apartment buildings and houses left standing. As a consequence, they had to accommodate 40 percent more people than they had before the earthquake.

The *San Francisco Chronicle* was not published for more than a month after the earthquake. When the newspaper reappeared on May 24, 1906, the city's housing shortage—what would seem to be a major news item that would still be of grave importance—was not mentioned. Milton Friedman and George Stigler describe the situation:

> *There is not a single mention of a housing shortage!* The classified advertisements listed sixty-four offers of flats and houses for rent, and nineteen of houses for sale, against five advertisements of flats or houses wanted. Then and thereafter a considerable number of all types of accommodation except hotel rooms were offered for rent.[2]

How did San Francisco cope with such a devastating reduction in the supply of housing?

---

[1] Reported in Milton Friedman and George J. Stigler, "Roofs or Ceilings? The Current Housing Problem," in *Popular Essays on Current Problems*, vol. 1, no. 2 (New York: Foundation for Economic Education, 1946), pp. 3–159.

[2] *Ibid.*, p. 3.

The Market Response to a Decrease in Supply

Figure 6.1 shows the market for housing in San Francisco. The demand curve for housing is *D*. There is a short-run supply curve, labelled *SS*, and a long-run supply curve, labelled *LS*.

The short-run supply curve shows the change in the quantity of housing supplied as the rent changes while the number of houses and apartment buildings remains constant. The short-run supply response arises from changes in the intensity with which existing buildings are used. The quantity of housing supplied increases if families rent out rooms that they previously used themselves, and it decreases if families use rooms that they previously rented out to others.

The long-run supply curve shows how the quantity of housing supplied responds to a change in price after enough time has elapsed for new apartment buildings and houses to be erected or for existing ones to be destroyed. In Fig. 6.1, the long-run supply curve is *perfectly elastic*. We do not actually know that the long-run supply curve is perfectly elastic, but it is a reasonable assumption. It implies that the cost of building an apartment is pretty much the same regardless of whether there are 50,000 or 150,000 apartments in existence.

The equilibrium price (rent) and quantity are determined at the point of intersection of the *short-run* supply curve and the demand curve. Before the earthquake, the equilibrium rent is $16 a month and the quantity is 100,000 units of housing.

Figure 6.1(a) shows the situation immediately after the earthquake. The destruction of buildings decreases the supply of housing and shifts the short-run supply curve *SS* leftward to *SS_A*. If the rent remains at $16 a month, only 44,000 units of housing are available. But with only 44,000 units of housing available, the maximum rent that someone is willing to pay for the last available apartment is $24 a month. So rents rise. In Fig. 6.1(a), the rent rises to $20 a month.

As the rent rises, the quantity of housing demanded decreases and the quantity supplied increases to 72,000 units. These changes occur because people economize on their use of space and make spare rooms, attics, and basements available to others. The higher rent allocates the scarce housing to the people who value it most highly and are willing to pay the most for it.

But the higher rent has other, long-run effects. Let's look at these long-run effects.

Long-Run Adjustments

With sufficient time for new apartments and houses to be constructed, supply increases. The long-run supply curve tells us that in the long run, housing is supplied at a rent of $16 a month. Because the rent of $20 a month exceeds the long-run supply price of $16 a month, there is a building boom. More apartments and houses are built, and the short-run supply curve shifts gradually rightward.

Figure 6.1(b) shows the long-run adjustment. As more housing is built, the short-run supply curve shifts gradually rightward and intersects the demand curve at lower rents and larger quantities. The market equilibrium follows the arrows down the demand curve. The building boom comes to an end when there is no further profit in building new apartments and houses. The process ends when the rent is back at $16 a month, and 100,000 units of housing are available.

We've just seen how a housing market responds to a decrease in supply. And we've seen that a key part of the adjustment process is a rise in the rent. Suppose the government passes a law to stop the rent from rising. What happens then?

A Regulated Housing Market

We're now going to study the effects of a price ceiling in the housing market. A **price ceiling** is a regulation that makes it illegal to charge a price higher than a specified level. When a price ceiling is applied to housing markets, it is called a **rent ceiling**. How does a rent ceiling affect the housing market?

The effect of a price (rent) ceiling depends on whether it is imposed at a level that is above or below the equilibrium price (rent). A price ceiling set *above* the equilibrium price has no effect. The reason is that the price ceiling does not constrain the market forces. The force of the law and the market forces are not in conflict. But a price ceiling *below* the equilibrium price has powerful effects on a market. The reason is that it attempts to prevent the price from regulating the quantities demanded and supplied. The force of the law and the market forces are in conflict, and one (or both) of these forces must yield to some degree. Let's study the effects of a price ceiling that is set below the equilibrium price by returning to San Francisco. What would have happened in San Francisco if a rent ceiling of $16 a month—the rent before the earthquake—had been imposed?

FIGURE 6.1 The San Francisco Housing Market in 1906

(a) After earthquake

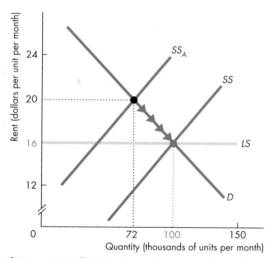

(b) Long-run adjustment

Part (a) shows that before the earthquake, 100,000 housing units were rented at $16 a month. After the earthquake, the short-run supply curve shifts from SS to SS_A. The rent rises to $20 a month, and the quantity of housing decreases to 72,000 units.

With rent at $20 a month, there is profit in building new apartments and houses. As the building proceeds, the short-run supply curve shifts rightward (part b). The rent gradually falls to $16 a month, and the quantity of housing increases to 100,000 units—as the arrowed line shows.

FIGURE 6.2   A Rent Ceiling

A rent above $16 a month is illegal (in the grey-shaded illegal region). At a rent of $16 a month, the quantity of housing supplied after the earthquake is 44,000 units. Someone is willing to pay $24 a month for the 44,000th unit. Frustrated renters spend time searching for housing and frustrated renters and landlords make deals in a black market.

Figure 6.2 enables us to answer this question. A rent that exceeds $16 a month is in the grey-shaded illegal region in the figure. At a rent of $16 a month, the quantity of housing supplied is 44,000 units and the quantity demanded is 100,000 units. So there is a shortage of 56,000 units of housing.

But the story does not end here. Somehow, the 44,000 units of available housing must be allocated among people who demand 100,000 units. How is this allocation achieved? When a rent ceiling creates a housing shortage, two developments occur. They are

■ Search activity
■ Black markets

Search Activity

The time spent looking for someone with whom to do business is called **search activity.** We spend some time in search activity almost every time we buy something. You want the latest hot CD, and you know four stores that stock it. But which store has the best deal? You need to spend a few minutes on the telephone finding out. In some markets, we spend a lot of time searching. An example is the used

car market. People spend a lot of time checking out alternative dealers and cars.

But when a price is regulated and there is a shortage, search activity increases. In the case of a rent-controlled housing market, frustrated would-be renters scan the newspapers, not only for housing ads but also for death notices! Any information about newly available housing is useful. And they race to be first on the scene when news of a possible supplier breaks.

The *opportunity cost* of a good is equal not only to its price but also to the value of the search time spent finding the good. So the opportunity cost of housing is equal to the rent (a regulated price) plus the time and other resources spent searching for the restricted quantity available. Search activity is costly. It uses time and other resources, such as telephones, cars, and gasoline that could have been used in other productive ways. A rent ceiling controls the rent portion of the cost of housing, but it does not control the opportunity cost, which might even be *higher* than the rent would be if the market were unregulated.

Black Markets

A **black market** is an illegal market in which the price exceeds the legally imposed price ceiling. Black markets occur in rent-controlled housing, and scalpers run black markets in tickets for big sporting events and rock concerts.

When rent ceilings are in force, frustrated renters and landlords constantly seek ways of increasing rents. One common way is for a new tenant to pay a high price for worthless fittings, such as charging $2,000 for threadbare drapes. Another is for the tenant to pay an exorbitant price for new locks and keys—called "key money."

The level of a black market rent depends on how tightly the rent ceiling is enforced. With loose enforcement, the black market rent is close to the unregulated rent. But with strict enforcement, the black market rent is equal to the maximum price that renters are willing to pay.

With strict enforcement of the rent ceiling in the San Francisco example shown in Fig. 6.2, the quantity of housing available remains at 44,000 units. A small number of people offer housing for rent at $24 a month—the highest rent that someone is willing to pay—and the government detects and punishes some of these black market traders.

Inefficiency of Rent Ceilings

In an unregulated market, the market determines the rent at which the quantity demanded equals the quantity supplied. In this situation, scarce housing resources are allocated efficiently. *Marginal benefit* equals *marginal cost* (see Chapter 5, p. 110).

Figure 6.3 shows the inefficiency of a rent ceiling. If the rent is fixed at $16 per month, 44,000 units are supplied. Marginal benefit is $24 a month. The blue triangle above the supply curve and below the rent ceiling line shows producer surplus. Because the quantity of housing is less than the competitive quantity, there is a deadweight loss, shown by the grey triangle. This loss is borne by the consumers who can't find housing and by producers who can't supply housing at the new lower price. Consumers who do find housing at the controlled rent gain. If no one incurs search cost, consumer surplus is shown by the sum of the green triangle and the red rectangle. But search costs might eat up part of the consumer surplus, possibly as much as the entire amount that consumers are willing to pay for the available housing, (the red rectangle).

Equity? So rent ceilings prevent scarce resources from flowing to their highest-valued use. But don't rent ceilings ensure that scarce housing goes to the people whose need is greatest and make the allocation of scarce housing fair?

The complex ideas about fairness are explored in Chapter 5 (pp. 114–117). Blocking rent adjustments that bring the quantity of housing demanded into equality with the quantity supplied doesn't end scarcity. So when the law prevents rents from adjusting and blocks the price mechanism from allocating scarce housing, some other allocation mechanism must be used. One of these factors might be discrimination on the basis of race, ethnicity, or sex. Are these mechanisms fair?

Paris, New York, and Toronto are three cities that have rent ceilings; the best example is New York. One consequence of New York's rent ceilings is that families that have lived in the city for a long time—including some rich and famous ones—enjoy low rents, while newcomers pay high rents for hard-to-find apartments. At the same time, landlords in rent-controlled Harlem abandon entire city blocks to rats and drug dealers. Swedish economist Assar Lindbeck has suggested that rent ceilings are the most effective means yet for destroying cities, even more effective than the hydrogen bomb.

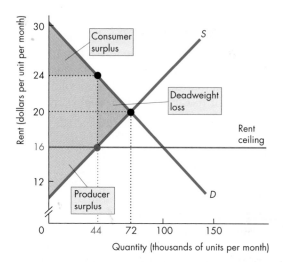

FIGURE 6.3   The Inefficiency of a Rent Ceiling

A rent ceiling of $16 a month decreases the quantity of housing supplied to 44,000 units. Producer surplus shrinks, and a deadweight loss arises. If people use no resources in search activity, consumer surplus is the green triangle plus the red rectangle. But if people use resources in search activity equal to the amount they are willing to pay for available housing (the red rectangle), the consumer surplus shrinks to the green triangle.

REVIEW QUIZ

1 How does a decrease in the supply of housing change the equilibrium rent in the short run?
2 What are the effects of a rise in rent? And who gets to consume the scarce housing resources?
3 What are the long-run effects of higher rents following a decrease in the supply of housing?
4 What is a rent ceiling and what are its effects if it is set above the equilibrium rent?
5 What are the effects of a rent ceiling that is set below the equilibrium rent?
6 How do scarce housing resources get allocated when a rent ceiling is in place?

You now know how a price ceiling works. Next, we'll learn about the effects of a price floor by studying minimum wages in the labour market.

The Labour Market and the Minimum Wage

FOR EACH ONE OF US, THE LABOUR MARKET IS the market that influences the jobs we get and the wages we earn. Firms decide how much labour to demand, and the lower the wage rate, the greater is the quantity of labour demanded. Households decide how much labour to supply, and the higher the wage rate, the greater is the quantity of labour supplied. The wage rate adjusts to make the quantity of labour demanded equal to the quantity supplied.

But the labour market is constantly hit by shocks, and wages and employment prospects constantly change. The most pervasive source of these shocks is the advance of technology.

New labour-saving technologies become available every year. As a result, the demand for some types of labour, usually the least-skilled types, decreases. During the 1980s and 1990s, for example, the demand for telephone operators and television repair technicians decreased. Throughout the past 200 years, the demand for low-skilled farm labourers has steadily decreased.

How does the labour market cope with this continuous decrease in the demand for low-skilled labour? Doesn't it mean that the wage rate of low-skilled workers is constantly falling?

To answer these questions, we must study the market for low-skilled labour. And just as we did when we studied the housing market, we must look at both the short run and the long run.

In the short run, there is a given number of people who have a given skill, training, and experience. Short-run supply of labour describes how the number of hours of labour supplied by this given number of workers changes as the wage rate changes. To get workers to work more hours, they must be offered a higher wage rate.

In the long run, people can acquire new skills and find new types of jobs. The number of people in the low-skilled labour market depends on the wage rate in this market compared with other opportunities. If the wage rate of low-skilled labour is high enough, people will enter this market. If the wage rate is too low, people will leave it. Some will seek training to enter higher-skilled labour markets, and others will stop working and stay at home or retire.

The long-run supply of labour is the relationship between the quantity of labour supplied and the wage rate after enough time has passed for people to enter or leave the low-skilled labour market. If people can freely enter and leave the low-skilled labour market, the long-run supply of labour is *perfectly elastic*.

Figure 6.4 shows the market for low-skilled labour. Other things remaining the same, the lower the wage rate, the greater is the quantity of labour demanded by firms. The demand curve for labour, D in part (a), shows this relationship between the wage rate and the quantity of labour demanded. Other things remaining the same, the higher the wage rate, the greater is the quantity of labour supplied by households. But the longer the period of adjustment, the greater is the *elasticity of supply* of labour. The short-run supply curve is SS, and the long-run supply curve is LS. In the figure, long-run supply is assumed to be perfectly elastic (the LS curve is horizontal). This market is in equilibrium at a wage rate of $5 an hour and 22 million hours of labour employed.

What happens if a labour-saving invention decreases the demand for low-skilled labour? Figure 6.4(a) shows the short-run effects of such a change. The demand curve before the new technology is introduced is the curve labelled D. After the introduction of the new technology, the demand curve shifts leftward to D_A. The wage rate falls to $4 an hour, and the quantity of labour employed decreases to 21 million hours. But this short-run effect on the wage rate and employment is not the end of the story.

People who are now earning only $4 an hour look around for other opportunities. They see many other jobs (in markets for other types of skills) that pay more than $4 an hour. One by one, workers decide to go back to school or take jobs that pay less but offer on-the-job training. As a result, the short-run supply curve begins to shift leftward.

Figure 6.4(b) shows the long-run adjustment. As the short-run supply curve shifts leftward, it intersects the demand curve D_A at higher wage rates and lower levels of employment. The process ends when workers have no incentive to leave the low-skilled labour market and the short-run supply curve has shifted all the way to SS_A. At this point, the wage rate has returned to $5 an hour and employment has decreased to 20 million hours a year.

Sometimes, the adjustment process that we've just described is rapid. At other times, it is slow and the wage rate remains low for a long period. To boost the incomes of the lowest-paid workers, the government intervenes in the labour market and sets the minimum wage that employers are required to pay. Let's look at the effects of the minimum wage.

FIGURE 6.4 A Market for Low-Skilled Labour

(a) After invention

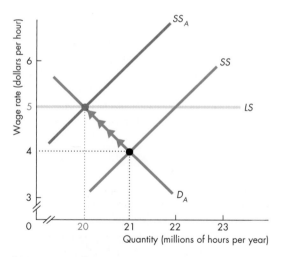

(b) Long-run adjustment

Part (a) shows the immediate effect of a labour-saving invention on the market for low-skilled labour. Initially, the wage rate is $5 an hour and 22 million hours a year are employed. A labour-saving invention shifts the demand curve from D to D_A. The wage rate falls to $4 an hour, and employment decreases to 21 million hours a year. With the lower wage rate, some workers leave this market, and the short-run supply curve starts to shift gradually leftward to SS_A (part b). The wage rate gradually rises, and the employment level decreases. In the long run, the wage rate returns to $5 an hour and employment decreases to 20 million hours a year.

The Minimum Wage

A **price floor** is a regulation that makes it illegal to trade at a price lower than a specified level. When a price floor is applied to labour markets, it is called a **minimum wage.** If the minimum wage is set *below* the equilibrium wage, the minimum wage has no effect. The minimum wage and market forces are not in conflict. If the minimum wage is set *above* the equilibrium wage, the minimum wage is in conflict with market forces and does have some effects on the labour market. Let's study these effects by returning to the market for low-skilled labour.

Suppose that with an equilibrium wage of $4 an hour (Fig. 6.4a), the government sets a minimum wage at $5 an hour. What are the effects of this minimum wage? Figure 6.5 answers this question. It shows the minimum wage as the horizontal red line labelled "Minimum wage." A wage below this level is in the grey-shaded illegal region. At the minimum wage rate, 20 million hours of labour are demanded (point *A*) and 22 million hours are supplied (point *B*), so 2 million hours of available labour are unemployed.

With only 20 million hours demanded, some workers are willing to supply that 20 millionth hour

FIGURE 6.5 Minimum Wage and Unemployment

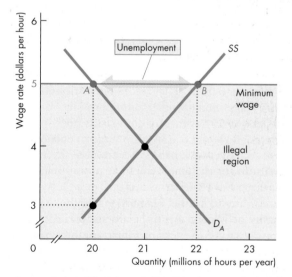

A wage below $5 an hour is illegal, in the grey-shaded illegal region. At the minimum wage of $5 an hour, 20 million hours are hired but 22 million hours are available. Unemployment—*AB*—of 2 million hours a year is created.

for $3. Frustrated unemployed workers spend time and other resources searching for hard-to-find jobs.

The Minimum Wage in Practice

Provincial governments in Canada set minimum wage rates. In 2003, minimum wage rates range from lows of $5.90 an hour in Alberta and $6.00 an hour in Newfoundland and Nova Scotia to highs of $8.00 an hour in British Columbia, $7.30 an hour in Quebec, and $7.20 an hour in the Yukon.

You saw in Fig. 6.5 that the minimum wage brings unemployment. But how much unemployment does it bring? Economists do not agree on the answer to this question. Until recently, most economists believed that the minimum wage was a big contributor to high unemployment among low-skilled young workers. But this view has recently been challenged and the challenge rebutted.

David Card, a Canadian economist who works at the University of California at Berkeley, and Alan Krueger of Princeton University say that increases in the minimum wage have not decreased employment and created unemployment. From their study of minimum wages in California, New Jersey, and Texas, Card and Krueger say that the employment rate of low-income workers increased following an increase in the minimum wage. They suggest three reasons why higher wages might increase employment. First, workers become more conscientious and productive. Second, workers are less likely to quit, so labour turnover, which is costly, is reduced. Third, managers make a firm's operations more efficient.

Most economists are skeptical about Card and Krueger's suggestions. They ask two questions. First, if higher wages make workers more productive and reduce labour turnover, why don't firms freely pay wage rates above the equilibrium wage to encourage more productive work habits? Second, are there other explanations for the employment responses that Card and Krueger have found?

According to Daniel Hamermesh of the University of Texas at Austin, Card and Krueger got the timing wrong and fell into the trap of the *post hoc* fallacy (see pp. 13–14). Hamermesh says that firms cut employment *before* the minimum wage is increased in anticipation of the increase. If he is correct, looking for the effects of an increase *after* it has occurred misses its main effects. Finis Welch of Texas A&M University and Kevin Murphy of the University of Chicago say the employment effects

that Card and Krueger found are caused by regional differences in economic growth, not by changes in the minimum wage.

One effect of the minimum wage, according to Fig. 6.5, is an increase in the quantity of labour supplied. If this effect occurs, it might show up as an increase in the number of people who quit school before completing high school to look for work. Some economists say that this response does occur.

Inefficiency of the Minimum Wage

An unregulated labour market allocates scarce labour resources to the jobs in which they are valued most highly. The minimum wage frustrates the market mechanism and results in unemployment—wasted labour resources—and an inefficient amount of job search.

In Fig. 6.5, with firms employing only 20 million hours of labour at the minimum wage, many people who are willing to supply labour are unable to get hired. You can see that the 20 millionth hour of labour is available for $3. That is, the lowest wage at which someone is willing to supply the 20 millionth hour— read off from the supply curve—is $3. Someone who manages to find a job earns $5 an hour—$2 an hour more than the lowest wage rate at which someone is willing to work. So it pays unemployed people to spend time and effort looking for work.

REVIEW QUIZ

1 How does a decrease in the demand for low-skilled labour change the wage rate in the short run?
2 What are the long-run effects of a lower wage rate for low-skilled labour?
3 What is a minimum wage? What are the effects of a minimum wage set below the equilibrium wage?
4 What is the effect of a minimum wage that is set above the equilibrium wage?

Next we're going to study a more widespread government action in markets: taxes, such as the sales taxes that most provinces impose. We'll see how taxes change prices and quantities and discover that usually a sales tax is not paid entirely by the buyer. And we'll see that a tax usually creates a deadweight loss.

Taxes

ALMOST EVERYTHING YOU BUY IS TAXED. But who really pays the tax? Because the sales tax is added to the price of a good or service when it is sold, isn't it obvious that the *buyer* pays the tax? Isn't the price higher than it otherwise would be by an amount equal to the tax? It can be, but usually it isn't. And it is even possible that the buyer actually pays none of the tax! Let's see how we can make sense of these apparently absurd statements.

Who Pays a Sales Tax?

Suppose the government puts a $10 sales tax on CD players. What are the effects of the sales tax on the price and quantity of CD players? To answer this question, we need to work out what happens to demand and supply in the market for CD players.

Figure 6.6 shows this market. The demand curve is *D*, and the supply curve is *S*. With no sales tax, the equilibrium price is $100 per CD player and 5,000 CD players are bought and sold each week.

When a good is taxed, it has two prices: a price that excludes the tax and a price that includes the tax. Buyers respond only to the price that includes the tax, because that is the price they pay. Sellers respond only to the price that excludes the tax, because that is the price they receive. The tax is like a wedge between these two prices.

Think of the price on the vertical axis of Fig. 6.6 as the price paid by buyers—the price that *includes* the tax. When a tax is imposed and the price changes, there is a change in the quantity demanded but no change in demand. That is, there is a movement along the demand curve and no shift of the demand curve.

But supply changes, and the supply curve shifts. The sales tax is like an increase in cost, so supply decreases and the supply curve shifts leftward to *S* + *tax*. To determine the position of this new supply curve, we add the tax to the minimum price that sellers are willing to accept for each quantity sold. For example, with no tax, sellers are willing to offer 5,000 CD players a week for $100 a player. So with a $10 tax, they will supply 5,000 CD players a week for $110—a price that includes the tax. The curve *S* + *tax* describes the terms under which sellers are willing to offer CD players for sale now that there is a $10 tax.

Equilibrium occurs where the new supply curve intersects the demand curve—at a price of $105 and

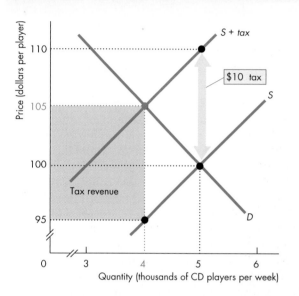

FIGURE 6.6   A Sales Tax

With no sales tax, 5,000 CD players a week are bought and sold at $100 each. A sales tax of $10 a CD player is imposed, and the supply curve shifts leftward to S + *tax*. In the new equilibrium, the price rises to $105 a CD player and the quantity decreases to 4,000 CD players a week. The sales tax raises the price by less than the tax, lowers the price received by the seller, and decreases the quantity. The sales tax brings in revenue to the government equal to the purple rectangle.

a quantity of 4,000 CD players a week. The $10 sales tax increases the price paid by the buyer by $5 a CD player and it decreases the price received by the seller by $5 a CD player. So the buyer and the seller pay the $10 tax equally.

The tax brings in tax revenue to the government equal to the tax per item multiplied by the number of items sold. The purple area in Fig. 6.6 illustrates the tax revenue. The $10 tax on CD players brings in tax revenue of $40,000 a week.

In this example, the buyer and the seller split the tax equally: The buyer pays $5 a CD player, and so does the seller. This equal sharing of the tax is a special case and does not usually occur. But some sharing of the tax between the buyer and seller is usual. And in other special cases, either the buyer or the seller pays the entire tax. The division of the tax between the buyer and the seller depends on the elasticities of demand and supply.

Tax Division and Elasticity of Demand

The division of the tax between the buyer and the seller depends in part on the elasticity of demand. There are two extreme cases:

- Perfectly inelastic demand—buyer pays.
- Perfectly elastic demand—seller pays.

Perfectly Inelastic Demand Figure 6.7(a) shows the market for insulin, a vital daily medication of diabetics. Demand is perfectly inelastic at 100,000 doses a day, regardless of the price, as shown by the vertical curve *D*. That is, a diabetic would sacrifice all other goods and services rather than not consume the insulin dose that provides good health. The supply curve of insulin is *S*. With no tax, the price is $2 a dose and the quantity is 100,000 doses a day.

If insulin is taxed at 20¢ a dose, we must add the tax to the minimum price at which drug companies are willing to sell insulin. The result is the new supply curve *S* + *tax*. The price rises to $2.20 a dose, but the quantity does not change. The buyer pays the entire sales tax of 20¢ a dose.

Perfectly Elastic Demand Figure 6.7(b) shows the market for pink marker pens. Demand is perfectly elastic at $1 a pen, as shown by the horizontal curve *D*. If pink pens are less expensive than the others, everyone uses pink. If pink pens are more expensive than the others, no one uses pink. The supply curve is *S*. With no tax, the price of a pink marker is $1, and the quantity is 4,000 pens a week.

If a sales tax of 10¢ a pen is imposed on pink marker pens but not on other colours, we add the tax to the minimum price at which sellers are willing to offer pink pens for sale, and the new supply curve is *S* + *tax*. The price remains at $1 a pen, and the quantity decreases to 1,000 a week. The 10¢ sales tax leaves the price paid by the buyer unchanged but lowers the amount received by the seller by the full amount of the sales tax. The seller pays the entire tax. As a result, sellers decrease the quantity offered for sale.

We've seen that when demand is perfectly inelastic, the buyer pays the entire tax and when demand is perfectly elastic, the seller pays it. In the usual case, demand is neither perfectly inelastic nor perfectly elastic and the tax is split between the buyer and the seller. But the division depends on the elasticity of demand. The more inelastic the demand, the larger is the amount of the tax paid by the buyer.

FIGURE 6.7   Sales Tax and the Elasticity of Demand

(a) Perfectly inelastic demand

(b) Perfectly elastic demand

Part (a) shows the market for insulin, where demand is perfectly inelastic. With no tax, the price is $2 a dose and the quantity is 100,000 doses a day. A sales tax of 20¢ a dose shifts the supply curve to *S* + *tax*. The price rises to $2.20 a dose, but the quantity bought does not change. The buyer pays the entire tax.

Part (b) shows the market for pink pens. The demand for pink pens is perfectly elastic. With no tax, the price of a pen is $1 and the quantity is 4,000 pens a week. A sales tax of 10¢ a pink pen shifts the supply curve to *S* + *tax*. The price remains at $1 a pen, and the quantity of pink pens sold decreases to 1,000 a week. The seller pays the entire tax.

Tax Division and Elasticity of Supply

The division of the tax between the buyer and the seller also depends, in part, on the elasticity of supply. Again, there are two extreme cases:

■ Perfectly inelastic supply—seller pays.
■ Perfectly elastic supply—buyer pays.

Perfectly Inelastic Supply   Figure 6.8(a) shows the market for water from a mineral spring that flows at a constant rate that can't be controlled. Supply is perfectly inelastic at 100,000 bottles a week, as shown by the supply curve *S*. The demand curve for the water from this spring is *D*. With no tax, the price is 50¢ a bottle and the 100,000 bottles that flow from the spring are bought.

Suppose this spring water is taxed at 5¢ a bottle. The supply curve does not change because the spring owners still produce 100,000 bottles a week even though the price they receive falls. But buyers are willing to buy the 100,000 bottles only if the price is 50¢ a bottle. So the price remains at 50¢ a bottle. The sales tax reduces the price received by sellers to 45¢ a bottle, and the seller pays the entire tax.

Perfectly Elastic Supply   Figure 6.8(b) shows the market for sand from which computer-chip makers extract silicon. Supply of this sand is perfectly elastic at a price of 10¢ a kilogram, as shown by the supply curve *S*. The demand curve for sand is *D*. With no tax, the price is 10¢ a kilogram and 5,000 kilograms a week are bought.

If this sand is taxed at 1¢ a kilogram, we must add the tax to the minimum supply-price. Sellers are now willing to offer any quantity at 11¢ a kilogram along the curve *S* + *tax*. A new equilibrium is determined where the new supply curve intersects the demand curve: at a price of 11¢ a kilogram and a quantity of 3,000 kilograms a week. The sales tax has increased the price paid by the buyer by the full amount of the tax—1¢ a kilogram—and has decreased the quantity sold. The buyer pays the entire tax.

We've seen that when supply is perfectly inelastic, the seller pays the entire tax, and when supply is perfectly elastic, the buyer pays it. In the usual case, supply is neither perfectly inelastic nor perfectly elastic and the tax is split between the buyer and the seller. But the division between the buyer and the seller depends on the elasticity of supply. The more elastic the supply, the larger is the amount of the tax paid by the buyer.

FIGURE 6.8   Sales Tax and the Elasticity of Supply

(a) Perfectly inelastic supply

(b) Perfectly elastic supply

Part (a) shows the market for water from a mineral spring. Supply is perfectly inelastic. With no tax, the price is 50¢ a bottle. With a sales tax of 5¢ a bottle, the price remains at 50¢ a bottle. The number of bottles bought remains the same, but the price received by sellers decreases to 45¢ a bottle. The seller pays the entire tax.

Part (b) shows the market for sand. Supply is perfectly elastic. With no tax, the price is 10¢ a kilogram. A sales tax of 1¢ a kilogram increases the minimum supply-price to 11¢ a kilogram. The supply curve shifts to *S* + *tax*. The price increases to 11¢ a kilogram. The buyer pays the entire tax.

Sales Taxes in Practice

We've looked at the range of possible effects of a sales tax by studying the extreme cases. In practice, supply and demand are rarely perfectly elastic or perfectly inelastic. They lie somewhere in between. But some items tend towards one of the extremes. For example, a heavily taxed item such as alcohol, tobacco, or gasoline has a low elasticity of demand. Consequently, the buyer pays most of the tax. Also, because demand is inelastic, the quantity bought does not decrease much and the government collects a large tax revenue.

It is unusual to tax an item heavily if its demand is elastic. Such a good or service has close substitutes. If a tax is levied on such a good or service, people will reduce their purchases of the taxed good and increase their purchases of an untaxed substitute. That is, the quantity of the taxed good bought decreases by a large amount and the government will not collect much tax revenue. This explains why the items that are taxed are those that have inelastic demands and why buyers pay most of the taxes.

Taxes and Efficiency

You've seen that a sales tax places a wedge between the price paid by buyers and the price received by sellers. The price paid by buyers is also the buyers' willingness to pay, which measures marginal benefit. And the price received by sellers is the sellers' minimum supply-price, which equals marginal cost.

So because a tax places a wedge between the buyers' price and the sellers' price, it also puts a wedge between marginal benefit and marginal cost and creates inefficiency. With a higher buying price and a lower selling price, the tax decreases the quantity produced and consumed and a deadweight loss arises. Figure 6.9 shows the inefficiency of a sales tax. With a sales tax, both consumer surplus and producer surplus shrink. Part of each surplus goes to the government in tax revenue—the purple area in the figure. And part of each surplus becomes a deadweight loss—the grey area.

In the extreme cases of perfectly inelastic demand and perfectly inelastic supply, the quantity does not change and there is no deadweight loss. The more inelastic is either demand or supply, the smaller is the decrease in quantity and the smaller is the deadweight loss. When demand or supply is perfectly inelastic, the quantity remains constant and there is no deadweight loss.

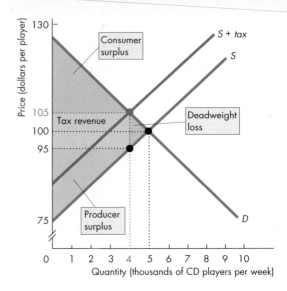

FIGURE 6.9   Taxes and Efficiency

With no sales tax, 5,000 CD players a week are bought and sold at $100 each. With a sales tax of $10 a CD player, the buyer's price rises to $105 a player, the seller's price falls to $95 a player, and the quantity decreases to 4,000 CD players a week. Consumer surplus shrinks to the green area, and the producer surplus shrinks to the blue area. Part of the loss of consumer surplus and producer surplus goes to the government as tax revenue, which is shown as the purple area. A deadweight loss arises, which is shown by the grey area.

REVIEW QUIZ

1 How does the elasticity of demand influence the effect of a sales tax on the price paid by the buyer, the price received by the seller, the quantity, the tax revenue, and the deadweight loss?
2 How does the elasticity of supply influence the effect of a sales tax on the price paid by the buyer, the price received by the seller, the quantity, the tax revenue, and the deadweight loss?
3 Why does a tax create a deadweight loss?

Governments make some types of goods, such as drugs, illegal. Let's see how the market works when trade in an illegal good takes place.

Markets for Illegal Goods

THE MARKETS FOR MANY GOODS AND SERVICES are regulated, and buying and selling some goods is illegal. The best-known examples of such goods are drugs, such as marijuana, cocaine, Ecstasy, and heroin.

Despite the fact that these drugs are illegal, trade in them is a multibillion-dollar business. This trade can be understood by using the same economic model and principles that explain trade in legal goods. To study the market for illegal goods, we're first going to examine the prices and quantities that would prevail if these goods were not illegal. Next, we'll see how prohibition works. Then we'll see how a tax might be used to limit the consumption of these goods.

A Free Market for Drugs

Figure 6.10 shows the market for drugs. The demand curve, D, shows that, other things remaining the same, the lower the price of drugs, the larger is the quantity of drugs demanded. The supply curve, S, shows that, other things remaining the same, the lower the price of drugs, the smaller is the quantity supplied. If drugs were not illegal, the quantity bought and sold would be Q_C and the price would be P_C.

A Market for Illegal Drugs

When a good is illegal, the cost of trading in the good increases. By how much the cost increases and on whom the cost falls depend on the penalties for violating the law and the effectiveness with which the law is enforced. The larger the penalties and the more effective the policing, the higher are the costs. Penalties might be imposed on sellers, buyers, or both.

Penalties on Sellers Drug dealers in Canada face large penalties if their activities are detected. For example, a marijuana dealer could pay a $200,000 fine and serve a 15-year prison term. A heroin dealer could pay a $500,000 fine and serve a 20-year prison term. These penalties are part of the cost of supplying illegal drugs, and they bring a decrease in supply—a leftward shift in the supply curve. To determine the new supply curve, we add the cost of breaking the law to the minimum price that drug dealers are willing to accept. In Fig. 6.10, the cost of breaking the law by selling drugs (CBL) is added to the minimum

FIGURE 6.10 A Market for an Illegal Good

The demand curve for drugs is D, and the supply curve is S. If drugs are not illegal, the quantity bought and sold is Q_C at a price of P_C—point E. If selling drugs is illegal, the cost of breaking the law by selling drugs (CBL) is added to the minimum supply-price and supply decreases to $S + CBL$. The market moves to point F. If buying drugs is illegal, the cost of breaking the law is subtracted from the maximum price that buyers are willing to pay, and demand decreases to $D - CBL$. The market moves to point G. With both buying and selling illegal, the supply curve and the demand curve shift and the market moves to point H. The market price remains at P_C but the market price plus the penalty for buying rises to P_B—point J—and the market price minus the penalty for sellers falls to P_S—point K.

price that dealers will accept and the supply curve shifts leftward to $S + CBL$. If penalties were imposed only on sellers, the market would move from point E to point F.

Penalties on Buyers In Canada, it is illegal to *possess* drugs such as marijuana, cocaine, Ecstasy, and heroin. For example, possession of marijuana can bring a prison term of 1 year, and possession of heroin can bring a prison term of 2 years. Penalties fall on buyers, and the cost of breaking the law must be subtracted from the value of the good to determine the maximum price buyers are willing to pay for the drugs. Demand decreases, and the demand curve shifts leftward. In Fig. 6.10, the demand curve shifts to $D - CBL$. If penalties were imposed only on buyers, the market would move from point E to point G.

Penalties on Both Sellers and Buyers

Because penalties are imposed on both sellers *and* buyers, supply and demand decrease and the supply curve and the demand curve shift. In Fig. 6.10 the costs of breaking the law are the same for both buyers and sellers, so both curves shift leftward by the same amount. The market moves to point H. The market price remains at the competitive market price P_C, but the quantity bought decreases to Q_P. The buyer pays P_C plus the cost of breaking the law, which is P_B. And the seller receives P_C minus the cost of breaking the law, which is P_S.

The larger the penalties and the greater the degree of law enforcement, the larger is the decrease in demand and/or supply, the smaller is the equilibrium quantity, and the higher is the total price paid by the buyer. That total price is the market price plus the cost of breaking the law imposed on the buyer. But the market price itself might be greater than or less than the free market price P_C. In Canada, the penalties on sellers are much larger than those on buyers, so the quantity of drugs traded decreases and the price increases compared with a free market.

With high enough penalties and effective law enforcement, it is possible to decrease demand and/or supply to the point at which the quantity bought is zero. But in reality, such an outcome is unusual. It does not happen in Canada in the case of illegal drugs. The key reason is the high cost of law enforcement and insufficient resources for the police to achieve effective enforcement. Because of this situation, some people suggest that drugs (and other illegal goods) should be legalized and sold openly but should also be taxed at a high rate in the same way that legal drugs such as alcohol are taxed. How would such an arrangement work?

Legalizing and Taxing Drugs

From your study of the effects of taxes, it is easy to see that the quantity of drugs bought could be decreased if drugs were legalized and taxed. A sufficiently high tax could be imposed to decrease supply, raise the price, and achieve the same decrease in the quantity bought as with a prohibition on drugs. The government would collect a large tax revenue.

Illegal Trading to Evade the Tax

It is likely that an extremely high tax rate would be needed to cut the quantity of drugs bought to the level prevailing with a prohibition. It is also likely that many drug dealers and consumers would try to cover up their activities to evade the tax. If they did act in this way, they would face the cost of breaking the law—the tax law. If the penalty for tax law violation is as severe and as effectively policed as drug-dealing laws, the analysis we've already conducted applies also to this case. The quantity of drugs bought would depend on the penalties for law breaking and on the way in which the penalties are assigned to buyers and sellers.

Taxes Versus Prohibition: Some Pros and Cons

Which is more effective: prohibition or taxes? In favour of taxes and against prohibition is the fact that the tax revenue can be used to make law enforcement more effective. It can also be used to run a more effective education campaign against illegal drug use. In favour of prohibition and against taxes is the fact that prohibition sends a signal that might influence preferences, decreasing the demand for illegal drugs. Also, some people intensely dislike the idea of the government profiting from trade in harmful substances.

REVIEW QUIZ

1. How does the imposition of a penalty for selling an illegal drug influence demand, supply, price, and the quantity of the drug consumed?
2. How does the imposition of a penalty for possessing an illegal drug influence demand, supply, price, and the quantity of the drug consumed?
3. How does the imposition of a penalty for selling *or* possessing an illegal drug influence demand, supply, price, and the quantity of the drug consumed?
4. Is there any case for legalizing drugs?

You've seen how government action in markets in the form of price ceilings, minimum wages, and taxes limits the quantity and create inefficient resource use. You've also seen how in a market for an illegal good, the quantity can be decreased by imposing penalties on either buyers or sellers or by legalizing and taxing the good. Next, we look at agricultural markets and see how governments try to stabilize farm revenues.

Stabilizing Farm Revenues

EARLY FROST, DROUGHT, HEAVY RAIN, AND flooding all fill the lives of farmers with uncertainty. Fluctuations in the weather bring big fluctuations in farm output. How do changes in farm output affect farm prices and farm revenues? And how might farm revenues be stabilized? Let's begin to answer these questions by looking at an agricultural market.

An Unregulated Agricultural Market

Figure 6.11 shows the market for wheat. In both parts, the demand curve for wheat is *D*. Once farmers have harvested their crop, they have no control over the quantity supplied, and supply is inelastic along a *momentary supply curve*. In normal climate conditions, the momentary supply curve is MS_0 (in both parts of the figure).

The price is determined at the point of intersection of the momentary supply curve and the demand curve. In normal conditions, the price is $200 a tonne. The quantity of wheat produced is 20 million tonnes, and farm revenue is $4 billion. Suppose the opportunity cost to farmers of producing wheat is also $4 billion. Then in normal conditions, farmers just cover their opportunity cost.

Poor Harvest Suppose there is a bad growing season, resulting in a poor harvest. What happens to the price of wheat and the revenue of farmers? These questions are answered in Fig. 6.11(a). The poor harvest decreases supply to 15 million tonnes of wheat, and the momentary supply curve shifts leftward to MS_1. With a decrease in supply, the price rises to $300 a tonne.

What happens to total farm revenue? It *increases* to $4.5 billion. A decrease in supply has brought an increase in price and an increase in farm revenue. It does so because the demand for wheat is *inelastic*. The percentage decrease in the quantity demanded is less than the percentage increase in price. You can verify this fact by noticing in Fig. 6.11(a) that the increase in revenue from the higher price ($1.5 billion—the light blue area) exceeds the decrease in revenue from the smaller quantity ($1.0 billion—the red area). Farmers now make revenue in excess of their opportunity cost.

Although total farm revenue increases when there is a poor harvest, some farmers, whose entire crop is wiped out, suffer a decrease in revenue. Others, whose crop is unaffected, make an enormous gain.

FIGURE 6.11   Harvests, Farm Prices, and Farm Revenue

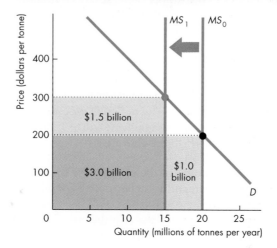

(a) Poor harvest: revenue increases

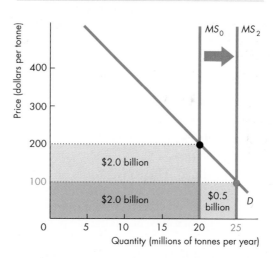

(b) Bumper harvest: revenue decreases

The demand curve for wheat is *D*. In normal times, the supply curve is MS_0 and 20 million tonnes are sold for $200 a tonne. In part (a), a poor harvest decreases supply to MS_1. The price rises to $300 a tonne, and farm revenue increases to $4.5 billion—the $1.5 billion increase from the higher price (light blue area) exceeds the $1.0 billion decrease from the smaller quantity (red area).

In part (b), a bumper harvest increases supply to MS_2. The price falls to $100 a tonne, and farm revenue decreases to $2.5 billion—the $2.0 billion decrease from the lower price (red area) exceeds the $0.5 billion increase from the increase in the quantity sold (light blue area).

Bumper Harvest Figure 6.11(b) shows what happens in the opposite situation, when there is a bumper harvest. Now supply increases to 25 million tonnes, and the momentary supply curve shifts rightward to MS_2. With the increased quantity supplied, the price falls to $100 a tonne. Farm revenue decreases to $2.5 billion. It does so because the demand for wheat is inelastic. To see this fact, notice in Fig. 6.11(b) that the decrease in revenue from the lower price ($2.0 billion—the red area) exceeds the increase in revenue from the increase in the quantity sold ($0.5 billion—the light blue area).

Elasticity of Demand In the example we've just worked through, demand is inelastic. If demand is elastic, the price fluctuations go in the same directions as those we've worked out but revenue fluctuates in the opposite direction. Bumper harvests increase revenue, and poor harvests decrease it. But the demand for most agricultural products is inelastic, and the case we've studied is the relevant one.

Because farm prices fluctuate, institutions have evolved to stabilize them. There are two types of institutions:

- Speculative markets in inventories
- Farm marketing boards

Speculative Markets in Inventories

Many goods, including a wide variety of agricultural products, can be stored. These inventories provide a cushion between production and consumption. If production decreases, goods can be sold from inventory; if production increases, goods can be put into inventory.

In a market that has inventories, we must distinguish production from supply. The quantity produced is *not* the same as the quantity supplied. The quantity supplied exceeds the quantity produced when goods are sold from inventory. And the quantity supplied is less than the quantity produced when goods are put into inventory. Supply therefore depends on the behaviour of inventory holders.

The Behaviour of Inventory Holders Inventory holders speculate. They hope to buy at a low price and sell at a high price. That is, they hope to buy goods and put them into inventory when the price is low and sell them from inventory when the price is high. They make a profit or incur a loss equal to their

selling price minus their buying price and minus the cost of storage.

But how do inventory holders know when to buy and when to sell? How do they know whether the price is high or low? To decide whether a price is high or low, inventory holders forecast the future price. If the current price is above the forecasted future price, inventory holders sell goods from inventory. If the current price is below the forecasted future price, inventory holders buy goods to put into inventory. This behaviour by inventory holders makes the supply of the good perfectly elastic at the price forecasted by inventory holders.

Let's work out what happens to price and quantity in a market in which inventories are held when production fluctuates. Let's look again at the wheat market.

Fluctuations in Production In Fig. 6.12, the demand curve for wheat is D. Inventory holders expect the future price to be $200 a tonne. The supply curve is S—supply is perfectly elastic at the price expected by inventory holders. Production fluctuates between Q_1 and Q_2.

When production fluctuates and there are no inventories, the price and the quantity fluctuate. We saw this result in Fig. 6.11. But if there are inventories, the price does not fluctuate. When production decreases to Q_1, or 15 million tonnes, inventory holders sell 5 million tonnes from inventory and the quantity bought by consumers is 20 million tonnes. The price remains at $200 a tonne. When production increases to Q_2, or 25 million tonnes, inventory holders buy 5 million tonnes and consumers continue to buy 20 million tonnes. Again, the price remains at $200 a tonne. The actions of inventory holders reduce price fluctuations. In Fig. 6.12, the price fluctuations are entirely eliminated. When there are costs of carrying inventories and when inventories become almost depleted, some price fluctuations do occur, but these fluctuations are smaller than those occurring in a market without inventories.

Farm Revenue Even if inventory speculation succeeds in stabilizing the price, it does not stabilize farm revenue. With the price stabilized, farm revenue fluctuates as production fluctuates. But now bumper harvests always bring larger revenues than poor harvests do because the price remains constant and only the quantity fluctuates.

FIGURE 6.12   How Inventories Limit Price Changes

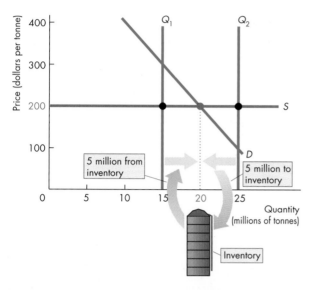

Inventory holders sell wheat from inventory if the price rises above $200 a tonne, and they buy wheat to hold in inventory if the price falls below $200 a tonne, which makes supply (S) perfectly elastic. When production decreases to Q_1, 5 million tonnes are sold from inventory; when production increases to Q_2, 5 million tonnes are added to inventory. The price remains at $200 a tonne.

Farm Marketing Boards

Most governments intervene in agricultural markets. The most extensive such intervention occurs in the European Union and Japan. Farm price intervention is not as extensive in Canada and the United States. But government regulations influence the prices of some agricultural products that include grains, milk, eggs, tobacco, rice, peanuts, cotton, and poultry meats.

In Canada, more than 100 farm marketing boards operate and influence more than one-half of total farm sales. A **farm marketing board** is a regulatory agency that intervenes in an agricultural market to stabilize the price of an agricultural product. Farm marketing boards are often supported by governments. How do agricultural markets work when a stabilization program is in place? The answer depends on which type of intervention takes place. There are three types of intervention:

- Price floor
- Quota
- Subsidy

Price Floor A *price floor* operates in an agricultural market in much the same way that it operates in other markets. Earlier in this chapter, we examined a price floor in the labour market when we studied the effect of minimum wages. The principles are the same in the case of agricultural markets.

Figure 6.13 shows how a price floor works in the market for skim milk powder. The competitive equilibrium price of skim milk powder is $3 a tonne, and 16 million tonnes are produced and bought. If the Canadian Dairy Commission imposes a price floor of $4 a tonne, then the price increases to $4 a tonne and the quantity demanded decreases to 14 million tonnes.

FIGURE 6.13 A Price Floor

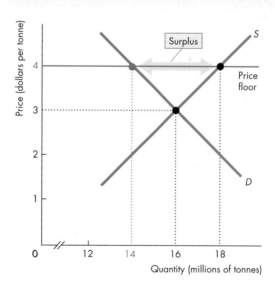

A competitive equilibrium price is $3 a tonne and the equivalent quantity produced and bought is 16 million tonnes. A price floor of $4 a tonne increases the price to $4 a tonne, decreases the quantity sold to 14 million tonnes, and increases the quantity produced to 18 million tonnes. The price floor creates a surplus of 4 million tonnes. If the Canadian Dairy Commission does not buy the surplus and allows farmers to find their own market, the price will return to its competitive level of $3 a tonne.

The quantity supplied increases to 18 million tonnes. Farmers produce a surplus of 4 million tonnes.

This method of supporting the price of an agricultural product will fail unless there is some method of taking up the surplus produced. If farmers are left to find a market for their surplus, then the price will fall below the price floor to the competitive price—$3 a tonne. If, on the other hand, the Canadian Dairy Commission purchases the surplus at the price floor, then the price will remain at the price floor. If the marketing board systematically buys more than it sells, then it will end up with a large inventory. Such has been the outcome in the European Union, where stabilization agencies have mountains of butter and lakes of wine! The cost of buying and storing the inventory falls on taxpayers, and the main gainers from a price floor are the large, efficient farms.

Quota A **quota** is a restriction on the quantity of a good that a farm is permitted to produce. If a quota restricts farm production, then the supply curve becomes perfectly inelastic at the quota quantity.

Figure 6.14 illustrates how a quota works in the market for skim milk. The competitive price is $3 a tonne and the competitive quantity is 16 million tonnes. If the Canadian Dairy Commission imposes a quota that restricts total production to 14 million tonnes, the supply curve becomes the vertical line labelled "Quota." With output restricted by the quota, the quantity produced is now 14 million tonnes and the price increases to $4 a tonne.

But this might not be the end of the story. Farmers are willing to produce skim milk at $2 a tonne, so at a market price of $4 a tonne, they will want to increase their output. If the Canadian Dairy Commission does not prevent quotas from being exceeded, a gradual increase in the quantity of skim milk supplied will eventually restore the competitive equilibrium.

Subsidy A **subsidy** is a payment made by the government to the producer. A subsidy is like a tax—a payment made by a producer to the government—but it goes in the reverse direction. Therefore a subsidy works in a similar way to a tax, but instead of adding something to the price paid by the consumer, a subsidy lowers the price to below what it would be in the absence of a subsidy.

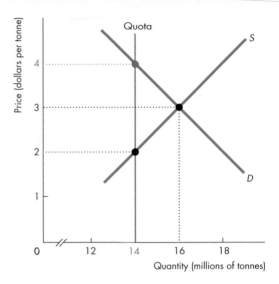

FIGURE 6.14   A Quota

The competitive equilibrium price is $3 a tonne and the equilibrium quantity produced and bought is 16 million tonnes. A quota is set at 14 million tonnes. As a result, the price rises to $4 a tonne and the quantity sold decreases to 14 million tonnes. Producers are willing to supply 14 million tonnes at $2 a tonne, so they will want to increase the quantity that they supply. If the regulatory agency cannot control the quantity produced, then the quantity produced will increase and the price will fall to its competitive level of $3 a tonne.

Figure 6.15 illustrates how a subsidy works in the market for (liquid) milk. The competitive equilibrium is at 30¢ a litre with 16 billion litres produced and bought. The Canadian Dairy Commission then offers a subsidy of 10¢ a litre. The subsidy increases the supply of milk and shifts the supply curve rightward. The magnitude of the shift depends on the size of the subsidy. In this case, farmers are willing to sell each litre for 10¢ less than they would be willing to accept in the absence of a subsidy. The equilibrium price falls to 25¢ a litre, and the quantity produced and bought increases to 17 billion litres. Farmers receive 35¢ a litre, which is the market price of 25¢ a litre plus the subsidy of 10¢ a litre. Thus farmers gain, but taxpayers pay the subsidy. The total subsidy paid is $1.7 billion, which is the 10¢ a litre subsidy

FIGURE 6.15 A Subsidy

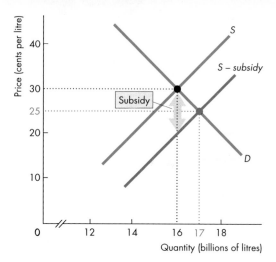

The competitive equilibrium price is 30¢ a litre and the equilibrium quantity produced and bought is 16 billion litres. The Canadian Dairy Commission introduces a subsidy of 10¢ a litre. As a result, producers are now willing to supply each quantity at 10¢ a litre less. The supply curve shifts rightward such that the vertical distance between the supply curve S and the supply curve S – subsidy is 10¢ a litre. The price falls to 25¢ a litre, and the quantity produced and sold increases to 17 billion litres. Producers receive 35¢ a litre, which is the market price of 25¢ a litre plus the subsidy of 10¢ a litre. The total subsidy paid is $1.7 billion, which taxpayers will have to pay.

multiplied by the 17 billion litres of milk produced. This method of agricultural support can impose major costs on taxpayers.

Efficiency and Equity in Farm Markets

Are farm marketing boards efficient, and are they fair? It is easy to answer the first question: farm marketing boards are generally inefficient. It is harder to answer the second question, about their fairness.

Inefficiency of Farm Marketing Boards You can see that farm marketing boards are inefficient by looking at what they do to the relationship between marginal cost and marginal benefit. A price floor that exceeds the competitive equilibrium price decreases

the quantity demanded and results in a price that equals marginal benefit but exceeds marginal cost. So both consumer surplus and producer surplus shrink and there is a deadweight loss.

A quota restricts output below the quantity that maximizes the sum of consumer surplus and producer surplus. So it, too, creates deadweight loss.

A subsidy increases production above the competitive level. So it results in marginal cost exceeding marginal benefit and creates deadweight loss. All the methods of intervention, then, are inefficient. But are they fair?

Equity of Farm Marketing Boards Farm marketing boards increase the incomes of farmers and decrease the incomes of taxpayers and consumers of farm products compared with what the unregulated market would provide. Because the actions of farm marketing boards create deadweight loss, the gains by farmers are smaller than the losses borne by everyone else.

Whether this redistribution of economic well-being towards farmers is fair is a controversial matter. Most farmers probably think it perfectly fair and most other people probably have their doubts. Whatever the merits of either view, it is a curious and perhaps surprising fact that farmers throughout the world manage to persuade the non-farming majority that redistribution towards the farmers is necessary.

REVIEW QUIZ

1 How do poor harvests and bumper harvests influence farm prices and farm revenues?
2 Explain how inventories and speculation influence farm prices and farm revenues.
3 What are the main actions that farm marketing boards take and how do these actions influence farm prices and farm revenues?

◆ You now know how to use the demand and supply model to predict prices, to study government actions in markets, and to study the sources and costs of inefficiency. Before you leave this topic, take a look at *Reading Between the Lines* on pp. 142–143 and see how the market for air travel has been affected by the new airport security tax.

Who Pays the Airport Security Tax?

THE GLOBE AND MAIL, AUGUST 2, 2002

Impact of air security tax known

The federal government knew its $24 security surcharge could seriously impair passenger traffic before it started collecting the fee on April 1, according to a document obtained by *The Globe and Mail.*

The report, which was prepared for the Department of Finance by investment bank N.M. Rothschild & Sons, reviewed prior studies into price elasticity of air fares and determined there was a potential for a drop in traffic on the short-haul, low-cost market.

"Taken alone, the elasticities imply that a change in the price of air travel of 1 per cent, would result, on average, in an approximately 0.7-percent to 2.1-per-cent decline in the demand for air travel services," said the Feb. 19 report, which was released under the Access to Information Act.

However, the report suggests that enhanced security, made possible through the security surcharge, could counteract the drop in traffic by making people feel safer about flying.

Montreal-based Air Canada and Calgary-based WestJet Airlines Ltd. have both complained that the surcharge—$12 on a one-way fare or $24 round-trip—has affected passenger traffic on short-haul routes. ...

WestJet's load factor on Calgary-Edmonton flights fell to 60.5 per cent from 76.2 last year. ... WestJet is selling tickets for fall travel from Calgary to Edmonton for $52.50. Taxes and surcharges bring the total price of the ticket to $89.08. That means the security surcharge, and related GST, raise the total price by 17 per cent.

According to the assumptions in the Rothschild report, that would translate into an anticipated drop in traffic of between 12 per cent and 35 per cent, aside from any increase in traffic as a result of safer skies. ...

Reprinted with permission from *The Globe and Mail.*

Essence of the Story

■ Investment bank N.M. Rothschild & Sons has reviewed studies on the price elasticity of demand for air travel for the Department of Finance.

■ Estimates of these elasticities range between 0.7 and 2.1.

■ The report says that enhanced security made possible through the security surcharge might increase the demand for air travel.

■ Airlines complain that the surcharge—$12 on a one-way fare or $24 round-trip—has a big effect on short-haul routes.

■ WestJet says that on Calgary–Edmonton flights it is carrying 60.5 percent of its capacity, down from 76.2 percent of capacity the previous year.

■ WestJet's base fare for fall travel from Calgary to Edmonton is $52.50, but taxes and surcharges raise the price to $89.08 —17 percent above the base—which means a decrease in traffic between 12 percent and 35 percent, other things remaining the same.

Economic Analysis

■ Who pays the airport security tax depends on the elasticities of demand for and supply of air transportation.

■ The elasticity of demand for air travel as reported in the news article is estimated to be between 0.7 and 2.1.

■ Notice that in reporting the range of elasticity estimates, the news article misuses the term "demand." The elasticity of demand tells us how the *quantity demanded* changes when the price changes for a *given demand*. It does not tell us how demand changes!

■ The range of estimates reported in the article is large and implies that demand might be inelastic (0.7) or elastic (2.1).

■ The news article does *not* report estimates of the elasticity of supply of air transportation. But the article says that the price will rise by the amount of the tax—the buyer pays the entire tax. So it implicitly assumes that the elasticity of supply is infinite—perfectly elastic.

■ Figure 1 shows the possible results of the airport security tax if the elasticity of supply is indeed infinite. The numbers are approximately based on WestJet's Calgary–Edmonton route.

■ If the elasticity of demand is 0.7, the demand curve is D_0. If the elasticity of demand is 2.1, the demand curve is D_1. The elasticity of supply is assumed to be infinite, so the supply curve is S.

■ With no tax, the fare is $60 a trip and 1,400 passengers a day travel the route.

■ The tax shifts the supply curve to $S + tax$—a position $12 above the original supply curve.

■ The price rises by the full $12 of the tax and the quantity decreases to 1,230 if demand is inelastic or to 950 if demand is elastic.

■ Figure 2 shows the importance of knowing the elasticity of supply. It shows the outcome if supply is unit elastic.

■ Again, with no tax, the fare is $60 a trip and 1,400 passengers a day travel the route.

■ The tax shifts the supply curve to $S + tax$—a position $12 above the original supply curve.

■ Now the price rises by between $4 and $7 depending on whether demand is elastic or inelastic.

■ The effects of the tax on the price and quantity of air travel depend crucially on the elasticity of supply as well as the elasticity of demand.

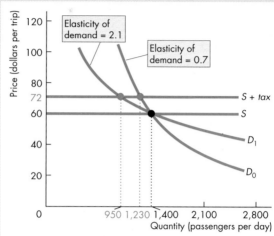

Figure 1 Supply perfectly elastic

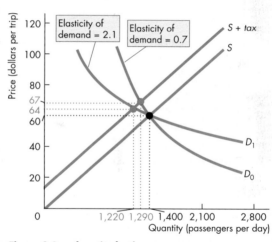

Figure 2 Supply unit elastic

You're The Voter

■ Would you vote for an airport security tax? Why or why not?

■ Do you think the airport security tax should be a percentage of the fare rather than a fixed number of dollars? Why or why not?

143

SUMMARY

KEY POINTS

Housing Markets and Rent Ceilings (pp. 124–127)

- A decrease in the supply of housing raises rents.
- Higher rents stimulate building, and in the long run, the quantity of housing increases and rents fall.
- A rent ceiling that is set below the equilibrium rent creates a housing shortage, wasteful search, and a black market.

The Labour Market and the Minimum Wage (pp. 128–130)

- A decrease in the demand for low-skilled labour lowers the wage rate and reduces employment.
- The lower wage rate encourages low-skilled people to acquire more skills, which decreases the supply of low-skilled labour and, in the long run, raises their wage rate.
- A minimum wage set above the equilibrium wage rate creates unemployment and increases the amount of time people spend searching for a job.
- A minimum wage hits low-skilled young people hardest.

Taxes (pp. 131–134)

- A sales tax raises price but usually by less than the tax.
- The shares of a tax paid by the buyer and by the seller depend on the elasticity of demand and the elasticity of supply.
- The less elastic the demand and the more elastic the supply, the greater is the price increase, the smaller is the quantity decrease, and the larger is the share of the tax paid by the buyer.
- If demand is perfectly elastic or supply is perfectly inelastic, the seller pays the entire tax. And if demand is perfectly inelastic or supply is perfectly elastic, the buyer pays the entire tax.

Markets for Illegal Goods (pp. 135–136)

- Penalties on sellers of an illegal good increase the cost of selling the good and decrease its supply. Penalties on buyers decrease their willingness to pay and decrease the demand for the good.
- The higher the penalties and the more effective the law enforcement, the smaller is the quantity bought.
- A tax that is set at a sufficiently high rate will decrease the quantity of drug consumed, but there will be a tendency for the tax to be evaded.

Stabilizing Farm Revenues (pp. 137–141)

- Farm revenues fluctuate because supply fluctuates.
- The demand for most farm products is inelastic, so a decrease in supply increases the price and increases farm revenues, while an increase in supply decreases price and decreases farm revenues.
- Inventory holders and farm marketing boards act to stabilize farm prices and revenues.

KEY FIGURES

Figure 6.2   A Rent Ceiling, 126
Figure 6.3   The Inefficiency of a Rent Ceiling, 127
Figure 6.5   Minimum Wage and Unemployment, 129
Figure 6.6   A Sales Tax, 131
Figure 6.9   Taxes and Efficiency, 134
Figure 6.10   A Market for an Illegal Good, 135
Figure 6.11   Harvests, Farm Prices, and Farm Revenue, 137

KEY TERMS

Black market, 126
Farm marketing board, 139
Minimum wage, 129
Price ceiling, 125
Price floor, 129
Rent ceiling, 125
Quota, 140
Search activity, 126
Subsidy, 140

PROBLEMS

*1. The figure shows the demand for and supply of rental housing in the Village.

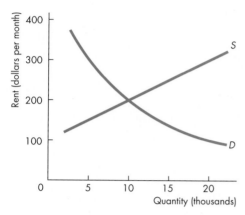

a. What are the equilibrium rent and equilibrium quantity of rental housing?

If a rent ceiling is set at $150 a month, what is
b. The quantity of housing rented?
c. The shortage of housing?
d. The maximum price that someone is willing to pay for the last unit of housing available?

2. The figure shows the demand for and supply of rental housing in Townsville.

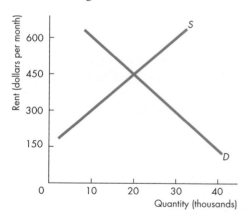

a. What are the equilibrium rent and equilibrium quantity of rental housing?

If a rent ceiling is set at $300 a month, what is
b. The quantity of housing rented?
c. The shortage of housing?
d. The maximum price that someone is willing to pay for the last unit available?

*3. The table gives the demand for and supply of teenage labour.

Wage rate (dollars per hour)	Quantity demanded	Quantity supplied
	(hours per month)	
2	3,000	1,000
3	2,500	1,500
4	2,000	2,000
5	1,500	2,500
6	1,000	3,000

a. What are the equilibrium wage rate and level of employment?
b. What is the quantity of unemployment?
c. If a minimum wage of $3 an hour is set for teenagers, how many hours do they work?
d. With a minimum wage of $3 an hour, how many hours are unemployed?
e. If a minimum wage is set at $5 an hour for teenagers, what are quantities of employment and unemployment?
f. If a minimum wage is set at $5 an hour and demand increases by 500 hours a month, what is the wage rate paid to teenagers and how many hours of their labour are unemployed?

4. The table gives the demand for and supply of labour of high school graduates.

Wage rate (dollars per hour)	Quantity demanded	Quantity supplied
	(hours per month)	
6	10,000	4,000
7	8,000	6,000
8	6,000	8,000
9	4,000	10,000
10	2,000	12,000

a. On a graph, mark in the equilibrium wage rate and level of employment.
b. What is the level of unemployment?
c. If a minimum wage is set at $7 an hour, how many hours do high school graduates work?
d. If a minimum wage is set at $7 an hour, how many hours of labour are unemployed?
e. If a minimum wage is set at $8 an hour, what are employment and unemployment?
f. If the minimum wage is $8 an hour and demand decreases by 2,000 hours a month, what are the wage rate and employment?

*5. The table gives the demand and supply schedules for chocolate brownies.

Price (cents per brownie)	Quantity demanded	Quantity supplied
	(millions per day)	
50	5	3
60	4	4
70	3	5
80	2	6
90	1	7

a. If brownies are not taxed, what is the price of a brownie and how many are consumed?

b. If brownies are taxed at 20¢ each, what is the price and how many brownies are consumed? Who pays the tax?

6. The demand and supply schedules for roses are

Price (dollars per bunch)	Quantity demanded	Quantity supplied
	(bunches per week)	
10	100	40
12	90	60
14	80	80
16	70	100
18	60	120

a. If there is no tax on roses, what is the price and how many bunches are bought?

b. If a tax of $6 a bunch is introduced, what is the price and how many bunches are bought? Who pays the tax?

*7. The demand and supply schedules for rice are

Price (dollars per box)	Quantity demanded	Quantity supplied
	(boxes per week)	
1.20	3,000	500
1.30	2,750	1,500
1.40	2,500	2,500
1.50	2,250	3,500
1.60	2,000	4,500

A storm destroys part of the crop and decreases supply by 500 boxes a week.

a. What do inventory holders do?

b. What is the price and what is farm revenue?

8. In problem 7, instead of a storm, good weather increases supply by 250 boxes a week.

a. What do inventory holders do?

b. What is the price and what is farm revenue?

CRITICAL THINKING

1. Study *Reading Between the Lines* on the airport security tax on pp. 142–143 and answer the following questions:

a. The airport security tax is a fixed number of dollars per trip. Is this arrangement the best one or would a tax calculated as a percentage of the ticket price work better?

b. Why do the airlines complain about the airport security tax?

c. How might the airport security tax increase the demand for air travel?

d. Do you think the airlines will absorb the tax into their costs and keep ticket prices unchanged? If this outcome did occur, what would it imply about the elasticity of supply of air travel?

e. Suppose that instead of introducing the airport security tax, the government had put a surcharge on airline fuel to cover the cost of increased security. How would such a tax have affected the price and quantity of air travel? Would it change the distribution of the tax between the traveller and the airlines?

WEB EXERCISES

1. Use the links on the Parkin–Bade Web site to obtain information about cigarette tax rates, tax revenues, purchases, population, and income. Then answer the following questions about the relationship between the number of packs of cigarettes purchased and the price of a pack across Canada.

a. How would you describe the relationship?

b. What does the relationship tell you about the demand for cigarettes?

c. What does the relationship tell you about the amount of cigarette smuggling?

2. Use the links on the Parkin–Bade Web site to obtain information about farm marketing boards in Canada. What are their effects on the quantities of farm products, their prices, and economic efficiency?

The Amazing Market

The four chapters that you've just studied explain how markets work. The market is an amazing instrument. It enables people who have never met and who know nothing about each other to interact and do business. It also enables us to allocate our scarce resources to the uses that we value most highly. Markets can be very simple or highly organized. ◆ A simple market is one that the American historian Daniel J. Boorstin describes in *The Discoverers* (p. 161). In the late fourteenth century,

The Muslim caravans that went southward from Morocco across the Atlas Mountains arrived after twenty days at the shores of the Senegal River. There the Moroccan traders laid out separate piles of salt, of beads from Ceutan coral, and cheap manufactured goods. Then they retreated out of sight. The local tribesmen, who lived in the strip mines where they dug their gold, came to the shore and put a heap of gold beside each pile of Moroccan goods. Then they, in turn, went out of view, leaving the Moroccan traders either to take the gold offered for a particular pile or to reduce the pile of their merchandise to suit the offered price in gold. Once again the Moroccan traders withdrew, and the process went on. By this system of commercial etiquette, the Moroccans collected their gold.

An organized market is the Toronto Stock Exchange, which trades many millions of stocks each day. Another is an auction at which a government sells rights to broadcasters and cellular telephone companies for the use of the airwaves. ◆ All of these markets determine the prices at which exchanges take place and enable both buyers and sellers to benefit. ◆ Everything and anything that can be exchanged is traded in markets. There are markets for goods and services; for resources such as labour, capital, and raw materials; for dollars, pounds, and yen; for goods to be delivered now and for goods to be delivered in the future. Only the imagination places limits on what can be traded in markets. ◆ You began your study of markets in Chapter 3 by learning about the laws of demand and supply. There, you discovered the forces that make prices adjust to coordinate buying plans and selling plans. In Chapter 4, you learned how to calculate and use the concept of elasticity to predict the responsiveness of prices and quantities to changes in supply and demand. In Chapter 5, you studied efficiency and discovered the conditions under which a competitive market sends resources to uses in which they are valued most highly. And finally, in Chapter 6, you studied markets in action. There, you learned how markets cope with change and discovered how they operate when governments intervene to fix prices, impose taxes, or make some goods illegal. ◆ The laws of demand and supply that you've learned and used in these four chapters were discovered during the nineteenth century by some remarkable economists. We conclude our study of demand and supply and markets by looking at the lives and times of some of these economists and by talking to one of today's most influential economists who studies and creates sophisticated auction markets.

147

Discovering the Laws of Demand and Supply

THE ECONOMIST

"The forces to be dealt with are ... so numerous, that it is best to take a few at a time .... Thus we begin by isolating the primary relations of supply, demand, and price."

ALFRED
MARSHALL,
*The Principles
of Economics*

ALFRED MARSHALL *(1842–1924) grew up in an England that was being transformed by the railroad and by the expansion of manufacturing. Mary Paley was one of Marshall's students at Cambridge, and when Alfred and Mary married, in 1877, celibacy rules barred Alfred from continuing to teach at Cambridge. By 1884, with more liberal rules, the Marshalls returned to Cambridge, where Alfred became Professor of Political Economy.*

Many others had a hand in refining the theory of demand and supply, but the first thorough and complete statement of the theory as we know it today was set by Alfred Marshall, with the acknowledged help of Mary Paley Marshall. Published in 1890, this monumental treatise, The Principles of Economics, *became the textbook on economics on both sides of the Atlantic for almost half a century. Marshall was an outstanding mathematician, but he kept mathematics and even diagrams in the background. His supply and demand diagram appears only in a footnote.*

THE ISSUES

The laws of demand and supply that you studied in Chapter 3 were discovered during the 1830s by Antoine-Augustin Cournot (1801–1877), a professor of mathematics at the University of Lyon, France. Although Cournot was the first to use demand and supply, it was the development and expansion of the railroads during the 1850s that gave the newly emerging theory its first practical applications. Railroads then were at the cutting edge of technology just as airlines are today. And as in the airline industry today, competition among the railroads was fierce.

Dionysius Lardner (1793–1859), an Irish professor of philosophy at the University of London, used demand and supply to show railroad companies how they could increase their profits by cutting rates on long-distance business on which competition was fiercest and by raising rates on short-haul business on which they had less to fear from other transportation suppliers. Today, economists use the principles that Lardner worked out during the 1850s to calculate the freight rates and passenger fares that will give airlines the largest possible profit. And the rates calculated have a lot in common with the railroad rates of the nineteenth century. On local routes on which there is little competition, fares per kilometre are highest, and on long-distance routes on which the airlines compete fiercely, fares per kilometre are lowest.

Known satirically among scientists of the day as "Dionysius Diddler," Lardner worked on an amazing range of problems from astronomy to railway engineering to economics. A colourful character, he would have been a regular guest if late-night talk shows had been around in the 1850s. Lardner visited the École des Ponts et Chaussées (School of Bridges and Roads) in Paris and must have learned a great deal from Jules Dupuit.

In France, Jules Dupuit (1804–1866), a French engineer/economist, used demand to calculate the benefits from building a bridge and, once the bridge was built, for calculating the toll to charge for its use. His work was the forerunner of what is today called *cost-benefit analysis*. Working with the principles invented by Dupuit, economists today calculate the costs and benefits of highways and airports, dams, and power stations.

Now

Today, using the same principles that Dupuit devised, economists calculate whether the benefits of expanding airports and air-traffic control facilities are sufficient to cover their costs. Airline companies use the principles developed by Lardner to set their prices and to decide when to offer "seat sales." Like the railroads before them, the airlines charge a high price per kilometre on short flights, for which they face little competition, and a low price per kilometre on long flights, for which competition is fierce.

THEN

Dupuit used the law of demand to determine whether a bridge or canal would be valued enough by its users to justify the cost of building it. Lardner first worked out the relationship between the cost of production and supply and used demand and supply theory to explain the costs, prices, and profits of railroad operations. He also used the theory to discover ways of increasing revenue by raising rates on short-haul business and lowering them on long-distance freight.

Markets do an amazing job. And the laws of demand and supply help us to understand how markets work. But in some situations, a market must be designed and institutions must be created to enable the market to operate. In recent years, economists have begun to use their tools to design and create markets. And one of the chief architects of new-style markets is John McMillan, whom you can meet on the following pages.

149

TALKING WITH

JOHN MCMILLAN *holds the Jonathan B. Lovelace Chair and teaches international management and economics in the Graduate School of Business at Stanford University. Born in Christchurch, New Zealand in 1951, he was an undergraduate at the University of Canterbury, where he studied first mathematics and then economics. For graduate school, he went to the University of New South Wales. John McMillan's research focuses on the way markets work. He wants to dig more deeply than demand and supply and explain how prices get determined, how markets are organized, why some use auctions and some don't, and why different types of auctions get used in different situations. His work has found practical application in the design of mechanisms for selling rights to the electromagnetic spectrum—the air waves that carry your cell-phone messages. His recent book,* Reinventing the Bazaar: A Natural History of Markets *(New York, W.W. Norton, 2002), provides a fascinating account of the rich diversity of market arrangements that have been used through the ages.*

Michael Parkin and Robin Bade talked with John McMillan about his career and the

John McMillan

progress that economists have made in understanding markets since the pioneering work of Alfred Marshall.

Professor McMillan, how does Alfred Marshall's assessment of how competitive markets work look today in the light of the progress that economists have made?

Supply and demand is still our basic tool of analysis, but modern microeconomics has dug deeper than Marshall was able to. The supply-demand diagram tells us what prices can do, but it sidesteps the question of where prices come from.

The main insight underlying much of modern microeconomics (and discussed in my book *Reinventing the Bazaar*) is that transaction costs can impede the smooth functioning of markets. Transaction costs include the time and money spent locating trading partners, assessing their reliability, negotiating an agreement, and monitoring performance.

Information is a major source of transaction costs. Often information is unevenly distributed: the seller knows more about the quality of the item for sale than the potential buyer; the buyer knows her willingness to pay but the seller doesn't. Informational asymmetries such as these can mean that transactions that would be mutually beneficial might fail to be realized.

The tools for analyzing the details of deal-making are game theory (as developed by John Nash, the hero of the motion picture *A Beautiful Mind*), and information economics (which was recognized by the Nobel committee in its 2001 economics award to George Akerlof, Michael Spence, and Joseph Stiglitz).

Marshall's economics is like physics without friction. For some questions, the assumption of a frictionless world is a useful short cut: for analyzing, say, the effects of rent controls or minimum-wage laws. For other questions, we need to examine the frictions explicitly. For example, to understand why financial markets are organized as they are we need to bring information asymmetries and transaction costs into the picture.

> *"The main insight underlying much of modern microeconomics... is that transaction costs can impede the smooth functioning of markets."*

The focus on the costs of transacting has brought a recognition that markets can't operate in thin air. A market is a social construction. To operate well, with transaction costs minimized, any market needs rules and procedures. Some of these rules, perhaps most of them, arise from the bottom up; that is, they evolve through the everyday trial and error of the market participants. Others are set from the top down: government-set laws and regulations can help foster efficient transacting.

Are there any contemporary or recent examples that illustrate the way markets get created, and that perhaps hold some lessons about what works and what doesn't?

Yes. An experiment in the creation of markets is offered to us by the ex-communist countries. In the early 1990s, a common view among those advising Russia, for example, was that the overriding objective was to get the government out. Russia's approach to reform was to abolish all the mechanisms that had run the planned economy and to start with a clean slate. Once the prohibitions on market activity were abolished, the reformers believed, the private sector would quickly take over. Later, in light of Russia's grim performance in the 1990s, this simple view was supplanted by recognition that building a market economy is exceedingly hard. Success requires a complex package of microeconomic reform, macroeconomic stability, and institution-building. Markets don't operate well in an institutional vacuum.

China provides a telling contrast to Russia. China's reforms consisted of leaving the old institutions of the planned economy in place and letting markets grow up around the plan. China boomed during reform; its spectacular economic growth lifted millions out of dire poverty. This growth resulted from the emergence and expansion of the scope of markets and the gradual erosion of the formerly planned economy.

Markets developed in China, paradoxically, in the absence of any laws of contract and of any formal recognition of property rights. In place of the usual market-economy institutions, the pre-existing mechanisms of the planned economy served as a transitional substitute. Highly imperfect as these institutions were, they were enough to support the rapid development of markets. The lesson from the Russia-China comparison is that, for markets to work well, some institutions are better than none.

What is the most remarkable market that you've encountered?

In the Dutch village of Aalsmeer, just outside Amsterdam, operates a flower market of almost unbelievable size and complexity. Its warehouses, full of flowers, cover an area the size of 125 soccer fields. Each morning, 2,000 or so buyers bid around US$5 million for the flowers. The flowers are flown in from far away, from places like Israel, Colombia, and Zimbabwe, and are later dispatched to buyers around the globe.

Sophisticated technology is needed to operate a global market in as perishable an item as cut flowers. The flower auctions are run via a giant clock at the front of the bidding hall, which winds down to successively lower prices. The bidders can stop the clock by pushing a button, meaning they have bought the flowers at the price shown on the clock. Computers then automatically organize the flowers' delivery to the buyer's address.

The auction that you've just described, appropriately called a Dutch auction, starts at a high price and goes down until someone accepts the price. It contrasts with a so-called English

auction, where the price starts low and rises until only one buyer is left. Which works best?

The Dutch auction is used at Aalsmeer because of its speed: a huge volume of flowers must be sold in a few hours. Both buyers and sellers value the speed of the Dutch auction. In other circumstances, the English auction works better from the seller's point of view, but not necessarily from the buyer's point of view.

Consider a situation where there is significant uncertainty about the value of the item for sale. The items has the same value whichever bidder ends up owning it, but at the time of bidding each of the bidders has a different estimate of the value. (This describes, for example, bidding for the right to drill for oil on a tract of land, and each of the bidders has an imperfect estimate of the amount of oil there.) In this situation, there is a risk of what is called the "winner's curse." The bidder who wins is the one with the highest value estimate, which might well be an overestimate. Winning thus conveys bad news: it tells the winner that everyone else believed the item was worth less than the winner believed.

Bidders who understand the winner's curse tend to bid cautiously. But they tend to bid less cautiously—that is, higher—in an English auction than in a Dutch auction. This is because they can see and react to each other's bids. The bids, as they ascend, convey some information about how highly the others value the item, mitigating the winner's curse and thereby usually inducing a higher price. The higher bids induced by the English auction than the other forms of auction are probably the reason that the English auction is the most commonly used auction form around the world.

What is special about selling airwaves that enables expensive economic consultants like you to show governments how to do it?

The spectrum auctions were unusually complex. Thousands of licences were offered. The sale procedure had to recognize complementarities among the licences: that is, the value to a bidder of a licence covering, say, New Jersey, was probably higher if that bidder was going to end up owning a New York licence as well (because the firm could spread its marketing costs across the wider region and in other ways offer more efficient service). None of the tried-and-true

auction forms allowed the bidding process to encompass such complementarities. As Vice President Al Gore said at the opening ceremony of one of the auctions, "They couldn't just go look it up in a book."

The auction form that we economists recommend and the government adopted was what came to be known as the "simultaneous ascending auction." Multiple licences were offered for sale at the same time. The ascending bids allowed the bidders to avoid the winner's curse, and the simultaneous bidding on multiple licences allowed the bidders to express their demands for packages of complementary licences. The new auction form has raised many billions of dollars.

What does the Internet mean for markets today? Is it creating gains from trade that were previously unattainable?

It certainly has. By lowering transaction costs—especially the cost of search—to close to zero, it has created global markets in goods that before, because of their lower value, previously had only a local sale. Before the Internet, if you wanted some obscure object, you had to hunt in antique shops, flea markets, and so on. Now you simply use your Internet search engine. Buyers and sellers can quickly and easily contact each other where before it would have been prohibitively expensive. The result is better matches of buyer and seller—and larger gains from trade.

You began your university life studying math. Why did you switch to economics?

I was intrigued that mathematics could be used to help understand how the world works. Of course, as I was to learn, any good piece of economic analysis contains much more than just mathematics, but the mathematics lends the study rigour and precision.

What other subjects work well with economics?

Almost any subject. Mathematics is essential; you can't get to the frontiers of economics research without it. But that's not the only discipline of relevance. Economics uses ideas from fields like biology (for example, natural selection), history (the origins of institutions), sociology (networks and social capital), and philosophy (what is meant by fairness).

UTILITY AND DEMAND

Water, Water, Everywhere

We need water to live. We don't need diamonds for much besides decoration. If the benefits of water far outweigh the benefits of diamonds, why does water cost practically nothing while diamonds are expensive? ◆ When a winter storm cuts off the power supply, the prices of alternative sources of heat and light, such as firewood and candles, rise dramatically. But people buy as much firewood and as many candles as they can get their hands on. Our demand for goods that provide heat and light is price inelastic. Why? ◆ When the personal computer (PC) was introduced in 1980, it cost more than $5,000 and consumers didn't buy very many. Since then, the price has tumbled and people are buying PCs in enormous quantities. Our demand for PCs is price elastic. What makes the demand for some things price elastic, while the demand for others is price inelastic? ◆ When you buy a monthly transit pass, each additional ride you take is free. What limits the quantity bought when something is "free"?

◈ In the preceding four chapters, we saw that demand has an important effect on the price of a good. But we did not analyze what exactly shapes a person's demand. This chapter examines household behaviour and its influence on demand. It explains why demand for some goods is elastic and the demand for other goods is inelastic. It also explains why the prices of some things, such as diamonds and water, are so out of proportion to their total benefits. And in *Reading Between the Lines* at the end of the chapter, we look at demand when you can buy a monthly pass so the price of an additional unit is zero.

After studying this chapter, you will be able to

- **Describe preferences using the concept of utility and distinguish between total utility and marginal utility**

- **Explain the marginal utility theory of consumer choice**

- **Use marginal utility theory to predict the effects of changing prices and incomes**

- **Explain the paradox of value**

Household Consumption Choices

A HOUSEHOLD'S CONSUMPTION CHOICES ARE determined by many factors, but we can summarize all of these factors in terms of two concepts:

■ Consumption possibilities
■ Preferences

Consumption Possibilities

A household's consumption choices are constrained by the household's income and by the prices of the goods and services it buys. The household has a given amount of income to spend and cannot influence the prices of the goods and services it buys.

A household's *budget line* describes the limits to its consumption choices. Let's consider Lisa's household. Lisa has an income of $30 a month, and she plans to buy only two goods: movies and pop. The price of a movie is $6; the price of pop is $3 a six-pack. If Lisa spends all her income, she will reach the limits to her consumption of movies and pop.

Figure 7.1 illustrates Lisa's possible consumption of movies and pop. Rows *A* through *F* in the table show six possible ways of allocating $30 to these two goods. For example, Lisa can see 2 movies for $12 and buy 6 six-packs of pop for $18 (row *C*). Points *A* through *F* in the figure illustrate the possibilities presented in the table. The line passing through these points is Lisa's budget line.

Lisa's budget line is a constraint on her choices. It marks the boundary between what she can afford and what she cannot afford. She can afford all the points on the line and inside it. She cannot afford the points outside the line. Lisa's consumption possibilities depend on the price of a movie, the price of pop, and her income. Her consumption possibilities change when the price of a movie, the price of a six-pack of pop, or her income changes.

Preferences

How does Lisa divide her $30 between these two goods? The answer depends on her likes and dislikes—her *preferences*. Economists use the concept of utility to describe preferences. The benefit or satisfaction that a person gets from the consumption of a good or service is called **utility**. Let's now see how we can use the concept of utility to describe preferences.

FIGURE 7.1   Consumption Possibilities

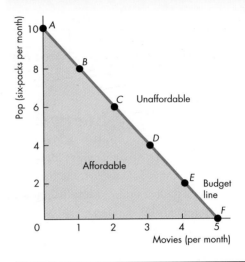

Possibility	Movies		Pop	
	Quantity	Expenditure (dollars)	Six-packs	Expenditure (dollars)
A	0	0	10	30
B	1	6	8	24
C	2	12	6	18
D	3	18	4	12
E	4	24	2	6
F	5	30	0	0

Rows *A* through *F* in the table show six possible ways in which Lisa can allocate $30 to movies and pop. For example, Lisa can buy 2 movies and 6 six-packs of pop (row *C*). The combination in each row costs $30. These possibilities are points *A* through *F* in the figure. The line through those points, the budget line, is a boundary between what Lisa can afford and what she cannot afford. Her choices must lie along the line *AF* or inside the orange area.

Total Utility

Total utility is the total benefit that a person gets from the consumption of goods and services. Total utility depends on the level of consumption—more consumption generally gives more total utility. The units of utility are arbitrary. Suppose we tell Lisa that we want to measure her utility. We're going to call the utility from no consumption zero. And we are going

TABLE 7.1	Lisa's Total Utility from Movies and Pop		
Movies		**Pop**	
Quantity per month	Total utility	Six-packs per month	Total utility
0	0	0	0
1	50	1	75
2	88	2	117
3	121	3	153
4	150	4	181
5	175	5	206
6	196	6	225
7	214	7	243
8	229	8	260
9	241	9	276
10	250	10	291
11	256	11	305
12	259	12	318
13	261	13	330
14	262	14	341

to call the utility she gets from 1 movie a month 50 units. We then ask her to tell us, on the same scale, how much she would like 2, 3, and more movies up to 14 a month. We also ask her to tell us, on the same scale, how much she would like 1 six-pack of pop a month, 2 six-packs, and more up to 14 six-packs a month. Table 7.1 shows Lisa's answers.

Marginal Utility

Marginal utility is the change in total utility that results from a one-unit increase in the quantity of a good consumed. When the number of six-packs Lisa buys increases from 4 to 5 a month, her total utility from pop increases from 181 units to 206 units. Thus for Lisa, the marginal utility of consuming a fifth six-pack each month is 25 units. The table in Fig. 7.2 shows Lisa's marginal utility from pop. Notice that marginal utility appears midway between the quantities of pop. It does so because it is the change in consumption from 4 to 5 six-packs that produces the marginal utility of 25 units. The table displays calculations of marginal utility for each number of six-

packs that Lisa buys from 1 to 5.

Figure 7.2(a) illustrates the total utility that Lisa gets from pop. The more pop Lisa drinks in a month, the more total utility she gets. Figure 7.2(b) illustrates her marginal utility. This graph tells us that as Lisa drinks more pop, the marginal utility that she gets from pop decreases. For example, her marginal utility decreases from 75 units for the first six-pack to 42 units for the second six-pack and to 36 units for the third. We call this decrease in marginal utility as the quantity of the good consumed increases the principle of **diminishing marginal utility.**

Marginal utility is positive but diminishes as consumption of a good increases. Why does marginal utility have these two features? In Lisa's case, she likes pop, and the more she drinks the better. That's why marginal utility is positive. The benefit that Lisa gets from the last six-pack consumed is its marginal utility. To see why marginal utility diminishes, think about the following two situations: In one, you've just been studying all through the day and evening and you've been too busy finishing an assignment to go shopping. A friend drops by with a six-pack of pop. The utility you get from that pop is the marginal utility from one six-pack. In the second situation, you've been on a pop binge. You've been working on an assignment all day but you've guzzled three six-packs while doing so. You are up to your eyeballs in pop. You are happy enough to have one more can. But the thrill that you get from it is not very large. It is the marginal utility of the nineteenth can in a day.

Temperature: An Analogy

Utility is similar to temperature. Both are abstract concepts, and both have units of measurement that are arbitrary. You know when you feel hot, and you know when you feel cold. But you can't *observe* temperature. You can observe water turning to steam if it is hot enough or turning to ice if it is cold enough. And you can construct an instrument—a thermometer—that can help you to predict when such changes will occur. We call the scale on the thermometer temperature, and we call the units of temperature degrees. But these degree units are arbitrary. For example, we can accurately predict that when a Celsius thermometer shows a temperature of 0, water will turn to ice. This same event occurs when a Fahrenheit thermometer shows a temperature of 32. So the units of measurement of temperature don't matter.

The concept of utility helps us make predictions

FIGURE 7.2   Total Utility and Marginal Utility

Quantity	Total utility	Marginal utility
0	0	
		75
1	75	
		42
2	117	
		36
3	153	
		28
4	181	
		25
5	206	

(a) Total utility

(b) Marginal utility

The table shows that as Lisa drinks more pop, her total utility from pop increases. The table also shows her marginal utility—the change in total utility resulting from the last six-pack she consumes. Marginal utility declines as consumption increases. The figure graphs Lisa's total utility and marginal utility from pop. Part (a) shows her total utility. It

also shows as a bar the extra total utility she gains from each additional six-pack—her marginal utility. Part (b) shows how Lisa's marginal utility from pop diminishes by placing the bars shown in part (a) side by side as a series of declining steps.

about consumption choices in much the same way that the concept of temperature helps us make predictions about physical phenomena.

Admittedly, marginal utility theory does not enable us to predict how buying plans change with the same precision that a thermometer enables us to predict when water will turn to ice or steam. But the theory provides important insights into buying plans and has some powerful implications, as you are about to discover. It helps us to understand why people buy more of a good or service when its price falls, why people buy more of most goods when their incomes increase, and it resolves the paradox of value.

REVIEW QUIZ

1. Explain how a consumer's income and the prices of goods limit consumption possibilities.
2. What is utility and how do we use the concept of utility to describe a consumer's preferences?
3. What is the distinction between total utility and marginal utility?
4. What is the key assumption about marginal utility?

Maximizing Utility

A HOUSEHOLD'S INCOME AND THE PRICES THAT the household faces limit its consumption choices, and the household's preferences determine the utility that it can obtain from each consumption possibility. The key assumption of marginal utility theory is that the household chooses the consumption possibility that maximizes its total utility. This assumption of utility maximization is a way of expressing the fundamental economic problem: scarcity. People's wants exceed the resources available to satisfy those wants, so they must make hard choices. In making choices, they try to get the maximum attainable benefit—they try to maximize total utility.

Let's see how Lisa allocates $30 a month between movies and pop to maximize her total utility. We'll continue to assume that the price of a movie is $6 each and the price of pop is $3 a six-pack.

The Utility-Maximizing Choice

The most direct way of calculating how Lisa spends her income to maximize her total utility is by making a table like Table 7.2. The rows of this table show the affordable combinations of movies and pop that lie along Lisa's budget line in Fig. 7.1. The table records three things: first, the number of movies seen and the total utility derived from them (the left side of the table); second, the number of six-packs consumed and the total utility derived from them (the right side of the table); and third, the total utility derived from both movies and pop (the centre column).

The first row of Table 7.2 records the situation when Lisa watches no movies and buys 10 six-packs. In this case, Lisa gets no utility from movies and 291 units of total utility from pop. Her total utility from movies and pop (the centre column) is 291 units. The rest of the table is constructed in the same way.

The consumption of movies and pop that maximizes Lisa's total utility is highlighted in the table. When Lisa sees 2 movies and buys 6 six-packs of pop, she gets 313 units of total utility. This is the best Lisa can do, given that she has only $30 to spend and given the prices of movies and pop. If she buys 8 six-packs of pop, she can see only 1 movie. She gets 310 units of total utility, 3 less than the maximum attainable. If she sees 3 movies, she can drink only 4 six-packs. She gets 302 units of total utility, 11 less than the maximum attainable.

TABLE 7.2 Lisa's Utility-Maximizing Combinations

	Movies		Total utility from movies and pop	Pop	
	Quantity per month	Total utility		Total utility	Six-packs per month
A	0	0	291	291	10
B	1	50	310	260	8
C	2	88	313	225	6
D	3	121	302	181	4
E	4	150	267	117	2
F	5	175	175	0	0

We've just described Lisa's consumer equilibrium. A **consumer equilibrium** is a situation in which a consumer has allocated all his or her available income in the way that, given the prices of goods and services, maximizes his or her total utility. Lisa's consumer equilibrium is 2 movies and 6 six-packs.

In finding Lisa's consumer equilibrium, we measured her *total* utility from movies and pop. But there is a better way of determining a consumer equilibrium, which uses the idea you first met in Chapter 1 that choices are made at the margin. Let's look at this alternative.

Equalizing Marginal Utility per Dollar Spent

A consumer's total utility is maximized by following the rule:

Spend all the available income and equalize the marginal utility per dollar spent on all goods.

The **marginal utility per dollar spent** is the marginal utility from a good divided by its price. For example, Lisa's marginal utility from seeing 1 movie a month, MU_M, is 50 units of utility. The price of a movie, P_M, is $6, which means that the marginal utility per dollar spent on 1 movie a month, MU_M/P_M, is 50 units divided by $6, or 8.33 units of utility per dollar.

You can see why following this rule maximizes total utility by thinking about a situation in which Lisa has spent all her income but the marginal utilities per dollar spent are not equal. Suppose that Lisa's marginal utility per dollar spent on pop, MU_P/P_P, exceeds that on movies. By spending a dollar more on pop and a dollar less on movies, her total utility from pop rises and her total utility from movies falls. But her utility gain from pop exceeds her utility loss from movies, so her total utility increases. Because she's consuming more pop, her marginal utility from pop has fallen. And because she sees fewer movies, her marginal utility from movies has risen. Lisa keeps increasing her consumption of pop and decreasing her consumption of movies until the two marginal utilities per dollar spent are equal, or when

$$\frac{MU_M}{P_M} = \frac{MU_P}{P_P}.$$

Table 7.3 calculates Lisa's marginal utility per dollar spent on each good. Each row exhausts Lisa's income of $30. In row B, Lisa's marginal utility from movies is 50 units (use Table 7.1 to calculate the marginal utilities). Because the price of a movie is $6, Lisa's marginal utility per dollar spent on movies is 50 units divided by $6, which is 8.33. Marginal utility per dollar spent on each good, like marginal utility, decreases as more of the good is consumed.

Lisa maximizes her total utility when the marginal utility per dollar spent on movies is equal to the marginal utility per dollar spent on pop—possibility C. Lisa consumes 2 movies and 6 six-packs.

Figure 7.3 shows why the rule "equalize marginal utility per dollar spent on all goods" works. Suppose

that instead of consuming 2 movies and 6 six-packs (possibility C), Lisa consumes 1 movie and 8 six-packs (possibility B). She then gets 8.33 units of utility per dollar spent on movies and 5.67 units per dollar spent on pop. Lisa can increase her total utility by buying less pop and seeing more movies. If she sees one additional movie and spends less on pop, her total utility from movies increases by 8.33 units per dollar and her total utility from pop decreases by 5.67 units per dollar. Her total utility increases by 2.66 units per dollar, as shown by the blue area.

Or suppose that Lisa consumes 3 movies and 4 six-packs (possibility D). In this situation, her mar-

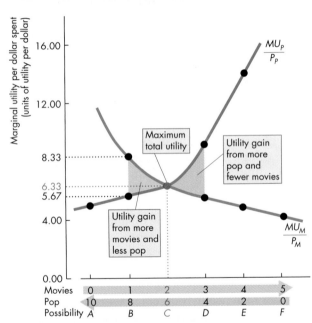

FIGURE 7.3   Equalizing Marginal Utilities per Dollar Spent

If Lisa consumes 1 movie and 8 six-packs (possibility B), she gets 8.33 units of utility from the last dollar spent on movies and 5.67 units of utility from the last dollar spent on pop. She can get more total utility by seeing one more movie and drinking less pop. If she consumes 4 six-packs and sees 3 movies (possibility D), she gets 5.50 units of utility from the last dollar spent on movies and 9.33 units of utility from the last dollar spent on pop. She can increase her total utility by seeing one fewer movie and drinking more pop. When Lisa's marginal utilities per dollar spent on both goods are equal, her total utility is maximized.

TABLE 7.3   Equalizing Marginal Utilities per Dollar Spent

	Movies ($6 each)			Pop ($3 per six-pack)		
	Quantity	Marginal utility	Marginal utility per dollar spent	Six-packs	Marginal utility	Marginal utility per dollar spent
A	0	0		10	15	5.00
B	1	50	8.33	8	17	5.67
C	2	38	6.33	6	19	6.33
D	3	33	5.50	4	28	9.33
E	4	29	4.83	2	42	14.00
F	5	25	4.17	0	0	

ginal utility per dollar spent on movies (5.50) is less than her marginal utility per dollar spent on pop (9.33). Lisa can now increase her total utility by seeing one fewer movie and spending more on pop, as the green area shows.

The Power of Marginal Analysis The method we've just used to find Lisa's utility-maximizing choice of movies and pop is an example of the power of marginal analysis. By comparing the marginal gain from having more of one good with the marginal loss from having less of another good, Lisa is able to ensure that she gets the maximum attainable utility.

The rule to follow is simple: If the marginal utility per dollar spent on movies exceeds the marginal utility per dollar spent on pop, see more movies and buy less pop; if the marginal utility per dollar spent on pop exceeds the marginal utility per dollar spent on movies, buy more pop and see fewer movies.

More generally, if the marginal gain from an action exceeds the marginal loss, take the action. You will meet this principle time and again in your study of economics. And you will find yourself using it when you make your own economic choices, especially when you must make a big decision.

Units of Utility In maximizing total utility by making the marginal utilities per dollar spent equal for both goods, the units in which utility is measured do not matter. Any arbitrary units will work. It is in this respect that utility is like temperature. Predictions about the freezing point of water don't depend on the temperature scale; and predictions about a household's consumption choices don't depend on the units of utility.

REVIEW QUIZ

1 What is Lisa's goal when she chooses the quantities of movies and pop to consume?
2 What two conditions are met if a consumer is maximizing utility?
3 Explain why equalizing the marginal utilities of both goods does *not* maximize utility.
4 Explain why equalizing the marginal utilities per dollar spent on both goods *does* maximize utility.

Predictions of Marginal Utility Theory

WE'RE NOW GOING TO USE MARGINAL UTILITY theory to make some predictions. In Chapter 3, we assumed that a fall in the price of a good, other things remaining the same, brings an increase in the quantity demanded of that good—the law of demand. We also assumed that a fall in the price of a substitute decreases demand and a rise in income increases demand for a normal good. We're now going to see that these assumptions are predictions of marginal utility theory.

A Fall in the Price of a Movie

A fall in the price of a movie, other things remaining the same, changes the quantity of movies demanded and brings a movement along the demand curve for movies. We've already found one point on Lisa's demand curve for movies: When the price of a movie is $6, Lisa sees 2 movies a month. Figure 7.4 shows this point on Lisa's demand curve for movies.

To find another point on her demand curve for movies, we need to work out what Lisa buys when the price of a movie changes. Suppose that the price of a movie falls from $6 to $3 and nothing else changes.

To work out the effect of this change in price of a movie on Lisa's buying plans, we must first determine the combinations of movies and pop that she can afford at the new prices. Then we calculate the new marginal utilities per dollar spent. Finally, we determine the combination that makes the marginal utilities per dollar spent on movies and pop equal.

The rows of Table 7.4 show the combinations of movies and pop that exhaust Lisa's $30 of income when the price of a movie is $3 and the price of a six-pack is $3. Lisa's preferences do not change when prices change, so her marginal utility schedule remains the same as that in Table 7.3. Divide her marginal utility from movies by $3 to get the marginal utility per dollar spent on movies.

Lisa now sees 5 movies and drinks 5 six-packs. She *substitutes* movies for pop. Figure 7.4 shows both of these effects. In part (a), we've found another point on Lisa's demand curve for movies. And we've discovered that her demand curve obeys the law of demand. In part (b), we see that a fall in the price of a movie decreases the demand for pop. The demand curve for pop shifts leftward. For Lisa, pop and movies are substitutes.

TABLE 7.4   How a Change in the Price of a Movie Affects Lisa's Choices

	Movies ($3 each)		Pop ($3 per six-pack)	
Quantity	Marginal utility per dollar spent	Six-packs	Marginal utility per dollar spent	
0		10	5.00	
1	16.67	9	5.33	
2	12.67	8	5.67	
3	11.00	7	6.00	
4	9.67	6	6.33	
5	8.33	5	8.33	
6	7.00	4	9.33	
7	6.00	3	12.00	
8	5.00	2	14.00	
9	4.00	1	25.00	
10	3.00	0		

FIGURE 7.4   A Fall in the Price of a Movie

(a) Demand for movies

(b) Demand for pop

When the price of a movie falls and the price of pop remains the same, the quantity of movies demanded by Lisa increases, and in part (a), Lisa moves along her demand curve for movies. Also when the price of a movie falls, Lisa's demand for pop decreases, and in part (b), her demand curve for pop shifts leftward.

A Rise in the Price of Pop

In Fig. 7.4(b), we know only one point on Lisa's demand curve for pop when the price of a movie is $3. To find Lisa's demand curve for pop, we must see how Lisa responds to a change in the price of pop. Suppose that the price of pop rises from $3 to $6 a six-pack. The rows of Table 7.5 show the combinations of movies and pop that exhaust Lisa's $30 of income when the price of a movie is $3 and the price of a six-pack is $6. Again, Lisa's preferences don't change when the price changes. Divide Lisa's marginal utility from pop by $6 to get her marginal utility per dollar spent on pop.

Lisa now drinks 2 six-packs a month and sees 6 movies a month. Lisa *substitutes* movies for pop. Figure 7.5 shows both of these effects. In part (a), we've found another point on Lisa's demand curve for pop. And we've confirmed that this demand curve obeys the law of demand. In part (b), we see that Lisa increases the number of movies that she sees when the price of pop rises and the price of a movie

remains constant. The demand curve for movies shifts rightward. For Lisa, movies and pop are substitutes.

TABLE 7.5	How a Change in the Price of Pop Affects Lisa's Choices			
Movies ($3 each)			**Pop** ($6 per six-pack)	
Quantity	Marginal utility per dollar spent		Six-packs	Marginal utility per dollar spent
0			5	4.17
2	12.67		4	4.67
4	9.67		3	6.00
6	7.00		2	7.00
8	5.00		1	12.50
10	3.00		0	

Marginal utility theory predicts these two results:

- When the price of a good rises, the quantity demanded of that good decreases.
- If the price of one good rises, the demand for another good that can serve as a substitute increases.

These predictions of marginal utility theory sound familiar because they correspond to the assumptions that we made about demand in Chapter 3. There, we assumed that the demand curve for a good slopes downward and that a rise in the price of a substitute increases demand.

We have now seen that marginal utility theory predicts how the quantities of goods and services that people demand respond to price changes. The theory enables us to derive the consumer's demand curve and predict how the demand curve for one good shifts when the price of another good changes.

Marginal utility theory also helps us to predict how demand changes when income changes. Let's study the effects of a change in income on demand.

FIGURE 7.5   A Rise in the Price of Pop

(a) Demand for pop

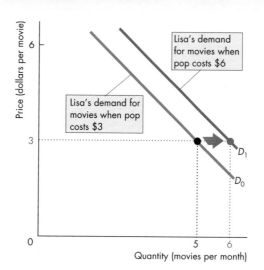

(b) Demand for movies

When the price of pop rises and the price of a movie remains the same, the quantity of pop demanded by Lisa decreases, and in part (a), Lisa moves along her demand curve for pop. Also when the price of pop rises, Lisa's demand for movies increases, and in part (b), her demand curve for movies shifts rightward.

A Rise in Income

Let's suppose that Lisa's income increases to $42 a month, and that the price of a movie is $3 and the price of a six-pack is $3. We saw in Table 7.4 that with these prices and with an income of $30 a month, Lisa sees 5 movies and drinks 5 six-packs a month. We want to compare this choice of movies and pop with Lisa's choice when her income is $42. Table 7.6 shows the calculations needed to make the comparison. With $42, Lisa can see 14 movies a month and buy no pop, or buy 14 six-packs a month and see no movies, or choose any combination of the two goods in the rows of the table. We calculate the marginal utility per dollar spent in exactly the same way as we did before and find the quantities at which the marginal utility per dollar spent on movies and

the marginal utility per dollar spent on pop are equal. When Lisa's income is $42, the marginal utilities per dollar spent on both goods are equal when she sees 7 movies and drinks 7 six-packs of pop a month.

By comparing this situation with that in Table 7.4, we see that with an additional $12 a month, Lisa buys 2 more six-packs and sees 2 more movies a month. Lisa's response arises from her preferences, as described by her marginal utilities. Different preferences would produce different quantitative responses. With a larger income, the consumer always buys more of a *normal* good and less of an *inferior* good. For Lisa, pop and movies are normal goods. When her income increases, Lisa buys more of both goods.

You have now completed your study of the marginal utility theory of a household's consumption choices. Table 7.7 summarizes the key assumptions, implications, and predictions of the theory.

TABLE 7.6   Lisa's Choices with an Income of $42 a Month

Movies ($3 each)		Pop ($3 per six-pack)	
Quantity	Marginal utility per dollar spent	Six-packs	Marginal utility per dollar spent
0		14	3.67
1	16.67	13	4.00
2	12.67	12	4.33
3	11.00	11	4.67
4	9.67	10	5.00
5	8.33	9	5.33
6	7.00	8	5.67
7	6.00	7	6.00
8	5.00	6	6.33
9	4.00	5	8.33
10	3.00	4	9.33
11	2.00	3	12.00
12	1.00	2	14.00
13	0.67	1	25.00
14	0.33	0	

TABLE 7.7   Marginal Utility Theory

Assumptions

- A consumer derives utility from the goods consumed.
- Each additional unit of consumption yields additional total utility—marginal utility is positive.
- As the quantity of a good consumed increases, marginal utility decreases.
- A consumer's aim is to maximize total utility.

Implication

- Total utility is maximized when all the available income is spent and when the marginal utility per dollar spent is equal for all goods.

Predictions

- Other things remaining the same, the higher the price of a good, the smaller is the quantity demanded (the law of demand).
- The higher the price of a good, the greater is the quantity bought of substitutes for that good.
- The larger the consumer's income, the greater is the quantity demanded of normal goods.

Individual Demand and Market Demand

Marginal utility theory explains how an individual household spends its income and enables us to derive an individual household's demand curve. In the earlier chapters, we've used *market* demand curves. We can derive a market demand curve from individual demand curves. Let's see how.

The relationship between the total quantity demanded of a good and its price is called **market demand.** The market demand curve is what you studied in Chapter 3. The relationship between the quantity demanded of a good by a single individual and its price is called *individual demand.*

Figure 7.6 illustrates the relationship between individual demand and market demand. In this example, Lisa and Chuck are the only people. The market demand is the total demand of Lisa and Chuck. At $3 a movie, Lisa demands 5 movies a month and Chuck demands 2, so the total quantity demanded by the market is 7 movies a month. Lisa's demand curve for movies in part (a) and Chuck's in part (b) sum *horizontally* to give the market demand curve in part (c).

The market demand curve is the horizontal sum of the individual demand curves and is formed by adding the quantities demanded by each individual at each price.

Because marginal utility theory predicts that individual demand curves slope downward, it also predicts that market demand curves slope downward.

FIGURE 7.6   Individual and Market Demand Curves

(a) Lisa's demand   (b) Chuck's demand   (c) Market demand

Price	Quantity of movies demanded		
(dollars per movie)	Lisa	Chuck	Market
7	1	0	1
6	2	0	2
5	3	0	3
4	4	1	5
3	5	2	7
2	6	3	9

The table and figure illustrate how the quantity of movies demanded varies as the price of a movie varies. In the table, the market demand is the sum of the individual demands. For example, at a price of $3 a movie, Lisa demands 5 movies and Chuck demands 2 movies, so the total quantity demanded in the market is 7 movies. In the figure, the market demand curve is the horizontal sum of the individual demand curves. Thus when the price is $3 a movie, the market demand curve shows that the quantity demanded is 7 movies, the sum of the quantities demanded by Lisa and Chuck.

Marginal Utility and Elasticity

At the beginning of this chapter, we asked why the demand for some things is price elastic while the demand for others is price inelastic. The main answer in Chapter 4 (p. 89) is that a good with close substitutes has an elastic demand and a good with poor substitutes has an inelastic demand. This answer is correct. But you can now provide a deeper answer based on marginal utility theory.

You know that for any pair of goods, X and Y, the consumer maximizes utility when

$$\frac{MU_X}{P_X} = \frac{MU_Y}{P_Y}.$$

If the price of X falls, the consumer will buy more of X to drive the marginal utility of X, MU_X, down. If MU_X diminishes only slightly as the quantity of X consumed increases, then a large increase in the quantity of X restores consumer equilibrium and the demand for X is elastic. If the MU_X diminishes steeply as the quantity of X consumed increases, then a small increase in the quantity of X restores consumer equilibrium and the demand for X is inelastic.

If X has close substitutes, the marginal utility of X diminishes slightly as its quantity consumed increases. If X has poor substitutes, its marginal utility diminishes steeply as its quantity consumed increases.

REVIEW QUIZ

1 When the price of a good falls and the prices of other goods and a consumer's income remain the same, what happens to the consumption of the good whose price has fallen and to the consumption of other goods?
2 Elaborate on your answer to the previous question by using demand curves. For which good does demand change, and for which good does quantity demanded change?
3 If a consumer's income increases and if all goods are normal goods, how does the quantity bought of each good change?

We're going to end this chapter by returning to a recurring theme throughout your study of economics: the concept of efficiency and the distinction between price and value.

Efficiency, Price, and Value

MARGINAL UTILITY THEORY HELPS US TO DEEPEN our understanding of the concept of efficiency and also helps us to see more clearly the distinction between value and price. Let's find out how.

Consumer Efficiency and Consumer Surplus

When Lisa allocates her limited budget to maximize utility, she is using her resources efficiently. Any other allocation of her budget wastes some resources.

But when Lisa has allocated her limited budget to maximize utility, she is *on* her demand curve for each good. A demand curve is a description of the quantity demanded at each price when utility is maximized. When we studied efficiency in Chapter 5, we learned that value equals marginal benefit and that a demand curve is also a willingness-to-pay curve. It tells us a consumer's *marginal benefit*—the benefit from consuming an additional unit of a good. You can now give the idea of marginal benefit a deeper meaning:

Marginal benefit is the maximum price a consumer is willing to pay for an extra unit of a good or service when utility is maximized.

The Paradox of Value

For centuries, philosophers have been puzzled by a paradox that we raised at the start of this chapter. Water, which is essential to life itself, costs little, but diamonds, which are useless in comparison to water, are expensive. Why? Adam Smith tried to solve this paradox. But not until the theory of marginal utility had been developed could anyone give a satisfactory answer.

You can solve this puzzle by distinguishing between *total* utility and *marginal* utility. The total utility that we get from water is enormous. But remember, the more we consume of something, the smaller is its marginal utility. We use so much water that its marginal utility—the benefit we get from one more glass of water—diminishes to a small value. Diamonds, on the other hand, have a small total utility relative to water, but because we buy few diamonds, they have a high marginal utility. When a household has maximized its total utility, it has allocated its budget in the way that makes the marginal

FIGURE 7.7   The Paradox of Value

(a) Water

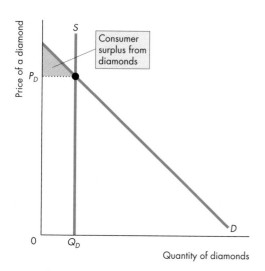

(b) Diamonds

Part (a) shows the demand for water, D, and the supply of water, S. The supply is assumed to be perfectly elastic at the price P_W. At this price, the quantity of water consumed is Q_W and the consumer surplus from water is the large green triangle. Part (b) shows the demand for diamonds, D, and the supply of diamonds, S. The supply is assumed to be perfectly inelastic at the quantity Q_D. At this quantity, the price of diamonds is P_D and the consumer surplus from diamonds is the small green triangle. Water is valuable—it has a large consumer surplus—but cheap. Diamonds are less valuable than water—they have a smaller consumer surplus—but are expensive.

utilities per dollar spent equal for all goods. That is, the marginal utility from a good divided by the price of the good is equal for all goods. This equality of marginal utilities per dollar spent holds true for diamonds and water: Diamonds have a high price and a high marginal utility. Water has a low price and a low marginal utility. When the high marginal utility of diamonds is divided by the high price of diamonds, the result is a number that equals the low marginal utility of water divided by the low price of water. The marginal utility per dollar spent is the same for diamonds as for water.

Another way to think about the paradox of value uses *consumer surplus*. Figure 7.7 explains the paradox of value by using this idea. The supply of water (part a) is perfectly elastic at price P_W, so the quantity of water consumed is Q_W and the consumer surplus from water is the large green area. The supply of diamonds (part b) is perfectly inelastic at price Q_D, so the price of diamonds is P_D and the consumer surplus from diamonds is the small green area. Water is cheap but brings a large consumer surplus, while diamonds are expensive but bring a small consumer surplus.

REVIEW QUIZ

1 Can you explain why, along a demand curve, a consumer's choices are efficient?
2 Can you explain the paradox of value?
3 Does water or do diamonds have the greater marginal utility? Does water or do diamonds have the greater total utility? Does water or do diamonds have the greater consumer surplus?

◆ You have now completed your study of the marginal utility theory. And you've seen how the theory can be used to explain our real-world consumption choices. You can see the theory in action once again in *Reading Between the Lines* on pp. 166–167, where it is used to interpret how commuters in Winnipeg will use the new network of water buses along the Assiniboine and Red Rivers.

The next chapter presents an alternative theory of household behaviour. To help you see the connection between the two theories of consumer behaviour, we'll continue with the same example. We'll meet Lisa again and discover another way of understanding how she gets the most out of her $30 a month.

What's the Marginal Utility of a Boat Ride?

WINNIPEG FREE PRESS, July 25, 2001

New network of transit boats invite all aboard

With the city skyline behind him, Mayor Glen Murray rode to work yesterday morning, one of the first passengers in the city's new water transit boat.

"This is a fast, hassle-free and affordable way to travel that avoids traffic congestion," Murray said as the system's inaugural ride was filmed and photographed by the media.

The water bus shuttle links six public docks along the Assiniboine and Red Rivers.

Murray boarded the shuttle near his home, a new dock at the foot of Hugo Street, off Wellington Crescent. A 14–minute ride took Murray to the newly constructed dock in Stephen Juba Park at the end of Bannatyne Avenue, where he then walked to city hall.

The new service links the east Exchange area with the Corydon Avenue strip from the Hugo Street dock, with stops in between at The Forks, Tache, the Midtown bridge, and docks at the Legislature and the Osborne Street bridge.

…

For a $2 fee, riders can travel from dock to dock. Passengers are not given life jackets but they will be offered to children. Monthly commuter passes for rush-hour service costs $100. Day passes are $7; $6 for seniors and youths.

The shuttle will operate seven days a week; weekday service has rush-hour departures at eight-minute intervals from 7–9:30 a.m. and 4–6 p.m., with regular 15-minute departures until 11 p.m. On weekends, the service will have departures at 15-minute intervals from 10 a.m.–11 p.m.

The 12-passenger boats travel fully loaded at a maximum speed of about 40 kilometres per hour.

…

Essence of the Story

■ A water bus shuttle links six public docks along the Assiniboine and Red Rivers in Winnipeg.

■ The price of a one-way trip is $2. The price of a one-day pass is $7 ($6 for seniors and youths). The price of a one-month rush-hour pass is $100.

■ The shuttle operates seven days a week. On weekdays boats depart at 15-minute intervals and at eight-minute intervals during rush hours.

■ A boat carries 12 passengers at a maximum speed of 40 kilometres per hour.

Economic Analysis

■ The people who live in the region served by the Winnipeg water bus shuttle choose the method of transportation and number of trips that maximize utility.

■ The price of each trip is $2 (no special passes), so each person takes the number of trips that makes the marginal utility per dollar spent on boat trips equal to the marginal utility per dollar spent on other goods.

■ The table illustrates a person's choice if the amount available is $160, the price of a boat ride is $2, and the price of a unit of other goods is $10.

■ The person maximizes utility in this example by taking 20 boat trips and consuming 12 units of other goods.

■ But a Winnipeg commuter must make a more complicated choice because the boat company offers special passes. We'll consider just the $100 monthly pass.

■ Figure 1 shows the consumption possibilities that face the commuter. The commuter can pay $2 a trip or $100 for a month of "free" trips.

■ You can see that the person who takes fewer than 50 trips a month

can buy more other goods by paying $2 a trip. The person who takes more than 50 trips a month can buy more other goods by paying $100 for the trips.

■ To decide whether to buy a monthly commuter pass for $100 or pay $2 per trip, the commuter must make two calculations, each similar to the one you've just seen, but with a twist.

■ If the utility-maximizing number of trips at $2 a trip turns out to be greater than 50 a month, the choice is easy: buy a commuter pass and save some money that can be spent on other goods.

■ If the utility-maximizing number of trips at $2 a trip turns out to be less than 50 a month, the commuter needs to reason as follows.

■ If I buy a commuter pass for $100, I can take any number of trips I choose and the cost of one marginal trip is zero. So I will take a trip if its marginal utility is positive.

■ The total utility that I get from these trips is the marginal utility from a commuter pass—it is the change in total utility that results from the decision to buy the pass.

■ So I will buy a commuter pass when the change in total utility that results from the decision to buy the pass divided by $100 is greater than or equal to the marginal utility per dollar spent on other goods.

■ In this case, I will take boat rides until the marginal utility of a ride is zero.

Winnipeg Traveller's Choices at $2 a Trip

	Boat trips ($2 each)			Other goods ($10 each)		
	Quantity	Marginal utility	Marginal utility per dollar spent	Quantity	Marginal utility	Marginal utility per dollar spent
A	0			16	10	1.00
B	10	10	5.00	14	20	2.00
C	20	8	4.00	12	40	4.00
D	30	6	3.00	10	60	6.00
E	40	4	2.00	8	80	8.00
F	50	3	1.50	6	100	10.00
G	60	2	1.00	4	120	12.00
H	70	1	0.50	2	140	14.00
I	80	0	0	0		

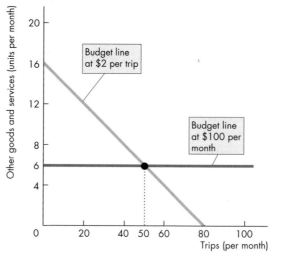

Figure 1 Budget lines for boat trips and other goods

167

SUMMARY

KEY POINTS

Household Consumption Choices (pp. 154–156)

- A household's choices are determined by its consumption possibilities and preferences.
- A household's consumption possibilities are constrained by its income and by the prices of goods and services. Some combinations of goods and services are affordable, and some are not affordable.
- A household's preferences can be described by marginal utility.
- The key assumption of marginal utility theory is that the marginal utility of a good or service decreases as consumption of the good or service increases.
- Marginal utility theory assumes that people buy the affordable combination of goods and services that maximizes their total utility.

Maximizing Utility (pp. 157–159)

- Total utility is maximized when all the available income is spent and when the marginal utilities per dollar spent on all goods are equal.
- If the marginal utility per dollar spent on good A exceeds that on good B, total utility increases if the quantity purchased of good A increases and the quantity purchased of good B decreases.

Predictions of Marginal Utility Theory (pp. 159–164)

- Marginal utility theory predicts the law of demand. That is, other things remaining the same, the higher the price of a good, the smaller is the quantity demanded of that good.
- Marginal utility theory also predicts that, other things remaining the same, the larger the consumer's income, the larger is the quantity demanded of a normal good.
- The market demand curve is found by summing horizontally all the individual demand curves.

Efficiency, Price, and Value (pp. 164–165)

- When a consumer maximizes utility, he or she is using resources efficiently.
- Marginal utility theory resolves the paradox of value.
- When we talk loosely about value, we are thinking of *total* utility or consumer surplus. But price is related to *marginal* utility.
- Water, which we consume in large amounts, has a high total utility and a large consumer surplus, but the price of water is low and the marginal utility from water is low.
- Diamonds, which we consume in small amounts, have a low total utility and a small consumer surplus, but the price of a diamond is high and the marginal utility from diamonds is high.

KEY FIGURES AND TABLE

Figure 7.1   Consumption Possibilities, 154
Figure 7.2   Total Utility and Marginal Utility, 156
Figure 7.3   Equalizing Marginal Utilities per Dollar Spent, 158
Figure 7.4   A Fall in the Price of a Movie, 160
Figure 7.5   A Rise in the Price of Pop, 161
Figure 7.6   Individual and Market Demand Curves, 163
Figure 7.7   The Paradox of Value, 165
Table 7.7   Marginal Utility Theory, 162

KEY TERMS

Consumer equilibrium, 157
Diminishing marginal utility, 155
Marginal utility, 155
Marginal utility per dollar spent, 157
Market demand, 163
Total utility, 154
Utility, 154

PROBLEMS

*1. Jason enjoys rock CDs and spy novels and spends $60 a month on them. The table shows the utility he gets from each good.

Quantity per month	Utility from rock CDs	Utility from spy novels
1	60	20
2	110	38
3	150	53
4	180	64
5	200	70
6	206	75

a. Draw graphs that show Jason's utility from rock CDs and utility from spy novels.
b. Compare the two utility graphs. Can you say anything about Jason's preferences?
c. Draw graphs that show Jason's marginal utility from rock CDs and marginal utility from spy novels.
d. What do the two marginal utility graphs tell you about Jason's preferences?
e. If the price of a rock CD is $10 and the price of a spy novel is $10, how does Jason spend the $60?

2. Martha enjoys classical CDs and travel books and spends $75 a month on them. The table shows the utility she gets from each good.

Quantity per month	Utility from classical CDs	Utility from travel books
1	90	120
2	110	136
3	126	148
4	138	152
5	146	154

a. Draw graphs that show Martha's utility from classical CDs and utility from travel books.
b. Compare the two utility graphs. Can you say anything about Martha's preferences?
c. Draw graphs that show Martha's marginal utility from classical CDs and from travel books.
d. What do the two marginal utility graphs tell you about Martha's preferences?
e. If the price of a classical CD is $15 and the price of a travel book is $15, how does Martha spend the $75 a month?

*3. Max enjoys windsurfing and snorkelling. The table shows the marginal utility he gets from each activity.

Hours per day	Marginal utility from windsurfing	Marginal utility from snorkelling
1	120	40
2	100	36
3	80	30
4	60	22
5	40	12
6	12	10
7	10	8

Max has $35 to spend, and he can spend as much time as he likes on his leisure pursuits. Windsurfing equipment rents for $10 an hour, and snorkelling equipment rents for $5 an hour.

How long does Max spend windsurfing and how long does he spend snorkelling?

4. Pete enjoys rock concerts and the opera. The table shows the marginal utility he gets from each event.

Events per month	Marginal utility from rock concerts	Marginal utility from operas
1	120	200
2	100	160
3	80	120
4	60	80
5	40	40
6	20	0

Pete has $200 a month to spend on these events. The price of a rock concert ticket is $20, and the price of an opera ticket is $40.

How many rock concerts and how many operas does Pete attend?

*5. In problem 3, Max's sister gives him $20 to spend on his leisure pursuits, so he now has a total of $55.
a. Draw a graph that shows Max's consumption possibilities.
b. How many hours does Max choose to windsurf and how many hours does he choose to snorkel now that he has $55 to spend?

6. In problem 4, Pete's uncle gives him $60 to spend on event tickets, so he now has $260.
   a. Draw a graph that shows Pete's budget line.
   b. How many rock concerts and how many operas does Pete now attend?

*7. In problem 5, if the rent on windsurfing equipment decreases to $5 an hour, how many hours does Max now windsurf and how many hours does he snorkel?

8. In Problem 4, if the price of an opera ticket decreases to $20, how many rock concerts and how many operas will Pete attend?

*9. Max, in Problem 3, takes a Club Med vacation, the cost of which includes unlimited sports activities. There is no extra charge for equipment. If Max windsurfs and snorkels for 6 hours a day, how many hours does he windsurf and how many hours does he snorkel?

10. Pete, in Problem 4, wins a prize and has more than enough money to satisfy his desires for rock concerts and operas. He decides to buy a total of 7 tickets each month. How many rock concerts and how many operas does he now attend?

*11. Shirley and Dan are the only two individuals and their demand schedules for popcorn are

| Price (cents per carton) | Quantity demanded by | |
| | Shirley | Dan |
	(cartons per week)	
10	12	6
30	9	5
50	6	4
70	3	3
90	1	2

What is the market demand for popcorn?

12. Lee's and Lou's demand schedules for CDs are

| Price (dollars per CD) | Quantity demanded by | |
| | Lee | Lou |
	(CDs per year)	
6	12	10
8	9	8
10	6	6
12	3	4
14	0	2

If Lee and Lou are the only two individuals, what is the market demand for CDs?

CRITICAL THINKING

1. Study *Reading Between the Lines* on pp. 166–167 on the Winnipeg water transit boats and then answer the following questions:
   a. If the price of a ride is $2 and the price of a day pass is $6, how does a person decide whether to buy the pass or pay for each ride?
   b. List the components of the opportunity cost of a ride other than the cost of the ticket.
   c. What does marginal utility theory predict will happen to the demand for public transit as incomes rise?

2. Smoking is banned on most airline flights. Use marginal utility theory to explain
   a. The effect of the ban on the utility of smokers.
   b. How the ban influences the decisions of smokers.
   c. The effects of the ban on the utility of non-smokers.
   d. How the ban influences the decisions of non-smokers.

WEB EXERCISES

1. Use the links on the Parkin–Bade Web site and read what Henry Schimberg, former CEO of Coca-Cola, said about the market for bottled water. Use marginal utility theory to explain and interpret his remarks.

2. Use the links on the Parkin–Bade Web site and obtain information about the prices on the Toronto Transit system.
   a. Show the effects of the different ticket options on the consumer's budget line.
   b. How would a person decide whether to pay for each trip, to buy a day pass, or to buy a pass for a longer period? Use marginal utility theory to answer this question.
   c. How do you think the number of riders would change if the price of a single trip fell and the price of a day pass increased?

POSSIBILITIES, PREFERENCES, AND CHOICES

CHAPTER 8

Subterranean Movements

Like the continents floating on the earth's mantle, our spending patterns change steadily over time. On such subterranean movements, business empires rise and fall. One of these movements is occurring with the expansion of Internet access. We now can choose whether to buy a book in the normal way—a regular previously printed and bound book—or to buy a print-on-demand book or an e-book. The price of a print-on-demand book is a bit higher than a regular book, but the buyer can customize the cover and make other custom choices. People are increasingly buying print-on-demand books, but they are still a small part of the overall market for books. Will print-on-demand and other technologies expand and eventually displace the traditional book? ◆ Subterranean movements also govern the way we spend our time. The average workweek has fallen steadily from 70 hours a week in the nineteenth century to 35 hours a week today. While the average workweek is now much shorter than it once was, far more people now have jobs. Why has the average workweek declined?

◆ In this chapter, we're going to study a model of choice that predicts the effects of changes in prices and incomes on what people buy and that explains how much work people do. *Reading Between the Lines* explains why we buy print-on-demand books even though they cost a bit more than regular books.

After studying this chapter, you will be able to

- **Describe a household's budget line and show how it changes when a price or income changes**

- **Make a map of preferences by using indifference curves and explain the principle of diminishing marginal rate of substitution**

- **Predict the effects of changes in prices and income on consumption choices**

- **Predict the effects of changes in wage rates on work–leisure choices**

Consumption Possibilities

CONSUMPTION CHOICES ARE LIMITED BY INCOME and by prices. A household has a given amount of income to spend and cannot influence the prices of the goods and services it buys. A household's **budget line** describes the limits to its consumption choices.

Let's look at Lisa's budget line.[1] Lisa has an income of $30 a month to spend. She buys two goods: movies and pop. The price of a movie is $6, and the price of pop is $3 a six-pack. Figure 8.1 shows alternative affordable ways for Lisa to consume movies and pop. Row *A* says that she can buy 10 six-packs of pop and see no movies, a combination of movies and pop that exhausts her monthly income of $30. Row *F* says that Lisa can watch 5 movies and drink no pop—another combination that exhausts the $30 available. Each of the other rows in the table also exhausts Lisa's income. (Check that each of the other rows costs exactly $30.) The numbers in the table define Lisa's consumption possibilities. We can graph Lisa's consumption possibilities as points *A* through *F* in Fig. 8.1.

Divisible and Indivisible Goods Some goods—called divisible goods—can be bought in any quantity desired. Examples are gasoline and electricity. We can best understand household choice if we suppose that all goods and services are divisible. For example, Lisa can consume a half a movie a month on the average by seeing one movie every two months. When we think of goods as being divisible, the consumption possibilities are not just the points *A* through *F* shown in Fig. 8.1, but those points plus all the intermediate points that form the line running from *A* to *F*. Such a line is a budget line.

Lisa's budget line is a constraint on her choices. It marks the boundary between what is affordable and what is unaffordable. She can afford any point on the line and inside it. She cannot afford any point outside the line. The constraint on her consumption depends on prices and her income, and the constraint changes when prices or her income changes. Let's see how by studying the budget equation.

---

[1] If you have studied Chapter 7 on marginal utility theory, you have already met Lisa. This tale of her thirst for pop and zeal for movies will sound familiar to you—up to a point. But in this chapter, we're going to use a different method for representing preferences—one that does not require us to resort to the idea of utility.

FIGURE 8.1   The Budget Line

Income	$30
Movies	$6 each
Pop	$3 a six-pack

Consumption possibility	Movies (per month)	Pop (six-packs per month)
A	0	10
B	1	8
C	2	6
D	3	4
E	4	2
F	5	0

Lisa's budget line shows the boundary between what she can and cannot afford. The rows of the table list Lisa's affordable combinations of movies and pop when her income is $30, the price of pop is $3 a six-pack, and the price of a movie is $6. For example, row A tells us that Lisa exhausts her $30 income when she buys 10 six-packs and sees no movies. The figure graphs Lisa's budget line. Points A through F on the graph represent the rows of the table. For divisible goods, the budget line is the continuous line AF. To calculate the equation for Lisa's budget line, start with expenditure equal to income:

$$\$3Q_P + \$6Q_M = \$30.$$

Divide by $3 to obtain

$$Q_P + 2Q_M = 10.$$

Subtract $2Q_M$ from both sides to obtain

$$Q_P = 10 - 2Q_M.$$

The Budget Equation

We can describe the budget line by using a *budget equation*. The budget equation starts with the fact that

$$\text{Expenditure} = \text{Income.}$$

Expenditure is equal to the sum of the price of each good multiplied by the quantity bought. For Lisa,

Expenditure = (Price of pop × Quantity of pop) + (Price of movie × Quantity of movies).

Call the price of pop P_P, the quantity of pop Q_P, the price of a movie P_M, the quantity of movies Q_M, and income Y. We can now write Lisa's budget equation as

$$P_P Q_P + P_M Q_M = Y.$$

Or, using the prices Lisa faces, $3 for a six-pack and $6 for a movie, and Lisa's income, $30, we get

$$\$3 Q_P + \$6 Q_M = \$30.$$

Lisa can choose any quantities of pop (Q_P) and movies (Q_M) that satisfy this equation. To find the relationship between these quantities, divide both sides of the equation by the price of pop (P_P) to get

$$Q_P + \frac{P_M}{P_P} \times Q_M = \frac{Y}{P_P}.$$

Now subtract the term $P_M/P_P \times Q_M$ from both sides of this equation to get

$$Q_P = \frac{Y}{P_P} - \frac{P_M}{P_P} \times Q_M.$$

For Lisa, income (Y) is $30, the price of a movie (P_M) is $6, and the price of pop (P_P) is $3 a six-pack. So Lisa must choose the quantities of movies and pop to satisfy the equation

$$Q_P = \frac{\$30}{\$3} - \frac{\$6}{\$3} \times Q_M,$$

or

$$Q_P = 10 - 2 Q_M.$$

To interpret the equation, look at the budget line in Fig. 8.1 and check that the equation delivers that budget line. First, set Q_M equal to zero. The budget equation tells us that Q_P, the quantity of pop, is Y/P_P, which is 10 six-packs. This combination of Q_M and Q_P is the one shown in row A of the table in Fig. 8.1. Next set Q_M equal to 5. Q_P now equals zero (row F of the table). Check that you can derive the other rows.

The budget equation contains two variables chosen by the household (Q_M and Q_P) and two variables (Y/P_P and P_M/P_P) that the household takes as given. Let's look more closely at these variables.

Real Income A household's **real income** is the household's income expressed as a quantity of goods the household can afford to buy. Expressed in terms of pop, Lisa's real income is Y/P_P. This quantity is the maximum number of six-packs that she can buy. It is equal to her money income divided by the price of pop. Lisa's income is $30 and the price of pop is $3 a six-pack, so her real income in terms of pop is 10 six-packs, which is shown in Fig. 8.1 as the point at which the budget line intersects the y-axis.

Relative Price A **relative price** is the price of one good divided by the price of another good. In Lisa's budget equation, the variable P_M/P_P is the relative price of a movie in terms of pop. For Lisa, P_M is $6 a movie and P_P is $3 a six-pack, so P_M/P_P is equal to 2 six-packs per movie. That is, to see 1 more movie, Lisa must give up 2 six-packs.

You've just calculated Lisa's opportunity cost of a movie. Recall that the opportunity cost of an action is the best alternative forgone. For Lisa to see 1 more movie a month, she must forgo 2 six-packs. You've also calculated Lisa's opportunity cost of pop. For Lisa to consume 2 more six-packs a month, she must give up seeing 1 movie. So her opportunity cost of 2 six-packs is 1 movie.

The relative price of a movie in terms of pop is the magnitude of the slope of Lisa's budget line. To calculate the slope of the budget line, recall the formula for slope (see the Chapter 1 Appendix): Slope equals the change in the variable measured on the y-axis divided by the change in the variable measured on the x-axis as we move along the line. In Lisa's case (Fig. 8.1), the variable measured on the y-axis is the quantity of pop, and the variable measured on the x-axis is the quantity of movies. Along Lisa's budget line, as pop decreases from 10 to 0 six-packs, movies increase from 0 to 5. So the magnitude of the slope of the budget line is 10 six-packs divided by 5 movies, or 2 six-packs per movie. The magnitude of this slope is exactly the same as the relative price we've just calculated. It is also the opportunity cost of a movie.

A Change in Prices When prices change, so does the budget line. The lower the price of the good measured on the horizontal axis, other things remain

FIGURE 8.2   Changes in Prices and Income

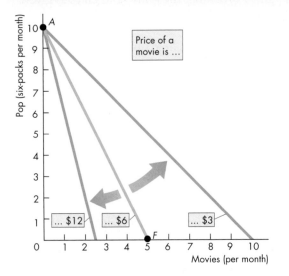

(a) A change in price

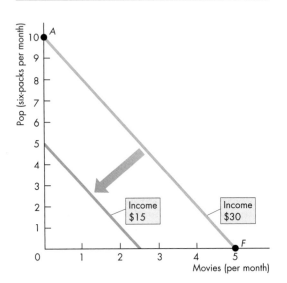

(b) A change in income

In part (a), the price of a movie changes. A fall in the price from $6 to $3 a movie rotates the budget line outward and makes it flatter. A rise in the price from $6 to $12 a movie rotates the budget line inward and makes it steeper.

In part (b), income falls from $30 to $15 while the prices of movies and pop remain constant. The budget line shifts leftward, but its slope does not change.

ing the same, the flatter is the budget line. For example, if the price of a movie falls from $6 to $3, real income in terms of pop does not change but the relative price of a movie falls. The budget line rotates outward and becomes flatter, as Fig. 8.2(a) illustrates. The higher the price of the good measured on the horizontal axis, other things remaining the same, the steeper is the budget line. For example, if the price of a movie rises from $6 to $12, the relative price of a movie increases. The budget line rotates inward and becomes steeper, as Fig. 8.2(a) illustrates.

A Change in Income A change in money income changes real income but does not change relative prices. The budget line shifts, but its slope does not change. The bigger a household's money income, the bigger is real income and the farther to the right is the budget line. The smaller a household's money income, the smaller is real income and the farther to the left is the budget line. Figure 8.2(b) shows the effect of a change in money income on Lisa's budget line. The initial budget line when Lisa's income is $30 is the same one that we began with in Fig. 8.1. The new budget line shows how much Lisa can consume if her income falls to $15 a month. The two budget lines have the same slope because they have the same relative price. The new budget line is closer to the origin than the initial one because Lisa's real income has decreased.

REVIEW QUIZ

1 What does a household's budget line show?
2 How does the relative price and a household's real income influence its budget line?
3 If a household has an income of $40 and buys only bus rides at $4 each and magazines at $2 each, what is the equation of the household's budget line?
4 If the price of one good changes, what happens to the relative price and to the slope of the household's budget line?
5 If a household's money income changes and prices do not change, what happens to the household's real income and budget line?

We've studied the limits to what a household can consume. Let's now learn how we can describe preferences and make a map that contains a lot of information about a household's preferences.

Preferences and Indifference Curves

YOU ARE GOING TO DISCOVER A VERY NEAT IDEA: that of drawing a map of a person's preferences. A preference map is based on the intuitively appealing assumption that people can sort all the possible combinations of goods into three groups: preferred, not preferred, and indifferent. To make this idea more concrete, let's ask Lisa to tell us how she ranks various combinations of movies and pop.

Figure 8.3(a) shows part of Lisa's answer. She tells us that she currently consumes 2 movies and 6 six-packs a month at point *C*. She then lists all the combinations of movies and pop that she says are just as acceptable to her as her current consumption. When we plot these combinations of movies and pop, we get the green curve in Fig. 8.3(a). This curve is the key element in a map of preferences and is called an indifference curve.

An **indifference curve** is a line that shows combinations of goods among which a consumer is *indifferent*. The indifference curve in Fig. 8.3(a) tells us that Lisa is just as happy to consume 2 movies and 6 six-packs a month at point *C* as she is to consume the combination of movies and pop at point *G* or at any other point along the curve.

Lisa also says that she prefers all the combinations of movies and pop above the indifference curve in Fig. 8.3(a)—the yellow area—to those on the indifference curve. And she prefers any combination on the indifference curve to any combination in the grey area below the indifference curve.

The indifference curve in Fig. 8.3(a) is just one of a whole family of such curves. This indifference curve appears again in Fig. 8.3(b) labelled I_1. The curves labelled I_0 and I_2 are two other indifference curves. Lisa prefers any point on indifference curve I_2 to any point on indifference curve I_1, and she prefers any point on I_1 to any point on I_0. We refer to I_2 as being a higher indifference curve than I_1 and I_1 as being higher than I_0.

A preference map is a series of indifference curves that resembles the contour lines on a map. By looking at the shape of the contour lines on a map, we can draw conclusions about the terrain. Similarly, by looking at the shape of indifference curves, we can draw conclusions about a person's preferences.

Let's learn how to "read" a preference map.

FIGURE 8.3 A Preference Map

(a) An indifference curve

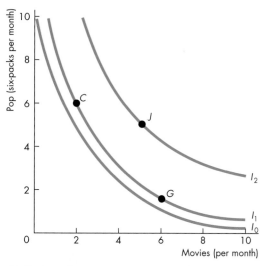

(b) Lisa's preference map

In part (a), Lisa consumes 6 six-packs of pop and 2 movies a month at point *C*. She is indifferent between all the points on the green indifference curve such as *C* and *G*. She prefers any point above the indifference curve (the yellow area) to any point on it, and she prefers any point on the indifference curve to any point below it (the grey area). A preference map is a number of indifference curves. Part (b) shows three indifference curves—I_0, I_1, and I_2—that are part of Lisa's preference map. She prefers point *J* to point *C* or *G*, and so she prefers any point on I_2 to any point on I_1.

Marginal Rate of Substitution

The **marginal rate of substitution** (*MRS*) is the rate at which a person will give up good *y* (the good measured on the *y*-axis) to get an additional unit of good *x* (the good measured on the *x*-axis) and at the same time remain indifferent (remain on the same indifference curve). The magnitude of the slope of an indifference curve measures the marginal rate of substitution.

- If the indifference curve is *steep*, the marginal rate of substitution is *high*. The person is willing to give up a large quantity of good *y* to get an additional unit of good *x* while remaining indifferent.

- If the indifference curve is *flat*, the marginal rate of substitution is *low*. The person is willing to give up a small amount of good *y* to get an additional unit of good *x* while remaining indifferent.

Figure 8.4 shows you how to calculate the marginal rate of substitution. Suppose that Lisa drinks 6 six-packs and sees 2 movies at point *C* on indifference curve *I*₁. To calculate her marginal rate of substitution, we measure the magnitude of the slope of the indifference curve at point *C*. To measure this magnitude, place a straight line against, or tangent to, the indifference curve at point *C*. Along that line, as the quantity of pop decreases by 10 six-packs, the number of movies increases by 5—an average of 2 six-packs per movie. So at point *C*, Lisa is willing to give up pop for movies at the rate of 2 six-packs per movie—a marginal rate of substitution of 2.

Now suppose that Lisa drinks 1.5 six-packs and sees 6 movies at point *G* in Fig. 8.4. Her marginal rate of substitution is now measured by the slope of the indifference curve at point *G*. That slope is the same as the slope of the tangent to the indifference curve at point *G*. Here, as the quantity of pop decreases by 4.5 six-packs, the number of movies increases by 9—an average of 1/2 six-pack per movie. So at point *G*, Lisa is willing to give up pop for movies at the rate of 1/2 six-pack per movie—a marginal rate of substitution of 1/2.

As Lisa sees more movies and drinks less pop, her marginal rate of substitution diminishes. Diminishing marginal rate of substitution is the key assumption of consumer theory. A **diminishing marginal rate of substitution** is a general tendency for a person to be willing to give up less of good *y* to get one more unit of good *x*, and at the same time remain indifferent, as the quantity of *x* increases. In Lisa's case, she is less willing to give up pop to see one more movie, the more movies she sees.

FIGURE 8.4   The Marginal Rate of Substitution

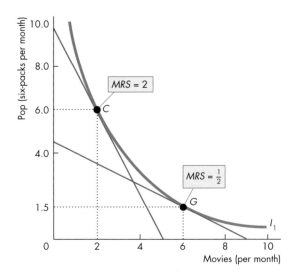

The magnitude of the slope of an indifference curve is called the marginal rate of substitution (*MRS*). The red line at point *C* tells us that Lisa is willing to give up 10 six-packs to see 5 movies. Her marginal rate of substitution at point *C* is 10 divided by 5, which equals 2. The red line at point *G* tells us that Lisa is willing to give up 4.5 six-packs to see 9 movies. Her marginal rate of substitution at point *G* is 4.5 divided by 9, which equals 1/2.

Your Own Diminishing Marginal Rate of Substitution Think about your own diminishing marginal rate of substitution. Imagine that in a week, you drink 10 six-packs of pop and see no movies. Most likely, you are willing to give up a lot of pop so that you can see just 1 movie. But now imagine that in a week, you drink 1 six-pack and see 6 movies. Most likely, you will now not be willing to give up much pop to see a seventh movie. As a general rule, the greater the number of movies you see, the smaller is the quantity of pop you are willing to give up to see one additional movie.

The shape of a person's indifference curves incorporates the principle of the diminishing marginal rate of substitution because the curves are bowed towards the origin. The tightness of the bend of an indifference curve tells us how willing a person is to substitute one good for another while remaining indifferent. Let's look at some examples that make this point clear.

Degree of Substitutability

Most of us would not regard movies and pop as being close substitutes. We probably have some fairly clear ideas about how many movies we want to see each month and how many cans of pop we want to drink. But to some degree, we are willing to substitute between these two goods. No matter how big a pop freak you are, there is surely some increase in the number of movies you can see that will compensate you for being deprived of a can of pop. Similarly, no matter how addicted you are to the movies, surely some number of cans of pop will compensate you for being deprived of seeing one movie. A person's indifference curves for movies and pop might look something like those shown in Fig. 8.5(a).

Close Substitutes   Some goods substitute so easily for each other that most of us do not even notice which we are consuming. The different brands of personal computers are an example. As long as it has an "Intel inside" and runs Windows, most of us don't care whether our PC is a Dell, a Compaq, a Sony, or any of a dozen other brands. The same holds true for

marker pens. Most of us don't care whether we use a marker pen from the campus bookstore or one from the local supermarket. When two goods are perfect substitutes, their indifference curves are straight lines that slope downward, as Fig. 8.5(b) illustrates. The marginal rate of substitution is constant.

Complements   Some goods cannot substitute for each other at all. Instead, they are complements. The complements in Fig. 8.5(c) are left and right running shoes. Indifference curves of perfect complements are L–shaped. One left running shoe and one right running shoe are as good as one left shoe and two right ones. Having two of each is preferred to having one of each, but having two of one and one of the other is no better than having one of each.

The extreme cases of perfect substitutes and perfect complements shown here don't often happen in reality. But they do illustrate that the shape of the indifference curve shows the degree of substitutability between two goods. The more perfectly substitutable the two goods, the more nearly are their indifference curves straight lines and the less quickly does the

---

FIGURE 8.5   The Degree of Substitutability

  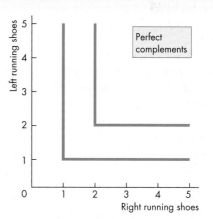

(a) Ordinary goods   **(b) Perfect substitutes**   **(c) Perfect complements**

The shape of the indifference curves reveals the degree of substitutability between two goods. Part (a) shows the indifference curves for two ordinary goods: movies and pop. To drink less pop and remain indifferent, one must see more movies. The number of movies that compensates for a reduction in pop increases as less pop is consumed. Part (b) shows the indifference curves for two perfect substitutes. For the consumer to remain indifferent, one fewer marker pen from the local supermarket must be replaced by one extra marker pen from the campus bookstore. Part (c) shows two perfect complements—goods that cannot be substituted for each other at all. Having two left running shoes with one right running shoe is no better than having one of each. But having two of each is preferred to having one of each.

"With the pork I'd recommend an Alsatian white or a Coke."

marginal rate of substitution diminish. Poor substitutes for each other have tightly curved indifference curves, approaching the shape of those shown in Fig. 8.5(c).

As you can see in the cartoon, according to the waiter's preferences, Coke and Alsatian white wine are perfect substitutes and each is a complement of pork. We hope the customers agree with him.

REVIEW QUIZ

1 What is an indifference curve and how does a preference map show preferences?

2 Why does an indifference curve slope downward and why is it bowed towards the origin?

3 What do we call the magnitude of the slope of an indifference curve?

4 What is the key assumption about a consumer's marginal rate of substitution?

The two components of the model of household choice are now in place: the budget line and the preference map. We will now use these components to work out the household's choice and to predict how choices change when prices and income change.

Predicting Consumer Behaviour

WE ARE NOW GOING TO PREDICT THE QUANTITIES of movies and pop that Lisa chooses to buy. Figure 8.6 shows Lisa's budget line from Fig. 8.1 and her indifference curves from Fig. 8.3(b). We assume that Lisa consumes at her best affordable point, which is 2 movies and 6 six-packs—at point *C*. Here, Lisa

■ Is on her budget line.

■ Is on her highest attainable indifference curve.

■ Has a marginal rate of substitution between movies and pop equal to the relative price.

For every point inside the budget line, such as point *I*, there are points *on* the budget line that Lisa prefers. For example, she prefers all the points on the

FIGURE 8.6   The Best Affordable Point

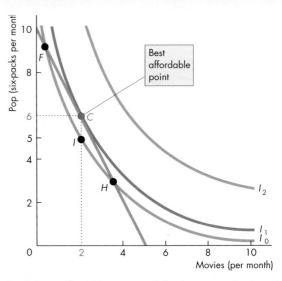

Lisa's best affordable point is *C*. At that point, she is on her budget line and also on the highest attainable indifference curve. At a point such as *H*, Lisa is willing to give up more movies in exchange for pop than she has to. She can move to point *I*, which is just as good as point *H*, and have some unspent income. She can spend that income and move to *C*, a point that she prefers to point *I*.

budget line between *F* and *H* to point *I*. So she chooses a point on the budget line.

Every point on the budget line lies on an indifference curve. For example, point *H* lies on the indifference curve I_0. At point *H*, Lisa's marginal rate of substitution is less than the relative price. Lisa is willing to give up more movies in exchange for pop than the budget line says she must. So she moves along her budget line from *H* towards *C*. As she does so, she passes through a number of indifference curves (not shown in the figure) located between indifference curves I_0 and I_1. All of these indifference curves are higher than I_0, and therefore Lisa prefers any point on them to point *H*. But when Lisa gets to point *C*, she is on the highest attainable indifference curve. If she keeps moving along the budget line, she starts to encounter indifference curves that are lower than I_1. So Lisa chooses point *C*.

At the chosen point, the marginal rate of substitution (the magnitude of the slope of the indifference curve) equals the relative price (the magnitude of the slope of the budget line).

Let's use this model of household choice to predict the effects on consumption of changes in prices and income. We'll begin by studying the effect of a change in price.

A Change in Price

The effect of a change in the price on the quantity of a good consumed is called the **price effect.** We will use Fig. 8.7(a) to work out the price effect of a fall in the price of a movie. We start with the price of a movie at $6, the price of pop at $3 a six-pack, and Lisa's income at $30 a month. In this situation, she drinks 6 six-packs and sees 2 movies a month at point *C*.

Now suppose that the price of a movie falls to $3. With a lower price of a movie, the budget line rotates outward and becomes flatter. (Check back to Fig. 8.2(a) for a refresher on how a price change affects the budget line.) The new budget line is the dark orange one in Fig. 8.7(a).

Lisa's best affordable point is now point *J*, where she sees 5 movies and drinks 5 six-packs of pop. Lisa drinks less pop and watches more movies now that movies are cheaper. She cuts her pop consumption from 6 to 5 six-packs and increases the number of movies she sees from 2 to 5 a month. Lisa substitutes movies for pop when the price of a movie falls and the price of pop and her income remain constant.

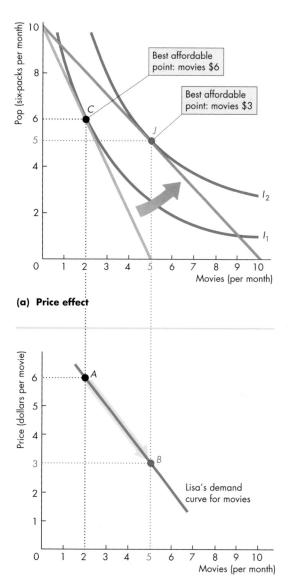

FIGURE 8.7   Price Effect and Demand Curve

(a) Price effect

(b) Demand curve

Initially, Lisa consumes at point *C* (part a). If the price of a movie falls from $6 to $3, Lisa consumes at point *J*. The move from *C* to *J* is the price effect.

At a price of $6 a movie, Lisa sees 2 movies a month—at point *A* in part (b). At a price of $3 a movie, she sees 5 movies a month—at point *B*. Lisa's demand curve traces out her best affordable quantity of movies as the price of a movie varies.

The Demand Curve In Chapter 3, we asserted that the demand curve slopes downward. We can now derive a demand curve from a consumer's budget line and indifference curves. By doing so, we can see that the law of demand and the downward-sloping demand curve are consequences of the consumer's choosing his or her best affordable combination of goods.

To derive Lisa's demand curve for movies, lower the price of a movie and find her best affordable point at different prices. We've just done this for two movie prices in Fig. 8.7(a). Figure 8.7(b) highlights these two prices and two points that lie on Lisa's demand curve for movies. When the price of a movie is $6, Lisa sees 2 movies a month at point *A*. When the price falls to $3, she increases the number of movies she sees to 5 a month at point *B*. The demand curve is made up of these two points plus all the other points that tell us Lisa's best affordable consumption of movies at each movie price, given the price of pop and Lisa's income. As you can see, Lisa's demand curve for movies slopes downward—the lower the price of a movie, the more movies she watches each month. This is the law of demand.

Next, let's see how Lisa changes her consumption of movies and pop when her income changes.

A Change in Income

The effect of a change in income on consumption is called the **income effect.** Let's work out the income effect by examining how consumption changes when income changes and prices remain constant. Figure 8.8(a) shows the income effect when Lisa's income falls. With an income of $30 and with the price of a movie at $3 and the price of pop at $3 a six-pack, she consumes at point *J*—she sees 5 movies and drinks 5 six-packs. If her income falls to $21, she consumes at point *K*—she sees 4 movies and drinks 3 six-packs. When Lisa's income falls, she consumes less of both goods. Movies and pop are normal goods.

The Demand Curve and the Income Effect A change in income leads to a shift in the demand curve, as shown in Fig. 8.8(b). With an income of $30, Lisa's demand curve for movies is D_0, the same as in Fig. 8.7(b). But when her income falls to $21, she plans to see fewer movies at each price, so her demand curve for movies shifts leftward to D_1.

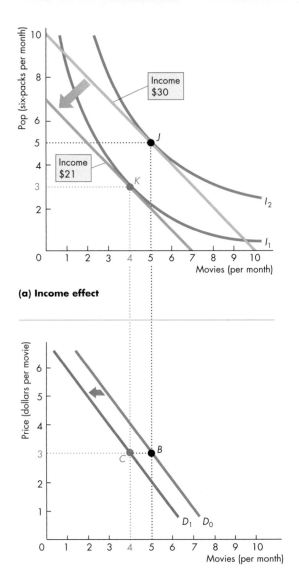

FIGURE 8.8   Income Effect and Change in Demand

(a) Income effect

(b) Demand curve

A change in income shifts the budget line and changes the best affordable point and changes consumption. In part (a), when Lisa's income decreases from $30 to $21, she consumes less of both movies and pop. In part (b), Lisa's demand curve for movies when her income is $30 is D_0. When Lisa's income decreases to $21, her demand curve for movies shifts leftward to D_1. Lisa's demand for movies decreases because she now sees fewer movies at each price.

Substitution Effect and Income Effect

For a normal good, a fall in price *always* increases the quantity bought. We can prove this assertion by dividing the price effect into two parts:

- Substitution effect
- Income effect

Figure 8.9(a) shows the price effect, and Fig. 8.9(b) divides the price effect into its two parts.

Substitution Effect The **substitution effect** is the effect of a change in price on the quantity bought when the consumer (hypothetically) remains indifferent between the original situation and the new one. To work out Lisa's substitution effect, when the price of a movie falls, we cut her income by enough to leave her on the same indifference curve as before.

When the price of a movie falls from $6 to $3, suppose (hypothetically) that we cut Lisa's income to $21. What's special about $21? It is the income that is just enough, at the new price of a movie, to keep Lisa's best affordable point on the same indifference curve as her original consumption point *C*. Lisa's budget line is now the light orange line in Fig. 8.9(b). With the lower price of a movie and a smaller income, Lisa's best affordable point is *K* on indifference curve I_1. The move from *C* to *K* is the substitution effect of the price change. The substitution effect of the fall in the price of a movie is an increase in the consumption of movies from 2 to 4. The direction of the substitution effect never varies: When the relative price of a good falls, the consumer substitutes more of that good for the other good.

Income Effect To calculate the substitution effect, we gave Lisa a $9 pay cut. To calculate the income effect, we give Lisa her $9 back. The $9 increase in income shifts Lisa's budget line outward, as shown in Fig. 8.9(b). The slope of the budget line does not change because both prices remain constant. This change in Lisa's budget line is similar to the one illustrated in Fig. 8.8. As Lisa's budget line shifts outward, her consumption possibilities expand and her best affordable point becomes *J* on indifference curve I_2. The move from *K* to *J* is the income effect of the price change. In this example, as Lisa's income increases, she increases her consumption of movies. For Lisa, a movie is a normal good. For a normal good, the income effect reinforces the substitution effect.

FIGURE 8.9 Substitution Effect and Income Effect

(a) Price effect

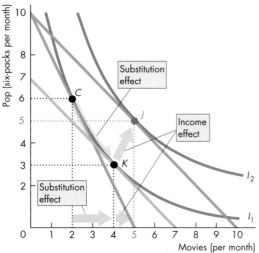

(b) Substitution effect and income effect

The price effect in part (a) can be separated into a substitution effect and an income effect in part (b). To isolate the substitution effect, we confront Lisa with the new price but keep her on her original indifference curve, I_1. The substitution effect is the move from *C* to *K*. To isolate the income effect, we confront Lisa with the new price of a movie but increase her income so that she can move from the original indifference curve, I_1, to the new one, I_2. The income effect is the move from *K* to *J*.

Inferior Goods The example that we have just studied is that of a change in the price of a normal good. The effect of a change in the price of an inferior good is different. Recall that an inferior good is one whose consumption decreases as income increases. For an inferior good, the income effect is negative. Thus for an inferior good, a lower price does not always lead to an increase in the quantity demanded. The lower price has a substitution effect that increases the quantity demanded. But the lower price also has a negative income effect that reduces the demand for the inferior good. Thus the income effect offsets the substitution effect to some degree. If the negative income effect exceeded the positive substitution effect, the demand curve would slope upward. This case does not appear to occur in the real world.

Back to the Facts

We started this chapter by observing how consumer spending has changed over the years. The indifference curve model explains those changes. Spending patterns are determined by best affordable choices. Changes in prices and incomes change the best affordable choice and change consumption patterns.

REVIEW QUIZ

1 When a consumer chooses the combination of goods and services to buy, what is she or he trying to achieve?
2 Can you explain the conditions that are met when a consumer has found the best affordable combination of goods to buy? (Use the terms budget line, marginal rate of substitution, and relative price in your explanation.)
3 If the price of a normal good falls, what happens to the quantity demanded of that good?
4 Into what two effects can we divide the effect of a price change?
5 For a normal good, does the income effect reinforce the substitution effect or does it partly offset the substitution effect?

The model of household choice can explain many other household choices. Let's look at one of them.

Work–Leisure Choices

HOUSEHOLDS MAKE MANY CHOICES OTHER THAN those about how to spend their income on the various goods and services available. We can use the model of household choice to understand many other household choices. Some of these choices are discussed in the part closer on pp. 190–194. Here we'll study a key choice: how much labour to supply.

Labour Supply

Every week, we allocate our 168 hours between working—called *labour*—and all other activities—called *leisure*. How do we decide how to allocate our time between labour and leisure? We can answer this question by using the theory of household choice.

The more hours we spend on *leisure,* the smaller is our income. The relationship between leisure and income is described by an *income–time budget line.* Figure 8.10(a) shows Lisa's income–time budget line. If Lisa devotes the entire week to leisure—168 hours—she has no income and is at point Z. By supplying labour in exchange for a wage, she can convert hours into income along the income–time budget line. The slope of that line is determined by the hourly wage rate. If the wage rate is $5 an hour, Lisa faces the flattest budget line. If the wage rate is $10 an hour, she faces the middle budget line. And if the wage rate is $15 an hour, she faces the steepest budget line.

Lisa buys leisure by not supplying labour and by forgoing income. The opportunity cost of an hour of leisure is the hourly wage rate forgone.

Figure 8.10(a) also shows Lisa's indifference curves for income and leisure. Lisa chooses her best attainable point. This choice of income and time allocation is just like her choice of movies and pop. She gets onto the highest possible indifference curve by making her marginal rate of substitution between income and leisure equal to her wage rate. Lisa's choice depends on the wage rate she can earn. At a wage rate of $5 an hour, Lisa chooses point A and works 20 hours a week (168 minus 148) for an income of $100 a week. At a wage rate of $10 an hour, she chooses point B and works 35 hours a week (168 minus 133) for an income of $350 a week. And at a wage rate of $15 an hour, she chooses point C and works 30 hours a week (168 minus 138) for an income of $450 a week.

FIGURE 8.10   The Supply of Labour

(a) Time allocation decision

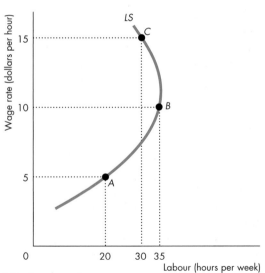

(b) Labour supply curve

In part (a), at a wage rate of $5 an hour, Lisa takes 148 hours of leisure and works 20 hours a week at point A. If the wage rate increases from $5 to $10, she decreases her leisure to 133 hours and increases her work to 35 hours a week at point B. But if the wage rate increases from $10 to $15, Lisa *increases* her leisure to 138 hours and *decreases* her work to 30 hours a week at point C. Part (b) shows Lisa's labour supply curve. Points A, B, and C on the supply curve correspond to Lisa's choices on her income–time budget line in part (a).

The Labour Supply Curve

Figure 8.10(b) shows Lisa's labour supply curve. This curve shows that as the wage rate increases from $5 to $10 an hour, Lisa increases the quantity of labour supplied from 20 hours to 35 hours a week. But when the wage rate increases to $15 an hour, she decreases her quantity of labour supplied to 30 hours a week.

Lisa's supply of labour is similar to that described for the economy as a whole at the beginning of this chapter. As wage rates have increased, work hours have decreased. At first, this pattern seems puzzling. We've seen that the hourly wage rate is the opportunity cost of leisure. So a higher wage rate means a higher opportunity cost of leisure. This fact on its own leads to a decrease in leisure and an increase in work hours. But instead, we've cut our work hours. Why? Because our incomes have increased. As the wage rate increases, incomes increase, so people demand more of all normal goods. Leisure is a normal good, so as incomes increase, people demand more leisure.

The higher wage rate has both a *substitution effect* and an *income effect*. The higher wage rate increases the opportunity cost of leisure and so leads to a substitution effect away from leisure. And the higher wage rate increases income and so leads to an income effect towards more leisure. This outcome of rational household choice explains why the average workweek has fallen steadily as wage rates have increased. With higher wage rates, people have decided to use their higher incomes in part to consume more leisure.

REVIEW QUIZ

1 What is the opportunity cost of leisure?
2 Why might a rise in the wage rate lead to an increase in leisure and a decrease in work hours?

◆ *Reading Between the Lines* on pp. 184–185 shows you how the theory of household choice explains why people buy print-on-demand books even though they cost more than regular books and what might happen in the market for books as the price of a print-on-demand book gets closer to the price of a regular book.

In the chapters that follow, we study firms' choices. We'll see how, in the pursuit of profit, firms make choices that determine the supply of goods and services and the demand for productive resources.

Regular Books versus Print-on-Demand Books

THE GLOBE AND MAIL, APRIL 5, 2002

E-books a new chapter in publishing

Audrey McNeill is an avid reader, so when she heard that her favourite book store in Cambridge, Ont., was selling some tough-to-find classics in a new print-on-demand format, she jumped at the opportunity.

Last week, Ms. McNeill bought three books-on-demand from Books Express as birthday gifts for her daughter: a two-volume set of George Eliot's *Adam Bede* for $20, and Anne Bronte's *Agnes Grey* at $12.50.

It took the retailer five minutes to produce each tome, by downloading the content from a computer, printing the pages, trimming and mechanically binding them together—all at the book seller's new "InstaBook" counter.

A big perk of the InstaBook invention was that it allowed Ms. McNeill to personalize the cover by having her daughter's name printed on it.

"The books weren't available in the store," says the Kitchener resident, who paid slightly more for the books than they would cost in regular paperback. "I wanted to get something personalized. ... My daughter was thrilled."

InstaBook is one of a number of print-on-demand systems slowly coming on stream in North America. Some observers see the technology as an integral step to publishers and book buyers alike becoming more comfortable with electronic books— hyped heavily a couple of years ago but slow to find acceptance.

... Daniel O'Brien, a senior analyst at U.S.-based Forrester Research ... sees potential in print-on-demand books as well as textbooks and technical books in digital form. His research has forecast that print-on-demand will be a $3.9-billion (U.S.) market in the United States by 2005 from a projected $244-million in 2000.

Over all, Forrester expects custom publishing, digital textbooks and consumer e-books to reach $7.8-billion in sales, or 17.5 per cent of the U.S. publishing industry, by 2005.

...

Essence of the Story

■ Audrey McNeill bought three books-on-demand from Books Express.

■ It took five minutes to produce each book at the book seller's "InstaBook" counter.

■ InstaBook allows the consumer to personalize the book's cover.

■ The price of an Insta-Book is slightly higher than the price of a regular paperback.

■ One analyst predicts that print-on-demand will be a $3.9-billion (U.S.) market in the United States by 2005 from a projected $244 million in 2000 and that custom publishing, digital textbooks, and consumer e-books will reach $7.8 billion or 17.5 per cent of total revenue in the U.S. publishing industry, by 2005.

Economic Analysis

■ Regular books and print-on-demand books are good substitutes, but probably not perfect substitutes for most people.

■ When two goods are close substitutes, the marginal rate of substitution doesn't change much as the quantities consumed change, so the indifference curves are relatively straight and a small change in the relative price brings a large change in the quantities bought.

■ Figure 1 shows an example of what Audrey McNeill's indifference curves for regular books and print-on-demand books might look like.

■ The figure also shows two budget lines, the line AB and the line AC.

■ Along the budget line AC, the price of a regular book is the same as the price of a print-on-demand book.

■ Along the budget line AB, the price of a print-on-demand book is higher than the price of a regular book.

■ Suppose that Audrey has a budget for books that enables her to buy 9 regular books a year and no print-on-demand books.

■ Because the price of a print-on-demand book is greater than the price of a regular book, she faces the budget line AB.

■ Audrey's best affordable point, where her budget line just touches her indifference curve I_0, is where she buys 5 regular books and 3 print-on-demand books a year.

■ If print-on-demand technology improves and the price of a print-on-demand book falls to that of a regular book, Audrey's budget line rotates outward to become the budget line AC.

■ With the lower relative price of a print-on-demand book, she substitutes in favour of that type of book.

■ Audrey's best affordable point now becomes that at which she buys 6 print-on-demand books and 3 regular books a year.

■ If print-on-demand books and regular books are indeed close substitutes, the growth in revenue from print-on-demand and other new technologies predicted in the news article does seem likely.

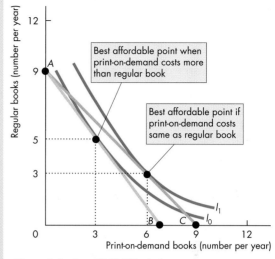

Figure 1 Audrey McNeill's choices

SUMMARY

KEY POINTS

Consumption Possibilities (pp. 172–174)

- The budget line is the boundary between what the household can and cannot afford given its income and the prices of goods.
- The point at which the budget line intersects the y-axis is the household's real income in terms of the good measured on that axis.
- The magnitude of the slope of the budget line is the relative price of the good measured on the x-axis in terms of the good measured on the y-axis.
- A change in price changes the slope of the budget line. A change in income shifts the budget line but does not change its slope.

Preferences and Indifference Curves (pp. 175–178)

- A consumer's preferences can be represented by indifference curves. An indifference curve joins all the combinations of goods among which the consumer is indifferent.
- A consumer prefers any point above an indifference curve to any point on it and any point on an indifference curve to any point below it.
- The magnitude of the slope of an indifference curve is called the marginal rate of substitution.
- The marginal rate of substitution diminishes as consumption of the good measured on the y-axis decreases and consumption of the good measured on the x-axis increases.

Predicting Consumer Behaviour (pp. 178–182)

- A household consumes at its best affordable point. This point is on the budget line and on the highest attainable indifference curve and has a marginal rate of substitution equal to relative price.
- The effect of a price change (the price effect) can be divided into a substitution effect and an income effect.
- The substitution effect is the effect of a change in price on the quantity bought when the consumer

(hypothetically) remains indifferent between the original and the new situation.
- The substitution effect always results in an increase in consumption of the good whose relative price has fallen.
- The income effect is the effect of a change in income on consumption.
- For a normal good, the income effect reinforces the substitution effect. For an inferior good, the income effect works in the opposite direction to the substitution effect.

Work–Leisure Choices (pp. 182–183)

- The indifference curve model of household choice enables us to understand how a household allocates its time between work and leisure.
- Work hours have decreased and leisure hours have increased because the income effect on the demand for leisure has been greater than the substitution effect.

KEY FIGURES

Figure 8.1   The Budget Line, 172
Figure 8.2   Changes in Prices and Income, 174
Figure 8.3   A Preference Map, 175
Figure 8.4   The Marginal Rate of Substitution, 176
Figure 8.6   The Best Affordable Point, 178
Figure 8.7   Price Effect and Demand Curve, 179
Figure 8.8   Income Effect and Change in Demand, 180
Figure 8.9   Substitution Effect and Income Effect, 181

KEY TERMS

Budget line, 172
Diminishing marginal rate of substitution, 176
Income effect, 180
Indifference curve, 175
Marginal rate of substitution, 176
Price effect, 179
Real income, 173
Relative price, 173
Substitution effect, 181

PROBLEMS

⬚ *1. Sara's income is $12 a week. The price of popcorn is $3 a bag, and the price of cola is $3 a can.
   a. What is Sara's real income in terms of cola?
   b. What is her real income in terms of popcorn?
   c. What is the relative price of cola in terms of popcorn?
   d. What is the opportunity cost of a can of cola?
   e. Calculate the equation for Sara's budget line (placing bags of popcorn on the left side of the equation).
   f. Draw a graph of Sara's budget line with cola on the x-axis.
   g. In part (f), what is the slope of Sara's budget line? What determines its value?

2. Rashid's income is $100 per week. The price of a CD is $10, and the price of a book is $20.
   a. What is Rashid's real income in terms of CDs?
   b. What is his real income in terms of books?
   c. What is the relative price of a CD in terms of books?
   d. What is the opportunity cost of a book?
   e. Calculate the equation for Rashid's budget line (placing books on the left side of the equation).
   f. Draw a graph of Rashid's budget line with CDs on the x-axis.
   g. In part (f), what is the slope of Rashid's budget line? What determines its value?

*3. Sara's income and the prices of popcorn and cola are the same as those in problem 1. The figure illustrates Sara's preferences.

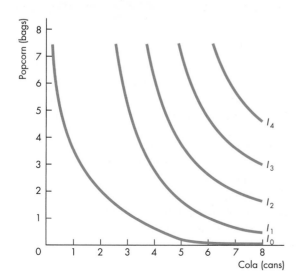

   a. What quantities of popcorn and cola does Sara buy?
   b. What is Sara's marginal rate of substitution at the point at which she consumes?

4. Rashid's income and the prices of CDs and books are the same as those in problem 2. The figure illustrates his preferences.

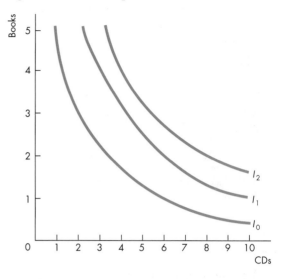

   a. What quantities of CDs and books does Rashid buy?
   b. What is Rashid's marginal rate of substitution at the point at which he consumes?

*5. Now suppose that in problem 3, the price of cola falls to $1.50 a can and the price of popcorn and Sara's income remain the same.
   a. What quantities of cola and popcorn does Sara now buy?
   b. Find two points on Sara's demand curve for cola.
   c. Find the substitution effect of the price change.
   d. Find the income effect of the price change.
   e. Is cola a normal good or an inferior good for Sara?

6. Now suppose that in problem 4, the price of a CD rises to $20 and the price of a book and Rashid's income remain the same.
   a. What quantities of CDs and books does Rashid now buy?
   b. Find two points on Rashid's demand curve for CDs.
   c. Find the substitution effect of the price change.
   d. Find the income effect of the price change.
   e. Is a CD a normal good or an inferior good for Rashid?

*7. Pam buys cookies and comic books. The price of a cookie is $1, and the price of a comic book is $2. Each month, Pam spends all of her income and buys 30 cookies and 5 comic books. Next month, the price of a cookie will fall to 50¢ and the price of a comic book will rise to $5. Assume that Pam's preference map is similar to that in Fig. 8.5(a). Use a graph to answer the following questions.
   a. Will Pam be able to buy 30 cookies and 5 comic books next month?
   b. Will Pam want to buy 30 cookies and 5 comic books?
   c. Which situation does Pam prefer: cookies at $1 and comic books at $2, or cookies at 50¢ and comic books at $3?
   d. If Pam changes the quantities that she buys next month, which good will she buy more of and which will she buy less of?
   e. When the prices change next month, will there be both an income effect and a substitution effect at work or just one of them?

8. Yangjie buys smoothies and sushi. The price of a smoothie is $5, and the price of sushi is $1 a piece. Each month, Yangjie spends all of her income and buys 10 smoothies and 20 pieces of sushi. Next month, the price of a smoothie will fall to $3 and the price of sushi will rise to $2 a piece. Assume that Yangjie's preference map is similar to that in Fig. 8.5(a). Use a graph to answer the following questions.
   a. Will Yangjie be able to buy 10 smoothies and 20 pieces of sushi next month?
   b. Will Yangjie want to buy 10 smoothies and 20 pieces of sushi? Explain why.
   c. Which situation does Yangjie prefer: smoothies at $5 each and sushi at $1 a piece or smoothies at $3 each and sushi at $2 a piece?
   d. If Yangjie changes the quantities that she buys next month, which good will she buy more of and which will she buy less of?
   e. When the prices change next month, will there be both an income effect and a substitution effect at work or just one of them? Explain.

CRITICAL THINKING

1. Study *Reading Between the Lines* about print-on-demand books on pp. 184–185, and then answer the following questions.
   a. How do you buy books?
   b. Sketch your budget constraint for books and other items.
   c. Sketch your indifference curves for books and other goods.
   d. What do you predict would happen to the way that you buy books if the price of a conventional book increased and the price of a print-on-demand book decreased, leaving you able to buy exactly the same quantity of books as you buy now?

2. Some people say that the GST should be scrapped. If the GST, a tax on both goods and services, were replaced by a higher rate of provincial sales tax, a tax on goods but not on services
   a. What would happen to the relative price of CD-Rs and haircuts?
   b. What would happen to the budget line that shows the quantities of CD-Rs and haircuts you can afford to buy?
   c. How would you change your purchases of CD-Rs and haircuts?
   d. Which type of tax is better for the consumer and why?
   Use a graph to illustrate your answers and to show the substitution effect and the income effect of the price change.

WEB EXERCISES

1. Use the links on the Parkin–Bade Web site to obtain information about the prices of cell phone service and first-class mail.
   a. Sketch the budget constraint for a consumer who spent $50 a month on these two goods in 1999 and 2001.
   b. Can you say whether the consumer was better off or worse off in 2001 than in 1999?
   c. Sketch some indifference curves for cell phone calls and first-class letters mailed, and show the income effect and the substitution effect of the changes in prices that occurred between 1999 and 2001.

UNDERSTANDING HOUSEHOLDS' CHOICES

PART 3

Making the Most of Life

The powerful forces of demand and supply shape the fortunes of families, businesses, nations, and empires in the same unrelenting way that the tides and winds shape rocks and coastlines. You saw in Chapters 3 through 6 how these forces raise and lower prices, increase and decrease quantities bought and sold, cause revenues to fluctuate, and send resources to their most valuable uses. ◆ These powerful forces begin quietly and privately with the choices that each one of us makes. Chapters 7 and 8 probe these individual choices. Chapter 7 explores the marginal utility theory of human decisions. This theory explains people's consumption of leisure time and its flip side, the supply of work time. Marginal utility theory can even be used to explain "non-economic" choices, such as whether to marry and how many children to have. In a sense, there are no non-economic choices. If there is scarcity, there must be choice. And economics studies all such choices. Chapter 8 describes a tool that enables us to make a map of people's likes and dislikes, a tool called an *indifference curve.* Indifference curves are considered an advanced topic, so this chapter is *strictly optional.* But the presentation of indifference curves in Chapter 8 is the clearest and most straightforward available, so if you want to learn about this tool, this chapter is the place to do so. ◆ The earliest economists (Adam Smith and his contemporaries) did not have a very deep understanding of households' choices. It was not until the nineteenth century that progress was made in this area. On the following pages, you can spend some time with Jeremy Bentham, the person who pioneered the use of the concept of utility to the study of human choices, and with Gary Becker of the University of Chicago, who is one of today's most influential students of human behaviour.

PROBING THE IDEAS

People as Rational Decision Makers

"*... It is the greatest happiness of the greatest number that is the measure of right and wrong.*"

JEREMY
BENTHAM
*Fragment on
Government*

JEREMY BENTHAM *(1748–1832), who lived in London, was the son and grandson of a lawyer and was himself trained as a barrister. But he rejected the opportunity to maintain the family tradition and, instead, spent his life as a writer, activist, and Member of Parliament in the pursuit of rational laws that would bring the greatest happiness to the greatest number of people.*

Bentham, whose embalmed body is preserved to this day in a glass cabinet in the University of London, was the first person to use the concept of utility to explain human choices. But in Bentham's day, the distinction between explaining and prescribing was not a sharp one, and Bentham was ready to use his ideas to tell people how they ought to behave. He was one of the first to propose pensions for the retired, guaranteed employment, minimum wages, and social benefits such as free education and free medical care.

The economic analysis of human behaviour in the family, the workplace, the markets for goods and services, the markets for labour services, and financial markets is based on the idea that our behaviour can be understood as a response to scarcity. Everything we do can be understood as a choice that maximizes total benefit subject to the constraints imposed by our limited resources and technology. If people's preferences are stable in the face of changing constraints, then we have a chance of predicting how they will respond to an evolving environment.

The economic approach explains the incredible change that has occurred during the past 100 years in the way women allocate their time as the consequences of changing constraints, not of changing attitudes. Technological advances have equipped the nation's farms and factories with machines that have increased the productivity of both women and men, thereby raising the wages they can earn. The increasingly technological world has increased the return to education for both women and men and has led to a large increase in high school and college graduates of both sexes. And equipped with an ever-widening array of gadgets and appliances that cut the time taken to do household jobs, an increasing proportion of women have joined the labour force.

The economic explanation might not be correct, but it is a powerful one. And if it is correct, the changing attitudes are a consequence, not a cause, of the economic advancement of women.

THEN

Economists explain people's actions as the consequences of choices that maximize total utility subject to constraints. In the 1890s, fewer than 20 percent of women chose market employment, and most of those who did had low-paying and unattractive jobs. The other 80 percent of women chose nonmarket work in the home. What constraints led to these choices?

Now

By 2002, more that 60 percent of women were in the labour force, and although many had low-paying jobs, women were increasingly found in the professions and in executive positions. What brought about this dramatic change compared with 100 years earlier? Was it a change in preferences or a change in the constraints that women face?

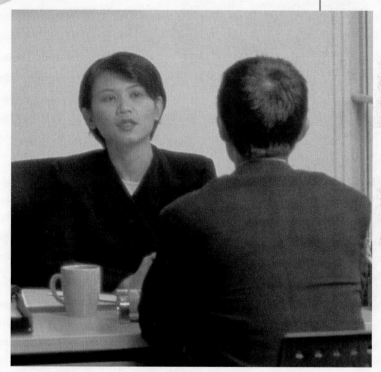

Today, one economist who stands out above all others and who stands on the shoulders of Jeremy Bentham is Gary Becker of the University of Chicago. Professor Becker has transformed the way we think about human choices. You can meet him on the following pages.

191

GARY S. BECKER *is Professor of Economics and Sociology at the University of Chicago. Born in 1930 in Pottsville, Pennsylvania, he was an undergraduate at Princeton University and a graduate student at the University of Chicago. His graduate supervisor was Milton Friedman, and his Ph.D. thesis became the book* The Economics of Discrimination, *a work that profoundly changed the way we think about discrimination and economic ways of reducing it.*

Professor Becker's other major book, Human Capital, *first published in 1964, has become a classic that influenced the thinking of the Clinton Administration on education issues. In 1992, he was awarded the Nobel Prize for Economic Science for his work on human capital.*

Professor Becker has revolutionized the way we think about human decisions in all aspects of life. Michael Parkin and Robin Bade talked with Professor Becker about his work and how it uses and builds on the work of Jeremy Bentham.

Professor Becker, why are you an economist?

When I went to Princeton, I was interested in mathematics, but I wanted to do something for society. I took economics in my freshman year by accident, and it was a lucky accident. I found economics to be tremendously exciting intellectually because it could be used to understand the difference between capitalism and socialism, what determined wages, and how people are taxed. This was so exciting to me that I didn't even worry about job opportunities at the time.

Can we really hope to explain all human choices by using models that were invented initially to explain and predict choices about the allocation of income among alternative consumer goods and services?

I think we can hope to explain all human choices. All choices involve making comparisons and assessing how to allocate our time between work, leisure, and taking care of children. These are choices that are not in principle very different from the type of choices involved in allocating income. Whether economists succeed at the goal of explaining everything, of course, remains to be seen. We certainly haven't done that yet, but I think we've made considerable progress in expanding our horizons with the theory of choice.

You are a professor of both economics and sociology. Do you see these same techniques being used to address questions that are the traditional domain of the sociologist? Or is sociology just a totally different discipline?

Sociology is a discipline with many different approaches. There is a small but growing and vocal group of sociologists who believe in what they call *rational choice theory*, which is the theory economists have used to explain choices in markets. My late colleague, James Coleman, was the leader of that group. One of the issues they deal with is the influence of peers on behaviour. For example, imagine that I am a teenager facing choices of getting

Gary S. Becker

192

involved with drugs or heavy drinking or smoking because of peer pressure. How would rational choice theorists incorporate this peer pressure into an analysis of these choices? The simple approach they take is that my utility, or pleasure, depends not only on what I'm consuming but also on what my peers are doing. If they're doing something very different from what I'm doing, that reduces my utility partly because I receive less respect from them and feel less part of the group.

Therefore when I am trying to get as much utility as possible, I take into account what my peers are doing. But since we're all doing that, this leads to some equilibrium in this peer market. Instead of us all behaving independently, we are all behaving interdependently. I think economists have given social structures such as peer pressure far too little attention. One of the things I learned during my association with Coleman and other sociologists is a better appreciation of the importance of social factors in individual behaviour.

Can you identify the historical figures that have been most influential to your thinking and your career?

Economics is a cumulative field in which we build on the giants who went earlier, and we try to add a little bit. And then other people build on our generation's contributions. The view I take of the broad scope of the economic approach has had a number of major practitioners, including Jeremy Bentham, who stated and applied a very general view of utility-maximizing behaviour to many problems, such as the factors that reduce crime.

Very few people's work, certainly not mine, spring out of nowhere. They have continuity with the past. What we do is try to build on the work of past economists and do a little more and a little better than what they did.

Other nineteenth century people like Wicksteed and Marshall highlighted the rational choice aspect of economics. In the eighteenth century, Adam Smith already applied economic reasoning to political behaviour. My work on human capital was very much influenced by Irving Fisher, Alfred Marshall, Milton Friedman, and Ted Schultz. Very few people's work, certainly not mine, spring out of nowhere. They have continuity with the past. What we do is try to build on the work of past economists and do a little more and a little better than what they did.

How would you characterize the major achievements of the economics of human behaviour? What questions, for example, would have convincing answers?

The area of law and economics has been very successful in analyzing criminal behaviour. Work by many lawyers and economists, particularly Judge Richard Posner and William Landes of the University of Chicago Law School, has produced many successful applications. The question that economics of crime seeks to answer is: What determines the amount of crime that we have and how effective are various actions that governments can take in reducing the amount of crime? This analysis discusses apprehending and punishing criminals, giving better education to people who might commit crimes, reducing unemployment, and so on. They have basically said that fundamentally, the factors determining criminal behaviour are not so different from the factors determining whether people become professors or not. People make choices, and these choices are conditional on their expected benefits and the cost. You can affect the number of people who decide to enter criminal activities by affecting the benefits and costs. To the extent that people make these calculations, they are more likely to enter crime when benefits are high relative to the cost.

One way to affect costs is to make it more likely that if somebody commits a crime they'll be captured, apprehended, convicted, and punished. That raises the cost and reduces crime. I think now that people accept this conclusion for most crimes.

But the economic approach is not simply a law and order approach. It also says that if you can increase the attractiveness to people of working at legal activities rather than illegal or criminal activities, you will also have less crime. One way to increase the attractiveness is to make it easier for people to find jobs and to earn more by improving their skills, their education, and their training and also by improving the functioning of labour markets.

You've made a significant contribution to demographic economics. Nearly 40 years ago, you introduced the idea of children being durable goods. Can you talk about the evolution of this idea?

Demographers initially were extremely hostile to my point of view. However, I recently received the Irene Taeuber Award from the Population Association of America, their most prestigious demographic award. It was given to me in recognition of the value of the economic way of looking at demographic questions, including birth and marriage rates. Over time, the cumulative work of many economists working on population problems around the world made an impact.

The main payoffs from this work have been in our understanding of fertility. The conclusions from the economic approach are that the number of children people have is very much a function of two variables: costs and choices. Costs depend not only on how much food and shelter you give children, but also on the time of parents. In most societies, most of that time is the mother's time, which has a value. As we have become richer, and as women have become better educated and are working outside the home more, the cost to them of spending time on children has risen.

> *There are about 15 countries of the world that now have birth rates well below replacement levels. If families continue with these rates, the populations will eventually decline—and decline rapidly.*

As these costs have risen, families are deterred from having as many children as they had in the past. So one of the factors explaining the big decline in birth rates is the increasing costs of children.

The second variable that economists recognize is that families are making choices about the quality of children's lives in terms of their education, training, and health. In modern economies, this quality component has become very important because the emphasis in modern economies is on knowledge, technology, and skills. But there is a tradeoff. If you spend more on each child's skills, education, and training, you make children more costly and you are likely to have fewer

children. Over the past 30 years, birth rates have been decreasing in most countries of the world, including India, China, parts of Asia, Latin America, some parts of Africa, Europe, Canada, and the United States.

How do you respond to people who feel that explaining choices such as how many children to raise is deeply personal and that it is therefore immoral to think of children in these terms?

I think morality is misplaced in this area. We are trying to understand very major changes in the world. There are about 15 countries of the world that now have birth rates well below replacement levels. If families continue with these rates, these populations will eventually decline—and decline rapidly. This includes Germany, Italy, Spain, Portugal, France, and Japan. It is important to understand why birth rates are going down. If this way of looking at it is a powerful tool for understanding why families have made these choices, then it would be immoral, I believe, to neglect this approach. If we are concerned about low birth rates, how can we go about raising them? Or if we want to understand what to expect in other countries that are experiencing significant economic development, we will miss out if we neglect an important set of considerations that help us to understand what's going on.

Is economics a subject that a young person can happily enter today? What are the major incentives for pursuing economics as an undergraduate?

I would certainly encourage a young person to enter economics for several reasons. There are many employment opportunities in economics, and it is also valuable if you decide to go into other areas such as the law, business, or even medicine. Economic issues, including the budget deficit, entitlement programs, minimum wages, and how to subsidize the elderly, are extremely important public policy issues.

I want to stress that economics is a wonderful intellectual activity. To be able to take this very mysterious world we live in and to illuminate parts of it, important parts of it, through the use of economics is enormously intellectually satisfying and challenging for an undergraduate or for anybody else. So I would say it's both practical and satisfying. Who can ask for a better combination?

PART 4 FIRMS AND MARKETS

ORGANIZING PRODUCTION

CHAPTER 9

Spinning a Web

In the fall of 1990, a British scientist named Tim Berners-Lee invented the World Wide Web. This remarkable idea paved the way for the creation and growth of thousands of profitable businesses. One of these businesses is Nortel Networks, founded as Northern Electric and Manufacturing Company Limited at the start of the telephone era more than 100 years ago. ◆ How do Nortel and the other 2 million firms in Canada make their business decisions? How do they operate efficiently? ◆ Businesses range from multinational giants like Nortel to small family restaurants and local Internet service providers. Three-quarters of all firms are operated by their owners. But corporations (such as Nortel) account for 90 percent of all business sales. What are the different forms a firm can take? Why do some firms remain small while others become giants? Why are most firms owner-operated? ◆ Many businesses operate in a highly competitive environment and struggle to make a profit. Others, like Microsoft, seem to have cornered the market for their products and make a large profit. What are the different types of markets in which firms operate? Why is it harder to make a profit in some markets than in others? ◆ GM, Ford, and DaimlerChrysler are household names and we think of them as the makers of our cars. But almost all of the *components* of a car are made by other firms, most of which you've never heard. One firm makes the engine casting, another makes the body panels, and yet another makes the transmission system. Other firms make the windshield, the tires, brakes, and so on. Why doesn't GM make all its own auto components? Why does it leave these activities to other firms and buy from them in markets? How do firms decide what to make themselves and what to buy in the marketplace from other firms?

◇ In this chapter, we are going to learn about firms and the choices they make to cope with scarcity. We begin by studying the economic problems and choices that all firms face.

After studying this chapter, you will be able to

- Explain what a firm is and describe the economic problems that *all* firms face

- Distinguish between technological efficiency and economic efficiency

- Define and explain the principal–agent problem and describe how different types of business organizations cope with this problem

- Describe and distinguish between different types of markets in which firms operate

- Explain why markets coordinate some economic activities and firms coordinate others

195

The Firm and Its Economic Problem

THE 2 MILLION FIRMS IN CANADA DIFFER IN SIZE and in the scope of what they do. But they all perform the same basic economic functions. Each **firm** is an institution that hires factors of production and organizes those factors to produce and sell goods and services.

Our goal is to predict firms' behaviour. To do so, we need to know a firm's goals and the constraints it faces. We begin with the goals.

The Firm's Goal

If you asked a group of entrepreneurs what they are trying to achieve, you would get many different answers. Some would talk about making a high-quality product, others about business growth, others about market share, and others about the job satisfaction of their work force. All of these goals might be pursued, but they are not the fundamental goal. They are means to a deeper goal.

A firm's goal is to maximize profit. A firm that does not seek to maximize profit is either eliminated or bought out by firms that do seek to maximize profit.

What exactly is the profit that a firm seeks to maximize? To answer this question, let's look at Sidney's Sweaters.

Measuring a Firm's Profit

Sidney runs a successful business that makes sweaters. Sidney's Sweaters receives $400,000 a year for the sweaters it sells. Its expenses are $80,000 a year for wool, $20,000 for utilities, $120,000 for wages, and $10,000 in interest on a bank loan. With receipts of $400,000 and expenses of $230,000, Sidney's Sweaters' annual surplus is $170,000.

Sidney's accountant lowers this number by $20,000, which he says is the depreciation (fall in value) of the firm's buildings and knitting machines during the year. (Accountants use Canada Customs and Revenue Agency rules based on standards established by the accounting profession to calculate the depreciation.) So the accountant reports that the profit of Sidney's Sweaters is $150,000 a year.

Sidney's accountant measures cost and profit to ensure that the firm pays the correct amount of income tax and to show the bank how its loan has been used. But we want to predict the decisions that a firm makes. These decisions respond to *opportunity cost* and *economic profit*.

Opportunity Cost

The *opportunity cost* of any action is the highest-valued alternative forgone. The action that you choose not to take—the highest-valued alternative forgone—is the cost of the action that you choose to take. For a firm, the opportunity cost of production is the value of the firm's best alternative use of its resources.

Opportunity cost is a real alternative forgone. But so that we can compare the cost of one action with that of another action, we express opportunity cost in money units. A firm's opportunity cost includes both

- Explicit costs
- Implicit costs

Explicit Costs Explicit costs are paid in money. The amount paid for a resource could have been spent on something else, so it is the opportunity cost of using the resource. For Sidney, his expenditures on wool, utilities, wages, and bank interest are explicit costs.

Implicit Costs A firm incurs implicit costs when it forgoes an alternative action but does not make a payment. A firm incurs implicit costs when it

1. Uses its own capital.
2. Uses its owner's time or financial resources.

The cost of using its own capital is an implicit cost—and an opportunity cost—because the firm could rent the capital to another firm. The rental income forgone is the firm's opportunity cost of using its own capital. This opportunity cost is called the **implicit rental rate** of capital.

People rent houses, apartments, cars, and videotapes. And firms rent photocopiers, earth-moving equipment, satellite-launching services, and so on. If a firm rents capital, it incurs an explicit cost. If a firm buys the capital it uses, it incurs an implicit cost. The implicit rental rate of capital is made up of

1. Economic depreciation
2. Interest forgone

Economic depreciation is the change in the *market* value of capital over a given period. It is calculated as the market price of the capital at the beginning of the period minus its market price at the end of the period. For example, suppose that Sidney could have sold his buildings and knitting machines on December 31, 2001, for $400,000. If he can sell the same capital on December 31, 2002, for $375,000, his economic depreciation during 2002 is $25,000—the fall in the market value of the machines. This $25,000 is an implicit cost of using the capital during 2002.

The funds used to buy capital could have been used for some other purpose. And in their next best use, they would have yielded a return—an interest income. This forgone interest is part of the opportunity cost of using the capital. For example, Sidney's Sweaters could have bought government bonds instead of a knitting factory. The interest forgone on the government bonds is an implicit cost of operating the knitting factory.

Cost of Owner's Resources A firm's owner often supplies entrepreneurial ability—the factor of production that organizes the business, makes business decisions, innovates, and bears the risk of running the business. The return to entrepreneurship is profit, and the return that an entrepreneur can expect to receive on the average is called **normal profit.** Normal profit is part of a firm's opportunity cost because it is the cost of a forgone alternative—running another firm. If normal profit in the textile business is $50,000 a year, this amount must be added to Sidney's costs to determine his opportunity cost.

The owner of a firm also can supply labour (in addition to entrepreneurship). The return to labour is a wage. And the opportunity cost of the owner's time spent working for the firm is the wage income forgone by not working in the best alternative job. Suppose that Sidney could take another job that pays $40,000 a year. By working for his knitting business and forgoing this income, Sidney incurs an opportunity cost of $40,000 a year.

Economic Profit

What is the bottom line—the firm's profit or loss? A firm's **economic profit** is equal to its total revenue minus its opportunity cost. The firm's opportunity cost is the sum of its explicit costs and implicit costs. Implicit costs, remember, include *normal profit*. The return to entrepreneurial ability is greater than normal in a firm that makes a positive economic profit. And the return to entrepreneurial ability is less than

normal in a firm that makes a negative economic profit—a firm that incurs an economic loss.

Economic Accounting: A Summary

Table 9.1 summarizes the economic accounting concepts that you've just studied. Sidney's Sweaters' total revenue is $400,000. Its opportunity cost (explicit costs plus implicit costs) is $365,000. So its economic profit is $35,000.

To achieve the objective of maximum economic profit a firm must make five basic decisions:

1. What goods and services to produce and in what quantities
2. How to produce—the techniques of production to use
3. How to organize and compensate its managers and workers
4. How to market and price its products
5. What to produce itself and what to buy from other firms

In all these decisions, a firm's actions are limited by the constraints that it faces. Our next task is to learn about these constraints.

TABLE 9.1   Economic Accounting

Item		Amount
Total Revenue		**$400,000**
Opportunity Costs		
Wool	$80,000	
Utilities	20,000	
Wages paid	120,000	
Bank interest paid	10,000	
Total Explicit Costs		$230,000
Sidney's wages forgone	40,000	
Sidney's interest forgone	20,000	
Economic depreciation	25,000	
Normal profit	50,000	
Total Implicit Costs		$135,000
Total Cost		**$365,000**
Economic Profit		**$35,000**

The Firm's Constraints

Three features of its environment limit the maximum profit a firm can make. They are

- Technology constraints
- Information constraints
- Market constraints

Technology Constraints Economists define technology broadly. A **technology** is any method of producing a good or service. Technology includes the detailed designs of machines. It also includes the layout of the workplace. And it includes the organization of the firm. For example, the shopping mall is a technology for producing retail services. It is a different technology from the catalogue store, which in turn is different from the downtown store.

It might seem surprising that a firm's profits are limited by technology, for it seems that technological advances are constantly increasing profit opportunities. Almost every day, we learn about some new technological advance that amazes us. With computers that speak and recognize our own speech and cars that can find the address we need in a city we've never visited before, we are able to accomplish ever more.

Technology advances over time. But at each point in time, to produce more output and gain more revenue, a firm must hire more resources and incur greater costs. The increase in profit that the firm can achieve is limited by the technology available. For example, by using its current plant and work force, Ford can produce some maximum number of cars per day. To produce more cars per day, Ford must hire more resources, which increases Ford's costs and limits the increase in profit that Ford can make by selling the additional cars.

Information Constraints We never possess all the information we would like to have to make decisions. We lack information about both the future and the present. For example, suppose you plan to buy a new computer. When should you buy it? The answer depends on how the price is going to change in the future. Where should you buy it? The answer depends on the prices at hundreds of different computer shops. To get the best deal, you must compare the quality and prices in every shop. But the opportunity cost of this comparison exceeds the cost of the computer!

Similarly, a firm is constrained by limited information about the quality and effort of its work force, the current and future buying plans of its customers, and the plans of its competitors. Workers might slacken off when the manager believes they are working hard. Customers might switch to competing suppliers. Firms must compete against competition from a new firm.

Firms try to create incentive systems for workers to ensure that they work hard even when no one is monitoring their efforts. And firms spend millions of dollars on market research. But none of these efforts and expenditures eliminates the problems of incomplete information and uncertainty. And the cost of coping with limited information itself limits profit.

Market Constraints What each firm can sell and the price it can obtain are constrained by its customers' willingness to pay and by the prices and marketing efforts of other firms. Similarly, the resources that a firm can buy and the prices it must pay for them are limited by the willingness of people to work for and invest in the firm. Firms spend billions of dollars a year marketing and selling their products. Some of the most creative minds strive to find the right message that will produce a knockout television advertisement. Market constraints and the expenditures firms make to overcome them limit the profit a firm can make.

REVIEW QUIZ

1 Why do firms seek to maximize profit? What happens to firms that don't pursue this goal?
2 Why do accountants and economists calculate a firm's cost and profit in different ways?
3 What are the items that make opportunity cost differ from the accountant's cost measure?
4 Why is normal profit an opportunity cost?
5 What are the constraints that firms face? How does each constraint limit the firm's profit?

In the rest of this chapter and in Chapters 10 through 13, we study the decisions that firms make. We're going to learn how we can predict a firm's behaviour as the response to the constraints that it faces and to changes in those constraints. We begin by taking a closer look at the technology constraints, information constraints, and market constraints that firms face.

Technological and Economic Efficiency

MICROSOFT EMPLOYS A LARGE WORK FORCE, AND most Microsoft workers possess a large amount of human capital. But the firm uses a small amount of physical capital. In contrast, a coal-mining company employs a huge amount of mining equipment (physical capital) and almost no labour. Why? The answer lies in the concept of efficiency. There are two concepts of production efficiency: technological efficiency and economic efficiency. **Technological efficiency** occurs when the firm produces a given output by using the least amount of inputs. **Economic efficiency** occurs when the firm produces a given output at the least cost. Let's explore the two concepts of efficiency by studying an example.

Suppose that there are four alternative techniques for making TV sets:

A. *Robot production.* One person monitors the entire computer-driven process.
B. *Production line.* Workers specialize in a small part of the job as the emerging TV set passes them on a production line.
C. *Bench production.* Workers specialize in a small part of the job but walk from bench to bench to perform their tasks.
D. *Hand-tool production.* A single worker uses a few hand tools to make a TV set.

Table 9.2 sets out the amounts of labour and capital required by each of these four methods to make 10 TV sets a day.

Which of these alternative methods are technologically efficient?

Technological Efficiency

Recall that technological efficiency occurs when the firm produces a given output by using the least inputs. Inspect the numbers in the table and notice that method *A* uses the most capital but the least labour. Method *D* uses the most labour but the least capital. Method *B* and method *C* lie between the two extremes. They use less capital but more labour than method *A* and less labour but more capital than method *D*. Compare methods *B* and *C*. Method *C* requires 100 workers and 10 units of capital to produce 10 TV sets. Those same 10 TV

sets can be produced by method *B* with 10 workers and the same 10 units of capital. Because method *C* uses the same amount of capital and more labour than method *B*, method *C* is not technologically efficient.

Are any of the other methods not technologically efficient? The answer is no. Each of the other three methods is technologically efficient. Method *A* uses more capital but less labour than method *B*, and method *D* uses more labour but less capital than method *B*.

Which of the methods are economically efficient?

Economic Efficiency

Recall that economic efficiency occurs when the firm produces a given output at the least cost. Suppose that labour costs $75 per person-day and that capital costs $250 per machine-day. Table 9.3(a) calculates the costs of using the different methods. By inspecting the table, you can see that method *B* has the lowest cost. Although method *A* uses less labour, it uses too much expensive capital. And although method *D* uses less capital, it uses too much expensive labour.

Method *C*, which is technologically inefficient, is also economically inefficient. It uses the same amount of capital as method *B* but 10 times as much labour. So it costs more. A technologically inefficient method is never economically efficient.

Although *B* is the economically efficient method in this example, method *A* or *D* could be economically efficient with different input prices.

Suppose that labour costs $150 a person-day and capital costs only $1 a machine-day. Table 9.3(b) now shows the costs of making a TV set. In this case, method *A* is economically efficient. Capital is now so

---

TABLE 9.2 Four Ways of Making 10 TV Sets a Day

| | Method | Quantities of inputs | |
		Labour	Capital
A	Robot production	1	1,000
B	Production line	10	10
C	Bench production	100	10
D	Hand-tool production	1,000	1

TABLE 9.3   The Costs of Different Ways of Making 10 TV Sets a Day

(a) Four ways of making TVs

Method	Labour cost ($75 per day)		Capital cost ($250 per day)		Total cost	Cost per TV set
A	$75	+	$250,000	=	$250,075	$25,007.50
B	750	+	2,500	=	3,250	325.00
C	7,500	+	2,500	=	10,000	1,000.00
D	75,000	+	250	=	75,250	7,525.00

(b) Three ways of making TVs: High labour costs

Method	Labour cost ($150 per day)		Capital cost ($1 per day)		Total cost	Cost per TV set
A	$150	+	$1,000	=	$1,150	$115.00
B	1,500	+	10	=	1,510	151.00
D	150,000	+	1	=	150,001	15,000.10

(c) Three ways of making TVs: High capital costs

Method	Labour cost ($1 per day)		Capital cost ($1,000 per day)		Total cost	Cost per TV set
A	$1	+	$1,000,000	=	$1,000,001	$100,000.10
B	10	+	10,000	=	10,010	1,001.00
D	1,000	+	1,000	=	2,000	200.00

cheap relative to labour that the method that uses the most capital is the economically efficient method.

Next, suppose that labour costs only $1 a person-day while capital costs $1,000 a machine-day. Table 9.3(c) shows the costs in this case. Method D, which uses a lot of labour and little capital, is now the least-cost method and the economically efficient method.

From these examples, you can see that while technological efficiency depends only on what is feasible, economic efficiency depends on the relative costs of resources. The economically efficient method is the one that uses a smaller amount of a more expensive resource and a larger amount of a less expensive resource.

A firm that is not economically efficient does not maximize profit. Natural selection favours efficient firms and opposes inefficient firms. Inefficient firms go out of business or are taken over by firms with lower costs.

REVIEW QUIZ

1 How do we define technological efficiency? Is a firm technologically efficient if it uses the latest technology? Why or why not?

2 How do we define economic efficiency? Is a firm economically inefficient if it can cut costs by producing less? Why or why not?

3 Explain the key distinction between technological efficiency and economic efficiency.

4 Why do some firms use large amounts of capital and small amounts of labour, while others use small amounts of capital and large amounts of labour?

Next we study information constraints that firms face and the diversity of organization structures they generate.

Information and Organization

EACH FIRM ORGANIZES THE PRODUCTION OF goods and services by combining and coordinating the productive resources it hires. But there is variety across firms in how they organize production. Firms use a mixture of two systems:

- Command systems
- Incentive systems

Command Systems

A **command system** is a method of organizing production that uses a managerial hierarchy. Commands pass downward through the managerial hierarchy, and information passes upward. Managers spend most of their time collecting and processing information about the performance of the people under their control and making decisions about commands to issue and how best to get those commands implemented.

The military uses the purest form of command system. A commander-in-chief makes the big decisions about strategic objectives. Beneath this highest level, generals organize their military resources. Beneath the generals, successively lower ranks organize smaller and smaller units but pay attention to ever-increasing degrees of detail. At the bottom of the managerial hierarchy are the people who operate weapons systems.

Command systems in firms are not as rigid as those in the military, but they share some similar features. A chief executive officer (CEO) sits at the top of a firm's command system. Senior executives who report to and receive commands from the CEO specialize in managing production, marketing, finance, personnel, and perhaps other aspects of the firm's operations. Beneath these senior managers might be several tiers of middle management ranks that stretch downward to the managers who supervise the day-to-day operations of the business. Beneath these managers are the people who operate the firm's machines and who make and sell the firm's goods and services.

Small firms have one or two layers of managers, while large firms have several layers. As production processes have become ever more complex, management ranks have swollen. Today, more people have management jobs than ever before. But the information revolution of the 1990s slowed the growth of management, and in some industries, it reduced the number of layers of managers and brought a shakeout of middle managers.

Managers make enormous efforts to be well informed. And they try hard to make good decisions and issue commands that end up using resources efficiently. But managers always have incomplete information about what is happening in the divisions of the firm for which they are responsible. It is for this reason that firms use incentive systems as well as command systems to organize production.

Incentive Systems

An **incentive system** is a method of organizing production that uses a market-like mechanism inside the firm. Instead of issuing commands, senior managers create compensation schemes that will induce workers to perform in ways that maximize the firm's profit.

Selling organizations use incentive systems most extensively. Sales representatives who spend most of their working time alone and unsupervised are induced to work hard by being paid a small salary and a large performance-related bonus.

But incentive systems operate at all levels in a firm. CEOs' compensation plans include a share in the firm's profit, and factory floor workers sometimes receive compensation based on the quantity they produce.

Mixing the Systems

Firms use a mixture of commands and incentives. And they choose the mixture that maximizes profit. They use commands when it is easy to monitor performance or when a small deviation from an ideal performance is very costly. They use incentives when monitoring performance is either not possible or too costly to be worth doing.

For example, it is easy to monitor the performance of workers on a production line. If one person works too slowly, the entire line slows. So a production line is organized with a command system.

In contrast, it is costly to monitor a CEO. For example, what did John Roth (former CEO of Nortel) contribute to the initial success and subsequent problems of Nortel? This question can't be answered with certainty, yet Nortel's stockholders had to put someone in charge of the business and provide that person with an incentive to maximize their returns. The performance of Nortel illustrates the nature of this problem, known as the principal–agent problem.

The Principal–Agent Problem

The **principal–agent problem** is the problem of devising compensation rules that induce an *agent* to act in the best interest of a *principal*. For example, the stockholders of Nortel are *principals,* and the firm's managers are *agents.* The stockholders (the principals) must induce the managers (agents) to act in the stockholders' best interest. Similarly, Bill Gates (a principal) must induce the programmers who are working on the next generation of Windows (agents) to work efficiently.

Agents, whether they are managers or workers, pursue their own goals and often impose costs on a principal. For example, the goal of stockholders of CIBC (principals) is to maximize the firm's profit. But the firm's profit depends on the actions of its managers (agents) who have their own goals. Perhaps a manager takes a customer to a ball game on the pretense that she is building customer loyalty, when in fact she is simply enjoying on-the-job leisure. This same manager is also a principal, and her tellers are agents. The manager wants the tellers to work hard and attract new customers so that she can meet her operating targets. But the workers enjoy conversations with each other and take on-the-job leisure. Nonetheless, the firm constantly strives to find ways of improving performance and increasing profits.

Coping with the Principal–Agent Problem

Issuing commands does not address the principal–agent problem. In most firms, the shareholders can't monitor the managers and often the managers can't monitor the workers. Each principal must create incentives that induce each agent to work in the interests of the principal. Three ways of attempting to cope with the principal–agent problem are

- Ownership
- Incentive pay
- Long-term contracts

Ownership By assigning to a manager or worker ownership (or part-ownership) of a business, it is sometimes possible to induce a job performance that increases a firm's profits. Part-ownership schemes for senior managers are quite common, but they are less

common but not unknown for workers. For example, in 1995 Canadian Pacific Ltd. sold off CP Express and Transport, a coast-to-coast trucking operation, to its 3,500 employees.

Incentive Pay Incentive pay schemes—pay related to performance—are very common. They are based on a variety of performance criteria such as profits, production, or sales targets. Promoting an employee for good performance is another example of an incentive pay scheme.

Long-Term Contracts Long-term contracts tie the long-term fortunes of managers and workers (agents) to the success of the principal(s)—the owner(s) of the firm. For example, a multiyear employment contract for a CEO encourages that person to take a long-term view and devise strategies that achieve maximum profit over a sustained period.

These three ways of coping with the principal–agent problem give rise to different types of business organization. Each type of business organization is a different response to the principal–agent problem. Each type uses ownership, incentives, and long-term contracts in different ways. Let's look at the main types of business organization.

Types of Business Organization

The three main types of business organization are

- Sole proprietorship
- Partnership
- Corporation

Sole Proprietorship A *sole proprietorship* is a firm with a single owner—a proprietor—who has unlimited liability. *Unlimited liability* is the legal responsibility for all the debts of a firm up to an amount equal to the entire wealth of the owner. If a sole proprietorship cannot pay its debts, those to whom the firm owes money can claim the personal property of the owner. Some farmers, computer programmers, and artists are examples of sole proprietorships.

The proprietor makes management decisions, receives the firm's profits, and is responsible for its losses. The profits are taxed at the same rate as other sources of the proprietor's personal income.

Partnership A *partnership* is a firm with two or more owners who have unlimited liability. Partners must agree on an appropriate management structure and on how to divide the firm's profits among themselves. The profits of a partnership are taxed as the personal income of the owners. But each partner is legally liable for all the debts of the partnership (limited only by the wealth of that individual partner). Liability for the full debts of the partnership is called *joint unlimited liability*. Most law firms are partnerships.

Corporation A *corporation* is a firm owned by one or more limited liability stockholders. *Limited liability* means that the owners have legal liability only for the value of their initial investment. This limitation of liability means that if the corporation becomes bankrupt, its owners are not required to use their personal wealth to pay the corporation's debts.

Corporations' profits are taxed independently of stockholders' incomes. The stockholders pay tax on dividends and a capital gains tax on the profit they earn when they sell a stock for a higher price than they paid for it. Corporate stocks generate capital gains when a corporation retains some of its profit and reinvests it in profitable activities.

Pros and Cons of Different Types of Firms

The different types of business organization arise as different ways of trying to cope with the principal–agent problem. Each has advantages in particular situations. And because of its special advantages, each type continues to exist. Each type also has its disadvantages, which explains why it has not driven out the other two.

Table 9.4 summarizes these pros and cons of the different types of firms.

TABLE 9.4   The Pros and Cons of Different Types of Firms

Type of Firm	Pros	Cons
Sole proprietorship	■ Easy to set up ■ Simple decision making ■ Profits taxed only once as owner's income	■ Bad decisions not checked by need for consensus ■ Owner's entire wealth at risk ■ Firm dies with owner ■ Capital is expensive ■ Labour is expensive
Partnership	■ Easy to set up ■ Diversified decision making ■ Can survive withdrawal of partner ■ Profits taxed only once as owners' incomes	■ Achieving consensus may be slow and expensive ■ Owners' entire wealth at risk ■ Withdrawal of partner may create capital shortage ■ Capital is expensive
Corporation	■ Owners have limited liability ■ Large-scale, low-cost capital available ■ Professional management not restricted by ability of owners ■ Perpetual life ■ Long-term labour contracts cut labour costs	■ Complex management structure can make decisions slow and expensive ■ Profits taxed twice as company profit and as stockholders' income

FIGURE 9.1 Relative Importance of the Three Types of Firms

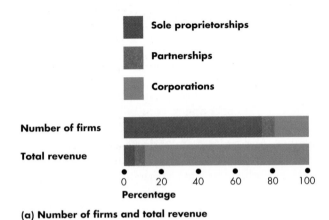

(a) Number of firms and total revenue

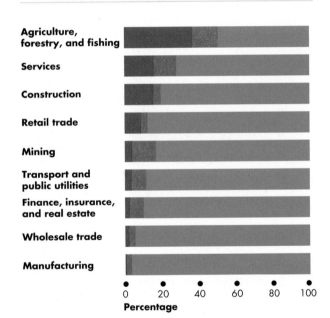

(b) Total revenue in various industries

The data shown are for the United States because we do not have comparable data for Canada. Three-quarters of all U.S. firms are sole proprietorships, almost one-fifth are corporations, and only a twentieth are partnerships. Corporations account for 86 percent of business revenue (part a). But sole proprietorships and partnerships account for a significant percentage of business revenue in some industries (part b).

Source: U.S. Bureau of the Census, *Statistical Abstract of the United States: 2001.*

The Relative Importance of Different Types of Firms

Figure 9.1(a) shows the relative importance of the three main types of firms in the U.S. economy. The figure also shows that the revenue of corporations is much larger than that of the other types of firms. Although only 18 percent of all firms are corporations, they generate 86 percent of revenue.

Figure 9.1(b) shows the percentage of revenue generated by the different types of firms in various industries. Sole proprietorships in agriculture, forestry, and fishing generate about 40 percent of the total revenue in those sectors. Sole proprietorships in the service sector, construction, and retail trades also generate a large percentage of total revenue. Partnerships in agriculture, forestry, and fishing generate about 15 percent of total revenue. Partnerships are more prominent in services; mining; and finance, insurance, and real estate than in other sectors. Corporations are important in all sectors and have the manufacturing field almost to themselves.

Why do corporations dominate the business scene? Why do the other types of business survive? And why are sole proprietorships and partnerships more prominent in some sectors? The answers to these questions lie in the pros and cons of the different types of business organization that are summarized in Table 9.4. Corporations dominate where a large amount of capital is used. But sole proprietorships dominate where flexibility in decision making is critical.

REVIEW QUIZ

1 Explain the distinction between a command system and an incentive system.
2 What is the principal–agent problem? What are the three ways in which firms try to cope with it?
3 What are the three types of firms? Explain the major advantages and disadvantages of each.
4 Why do all three types of firms survive and in which sectors is each type most prominent?

You've now seen how technology constraints influence a firm's use of capital and labour and how information constraints influence a firm's organization. We'll now look at market constraints and see how they influence the environment in which firms compete for business.

Markets and the Competitive Environment

THE MARKETS IN WHICH FIRMS OPERATE VARY A great deal. Some are highly competitive, and profits in these markets are hard to come by. Some appear to be almost free from competition, and firms in these markets earn large profits. Some markets are dominated by fierce advertising campaigns in which each firm seeks to persuade buyers that it has the best products. And some markets display a warlike character.

Economists identify four market types:

1. Perfect competition
2. Monopolistic competition
3. Oligopoly
4. Monopoly

Perfect competition arises when there are many firms, each selling an identical product, many buyers, and no restrictions on the entry of new firms into the industry. The many firms and buyers are all well informed about the prices of the products of each firm in the industry. The worldwide markets for corn, rice, and other grain crops are examples of perfect competition.

Monopolistic competition is a market structure in which a large number of firms compete by making similar but slightly different products. Making a product slightly different from the product of a competing firm is called **product differentiation**. Product differentiation gives the firm in monopolistic competition an element of market power. The firm is the sole producer of the particular version of the good in question. For example, in the market for running shoes, Nike, Reebok, Fila, New Balance, and Asics all make their own version of the perfect shoe. Each of these firms is the sole producer of a particular brand of shoe. Differentiated products are not necessarily different products. What matters is that consumers perceive them to be different. For example, different brands of aspirin are chemically identical (salicylic acid) and differ only in their packaging.

Oligopoly is a market structure in which a small number of firms compete. Computer software, airplane manufacture, and international air transportation are examples of oligopolistic industries. Oligopolies might produce almost identical products, such as the colas produced by Coke and Pepsi. Or they might produce differentiated products such as Chevrolet's Lumina and Ford's Taurus.

Monopoly arises when there is one firm, which produces a good or service that has no close substitutes and in which the firm is protected by a barrier preventing the entry of new firms. In some places, the phone, gas, electricity, and water suppliers are local monopolies—monopolies restricted to a given location. Microsoft Corporation, the software developer that created Windows, the operating system used by PCs, is an example of a global monopoly.

Perfect competition is the most extreme form of competition. Monopoly is the most extreme absence of competition. The other two market types fall between these extremes.

Many factors must be taken into account to determine which market structure describes a particular real-world market. One of these factors is the extent to which the market is dominated by a small number of firms. To measure this feature of markets, economists use indexes called measures of concentration. Let's look at these measures.

Measures of Concentration

Economists use two measures of concentration:

■ The four-firm concentration ratio
■ The Herfindahl–Hirschman Index

The Four-Firm Concentration Ratio The **four-firm concentration ratio** is the percentage of the value of sales accounted for by the four largest firms in an industry. The range of the concentration ratio is from almost zero for perfect competition to 100 percent for monopoly. This ratio is the main measure used to assess market structure.

Table 9.5 shows two calculations of the four-firm concentration ratio: one for tiremakers and one for

printers. In this example, 14 firms produce tires. The largest four have 80 percent of the sales, so the four-firm concentration ratio is 80 percent. In the printing industry, with 1,004 firms, the largest four firms have only 0.5 percent of the sales, so the four-firm concentration ratio is 0.5 percent.

A low concentration ratio indicates a high degree of competition, and a high concentration ratio indicates an absence of competition. A monopoly has a concentration ratio of 100 percent—the largest (and only) firm has 100 percent of the sales. A four-firm concentration ratio that exceeds 40 percent is regarded as an indication of a market that is highly concentrated and dominated by a few firms in an oligopoly. A ratio of less than 40 percent is regarded as an indication of a competitive market.

The Herfindahl–Hirschman Index The **Herfindahl–Hirschman Index**—also called the HHI—is the square of the percentage market share of each firm summed over the largest 50 firms (or summed over all the firms if there are fewer than 50) in a market. For example, if there are four firms in a market and the market shares of the firms are 50 percent, 25 percent, 15 percent, and 10 percent, the Herfindahl–Hirschman Index is

$$HHI = 50^2 + 25^2 + 15^2 + 10^2 = 3,450.$$

TABLE 9.5   Concentration Ratio Calculations

Tiremakers		Printers	
Firm	**Sales (millions of dollars)**	**Firm**	**Sales (millions of dollars)**
Top, Inc.	200	Fran's	2.5
ABC, Inc.	250	Ned's	2.0
Big, Inc.	150	Tom's	1.8
XYZ, Inc.	100	Jill's	1.7
Largest 4 firms	700	Largest 4 firms	8.0
Other 10 firms	175	Other 1,000 firms	1,592.0
Industry	875	Industry	**1,600.0**

Four-firm concentration ratios:

Tire makers: $\frac{700}{875} \times 100 = 80\%$ Printers: $\frac{8}{1,600} \times 100 = 0.5\%$

In perfect competition, the HHI is small. For example, if each of the largest 50 firms in an industry has a market share of 0.1 percent, then the HHI is $0.1^2 \times 50 = 0.5$. In a monopoly, the HHI is 10,000—the firm has 100 percent of the market: $100^2 = 10,000$.

The HHI can be used to classify markets across the spectrum of types. A market in which the HHI is less than 1,000 is regarded as being competitive and the smaller the number, the greater is the degree of competition. A market in which the HHI lies between 1,000 and 1,800 is regarded as being moderately competitive—a form of monopolistic competition. Although the HHI of 10,000 is needed for pure monopoly, a market in which the HHI exceeds 1,800 is regarded as being uncompetitive and a potential matter for concern by competition regulators.

Concentration Measures for the Canadian Economy

Figure 9.2 shows a selection of concentration ratios for Canada that Statistics Canada has calculated.

Industries that produce tobacco products, petroleum and coal products, transport equipment, communications, and beverages have a high degree of concentration and are oligopolies. Services, clothing, furniture, retail trade, and knitting mills have low concentration measures and are highly competitive. Industries that produce food and electrical products are moderately concentrated. These industries are examples of monopolistic competition.

Concentration measures are a useful indicator of the degree of competition in a market. But they must be supplemented by other information to determine a market's structure. Table 9.6 summarizes the range of other information, along with the measures of concentration, that determine which market structure describes a particular real-world market.

Limitations of Concentration Measures

The three main limitations of concentration measures alone as determinants of market structure are their failure to take proper account of

- The geographical scope of the market
- Barriers to entry and firm turnover
- The correspondence between a market and an industry

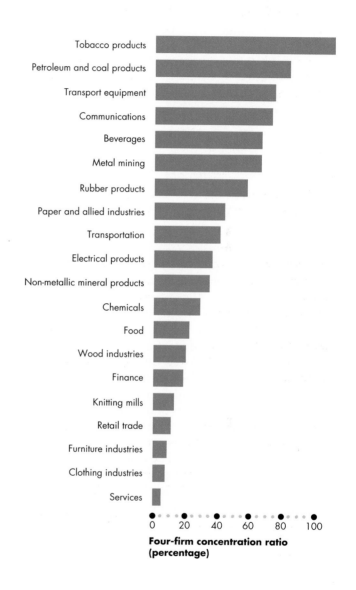

FIGURE 9.2 Concentration Measures in Canada

Four-firm concentration ratio (percentage)

The industries that produce tobacco products, petroleum and coal products, transport equipment, communications, and beverages are highly concentrated, while those that produce services, clothing, furniture, retail trade services, and knitwear are highly competitive. The industries that produce food and electrical products have an intermediate degree of concentration.

Source: Adapted from the Statistics Canada publication *CANSIM DISC,* 10F0007, March 1999.

TABLE 9.6   Market Structure

Characteristics	Perfect competition	Monopolistic competition	Oligopoly	Monopoly
Number of firms in industry	Many	Many	Few	One
Product	Identical	Differentiated	Either identical or differentiated	No close substitutes
Barriers to entry	None	None	Moderate	High
Firm's control over price	None	Some	Considerable	Considerable or regulated
Concentration ratio	0	Low	High	100
HHI (approx. ranges)	Less than 100	101 to 999	More than 1,000	10,000
Examples	Wheat, corn	Food, clothing	Automobiles, cereals	Local water supply

Geographical Scope of Market   Concentration measures take a national view of the market. Many goods are sold in a *national* market, but some are sold in a *regional* market and some in a *global* one. The newspaper industry consists of local markets. The concentration measures for newspapers are low, but there is a high degree of concentration in the newspaper industry in most cities. The auto industry has a global market. The three biggest North American car producers don't have much domestic competition, either in Canada or in the United States. But they face tough competition from foreign producers both here and more especially in foreign markets.

Barriers to Entry and Firm Turnover   Concentration measures don't measure barriers to entry. Some industries are highly concentrated but have easy entry and an enormous amount of turnover of firms. For example, many small towns have few restaurants, but there are no restrictions on opening a restaurant and many firms attempt to do so.

Also, an industry might be competitive because of *potential entry*—because a few firms in a market face competition from many firms that can easily enter the market and will do so if economic profits are available.

Market and Industry Correspondence   To calculate concentration ratios, Statistics Canada classifies each firm as being in a particular industry. But markets do not always correspond closely to industries for three reasons.

First, markets are often narrower than industries. For example, the pharmaceutical industry, which has a low concentration ratio, operates in many separate markets for individual products—for example, measles vaccines and AIDS-fighting drugs. These drugs do not compete with each other, so this industry, which looks competitive, includes firms that are monopolies (or near monopolies) in markets for individual drugs.

Second, most firms make several products. For example, Nortel produces telecommunication equipment and Internet database services, among other things. So this one firm operates in several separate markets. But Statistics Canada classifies Nortel as being in the telecommunication equipment industry. The fact that Nortel competes with other providers of e-commerce database services does not show up in the concentration data for that market.

Third, firms switch from one market to another depending on profit opportunities. For example, Canadian Pacific Ltd., which today produces hotel services, forest products, coal and petroleum products, as well as rail services, has diversified from being just a railroad company. Publishers of newspapers, magazines, and textbooks are today rapidly diversifying into Internet and multimedia products. These switches among industries show that there is much scope for entering and exiting an industry, and so measures of concentration have limited usefulness.

Despite their limitations, concentration measures do provide a basis for determining the degree of competition in an industry when they are combined with information about the geographical scope of the market, barriers to entry, and the extent to which large, multiproduct firms straddle a variety of markets.

Market Structures in the North American Economy

How competitive are the markets of North America? Do most firms operate in competitive markets or in non-competitive markets?

Figure 9.3 provides part of the answer to these questions. It shows the market structure of the U.S. economy and the trends in market structure between 1939 and 1980. (Unfortunately, comparable data for Canada alone and data for the 1980s and 1990s are not available.)

In 1980, three-quarters of the value of goods and services bought and sold in the United States were traded in markets that are essentially competitive—markets that have almost perfect competition or monopolistic competition. Monopoly and the dominance of a single firm accounted for about 5 percent of sales. Oligopoly, which is found mainly in manufacturing, accounted for about 18 percent of sales.

Over the period covered by the data in Fig. 9.3, the U.S. economy became increasingly competitive. You can see that the competitive markets have expanded most (the blue areas) and the oligopoly markets have shrunk most (the red areas).

But also during the past decades, the U.S. economy has become much more exposed to competition from the rest of the world. Figure 9.3 does not capture this international competition.

FIGURE 9.3 The Market Structure of the North American Economy

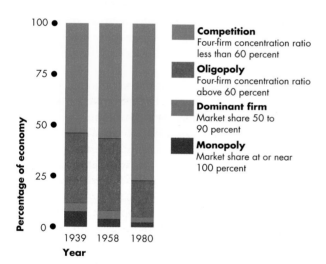

Competition
Four-firm concentration ratio less than 60 percent

Oligopoly
Four-firm concentration ratio above 60 percent

Dominant firm
Market share 50 to 90 percent

Monopoly
Market share at or near 100 percent

Three-quarters of the North American economy is effectively competitive (perfect competition or monopolistic competition), one-fifth is oligopoly, and the rest is monopoly. The economy became more competitive between 1939 and 1980. (Professor Shepherd, whose 1982 study remains the latest word on this topic, suspects that although some industries have become more concentrated, others have become less concentrated, so the net picture has probably not changed much since 1980.)

Source: William G. Shepherd, "Causes of Increased Competition in the U.S. Economy, 1939–1980," *Review of Economics and Statistics,* November 1982, pp. 613–626.

REVIEW QUIZ

1 What are the four market types? Explain the distinguishing characteristics of each.
2 What are the two measures of concentration? Explain how each measure is calculated.
3 Under what conditions do the measures of concentration give a good indication of the degree of competition in a market?
4 Is the North American economy competitive? Is it becoming more competitive or less competitive?

You now know the variety of market types and the way we classify firms and industries into the different market types. Our final question in this chapter is: What determines the things that firms decide to buy from other firms rather than produce for themselves?

Markets and Firms

AT THE BEGINNING OF THIS CHAPTER, WE defined a firm as an institution that hires productive resources and organizes them to produce and sell goods and services. To organize production, firms coordinate the economic decisions and activities of many individuals. But firms are not the only coordinators of economic decisions. You learned in Chapter 3 that markets coordinate decisions. They do so by adjusting prices and making the decisions of buyers and sellers consistent—making the quantity demanded equal to the quantity supplied for each good and service.

Market Coordination

Markets can coordinate production. For example, markets might coordinate the production of a rock concert. A promoter hires a stadium, some stage equipment, audio and video recording engineers and technicians, some rock groups, a superstar, a publicity agent, and a ticket agent—all market transactions—and sells tickets to thousands of rock fans, audio rights to a recording company, and video and broadcasting rights to a television network—another set of market transactions. Alternatively, if rock concerts were produced like cornflakes, the firm producing them would own all the capital used (stadiums, stage, sound and video equipment) and would employ all the labour needed (singers, engineers, salespeople, and so on).

Outsourcing—buying parts or products from other firms—is another example of market coordination. Dell uses outsourcing for all the components of the computers it produces. The major auto makers use outsourcing for windshields and windows, gearboxes, tires, and many other car parts.

What determines whether a firm or a market coordinates a particular set of activities? How does a firm decide whether to buy from another firm or manufacture an item itself? The answer is cost. Taking account of the opportunity cost of time as well as the costs of the other inputs, a firm uses the method that costs least. In other words, it uses the economically efficient method.

Firms coordinate economic activity when they can perform a task more efficiently than markets can. In such a situation, it is profitable to set up a firm. If markets can perform a task more efficiently than a firm can, people will use markets, and any attempt to

set up a firm to replace such market coordination will be doomed to failure.

Why Firms?

There are four key reasons why, in many instances, firms are more efficient than markets as coordinators of economic activity. Firms can achieve

- Lower transactions costs
- Economies of scale
- Economies of scope
- Economies of team production

Transactions Costs   The idea that firms exist because there are activities in which they are more efficient than markets was first suggested by University of Chicago economist and Nobel Laureate Ronald Coase. Coase focused on the firm's ability to reduce or eliminate transactions costs. **Transactions costs** are the costs that arise from finding someone with whom to do business, of reaching an agreement about the price and other aspects of the exchange, and of ensuring that the terms of the agreement are fulfilled. Market transactions require buyers and sellers to get together and to negotiate the terms and conditions of their trading. Sometimes, lawyers have to be hired to draw up contracts. A broken contract leads to still more expenses. A firm can lower such transactions costs by reducing the number of individual transactions undertaken.

Consider, for example, two ways of getting your creaking car fixed.

1. *Firm coordination:* You take the car to the garage. The garage owner coordinates parts and tools as well as the mechanic's time, and your car gets fixed. You pay one bill for the entire job.

2. *Market coordination:* You hire a mechanic, who diagnoses the problems and makes a list of the parts and tools needed to fix them. You buy the parts from the local wrecker's yard and rent the tools from ABC Rentals. You hire the mechanic again to fix the problems. You return the tools and pay your bills—wages to the mechanic, rental to ABC, and the cost of the parts used to the wrecker.

What determines the method that you use? The answer is cost. Taking account of the opportunity cost of your own time as well as the costs of the other inputs that you would have to buy, you will use the method that costs least. In other words, you will use the economically efficient method.

The first method requires that you undertake only one transaction with one firm. It's true that the firm has to undertake several transactions—hiring the labour and buying the parts and tools required to do the job. But the firm doesn't have to undertake those transactions simply to fix your car. One set of such transactions enables the firm to fix hundreds of cars. Thus there is an enormous reduction in the number of individual transactions that take place if people get their cars fixed at the garage rather than going through an elaborate sequence of market transactions.

Economies of Scale When the cost of producing a unit of a good falls as its output rate increases, **economies of scale** exist. Auto makers, for example, experience economies of scale because as the scale of production increases, the firm can use cost-saving equipment and highly specialized labour. An auto maker that produces only a few cars a year must use hand-tool methods that are costly. Economies of scale arise from specialization and the division of labour that can be reaped more effectively by firm coordination rather than by market coordination.

Economies of Scope A firm experiences **economies of scope** when it uses specialized (and often expensive) resources to produce a *range of goods and services*. For example, Microsoft hires specialist programmers, designers, and marketing experts and uses their skills across a range of software products. As a result, Microsoft coordinates the resources that produce software at a lower cost than can an individual who buys all these services in markets.

Economies of Team Production A production process in which the individuals in a group specialize in mutually supportive tasks is team production. Sport provides the best example of team activity. Some baseball team members specialize in pitching and some in batting, some basketball team members specialize in defence and some in offence. The production of goods and services offers many examples of team activity. For example, production lines in automobile and TV manufacturing plants work most efficiently when individual activity is organized in teams, each specializing in a small task. You can also think of an entire firm as being a team. The team has buyers of raw material and other inputs, production workers, and salespeople. There are even specialists within these various groups. Each individual member of the team specializes, but the value of the output of the team and the profit that it earns depend on the coordinated activities of all the team's

members. The idea that firms arise as a consequence of the economies of team production was first suggested by Armen Alchian and Harold Demsetz of the University of California at Los Angeles.

Because firms can economize on transactions costs, reap economies of scale and economies of scope, and organize efficient team production, it is firms rather than markets that coordinate most of our economic activity. But there are limits to the economic efficiency of firms. If a firm becomes too big or too diversified in the things that it seeks to do, the cost of management and monitoring per unit of output begins to rise, and at some point, the market becomes more efficient at coordinating the use of resources. IBM is an example of a firm that became too big to be efficient. In an attempt to restore efficient operations, IBM split up its large organization into a number of "Baby Blues," each of which specializes in a segment of the computer market.

Sometimes firms enter into long-term relationships with each other that effectively cut out ordinary market transactions and make it difficult to see where one firm ends and another begins. For example, GM has long-term relationships with suppliers of windows, tires, and other parts. Wal-Mart has long-term relationships with suppliers of the goods it sells in its stores. Such relationships make transactions costs lower than they would be if GM or Wal-Mart went shopping on the open market each time it wanted new supplies.

REVIEW QUIZ

1 What are the two ways in which economic activity can be coordinated?
2 What determines whether a firm or markets coordinates production?
3 What are the main reasons why firms can often coordinate production at a lower cost than markets can?

Reading Between the Lines on pp. 212–213 explores the economic problem faced by Nortel Networks. We continue to study firms and their decisions in the next four chapters. In Chapter 10, we learn about the relationships between cost and output at different output levels. These cost–output relationships are common to all types of firms in all types of markets. We then turn to problems that are specific to firms in different types of markets.

READING
BETWEEN
THE LINES

Nortel's Problem

THE CANADIAN PRESS, OCTOBER 3, 2001

Another 20,000 Nortel jobs lost: struggling high-tech giant cuts down to half its size

Nortel Networks is slashing another 20,000 jobs, hiring a new CEO and paring the company to half its size in the wake of another massive quarterly loss and warnings of continued weakness in the telecom industry.

The high-tech giant dropped another bombshell late yesterday, saying it will shrink its workforce by almost 20,000 more jobs to 45,000—less than half the total it started with this year after a spate of acquisitions.

Half of the cuts will be through the sale of assets and non-core businesses and will be completed by the end of this month.

Earlier this year, Nortel cut 30,000 jobs from its peak of 95,000 and reported a loss of $19.4 billion US, one of the biggest in corporate history. The latest cuts mean another 20,000 workers will leave the company, either through layoff or divestment.

Nortel, one of the world's major producers of fibre-optic communications equipment, also announced it will lose about $3.6 billion US in the third quarter, which ended Sunday. Much of that loss came from special charges, but the company also said it will lose $910 million US from operations.

Meanwhile, Nortel appointed its chief financial officer, Frank Dunn, to replace retiring chief executive John Roth, effective Nov. 1. Roth will stay on as vice-chairman until the end of 2002.

The Toronto-area company has been hit hard over the last year by a sharp drop in sales linked to the meltdown of the global technology industry. But stock-swap acquisitions at sky-high prices, overly aggressive expansion and quarterly forecasts it routinely failed to meet have helped batter its share price and produced massive losses.

...

"This has been a challenging period of adjustment," Roth told a telephone news conference, saying the company wants to break even at quarterly revenues of "well below" $4 billion US, down from $5 billion US in earlier estimates. The company is aiming to be at that level in the first quarter of 2002, he said.

...

The Canadian Press.

Essence of the Story

■ In 2001, Nortel, one of the world's major producers of fibre-optic communications equipment, announced a loss of $19.4 billion U.S., one of the biggest in corporate history.

■ The company cut its work force by 20,000 to 45,000—less than half the total it started the year with and hired a new CEO.

■ Half of the job cuts came from the sale of non-core businesses.

■ Earlier in 2001, Nortel cut 30,000 jobs from its peak of 95,000.

212

Economic Analysis

■ Nortel Networks is a very old Canadian corporation that was in business (under a different name) at the birth of the telephone.

■ Nortel produces a wide range of telecommunications equipment and services to customers in more than 150 countries. During the 1990s, Nortel grew to become the world's second largest telecommunications equipment producer (second to Lucent).

■ Nortel's goal is to maximize profit, and the news article illustrates the economic problem that confronted the company during 2001.

■ Nortel's main customers are telecommunications companies such as Bell, AT&T, World-Com, Global Crossing, and 360network.

■ Fundamentally, Nortel's problems stem from a shrinking market for its products.

■ During 2001, the global market for telecommunications equipment and services collapsed.

■ The collapse came partly from an over expansion as firms scrambled to dominate the $1 trillion global telecommunications market during the 1990s expansion.

■ Faced with a collapse in revenues, Nortel cut back its scale partly by selling assets in businesses outside its core activities and partly by cutting its work force.

■ Nortel also changed its CEO. This move was a change in its entrepreneurial resources.

■ Nortel's goal is to return to profitability but with a much smaller total revenue and total cost.

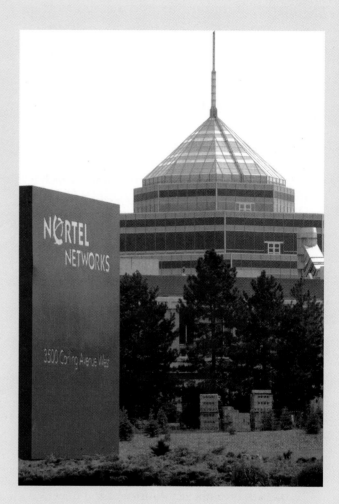

SUMMARY

KEY POINTS

The Firm and Its Economic Problem
(pp. 196–198)

- Firms hire factors of production and organize them to produce and sell goods and services.
- Firms seek to maximize economic profit, which is total revenue minus opportunity cost.
- Technology, information, and market constraints limit a firm's profit.

Technological and Economic Efficiency
(pp. 199–200)

- A method of production is technologically efficient when the firm produces a given output by using the least amount of inputs.
- A method of production is economically efficient when the cost of producing a given output is as low as possible.

Information and Organization (pp. 201–204)

- Firms use a combination of command systems and incentive systems to organize production.
- Faced with incomplete information and uncertainty, firms induce managers and workers to perform in ways that are consistent with the firm's goals.
- Sole proprietorships, partnerships, and corporations use ownership, incentives, and long-term contracts to cope with the principal–agent problem.

Markets and the Competitive Environment
(pp. 205–209)

- Perfect competition occurs when there are many buyers and sellers of an identical product and when new firms can easily enter a market.
- Monopolistic competition occurs when a large number of firms compete with each other by making slightly different products.
- Oligopoly occurs when a small number of producers compete with each other.

- Monopoly occurs when one firm produces a good or service for which there are no close substitutes and the firm is protected by a barrier that prevents the entry of competitors.

Markets and Firms (pp. 210–211)

- Firms coordinate economic activities when they can perform a task more efficiently—at lower cost—than markets can.
- Firms economize on transactions costs and achieve the benefits of economies of scale, economies of scope, and economies of team production.

KEY FIGURE AND TABLES

Figure 9.1   Relative Importance of the Three Types of Firms, 204
Table 9.4   The Pros and Cons of Different Types of Firms, 203
Table 9.5   Concentration Ratio Calculations, 206
Table 9.6   Market Structure, 208

KEY TERMS

Command system, 201
Economic depreciation, 196
Economic efficiency, 199
Economic profit, 197
Economies of scale, 211
Economies of scope, 211
Firm, 196
Four-firm concentration ratio, 206
Herfindahl–Hirschman Index, 206
Implicit rental rate, 196
Incentive system, 201
Monopolistic competition, 205
Monopoly, 205
Normal profit, 197
Oligopoly, 205
Perfect competition, 205
Principal–agent problem, 202
Product differentiation, 205
Technological efficiency, 199
Technology, 198
Transactions costs, 210

PROBLEMS

*1. One year ago, Jack and Jill set up a vinegar-bottling firm (called JJVB). Use the following information to calculate JJVB's explicit costs and implicit costs during its first year of operation:
   a. Jack and Jill put $50,000 of their own money into the firm.
   b. They bought equipment for $30,000.
   c. They hired one employee to help them for an annual wage of $20,000.
   d. Jack gave up his previous job, at which he earned $30,000, and spent all his time working for JJVB.
   e. Jill kept her old job, which paid $30 an hour, but gave up 10 hours of leisure each week (for 50 weeks) to work for JJVB.
   f. JJVB bought $10,000 of goods and services from other firms.
   g. The market value of the equipment at the end of the year was $28,000.

2. One year ago, Ms. Moffat and Mr. Spieder opened a cheese firm (called MSCF). Use the following information to calculate MSCF's explicit costs and implicit costs during its first year of operation:
   a. Moffat and Spieder put $70,000 of their own money into the firm.
   b. They bought equipment for $40,000.
   c. They hired one employee to help them for an annual wage of $18,000.
   d. Moffat gave up her previous job, at which she earned $22,000, and spent all her time working for MSCF.
   e. Spieder kept his old job, which paid $20 an hour, but gave up 20 hours of leisure each week (for 50 weeks) to work for MSCF.
   f. MSCF bought $5,000 of goods from other firms.
   g. The market value of the equipment at the end of the year was $37,000.

*3. Four methods for doing a tax return are with a personal computer, a pocket calculator, a pocket calculator with pencil and paper, and a pencil and paper. With a PC, the job takes an hour; with a pocket calculator, it takes 12 hours; with a pocket calculator and paper and pencil, it takes 12 hours; and with a pencil and paper, it takes 16 hours. The PC and its software cost

$1,000, the pocket calculator costs $10, and the pencil and paper cost $1.
   a. Which, if any, of the methods is technologically efficient?
   b. Which method is economically efficient if the wage rate is
      (i) $5 an hour?
      (ii) $50 an hour?
      (iii) $500 an hour?

4. Shawn is a part-time student and he can do his engineering assignment by using a personal computer, a pocket calculator, a pocket calculator and a pencil and paper, or a pencil and paper. With a PC, Shawn completes the job in 1 hour; with a pocket calculator, it takes 15 hours; with a pocket calculator and paper and pencil, it takes 7 hours; and with a pencil and paper, it takes 30 hours. The PC and its software cost $1,000, the pocket calculator costs $20, and the pencil and paper cost $5.
   a. Which, if any, of the methods is technologically efficient?
   b. Which method is economically efficient if Shawn's wage rate is
      (i) $10 an hour?
      (ii) $20 an hour?
      (iii) $250 an hour?

*5. Alternative ways of laundering 100 shirts are

Method	Labour (hours)	Capital (machines)
A	1	10
B	5	8
C	20	4
D	50	1

   a. Which methods are technologically efficient?
   b. Which method is economically efficient if the hourly wage rate and implicit rental rate of capital is
      (i) Wage rate is $1, rental rate is $100?
      (ii) Wage rate is $5, rental rate is $50?
      (iii) Wage rate is $50, rental rate is $5?

6. Four ways of making 10 surfboards a day are

Method	Labour (hours)	Capital (machines)
A	40	10
B	40	20
C	20	30
D	10	40

   a. Which methods are technologically efficient?

b. Which method is economically efficient if the hourly wage rate and implicit rental rate of capital are
   (i)   Wage rate is $1, rental rate $100?
   (ii) Wage rate is $5, rental rate is $50?
   (iii) Wage rate is $50, rental rate is $5?

*7. Sales of the firms in the tattoo industry are

Firm	Sales (dollars)
Bright Spots	450
Freckles	325
Love Galore	250
Native Birds	200
Other 15 firms	800

a. Calculate the four-firm concentration ratio.
b. What is the structure of the tattoo industry?

8. Sales of the firms in the dry cleaning industry are

Firm	Sales (thousands of dollars)
SqueakyClean, Inc.	15
Village Cleaners, Inc.	25
Plaza Cleaners, Inc.	30
The Cleanery, Inc.	40
Other 20 firms	300

a. Calculate the four-firm concentration ratio.
b. What is the structure of the industry?

*9. Market shares of chocolate makers are

Firm	Market Share (percent)
Mayfair, Inc.	15
Bond, Inc.	10
Magic, Inc.	20
All Natural, Inc.	15
Truffles, Inc.	25
Gold, Inc.	15

a. Calculate the Herfindahl–Hirschman Index.
b. What is the structure of the industry?

10. Market shares of orange juice suppliers are

Firm	Market Share (percent)
Natural Fresh, Inc.	75
Fresh Squeezed, Inc.	10
Juice-to-Go, Inc.	8
Juiced-Out, Inc.	7

a. Calculate the Herfindahl–Hirschman Index.
b. What is the structure of the industry?

CRITICAL THINKING

1. Study *Reading Between the Lines* about Nortel Network's economic problem on pp. 212–213, and then answer the following questions.
   a. What is the fundamental source of Nortel's economic problem?
   b. What actions did Nortel take in response to its falling revenues in 2001?
   c. How does Nortel seek to return to profitable operations in the face of falling revenues?
   d. Under what circumstances would you expect the firm to increase its work force back to its 2000 level?

2. What is the principal–agent problem? Do you think Nortel has such a problem? Describe the problem and explain how Nortel might cope with it.

3. Do you think that Nortel buys any services from other firms? If so, what types of services do you predict that Nortel buys? Why do you think Nortel doesn't produce these services for itself?

WEB EXERCISES

1. Use the link on your Parkin–Bade Web site and read James D. Miller's views on providing airport security services.
   a. What does Mr. Miller argue concerning the best way to organize airport security?
   b. Explain Mr. Miller's views using the principal–agent analysis. Who is the principal and who is the agent?
   c. What exactly is the principal–agent problem in providing airport security services?
   d. Why might a private provider offer better security than a public provider?
   e. Do you think that a private provider would operate at a lower cost than a public provider? Why or why not?

OUTPUT AND COSTS —— CHAPTER

10

What Does a Doughnut Cost?

More doughnuts are sold in Canada (per person) than anywhere else in the world. Tim Hortons, with its more than 2,000 outlets across Canada is the nation's leading producer. But competition has arrived from south of the border. In 2001, a Krispy Kreme outlet opened in Mississauga, Ontario, and more are springing up across the country. At the same time, Country Style is struggling and shrinking. Why? ◆ Firms differ in lots of ways from mom-and-pop convenience stores to multinational giants producing high-tech goods. But regardless of their size or what they produce, all firms must decide how much to produce and how to produce it. How are a firm's costs influenced by these decisions? ◆ Most automakers could produce more cars than they can sell. Why do automakers have expensive equipment lying around that isn't fully used? Electric utilities don't have enough capacity to meet demand on the coldest and hottest days and must buy power from other producers. Why don't these firms install more equipment so that they can supply the market themselves?

◆ We are going to answer these questions in this chapter. To do so, we are going to study the economic decisions of a small, imaginary firm: Cindy's Sweaters, Inc., a producer of knitted sweaters. By studying the economic problems of Cindy's Sweaters we will be able to get a clear view of the problems that face all firms—small ones like Cindy's Sweaters and a mom-and-pop convenience store as well as big firms such as banks, automakers, and electric utilities. We're going to begin by setting the scene and describing the time frames in which Cindy makes her business decisions. At the end of this chapter, in *Reading Between the Lines*, we'll return to Krispy Kreme and Country Style.

After studying this chapter, you will be able to

- Distinguish between the short run and the long run

- Explain the relationship between a firm's output and labour employed in the short run

- Explain the relationship between a firm's output and costs in the short run

- Derive and explain a firm's short-run cost curves

- Explain the relationship between a firm's output and costs in the long run

- Derive and explain a firm's long-run average cost curve

217

Decision Time Frames

PEOPLE WHO OPERATE FIRMS MAKE MANY decisions. And all of the decisions are aimed at one overriding objective: maximum attainable profit. But the decisions are not all equally critical. Some of the decisions are big ones. Once made, they are costly (or impossible) to reverse. If such a decision turns out to be incorrect, it might lead to the failure of the firm. Some of the decisions are small ones. They are easily changed. If one of these decisions turns out to be incorrect, the firm can change its actions and survive.

The biggest decision that any firm makes is what industry to enter. For most entrepreneurs, their background knowledge and interests drive this decision. But the decision also depends on profit prospects. No one sets up a firm without believing that it will be profitable—that total revenue will exceed opportunity cost (see Chapter 9, pp. 196–197).

The firm that we'll study has already chosen the industry in which to operate. It has also chosen its most effective method of organization, but it has not decided the quantity to produce, the quantities of resources to hire, or the price at which to sell its output.

Decisions about the quantity to produce and the price to charge depend on the type of market in which the firm operates. Perfect competition, monopolistic competition, oligopoly, and monopoly all confront the firm with their own special problems.

But decisions about how to produce a given output do not depend on the type of market in which the firm operates. These decisions are similar for *all* types of firms in *all* types of markets.

The actions that a firm can take to influence the relationship between output and cost depend on how soon the firm wants to act. A firm that plans to change its output rate tomorrow has fewer options than one that plans to change its output rate six months from now.

To study the relationship between a firm's output decision and its costs, we distinguish between two decision time frames:

- The short run
- The long run

The Short Run

The **short run** is a time frame in which the quantities of some resources are fixed. For most firms, the fixed resources are the firm's technology, buildings, and capital. The management organization is also fixed in the short run. We call the collection of fixed resources the firm's *plant*. So in the short run, a firm's plant is fixed.

For Cindy's Sweaters, the fixed plant is its factory building and its knitting machines. For an electric power utility, the fixed plant is its buildings, generators, computers, and control systems. For an airport, the fixed plant is the runways, terminal buildings, and traffic control facilities.

To increase output in the short run, a firm must increase the quantity of variable inputs it uses. Labour is usually the variable input. So to produce more output, Cindy's Sweaters must hire more labour and operate its knitting machines for more hours per day. Similarly, an electric power utility must hire more labour and operate its generators for more hours per day. And an airport must hire more labour and operate its runways, terminals, and traffic control facilities for more hours per day.

Short-run decisions are easily reversed. The firm can increase or decrease its output in the short run by increasing or decreasing the amount of labour it hires.

The Long Run

The **long run** is a time frame in which the quantities of *all* resources can be varied. That is, the long run is a period in which the firm can change its *plant*.

To increase output in the long run, a firm is able to choose whether to change its plant as well as whether to increase the quantity of labour it hires. Cindy's Sweaters can decide whether to install some additional knitting machines, use a new type of machine, reorganize its management, or hire more labour. An electric power utility can decide whether to install more generators. And an airport can decide whether to build more runways, terminals, and traffic control facilities.

Long-run decisions are *not* easily reversed. Once a plant decision is made, the firm usually must live with it for some time. To emphasize this fact, we call the past cost of buying a plant that has no resale value a **sunk cost**. A sunk cost is irrelevant to the firm's decisions. The only costs that influence its decisions are the short-run cost of changing its labour inputs and the long-run cost of changing its plant.

We're going to study costs in the short run and the long run. We begin with the short run and describe the technology constraint the firm faces.

Short-Run Technology Constraint

TO INCREASE OUTPUT IN THE SHORT RUN, A FIRM must increase the quantity of labour employed. We describe the relationship between output and the quantity of labour employed by using three related concepts:

1. Total product
2. Marginal product
3. Average product

These product concepts can be illustrated either by product schedules or by product curves. Let's look first at the product schedules.

Product Schedules

Table 10.1 shows some data that describe Cindy's Sweaters' total product, marginal product, and average product. The numbers tell us how Cindy's Sweaters' production increases as more workers are employed. They also tell us about the productivity of Cindy's Sweaters' workers.

Focus first on the columns headed "Labour" and "Total product." **Total product** is the total output produced. You can see from the numbers in these columns that as Cindy employs more labour, total product increases. For example, when Cindy employs 1 worker, total product is 4 sweaters a day, and when Cindy employs 2 workers, total product is 10 sweaters a day. Each increase in employment brings an increase in total product.

The **marginal product** of labour is the increase in total product that results from a one-unit increase in the quantity of labour employed with all other inputs remaining the same. For example, in Table 10.1, when Cindy increases the number of workers from 2 to 3 and keeps her capital the same, the marginal product of the third worker is 3 sweaters—total product goes from 10 to 13 sweaters.

Average product tells how productive workers are on the average. The **average product** of labour is equal to total product divided by the quantity of labour employed. For example, in Table 10.1, the average product of 3 workers is 4.33 sweaters per worker—13 sweaters a day divided by 3 workers.

If you look closely at the numbers in Table 10.1, you can see some patterns. As the number of workers increases, marginal product at first increases and then begins to decrease. For example, marginal product increases from 4 sweaters a day for the first worker to 6 sweaters a day for the second worker and then decreases to 3 sweaters a day for the third worker. Average product also increases at first and then decreases. You can see the relationships between employment and the three product concepts more clearly by looking at the product curves.

	Labour (workers per day)	Total product (sweaters per day)	Marginal product (sweaters per additional worker)	Average product (sweaters per worker)
A	0	0		
			4	
B	1	4		4.00
			6	
C	2	10		5.00
			3	
D	3	13		4.33
			2	
E	4	15		3.75
			1	
F	5	16		3.20

TABLE 10.1   Total Product, Marginal Product, and Average Product

Total product is the total amount produced. Marginal product is the change in total product that results from a one-unit increase in labour. For example, when labour increases from 2 to 3 workers a day (row C to row D), total product increases from 10 to 13 sweaters. The marginal product of going from 2 to 3 workers is 3 sweaters. Average product is total product divided by the quantity of labour employed. For example, the average product of 3 workers is 4.33 sweaters per worker (13 sweaters a day divided by 3 workers).

Product Curves

The product curves are graphs of the relationships between employment and the three product concepts you've just studied. They show how total product, marginal product, and average product change as employment changes. They also show the relationships among the three concepts. Let's look at the product curves.

Total Product Curve

Figure 10.1 shows Cindy's Sweaters' total product curve, *TP*. As employment increases, so does the number of sweaters knitted. Points *A* through *F* on the curve correspond to the same rows in Table 10.1.

The total product curve is similar to the *production possibilities frontier* (explained in Chapter 2). It separates the attainable output levels from those that are unattainable. All the points that lie above the curve are unattainable. Points that lie below the curve, in the orange area, are attainable. But they are inefficient—they use more labour than is necessary to produce a given output. Only the points *on* the total product curve are technologically efficient.

Notice especially the shape of the total product curve. As employment increases from zero to 1 to 2 workers per day, the curve becomes steeper. Then, as employment increases to 3, 4, and 5 workers a day, the curve becomes less steep. The steeper the slope of the total product curve, the greater is marginal product, as you are about to see.

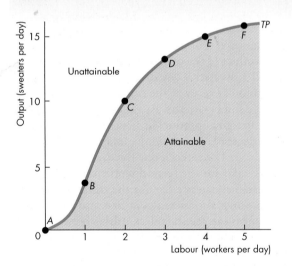

FIGURE 10.1 Total Product Curve

The total product curve, *TP*, is based on the data in Table 10.1. The total product curve shows how the quantity of sweaters changes as the quantity of labour employed changes. For example 2 workers can produce 10 sweaters a day (point *C*). Points *A* through *F* on the curve correspond to the rows of Table 10.1. The total product curve separates attainable outputs from unattainable outputs. Points below the *TP* curve are inefficient.

Marginal Product Curve

Figure 10.2 shows Cindy's Sweaters' marginal product of labour. Part (a) reproduces the total product curve from Fig. 10.1. Part (b) shows the marginal product curve, *MP*.

In part (a), the orange bars illustrate the marginal product of labour. The height of each bar measures marginal product. Marginal product is also measured by the slope of the total product curve. Recall that the slope of a curve is the change in the value of the variable measured on the *y*-axis—output—divided by the change in the variable measured on the *x*-axis—labour input—as we move along the curve. A one-unit increase in labour input, from 2 to 3 workers, increases output from 10 to 13 sweaters, so the slope from point *C* to point *D* is 3, the same as the marginal product that we've just calculated.

We've calculated the marginal product of labour for a series of unit increases in the quantity of labour. But labour is divisible into smaller units than one person. It is divisible into hours and even minutes. By varying the amount of labour in the smallest units imaginable, we can draw the marginal product curve shown in Fig. 10.2(b). The *height* of this curve measures the *slope* of the total product curve at a point. Part (a) shows that an increase in employment from 2 to 3 workers increases output from 10 to 13 sweaters (an increase of 3). The increase in output of 3 sweaters appears on the vertical axis of part (b) as the marginal product of going from 2 to 3 workers. We plot that marginal product at the midpoint between 2 and 3 workers. Notice that marginal product shown in Fig. 10.2(b) reaches a peak at 1.5 workers, and at that point, marginal product is 6. The peak occurs at 1.5 workers because the total product curve is steepest when employment increases from 1 worker to 2 workers.

The total product and marginal product curves are different for different firms and different types of goods. Ford Motor Company's product curves are different from those of Jim's Burger Stand, which in turn are different from those of Cindy's Sweaters. But the shapes of the product curves are similar because almost every production process has two features:

■ Increasing marginal returns initially
■ Diminishing marginal returns eventually

Increasing Marginal Returns Increasing marginal returns occur when the marginal product of an additional worker exceeds the marginal product of the

FIGURE 10.2   Marginal Product

(a) Total product

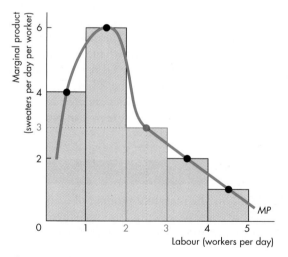

(b) Marginal product

Marginal product is illustrated by the orange bars. For example, when labour increases from 2 to 3, marginal product is the orange bar whose height is 3 sweaters. (Marginal product is shown midway between the labour inputs to emphasize that it is the result of *changing* inputs.) The steeper the slope of the total product curve (*TP*) in part (a), the larger is marginal product (*MP*) in part (b). Marginal product increases to a maximum (in this example when the second worker is employed) and then declines—diminishing marginal product.

previous worker. Increasing marginal returns arise from increased specialization and division of labour in the production process.

For example, if Cindy employs just one worker, that person must learn all the aspects of sweater production: running the knitting machines, fixing breakdowns, packaging and mailing sweaters, buying and checking the type and colour of the wool. All these tasks must be performed by that one person.

If Cindy hires a second person, the two workers can specialize in different parts of the production process. As a result, two workers produce more than twice as much as one. The marginal product of the second worker is greater than the marginal product of the first worker. Marginal returns are increasing.

Diminishing Marginal Returns   Most production processes experience increasing marginal returns initially. But all production processes eventually reach a point of *diminishing* marginal returns. **Diminishing marginal returns** occur when the marginal product of an additional worker is less than the marginal product of the previous worker.

Diminishing marginal returns arise from the fact that more and more workers are using the same capital and working in the same space. As more workers are added, there is less and less for the additional workers to do that is productive. For example, if Cindy hires a third worker, output increases but not by as much as it did when she hired the second worker. In this case, after two workers are hired, all the gains from specialization and the division of labour have been exhausted. By hiring a third worker, the factory produces more sweaters, but the equipment is being operated at a rate closer to its limits. There are even times when the third worker has nothing to do because the machines are running without the need for further attention. Hiring more and more workers continues to increase output but by successively smaller amounts. Marginal returns are diminishing. This phenomenon is such a pervasive one that it is called a "law"—the law of diminishing returns. The **law of diminishing returns** states that

As a firm uses more of a variable input, with a given quantity of fixed inputs, the marginal product of the variable input eventually diminishes.

You are going to return to the law of diminishing returns when we study a firm's costs. But before we do that, let's look at the average product of labour and the average product curve.

Average Product Curve

Figure 10.3 illustrates Cindy's Sweaters' average product of labour, *AP*. It also shows the relationship between average product and marginal product. Points *B* through *F* on the average product curve correspond to those same rows in Table 10.1. Average product increases from 1 to 2 workers (its maximum value at point *C*) but then decreases as yet more workers are employed. Notice also that average product is largest when average product and marginal product are equal. That is, the marginal product curve cuts the average product curve at the point of maximum average product. For the numbers of workers at which marginal product exceeds average product, average product is increasing. For the numbers of workers at which marginal product is less than average product, average product is decreasing.

The relationship between the average and marginal product curves is a general feature of the relationship between the average and marginal values of any variable. Let's look at a familiar example.

FIGURE 10.3   Average Product

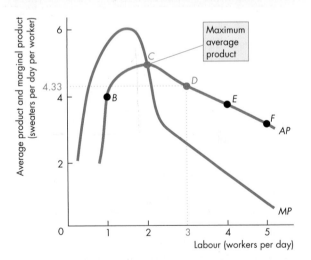

The figure shows the average product of labour and the connection between the average product and marginal product. With 1 worker per day, marginal product exceeds average product, so average product is increasing. With 2 workers per day, marginal product equals average product, so average product is at its maximum. With more than 2 workers per day, marginal product is less than average product, so average product is decreasing.

Marginal Grade and Grade Point Average

To see the relationship between average product and marginal product, think about the similar relationship between Cindy's average grade and marginal grade over five semesters. (Suppose Cindy is a part-time student who takes just one course each semester.) In the first semester, Cindy takes calculus and her grade is a C (2). This grade is her marginal grade. It is also her average grade—her GPA. In the next semester, Cindy takes French and gets a B (3). French is Cindy's marginal course, and her marginal grade is 3. Her GPA rises to 2.5. Because her marginal grade exceeds her average grade, it pulls her average up. In the third semester, Cindy takes economics and gets an A (4)—her new marginal grade. Because her marginal grade exceeds her GPA, it again pulls her average up. Cindy's GPA is now 3, the average of 2, 3, and 4. The fourth semester, she takes history and gets a B (3). Because her marginal grade is equal to her average, her GPA does not change. In the fifth semester, Cindy takes English and gets a D (2). Because her marginal grade, a 2, is below her GPA of 3, her GPA falls.

Cindy's GPA increases when her marginal grade exceeds her GPA. Her GPA falls when her marginal grade is below her GPA. And her GPA is constant when her marginal grade equals her GPA. The relationship between marginal product and average product is exactly the same as that between Cindy's marginal and average grades.

REVIEW QUIZ

1 Explain how the marginal product of labour and the average product of labour change as the quantity of labour employed increases (a) initially and (b) eventually.

2 What is the law of diminishing returns? Why does marginal product eventually diminish?

3 Explain the relationship between marginal product and average product. How does average product change when marginal product exceeds average product? How does average product change when average product exceeds marginal product? Why?

Cindy's Sweaters cares about its product curves because they influence its costs. Let's look at Cindy's Sweaters' costs.

Short-Run Cost

To produce more output in the short run, a firm must employ more labour, which means that it must increase its costs. We describe the relationship between output and cost by using three cost concepts:

- Total cost
- Marginal cost
- Average cost

Total Cost

A firm's **total cost** (*TC*) is the cost of the productive resources it uses. Total cost includes the cost of land, capital, and labour. It also includes the cost of entrepreneurship, which is *normal profit* (see Chapter 9, p. 197). We divide total cost into total fixed cost and total variable cost.

Total fixed cost (*TFC*) is the cost of the firm's fixed inputs. Because the quantity of a fixed input does not change as output changes, total fixed cost does not change as output changes.

Total variable cost (*TVC*) is the cost of the firm's variable inputs. Because to change its output a firm must change the quantity of variable inputs, total variable cost changes as output changes.

Total cost is the sum of total fixed cost and total variable cost. That is,

$$TC = TFC + TVC.$$

The table in Fig. 10.4 shows Cindy's total costs. With one knitting machine that Cindy rents for $25 a day, *TFC* is $25. To produce sweaters, Cindy hires labour, which costs $25 a day. *TVC* is the number of workers multiplied by $25. For example, to produce 13 sweaters a day, Cindy hires 3 workers and *TVC* is $75. *TC* is the sum of *TFC* and *TVC*, so to produce 13 sweaters a day, Cindy's total cost, *TC*, is $100. Check the calculation in each row of the table.

Figure 10.4 shows Cindy's total cost curves, which graph total cost against total product. The green total fixed cost curve (*TFC*) is horizontal because total fixed cost does not change when output changes. It is a constant at $25. The purple total variable cost curve (*TVC*) and the blue total cost curve (*TC*) both slope upward because total variable cost increases as output increases. The arrows highlight total fixed cost as the vertical distance between the *TVC* and *TC* curves.

Let's now look at Cindy's marginal cost.

FIGURE 10.4   Total Cost Curves

$$TC = TFC + TVC$$

	Labour (workers per day)	Output (sweaters per day)	Total fixed cost (TFC)	Total variable cost (TVC)	Total cost (TC)
			(dollars per day)		
A	0	0	25	0	25
B	1	4	25	25	50
C	2	10	25	50	75
D	3	13	25	75	100
E	4	15	25	100	125
F	5	16	25	125	150

Cindy rents a knitting machine for $25 a day. This amount is Cindy's total fixed cost. Cindy hires workers at a wage rate of $25 a day, and this cost is Cindy's total variable cost. For example, if Cindy employs 3 workers, total variable cost is 3 × $25, which equals $75. Total cost is the sum of total fixed cost and total variable cost. For example, when Cindy employs 3 workers, total cost is $100—total fixed cost of $25 plus total variable cost of $75. The graph shows Cindy's Sweaters' total cost curves. Total fixed cost (*TFC*) is constant—it graphs as a horizontal line—and total variable cost (*TVC*) increases as output increases. Total cost (*TC*) increases as output increases. The vertical distance between the total cost curve and the total variable cost curve is total fixed cost, as illustrated by the two arrows.

Marginal Cost

In Fig. 10.4, total variable cost and total cost increase at a decreasing rate at small outputs and then begin to increase at an increasing rate as output increases. To understand these patterns in the changes in total cost, we need to use the concept of *marginal cost*.

A firm's **marginal cost** is the increase in total cost that results from a one-unit increase in output. We calculate marginal cost as the increase in total cost divided by the increase in output. The table in Fig. 10.5 shows this calculation. When, for example, output increases from 10 sweaters to 13 sweaters, total cost increases from $75 to $100. The change in output is 3 sweaters, and the change in total cost is $25. The marginal cost of one of those 3 sweaters is ($25 ÷ 3), which equals $8.33.

Figure 10.5 graphs the marginal cost data in the table as the red marginal cost curve, *MC*. This curve is U-shaped because when Cindy hires a second worker, marginal cost decreases, but when she hires a third, a fourth, and a fifth worker, marginal cost successively increases.

Marginal cost decreases at low outputs because of economies from greater specialization. It eventually increases because of *the law of diminishing returns*. The law of diminishing returns means that each additional worker produces a successively smaller addition to output. So to get an additional unit of output, ever more workers are required. Because more workers are required to produce one additional unit of output, the cost of the additional output—marginal cost—must eventually increase.

Marginal cost tells us how total cost changes as output changes. The final cost concept tells us what it costs, on the average, to produce a unit of output. Let's now look at Cindy's Sweaters' average costs.

Average Cost

There are three average costs:

1. Average fixed cost
2. Average variable cost
3. Average total cost

Average fixed cost (*AFC*) is total fixed cost per unit of output. **Average variable cost** (*AVC*) is total variable cost per unit of output. **Average total cost** (*ATC*) is total cost per unit of output. The average

cost concepts are calculated from the total cost concepts as follows:

$$TC = TFC + TVC.$$

Divide each total cost term by the quantity produced, Q, to get,

$$\frac{TC}{Q} = \frac{TFC}{Q} + \frac{TVC}{Q}$$

or

$$ATC = AFC + AVC.$$

The table in Fig. 10.5 shows the calculation of average total cost. For example, when output is 10 sweaters, average fixed cost is ($25 ÷ 10), which equals $2.50, average variable cost is ($50 ÷ 10), which equals $5.00, and average total cost is ($75 ÷ 10), which equals $7.50. Note that average total cost is equal to average fixed cost ($2.50) plus average variable cost ($5.00).

Figure 10.5 shows the average cost curves. The green average fixed cost curve (*AFC*) slopes downward. As output increases, the same constant fixed cost is spread over a larger output. The blue average total cost curve (*ATC*) and the purple average variable cost curve (*AVC*) are U-shaped. The vertical distance between the average total cost and average variable cost curves is equal to average fixed cost—as indicated by the two arrows. That distance shrinks as output increases because average fixed cost declines with increasing output.

The marginal cost curve (*MC*) intersects the average variable cost curve and the average total cost curve at their minimum points. That is, when marginal cost is less than average cost, average cost is decreasing, and when marginal cost exceeds average cost, average cost is increasing. This relationship holds for both the *ATC* curve and the *AVC* curve and is another example of the relationship you saw in Fig. 10.3 for average product and marginal product and in Cindy's course grades.

Why the Average Total Cost Curve Is U-Shaped

Average total cost, *ATC*, is the sum of average fixed cost, *AFC*, and average variable cost, *AVC*. So the shape of the *ATC* curve combines the shapes of the *AFC* and *AVC* curves. The U shape of the average

FIGURE 10.5   Marginal Cost and Average Costs

Marginal cost is calculated as the change in total cost divided by the change in output. When output increases from 4 to 10, an increase of 6, total cost increases by $25 and marginal cost is $25 ÷ 6, which equals $4.17. Each average cost concept is calculated by dividing the related total cost by output. When 10 sweaters are produced, AFC is $2.50 ($25 ÷ 10), AVC is $5 ($50 ÷ 10), and ATC is $7.50 ($75 ÷ 10).

The graph shows that the marginal cost curve (MC) is U-shaped and intersects the average variable cost curve and the average total cost curve at their minimum points. Average fixed cost (AFC) decreases as output increases. The average total cost curve (ATC) and average variable cost curve (AVC) are U-shaped. The vertical distance between these two curves is equal to average fixed cost, as illustrated by the two arrows.

	Labour (workers per day)	Output (sweaters per day)	Total fixed cost (TFC)	Total variable cost (TVC)	Total cost (TC)	Marginal cost (MC) (dollars per additional sweater)	Average fixed cost (AFC)	Average variable cost (AVC)	Average total cost (ATC)
			(dollars per day)				(dollars per sweater)		
A	0	0	25	0	25		—	—	—
						6.25			
B	1	4	25	25	50		6.25	6.25	12.50
						4.17			
C	2	10	25	50	75		2.50	5.00	7.50
						8.33			
D	3	13	25	75	100		1.92	5.77	7.69
						12.50			
E	4	15	25	100	125		1.67	6.67	8.33
						25.00			
F	5	16	25	125	150		1.56	7.81	9.38

total cost curve arises from the influence of two opposing forces:

1. Spreading total fixed cost over a larger output
2. Eventually diminishing returns

When output increases, the firm spreads its total fixed cost over a larger output and so its average fixed cost decreases—its average fixed cost curve slopes downward.

Diminishing returns means that as output increases, ever-larger amounts of labour are needed to produce an additional unit of output. So average

variable cost eventually increases, and the AVC curve eventually slopes upward.

The shape of the average total cost curve combines these two effects. Initially, as output increases, both average fixed cost and average variable cost decrease, so average total cost decreases and the ATC curve slopes downward. But as output increases further and diminishing returns set in, average variable cost begins to increase. Eventually, average variable cost increases more quickly than average fixed cost decreases, so average total cost increases and the ATC curve slopes upward.

Cost Curves and Product Curves

The technology that a firm uses determines its costs. Figure 10.6 shows the links between the firm's technology constraint (its product curves) and its cost curves. The upper part of the figure shows the average product curve and the marginal product curve—like those in Fig. 10.3. The lower part of the figure shows the average variable cost curve and the marginal cost curve—like those in Fig. 10.5.

The figure highlights the links between technology and costs. As labour increases initially, marginal product and average product rise and marginal cost and average variable cost fall. Then, at the point of maximum marginal product, marginal cost is a minimum. As labour increases further, marginal product diminishes and marginal cost increases. But average product continues to rise, and average variable cost continues to fall. Then, at the point of maximum average product, average variable cost is a minimum. As labour increases further, average product diminishes and average variable cost increases.

Shifts in the Cost Curves

The position of a firm's short-run cost curves depend on two factors:

■ Technology
■ Prices of productive resources

Technology A technological change that increases productivity shifts the total product curve upward. It also shifts the marginal product curve and the average product curve upward. With a better technology, the same inputs can produce more output, so technological change lowers costs and shifts the cost curves downward.

For example, advances in robot production techniques have increased productivity in the automobile industry. As a result, the product curves of DaimlerChrysler, Ford, and GM have shifted upward, and their cost curves have shifted downward. But the relationships between their product curves and cost curves have not changed. These curves are still linked in the way shown in Fig. 10.6.

Often, a technological advance results in a firm using more capital (a fixed input) and less labour (a variable input). For example, today the telephone companies use computers to provide directory assistance in place of the human operators they used in

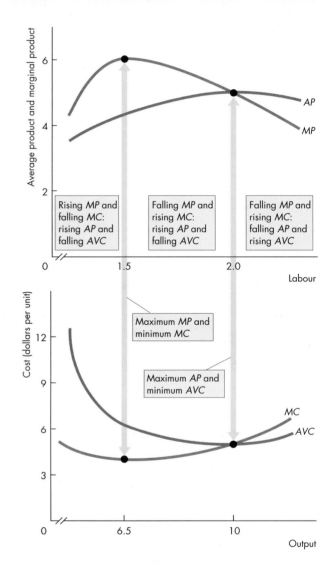

FIGURE 10.6 Product Curves and Cost Curves

A firm's marginal product curve is linked to its marginal cost curve. If marginal product rises, marginal cost falls. If marginal product is a maximum, marginal cost is a minimum. If marginal product diminishes, marginal cost rises. A firm's average product curve is linked to its average variable cost curve. If average product rises, average variable cost falls. If average product is a maximum, average variable cost is a minimum. If average product diminishes, average variable cost rises.

TABLE 10.2 A Compact Glossary of Costs

Term	Symbol	Definition	Equation
Fixed cost		Cost that is independent of the output level; cost of a fixed input	
Variable cost		Cost that varies with the output level; cost of a variable input	
Total fixed cost	TFC	Cost of the fixed inputs	
Total variable cost	TVC	Cost of the variable inputs	
Total cost	TC	Cost of all inputs	$TC = TFC + TVC$
Output (total product)	TP	Total quantity produced (output Q)	
Marginal cost	MC	Change in total cost resulting from a one-unit increase in total product	$MC = \Delta TC \div \Delta Q$
Average fixed cost	AFC	Total fixed cost per unit of output	$AFC = TFC \div Q$
Average variable cost	AVC	Total variable cost per unit of output	$AVC = TVC \div Q$
Average total cost	ATC	Total cost per unit of output	$ATC = AFC + AVC$

the 1980s. When such a technological change occurs, total cost decreases, but fixed costs increase and variable costs decrease. This change in the mix of fixed cost and variable cost means that at low output levels, average total cost might increase, while at high output levels, average total cost decreases.

Prices of Productive Resources An increase in the price of a productive resource increases costs and shifts the cost curves. But how the curves shift depends on which resource price changes. An increase in rent or some other component of *fixed* cost shifts the fixed cost curves (*TFC* and *AFC*) upward and shifts the total cost curve (*TC*) upward but leaves the variable cost curves (*AVC* and *TVC*) and the marginal cost curve (*MC*) unchanged. An increase in wages or some other component of *variable* cost shifts the variable cost curves (*TVC* and *AVC*) upward and shifts the marginal cost curve (*MC*) upward but leaves the fixed cost curves (*AFC* and *TFC*) unchanged. So, for example, if truck drivers' wages increase, the variable cost and marginal

cost of transportation services increase. If the interest expense paid by a trucking company increases, the fixed cost of transportation services increases.

You've now completed your study of short-run costs. All the concepts that you've met are summarized in a compact glossary in Table 10.2.

REVIEW QUIZ

1 What relationships do a firm's short-run cost curves show?
2 How does marginal cost change as output increases (a) initially and (b) eventually?
3 What does the law of diminishing returns imply for the shape of the marginal cost curve?
4 What is the shape of the average fixed cost curve and why?
5 What are the shapes of the average variable cost curve and the average total cost curve and why?

Long-Run Cost

IN THE SHORT RUN, A FIRM CAN VARY THE quantity of labour but the quantity of capital is fixed. So the firm has variable costs of labour and fixed costs of capital. In the long run, a firm can vary both the quantity of labour and the quantity of capital. So in the long run, all the firm's costs are variable. We are now going to study the firm's costs in the long run, when all costs are variable costs and when the quantities of labour and capital vary.

The behaviour of long-run cost depends on the firm's *production function*, which is the relationship between the maximum output attainable and the quantities of both labour and capital.

The Production Function

Table 10.3 shows Cindy's Sweaters' production function. The table lists total product schedules for four different quantities of capital. We identify the quantity of capital by the plant size. The numbers for Plant 1 are for a factory with 1 knitting machine—the case we've just studied. The other three plants have 2, 3, and 4 machines. If Cindy's Sweaters doubles its capital to 2 knitting machines, the various amounts of labour can produce the outputs shown in the second column of the table. The other two columns show the outputs of yet larger quantities of capital. Each column of the table could be graphed as a total product curve for each plant.

Diminishing Returns Diminishing returns occur at all four quantities of capital as the quantity of labour increases. You can check that fact by calculating the marginal product of labour in plants with 2, 3, and 4 machines. At each plant size, as the quantity of labour increases, its marginal product of labour (eventually) diminishes.

Diminishing Marginal Product of Capital
Diminishing returns also occur as the quantity of capital increases. You can check that fact by calculating the marginal product of capital at a given quantity of labour. The *marginal product of capital* is the change in total product divided by the change in capital when the quantity of labour is constant—equivalently, the change in output resulting from a one-unit increase in the quantity of capital. For example, if Cindy's has 3 workers and increases its capital from

TABLE 10.3   The Production Function

Labour (workers per day)	Output (sweaters per day)			
	Plant 1	Plant 2	Plant 3	Plant 4
1	4	10	13	15
2	10	15	18	20
3	13	18	22	24
4	15	20	24	26
5	16	21	25	27
Knitting machines (number)	1	2	3	4

The table shows the total product data for four quantities of capital. The greater the plant size, the larger is the total product for any given quantity of labour. But for a given plant size, the marginal product of labour diminishes. And for a given quantity of labour, the marginal product of capital diminishes.

1 machine to 2 machines, output increases from 13 to 18 sweaters a day. The marginal product of capital is 5 sweaters per day. If Cindy increases the number of machines from 2 to 3, output increases from 18 to 22 sweaters per day. The marginal product of the third machine is 4 sweaters per day, down from 5 sweaters per day for the second machine.

Let's now see what the production function implies for long-run costs.

Short-Run Cost and Long-Run Cost

Continue to assume that Cindy can hire a worker for $25 per day and rent a knitting machine for $25 per machine per day. Using these input prices and the data in Table 10.3, we can calculate and graph the average total cost curves for factories with 1, 2, 3, and 4 knitting machines. We've already studied the costs of a factory with 1 machine in Figs. 10.4 and 10.5. In Fig. 10.7, the average total cost curve for that case is ATC_1. Figure 10.7 also shows the average total cost curve for a factory with 2 machines, ATC_2, with 3 machines, ATC_3, and with 4 machines, ATC_4.

FIGURE 10.7   Short-Run Costs of Four Different Plants

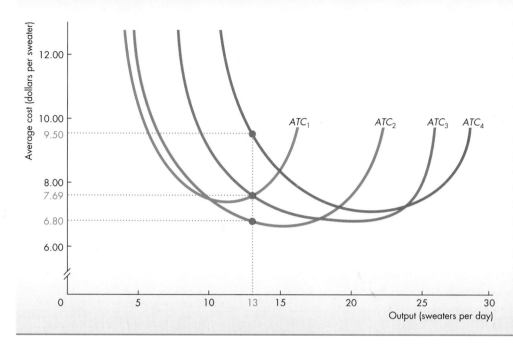

The figure shows short-run average total cost curves for four different quantities of capital. Cindy's can produce 13 sweaters a day with 1 knitting machine on ATC_1 or with 3 knitting machines on ATC_3 for an average cost of $7.69 per sweater. Cindy's can produce the same number of sweaters by using 2 knitting machines on ATC_2 for $6.80 per sweater or by using 4 machines on ATC_4 for $9.50 per sweater. If Cindy's produces 13 sweaters a day, the least-cost method of production—the long-run method—is with 2 machines on ATC_2.

You can see, in Fig. 10.7, that plant size has a big effect on the firm's average total cost. Two things stand out:

1. Each short-run ATC curve is U-shaped.
2. For each short-run ATC curve, the larger the plant, the greater is the output at which average total cost is a minimum.

Each short-run average total cost curve is U-shaped because, as the quantity of labour increases, its marginal product at first increases and then diminishes. And these patterns in the marginal product of labour, which we examined in some detail for the plant with 1 knitting machine on pp. 220–221, occur at all plant sizes.

The minimum average total cost for a larger plant occurs at a greater output than it does for a smaller plant because the larger plant has a higher total fixed cost and therefore, for any given output level, a higher average fixed cost.

Which short-run average cost curve Cindy's Sweaters operates on depends on its plant size. But in the long run, Cindy chooses the plant size. And which plant size she chooses depends on the output she plans to produce. The reason is that the average total cost of producing a given output depends on the plant size.

To see why, suppose that Cindy plans to produce 13 sweaters a day. With 1 machine, the average total cost curve is ATC_1 (in Fig. 10.7) and the average total cost of 13 sweaters a day is $7.69 per sweater. With 2 machines, on ATC_2, average total cost is $6.80 per sweater. With 3 machines, on ATC_3, average total cost is $7.69 per sweater, the same as with 1 machine. Finally, with 4 machines, on ATC_4, average total cost is $9.50 per sweater.

The economically efficient plant size for producing a given output is the one that has the lowest average total cost. For Cindy's Sweaters, the economically efficient plant to use to produce 13 sweaters a day is the one with 2 machines.

In the long run, Cindy's chooses the plant size that minimizes average total cost. When a firm is producing a given output at the least possible cost, it is operating on its *long-run average cost curve*.

The **long-run average cost curve** is the relationship between the lowest attainable average total cost and output when both the plant size and labour are varied.

The long-run average cost curve is a planning curve. It tells the firm the plant size and the quantity of labour to use at each output to minimize cost. Once the plant size is chosen, the firm operates on the short-run cost curves that apply to that plant size.

The Long-Run Average Cost Curve

Figure 10.8 shows Cindy's Sweaters' long-run average cost curve, *LRAC*. This long-run average cost curve is derived from the short-run average total cost curves in Fig. 10.7. For output rates up to 10 sweaters a day, average total cost is the lowest on ATC_1. For output rates between 10 and 18 sweaters a day, average total cost is the lowest on ATC_2. For output rates between 18 and 24 sweaters a day, average total cost is the lowest on ATC_3. And for output rates in excess of 24 sweaters a day, average total cost is the lowest on ATC_4. The segment of each of the four average total cost curves for which that quantity of capital has the lowest average total cost is highlighted in dark blue in Fig. 10.8. The scallop-shaped curve made up of these four segments is the long-run average cost curve.

Economies and Diseconomies of Scale

Economies of scale are features of a firm's technology that lead to falling long-run average cost as output increases. When economies of scale are present, the *LRAC* curve slopes downward. The *LRAC* curve in Fig. 10.8 shows that Cindy's Sweaters experiences economies of scale for outputs up to 15 sweaters a day.

With given input prices, economies of scale occur if the percentage increase in output exceeds the percentage increase in all inputs. For example, if when a firm increases its labour and capital by 10 percent, output increases by more than 10 percent, its average total cost falls. Economies of scale are present.

The main source of economies of scale is greater specialization of both labour and capital. For example, if GM produces 100 cars a week, each worker must perform many different tasks and the capital must be general-purpose machines and tools. But if GM produces 10,000 cars a week, each worker specializes and becomes highly proficient in a small number of tasks. Also, the capital is specialized and productive.

Diseconomies of scale are features of a firm's technology that lead to rising long-run average cost as output increases. When diseconomies of scale are present, the *LRAC* curve slopes upward. In Fig. 10.8, Cindy's Sweaters experiences diseconomies of scale at outputs greater than 15 sweaters a day.

With given input prices, diseconomies of scale occur if the percentage increase in output is less than the percentage increase in inputs. For example, if when a firm increases its labour and capital by 10 percent, output increases by less than 10 percent,

---

FIGURE 10.8   Long-Run Average Cost Curve

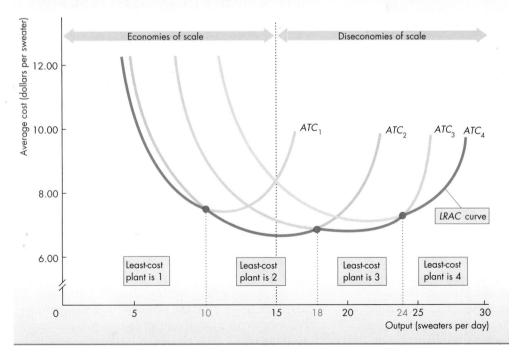

In the long run, Cindy's can vary both capital and labour inputs. The long-run average cost curve traces the lowest attainable average total cost of production. Cindy's produces on its long-run average cost curve if it uses 1 machine to produce up to 10 sweaters a day, 2 machines to produce between 10 and 18 sweaters a day, 3 machines to produce between 18 and 24 sweaters a day, and 4 machines to produce more than 24 sweaters a day. Within these ranges, Cindy's varies its output by varying its labour input.

its average total cost rises. Diseconomies of scale are present.

The main source of diseconomies of scale is the difficulty of managing a very large enterprise. The larger the firm, the greater is the challenge of organizing it and the greater is the cost of communicating both up and down the management hierarchy and among managers. Eventually, management complexity brings rising average cost.

Diseconomies of scale occur in all production processes but perhaps only at a very large output rate.

Constant returns to scale are features of a firm's technology that lead to constant long-run average cost as output increases. When constant returns to scale are present, the *LRAC* curve is horizontal.

Constant returns to scale occur if the percentage increase in output equals the percentage increase in inputs. For example, if when a firm increases its labour and capital by 10 percent, output increases by 10 percent, then constant returns to scale are present.

For example, General Motors can double its production of Cavaliers by doubling its production facility for those cars. It can build an identical production line and hire an identical number of workers. With the two identical production lines, GM produces exactly twice as many cars.

Minimum Efficient Scale A firm experiences economies of scale up to some output level. Beyond that level, it moves into constant returns to scale or diseconomies of scale. A firm's **minimum efficient scale** is the smallest quantity of output at which long-run average cost reaches its lowest level.

The minimum efficient scale plays a role in determining market structure, as you will learn in the next three chapters. The minimum efficient scale also helps to answer some questions about real businesses.

Economies of Scale at Cindy's Sweaters The production technology that Cindy's Sweaters uses, shown in Table 10.3, illustrates economies of scale and diseconomies of scale. If Cindy's Sweaters increases its inputs from 1 machine and 1 worker to 2 of each, a 100 percent increase in all inputs, output increases by more than 100 percent from 4 sweaters to 15 sweaters a day. Cindy's Sweaters experiences economies of scale, and its long-run average cost decreases. But if Cindy's Sweaters increases its inputs to 3 machines and 3 workers, a 50 percent increase, output increases to by less than 50 percent, from 15 sweaters to 22 sweaters a day. Now Cindy's Sweaters

experiences diseconomies of scale, and its long-run average cost increases. Its minimum efficient scale is at 15 sweaters a day.

Producing Cars and Generating Electric Power
Why do automakers have expensive equipment lying around that isn't fully used? You can now answer this question. An automaker uses the plant that minimizes the average total cost of producing the output that it can sell. But it operates below the efficient minimum scale. Its short-run average total cost curve looks like ATC_1 in Fig. 10.8. If it could sell more cars, it would produce more cars and its average total cost would fall.

Why do many electric utilities have too little production equipment to meet demand on the coldest and hottest days and have to buy power from other producers? You can now see why this happens and why an electric utility doesn't build more generating capacity. A power producer uses the plant size that minimizes the average total cost of producing the output that it can sell on a normal day. But it produces above the minimum efficient scale and experiences diseconomies of scale. Its short-run average total cost curve looks like ATC_3 in Fig. 10.8. With a larger plant size, its average total costs of producing its normal output would be higher.

REVIEW QUIZ

1 What does a firm's production function show and how is it related to a total product curve?
2 Does the law of diminishing returns apply to capital as well as to labour? Explain why or why not.
3 What does a firm's long-run average cost curve show? How is it related to the firm's short-run average cost curves?
4 What are economies of scale and diseconomies of scale? How do they arise? And what do they imply for the shape of the long-run average cost curve?
5 How is a firm's minimum efficient scale determined?

◆ *Reading Between the Lines* on pp. 232–233 applies what you've learned about a firm's cost curves. It looks at the cost curves of firms like Krispy Kreme and Country Style.

The Cost of a Doughnut

THE GLOBE AND MAIL, DECEMBER 12, 2001

Krispy Kreme store mobbed

It was a feeding frenzy yesterday as Krispy Kreme Doughnuts Inc. opened in Canada for the first time. ... And Krispy Kreme sold more than 25,000 doughnuts before 10 a.m., when the store officially opened in Mississauga. ...

That's quite all right with Scott Livengood, chairman, president and chief executive officer, who came up from head office in Winston-Salem, N.C., to oversee the launch. ...

The Krispy Kreme in Mississauga is charging $5.99 for a dozen of its doughnuts — $10.99 for two dozen. That's 35 per cent more than at least one of its competitors charges. ...

"Krispy Kreme is a cultural experience, a multidimensional experience," Mr. Livengood said. "People come for the aroma of coffee, the visual theatre. They come to watch the people.

"They see doughnuts rising through the proof box. It's almost a Circadian rhythm. It's a stimulating visual presentation."...

Mr. Livengood is confident that the formula will work — even in Canada, a country that has more doughnut shops per capita than anywhere in the world.

He has committed to building 31 more outlets over the next six years at a cost of $1.2-million (U.S.) each.

Reprinted with permission from *The Globe and Mail*.

EDMONTON JOURNAL, DECEMBER 15, 2001

Doughnut shop's demise comes as shock to owner

Country Style Food Services Inc. is closing 25 more stores under court-ordered bankruptcy protection so its struggling chain can restructure, the company said Friday.

Fifty stores that were "bleeding" the company's finances will no longer be operating by this weekend, says

Country Style, the third largest coffee and doughnut franchiser in Canada.

Dave Mills, the manager of the last Country Style Donut shop in the Edmonton area was shocked to learn Friday that his store was one of the bleeders that would be shut down this morning. ...

Reprinted with permission of the *Edmonton Journal*.

Essence of the Stories

■ Two news stories separated by only three days report the successful opening of a new doughnut shop and the closing of another.

■ Krispy Kreme is expanding its business into Canada and plans to open 31 more outlets over the next six years at a cost of $1.2 million (U.S.) each.

■ Country Style Food Services Inc., Canada's third largest coffee and doughnut franchiser, is closing 25 stores.

Economic Analysis

■ Doughnut producers must choose the styles and varieties of doughnuts to produce, the technology for producing them, and the scale of their production plants.

■ Krispy Kreme uses a secret formula to produce doughnuts and makes them in full view of its customers in a doughnut production theatre.

■ The Krispy Kreme technology is capital intensive and has high fixed costs.

■ To produce at a low enough average total cost (*ATC*), Krispy Kreme must produce a large output rate.

■ Figure 1 shows the average cost curves for a production process such as that of Krispy Kreme. (The numbers are assumed.)

■ Average fixed cost (*AFC*) is high and output must exceed 1,500 doughnuts an hour before it falls below 50¢ a doughnut.

■ Average variable cost (*AVC*) is low and is assumed to be constant for output rates up to 2,000 doughnuts an hour.

■ Average total cost (*ATC*) is at its minimum at an output rate of 2,500 doughnuts an hour.

■ Figure 2 shows the average cost curves for a production process such as that of Country Style. (Again, the numbers are assumed.)

■ Average fixed cost (*AFC*) is low and an output of 200 doughnuts an hour keeps it well below the price of a doughnut. But as the output rate falls to around 100 an hour, average costs rise steeply.

■ Average variable cost (*AVC*) is assumed to be constant for output rates up to 200 doughnuts an hour.

■ Average total cost (*ATC*) is at its minimum at an output rate of 300 doughnuts an hour.

■ If the output rate falls below 200 doughnuts an hour, *ATC* rises to exceed the market price of a doughnut and a firm like Country Style has a problem.

Figure 1 Krispy Kreme cost curves

Figure 2 Country Style cost curves

SUMMARY

KEY POINTS

Decision Time Frames (p. 218)

- In the short run, the quantity of some resources are fixed and the quantities of the other resources can be varied.
- In the long run, the quantities of all resources can be varied.

Short-Run Technology Constraint (pp. 219–222)

- A total product curve shows the quantity a firm can produce with a given quantity of capital and different quantities of labour.
- Initially, the marginal product of labour increases as the quantity of labour increases, but eventually, marginal product diminishes—the law of diminishing returns.
- Average product increases initially and eventually diminishes.

Short-Run Cost (pp. 223–227)

- As output increases, total fixed cost is constant, and total variable cost and total cost increase.
- As output increases, average fixed cost decreases and average variable cost, average total cost, and marginal cost decrease at low outputs and increase at high outputs. These cost curves are U-shaped.

Long-Run Cost (pp. 228–231)

- Long-run cost is the cost of production when all inputs—labour and capital—have been adjusted to their economically efficient levels.
- There is a set of short-run cost curves for each different plant size. There is one least-cost plant size for each output. The larger the output, the larger is the plant size that will minimize average total cost.

- The long-run average cost curve traces out the lowest attainable average total cost at each output when both capital and labour inputs can be varied.
- With economies of scale, the long-run average cost curve slopes downward. With diseconomies of scale, the long-run average cost curve slopes upward.

KEY FIGURES AND TABLE

Figure 10.2   Marginal Product, 221
Figure 10.3   Average Product, 222
Figure 10.5   Marginal Cost and Average Costs, 225
Figure 10.6   Product Curves and Cost Curves, 226
Figure 10.7   Short-Run Costs of Four Different Plants, 229
Figure 10.8   Long-Run Average Cost Curve, 230
Table 10.2   A Compact Glossary of Costs, 227

KEY TERMS

Average fixed cost, 224
Average product, 219
Average total cost, 224
Average variable cost, 224
Constant returns to scale, 231
Diminishing marginal returns, 221
Diseconomies of scale, 230
Economies of scale, 230
Law of diminishing returns, 221
Long run, 218
Long-run average cost curve, 229
Marginal cost, 224
Marginal product, 219
Minimum efficient scale, 231
Short run, 218
Sunk cost, 218
Total cost, 223
Total fixed cost, 223
Total product, 219
Total variable cost, 223

PROBLEMS

*1. Rubber Dinghies' total product schedule is

Labour (workers per week)	Output (dinghies per week)
1	1
2	3
3	6
4	10
5	15
6	21
7	26
8	30
9	33
10	35

a. Draw the total product curve.
b. Calculate the average product of labour and draw the average product curve.
c. Calculate the marginal product of labour and draw the marginal product curve.
d. What is the relationship between average product and marginal product when Rubber Dinghies produces (i) fewer than 30 dinghies a week and (ii) more than 30 dinghies a week?

2. Sue's SurfBoards' total product schedule is

Labour (workers per week)	Output (surfboards per week)
1	40
2	100
3	140
4	170
5	190
6	200

a. Draw the total product curve.
b. Calculate the average product of labour and draw the average product curve.
c. Calculate the marginal product of labour and draw the marginal product curve.
d. What is the relationship between the average product and marginal product when Sue's SurfBoards produces (i) less than 100 surfboards a week and (ii) more than 100 surfboards a week?

*3. In problem 1, the price of labour is $400 a week and total fixed cost is $1,000 a week.
a. Calculate total cost, total variable cost, and total fixed cost for each output and draw the short-run total cost curves.
b. Calculate average total cost, average fixed cost, average variable cost, and marginal cost at each output and draw the short-run average and marginal cost curves.

4. In problem 2, the price of labour is $100 per week and total fixed costs are $200 per week.
a. Calculate total cost, total variable cost, and total fixed costs for each level of output and draw the short-run total cost curves.
b. Calculate average total cost, average fixed cost, average variable cost, and marginal cost at each level of output and draw the short-run average and marginal cost curves.

*5. In problem 3, suppose that Rubber Dinghies' total fixed cost increases to $1,100 a week. Explain what changes occur in the short-run average and marginal cost curves.

6. In problem 4, suppose that the price of labour increases to $150 per week. Explain what changes occur in the short-run average and marginal cost curves.

*7. In problem 3, Rubber Dinghies buys a second plant and the total product of each quantity of labour doubles. The total fixed cost of operating each plant is $1,000 a week. The wage rate is $400 a week.
a. Set out the average total cost schedule when Rubber Dinghies operates two plants.
b. Draw the long-run average cost curve.
c. Over what output ranges is it efficient to operate one plant and two plants?

8. In problem 4, Sue's SurfBoards buys a second plant and the total product of each quantity of labour increases by 50 percent. The total fixed cost of operating each plant is $200 a week. The wage rate is $100 a week.
a. Set out the average total cost curve when Sue's SurfBoards operates two plants.
b. Draw the long-run average cost curve.
c. Over what output ranges is it efficient to operate one plant and two plants?

*9. The table shows the production function of
Bonnie's Balloon Rides.

Labour	Output (rides per day)			
(workers per day)	Plant 1	Plant 2	Plant 3	Plant 4
1	4	10	13	15
2	10	15	18	20
3	13	18	22	24
4	15	20	24	26
5	16	21	25	27
Balloons (number)	1	2	3	4

Bonnie pays $500 a day for each balloon she
rents and $250 a day for each balloon operator
she hires.
a. Find and graph the average total cost curve
   for each plant size.
b. Draw Bonnie's long-run average cost curve.
c. What is Bonnie's minimum efficient scale?
d. Explain how Bonnie uses her long-run average cost curve to decide how many balloons
   to rent.

10. The table shows the production function of
Cathy's Cakes.

Labour	Output (cakes per day)			
(workers per day)	Plant 1	Plant 2	Plant 3	Plant 4
1	20	40	55	65
2	40	60	75	85
3	65	75	90	100
4	65	85	100	110
Ovens (number)	1	2	3	4

Cathy pays $100 a day for each oven she rents
and $50 a day for each kitchen worker she
hires.
a. Find and graph the average total cost curve
   for each plant size.
b. Draw Cathy's long-run average cost curve.
c. Over what output range does Cathy experience economies of scale?
d. Explain how Cathy uses her long-run average cost curve to decide how many ovens to
   rent.

CRITICAL THINKING

1. Study *Reading Between the Lines* on pp. 232–233
   and then answer the following questions:
   a. What are the main differences in the cost
      curves of Krispy Kreme and Country Style?
   b. Why do you think Krispy Kreme is starting to
      operate in Canada?
   c. Would it ever make sense for Krispy Kreme to
      make its doughnuts using the same technology
      as Country Style uses?
   d. Would it ever make sense for Country Style to
      make its doughnuts using the same technology
      as Krispy Kreme uses?
   e. Suppose an advance in technology increases the
      productivity of a Krispy Kreme style doughnut
      production plant but has no effect on small-
      scale doughnut production. How would the
      technological change affect Krispy Kreme's
      costs and cost curves? Would it change the
      number of outlets and the number of people it
      employs? If so, how? Explain.

WEB EXERCISES

1. Use the link on your Parkin–Bade Web site to
   obtain information about the cost of producing
   pumpkins.
   a. List all the costs referred to on the Web page.
   b. For each item, say whether it is a fixed cost or a
      variable cost.
   c. Make some assumptions and sketch the average
      cost curves and the marginal cost curve for pro-
      ducing pumpkins.
2. Use the link on your Parkin–Bade Web site to
   obtain information about the cost of producing
   vegetables. For one of the vegetables (your choice):
   a. List all the costs referred to on the Web page.
   b. For each item, say whether it is a fixed cost or a
      variable cost.
   c. Sketch the average cost curves and the marginal
      cost curve for producing the vegetable you've
      chosen.

PERFECT COMPETITION

CHAPTER 11

Sweet Competition

Maple syrup is sweet, but producing it and selling it is a tough competitive business. Around 12,000 firms in Canada and the United States produce syrup. In 2000 and 2001, bumper crops sent the price of maple syrup tumbling. How did producers react to this drop in price? *Reading Between the Lines* at the end of the chapter answers this question. In recent years, new firms have entered the maple syrup business, while others have been squeezed out. Why do some firms enter an industry and others leave it? What are the effects on profits and prices of new firms entering and old firms leaving an industry? ◆ In September 2002, around 200,000 people were unemployed because they had been laid off by the firms that previously employed them. Why do firms lay off workers? Why do firms temporarily shut down? ◆ Over the past few years, there has been a dramatic fall in the prices of personal computers. For example, a slow computer cost almost $4,000 a few years ago, and a fast one costs only $1,000 today. What goes on in an industry when the price of its output falls sharply? What happens to the profits of the firms producing such goods? Ice cream, computers, and most other goods are produced by more than one firm, and these firms compete with each other for sales.

◆ To study competitive markets, we are going to build a model of a market in which competition is as fierce and extreme as possible—more extreme than in the examples we've just considered. We call this situation "perfect competition."

After studying this chapter, you will be able to

- Define perfect competition
- Explain how price and output are determined in perfect competition
- Explain why firms sometimes shut down temporarily and lay off workers
- Explain why firms enter and leave the industry
- Predict the effects of a change in demand and of a technological advance
- Explain why perfect competition is efficient

Competition

THE FIRMS THAT YOU STUDY IN THIS CHAPTER face the force of raw competition. We call this extreme form of competition perfect competition. **Perfect competition** is an industry in which

- Many firms sell identical products to many buyers.
- There are no restrictions on entry into the industry.
- Established firms have no advantage over new ones.
- Sellers and buyers are well informed about prices.

Farming, fishing, wood pulping and paper milling, the manufacture of paper cups and plastic shopping bags, grocery retailing, photo finishing, lawn service, plumbing, painting, dry cleaning, and the provision of laundry services are all examples of highly competitive industries.

How Perfect Competition Arises

Perfect competition arises if the minimum efficient scale of a single producer is small relative to the demand for the good or service. A firm's *minimum efficient scale* is the smallest quantity of output at which long-run average cost reaches is lowest level. (See Chapter 10, p. 231.) Where the minimum efficient scale of a firm is small relative to demand, there is room for many firms in an industry.

Second, perfect competition arises if each firm is perceived to produce a good or service that has no unique characteristics so that consumers don't care which firm they buy from.

Price Takers

Firms in perfect competition must make many decisions. But one thing they do *not* decide is the price at which to sell their output. Firms in perfect competition are said to be price takers. A **price taker** is a firm that cannot influence the price of a good or service.

The key reason why a perfectly competitive firm is a price taker is that it produces a tiny proportion of the total output of a particular good and buyers are well informed about the prices of other firms.

Imagine that you are a wheat farmer in Saskatchewan. You have 500 hectares under cultivation—which sounds like a lot. But compared to the thousands of hectares across the Canadian prairies and in the Dakotas, Nebraska, Colorado, Oklahoma, and Texas, as well as the thousands more in Argentina, Australia, and Ukraine, your 500 hectares is a drop in the ocean. Nothing makes your wheat any better than any other farmer's, and all the buyers of wheat know the price at which they can do business.

If everybody else sells their wheat for $300 a tonne and you want $310, why would people buy from you? They can go to the next farmer and the next and the one after that and buy all they need for $300 a tonne. This price is determined in the market for wheat, and you are a *price taker*.

A price taker faces a perfectly elastic demand. One farm's wheat is a *perfect substitute* for wheat from the farm next door or from any other farm. Note, though, that the *market* demand for wheat is not perfectly elastic. The market demand curve is downward sloping, and its elasticity depends on the substitutability of wheat for other grains such as barley, rye, corn, and rice.

Economic Profit and Revenue

A firm's goal is to maximize *economic profit*, which is equal to total revenue minus total cost. Total cost is the *opportunity cost* of production, which includes *normal profit*, the return that the entrepreneur can expect to receive on the average in an alternative business. (See Chapter 9, p. 197.)

A firm's **total revenue** equals the price of its output multiplied by the number of units of output sold (price × quantity). **Marginal revenue** is the change in total revenue that results from a one-unit increase in the quantity sold. Marginal revenue is calculated by dividing the change in total revenue by the change in the quantity sold.

Figure 11.1 illustrates these revenue concepts. Cindy's Sweaters is one of a thousand such small firms. Demand and supply in the sweater market determine the price of a sweater. Cindy must take this price. Cindy's Sweaters cannot influence the price by its own actions, so the price remains constant when Cindy changes the quantity of sweaters produced.

The table shows three different quantities of sweaters produced. As the quantity varies, the price remains constant—in this example, at $25 a sweater. Total revenue is equal to the price multiplied by the quantity sold. For example, if Cindy sells 8 sweaters, total revenue is 8 × $25, which equals $200.

Marginal revenue is the change in total revenue resulting from a one-unit change in quantity. For example, when the quantity sold increases from 8 to 9, total revenue increases from $200 to $225, so

FIGURE 11.1 Demand, Price, and Revenue in Perfect Competition

(a) Sweater market

(b) Cindy's marginal revenue

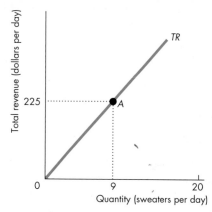

(c) Cindy's total revenue

Quantity sold (Q) (sweaters per day)	Price (P) (dollars per sweater)	Total revenue (TR = P × Q) (dollars)	Marginal revenue (MR = ΔTR/ΔQ) (dollars per additional sweater)
8	25	200	
			 25
9	25	225	
			 25
10	25	250	

Market demand and supply determine the market price. In part (a), the market price is $25 a sweater and 9,000 sweaters are bought and sold. The demand for Cindy's Sweaters is perfectly elastic at the market price of $25 a sweater. The table calculates total revenue and marginal revenue. Part (b) shows Cindy's Sweaters' marginal revenue curve (*MR*). This curve is also the demand curve for Cindy's sweaters. Part (c) shows Cindy's total revenue curve (*TR*). Point *A* corresponds to the second row of the table.

marginal revenue is $25 a sweater. (Notice that in the table, marginal revenue appears *between* the lines for the quantities sold to remind you that marginal revenue results from the *change* in the quantity sold.)

Because the price remains constant when the quantity sold changes, the change in total revenue resulting from a one-unit increase in the quantity sold equals price. Therefore in perfect competition, marginal revenue equals price.

Figure 11.1(b) shows Cindy's marginal revenue curve (*MR*). This curve tells us the change in total revenue that results from selling one more sweater. This curve is also the demand curve for Cindy's sweaters. The firm, being a price taker, can sell any quantity it chooses at the market price. The firm faces a perfectly elastic demand for its output.

The total revenue curve (*TR*) in Fig. 11.1(c) shows the total revenue at each quantity sold. For example, if Cindy sells 9 sweaters, total revenue is

$225 (point *A*). Because each additional sweater sold brings in a constant amount—$25—the total revenue curve is an upward-sloping straight line.

REVIEW QUIZ

1 Why is a firm in perfect competition a price taker?
2 In perfect competition, what is the relationship between the demand for the firm's output and the market demand?
3 In perfect competition, why is a firm's marginal revenue curve also the demand curve for the firm's output?
4 Why is the total revenue curve in perfect competition an upward-sloping straight line?

The Firm's Decisions in Perfect Competition

FIRMS IN A PERFECTLY COMPETITIVE INDUSTRY face a given market price and have the revenue curves that you've studied. These revenue curves summarize the market constraint faced by a perfectly competitive firm.

Firms also face a technology constraint, which is described by the product curves (total product, average product, and marginal product) that you studied in Chapter 10. The technology available to the firm determines its costs, which are described by the cost curves (total cost, average cost, and marginal cost) that you also studied in Chapter 10.

The task of the competitive firm is to make the maximum economic profit possible, given the constraints it faces. To achieve this objective, a firm must make four key decisions: two in the short run and two in the long run.

Short-Run Decisions The *short run* is a time frame in which each firm has a given plant and the number of firms in the industry is fixed. But many things can change in the short run, and the firm must react to these changes. For example, the price for which the firm can sell its output might have a seasonal fluctuation, or it might fluctuate with general business conditions. The firm must react to such short-run price fluctuations and decide

1. Whether to produce or to shut down
2. If the decision is to produce, what quantity to produce

Long-Run Decisions The *long run* is a time frame in which each firm can change the size of its plant and decide whether to leave the industry. Other firms can decide whether to enter the industry. So in the long run, both the plant size of each firm and the number of firms in the industry can change. Also in the long run, the constraints that firms face can change. For example, the demand for the good can permanently fall, or a technological advance can change the industry's costs. The firm must react to such long-run changes and decide

1. Whether to increase or decrease its plant size
2. Whether to stay in an industry or leave it

The Firm and the Industry in the Short Run and the Long Run To study a competitive industry, we begin by looking at an individual firm's short-run decisions. We then see how the short-run decisions of all firms in a competitive industry combine to determine the industry price, output, and economic profit. We then turn to the long run and study the effects of long-run decisions on the industry price, output, and economic profit. All the decisions we study are driven by the pursuit of a single objective: maximization of economic profit.

Profit-Maximizing Output

A perfectly competitive firm maximizes economic profit by choosing its output level. One way of finding the profit-maximizing output is to study a firm's total revenue and total cost curves and find the output level at which total revenue exceeds total cost by the largest amount. Figure 11.2 shows how to do this for Cindy's Sweaters. The table lists Cindy's total revenue and total cost at different outputs, and part (a) of the figure shows Cindy's total revenue and total cost curves. These curves are graphs of the numbers shown in the first three columns of the table. The total revenue curve (TR) is the same as that in Fig. 11.1(c). The total cost curve (TC) is similar to the one that you met in Chapter 10: As output increases, so does total cost.

Economic profit equals total revenue minus total cost. The fourth column of the table in Fig. 11.2 shows Cindy's economic profit, and part (b) of the figure illustrates these numbers as Cindy's profit curve. This curve shows that Cindy makes an economic profit at outputs between 4 and 12 sweaters a day. At outputs less than 4 sweaters a day, Cindy incurs an economic loss. She also incurs an economic loss if output exceeds 12 sweaters a day. At outputs of 4 sweaters and 12 sweaters a day, total cost equals total revenue and Cindy's economic profit is zero. An output at which total cost equals total revenue is called a *break-even point*. The firm's economic profit at a break-even point is zero. But because normal profit is part of total cost, a firm makes normal profit at a break-even point. That is, at the break-even point, the entrepreneur makes an income equal to the best alternative return forgone.

Notice the relationship between the total revenue, total cost, and profit curves. Economic profit is measured by the vertical distance between the total

FIGURE 11.2 Total Revenue, Total Cost, and Economic Profit

(a) Revenue and cost

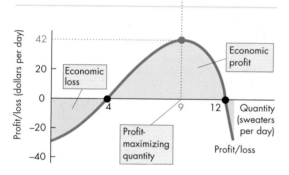

(b) Economic profit and loss

Quantity (Q) (sweaters per day)	Total revenue (TR) (dollars)	Total cost (TC) (dollars)	Economic profit (TR − TC) (dollars)
0	0	22	−22
1	25	45	−20
2	50	66	−16
3	75	85	−10
4	100	100	0
5	125	114	11
6	150	126	24
7	175	141	34
8	200	160	40
9	225	183	42
10	250	210	40
11	275	245	30
12	300	300	0
13	325	360	−35

The table lists Cindy's total revenue, total cost, and economic profit. Part (a) graphs the total revenue and total cost curves. Economic profit, in part (a), is the height of the blue area between the total cost and total revenue curves. Cindy's Sweaters makes maximum economic profit, $42 a day ($225 − $183), when it produces 9 sweaters—the output at which the vertical distance between the total revenue and total cost curves is at its largest. At outputs of 4

sweaters a day and 12 sweaters a day, Cindy makes zero economic profit—these are break-even points. At outputs less than 4 and greater than 12 sweaters a day, Cindy incurs an economic loss. Part (b) of the figure shows Cindy's profit curve. The profit curve is at its highest when economic profit is at a maximum and cuts the horizontal axis at the break-even points.

revenue and total cost curves. When the total revenue curve in part (a) is above the total cost curve, between 4 and 12 sweaters, the firm is making an economic profit and the profit curve in Fig. 11.2(b) is above the horizontal axis. At the break-even points, where the total cost and total revenue curves inter-

sect, the profit curve intersects the horizontal axis. The profit curve is at its highest when the distance between *TR* and *TC* is greatest. In this example, profit maximization occurs at an output of 9 sweaters a day. At this output, Cindy's economic profit is $42 a day.

Marginal Analysis

Another way of finding the profit-maximizing output is to use *marginal analysis* and compare marginal revenue, *MR*, with marginal cost, *MC*. As output increases, marginal revenue remains constant but marginal cost changes. At low output levels, marginal cost decreases, but it eventually increases. So where the marginal cost curve intersects the marginal revenue curve, marginal cost is rising.

If marginal revenue exceeds marginal cost (if *MR* > *MC*), then the extra revenue from selling one more unit exceeds the extra cost incurred to produce it. The firm makes an economic profit on the marginal unit, so its economic profit increases if output *increases.*

If marginal revenue is less than marginal cost (if *MR* < *MC*), then the extra revenue from selling one more unit is less than the extra cost incurred to produce it. The firm incurs an economic loss on the marginal unit, so its economic profit decreases if output increases and its economic profit increases if output *decreases.*

If marginal revenue equals marginal cost (if *MR* = *MC*), economic profit is maximized. The rule *MR* = *MC* is an example of marginal analysis. Let's check that this rule works to find the profit-maximizing output by returning to Cindy's Sweaters.

Look at Fig. 11.3. The table records Cindy's marginal revenue and marginal cost. Marginal revenue is a constant $25 a sweater. Over the range of outputs shown in the table, marginal cost increases from $19 a sweater to $35 a sweater.

Focus on the highlighted rows of the table. If Cindy increases output from 8 sweaters to 9 sweaters, marginal revenue is $25 and marginal cost is $23. Because marginal revenue exceeds marginal cost, economic profit increases. The last column of the table shows that economic profit increases from $40 to $42, an increase of $2. This economic profit from the ninth sweater is shown as the blue area in the figure.

If Cindy increases output from 9 sweaters to 10 sweaters, marginal revenue is still $25 but marginal cost is $27. Because marginal revenue is less than marginal cost, economic profit decreases. The last column of the table shows that economic profit decreases from $42 to $40. This loss from the tenth sweater is shown as the red area in the figure.

Cindy maximizes economic profit by producing 9 sweaters a day, the quantity at which marginal revenue equals marginal cost.

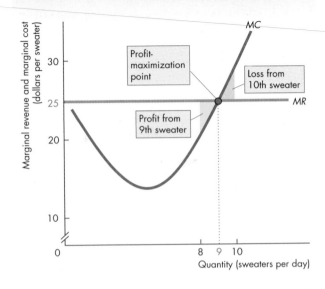

FIGURE 11.3 Profit-Maximizing Output

Quantity (Q) (sweaters per day)	Total revenue (TR) (dollars)	Marginal revenue (MR) (dollars per additional sweater)	Total cost (TC) (dollars)	Marginal cost (MC) (dollars per additional sweater)	Economic profit (TR – TC) (dollars)
7	175		141		34
		25		19	
8	200		160		40
		25		23	
9	225		183		42
		25		27	
10	250		210		40
		25		35	
11	275		245		30

Another way of finding the profit-maximizing output is to determine the output at which marginal revenue equals marginal cost. The table shows that if output increases from 8 to 9 sweaters, marginal cost is $23, which is less than the marginal revenue of $25. If output increases from 9 to 10 sweaters, marginal cost is $27, which exceeds the marginal revenue of $25. The figure shows that marginal cost and marginal revenue are equal when Cindy produces 9 sweaters a day. If marginal revenue exceeds marginal cost, an increase in output increases economic profit. If marginal revenue is less than marginal cost, an increase in output decreases economic profit. If marginal revenue equals marginal cost, economic profit is maximized.

Profits and Losses in the Short Run

In short-run equilibrium, although the firm produces the profit-maximizing output, it does not necessarily end up making an economic profit. It might do so, but it might alternatively break even (earn a normal profit) or incur an economic loss. To determine which of these outcomes occurs, we compare the firm's total revenue and total cost or, equivalently, we compare price with average total cost. If price equals average total cost, a firm breaks even—makes normal profit. If price exceeds average total cost, a firm makes an economic profit. If price is less than average total cost, a firm incurs an economic loss. Figure 11.4 shows these three possible short-run profit outcomes.

Three Possible Profit Outcomes In Fig. 11.4(a), the price of a sweater is $20. Cindy's profit-maximizing output is 8 sweaters a day. Average total cost is $20 a sweater, so Cindy breaks even and makes normal profit (zero economic profit).

In Fig. 11.4(b), the price of a sweater is $25. Profit is maximized when output is 9 sweaters a day. Here, price exceeds average total cost (*ATC*), so Cindy

makes an economic profit. This economic profit is $42 a day. It is made up of $4.67 per sweater ($25.00 − $20.33) multiplied by the number of sweaters ($4.67 × 9 = $42). The blue rectangle shows this economic profit. The height of that rectangle is profit per sweater, $4.67, and the length is the quantity of sweaters produced, 9 a day, so the area of the rectangle is Cindy's economic profit of $42 a day.

In Fig. 11.4(c), the price of a sweater is $17. Here, price is less than average total cost and Cindy incurs an economic loss. Price and marginal revenue are $17 a sweater, and the profit-maximizing (in this case, loss-minimizing) output is 7 sweaters a day. Cindy's total revenue is $119 a day (7 × $17). Average total cost is $20.14 a sweater, so the economic loss is $3.14 per sweater ($20.14 − $17.00). This loss per sweater multiplied by the number of sweaters is $22 ($3.14 × 7 = $22). The red rectangle shows this economic loss. The height of that rectangle is economic loss per sweater, $3.14, and the length is the quantity of sweaters produced, 7 a day, so the area of the rectangle is Cindy's economic loss of $22 a day.

FIGURE 11.4   Three Possible Profit Outcomes in the Short Run

(a) Normal profit

(b) Economic profit

(c) Economic loss

In the short run, the firm might break even (make a normal profit), make an economic profit, or incur an economic loss. If the price equals minimum average total cost, the firm breaks even and makes a normal profit (part a). If the price exceeds the average total cost of producing the profit-maximizing output, the firm makes an economic profit (the blue rectangle in part b). If the price is below minimum average total cost, the firm incurs an economic loss (the red rectangle in part c).

The Firm's Short-Run Supply Curve

A perfectly competitive firm's short-run supply curve shows how the firm's profit-maximizing output varies as the market price varies, other things remaining the same. Figure 11.5 shows how to derive Cindy's supply curve. Part (a) shows Cindy's Sweaters' marginal cost and average variable cost curves, and part (b) shows its supply curve. There is a direct link between the marginal cost and average variable cost curves and the supply curve. Let's see what that link is.

Temporary Plant Shutdown In the short run, a firm cannot avoid incurring its fixed cost. But the firm can avoid variable costs by temporarily laying off its workers and shutting down. If a firm shuts down, it produces no output and it incurs a loss equal to total fixed cost. This loss is the largest that a firm needs to incur. A firm shuts down if the price falls below minimum average variable cost. The **shutdown point** is the output and price at which the firm just covers its total variable cost—point T in Fig. 11.5(a). If the price is $17, the marginal revenue curve is MR_0 and the profit-maximizing output is 7 sweaters a day at point T. But both price and average variable cost equal $17, so Cindy's total revenue equals total variable cost. Cindy incurs an economic loss equal to total fixed cost. At a price below $17, no matter what quantity Cindy produces, average *variable* cost exceeds price and the firm's loss exceeds total fixed cost. At a price below $17, the firm shuts down temporarily.

The Short-Run Supply Curve If the price is above minimum average variable cost, Cindy maximizes profit by producing the output at which marginal cost equals price. We can determine the quantity produced at each price from the marginal cost curve. At a price of $25, the marginal revenue curve is MR_1 and Cindy maximizes profit by producing 9 sweaters. At a price of $31, the marginal revenue curve is MR_2 and Cindy produces 10 sweaters.

Cindy's short-run supply curve, shown in Fig. 11.5(b), has two separate parts: First, at prices that exceed minimum average variable cost, the supply curve is the same as the marginal cost curve above the shutdown point (T). Second, at prices below minimum average variable cost, Cindy shuts down and produces nothing. Its supply curve runs along the vertical axis. At a price of $17, Cindy is indifferent between shutting down and producing 7 sweaters a day. Either way, Cindy incurs a loss of $22 a day.

FIGURE 11.5   A Firm's Supply Curve

(a) Marginal cost and average variable cost

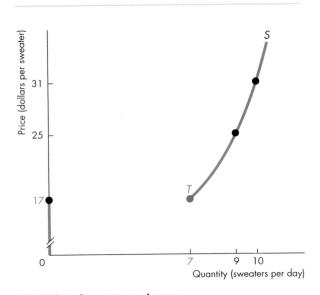

(b) Cindy's short-run supply curve

Part (a) shows Cindy's profit-maximizing output at various market prices. At $25 a sweater, Cindy produces 9 sweaters. At $17 a sweater, Cindy produces 7 sweaters. At any price below $17 a sweater, Cindy produces nothing. Cindy's shutdown point is T. Part (b) shows Cindy's supply curve—the number of sweaters Cindy will produce at each price. It is made up of the marginal cost curve (part a) at all points above minimum average variable cost and the vertical axis at all prices below minimum average variable cost.

Short-Run Industry Supply Curve

The **short-run industry supply curve** shows the quantity supplied by the industry at each price when the plant size of each firm and the number of firms remain constant. The quantity supplied by the industry at a given price is the sum of the quantities supplied by all firms in the industry at that price.

Figure 11.6 shows the supply curve for the competitive sweater industry. In this example, the industry consists of 1,000 firms exactly like Cindy's Sweaters. At each price, the quantity supplied by the industry is 1,000 times the quantity supplied by a single firm.

The table in Fig. 11.6 shows the firm's and the industry's supply schedule and how the industry supply curve is constructed. At prices below $17, every firm in the industry shuts down; the quantity supplied by the industry is zero. At a price of $17, each firm is indifferent between shutting down and producing nothing or operating and producing 7 sweaters a day. Some firms will shut down, and others will supply 7 sweaters a day. The quantity supplied by each firm is *either* 0 or 7 sweaters, but the quantity supplied by the industry is *between* 0 (all firms shut down) and 7,000 (all firms produce 7 sweaters a day each).

To construct the industry supply curve, we sum the quantities supplied by the individual firms. Each of the 1,000 firms in the industry has a supply schedule like Cindy's. At prices below $17, the industry supply curve runs along the price axis. At a price of $17, the industry supply curve is horizontal—supply is perfectly elastic. As the price rises above $17, each firm increases its quantity supplied and the quantity supplied by the industry increases by 1,000 times that of each firm.

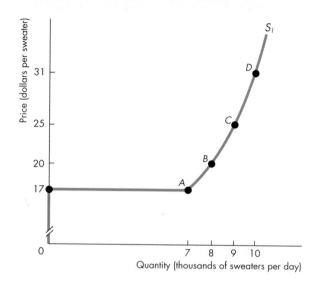

FIGURE 11.6   Industry Supply Curve

	Price (dollars per sweater)	Quantity supplied by Cindy's Sweaters (sweaters per day)	Quantity supplied by industry (sweaters per day)
A	17	0 or 7	0 to 7,000
B	20	8	8,000
C	25	9	9,000
D	31	10	10,000

The industry supply schedule is the sum of the supply schedules of all individual firms. An industry that consists of 1,000 identical firms has a supply schedule similar to that of the individual firm, but the quantity supplied by the industry is 1,000 times as large as that of the individual firm (see the table). The industry supply curve is S_I. Points A, B, C, and D correspond to the rows of the table. At the shutdown price of $17, each firm produces either 0 or 7 sweaters per day. The industry supply is perfectly elastic at the shutdown price.

So far, we have studied a single firm in isolation. We have seen that the firm's profit-maximizing actions depend on the market price, which the firm takes as given. But how is the market price determined? Let's find out.

Output, Price, and Profit in Perfect Competition

To determine the market price and the quantity bought and sold in a perfectly competitive market, we need to study how market demand and market supply interact. We begin this process by studying a perfectly competitive market in the short run when the number of firms is fixed and each firm has a given plant size.

Short-Run Equilibrium

Industry demand and supply determine the market price and industry output. Figure 11.7(a) shows a short-run equilibrium. The supply curve S is the same as S_I in Fig. 11.6. If demand is shown by the demand curve D_1, the equilibrium price is $20. Each firm takes this price as given and produces its profit-maximizing output, which is 8 sweaters a day. Because the industry has 1,000 firms, industry output is 8,000 sweaters a day.

A Change in Demand

Changes in demand bring changes to short-run industry equilibrium. Figure 11.7(b) shows these changes.

If demand increases, the demand curve shifts rightward to D_2. The price rises to $25. At this price, each firm maximizes profit by increasing output. The new output level is 9 sweaters a day for each firm and 9,000 sweaters a day for the industry.

If demand decreases, the demand curve shifts leftward to D_3. The price now falls to $17. At this price, each firm maximizes profit by decreasing its output. The new output level is 7 sweaters a day for each firm and 7,000 sweaters a day for the industry.

If the demand curve shifts farther leftward than D_3, the price remains constant at $17 because the industry supply curve is horizontal at that price. Some firms continue to produce 7 sweaters a day, and others temporarily shut down. Firms are indifferent between these two activities, and whichever they choose, they incur an economic loss equal to total fixed cost. The number of firms continuing to produce is just enough to satisfy the market demand at a price of $17.

FIGURE 11.7   Short-Run Equilibrium

(a) Equilibrium

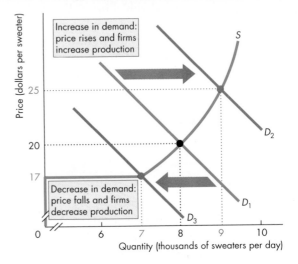

(b) Change in equilibrium

In part (a), the industry supply curve is S. Demand is D_1, and the price is $20. At this price, each firm produces 8 sweaters a day and the industry produces 8,000 sweaters a day. In part (b), when demand increases to D_2, the price rises to $25 and

each firm increases its output to 9 sweaters a day. Industry output is 9,000 sweaters a day. When demand decreases to D_3, the price falls to $17 and each firm decreases its output to 7 sweaters a day. Industry output is 7,000 sweaters a day.

Long-Run Adjustments

In short-run equilibrium, a firm might make an economic profit, incur an economic loss, or break even (make normal profit). Although each of these three situations is a short-run equilibrium, only one of them is a long-run equilibrium. To see why, we need to examine the forces at work in a competitive industry in the long run.

In the long run, an industry adjusts in two ways:

■ Entry and exit
■ Changes in plant size

Let's look first at entry and exit.

Entry and Exit

In the long run, firms respond to economic profit and economic loss by either entering or exiting an industry. Firms enter an industry in which firms are making an economic profit, and firms exit an industry in which firms are incurring an economic loss. Temporary economic profit and temporary economic loss do not trigger entry and exit. But the prospect of persistent economic profit or loss does.

Entry and exit influence price, the quantity produced, and economic profit. The immediate effect of these decisions is to shift the industry supply curve. If more firms enter an industry, supply increases and the industry supply curve shifts rightward. If firms exit an industry, supply decreases and the industry supply curve shifts leftward.

Let's see what happens when new firms enter an industry.

The Effects of Entry   Figure 11.8 shows the effects of entry. Suppose that all the firms in this industry have cost curves like those in Fig. 11.4. At any price greater than $20, firms make an economic profit. At any price less than $20, firms incur an economic loss. And at a price of $20, firms make zero economic profit. Also suppose that the demand curve for sweaters is D. If the industry supply curve is S_1, sweaters sell for $23, and 7,000 sweaters a day are produced. Firms in the industry make an economic profit. This economic profit is a signal for new firms to enter the industry.

As these events unfold, supply increases and the industry supply curve shifts rightward to S_0. With the greater supply and unchanged demand, the market price falls from $23 to $20 a sweater and the quantity

produced by the industry increases from 7,000 to 8,000 sweaters a day.

Industry output increases, but Cindy's Sweaters, like each other firm in the industry, moves down its supply curve and *decreases* output! Because the price falls, each firm produces less. But because the number of firms in the industry increases, the industry as a whole produces more.

Because price falls, each firm's economic profit decreases. When the price falls to $20, economic profit disappears and each firm makes a normal profit.

You have just discovered a key proposition:

As new firms enter an industry, the price falls and the economic profit of each existing firm decreases.

An example of this process occurred during the 1980s in the personal computer industry. When IBM introduced its first PC, there was little competition

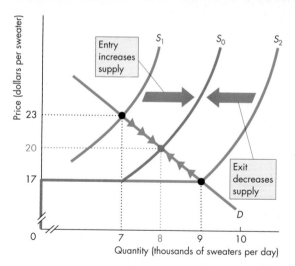

FIGURE 11.8   Entry and Exit

When new firms enter the sweater industry, the industry supply curve shifts rightward, from S_1 to S_0. The equilibrium price falls from $23 to $20, and the quantity produced increases from 7,000 to 8,000 sweaters.

When firms exit the sweater industry, the industry supply curve shifts leftward, from S_2 to S_0. The equilibrium price rises from $17 to $20, and the quantity produced decreases from 9,000 to 8,000 sweaters.

and the price of a PC gave IBM a big profit. But new firms such as Compaq, NEC, Dell, and a host of others entered the industry with machines that were technologically identical to IBM's. In fact, they were so similar that they came to be called "clones." The massive wave of entry into the personal computer industry shifted the supply curve rightward and lowered the price and the economic profit.

Let's now look at the effects of exit.

The Effects of Exit Figure 11.8 also shows the effects of exit. Suppose that firm's costs and market demand are the same as before. But now suppose the supply curve is S_2. The market price is $17, and 9,000 sweaters a day are produced. Firms in the industry now incur an economic loss. This economic loss is a signal for some firms to exit the industry. As firms exit, the industry supply curve shifts leftward to S_0. With the decrease in supply, industry output decreases from 9,000 to 8,000 sweaters and the price rises from $17 to $20.

As the price rises, Cindy's Sweaters, like each other firm in the industry, moves up along its supply curve and increases output. That is, for each firm that remains in the industry, the profit-maximizing output increases. Because the price rises and each firm sells more, economic loss decreases. When the price rises to $20, each firm makes a normal profit.

You've now discovered a second key proposition:

> As firms leave an industry, the price rises and the economic loss of each remaining firm decreases.

The same PC industry that saw a large amount of entry during the 1980s and 1990s is now beginning to see some exit. In 2001, IBM, the firm that first launched the PC, announced that it would no longer produce PCs. The intense competition from Compaq, NEC, Dell, and many others that entered the industry following IBM's lead has lowered the price and eliminated the economic profit on PCs. So IBM will now concentrate on servers and other parts of the computer market.

IBM exited the PC market because it was incurring losses on that line of business. Its exit decreased supply and made it possible for the remaining firms in the industry to earn normal profit.

You've now seen how economic profits induce entry, which in turn lowers profits. And you've seen how economic losses induce exit, which in turn eliminates losses. Let's now look at changes in plant size.

Changes in Plant Size

A firm changes its plant size if, by doing so, it can lower its costs and increase its economic profit. You can probably think of lots of examples of firms that have changed their plant size.

One example that has almost certainly happened near your campus in recent years is a change in the plant size of Kinko's or similar copy shops. Another is the number of FedEx vans that you see on the streets and highways. And another is the number of square feet of retail space devoted to selling computers and video games. These are examples of firms increasing their plant size to seek larger profits.

There are also many examples of firms that have decreased their plant size to avoid economic losses. One of these is Country Style Doughnuts. As competition from other coffee shops became tougher, Country Style Doughnuts closed 45 shops across Canada in late 2002. Many firms have scaled back in a process called *downsizing* in recent years.

Figure 11.9 shows a situation in which Cindy's Sweaters can increase its profit by increasing its plant size. With its current plant, Cindy's marginal cost curve is MC_0, and its short-run average total cost curve is $SRAC_0$. The market price is $25 a sweater, so Cindy's marginal revenue curve is MR_0, and Cindy maximizes profit by producing 6 sweaters a day.

Cindy's Sweaters' long-run average cost curve is $LRAC$. By increasing its plant size—installing more knitting machines—Cindy's Sweaters can move along its long-run average cost curve. As Cindy's Sweaters increases its plant size, its short-run marginal cost curve shifts rightward.

Recall that a firm's short-run supply curve is linked to its marginal cost curve. As Cindy's marginal cost curve shifts rightward, so does its supply curve. If Cindy's Sweaters and the other firms in the industry increase their plants, the short-run industry supply curve shifts rightward. With a given market demand for sweaters, the market price falls. The fall in the market price limits the extent to which Cindy's can profit from increasing its plant size.

Figure 11.9 also shows Cindy's Sweaters in a long-run competitive equilibrium. This situation arises when the market price has fallen to $20 a sweater. Marginal revenue is MR_1, and Cindy maximizes profit by producing 8 sweaters a day. In this situation, Cindy cannot increase her profit by changing the plant size. Cindy is producing at minimum long-run average cost (point M on $LRAC$).

FIGURE 11.9   Plant Size and Long-Run Equilibrium

Initially, Cindy's plant has marginal cost curve MC_0 and short-run average total cost curve $SRAC_0$. The market price is $25 a sweater, and Cindy's marginal revenue is MR_0. The short-run profit-maximizing quantity is 6 sweaters a day. Cindy can increase profit by increasing the plant size.

If all firms in the sweater industry increase their plant sizes, the short-run industry supply increases and the market price falls. In long-run equilibrium, a firm operates with the plant size that minimizes its average cost. Here, Cindy's Sweaters operates the plant with short-run marginal cost MC_1 and short-run average cost $SRAC_1$. Cindy's is also on its long-run average cost curve $LRAC$ and produces at point M. Its output is 8 sweaters a day, and its average total cost equals the price of a sweater: $20.

Because Cindy's Sweaters is producing at minimum long-run average cost, it has no incentive to change its plant size. Either a bigger plant or a smaller plant has a higher long-run average cost. If Fig. 11.9 describes the situation of all firms in the sweater industry, the industry is in long-run equilibrium. No firm has an incentive to change its plant size. Also, because each firm is making zero economic profit (normal profit), no firm has an incentive to enter the industry or to leave it.

Long-Run Equilibrium

Long-run equilibrium occurs in a competitive industry when economic profit is zero (when firms earn normal profit). If the firms in a competitive industry are making an economic profit, new firms enter the industry.

If firms can lower their costs by increasing their plant size, they expand. Each of these actions increases the industry supply, shifts the industry supply curve rightward, lowers the price, and decreases economic profit.

Firms continue to enter and profit decreases as long as firms in the industry are earning positive economic profits. When economic profit has been eliminated, firms stop entering the industry. And when firms are operating with the least-cost plant size, they stop expanding.

If the firms in a competitive industry are incurring an economic loss, some firms exit the industry. If firms can lower their costs by decreasing their plant size, they downsize. Each of these actions decreases industry supply, shifts the industry supply curve leftward, raises the price, and decreases economic loss.

Firms continue to exit and economic loss continues to decrease as long as firms in the industry are incurring economic losses. When economic loss has been eliminated, firms stop exiting the industry. And when firms are operating with the least-cost plant size, they stop downsizing.

So in long-run equilibrium in a competitive industry, firms neither enter nor exit the industry and old firms neither expand nor downsize. Each firm earns normal profit.

REVIEW QUIZ

1 When the market demand for the good decreases, explain how the price of the good and the output of each firm in perfect competition changes in the short run.
2 If the firms in a competitive industry earn an economic profit, what happens to supply, price, output, and economic profit in the long run?
3 If the firms in a competitive industry incur an economic loss, what happens to supply, price, output, and economic profit?

You've seen how a competitive industry adjusts towards its long-run equilibrium. But a competitive industry is rarely *in* a state of long-run equilibrium. A competitive industry is constantly and restlessly evolving towards such an equilibrium. But the constraints that firms in an industry face are constantly changing. The two most persistent sources of change are in tastes and technology. Let's see how a competitive industry reacts to such changes.

Changing Tastes and Advancing Technology

INCREASED AWARENESS OF THE HEALTH HAZARDS of smoking has caused a decrease in the demand for tobacco and cigarettes. The development of inexpensive car and air transportation has caused a huge decrease in the demand for long-distance trains and buses. Solid-state electronics have caused a large decrease in the demand for TV and radio repair. The development of good-quality inexpensive clothing has decreased the demand for sewing machines. What happens in a competitive industry when there is a permanent decrease in the demand for its products?

The development of the microwave oven has produced an enormous increase in demand for paper, glass, and plastic cooking utensils and for plastic wrap. The widespread use of the personal computer has brought a huge increase in the demand for CD-Rs. What happens in a competitive industry when the demand for its output increases?

Advances in technology are constantly lowering the costs of production. New biotechnologies have dramatically lowered the costs of producing many food and pharmaceutical products. New electronic technologies have lowered the cost of producing just about every good and service. What happens in a competitive industry when technological change lowers its production costs?

Let's use the theory of perfect competition to answer these questions.

A Permanent Change in Demand

Figure 11.10(a) shows a competitive industry that initially is in long-run equilibrium. The demand curve is D_0, the supply curve is S_0, the market price is P_0, and industry output is Q_0. Figure 11.10(b) shows a single firm in this initial long-run equilibrium. The firm produces q_0 and makes a normal profit and zero economic profit.

Now suppose that demand decreases and the demand curve shifts leftward to D_1, as shown in Fig. 11.10(a). The price falls to P_1, and the quantity supplied by the industry decreases from Q_0 to Q_1 as the industry slides down its short-run supply curve S_0. Fig. 11.10(b) shows the situation facing a firm. Price is now below the firm's minimum average total cost, so the firm incurs an economic loss. But to keep its loss to a minimum, the firm adjusts its output to

keep marginal cost equal to price. At a price of P_1, each firm produces an output of q_1.

The industry is now in short-run equilibrium but not long-run equilibrium. It is in short-run equilibrium because each firm is maximizing profit. But it is not in long-run equilibrium because each firm is incurring an economic loss—its average total cost exceeds the price.

The economic loss is a signal for some firms to leave the industry. As they do so, short-run industry supply decreases and the supply curve gradually shifts leftward. As industry supply decreases, the price rises. At each higher price, a firm's profit-maximizing output is greater, so the firms remaining in the industry increase their output as the price rises. Each firm slides up its marginal cost or supply curve in Fig. 11.10(b). That is, as firms exit the industry, industry output decreases but the output of the firms that remain in the industry increases. Eventually, enough firms leave the industry for the industry supply curve to have shifted to S_1 in Fig. 11.10(a). At this time, the price has returned to its original level, P_0. At this price, the firms remaining in the industry produce q_0, the same quantity that they produced before the decrease in demand. Because firms are now making normal profit (zero economic profit), no firm wants to enter or exit the industry. The industry supply curve remains at S_1, and industry output is Q_2. The industry is again in long-run equilibrium.

The difference between the initial long-run equilibrium and the final long-run equilibrium is the number of firms in the industry. A permanent decrease in demand has decreased the number of firms. Each remaining firm produces the same output in the new long-run equilibrium as it did initially and earns a normal profit. In the process of moving from the initial equilibrium to the new one, firms incur economic losses.

We've just worked out how a competitive industry responds to a permanent *decrease* in demand. A permanent increase in demand triggers a similar response, except in the opposite direction. The increase in demand brings a higher price, economic profit, and entry. Entry increases industry supply and eventually the price falls to its original level and economic profit returns to normal profit.

The demand for airline travel in the world economy increased permanently during the 1990s and the deregulation of the airlines freed up firms to seek profit opportunities in this industry. The result was a

FIGURE 11.10   A Decrease in Demand

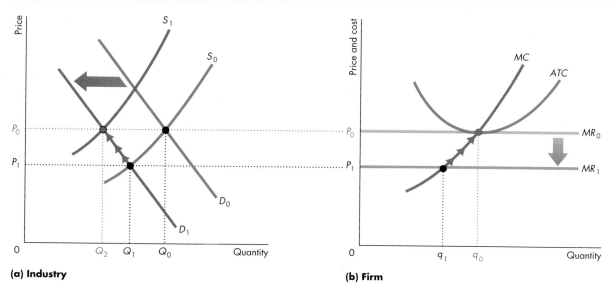

(a) Industry

(b) Firm

An industry starts out in long-run competitive equilibrium. Part (a) shows the industry demand curve D_0, the industry supply curve S_0, the equilibrium quantity Q_0, and the market price P_0. Each firm sells its output at price P_0, so its marginal revenue curve is MR_0 in part (b). Each firm produces q_0 and makes a normal profit. Demand decreases permanently from D_0 to D_1 (part a). The equilibrium price falls to P_1, each firm decreases its output to q_1 (part b), and indus-

try output decreases to Q_1 (part a).

In this new situation, firms incur economic losses and some firms leave the industry. As they do so, the industry supply curve gradually shifts leftward, from S_0 to S_1. This shift gradually raises the market price from P_1 back to P_0. Once the price has returned to P_0, each firm makes a normal profit. Firms have no further incentive to leave the industry. Each firm produces q_0, and industry output is Q_2.

massive rate of entry of new airlines. The process of competition and change in the airline industry is similar to what we have just studied (but with an increase in demand rather than a decrease in demand).

We've now studied the effects of a permanent change in demand for a good. To study these effects, we began and ended in a long-run equilibrium and examined the process that takes a market from one equilibrium to another. It is this process, not the equilibrium points, that describes the real world.

One feature of the predictions that we have just generated seems odd: In the long run, regardless of whether demand increases or decreases, the price returns to its original level. Is this outcome inevitable? In fact, it is not. It is possible for the long-run equilibrium price to remain the same, rise, or fall.

External Economies and Diseconomies

The change in the long-run equilibrium price depends on external economies and external diseconomies. **External economies** are factors beyond the control of an individual firm that lower the firm's costs as the *industry* output increases. **External diseconomies** are factors outside the control of a firm that raise the firm's costs as industry output increases. With no external economies or external diseconomies, a firm's costs remain constant as the industry output changes.

Figure 11.11 illustrates these three cases and introduces a new supply concept: the long-run industry supply curve.

A **long-run industry supply curve** shows how the quantity supplied by an industry varies as the market price varies after all the possible adjustments have been made, including changes in plant size and the number of firms in the industry.

Figure 11.11(a) shows the case we have just studied—no external economies or diseconomies. The long-run industry supply curve (LS_A) is horizontal. In this case, a permanent increase in demand from D_0 to D_1 has no effect on the price in the long run. The increase in demand brings a temporary increase in price to P_S and a short-run quantity increase from Q_0 to Q_S. Entry increases short-run supply from S_0 to S_1, which lowers the price to its original level, P_0, and increases the quantity to Q_1.

Figure 11.11(b) shows the case of external diseconomies. The long-run supply industry curve (LS_B) slopes upward. A permanent increase in demand from D_0 to D_1 increases the price in both the short run and the long run. As in the previous case, the increase in demand brings a temporary increase in price to P_S and a short-run quantity increase from Q_0 to Q_S. Entry increases short-run supply from S_0 to S_2, which lowers the price to P_2 and increases the quantity to Q_2.

One source of external diseconomies is congestion. The airline industry provides a good example. With bigger airline industry output, there is more congestion of airports and airspace, which results in longer delays and extra waiting time for passengers and airplanes. These external diseconomies mean that as the output of air transportation services increases (in the absence of technological advances), average cost increases. As a result, the long-run supply curve is upward sloping. So a permanent increase in demand brings an increase in quantity and a rise in the price. (Industries with external diseconomies might nonetheless have a falling price because technological advances shift the long-run supply curve downward.)

Figure 11.11(c) shows the case of external economies. In this case, the long-run industry supply curve (LS_C) slopes downward. A permanent increase in demand from D_0 to D_1 increases the price in the short run and lowers it in the long run. Again, the increase in demand brings a temporary increase in price to P_S, and a short-run quantity increase from Q_0 to Q_S. Entry increases short-run supply from S_0 to S_3, which lowers the price to P_3 and increases the quantity to Q_3.

FIGURE 11.11   Long-Run Changes in Price and Quantity

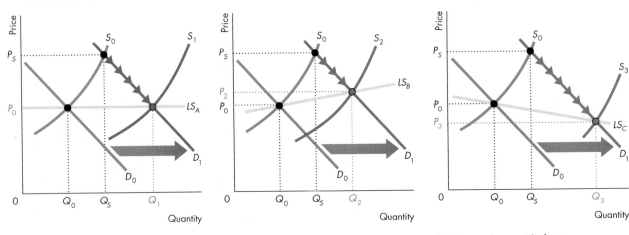

(a) Constant-cost industry   **(b) Increasing-cost industry**   **(c) Decreasing-cost industry**

Three possible changes in price and quantity occur in the long run. When demand increases from D_0 to D_1, entry occurs and the industry supply curve gradually shifts rightward from S_0 to S_1.

In part (a), the long-run supply curve, LS_A, is horizontal. The quantity increases from Q_0 to Q_1, and the price remains constant at P_0. In part (b), the long-run supply curve is LS_B; the price rises to P_2, and the quantity increases to Q_2. This case occurs in industries with external diseconomies. In part (c), the long-run supply curve is LS_C; the price falls to P_3, and the quantity increases to Q_3. This case occurs in an industry with external economies.

An example of external economies is the growth of specialist support services for an industry as it expands. As farm output increased in the nineteenth and early twentieth centuries, the services available to farmers expanded. New firms specialized in the development and marketing of farm machinery and fertilizers. As a result, average farm costs decreased. Farms enjoyed the benefits of external economies. As a consequence, as the demand for farm products increased, the output increased but the price fell.

Over the long term, the prices of many goods and services have fallen, not because of external economies but because of technological change. Let's now study this influence on a competitive market.

Technological Change

Industries are constantly discovering lower-cost techniques of production. Most cost-saving production techniques cannot be implemented, however, without investing in new plant and equipment. As a consequence, it takes time for a technological advance to spread through an industry. Some firms whose plants are on the verge of being replaced will be quick to adopt the new technology, while other firms whose plants have recently been replaced will continue to operate with an old technology until they can no longer cover their average variable cost. Once average variable cost cannot be covered, a firm will scrap even a relatively new plant (embodying an old technology) in favour of a plant with a new technology.

New technology allows firms to produce at a lower cost. As a result, as firms adopt a new technology, their cost curves shift downward. With lower costs, firms are willing to supply a given quantity at a lower price or, equivalently, they are willing to supply a larger quantity at a given price. In other words, industry supply increases, and the industry supply curve shifts rightward. With a given demand, the quantity produced increases and the price falls.

Two forces are at work in an industry undergoing technological change. Firms that adopt the new technology make an economic profit. So there is entry by new-technology firms. Firms that stick with the old technology incur economic losses. They either exit the industry or switch to the new technology.

As old-technology firms disappear and new-technology firms enter, the price falls and the quantity produced increases. Eventually, the industry arrives at

a long-run equilibrium in which all the firms use the new technology and make a zero economic profit (a normal profit). Because in the long run competition eliminates economic profit, technological change brings only temporary gains to producers. But the lower prices and better products that technological advances bring are permanent gains for consumers.

The process that we've just described is one in which some firms experience economic profits and others experience economic losses. It is a period of dynamic change for an industry. Some firms do well, and others do badly. Often, the process has a geographical dimension—the expanding new-technology firms bring prosperity to what was once the boondocks, and traditional industrial regions decline. Sometimes, the new-technology firms are in a foreign country, while the old-technology firms are in the domestic economy. The information revolution of the 1990s produced many examples of changes like these. The computer programming industry, traditionally concentrated in the United States, now flourishes in Canada, the United Kingdom, and India. Television shows and movies, traditionally made in Los Angeles and New York, are now made in large numbers in Toronto and Vancouver.

Technological advances are not confined to the information and entertainment industries. Even milk production is undergoing a major technological change because of genetic engineering.

REVIEW QUIZ

1 Describe the course of events in a competitive industry following a permanent decrease in demand. What happens to output, price, and economic profit in the short run and in the long run?

2 Describe the course of events in a competitive industry following a permanent increase in demand. What happens to output, price, and economic profit in the short run and in the long run?

3 Describe the course of events in a competitive industry following the adoption of a new technology. What happens to output, price, and economic profit in the short run and in the long run?

Competition and Efficiency

A COMPETITIVE INDUSTRY CAN ACHIEVE AN efficient use of resources. You studied efficiency in Chapter 5 using only the concepts of demand, supply, consumer surplus, and producer surplus. But now that you have learned what lies behind the demand and supply curves of a competitive market, you can gain a deeper understanding of how the competitive market achieves efficiency.

Efficient Use of Resources

Recall that resource use is efficient when we produce the goods and services that people value most highly (see Chapter 5, pp. 104–105). If someone can become better off without anyone else becoming worse off, resources are *not* being used efficiently. For example, suppose we produce a computer that no one wants and that no one will ever use. Suppose also that some people are clamouring for more video games. If we produce one less computer and reallocate the unused resources to produce more video games, some people will become better off and no one will be worse off. So the initial resource allocation was inefficient.

In the more technical language that you have learned, resource use is efficient when marginal benefit equals marginal cost. In the computer and video games example, the marginal benefit of video games exceeds the marginal cost. And the marginal cost of a computer exceeds its marginal benefit. So by producing fewer computers and more video games, we move resources towards a higher-valued use.

Choices, Equilibrium, and Efficiency

We can use what you have learned about the decisions made by consumers and competitive firms and market equilibrium to describe an efficient use of resources.

Choices Consumers allocate their budgets to get the most possible value out of them. And we derive a consumer's demand curve by finding how the best budget allocation changes as the price of a good changes. So consumers get the most value out of their resources at all points along their demand curves, which are also their marginal benefit curves.

Competitive firms produce the quantity that maximizes profit. And we derive the firm's supply curve by finding the profit-maximizing quantities at each price. So firms get the most value out of their resources at all points along their supply curves, which are also their marginal cost curves. (On their supply curves, firms are *technologically efficient*—they get the maximum possible output from given inputs—and *economically efficient*—they combine resources to minimize cost. See Chapter 9, pp. 199–200.)

Equilibrium In competitive equilibrium, the quantity demanded equals the quantity supplied. So the price equals the consumers' marginal benefit and the producers' marginal cost. In this situation, the gains from trade between consumers and producers are maximized. These gains from trade are the consumer surplus plus the producer surplus.

The gains from trade for consumers are measured by *consumer surplus*, which is the area below the demand curve and above the price paid. (See Chapter 5, p. 107.) The gains from trade for producers are measured by *producer surplus*, which is the area above the marginal cost curve and below the price received. (See Chapter 5, p. 109.) The total gains from trade are the sum of consumer surplus and producer surplus.

Efficiency If the people who consume and produce a good or service are the only ones affected by it and if the market for the good or service is in equilibrium, then resources are being used efficiently. They cannot be reallocated to increase their value.

In such a situation, there are no external benefits or external costs. **External benefits** are benefits that accrue to people other than the buyer of a good. For example, you might get a benefit from your neighbour's expenditure on her garden. Your neighbour buys the quantities of garden plants that make *her* as well off as possible, not her *and* you.

In the absence of external benefits, the market demand curve measures marginal *social* benefit—the value that *everyone* places on one more unit of a good or service.

External costs are costs that are borne not by the producer of a good or service but by someone else. For example, a firm might lower its costs by polluting. The cost of pollution is an external cost. Firms produce the output level that maximizes their own profit, and they do not count the cost of pollution as a charge against their profit.

In the absence of external costs, the market supply curve measures marginal *social* cost—the entire marginal cost that *anyone* bears to produce one more unit of a good or service.

An Efficient Allocation Figure 11.12 shows an efficient allocation. Consumers are efficient at all points on the demand curve, D (which is also the marginal benefit curve MB). Producers are efficient at all points on the supply curve, S (which is also the marginal cost curve MC). Resources are used efficiently at the quantity Q^* and price P^*. Marginal benefit equals marginal cost, and the sum of producer surplus (blue area) and consumer surplus (green area) is maximized.

If output is Q_0, marginal cost is C_0 and marginal benefit is B_0. Producers can supply more of the good for a cost lower than the price that consumers are willing to pay, and everyone gains by increasing the quantity produced. If output is greater than Q^*, marginal cost exceeds marginal benefit. It costs producers more to supply the good than the price that consumers are willing to pay, and everyone gains by decreasing the quantity produced.

FIGURE 11.12   Efficiency of Competition

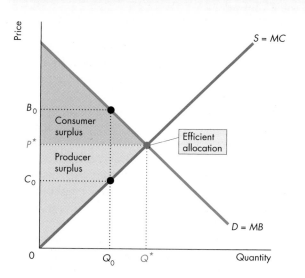

The efficient use of resources requires: consumers to be efficient, which occurs when they are on their demand curves; firms to be efficient, which occurs when they are on their supply curves; and the market to be in equilibrium, with no external benefits or external costs. Resources are used efficiently at the quantity Q^* and the price P^*. With no external benefits or external costs, perfect competition achieves an efficient use of resources. If output is Q_0, the cost of producing one more unit, C_0, is less than its marginal benefit, B_0, and resources are not used efficiently.

Efficiency of Perfect Competition

Perfect competition achieves efficiency if there are no external benefits and external costs. In such a case, the benefits accrue to the buyers of the good and the costs are borne by its producer. In Fig. 11.12, the equilibrium quantity Q^* at the price P^* is efficient.

There are three main obstacles to efficiency:

1. Monopoly
2. Public goods
3. External costs and external benefits

Monopoly Monopoly (Chapter 12) restricts output below its competitive level to raise price and increase profit. Government policies (Chapter 17) arise to limit such use of monopoly power.

Public Goods Goods such as national security, the enforcement of law and order, the provision of clean drinking water, and the disposal of sewage and garbage are examples of public goods. Left to competitive markets, too small a quantity of them would be produced. Government institutions and policies (Chapter 16) help to overcome the problem of providing an efficient quantity of public goods.

External Costs and External Benefits The production of steel and chemicals can generate air and water pollution, and perfect competition might produce too large a quantity of these goods. Government policies (Chapter 18) attempt to cope with external costs and benefits.

◆ You've now completed your study of perfect competition. And *Reading Between the Lines* on pp. 256–257 gives you an opportunity to use what you have learned to understand recent events in the highly competitive maple syrup market.

Although many markets approximate the model of perfect competition, many do not. Your next task is to study markets at the opposite extreme of market power: monopoly. Then, in Chapter 13, we'll study markets that lie between perfect competition and monopoly: monopolistic competition (competition with monopoly elements) and oligopoly (competition among a few producers). When you have completed this study, you'll have a tool kit that will enable you to understand the variety of real-world markets.

Perfect Competition in Maple Syrup

MONTREAL GAZETTE, MARCH 14, 2001

Maple syrup sits unsold in warehouses

A sticky turf war has boiled over in Canada's sugar patch, with farmers and processors feuding over what to do with a glut of maple syrup. ...

... after two bumper crops in a row, producers wonder if it's worth the effort to tap all their trees.

"People naturally aren't encouraged by the prices," said Stanley Holmes, a farmer and maple-syrup producer from Ayer's Cliff who also buys syrup in bulk from neighbouring producers on behalf of Ontario-based processor Delta Foods International.

"Really what they need is less production to get rid of some of this surplus that's hanging over the industry."

Prices alone won't dictate supply, though. Operating conditions, particularly the deep snow still lying in the woods across the province, could also influence the number of trees farmers tap this spring, Holmes said.

"With the snow it's very difficult to get around, and when your prices aren't good, if you have hard conditions like that to overcome, that's another reason not to tackle the job."

Holmes's own sugarbush has a production capacity of 10,000 taps with three-quarters of his trees connected to a pipeline and the rest on buckets. He said he may forego bringing into production those trees that are difficult to reach, especially those not already hooked to a pipeline. ...

The average floor price for syrup has tumbled from a high of around $2.50 per pound in 1997 and 1998 to $1.56 in 2000 and is not expected to be any higher in 2001.

Reprinted by permission of Dwane Wilkin.

Essence of the Story

■ Two back-to-back bumper maple syrup crops have lowered the price of syrup from $2.50 per pound to $1.56.

■ At this low price, producers are decreasing the number of trees they tap.

■ Supply is influenced by snow, which makes it difficult for producers to tap some of their trees.

■ Stanley Holmes has a production capacity of 10,000 taps. 7,500 of these are connected to a pipeline and the rest on buckets.

■ At today's low price, Stanley Holmes says he may forego the production on those trees that are difficult to reach and not already hooked to a pipeline.

Economic Analysis

■ Maple syrup—the real kind, not the synthetic syrup such as Aunt Jemima—is produced in Canada and the United States by about 12,000 firms.

■ The market for maple syrup is close to perfectly competitive.

■ Before the bumper crop, the price of maple syrup (in the news article) was $2.50 a pound.

■ After the bumper crop, the price fell to $1.56 a pound.

■ Figure 1 shows why the price fell. The demand curve for maple syrup is D, and before the bumper harvest, the supply curve was S_0. The equilibrium price was $2.50 a pound.

■ The bumper harvest shifted the supply curve rightward to S_1. At the price of $2.50 a pound, there was a surplus of syrup, so the price fell. The new equilibrium price is $1.56 a pound.

■ Figure 2 shows the situation facing Stanley Holmes. Stanley is a price taker and maximizes his profit by producing the quantity at which marginal cost (MC) equals marginal revenue (MR).

■ The figure shows Stanley's cost curves—average total cost curve, ATC, average variable cost curve, AVC, and marginal cost curve, MC.

■ We don't know the exact position of these curves, and those in the figure are assumed. But we do know from Stanley's description of his supply conditions that his marginal cost curve slopes upward.

■ When Stanley says, "With the snow it's very difficult to get around, and when your prices aren't good, if you have hard conditions like that to overcome, that's another reason not to tackle the job," the marginal cost of tapping all his trees is greater than the price he would receive.

■ The figure also shows Stanley's marginal revenue curves before, MR_0, and after, MR_1, the bumper harvest.

■ At $2.50 a pound, Stanley would tap all his trees (10,000 taps according to the news article). At $1.56 a pound, Stanley doesn't bother to tap the distant trees that are not connected to the pipeline.

■ Although the price is low, Stanley says that he

will produce from his 7,500 taps that are connected to the pipeline. This fact implies, as the figure shows, that the price of $1.56 exceeds average variable cost. If it didn't, Stanley would temporarily shut down.

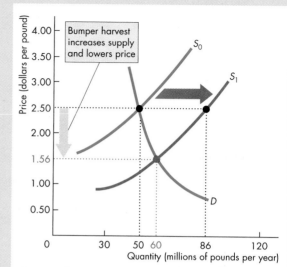

Figure 1 The maple syrup market

Figure 2 Stanley Holmes' maple farm

SUMMARY

KEY POINTS

Competition (pp. 238–239)

■ A perfectly competitive firm is a price taker.

The Firm's Decisions in Perfect Competition (pp. 240–245)

■ The firm produces the output at which marginal revenue (price) equals marginal cost.
■ In short-run equilibrium, a firm can make an economic profit, incur an economic loss, or make normal profit.
■ If price is less than minimum average variable cost, the firm temporarily shuts down.
■ A firm's supply curve is the upward-sloping part of its marginal cost curve above minimum average variable cost.
■ An industry supply curve shows the sum of the quantities supplied by each firm at each price.

Output, Price, and Profit in Perfect Competition (pp. 246–249)

■ Market demand and market supply determine price.
■ Persistent economic profit induces entry. Persistent economic loss induces exit.
■ Entry and plant expansion increase supply and lower price and profit. Exit and downsizing decrease supply and raise price and profit.
■ In long-run equilibrium, economic profit is zero (firms earn normal profit). There is no entry, exit, plant expansion, or downsizing.

Changing Tastes and Advancing Technology (pp. 250–253)

■ A permanent decrease in demand leads to a smaller industry output and a smaller number of firms.
■ A permanent increase in demand leads to a larger industry output and a larger number of firms.

■ The long-run effect of a change in demand on price depends on whether there are external economies (the price falls) or external diseconomies (the price rises) or neither (the price remains constant).
■ New technologies increase supply and in the long run lower the price and increase the quantity.

Competition and Efficiency (pp. 254–255)

■ Resources are used efficiently when we produce goods and services in the quantities that people value most highly.
■ When there are no external benefits and external costs, perfect competition achieves an efficient allocation. Marginal benefit equals marginal cost, and the sum of consumer surplus and producer surplus is maximized.
■ The existence of monopoly, public goods, and external costs and external benefits presents obstacles to efficiency.

KEY FIGURES

Figure 11.2   Total Revenue, Total Cost, and Economic Profit, 241
Figure 11.3   Profit-Maximizing Output, 242
Figure 11.4   Three Possible Profit Outcomes in the Short Run, 243
Figure 11.5   A Firm's Supply Curve, 244
Figure 11.7   Short-Run Equilibrium, 246
Figure 11.8   Entry and Exit, 247
Figure 11.12 Efficiency of Competition, 255

KEY TERMS

External benefits, 254
External costs, 254
External diseconomies, 251
External economies, 251
Long-run industry supply curve, 251
Marginal revenue, 238
Perfect competition, 238
Price taker, 238
Short-run industry supply curve, 245
Shutdown point, 244
Total revenue, 238

PROBLEMS

*1. Quick Copy is one of the many copy shops near the campus. The figure shows Quick Copy's cost curves.

a. If the market price of copying one page is 10 cents, what is Quick Copy's profit-maximizing output?

b. Calculate Quick Copy's profit.

c. With no change in demand or technology, how will the price change in the long run?

2. Jerry's is one of many ice cream stands along the beach. The figure shows Jerry's cost curves.

a. If the market price of an ice cream cone is $3, what is Jerry's profit-maximizing output?

b. Calculate Jerry's profit.

c. With no change in demand or technology, how will the price change in the long run?

*3. Pat's Pizza Kitchen is a price taker. Its costs are

Output (pizzas per hour)	Total cost (dollars per hour)
0	10
1	21
2	30
3	41
4	54
5	69

a. What is Pat's profit-maximizing output and how much economic profit does Pat make if the market price is (i) $14, (ii) $12, and (iii) $10?

b. What is Pat's shutdown point?

c. Derive Pat's supply curve.

d. At what price will Pat exit the pizza industry?

4. Luigi's Lasagna is a price taker. Its costs are

Output (plates per day)	Total cost (dollars per day)
0	14
1	38
2	48
3	62
4	80
5	102
6	128

a. What is Luigi's profit-maximizing output and how much profit does Luigi make if the market price is (i) $24 a plate, (ii) $20 a plate, and (iii) $12 a plate?

b. What is Luigi's shutdown point?

c. What is Luigi's profit at the shutdown point?

d. At what prices will firms with costs the same as Luigi's enter the lasagna market?

*5. The market demand schedule for cassettes is

Price (dollars per cassette)	Quantity demanded (thousands of cassettes per week)
3.65	500
5.20	450
6.80	400
8.40	350
10.00	300
11.60	250
13.20	200
14.80	150

The market is perfectly competitive, and each firm has the following cost structure:

Output (cassettes per week)	Marginal cost (dollars per additional cassette)	Average variable cost (dollars per cassette)	Average total cost (dollars per cassette)
150	6.00	8.80	15.47
200	6.40	7.80	12.80
250	7.00	7.00	11.00
300	7.65	7.10	10.43
350	8.40	7.20	10.06
400	10.00	7.50	10.00
450	12.40	8.00	10.22
500	20.70	9.00	11.00

There are 1,000 firms in the industry.

a. What is the market price?
b. What is the industry's output?
c. What is the output produced by each firm?
d. What is the economic profit made by each firm?
e. Do firms enter or exit the industry?
f. What is the number of firms in the long run?

6. The same demand conditions as those in problem 5 prevail and there are 1,000 firms in the industry, but fixed costs increase by $980. What now are your answers to the questions in problem 5?

*7. In problem 5, the price of compact discs permanently decreases the demand for cassettes and the demand schedule becomes

Price (dollars per cassette)	Quantity demanded (thousands of cassettes per week)
2.95	500
4.13	450
5.30	400
6.48	350
7.65	300
8.83	250
10.00	200
11.18	150

What now are your answers to the questions in problem 5?

8. In problem 6, the price of compact discs permanently decreases the demand for cassettes and the demand schedule becomes that given in the table in problem 7. What now are your answers to the questions in problem 6?

CRITICAL THINKING

1. After you have studied *Reading Between the Lines* on pp. 256–257, answer the following questions.
   a. What are the features of the market for maple syrup that make it an example of perfect competition?
   b. During the 1980s, the technology for extracting sap advanced. What effect do you predict that this development had on the price of syrup and the number of firms that produce it?
   c. Suppose that Aunt Jemima invents a syrup that no one can distinguish (in a blind test) from the real thing and can produce it for half the price of real maple syrup. What effect would you expect this development to have on the market for real maple syrup?

2. Why have the prices of pocket calculators and VCRs fallen? What do you think has happened to the costs and economic profits of the firms that make these products?

3. What has been the effect of an increase in world population on the wheat market and the individual wheat farmer?

4. How has the diaper service industry been affected by the decrease in the Canadian birth rate and the development of disposable diapers?

WEB EXERCISES

1. Use the link on the Parkin–Bade Web site and study the *Web Reading Between the Lines*, "Dumping Steel." Then answer the following questions:
   a. What is the argument in the news article about limiting steel imports?
   b. Do you agree with the argument? Why or why not?
   c. Why do Canada and the United States claim that foreign steel is being dumped in North America? (Use the links in the *Web Reading Between the Lines* to answer this question.)

The Profits of Generosity

If you take a trip by air in Canada, it is most likely that you will be flying with Air Canada. Since the disappearance of Canadian Airlines a few years ago, Air Canada has become the only national airline on many major Canadian air routes. Air Canada is obviously not like the firms in perfect competition. It doesn't face a market-determined price. It can choose its own price. How do Air Canada and the firms like it behave? How do these firms choose the quantity to produce and the price at which to sell it? How does their behaviour compare with that of firms in perfectly competitive industries? Do these firms charge prices that are too high and that damage the interests of consumers? Do they bring any benefits? ◆ As a student, you get lots of discounts: when you get your hair cut, go to a museum, or go to a movie. When you take a trip by air, you almost never pay the full fare. Instead, you buy a discounted ticket. Are the people who operate barber shops, museums, movie theatres, and airlines simply generous folks who don't maximize profit? Aren't they throwing profit away by offering discounts?

◆ In this chapter, we study markets in which the firm can influence the price. We also compare the performance of the firm in such a market with that of a competitive market and examine whether monopoly is as efficient as competition. In *Reading Between the Lines* at the end of the chapter, we'll return to Air Canada's monopoly in air travel.

After studying this chapter, you will be able to

- Explain how monopoly arises and distinguish between single-price monopoly and price-discriminating monopoly
- Explain how a single-price monopoly determines its output and price
- Compare the performance and efficiency of single-price monopoly and competition
- Define rent seeking and explain why it arises
- Explain how price discrimination increases profit
- Explain how monopoly regulation influences output, price, economic profit, and efficiency

Market Power

MARKET POWER AND COMPETITION ARE THE TWO forces that operate in most markets. **Market power** is the ability to influence the market, and in particular the market price, by influencing the total quantity offered for sale.

The firms in perfect competition that you studied in Chapter 11 have no market power. They face the force of raw competition and are price takers. The firms that we study in this chapter operate at the opposite extreme. They face no competition and exercise raw market power. We call this extreme monopoly. A **monopoly** is an industry that produces a good or service for which no close substitute exists and in which there is one supplier that is protected from competition by a barrier preventing the entry of new firms.

Examples of monopoly include your local phone, gas, electricity, and water suppliers, as well as De Beers, the South African diamond producer, and Microsoft Corporation, the software developer that created the Windows operating system.

How Monopoly Arises

Monopoly has two key features:

- No close substitutes
- Barriers to entry

No Close Substitutes If a good has a close substitute, even though only one firm produces it, that firm effectively faces competition from the producers of substitutes. Water supplied by a local public utility is an example of a good that does not have close substitutes. While it does have a close substitute for drinking—bottled spring water—it has no effective substitutes for showering or washing a car.

Monopolies are constantly under attack from new products and ideas that substitute for products produced by monopolies. For example, FedEx, Purolator, the fax machine, and e-mail have weakened the monopoly of Canada Post. Similarly, the satellite dish has weakened the monopoly of cable television companies.

But new products also are constantly creating monopolies. An example is Microsoft's monopoly in the DOS operating system during the 1980s and in the Windows operating system today.

Barriers to Entry Legal or natural constraints that protect a firm from potential competitors are called **barriers to entry**. A firm can sometimes create its own barrier to entry by acquiring a significant portion of a key resource. For example, De Beers controls more than 80 percent of the world's supply of natural diamonds. But most monopolies arise from two other types of barriers: legal barriers and natural barriers.

Legal Barriers to Entry Legal barriers to entry create legal monopoly. A **legal monopoly** is a market in which competition and entry are restricted by the granting of a public franchise, government licence, patent, or copyright.

A *public franchise* is an exclusive right granted to a firm to supply a good or service. An example is Canada Post, which has the exclusive right to carry first-class mail. A *government licence* controls entry into particular occupations, professions, and industries. Examples of this type of barrier to entry occur in medicine, law, dentistry, schoolteaching, architecture, and many other professional services. Licensing does not always create monopoly, but it does restrict competition.

A *patent* is an exclusive right granted to the inventor of a product or service. A *copyright* is an exclusive right granted to the author or composer of a literary, musical, dramatic, or artistic work. Patents and copyrights are valid for a limited time period that varies from country to country. In Canada, a patent is valid for 20 years. Patents encourage the *invention* of new products and production methods. They also stimulate *innovation*—the use of new inventions—by encouraging inventors to publicize their discoveries and offer them for use under licence. Patents have stimulated innovations in areas as diverse as soybean seeds, pharmaceuticals, computer memory chips, and video games.

Natural Barriers to Entry Natural barriers to entry create **natural monopoly**, which is an industry in which one firm can supply the entire market at a lower price than two or more firms can.

Figure 12.1 shows a natural monopoly in the distribution of electric power. Here, the market demand curve for electric power is *D*, and the average total cost curve is *ATC*. Because average total cost decreases as output increases, economies of scale prevail over the entire length of the *ATC* curve. One firm can produce 4 million kilowatt-hours at 5 cents a kilowatt-hour. At this price, the quantity demanded is 4 million kilowatt-hours. So if the price were 5 cents, one firm could supply the entire market. If two firms shared the market, it would cost each of them 10 cents a kilowatt-hour to produce a total of 4 million kilowatt-hours. If four firms shared the market, it would cost each of them 15 cents a kilowatt-hour to produce a total of 4 million kilowatt-hours. So in conditions like those shown in Fig. 12.1, one firm can supply the entire market at a lower cost than two or more firms can. The distribution of electric power is an example of natural monopoly. So is the distribution of water and gas.

Most monopolies are regulated in some way by government agencies. We will study such regulation at the end of this chapter. But for two reasons, we'll first study unregulated monopoly. First, we can better understand why governments regulate monopolies and the effects of regulation if we also know how an unregulated monopoly behaves. Second, even in industries with more than one producer, firms often

have a degree of monopoly power, and the theory of monopoly sheds light on the behaviour of such firms and industries.

A major difference between monopoly and competition is that a monopoly sets its own price. But in doing so, it faces a market constraint. Let's see how the market limits a monopoly's pricing choices.

Monopoly Price-Setting Strategies

All monopolies face a tradeoff between price and the quantity sold. To sell a larger quantity, the monopolist must charge a lower price. But there are two broad monopoly situations that create different tradeoffs. They are

- Price discrimination
- Single price

Price Discrimination Many firms price discriminate and most are *not* monopolies. Airlines offer a dizzying array of different prices for the same trip. Pizza producers charge one price for a single pizza and almost give away a second pizza. These are examples of *price discrimination*. **Price discrimination** is the practice of selling different units of a good or service for different prices. Different customers might pay different prices (like airline passengers), or one customer might pay different prices for different quantities bought (like the bargain price for a second pizza).

When a firm price discriminates, it looks as though it is doing its customers a favour. In fact, it is charging the highest possible price for each unit sold and making the largest possible profit.

Not all monopolies can price discriminate. The main obstacle to price discrimination is resale by customers who buy for a low price. Because of resale possibilities, price discrimination is limited to monopolies that sell services that cannot be resold.

Single Price De Beers sells diamonds (of a given size and quality) for the same price to all its customers. If it tried to sell at a low price to some customers and at a higher price to others, only the low-price customers would buy from De Beers. Others would buy from De Beers' low-price customers.

De Beers is a *single-price* monopoly. A **single-price monopoly** is a firm that must sell each unit of its output for the same price to all its customers.

We'll look first at single-price monopoly.

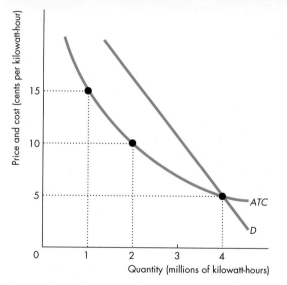

FIGURE 12.1 Natural Monopoly

The market demand curve for electric power is *D*, and the average total cost curve is *ATC*. Economies of scale exist over the entire *ATC* curve. One firm can distribute 4 million kilowatt-hours at a cost of 5 cents a kilowatt-hour. This same total output costs 10 cents a kilowatt-hour with two firms and 15 cents a kilowatt-hour with four firms. So one firm can meet the market demand at a lower cost than two or more firms can, and the market is a natural monopoly.

A Single-Price Monopoly's Output and Price Decision

To understand how a single-price monopoly makes its output and price decision, we must first study the link between price and marginal revenue.

Price and Marginal Revenue

Because in a monopoly there is only one firm, the demand curve facing the firm is the market demand curve. Let's look at Bobbie's Barbershop, the sole supplier of haircuts in Trout River, Newfoundland. The table in Fig. 12.2 shows the market demand schedule. At a price of $20, Bobbie sells no haircuts. The lower the price, the more haircuts per hour Bobbie can sell. For example, at $12, consumers demand 4 haircuts per hour (row *E*).

Total revenue (*TR*) is the price (*P*) multiplied by the quantity sold (*Q*). For example, in row *D*, Bobbie sells 3 haircuts at $14 each, so total revenue is $42. *Marginal revenue* (*MR*) is the change in total revenue (Δ*TR*) resulting from a one-unit increase in the quantity sold. For example, if the price falls from $16 (row *C*) to $14 (row *D*), the quantity sold increases from 2 to 3 haircuts. Total revenue rises from $32 to $42, so the change in total revenue is $10. Because the quantity sold increases by 1 haircut, marginal revenue equals the change in total revenue and is $10. Marginal revenue is placed between the two rows to emphasize that marginal revenue relates to the *change* in the quantity sold.

Figure 12.2 shows the market demand curve and marginal revenue curve (*MR*) and also illustrates the calculation we've just made. Notice that at each level of output, marginal revenue is *less* than price—the marginal revenue curve lies below the demand curve. Why is marginal revenue less than price? It is because when the price is lowered to sell one more unit, two opposing forces affect total revenue. The lower price results in a revenue loss, and the increased quantity sold results in a revenue gain. For example, at a price of $16, Bobbie sells 2 haircuts (point *C*). If she lowers the price to $14, she sells 3 haircuts and has a revenue gain of $14 on the third haircut. But she now receives only $14 on the first two—$2 less than before. As a result, she loses $4 of revenue on the first 2 haircuts. To calculate marginal revenue, she must deduct this amount from the revenue gain of $14. So her marginal revenue is $10, which is less than the price.

FIGURE 12.2   Demand and Marginal Revenue

	Price (P) (dollars per haircut)	Quantity demanded (Q) (haircuts per hour)	Total revenue (TR = P × Q) (dollars)	Marginal revenue (MR = ΔTR/ΔQ) (dollars per haircut)
A	20	0	0	
				18
B	18	1	18	
				14
C	16	2	32	
				10
D	14	3	42	
				6
E	12	4	48	
				2
F	10	5	50	

The table shows the demand schedule. Total revenue (*TR*) is price multiplied by quantity sold. For example, in row *C*, the price is $16 a haircut, Bobbie sells 2 haircuts and total revenue is $32. Marginal revenue (*MR*) is the change in total revenue that results from a one-unit increase in the quantity sold. For example, when the price falls from $16 to $14 a haircut, the quantity sold increases by 1 haircut and total revenue increases by $10. Marginal revenue is $10. The demand curve and the marginal revenue curve, *MR*, are based on the numbers in the table and illustrate the calculation of marginal revenue when the price of a haircut falls from $16 to $14.

Marginal Revenue and Elasticity

A single-price monopoly's marginal revenue is related to the *elasticity of demand* for its good. The demand for a good can be *elastic* (the elasticity of demand is greater than 1), *inelastic* (the elasticity of demand is less than 1), or *unit elastic* (the elasticity of demand is equal to 1). Demand is *elastic* if a 1 percent fall in price brings a greater than 1 percent increase in the quantity demanded. Demand is *inelastic* if a 1 percent fall in price brings a less than 1 percent increase in the quantity demanded. And demand is *unit elastic* if a 1 percent fall in price brings a 1 percent increase in the quantity demanded. (See Chapter 4, pp. 86–87.)

If demand is elastic, a fall in price brings an increase in total revenue—the increase in revenue from the increase in quantity sold outweighs the decrease in revenue from the lower price—and marginal revenue is positive. If demand is inelastic, a fall in price brings a decrease in total revenue—the increase in revenue from the increase in quantity sold is outweighed by the decrease in revenue from the lower price—and marginal revenue is negative. If demand is unit elastic, total revenue does not change—the increase in revenue from the increase in quantity sold offsets the decrease in revenue from the lower price—and marginal revenue is zero. (The relationship between total revenue and elasticity is explained in Chapter 4, on p. 88.)

Figure 12.3 illustrates the relationship between marginal revenue, total revenue, and elasticity. As the price of a haircut gradually falls from $20 to $10, the quantity of haircuts demanded increases from 0 to 5 an hour. Over this output range, marginal revenue is positive (part a), total revenue increases (part b), and the demand for haircuts is elastic. As the price falls from $10 to $0 a haircut, the quantity of haircuts demanded increases from 5 to 10 an hour. Over this output range, marginal revenue is negative (part a), total revenue decreases (part b), and the demand for haircuts is inelastic. When the price is $10 a haircut, marginal revenue is zero, total revenue is a maximum, and the demand for haircuts is unit elastic.

In Monopoly, Demand Is Always Elastic The relationship between marginal revenue and elasticity that you've just discovered implies that a profit-maximizing monopoly never produces an output in the inelastic range of its demand curve. If it did so, it could charge a higher price, produce a smaller quantity, and increase its profit. Let's now look more closely at a monopoly's output and price decision.

FIGURE 12.3 Marginal Revenue and Elasticity

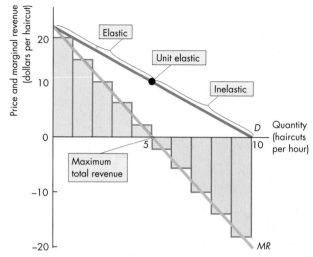

(a) Demand and marginal revenue curves

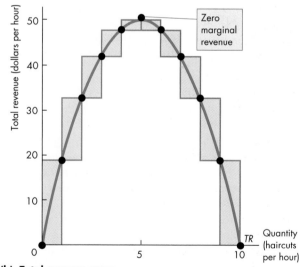

(b) Total revenue curve

In part (a), the demand curve is *D* and the marginal revenue curve is *MR*. In part (b), the total revenue curve is *TR*. Over the range from 0 to 5 haircuts an hour, a price cut increases total revenue, so marginal revenue is positive—as shown by the blue bars. Demand is elastic. Over the range 5 to 10 haircuts an hour, a price cut decreases total revenue, so marginal revenue is negative—as shown by the red bars. Demand is inelastic. At 5 haircuts an hour, total revenue is maximized and marginal revenue is zero. Demand is unit elastic.

Output and Price Decision

To determine the output level and price that maximize a monopoly's profit, we need to study the behaviour of both revenue and costs as output varies. A monopoly faces the same types of technology and cost constraints as a competitive firm. But it faces a different market constraint. The competitive firm is a price taker, whereas the monopoly's output decision influences the price it receives. Let's see how.

Bobbie's revenue, which we studied in Fig. 12.2, is shown again in Table 12.1. The table also contains information on Bobbie's costs and economic profit. Total cost (*TC*) rises as output increases, and so does total revenue (*TR*). Economic profit equals total revenue minus total cost. As you can see in the table, the maximum profit ($12) occurs when Bobbie sells 3 haircuts for $14 each. If she sells 2 haircuts for $16 each or 4 haircuts for $12 each, her economic profit will be only $8.

You can see why 3 haircuts is Bobbie's profit-maximizing output by looking at the marginal revenue and marginal cost columns. When Bobbie increases output from 2 to 3 haircuts, her marginal revenue is $10 and her marginal cost is $6. Profit increases by the difference—$4 an hour. If Bobbie increases output yet further, from 3 to 4 haircuts, her marginal revenue is $6 and her marginal cost is $10. In this case, marginal cost exceeds marginal revenue by $4, so profit decreases by $4 an hour. When marginal revenue exceeds marginal cost, profit increases if output increases. When marginal cost exceeds marginal revenue, profit increases if output decreases. When marginal cost and marginal revenue are equal, profit is maximized.

The information set out in Table 12.1 is shown graphically in Fig. 12.4. Part (a) shows Bobbie's total revenue curve (*TR*) and total cost curve (*TC*). Economic profit is the vertical distance between *TR* and *TC*. Bobbie maximizes her profit at 3 haircuts an hour—economic profit is $42 minus $30, or $12.

A monopoly, like a competitive firm, maximizes profit by producing the output at which marginal cost equals marginal revenue. Figure 12.4(b) shows the market demand curve (*D*), Bobbie's marginal revenue curve (*MR*), and her marginal cost curve (*MC*) and average total cost curve (*ATC*). Bobbie maximizes her profit by doing 3 haircuts an hour. But what price does she charge for a haircut? To set the price, the monopolist uses the demand curve and finds the highest price at which she can sell the profit-maximizing output. In Bobbie's case, the highest price at which she can sell 3 haircuts an hour is $14 per haircut.

TABLE 12.1   A Monopoly's Output and Price Decision

Price (P) (dollars per haircut)	Quantity demanded (Q) (haircuts per hour)	Total revenue (TR = P × Q) (dollars)	Marginal revenue (MR = ΔTR/ΔQ) (dollars per haircut)	Total cost (TC) (dollars)	Marginal cost (MC = ΔTC/ΔQ) (dollars per haircut)	Economic profit (TR − TC) (dollars)
20	0	0		20		−20
			18		1	
18	1	18		21		−3
			14		3	
16	2	32		24		+8
			10		6	
14	3	42		30		+12
			6		10	
12	4	48		40		+8
			2		15	
10	5	50		55		−5

This table gives the information needed to find the profit-maximizing output and price. Total revenue (*TR*) equals price multiplied by the quantity sold. Profit equals total revenue minus total cost (*TC*). Profit is maximized when 3 haircuts are sold at $14 a haircut. Total revenue is $42, total cost is $30, and economic profit is $12 ($42 − $30).

FIGURE 12.4 A Monopoly's Output and Price

(a) Total revenue and total cost curves

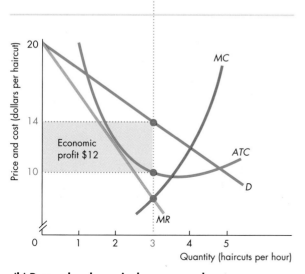

(b) Demand and marginal revenue and cost curves

In part (a), economic profit is the vertical distance equal to total revenue (*TR*) minus total cost (*TC*) and economic profit is maximized at 3 haircuts an hour. In part (b), economic profit is maximized when marginal cost (*MC*) equals marginal revenue (*MR*). The profit-maximizing output is 3 haircuts an hour. The price is determined by the demand curve (*D*) and is $14 a haircut. Her average total cost is $10 a haircut, so economic profit, the blue rectangle, is $12—the profit per haircut ($4) multiplied by 3 haircuts.

All firms maximize profit by producing the output at which marginal revenue equals marginal cost. For a competitive firm, price equals marginal revenue, so price also equals marginal cost. For a monopoly, price exceeds marginal revenue, so price also exceeds marginal cost.

A monopoly charges a price that exceeds marginal cost, but does it always make an economic profit? In Bobbie's case, when she produces 3 haircuts an hour, her average total cost is $10 (read from the *ATC* curve) and her price is $14 (read from the *D* curve). Her profit per haircut is $4 ($14 – $10). Bobbie's economic profit is shown by the blue rectangle, which equals the profit per haircut ($4) multiplied by the number of haircuts (3), for a total of $12.

If firms in a perfectly competitive industry make a positive economic profit, new firms enter. That does not happen in monopoly. Barriers to entry prevent new firms from entering an industry in which there is a monopoly. So a monopoly can make a positive economic profit and continue to do so indefinitely. Sometimes that profit is large, as in the international diamond business.

Bobbie makes a positive economic profit. But suppose that the owner of the shop that Bobbie rents increases Bobbie's rent. If Bobbie pays an additional $12 an hour for rent, her fixed cost increases by $12 an hour. Her marginal cost and marginal revenue don't change, so her profit-maximizing output remains at 3 haircuts an hour. Her profit decreases by $12 an hour to zero. If Bobbie pays more than an additional $12 an hour for her shop rent, she incurs an economic loss. If this situation were permanent, Bobbie would go out of business. But entrepreneurs are a hardy lot, and Bobbie might find another shop where the rent is less.

REVIEW QUIZ

1 What is the relationship between marginal cost and marginal revenue when a single-price monopoly maximizes profit?

2 How does a single-price monopoly determine the price it will charge its customers?

3 What is the relationship between price, marginal revenue, and marginal cost when a single-price monopoly is maximizing profit?

4 Why can a monopoly make a positive economic profit even in the long run?

Single-Price Monopoly and Competition Compared

IMAGINE AN INDUSTRY THAT IS MADE UP OF MANY small firms operating in perfect competition. Then imagine that a single firm buys out all these small firms and creates a monopoly.

What will happen in this industry? Will the price rise or fall? Will the quantity produced increase or decrease? Will economic profit increase or decrease? Will either the original competitive situation or the new monopoly situation be efficient?

These are the questions we're now going to answer. First, we look at the effects of monopoly on the price and quantity produced. Then we turn to the questions about efficiency.

Comparing Output and Price

Figure 12.5 shows the market we'll study. The market demand curve is *D*. The demand curve is the same regardless of how the industry is organized. But the supply side and the equilibrium are different in monopoly and competition. First, let's look at the case of perfect competition.

Perfect Competition Initially, with many small perfectly competitive firms in the market, the market supply curve is **S**. This supply curve is obtained by summing the supply curves of all the individual firms in the market.

In perfect competition, equilibrium occurs where the supply curve and the demand curve intersect. The quantity produced by the industry is Q_C, and the price is P_C. Each firm takes the price P_C and maximizes its profit by producing the output at which its own marginal cost equals the price. Because each firm is a small part of the total industry, there is no incentive for any firm to try to manipulate the price by varying its output.

Monopoly Now suppose that this industry is taken over by a single firm. Consumers do not change, so the demand curve remains the same as in the case of perfect competition. But now the monopoly recognizes this demand curve as a constraint on its sales. The monopoly's marginal revenue curve is *MR*.

e monopoly maximizes profit by producing
antity at which marginal revenue equals mar-
cost. To find the monopoly's marginal cost

curve, first recall that in perfect competition, the industry supply curve is the sum of the supply curves of the firms in the industry. Also recall that each firm's supply curve is its marginal cost curve (see Chapter 11, pp. 244–245). So when the industry is taken over by a single firm, the competitive industry's supply curve becomes the monopoly's marginal cost curve. To remind you of this fact, the supply curve is also labelled *MC*.

The output at which marginal revenue equals marginal cost is Q_M. This output is smaller than the competitive output Q_C. And the monopoly charges the price P_M, which is higher than P_C. We have established that

> Compared to a perfectly competitive industry, a single-price monopoly restricts its output and charges a higher price.

We've seen how the output and price of a monopoly compare with those in a competitive industry. Let's now compare the efficiency of the two types of markets.

FIGURE 12.5 Monopoly's Smaller Output and Higher Price

A competitive industry produces the quantity Q_C at price P_C. A single-price monopoly produces the quantity Q_M at which marginal revenue equals marginal cost and sells that quantity for the price P_M. Compared to perfect competition, a single-price monopoly restricts output and raises the price.

Efficiency Comparison

When we studied efficiency in perfect competition, (see Chapter 11, pp. 254–255), we discovered that if there are no external costs and benefits, perfect competition is efficient. Along the demand curve, consumers are efficient. Along the supply curve, producers are efficient. And where the curves intersect—the competitive equilibrium—both consumers and producers are efficient. Price, which measures marginal benefit, equals marginal cost.

Monopoly restricts output below the competitive level and is inefficient. If a monopoly increases its output by one unit, consumers' marginal benefit exceeds the monopoly's marginal cost and resource use will be more efficient.

Figure 12.6 illustrates the inefficiency of monopoly and shows the loss of consumer and producer surpluses in a monopoly. In perfect competition (part a), consumers pay P_C for each unit. The marginal benefit to consumers is shown by the demand curve ($D = MB$). So the price P_C measures the value of the good to the consumer. Value minus the price paid equals *consumer surplus* (see Chapter 5, p. 107). In Fig. 12.6(a), consumer surplus is shown by the green triangle.

The marginal cost of production (opportunity cost) in perfect competition is shown by the supply curve ($S = MC$). The amount received by the producer in excess of this marginal cost is *producer surplus*. In Fig. 12.6(a), the blue area shows producer surplus. At the competitive equilibrium, marginal benefit equals marginal cost and the sum of consumer surplus and producer surplus is maximized. Resource use is efficient.

In Fig. 12.6(b), a monopoly restricts output to Q_M and sells that output for P_M. Consumer surplus decreases to the smaller green triangle. Consumers lose partly by having to pay more for the good and partly by getting less of it. Part of the original producer surplus is also lost. The total loss resulting from the smaller monopoly output (Q_M) is the grey area. The part of the grey area above P_C is the loss of consumer surplus, and the part of the area below P_C is the loss of producer surplus. The entire grey area measures the loss of consumer surplus plus producer surplus. This loss is called the *deadweight loss*. The smaller output and higher price drive a wedge between marginal benefit and marginal cost and eliminate the producer surplus and the consumer surplus on the output that a competitive industry would have produced but the monopoly does not.

FIGURE 12.6   Inefficiency of Monopoly

(a) Perfect competition

(b) Monopoly

In perfect competition (part a), the quantity Q_C is sold at the price P_C. Consumer surplus is shown by the green triangle. In long-run equilibrium, firms' economic profits are zero and consumer surplus is maximized.

A single-price monopoly (part b) restricts output to Q_M and increases the price to P_M. Consumer surplus is the smaller green triangle. The monopoly takes the darker blue rectangle and creates a deadweight loss (the grey area).

Redistribution of Surpluses

You've seen that monopoly is inefficient because marginal benefit exceeds marginal cost and there is dead-weight loss—a social loss. But monopoly also brings a *redistribution* of surpluses.

Some of the lost consumer surplus goes to the monopoly. In Fig. 12.6, the monopoly gets the difference between the higher price, P_M, and the competitive price, P_C, on the quantity sold, Q_M. So the monopoly takes the part of the consumer surplus shown by the darker blue rectangle. This portion of the loss of consumer surplus is not a loss to society. It is redistribution from consumers to the monopoly producer.

Rent Seeking

You've seen that monopoly creates a deadweight loss and so is inefficient. But the social cost of monopoly exceeds the deadweight loss because of an activity called rent seeking. **Rent seeking** is any attempt to capture a consumer surplus, a producer surplus, or an economic profit. The activity is not confined to monopoly. But attempting to capture the economic profit of a monopoly is a major form of rent seeking.

You've seen that a monopoly makes its economic profit by diverting part of consumer surplus to itself. Thus the pursuit of an economic profit by a monopolist is rent seeking. It is the attempt to capture consumer surplus.

Rent seekers pursue their goals in two main ways. They might

- Buy a monopoly
- Create a monopoly

Buy a Monopoly To rent seek by buying a monopoly, a person searches for a monopoly that is for sale at a lower price than the monopoly's economic profit. Trading of taxicab licences is an example of this type of rent seeking. In some cities, taxicabs are regulated. The city restricts both the fares and the number of taxis that can operate so that operating a taxi results in economic profit, or rent. A person who wants to operate a taxi must buy a licence from someone who already has one. People rationally devote their time and effort to seeking out profitable monopoly businesses to buy. In the process, they use scarce resources that could otherwise have been employed to produce goods and services. The value of this lost production is part of the social cost of monopoly. The amount

paid for a monopoly is not a social cost because the payment is just a transfer of an existing producer surplus from the buyer to the seller.

Create a Monopoly Rent seeking by creating monopoly is mainly a political activity. It takes the form of lobbying and trying to influence the political process. Such influence might be sought by making campaign contributions in exchange for legislative support or by seeking to influence political outcomes indirectly through publicity in the media or more direct contacts with politicians and bureaucrats. An example of a monopoly right created in this way is the cable television monopoly created and regulated by the Canadian Radio-Television and Telecommunications Commission (CRTC). Another is a regulation that restricts "split-run" magazines. These regulations restrict output and increase price.

This type of rent seeking is a costly activity that uses up scarce resources. Taken together, firms spend billions of dollars lobbying MPs, MPPs, and bureaucrats in the pursuit of licences and laws that create barriers to entry and establish a monopoly right. Everyone has an incentive to rent seek, and because there are no barriers to entry into the rent-seeking activity, there is a great deal of competition for new monopoly rights.

Rent-Seeking Equilibrium

Barriers to entry create monopoly. But there is no barrier to entry into rent seeking. Rent seeking is like perfect competition. If an economic profit is available, a new rent seeker will try to get some of it. And competition among rent seekers pushes up the price that must be paid for a monopoly right to the point at which only a normal profit can be made by operating the monopoly. For example, competition for the right to operate a taxi in Toronto leads to a price of more than $80,000 for a taxi licence, which is sufficiently high to eliminate economic profit for taxi operators and leave them with normal profit.

Figure 12.7 shows a rent-seeking equilibrium. The cost of rent seeking is a fixed cost that must be added to a monopoly's other costs. Rent seeking and rent-seeking costs increase to the point at which no economic profit is made. The average total cost curve, which includes the fixed cost of rent seeking, shifts upward until it just touches the demand curve. Economic profit is zero. It has been lost in rent seeking. Consumer surplus is unaffected. But the

FIGURE 12.7 Rent-Seeking Equilibrium

With competitive rent seeking, a monopoly uses all its economic profit to prevent another firm from taking its economic rent. The firm's rent-seeking costs are fixed costs. They add to total fixed cost and to average total cost. The ATC curve shifts upward until, at the profit-maximizing price, the firm breaks even.

deadweight loss of monopoly now includes the original deadweight loss triangle plus the lost producer surplus, shown by the enlarged grey area in the figure.

REVIEW QUIZ

1 Why does a single-price monopoly produce a smaller output and charge a higher price than what would prevail if the industry were perfectly competitive?
2 How does a monopoly transfer consumer surplus to itself?
3 Why is a single-price monopoly inefficient?
4 What is rent seeking and how does it influence the inefficiency of monopoly?

So far, we've considered only a single-price monopoly. But many monopolies do not operate with a single price. Instead, they price discriminate. Let's now see how a price-discriminating monopoly works.

Price Discrimination

PRICE DISCRIMINATION—SELLING A GOOD OR service at a number of different prices—is widespread. You encounter it when you travel, go to the movies, get your hair cut, buy pizza, or visit an art museum. Most price discriminators are not monopolies, but monopolies price discriminate when they can do so.

To be able to price discriminate, a monopoly must

1. Identify and separate different buyer types.
2. Sell a product that cannot be resold.

Price discrimination is charging different prices for a single good or service because of differences in buyers' willingness to pay and not because of differences in production costs. So not all price *differences* are price *discrimination*. Some goods that are similar but not identical have different prices because they have different production costs. For example, the cost of producing electricity depends on the time of day. If an electric power company charges a higher price during the peak consumption periods from 7:00 to 9:00 in the morning and from 4:00 to 7:00 in the evening than it does at other times of the day, it is not price discriminating.

At first sight, it appears that price discrimination contradicts the assumption of profit maximization. Why would a movie theatre allow children to see movies at half price? Why would a hairdresser charge students and senior citizens less? Aren't these firms losing profit by being nice to their customers?

Deeper investigation shows that far from losing profit, price discriminators make a bigger profit than they would otherwise. So a monopoly has an incentive to find ways of discriminating and charging each buyer the highest possible price. Some people pay less with price discrimination, but others pay more.

Price Discrimination and Consumer Surplus

The key idea behind price discrimination is to convert consumer surplus into economic profit. Demand curves slope downward because the value that people place on any good decreases as the quantity consumed of that good increases. When all the units consumed are sold for a single price, consumers benefit. The benefit is the value the consumers get from each unit of the good minus the price actually paid for it. This benefit is *consumer surplus*. Price discrimination is an attempt by a monopoly to capture as much of the consumer surplus as possible for itself.

To extract every dollar of consumer surplus from every buyer, the monopoly would have to offer each individual customer a separate price schedule based on that customer's own willingness to pay. Clearly, such price discrimination cannot be carried out in practice because a firm does not have enough information about each consumer's demand curve.

But firms try to extract as much consumer surplus as possible, and to do so, they discriminate in two broad ways:

■ Among units of a good
■ Among groups of buyers

Discriminating Among Units of a Good One method of price discrimination charges each buyer a different price on each unit of a good bought. A discount for bulk buying is an example of this type of discrimination. The larger the quantity bought, the larger is the discount—and the lower is the price. (Note that some discounts for bulk arise from lower costs of production for greater bulk. In these cases, such discounts are not price discrimination.)

Discriminating Among Groups of Buyers Price discrimination often takes the form of discriminating between different groups of consumers on the basis of age, employment status, or some other easily distinguished characteristic. This type of price discrimination works when each group has a different average willingness to pay for the good or service.

For example, a face-to-face sales meeting with a customer might bring a large and profitable order. For salespeople and other business travellers, the marginal benefit from a trip is large and the price that such a traveller will pay for a trip is high. In contrast, for a vacation traveller, any of several different trips and even no vacation trip are options. So for vacation travellers, the marginal benefit of a trip is small and the price that such a traveller will pay for a trip is low. Because business travellers are willing to pay more than vacation travellers are, it is possible for an airline to profit by price discriminating between these two groups. Similarly, because students have a lower willingness to pay for a haircut than a working person does, it is possible for a hairdresser to profit by price discriminating between these two groups.

Let's see how an airline exploits the differences in demand by business and vacation travellers and increases its profit by price discriminating.

Profiting by Price Discriminating

Global Air has a monopoly on an exotic route. Figure 12.8 shows the demand curve (*D*) and the marginal revenue curve (*MR*) for travel on this route. It also shows Global Air's marginal cost curve (*MC*) and average total cost curve (*ATC*).

Initially, Global is a single-price monopoly and maximizes its profit by producing 8,000 trips a year (the quantity at which *MR* equals *MC*). The price is $1,200 per trip. The average total cost of producing a trip is $600, so economic profit is $600 a trip. On 8,000 trips, Global's economic profit is $4.8 million a year, shown by the blue rectangle. Global's customers enjoy a consumer surplus shown by the green triangle.

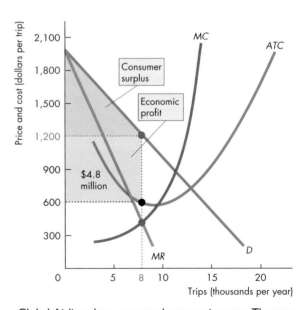

FIGURE 12.8   A Single Price of Air Travel

Global Airlines has a monopoly on an air route. The market demand curve is *D*, and marginal revenue curve is *MR*. Global Air's marginal cost curve is *MC*, and its average total cost curve is *ATC*. As a single-price monopoly, Global maximizes profit by selling 8,000 trips a year at $1,200 a trip. Its profit is $4.8 million a year—the blue rectangle. Global's customers enjoy a consumer surplus—the green triangle.

Global is struck by the fact that many of its customers are business travellers, and Global suspects that they are willing to pay more than $1,200 a trip. So Global does some market research, which tells Global that some business travellers are willing to pay as much as $1,800 a trip. Also, these customers frequently change their travel plans at the last moment. Another group of business travellers is willing to pay $1,600. These customers know one week ahead when they will travel, and they never want to stay over a weekend. Yet another group would pay up to $1,400. These travellers know two weeks ahead when they will travel and don't want to stay over a weekend.

So Global announces a new fare schedule: no restrictions, $1,800; 7-day advance purchase, no cancellation, $1,600; 14-day advance purchase, no cancellation, $1,400; 14-day advance purchase, must stay over a weekend, $1,200.

Figure 12.9 shows the outcome with this new

fare structure and also shows why Global is pleased with its new fares. It sells 2,000 seats at each of its fare structure and also shows why Global is pleased four prices. Global's economic profit increases by the dark blue steps in Fig. 12.9. Its economic profit is now its original $4.8 million a year plus an additional $2.4 million from its new higher fares. Consumer surplus has shrunk to the smaller green area.

Perfect Price Discrimination

But Global reckons that it can do even better. It plans to achieve **perfect price discrimination**, which extracts the entire consumer surplus. To do so, Global must get creative and come up with a host of additional fares—ranging between $2,000 and $1,200, each of which appeals to a small segment of the business market—that will extract the entire consumer surplus from the business travellers.

With perfect price discrimination, something special happens to marginal revenue. For the perfect price discriminator, the market demand curve becomes the marginal revenue curve. The reason is that when the price is cut to sell a larger quantity, the firm sells only the marginal unit at the lower price. All the other units continue to be sold for the highest price that each buyer is willing to pay. So for the perfect price discriminator, marginal revenue *equals* price and the demand curve becomes the marginal revenue curve.

With marginal revenue equal to price, Global can obtain yet greater profit by increasing output up to the point at which price (and marginal revenue) is equal to marginal cost.

So Global now seeks additional travellers who will not pay as much as $1,200 a trip but who will pay more than marginal cost. More creative pricing comes up with vacation specials and other fares that have combinations of advance reservation, minimum stay, and other restrictions that make these fares unattractive to its existing customers but attractive to a further group of travellers. With all these fares and specials, Global increases sales, extracts the entire consumer surplus, and maximizes economic profit. Figure 12.10 shows the outcome with perfect price discrimination. The dozens of fares paid by the original travellers who are willing to pay between $1,200 and $2,000 have extracted the entire consumer surplus from this group and converted it into economic profit for Global.

The new fares between $900 and $1,200 have attracted 3,000 additional travellers but taken their entire consumer surplus also. Global is earning an economic profit of more than $9 million.

FIGURE 12.9   Price Discrimination

Global revises its fare structure: no restrictions at $1,800, 7-day advance purchase at $1,600, 14-day advance purchase at $1,400, and must stay over a weekend at $1,200. Global sells 2,000 trips at each of its four new fares. Its economic profit increases by $2.4 million a year to $7.2 million a year, which is shown by the original blue rectangle plus the dark blue steps. Global's customers' consumer surplus shrinks.

FIGURE 12.10 Perfect Price Discrimination

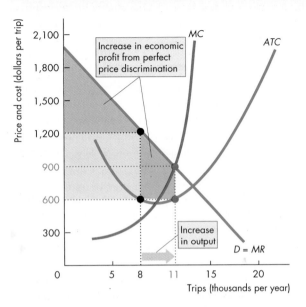

Dozens of fares discriminate among many different types of business travellers, and many new low fares with restrictions appeal to vacation travellers. With perfect price discrimination, Global's demand curve becomes its marginal revenue curve. Economic profit is maximized when the lowest price equals marginal cost. Here, Global sells 11,000 trips and makes an economic profit of $9.35 million a year.

Real-world airlines are just as creative as Global, as you can see in the cartoon!

Would it bother you to hear how little I paid for this flight?

From William Hamilton, "Voodoo Economics," © 1992 by Chronicle Books. Published by Chronicle Books LLC, San Francisco. Used with permission. Visit http://www.chroniclebooks.com.

Efficiency and Rent Seeking with Price Discrimination

With perfect price discrimination, output increases to the point at which price equals marginal cost—where the marginal cost curve intersects the demand curve. This output is identical to that of perfect competition. Perfect price discrimination pushes consumer surplus to zero but increases producer surplus to equal the sum of consumer surplus and producer surplus in perfect competition. Deadweight loss with perfect price discrimination is zero. So perfect price discrimination achieves efficiency.

The more perfectly the monopoly can price discriminate, the closer its output gets to the competitive output and the more efficient is the outcome.

But there are two differences between perfect competition and perfect price discrimination. First, the distribution of the surplus is different. It is shared by consumers and producers in perfect competition, while the producer gets it all with perfect price discrimination. Second, because the producer grabs the surplus, rent seeking becomes profitable.

People use resources in pursuit of rents, and the bigger the rents, the more resources get used in pursuing them. With free entry into rent seeking, the long-run equilibrium outcome is that rent seekers use up the entire producer surplus.

REVIEW QUIZ

1 What is price discrimination and how is it used to increase a monopoly's profit?
2 Explain how consumer surplus changes when a monopoly price discriminates.
3 Explain how consumer surplus, economic profit, and output change when a monopoly perfectly price discriminates.
4 What are some of the ways in which real-world airlines price discriminate?

You've seen that monopoly is profitable for the monopolist but costly for other people. It results in inefficiency. Because of these features of monopoly, it is subject to policy debate and regulation. We'll now study the key monopoly policy issues.

Monopoly Policy Issues

MONOPOLY LOOKS BAD WHEN WE COMPARE IT with competition. Monopoly is inefficient, and it captures consumer surplus and converts it into producer surplus or pure waste in the form of rent-seeking costs. If monopoly is so bad, why do we put up with it? Why don't we have laws that crack down on monopoly so hard that it never rears its head? We do indeed have laws that limit monopoly power and regulate the prices that monopolies are permitted to charge. But monopoly also brings some benefits. We begin this review of monopoly policy issues by looking at the benefits of monopoly. We then look at monopoly regulation.

Gains from Monopoly

The main reason why monopoly exists is that it has potential advantages over a competitive alternative. These advantages arise from

- Incentives to innovation
- Economies of scale and economies of scope

Incentives to Innovation Invention leads to a wave of innovation as new knowledge is applied to the production process. Innovation may take the form of developing a new product or a lower-cost way of making an existing product. Controversy has raged over whether large firms with market power or small competitive firms lacking such market power are the most innovative. It is clear that some temporary market power arises from innovation. A firm that develops a new product or process and patents it obtains an exclusive right to that product or process for the term of the patent.

But does the granting of a monopoly, even a temporary one, to an innovator increase the pace of innovation? One line of reasoning suggests that it does. Without protection, an innovator is not able to enjoy the profits from innovation for very long. Thus the incentive to innovate is weakened. A contrary argument is that monopolies can afford to be lazy while competitive firms cannot. Competitive firms must strive to innovate and cut costs even though they know that they cannot hang onto the benefits of their innovation for long. But that knowledge spurs them on to greater and faster innovation.

The evidence on whether monopoly leads to greater innovation than competition is mixed. Large firms do more research and development than do small firms. But research and development are inputs into the process of innovation. What matters is not input but output. Two measures of the output of research and development are the number of patents and the rate of productivity growth. On these measures, it is not clear that bigger is better. But as a new process or product spreads through an industry, the large firms adopt the new process or product more quickly than do small firms. So large firms help to speed the process of diffusion of technological change.

Economies of Scale and Economies of Scope

Economies of scale and economies of scope can lead to natural monopoly. As you saw at the beginning of this chapter, in a natural monopoly, a single firm can produce at a lower average total cost than can a number of firms.

A firm experiences *economies of scale* when an increase in its output of a good or service brings a decrease in the average total cost of producing it (see Chapter 10, pp. 230–231). A firm experiences *economies of scope* when an increase in the *range of the goods produced* brings a decrease in average total cost (see Chapter 9, p. 211). Economies of scope occur when different goods can share specialized (and usually costly) capital resources. For example, McDonald's can produce both hamburgers and french fries at a lower average total cost than can two separate firms—a burger firm and a french fry firm—because at McDonald's, hamburgers and french fries share the use of specialized food storage and preparation facilities. A firm that produces a wide range of products can hire specialist designers and marketing experts whose skills can be used across the product range, thereby spreading the costs and lowering the average total cost of production of each of the goods.

There are many examples in which combinations of economies of scale and economies of scope arise, but not all of them lead to monopoly. Some examples are the brewing of beer, the manufacture of refrigerators and other household appliances, the manufacture of pharmaceuticals, and the refining of petroleum.

Examples of industries in which economies of scale are so significant that they lead to a natural monopoly are becoming rare. Public utilities such as gas, electric power, local telephone service, and garbage collection once were natural monopolies. But technological advances now enable us to separate the *production* of electric power or natural gas from its *distribution*. The provision of water, though, remains a natural monopoly.

A large-scale firm that has control over supply and can influence price—and therefore behaves like the monopoly firm that you've studied in this chapter—can reap these economies of scale and scope. Small, competitive firms cannot. Consequently, there are situations in which the comparison of monopoly and competition that we made earlier in this chapter is not valid. Recall that we imagined the takeover of a large number of competitive firms by a monopoly firm. But we also assumed that the monopoly would use exactly the same technology as the small firms and have the same costs. If one large firm can reap economies of scale and economies of scope, its marginal cost curve will lie below the supply curve of a competitive industry made up of many small firms. It is possible for such economies of scale and economies of scope to be so large as to result in a larger output and lower price under monopoly than a competitive industry would achieve.

Where significant economies of scale and economies of scope exist, it is usually worth putting up with monopoly and regulating its price.

Regulating Natural Monopoly

Where demand and cost conditions create a natural monopoly, a federal, provincial, or local government agency usually steps in to regulate the prices of the monopoly. By regulating a monopoly, some of the worst aspects of monopoly can be avoided or at least moderated. Let's look at monopoly price regulation.

Figure 12.11 shows the demand curve *D*, the marginal revenue curve *MR*, the long-run average cost curve *ATC*, and the marginal cost curve *MC* for a natural gas distribution company that is a natural monopoly.

The firm's marginal cost is constant at 10 cents per cubic metre. But average total cost decreases as output increases. The reason is that the natural gas company has a large investment in pipelines and so has high fixed costs. These fixed costs are part of the company's average total cost and so appear in the *ATC* curve. The average total cost curve slopes downward because as the number of cubic metres sold increases, the fixed cost is spread over a larger number of units. (If you need to refresh your memory on how the average total cost curve is calculated, look back at Chapter 10, pp. 224–225.)

This one firm can supply the entire market at a lower cost than two firms can because average total cost is falling even when the entire market is supplied. (Refer back to p. 262–263 if you need a quick refresher on natural monopoly.)

Profit Maximization Suppose the natural gas company is not regulated and instead maximizes profit. Figure 12.11 shows the outcome. The company produces 2 million cubic metres a day, the quantity at which marginal cost equals marginal revenue. It prices the gas at 20 cents a cubic metre and makes an economic profit of 2 cents a cubic metre, or $40,000 a day.

This outcome is fine for the gas company, but it is inefficient. The price of gas is 20 cents a cubic metre when its marginal cost is only 10 cents a cubic metre. Also, the gas company is making a big profit. What can regulation do to improve this outcome?

The Efficient Regulation If the monopoly regulator wants to achieve an efficient use of resources, it must require the gas monopoly to produce the quantity of gas that brings marginal benefit into equality with marginal cost. Marginal benefit is what the consumer is willing to pay and is shown by the demand curve. Marginal cost is shown by the firm's marginal cost curve. You can see in Fig. 12.11 that this outcome occurs if the price is regulated at 10 cents per cubic metre and if 4 million cubic metres per day are produced. The regulation that produces this outcome is called a marginal cost pricing rule. A **marginal cost pricing rule** sets price equal to marginal cost. It maximizes total surplus in the regulated industry. In this example, that surplus is all consumer surplus and it equals the area of the triangle beneath the demand curve and above the marginal cost curve.

The marginal cost pricing rule is efficient. But it leaves the natural monopoly incurring an economic loss. Because average total cost is falling as output increases, marginal cost is below average total cost. And because price equals marginal cost, price is below average total cost. Average total cost minus price is the loss per unit produced. It's pretty obvious that a natural gas company that is required to use a marginal cost pricing rule will not stay in business for long. How can a company cover its costs and, at the same time, obey a marginal cost pricing rule?

One possibility is price discrimination in which the firm produces the quantity at which price equals marginal cost but sells some units to some buyers at a higher price (see p. 274).

FIGURE 12.11   Regulating a Natural Monopoly

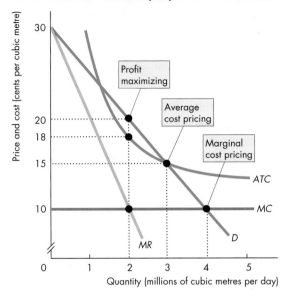

A natural monopoly is an industry in which average total cost is falling even when the entire market demand is satisfied. A natural gas producer faces the demand curve D. The firm's marginal cost is constant at 10 cents per cubic metre, as shown by the curve labelled MC. Fixed costs are large, and the average total cost curve, which includes average fixed cost, is shown as ATC. A marginal cost pricing rule sets the price at 10 cents per cubic metre. The monopoly produces 4 million cubic metres per day and incurs an economic loss. An average cost pricing rule sets the price at 15 cents per cubic metre. The monopoly produces 3 million cubic metres per day and makes normal profit.

Another possibility is to use a two-part price (called a two-part tariff). For example, the gas company might charge a monthly fixed fee that covers its fixed cost and then charge for gas consumed at marginal cost.

But a natural monopoly cannot always cover its costs in these ways. If a natural monopoly cannot cover its total cost from its customers and if the government wants it to follow a marginal cost pricing rule, then the government must give the firm a subsidy. In such a case, the government raises the revenue for the subsidy by taxing some other activity. But as we saw in Chapter 6, taxes themselves generate deadweight loss. Thus the deadweight loss resulting from additional taxes must be subtracted from the efficiency gained by forcing the natural monopoly to adopt a marginal cost pricing rule.

Average Cost Pricing Regulators almost never impose efficient pricing because of its consequences for the firm's profit. Instead, they compromise by permitting the firm to cover its costs and to earn a normal profit. Recall that normal profit is a cost of production and we include it along with the firm's other fixed costs in the average total cost curve. So pricing to cover cost including normal profit means setting price equal to average total cost—called an **average cost pricing rule**.

Figure 12.11 shows the average cost pricing outcome. The natural gas company charges 15 cents a cubic metre and sells 3 million cubic metres per day. This outcome is better for consumers than the unregulated profit-maximizing outcome. The price is 5 cents a cubic metre lower, and the quantity consumed is 1 million cubic metres per day more. And the outcome is better for the producer than the marginal cost pricing rule outcome. The firm earns normal profit. The outcome is inefficient but less so than the unregulated profit-maximizing outcome.

REVIEW QUIZ

1 What are the two main reasons why monopoly is worth tolerating?
2 Can you provide some examples of economies of scale and economies of scope?
3 Why might the incentive to innovate be greater for a monopoly than for a small competitive firm?
4 What is the price that achieves an efficient outcome for a regulated monopoly? And what is the problem with this price?
5 Compare the consumer surplus, producer surplus, and deadweight loss that arise from average cost pricing with those that arise from profit-maximization pricing and marginal cost pricing.

You've now studied perfect competition and monopoly. *Reading Between the Lines* on pp. 278–279 looks at market power in Canadian air travel. In the next chapter, we study markets that lie between the extremes of perfect competition and monopoly and that blend elements of the two.

Domestic Airline Monopoly

OTTAWA CITIZEN, AUGUST 13, 2002

Air Canada needs to compete, poll says

A majority of Canadians want to end Air Canada's virtual monopoly, preferring free competition in the country's skies even if it means the end of all major Canadian-owned airlines, a newly released poll indicates.

The survey, conducted for Transport Canada earlier this year, suggests 55 per cent believe that even if opening up the air industry further to U.S.-based airlines means the end of Air Canada and other major Canadian airlines, this is better than having a monopoly.

The comprehensive national poll found great willingness to open up Canadian skies to foreign competitors, with 84 per cent saying they would accept Canadian and American airlines if it meant they could fly all over North America. And a surprising 71 per cent said they would accept U.S.-based airlines in Canada even without equal access for Canadian airlines in the U.S., if it meant lower fares for passengers. This number dropped to 44 per cent, however, if it also meant less service to remote areas in Canada.

The poll indicated that only 15 per cent of Canadians felt the country's airline industry is working well. This is half the number of respondents who said they were satisfied flyers in 1999 when the last survey was performed.

"Overall, Canadians want safety and affordable air fares. They are not happy with the industry as it exists today, and they want to see it fixed," said the poll report. Goldfarb Consultants interviewed 2,083 adult Canadians by telephone between March 5 and 20. It has a margin of error within 2.2 percentage points, 19 times out of 20.

When asked about the problems plaguing the industry, almost two in five respondents mentioned a decline in competition and Air Canada's near monopoly. The report says the second most cited problem—35 per cent mentioned rising airfares and surcharges—may be related to the first.

Laura Cooke, a spokesperson for Air Canada, said she could not offer specific comments about the poll until she had read it, but added that the airline favours free competition with the U.S. airlines in Canada as long as there is a reciprocal deal for Air Canada in the U.S.

"It does not make sense to give up rights or ensure that U.S. carriers have unfettered access to Canada if we were not granted the same consideration in the United States."

Jack Aubrey/*Ottawa Citizen.*

Essence of the Story

■ Consultants interviewed 2,083 adult Canadians by telephone in March 2002. The poll has a margin of error within 2.2 percentage points, 19 times out of 20.

■ The survey found that 55 percent of Canadians want to end Air Canada's monopoly in domestic air travel.

■ The survey found that 84 percent of Canadians are willing to open Canadian skies to foreign competitors.

■ The poll found that 71 percent of Canadians say they would accept U.S.-based airlines in Canada even without equal access for Canadian airlines in the United States if it meant lower fares.

■ Rising airfares and surcharges give Canadians great concern.

■ An Air Canada spokesperson said that the airline favours free competition with U.S. airlines, but only if Air Canada gets the same access to the United States that U.S. carriers get in Canada.

Economic Analysis

■ The market for domestic air travel in Canada is effectively a monopoly on many routes.

■ The market for international travel is competitive.

■ On a day in September 2002, Air Canada quoted the following fares for economy class travel: Toronto–Vancouver round trip, $3,383.80; Toronto–Los Angeles round trip, $2,865.27.

■ The distances between Toronto and Vancouver and Toronto and Los Angeles are similar and the price difference represents the difference between competition on the international route and monopoly on the domestic route.

■ Figure 1 shows the monopoly outcome on a route on which Air Canada has a monopoly. The quantity of trips is that at which marginal cost, MC, equals marginal revenue, MR, and the price is the highest that the consumer is willing to pay for this quantity—$1,750 in this example.

■ Figure 2 shows the outcome if Air Canada is regulated to price its services at the competitive level. The quantity of trips increases to that at which marginal cost, MC, equals price, and the price falls to $1,250 in this example.

■ Figure 3 shows the outcome if other airlines are permitted to compete with Air Canada. With just two airlines similar in size to Air Canada, marginal cost for the route falls from MC_0 to MC_1, and in this example the price falls to $900 a trip.

■ By comparing the outcomes in these three examples, you can see why most Canadians would like to see competition and open skies. You can also see why Air Canada has a different view!

You're The Voter

■ Do you think that the federal government should open Canada's skies to competition from foreign-based airlines?

■ Do you think the service to remote parts of Canada would suffer if competition replaced monopoly in Canadian air transportation?

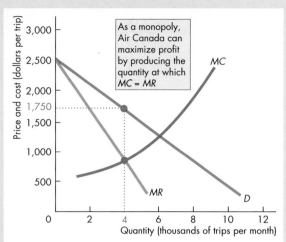

Figure 1 Air Canada operates as a monopoly

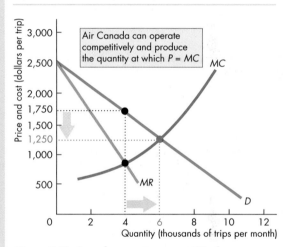

Figure 2 Air Canada operates competitively

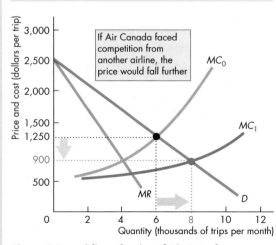

Figure 3 Two airlines the size of Air Canada operate competitively

279

SUMMARY

KEY POINTS

Market Power (pp. 262–263)

- A monopoly is an industry in which there is a single supplier of a good or service that has no close substitutes and in which barriers to entry prevent competition.
- Barriers to entry may be legal (public franchise, licence, patent, copyright, firm owns control of a resource) or natural (created by economies of scale).
- A monopoly might be able to price discriminate when there is no resale possibility.
- Where resale is possible, a firm charges one price.

A Single-Price Monopoly's Output and Price Decision (pp. 264–267)

- A monopoly's demand curve is the market demand curve, and a single-price monopoly's marginal revenue is less than price.
- A monopoly maximizes profit by producing the output at which marginal revenue equals marginal cost and by charging the maximum price that consumers are willing to pay for that output.

Single-Price Monopoly and Competition Compared (pp. 268–271)

- A single-price monopoly charges a higher price and produces a smaller quantity than a perfectly competitive industry.
- A single-price monopoly restricts output and creates a deadweight loss.
- Monopoly imposes costs that equal its deadweight loss plus the cost of the resources devoted to rent seeking.

Price Discrimination (pp. 271–274)

- Price discrimination is an attempt by the monopoly to convert consumer surplus into economic profit.
- Perfect price discrimination extracts the entire consumer surplus. Such a monopoly charges a different price for each unit sold and obtains the maximum price that each consumer is willing to pay for each unit bought.

- With perfect price discrimination, the monopoly produces the same output as would a perfectly competitive industry.
- Rent seeking with perfect price discrimination might eliminate the entire consumer surplus and producer surplus.

Monopoly Policy Issues (pp. 275–277)

- A monopoly with large economies of scale and economies of scope can produce a larger quantity at a lower price than a competitive industry can achieve, and a monopoly might be more innovative than small competitive firms.
- Efficient regulation requires a monopoly to charge a price equal to marginal cost, but for a natural monopoly, such a price is less than average total cost.
- Average cost pricing is a compromise pricing rule that covers a firm's costs and provides a normal profit but is not efficient. It is more efficient than unregulated profit maximization.

KEY FIGURES AND TABLE

Figure 12.2   Demand and Marginal Revenue, 264
Figure 12.3   Marginal Revenue and Elasticity, 265
Figure 12.4   A Monopoly's Output and Price, 267
Figure 12.5   Monopoly's Smaller Output and Higher Price, 268
Figure 12.6   Inefficiency of Monopoly, 269
Figure 12.9   Price Discrimination, 273
Figure 12.10   Perfect Price Discrimination, 274
Figure 12.11   Regulating a Natural Monopoly, 277
Table 12.1   A Monopoly's Output and Price Decision, 266

KEY TERMS

Average cost pricing rule, 277
Barriers to entry, 262
Legal monopoly, 262
Marginal cost pricing rule, 276
Market power, 262
Monopoly, 262
Natural monopoly, 262
Perfect price discrimination, 273
Price discrimination, 263
Rent seeking, 270
Single-price monopoly, 263

PROBLEMS

*1. Minnie's Mineral Springs, a single-price monopoly, faces the demand schedule.

Price (dollars per bottle)	Quantity demanded (bottles per hour)
10	0
8	1
6	2
4	3
2	4
0	5

a. Calculate Minnie's total revenue schedule.
b. Calculate its marginal revenue schedule.

2. Burma Ruby Mines, a single-price monopoly, faces the demand schedule.

Price (dollars per ruby)	Quantity demanded (rubies per day)
1,100	0
900	1
700	2
500	3
300	4

a. Calculate Burma's total revenue schedule.
b. Calculate its marginal revenue schedule.

*3. Minnie's Mineral Springs in problem 1 has the following total cost:

Quantity produced (bottles per hour)	Total cost (dollars)
0	1
1	3
2	7
3	13
4	21
5	31

a. Calculate the marginal cost of producing each output in the table.
b. Calculate the profit-maximizing output and price.
c. Calculate the economic profit.
d. Does Minnie's use resources efficiently? Explain your answer.

4. Burma Ruby Mines in problem 2 has the following total cost:

Quantity produced (rubies per day)	Total cost (dollars)
1	1,220
2	1,300
3	1,400
4	1,520

a. Calculate the marginal cost of producing each quantity listed in the table.
b. Calculate the profit-maximizing output and price.
c. Calculate the economic profit.
d. Does Burma Ruby Mines use its resources efficiently? Explain your answer.

*5. The figure illustrates the situation facing the publisher of the only newspaper containing local news in an isolated community.

a. On the graph, draw the publisher's marginal revenue curve.
b. What are the profit-maximizing quantity and price?
c. What is the publisher's daily total revenue?
d. At the price charged, is the demand for newspapers elastic or inelastic? Why?
e. On the graph, mark in the consumer surplus and deadweight loss.
f. Might the newspaper try to price discriminate? Explain why or why not.

6. The figure illustrates the situation facing the only coffee shop in an isolated community.

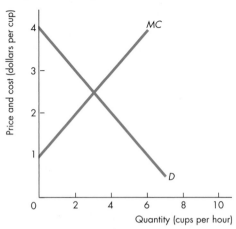

a. What are the profit-maximizing quantity and price of coffee?
b. On the graph, mark the coffee shop's profit.
c. What are consumer surplus and deadweight loss?
d. What is the efficient quantity? Explain your answer.
e. Might the coffee shop try to price discriminate? Explain why or why not.

*7. The figure shows the situation facing a natural monopoly that cannot price discriminate.

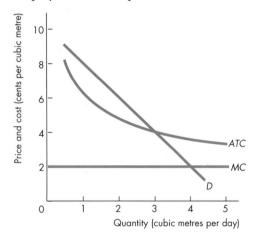

What quantity will be produced and what will be the deadweight loss if the firm is
a. An unregulated profit maximizer?
b. Regulated to earn only normal profit?
c. Regulated to be efficient?

8. If, in problem 7, marginal cost doubles, what now are your answers?

CRITICAL THINKING

1. Study *Reading Between the Lines* on pp. 278–279 and then answer the following questions.
   a. Is it correct to call Air Canada a monopoly?
   b. How would the arrival of a viable alternative airline affect Air Canada?
   c. How would you regulate the air travel industry to ensure that resources are used efficiently?
   d. "Anyone is free to buy stock in Air Canada, so everyone is free to share in Air Canada's economic profit, and the bigger that economic profit, the better for all." Evaluate this statement.

WEB EXERCISES

1. Use the links on the Parkin–Bade Web site to read the statement by Ralph Nader about Microsoft.
   a. What are Ralph Nader's main claims about Microsoft?
   b. Do you agree with Ralph Nader? Why or why not?
   c. If some other operating systems are better than Windows, why don't they take off?
   d. Does Ralph Nader identify the main costs to the consumer of Microsoft's practices? Explain why or why not.
2. Use the link on the Parkin–Bade Web site to study the market for computer chips.
   a. Is it correct to call Intel a monopoly? Why or why not?
   b. How does Intel try to raise barriers to entry in this market?
3. Use the link on the Parkin–Bade Web site to learn about developments in the Canadian railroad industry of the 1880s.
   a. Was Canadian Pacific a monopoly? Why or why not?
   b. What other elements of market power are discussed on this Web page?
   c. Do you think monopoly was a bigger problem in the 1880s than it is today? Why or why not?

MONOPOLISTIC COMPETITION AND OLIGOPOLY — CHAPTER 13

PC War Games

Since the fall of 2000, our newspapers and magazines have been stuffed with advertising by the big-name PC makers announcing yet lower prices and yet better products and value for money. How do firms like PC makers that are locked in fierce competition with each other set their prices, pick their product lines, and choose the quantities to produce? How are the profits of such firms affected by the actions of other firms? ◆ During the 1990s, a large bookseller, Chapters, began buying up and competing fiercely with smaller independent booksellers. Seeing Chapters' success, another firm with big ideas, Indigo, started to compete with Chapters. Then Indigo bought Chapters! The most recent event in the saga of Canadian book selling was the launch of Amazon.ca, a new online competitor for Indigo, in the summer of 2002. We'll look further at this development in *Reading Between the Lines* at the end of this chapter. How do markets work when only a small number of firms compete for the business?

◆ The theories of monopoly and perfect competition do not predict the kind of behaviour that we've just described. There are no newspaper ads, best brands, or price wars in perfect competition because all firms produce an identical product and each firm is a price taker. And there are none in monopoly because each monopoly firm has the entire market to itself. To understand advertising and price wars, we need the richer models that are explained in this chapter.

After studying this chapter, you will be able to

- **Define and identify monopolistic competition**
- **Explain how output and price are determined in a monopolistically competitive industry**
- **Explain why advertising costs are high in a monopolistically competitive industry**
- **Explain why the price might be sticky in oligopoly**
- **Explain how price and output are determined when there is one dominant firm and several smaller firms in a market**
- **Use game theory to make predictions about price wars and competition among a small number of firms**

Monopolistic Competition

YOU HAVE STUDIED TWO TYPES OF MARKET structure: perfect competition and monopoly. In perfect competition, a large number of firms produce identical goods, there are no barriers to entry, and each firm is a price taker. In the long run, there is no economic profit. In monopoly, a single firm is protected from competition by barriers to entry and can make an economic profit, even in the long run.

Many real-world markets are competitive but not as fiercely so as perfect competition because firms in these markets possess some power to set their prices as monopolies do. We call this type of market *monopolistic competition.*

Monopolistic competition is a market structure in which

- A large number of firms compete.
- Each firm produces a differentiated product.
- Firms compete on product quality, price, and marketing.
- Firms are free to enter and exit.

Large Number of Firms

In monopolistic competition, as in perfect competition, the industry consists of a large number of firms. The presence of a large number of firms has three implications for the firms in the industry.

Small Market Share In monopolistic competition, each firm supplies a small part of the total industry output. Consequently, each firm has only limited power to influence the price of its product. Each firm's price can deviate from the average price of other firms by a relatively small amount.

Ignore Other Firms A firm in monopolistic competition must be sensitive to the average market price of the product. But it does not pay attention to any one individual competitor. Because all the firms are relatively small, no one firm can dictate market conditions, and so no one firm's actions directly affect the actions of the other firms.

Collusion Impossible Firms in monopolistic competition would like to be able to conspire to fix a higher price—called collusion. But because there are many firms, collusion is not possible.

Product Differentiation

A firm practises **product differentiation** if it makes a product that is slightly different from the products of competing firms. A differentiated product is one that is a close substitute but not a perfect substitute for the products of the other firms. Some people will pay more for one variety of the product, so when its price rises, the quantity demanded falls but it does not (necessarily) fall to zero. For example, Adidas, Asics, Diadora, Etonic, Fila, New Balance, Nike, Puma, and Reebok all make differentiated running shoes. Other things remaining the same, if the price of Adidas running shoes rises and the prices of the other shoes remain constant, Adidas sells fewer shoes and the other producers sell more. But sales of Adidas shoes don't disappear unless the price rises by a large enough amount.

Competing on Quality, Price, and Marketing

Product differentiation enables a firm to compete with other firms in three areas: product quality, price, and marketing.

Quality The quality of a product is the physical attributes that make it different from the products of other firms. Quality includes design, reliability, the service provided to the buyer, and the buyer's ease of access to the product. Quality lies on a spectrum that runs from high to low. Some firms—Dell Computers is an example—offer high-quality products. They are well designed and reliable, and the customer receives quick and efficient service. Other firms offer a lower-quality product that is less well designed, that might not work perfectly, and that the buyer must travel some distance to obtain.

Price Because of product differentiation, a firm in monopolistic competition faces a downward-sloping demand curve. So, like a monopoly, the firm can set its price. But there is a tradeoff between the product's quality and price: A firm that makes a high-quality product can charge a higher price than can a firm that makes a low-quality product.

Marketing Because of product differentiation, a firm in monopolistic competition must market its product. Marketing takes two main forms: advertising and packaging. A firm that produces a high-quality product wants to sell it for a suitably high price.

FIGURE 13.1   Examples of Monopolistic Competition

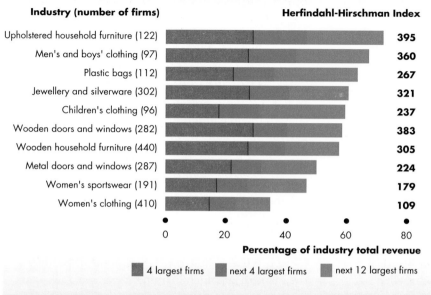

These industries operate in monopolistic competition. The number of firms in the industry is shown in parentheses after the name of the industry. The red bars show the percentage of industry sales by the largest 4 firms. The green bars show the percentage of industry sales by the next 4 largest firms, and the blue bars show the percentage of industry sales by the next 12 largest firms. So the entire length of the red, green, and blue bar combined shows the percentage of industry sales by the largest 20 firms. The Herfindahl–Hirschman Index is shown on the right.

Source: Statistics Canada, *Industrial Organization and Concentration in Manufacturing Industries*, Catalogue No. 31C0024.

To be able to do so, it must advertise and package its product in a way that convinces buyers that they are getting the higher quality for which they are paying a higher price. For example, pharmaceutical companies advertise and package their brand-name drugs to persuade buyers that these items are superior to the lower-priced generic alternatives. Similarly, a low-quality producer uses advertising and packaging to persuade buyers that although the quality is low, the low price more than compensates for this fact.

Entry and Exit

In monopolistic competition, there is free entry and free exit. Consequently, a firm cannot make an economic profit in the long run. When firms make an economic profit, new firms enter the industry. This entry lowers prices and eventually eliminates economic profit. When firms incur economic losses, some firms leave the industry. This exit increases prices and profits and eventually eliminates the economic loss. In long-run equilibrium, firms neither enter nor leave the industry and the firms in the industry make zero economic profit.

Examples of Monopolistic Competition

Figure 13.1 shows 10 industries that are examples of monopolistic competition. These industries have a large number of firms (shown in parentheses after the name of the industry). In the most concentrated of these industries, upholstered household furniture, the largest 4 firms produce 30 percent of the industry's total sales and the largest 20 firms produce 70 percent of total sales. The number on the right is the Herfindahl–Hirschman Index (p. 206–207). Producers of clothing, plastic bags, doors, and windows operate in monopolistic competition.

REVIEW QUIZ

1 What are the distinguishing characteristics of monopolistic competition?

2 How do firms in monopolistic competition compete?

3 In addition to the examples in Fig. 13.1, provide some examples of industries near your university that operate in monopolistic competition.

Output and Price in Monopolistic Competition

WE ARE NOW GOING TO LEARN HOW OUTPUT AND price are determined in monopolistic competition. First, we will suppose that the firm has already decided on the quality of its product and on its marketing program. For a given product and a given amount of marketing activity, the firm faces given costs and market conditions.

Figure 13.2 shows how a firm in monopolistic competition determines its price and output. Part (a) deals with the short run, and part (b) deals with the long run. We'll concentrate first on the short run.

Short Run: Economic Profit

The demand curve *D* shows the demand for the firm's product. It is the demand curve for Nautica jackets, not jackets in general. The curve labelled *MR*

is the marginal revenue curve associated with the demand curve. It is derived just like the marginal revenue curve of a single-price monopoly that you studied in Chapter 12. The figure also shows the firm's average total cost (*ATC*) and marginal cost (*MC*). These curves are similar to the cost curves that you first encountered in Chapter 10.

Nautica maximizes profit by producing the output at which marginal revenue equals marginal cost. In Fig. 13.2, this output is 150 jackets a day. Nautica charges the maximum price that buyers are willing to pay for this quantity, which is determined by the demand curve. This price is $190 a jacket. When Nautica produces 150 jackets a day, its average total cost is $140 a jacket, so Nautica makes a short-run economic profit of $7,500 a day ($50 a jacket multiplied by 150 jackets a day). The blue rectangle shows this economic profit.

So far, the firm in monopolistic competition looks just like a single-price monopoly. It produces the quantity at which marginal revenue equals mar-

---

FIGURE 13.2   Output and Price in Monopolistic Competition

(a) Short run

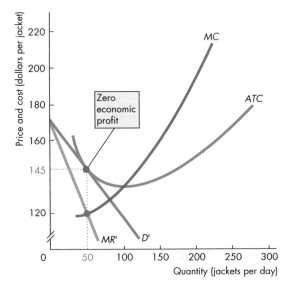

(b) Long run

Part (a) shows the short-run outcome. Profit is maximized by producing 150 jackets per day and selling them for a price of $190 per jacket. Average total cost is $140 per jacket, and the firm makes an economic profit (the blue rectangle) of $7,500 a day ($50 per jacket multiplied by 150 jackets).

Economic profit encourages new entrants in the long run, and part (b) shows the long-run outcome. The entry

of new firms decreases the demand for each firm's product and shifts the demand curve and marginal revenue curve leftward. When the demand curve has shifted to *D'*, the marginal revenue curve is *MR'* and the firm is in long-run equilibrium. The output that maximizes profit is 50 jackets a day, and the price is $145 per jacket. Average total cost is also $145 per jacket, so economic profit is zero.

ginal cost and then charges the highest price that buyers are willing to pay for that quantity, determined by the demand curve. The key difference between monopoly and monopolistic competition lies in what happens next.

Long Run: Zero Economic Profit

There is no restriction on entry in monopolistic competition, so economic profit attracts new entrants. As firms enter, each firm has a smaller market share and smaller demand for its product, which means that each firm's demand curve and marginal revenue curve shift leftward. Firms maximize short-run profit by producing the quantity at which marginal revenue equals marginal cost and by charging the highest price that buyers are willing to pay for this quantity. But as the demand for each firm's output decreases, the profit-maximizing quantity and price fall.

Figure 13.2(b) shows the long-run equilibrium. The demand curve for Nautica jackets has shifted leftward to D', and Nautica's marginal revenue curve has shifted leftward to MR'. Nautica produces 50 jackets a day and sells them at a price of $145 each. At this output level, Nautica's average total cost is also $145 a jacket. So Nautica is making zero economic profit.

When all the firms are earning zero economic profit, there is no incentive for new firms to enter the industry.

If demand is so low relative to costs that firms are incurring economic losses, exit will occur. As firms leave an industry, the demand for the remaining firms' products increases and their demand curves shift rightward. The exit process ends when all the firms are making zero economic profit.

Monopolistic Competition and Efficiency

When we studied a perfectly competitive industry, we discovered that in some circumstances, such an industry allocates resources efficiently. A key feature of efficiency is that marginal benefit equals marginal cost. Price measures marginal benefit, so efficiency requires price to equal marginal cost. When we studied monopoly, we discovered that such a firm creates an inefficient use of resources because it restricts output to a level at which price exceeds marginal cost. In such a situation, marginal benefit exceeds marginal cost and production is less than its efficient level.

Monopolistic competition shares this feature of monopoly. Even though there is zero economic profit in long-run equilibrium, the monopolistically competitive industry produces an output at which price equals average total cost but exceeds marginal cost. This outcome means that firms in monopolistic competition always have excess capacity in long-run equilibrium.

Excess Capacity A firm's **capacity output** is the output at which average total cost is a minimum—the output at the bottom of the U-shaped *ATC* curve. This output is 100 jackets a day in Fig. 13.3. Firms in monopolistic competition always have *excess capacity* in the long run. In Fig. 13.3, Nautica produces 50 jackets a day and has excess capacity of 50 jackets a day. That is, Nautica produces a smaller output than that which minimizes average total cost.

FIGURE 13.3   Excess Capacity

In long-run equilibrium, entry decreases demand to the point at which the firm makes zero economic profit. Nautica produces 50 jackets a day. A firm's capacity output is the output at which average total cost is a minimum. Nautica's capacity output is 100 jackets a day. Because the demand curve in monopolistic competition slopes downward, the profit-maximizing output in the long-run equilibrium is always less than capacity output. In long-run equilibrium, the firm operates with excess capacity.

Consequently, the consumer pays a price that exceeds minimum average total cost. This result arises from the fact that Nautica faces a downward-sloping demand curve. The demand curve slopes downward because of product differentiation, so product differentiation creates excess capacity.

You can see the excess capacity in monopolistic competition all around you. Family restaurants (except for the truly outstanding ones) almost always have some empty tables. You can always get a pizza delivered in less than 30 minutes. It is rare that every pump at a gas station is in use with customers waiting in line. There is always an abundance of realtors ready to help find or sell a home. These industries are examples of monopolistic competition. The firms have excess capacity. They could sell more by cutting their prices, but they would then incur losses.

Because in monopolistic competition price exceeds marginal cost, this market structure, like monopoly, is inefficient. The marginal cost of producing one more unit of output is less than the marginal benefit to the consumer, determined by the price the consumer is willing to pay. But the inefficiency of monopolistic competition arises from product differentiation—from product variety. Consumers value variety, but it is achievable only if firms make differentiated products. So the loss in efficiency that occurs in monopolistic competition must be weighed against the gain of greater product variety.

REVIEW QUIZ

1 How does a firm in monopolistic competition decide how much to produce and at what price to offer its product for sale?

2 Why can a firm in monopolistic competition earn an economic profit only in the short run?

3 Is monopolistic competition efficient?

4 Why do firms in monopolistic competition operate with excess capacity?

You've seen how the firm in monopolistic competition determines its output and price in the short run and the long run when it produces a given product and undertakes a *given* marketing effort. But how does the firm choose its product quality and marketing effort? We'll now study these decisions.

Product Development and Marketing

WHEN WE STUDIED A FIRM'S OUTPUT AND PRICE decision, we supposed that it had already made its product and marketing decisions. We're now going to study these decisions and the impact they have on the firm's output, price, and economic profit.

Innovation and Product Development

To enjoy economic profits, firms in monopolistic competition must be in a state of continuous product development. The reason is that wherever economic profits are earned, imitators emerge and set up business. So to maintain its economic profit, a firm must seek out new products that will provide it with a competitive edge, even if only temporarily. A firm that manages to introduce a new and differentiated variety will temporarily increase the demand for its product and will be able to increase its price temporarily. The firm will make an economic profit. Eventually, new firms that make close substitutes for the new product will enter and compete away the economic profit arising from this initial advantage. So to restore economic profit, the firm must again innovate.

The decision to innovate is based on the same type of profit-maximizing calculation that you've already studied. Innovation and product development are costly activities, but they also bring in additional revenues. The firm must balance the cost and benefit at the margin. At a low level of product development, the marginal revenue from a better product exceeds the marginal cost. When the marginal dollar of product development expenditure brings in a dollar of revenue, the firm is spending the profit-maximizing amount on product development.

For example, when Eidos Interactive released Tomb Raider: Lost Artifact, it was probably not the best game that Eidos could have created. Rather, it was the game that balanced the marginal benefit and willingness of the consumer to pay for further game enhancements against the marginal cost of these enhancements.

Efficiency and Product Innovation Is product innovation an efficient activity? Does it benefit the consumer? There are two views about these questions. One view is that monopolistic competition brings to market many improved products that bring great benefits to the consumer. Clothing, kitchen and other household appliances, computers, computer programs, cars, and many other products keep getting better every year, and the consumer benefits from these improved products.

But many so-called improvements amount to little more than changing the appearance of a product. And sometimes, the improvement is restricted to a different look in the packaging. In these cases, there is little objective benefit to the consumer.

But regardless of whether a product improvement is real or imagined, its value to the consumer is its marginal benefit, which equals the amount the consumer is willing to pay for the improvement. Whether the amount of product improvement is efficient or not depends on the marginal cost of the improvement. Only if the producers' marginal cost of product improvement equals the consumers' marginal benefit do we get the efficient amount of product innovation.

Marketing

Firms can achieve some product differentiation by designing and developing products that are actually different from those of the other firms. But firms also attempt to create a consumer perception of product differentiation even when actual differences are small. Advertising and packaging are the principal means used by firms to achieve this end. An American Express card is a different product from a Visa card. But the actual differences are not the main ones that American Express emphasizes in its marketing. The deeper message is that if you use an American Express card, which Tiger Woods uses, you'll be like Tiger Woods (or some other high-profile successful person).

Marketing Expenditures Firms in monopolistic competition incur huge costs to ensure that buyers appreciate and value the differences between their own products and those of their competitors. So a large proportion of the prices that we pay cover the cost of selling a good. And this proportion is increasing. The cost of advertising in newspapers, in magazines, and on radio and television is the main selling cost. But it is not the only one. Selling costs include the cost of shopping malls that look like movie sets, glossy catalogues and brochures, and the salaries, airfares, and hotel bills of salespeople.

The total scale of selling costs is hard to estimate, but some components can be measured. A survey conducted by a commercial agency suggested that for cleaning supplies and toys, around 15 percent of the price of an item is spent on advertising. Figure 13.4 shows some estimates for other industries.

For the North American economy as a whole, there are some 20,000 advertising agencies, which employ more than 200,000 people and have sales of $45 billion. But these numbers are only part of the total cost of advertising because firms have their own internal advertising departments, the cost of which we can only guess.

Marketing efforts affect a firm's profits in two ways: They increase costs, and if they are effective, they change demand. Let's look at these effects.

Selling Costs and Total Costs Selling costs such as advertising expenditures increase the costs of a monopolistically competitive firm above those of a competitive firm or a monopoly. Advertising costs and other selling costs are fixed costs. They do not vary as total output varies. So, just like fixed production costs, advertising costs per unit decrease as production increases.

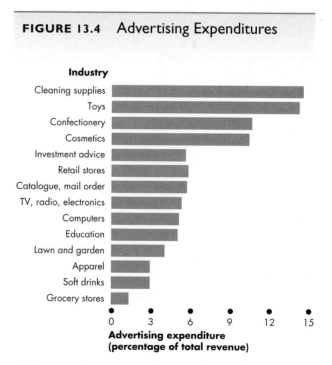

FIGURE 13.4   Advertising Expenditures

Advertising expenditures are a large part of the total revenue received by producers of cleaning supplies, toys, confectionery, and cosmetics.

Source: Schoenfeld & Associates, Lincolnwood, Illinois, reported at http://www.toolkit.cch.com/text/p03_7006.stm.

Figure 13.5 shows how selling costs and advertising expenditures change a firm's average total cost. The blue curve shows the average total cost of production. The red curve shows the firm's average total cost of production with advertising. The height of the red area between the two curves shows the average fixed cost of advertising. The *total* cost of advertising is fixed. But the *average* cost of advertising decreases as output increases.

The figure shows that if advertising increases the quantity sold by a large enough amount, it can lower average total cost. For example, if the quantity sold increases from 25 jackets a day with no advertising to 130 jackets a day with advertising, average total cost falls from $170 a jacket to $160 a jacket. The reason is that although the *total* fixed cost has increased, the greater fixed cost is spread over a greater output, so average total cost decreases.

Selling Costs and Demand Advertising and other selling efforts change the demand for a firm's prod-

uct. But does demand increase or decrease? The most natural answer is that advertising increases demand. By informing people about the quality of its products or by persuading people to switch from the products of other firms, a firm that advertises expects to increase the demand for its own products.

But all firms in monopolistic competition advertise. If advertising enables a firm to survive, it might increase the number of firms. To the extent that it increases the number of firms, advertising *decreases* the demand faced by any one firm.

Efficiency: The Bottom Line Selling costs that provide consumers with information that they value serve a useful purpose to the consumer and enable a better product choice to be made. But the opportunity cost of the additional services and information must be weighed against the gain to the consumer.

The bottom line on the question of efficiency of monopolistic competition is ambiguous. In some cases, the gains from extra product variety unquestionably offset the selling costs and the extra cost arising from excess capacity. The tremendous varieties of books and magazines, clothing, food, and drinks are examples of such gains. It is less easy to see the gains from being able to buy brand-name drugs that have a chemical composition identical to that of a generic alternative. But some people do willingly pay more for the brand-name alternative.

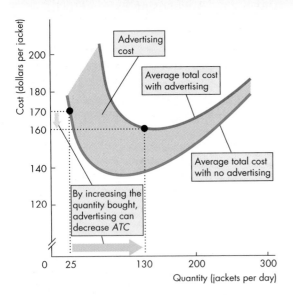

FIGURE 13.5   Selling Costs and Total Cost

Selling costs such as the cost of advertising are fixed costs, which increase average total cost. Selling costs increase average total cost by a greater amount at small outputs than at large outputs. If advertising enables sales to increase from 25 jackets a day to 130 jackets a day, average total cost *falls* from $170 to $160 a jacket.

Oligopoly

ANOTHER TYPE OF MARKET THAT LIES
between the extremes of perfect competition and
monopoly is oligopoly. **Oligopoly** is a market structure in which a small number of firms compete.

In oligopoly, the quantity sold by any one firm
depends on that firm's price *and* on the other firms'
prices and quantities sold. To see why, suppose you
run one of the three gas stations in a small town. If
you cut your price and your two competitors don't
cut theirs, your sales increase, and the sales of the
other two firms decrease. With lower sales, the other
firms most likely cut their prices too. If they do cut
their prices, your sales and profits take a tumble. So
before deciding to cut your price, you must predict
how the other firms will react and attempt to calculate the effects of those reactions on your own profit.

Several models have been developed to explain
the prices and quantities in oligopoly markets. But
no one theory has been found that can explain all the
different types of behaviour that we observe in such
markets. The models fall into two broad groups: traditional models and game theory models. We'll look
at examples of both types, starting with two traditional models.

The Kinked Demand Curve Model

The kinked demand curve model of oligopoly is
based on the assumption that each firm believes that

1. If it raises its price, others will not follow.
2. If it cuts its price, so will the other firms.

Figure 13.6 shows the demand curve (*D*) that a
firm believes it faces. The demand curve has a kink at
the current price, *P*, and quantity, *Q*. At prices above
P, a small price rise brings a big decrease in the quantity sold. The other firms hold their current price and
the firm has the highest price for the good, so it loses
market share. At prices below *P*, even a large price cut
brings only a small increase in the quantity sold. In
this case, other firms match the price cut, so the firm
gets no price advantage over its competitors.

The kink in the demand curve creates a break in
the marginal revenue curve (*MR*). To maximize
profit, the firm produces the quantity at which marginal cost equals marginal revenue. That quantity, *Q*,
is where the marginal cost curve passes through the
gap *AB* in the marginal revenue curve. If marginal

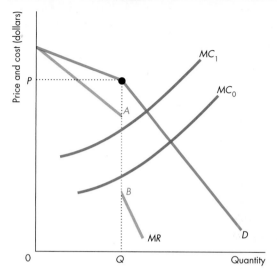

**FIGURE 13.6   The Kinked Demand Curve
Model**

The price in an oligopoly market is *P*. Each firm believes it
faces the demand curve *D*. At prices above *P*, a small price
rise brings a big decrease in the quantity sold because
other firms do not raise their prices. At prices below *P*,
even a big price cut brings only a small increase in the
quantity sold because other firms also cut their prices.
Because the demand curve is kinked, the marginal revenue
curve, *MR*, has a break, *AB*. Profit is maximized by producing *Q*. The marginal cost curve passes through the break in
the marginal revenue curve. Marginal cost changes inside
the range *AB* leave the price and quantity unchanged.

cost fluctuates between *A* and *B*, as the marginal cost
curves MC_0 and MC_1 illustrate, the firm does not
change its price or its output. Only if marginal cost
fluctuates outside the range *AB* does the firm change
its price and output. So the kinked demand curve
model predicts that price and quantity are insensitive
to small cost changes.

A problem with the kinked demand curve model
is that the firms' beliefs about the demand curve are
not always correct and firms can figure out that they
are not correct. If marginal cost increases by enough
to cause the firm to increase its price and if all firms
experience the same increase in marginal cost, they all
increase their prices together. The firm's belief that
others will not join it in a price rise is incorrect. A
firm that bases its actions on beliefs that are wrong
does not maximize profit and might even end up
incurring an economic loss.

Dominant Firm Oligopoly

A second traditional model explains a dominant firm oligopoly, which arises when one firm—the dominant firm—has a big cost advantage over the other firms and produces a large part of the industry output. The dominant firm sets the market price and the other firms are price takers. Examples of dominant firm oligopoly are a large gasoline retailer or a big video rental store that dominates its local market.

To see how a dominant firm oligopoly works, suppose that 11 firms operate gas stations in a city. Big-G is the dominant firm.

Figure 13.7 shows the market for gas in this city. In part (a), the demand curve D tells us the total quantity of gas demanded in the city at each price. The supply curve S_{10} is the supply curve of the 10 small suppliers.

Part (b) shows the situation facing Big-G. Its marginal cost curve is MC. Big-G faces the demand curve XD, and Big-G's marginal revenue curve is MR.

The demand curve XD shows the excess demand not met by the 10 small firms. For example, at a price of $1 a litre, the quantity demanded is 20,000 litres, the quantity supplied by the 10 small firms is 10,000 litres, so the excess quantity demanded is 10,000 litres, which the distance AB in both parts of the figure measures.

To maximize profit, Big-G operates like a monopoly. It sells 10,000 litres a week, where marginal revenue equals marginal cost, for a price of $1 a litre. The 10 small firms take the price of $1 a litre. They behave just like firms in perfect competition. The quantity of gas demanded in the entire city at $1 a litre is 20,000 litres, as shown in part (a). Of this amount, Big-G sells 10,000 litres and the 10 small firms each sell 1,000 litres.

The traditional theories of oligopoly do not enable us to understand all oligopoly markets and in recent years, economists have developed new models based on game theory. Let's now learn about game theory.

FIGURE 13.7   A Dominant Firm Oligopoly

(a) Ten small firms and market demand

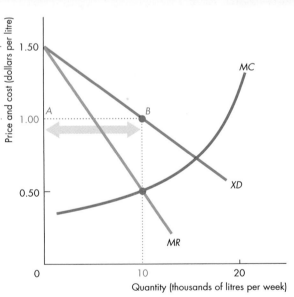

(b) Big-G's price and output decision

The demand curve for gas in a city is D in part (a). There are 10 small competitive firms that together have a supply curve of S_{10}. In addition, there is 1 large firm, Big-G, shown in part (b). Big-G faces the demand curve XD, determined as the market demand D minus the supply of the 10 small firms S_{10}—the demand that is not satisfied by the small firms.

Big-G's marginal revenue curve is MR, and its marginal cost curve is MC. Big-G sets its output to maximize profit by equating marginal cost and marginal revenue. This output is 10,000 litres per week. The price at which Big-G can sell this quantity is $1 a litre. The 10 small firms take this price, and each firm sells 1,000 litres per week, point A in part (a).

Oligopoly Games

ECONOMISTS THINK ABOUT OLIGOPOLY AS A game, and to study oligopoly markets they use a set of tools called game theory. **Game theory** is a tool for studying *strategic behaviour*—behaviour that takes into account the expected behaviour of others and the recognition of mutual interdependence. Game theory was invented by John von Neumann in 1937 and extended by von Neumann and Oskar Morgenstern in 1944. Today, it is one of the major research fields in economics.

Game theory seeks to understand oligopoly as well as all other forms of economic, political, social, and even biological rivalries by using a method of analysis specifically designed to understand games of all types, including the familiar games of everyday life. We will begin our study of game theory, and its application to the behaviour of firms, by thinking about familiar games.

What Is a Game?

What is a game? At first thought, the question seems silly. After all, there are many different games. There are ball games and parlour games, games of chance and games of skill. But what is it about all these different activities that makes them games? What do all these games have in common? All games share four features:

- Rules
- Strategies
- Payoffs
- Outcome

Let's see how these common features of games apply to a game called "the prisoners' dilemma." This game, it turns out, captures some of the essential features of oligopoly, and it gives a good illustration of how game theory works and how it generates predictions.

The Prisoners' Dilemma

Art and Bob have been caught red-handed, stealing a car. Facing airtight cases, they will receive a sentence of two years each for their crime. During his interviews with the two prisoners, the Crown attorney begins to suspect that he has stumbled on the two people who were responsible for a multimillion-dollar bank robbery some months earlier. But this is just a suspicion. The Crown attorney has no evidence on which he can convict them of the greater crime unless he can get them to confess. The Crown attorney decides to make the prisoners play a game with the following rules.

Rules Each prisoner (player) is placed in a separate room, and cannot communicate with the other player. Each is told that he is suspected of having carried out the bank robbery and that

- If both of them confess to the larger crime, each will receive a sentence of 3 years for both crimes.
- If he alone confesses and his accomplice does not, he will receive an even shorter sentence of 1 year while his accomplice will receive a 10-year sentence.

Strategies In game theory, **strategies** are all the possible actions of each player. Art and Bob each have two possible actions:

1. Confess to the bank robbery.
2. Deny having committed the bank robbery.

Payoffs Because there are two players, each with two strategies, there are four possible outcomes:

1. Both confess.
2. Both deny.
3. Art confesses and Bob denies.
4. Bob confesses and Art denies.

Each prisoner can work out exactly what happens to him—his *payoff*—in each of these four situations. We can tabulate the four possible payoffs for each of the prisoners in what is called a payoff matrix for the game. A **payoff matrix** is a table that shows the payoffs for every possible action by each player for every possible action by each other player.

Table 13.1 shows a payoff matrix for Art and Bob. The squares show the payoffs for each prisoner—the red triangle in each square shows Art's payoff and the blue triangle shows Bob's payoff. If both prisoners confess (top left), each gets a prison term of 3 years. If Bob confesses but Art denies (top right), Art gets a 10-year sentence and Bob gets a 1-year sentence. If Art confesses and Bob denies (bottom left), Art gets a 1-year sentence and Bob gets a 10-year sentence. Finally, if both of them deny (bottom right), neither can be convicted of the bank robbery charge but both are sentenced for the car theft—a 2-year sentence.

Outcome The choices of both players determine the outcome of the game. To predict that outcome, we use an equilibrium idea proposed by John Nash (of Princeton University) who received the Nobel Prize for Economic Science in 1994 and who was the subject of the 2001 movie *A Beautiful Mind*. In **Nash equilibrium**, player *A* takes the best possible action given the action of player *B* and player *B* takes the best possible action given the action of player *A*.

In the case of the prisoners' dilemma, the Nash equilibrium occurs when Art makes his best choice given Bob's choice and when Bob makes his best choice given Art's choice.

To find the Nash equilibrium, we compare all the possible outcomes associated with each choice and eliminate those that are dominated—that are not as good as some other choice. Let's find the Nash equilibrium for the prisoners' dilemma game.

Finding the Nash Equilibrium Look at the situation from Art's point of view. If Bob confesses, Art's best action is to confess because in that case, he is sentenced to 3 years rather than 10 years. If Bob does not confess, Art's best action is still to confess because in that case he receives 1 year rather than 2 years. So Art's best action is to confess.

Now look at the situation from Bob's point of view. If Art confesses, Bob's best action is to confess because in that case, he is sentenced to 3 years rather than 10 years. If Art does not confess, Bob's best action is still to confess because in that case, he receives 1 year rather than 2 years. So Bob's best action is to confess.

Because each player's best action is to confess, each does confess, each gets a 3-year prison term, and the Crown attorney has solved the bank robbery. This is the Nash equilibrium of the game.

The Dilemma Now that you have found the solution to the prisoners' dilemma, you can better see the dilemma. The dilemma arises as each prisoner contemplates the consequences of denying. Each prisoner knows that if both of them deny, they will each receive only a 2-year sentence for stealing the car. But neither has any way of knowing that his accomplice will deny. Each poses the following questions: Should I deny and rely on my accomplice to deny so that we will both get only 2 years? Or should I confess in the hope of getting just 1 year (provided that my accomplice denies) knowing that if my accomplice does con-

TABLE 13.1   Prisoners' Dilemma Payoff Matrix

Each square shows the payoffs for the two players, Art and Bob, for each possible pair of actions. In each square, the red triangle shows Art's payoff and the blue triangle shows Bob's. For example, if both confess, the payoffs are in the top left square. The equilibrium of the game is for both players to confess and each gets a 3-year sentence.

fess, we will both get 3 years in prison? The dilemma is resolved by finding the equilibrium of the game.

A Bad Outcome For the prisoners, the equilibrium of the game, with each confessing, is not the best outcome. If neither of them confesses, each gets only 2 years for the lesser crime. Isn't there some way in which this better outcome can be achieved? It seems that there is not, because the players cannot communicate with each other. Each player can put himself in the other player's place, and so each player can figure out that there is one best strategy for each of them. The prisoners are indeed in a dilemma. Each knows that he can serve 2 years only if he can trust the other to deny. But each prisoner also knows that it is not in the best interest of the other to deny. So each prisoner knows that he must confess, thereby delivering a bad outcome for both.

The firms in an oligopoly are in a similar situation to Art and Bob in the prisoners' dilemma game. Let's see how we can use this game to understand oligopoly.

An Oligopoly Price-Fixing Game

We can use game theory and a game like the prisoners' dilemma to understand price fixing, price wars, and other aspects of the behaviour of firms in oligopoly. We'll begin with a price-fixing game.

To understand how oligopolies fix prices, we're going to study a special case of oligopoly called duopoly. **Duopoly** is a market structure in which there are only two producers who compete. You can probably find some examples of duopoly near where you live. Many cities have only two suppliers of milk, two local newspapers, two taxi companies, two car rental firms, two copy centres, or two college bookstores. Duopoly captures the essence of all oligopoly situations. Our goal is to predict the prices charged and the quantities produced by the two firms.

Cost and Demand Conditions Two firms, Trick and Gear, produce switchgears. They have identical costs. Figure 13.8(a) shows their average total cost curve (*ATC*) and marginal cost curve (*MC*). Figure 13.8(b) shows the market demand curve for switchgears (*D*). The two firms produce identical switchgears, so one firm's switchgear is a perfect substitute for the other's. So the market prices of both firms' product are identical. The quantity demanded depends on that price—the higher the price, the smaller is the quantity demanded.

This industry is a natural duopoly. Two firms can produce this good at a lower cost than can either one firm or three firms. For each firm, average total cost is at its minimum when production is 3,000 units a week. And when price equals minimum average total cost, the total quantity demanded is 6,000 units a week. So two firms can just produce that quantity.

Collusion We'll suppose that Trick and Gear enter into a collusive agreement. A **collusive agreement** is an agreement between two (or more) producers to restrict output, raise the price, and increase profits. Such an agreement is illegal in Canada and is undertaken in secret. A group of firms that has entered into a collusive agreement to restrict output and increase prices and profits is called a **cartel**. The strategies that firms in a cartel can pursue are to

- Comply
- Cheat

A firm that complies carries out the agreement. A firm that cheats breaks the agreement to its own benefit and to the cost of the other firm.

Because each firm has two strategies, there are four possible combinations of actions for the firms:

1. Both firms comply.
2. Both firms cheat.
3. Trick complies and Gear cheats.
4. Gear complies and Trick cheats.

FIGURE 13.8   Costs and Demand

(a) Individual firm

(b) Industry

The average total cost curve for each firm is *ATC*, and the marginal cost curve is *MC* (part a). Minimum average total cost is $6,000 a unit, and it occurs at a production of 3,000 units a week. Part (b) shows the market demand curve. At a price of $6,000, the quantity demanded is 6,000 units per week. The two firms can produce this output at the lowest possible average cost. If the market had one firm, it would be profitable for another to enter. If the market had three firms, one would exit. There is room for only two firms in this industry. It is a natural duopoly.

Colluding to Maximize Profits Let's work out the payoffs to the two firms if they collude to make the maximum profit for the cartel by acting like a monopoly. The calculations that the two firms perform are the same calculations that a monopoly performs. (You can refresh your memory of these calculations by looking at Chapter 12, pp. 266–267.) The only thing that the duopolists must do beyond what a monopolist does is to agree on how much of the total output each of them will produce.

Figure 13.9 shows the price and quantity that maximize industry profit for the duopolists. Part (a) shows the situation for each firm, and part (b) shows the situation for the industry as a whole. The curve labelled *MR* is the industry marginal revenue curve. This marginal revenue curve is like that of a single-price monopoly (see Chapter 12, p. 264). The curve labelled MC_I is the industry marginal cost curve if each firm produces the same level of output. That curve is constructed by adding together the outputs of the two firms at each level of marginal cost. That is, at each level of marginal cost, industry output is twice as much as the output of each individual firm. Thus the curve MC_I in part (b) is twice as far to the right as the curve *MC* in part (a).

To maximize industry profit, the duopolists agree to restrict output to the rate that makes the industry marginal cost and marginal revenue equal. That output rate, as shown in part (b), is 4,000 units a week.

The highest price for which the 4,000 switchgears can be sold is $9,000 each. Trick and Gear agree to charge this price.

To hold the price at $9,000 a unit, production must not exceed 4,000 units a week. So Trick and Gear must agree on the production level for each of them that total 4,000 units a week. Let's suppose that they agree to split the market equally so that each firm produces 2,000 switchgears a week. Because the firms are identical, this division is the most likely.

The average total cost (*ATC*) of producing 2,000 switchgears a week is $8,000, so the profit per unit is $1,000 and economic profit is $2 million (2,000 units × $1,000 per unit). The economic profit of each firm is represented by the blue rectangle in Fig. 13.9(a).

We have just described one possible outcome for a duopoly game: The two firms collude to produce the monopoly profit-maximizing output and divide that output equally between themselves. From the industry point of view, this solution is identical to a monopoly. A duopoly that operates in this way is indistinguishable from a monopoly. The economic profit that is made by a monopoly is the maximum total profit that can be made by colluding duopolists.

But with price greater than marginal cost, either firm might think of trying to increase its profit by cheating on the agreement and producing more than the agreed amount. Let's see what happens if one of the firms does cheat in this way.

FIGURE 13.9   Colluding to Make Monopoly Profits

(a) Individual firm   (b) Industry

The industry marginal cost curve, MC_I in part (b), is the horizontal sum of the two firms' marginal cost curves, *MC*, in part (a). The industry marginal revenue curve is *MR*. To maximize profit, the firms produce 4,000 units a week (the quantity at which marginal revenue equals marginal cost). They sell that output for $9,000 a unit. Each firm produces 2,000 units a week. Average total cost is $8,000 a unit, so each firm makes an economic profit of $2 million (blue rectangle)—2,000 units multiplied by $1,000 profit a unit.

One Firm Cheats on a Collusive Agreement To set the stage for cheating on their agreement, Trick convinces Gear that demand has decreased and that it cannot sell 2,000 units a week. Trick tells Gear that it plans to cut its price in order to sell the agreed 2,000 units each week. Because the two firms produce an identical product, Gear matches Trick's price cut but still produces only 2,000 units a week.

In fact, there has been no decrease in demand. Trick plans to increase output, which it knows will lower the price, and Trick wants to ensure that Gear's output remains at the agreed level.

Figure 13.10 illustrates the consequences of Trick's cheating. Part (a) shows Gear (the complier); part (b) shows Trick (the cheat); and part (c) shows the industry as a whole. Suppose that Trick increases output to 3,000 units a week. If Gear sticks to the agreement to produce only 2,000 units a week, total output is 5,000 units a week, and given demand in part (c), the price falls to $7,500 a unit.

Gear continues to produce 2,000 units a week at a cost of $8,000 a unit and incurs a loss of $500 a unit, or $1 million a week. This economic loss is represented by the red rectangle in part (a). Trick produces 3,000 units a week at an average total cost of $6,000 each. With a price of $7,500, Trick makes a profit of $1,500 a unit and therefore an economic profit of $4.5 million. This economic profit is the blue rectangle in part (b).

We've now described a second possible outcome for the duopoly game: One of the firms cheats on the collusive agreement. In this case, the industry output is larger than the monopoly output and the industry price is lower than the monopoly price. The total economic profit made by the industry is also smaller than the monopoly's economic profit. Trick (the cheat) makes an economic profit of $4.5 million, and Gear (the complier) incurs an economic loss of $1 million. The industry makes an economic profit of $3.5 million. Thus the industry profit is $0.5 million less than the economic profit a monopoly would make. But the profit is distributed unevenly. Trick makes a bigger economic profit than it would under the collusive agreement, while Gear incurs an economic loss.

A similar outcome would arise if Gear cheated and Trick complied with the agreement. The industry profit and price would be the same, but in this case, Gear (the cheat) would make an economic profit of $4.5 million and Trick (the complier) would incur an economic loss of $1 million.

Let's next see what happens if both firms cheat.

FIGURE 13.10   One Firm Cheats

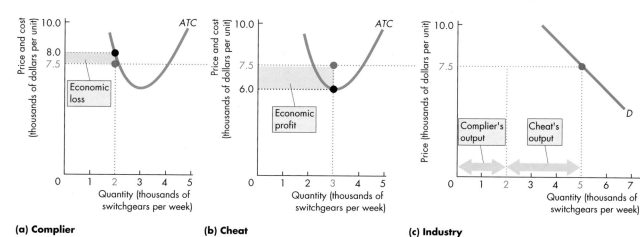

(a) Complier   **(b) Cheat**   **(c) Industry**

One firm, shown in part (a), complies with the agreement and produces 2,000 units. The other firm, shown in part (b), cheats on the agreement and increases its output to 3,000 units. Given the market demand curve, shown in part (c), and with a total production of 5,000 units a week, the price falls to $7,500. At this price, the complier in part (a) incurs an economic loss of $1 million ($500 per unit × 2,000 units), shown by the red rectangle. In part (b), the cheat makes an economic profit of $4.5 million ($1,500 per unit × 3,000 units), shown by the blue rectangle.

Both Firms Cheat Suppose that both firms cheat and that each behaves in the way that we have just analyzed. Each tells the other that it is unable to sell its output at the going price and that it plans to cut its price. But because both firms cheat, each will propose a successively lower price. As long as price exceeds marginal cost, each firm has an incentive to increase its production—to cheat. Only when price equals marginal cost is there no further incentive to cheat. This situation arises when the price has reached $6,000. At this price, marginal cost equals price. Also, price equals minimum average total cost. At a price less than $6,000, each firm incurs an economic loss. At a price of $6,000, each firm covers all its costs and makes zero economic profit (makes normal profit). Also, at a price of $6,000, each firm wants to produce 3,000 units a week, so the industry output is 6,000 units a week. Given the demand conditions, 6,000 units can be sold at a price of $6,000 each.

Figure 13.11 illustrates the situation just described. Each firm, in part (a), produces 3,000 units a week, and its average total cost is a minimum ($6,000 per unit). The market as a whole, in part (b), operates at the point at which the market demand curve (D) intersects the industry marginal cost curve (MC_I). Each firm has lowered its price and increased its output to try to gain an advantage over the other firm. Each has pushed this process as far as it can without incurring an economic loss.

We have now described a third possible outcome of this duopoly game: Both firms cheat. If both firms cheat on the collusive agreement, the output of each firm is 3,000 units a week and the price is $6,000. Each firm makes zero economic profit.

The Payoff Matrix Now that we have described the strategies and payoffs in the duopoly game, we can summarize the strategies and the payoffs in the form of the game's payoff matrix. Then we can find the Nash equilibrium.

Table 13.2 sets out the payoff matrix for this game. It is constructed in the same way as the payoff matrix for the prisoners' dilemma in Table 13.1. The squares show the payoffs for the two firms—Gear and Trick. In this case, the payoffs are profits. (For the prisoners' dilemma, the payoffs were losses.)

The table shows that if both firms cheat (top left), they achieve the perfectly competitive outcome—each firm makes zero economic profit. If both firms comply (bottom right), the industry makes the monopoly profit and each firm earns an economic profit of $2 million. The top right and bottom left squares show what happens if one firm cheats while the other complies. The firm that cheats collects an economic profit of $4.5 million, and the one that complies incurs a loss of $1 million.

Nash Equilibrium in the Duopolists' Dilemma
The duopolists have a dilemma like the prisoners' dilemma. Do they comply or cheat? To answer this question, we must find the Nash equilibrium.

FIGURE 13.11 Both Firms Cheat

(a) Individual firm

(b) Industry

If both firms cheat by increasing production, the collusive agreement collapses. The limit to the collapse is the competitive equilibrium. Neither firm will cut price below $6,000 (minimum average total cost) because to do so will result in losses. In part (a), both firms produce 3,000 units a week at an average total cost of $6,000 a unit. In part (b), with a total production of 6,000 units, the price falls to $6,000. Each firm now makes zero economic profit because price equals average total cost. This output and price are the ones that would prevail in a competitive industry.

TABLE 13.2   Duopoly Payoff Matrix

Gear's strategies

Each square shows the payoffs from a pair of actions. For example, if both firms comply with the collusive agreement, the payoffs are recorded in the bottom right square. The red triangle shows Gear's payoff, and the blue triangle shows Trick's. In Nash equilibrium, both firms cheat.

Look at things from Gear's point of view. Gear reasons as follows: Suppose that Trick cheats. If I comply, I will incur an economic loss of $1 million. If I also cheat, I will make zero economic profit. Zero is better than *minus* $1 million, so I'm better off if I cheat. Now suppose Trick complies. If I cheat, I will make an economic profit of $4.5 million, and if I comply, I will make an economic profit of $2 million. A $4.5 million profit is better than a $2 million profit, so I'm better off if I cheat. So regardless of whether Trick cheats or complies, it pays Gear to cheat. Cheating is Gear's best strategy.

Trick comes to the same conclusion as Gear because the two firms face an identical situation. So both firms cheat. The Nash equilibrium of the duopoly game is that both firms cheat. And although the industry has only two firms, they charge the same price and produce the same quantity as those in a competitive industry. Also, as in perfect competition, each firm makes zero economic profit.

This conclusion is not general and will not always arise. We'll see why not by looking first at some other games that are like the prisoners' dilemma. Then we'll broaden the types of games we consider.

Other Oligopoly Games

Firms in oligopoly must decide whether: to mount expensive advertising campaigns; to modify their product; to make their product more reliable and more durable; to price discriminate and, if so, among which groups of customers and to what degree; to undertake a large research and development (R&D) effort aimed at lowering production costs; and to enter or leave an industry.

All of these choices can be analyzed as games that are similar to the one that we've just studied. Let's look at one example: an R&D game.

An R&D Game

Disposable diapers were first marketed in 1966. The two market leaders from the start of this industry have been Procter & Gamble (the maker of Pampers) and Kimberly-Clark (the maker of Huggies). Procter & Gamble has about 40 percent of the total market, and Kimberly-Clark has about 33 percent. When the disposable diaper was first introduced in 1966, it had to be cost-effective in competition with reusable, laundered diapers. A costly research and development effort resulted in the development of machines that could make disposable diapers at a low enough cost to achieve that initial competitive edge. But new firms tried to get into the business and take market share away from the two industry leaders, and the industry leaders themselves battled each other to maintain or increase their own market share.

During the early 1990s, Kimberly-Clark was the first to introduce Velcro closures. And in 1996, Procter & Gamble was the first to introduce "breathable" diapers into the North American market.

The key to success in this industry (as in any other) is to design a product that people value highly relative to the cost of producing it. The firm that develops the most highly valued product and also develops the least-cost technology for producing it gains a competitive edge, undercutting the rest of the market, increasing its market share, and increasing its profit. But the R&D that must be undertaken to achieve product improvements and cost reductions is costly. So the cost of R&D must be deducted from the profit resulting from the increased market share that lower costs achieve. If no firm does R&D, every firm can be better off, but if one firm initiates the R&D activity, all must follow.

Table 13.3 illustrates the dilemma (with hypothetical numbers) for the R&D game that Kimberly-Clark and Procter & Gamble play. Each firm has two strategies: Spend $25 million a year on R&D or spend nothing on R&D. If neither firm spends on R&D, they make a joint profit of $100 million: $30 million for Kimberly-Clark and $70 million for Procter & Gamble (bottom right of the payoff matrix). If each firm conducts R&D, market shares are maintained but each firm's profit is lower by the amount spent on R&D (top left square of the payoff matrix). If Kimberly-Clark pays for R&D but Procter & Gamble does not, Kimberly-Clark gains a large part of Procter & Gamble's market. Kimberly-Clark profits, and Procter & Gamble loses (top right square of the payoff matrix). Finally, if Procter & Gamble conducts R&D and Kimberly-Clark does not, Procter & Gamble gains market share from Kimberly-Clark, increasing its profit, while Kimberly-Clark incurs a loss (bottom left square).

Confronted with the payoff matrix in Table 13.3, the two firms calculate their best strategies. Kimberly-Clark reasons as follows: If Procter & Gamble does not undertake R&D, we will make $85 million if we do and $30 million if we do not; so it pays us to conduct R&D. If Procter & Gamble conducts R&D, we will lose $10 million if we don't and make $5 million if we do. Again, R&D pays off. Thus conducting R&D is the best strategy for Kimberly-Clark. It pays, regardless of Procter & Gamble's decision.

Procter & Gamble reasons similarly: If Kimberly-Clark does not undertake R&D, we will make $70 million if we follow suit and $85 million if we conduct R&D. It therefore pays to conduct R&D. If Kimberly-Clark does undertake R&D, we will make $45 million by doing the same and lose $10 million by not doing R&D. Again, it pays us to conduct R&D. So for Procter & Gamble, conducting R&D is also the best strategy.

Because conducting R&D is the best strategy for both players, it is the Nash equilibrium. The outcome of this game is that both firms conduct R&D. They make less profit than they would if they could collude to achieve the cooperative outcome of no R&D.

The real-world situation has more players than Kimberly-Clark and Procter & Gamble. A large number of other firms share a small portion of the market, all of them ready to eat into the market share of Procter & Gamble and Kimberly-Clark. So the R&D effort by these two firms not only serves the purpose of maintaining shares in their own battle, but also helps to keep barriers to entry high enough to preserve their joint market share.

TABLE 13.3   Pampers versus Huggies: An R&D Game

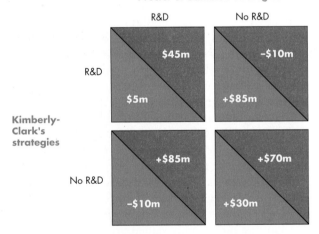

Procter & Gamble's strategies

	R&D	No R&D
R&D	$5m / $45m	+$85m / −$10m
No R&D	−$10m / +$85m	+$30m / +$70m

Kimberly-Clark's strategies

If both firms undertake R&D, their payoffs are those shown in the top left square. If neither firm undertakes R&D, their payoffs are in the bottom right square. When one firm undertakes R&D and the other one does not, their payoffs are in the top right and bottom left squares. The red triangle shows Procter & Gamble's payoff, and the blue triangle shows Kimberly-Clark's. The Nash equilibrium for this game is for both firms to undertake R&D. The structure of this game is the same as that of the prisoners' dilemma.

REVIEW QUIZ

1 What are the common features of all games?
2 Describe the prisoners' dilemma game and explain why the Nash equilibrium delivers a bad outcome for both players.
3 Why does a collusive agreement to restrict output and raise price create a game like the prisoners' dilemma?
4 What creates an incentive for firms in a collusive agreement to cheat and increase production?
5 What is the equilibrium strategy for each firm in a duopolists' dilemma and why do the firms not succeed in colluding to raise the price and profits?

Repeated Games and Sequential Games

THE GAMES THAT WE'VE STUDIED ARE PLAYED just once. In contrast, many real-world games are played repeatedly. This feature of games turns out to enable real-world duopolists to cooperate, collude, and earn a monopoly profit.

Another feature of the game that we've studied is that the players move simultaneously. But in many real-world situations, one player moves first and then the other moves—the play is sequential rather than simultaneous. This feature of real-world games creates a large number of possible outcomes.

We're now going to examine these two aspects of strategic decision making.

A Repeated Duopoly Game

If two firms play a game repeatedly, one firm has the opportunity to penalize the other for previous "bad" behaviour. If Gear cheats this week, perhaps Trick will cheat next week. Before Gear cheats this week, won't it take into account the possibility that Trick will cheat next week? What is the equilibrium of this game?

Actually, there is more than one possibility. One is the Nash equilibrium that we have just analyzed. Both players cheat, and each makes zero economic profit forever. In such a situation, it will never pay one of the players to start complying unilaterally because to do so would result in a loss for that player and a profit for the other. But a **cooperative equilibrium** in which the players make and share the monopoly profit is possible.

A cooperative equilibrium might occur if cheating is punished. There are two extremes of punishment. The smallest penalty is called "tit for tat." A *tit-for-tat strategy* is one in which a player cooperates in the current period if the other player cooperated in the previous period but cheats in the current period if the other player cheated in the previous period. The most severe form of punishment is called a trigger strategy. A *trigger strategy* is one in which a player cooperates if the other player cooperates but cheats forever thereafter if the other player cheats once.

In the duopoly game between Gear and Trick, a tit-for-tat strategy keeps both players cooperating and earning monopoly profits. Let's see why with an example.

Table 13.4 shows the economic profit that Trick and Gear will make over a number of periods under two alternative sequences of events: colluding and cheating with a tit-for-tat response by the other firm.

If both firms stick to the collusive agreement in period 1, each makes an economic profit of $2 million. Suppose that Trick contemplates cheating in period 1. The cheating produces a quick $4.5 million economic profit and inflicts a $1 million economic loss on Gear. But a cheat in period 1 produces a response from Gear in period 2. If Trick wants to get back into a profit-making situation, it must return to the agreement in period 2 even though it knows that Gear will punish it for cheating in period 1. So in period 2, Gear punishes Trick and Trick cooperates. Gear now makes an economic profit of $4.5 million, and Trick incurs an economic loss of $1 million. Adding up the profits over two periods of play, Trick would have made more profit by cooperating— $4 million compared with $3.5 million.

What is true for Trick is also true for Gear. Because each firm makes a larger profit by sticking with the collusive agreement, both firms do so and the monopoly price, quantity, and profit prevail.

In reality, whether a cartel works like a one-play game or a repeated game depends primarily on the

TABLE 13.4   Cheating with Punishment

Period of Play	Collude		Cheat with tit-for-tat	
	Trick's profit	Gear's profit	Trick's profit	Gear's profit
	(millions of dollars)		(millions of dollars)	
1	2	2	4.5	−1.0
2	2	2	−1.0	4.5
3	2	2	2.0	2.0
4	.	.	.	.

If duopolists repeatedly collude, each makes an economic profit of $2 million per period of play. If one player cheats in period 1, the other player plays a tit-for-tat strategy and cheats in period 2. The profit from cheating can be made for only one period and must be paid for in the next period by incurring a loss. Over two periods of play, the best that a duopolist can achieve by cheating is an economic profit of $3.5 million, compared to an economic profit of $4 million by colluding.

number of players and the ease of detecting and punishing cheating. The larger the number of players, the harder it is to maintain a cartel.

Games and Price Wars   A repeated duopoly game can help us understand real-world behaviour and, in particular, price wars. Some price wars can be interpreted as the implementation of a tit-for-tat strategy. But the game is a bit more complicated than the one we've looked at because the players are uncertain about the demand for the product.

Playing a tit-for-tat strategy, firms have an incentive to stick to the monopoly price. But fluctuations in demand lead to fluctuations in the monopoly price, and sometimes, when the price changes, it might seem to one of the firms that the price has fallen because the other has cheated. In this case, a price war will break out. The price war will end only when each firm is satisfied that the other is ready to cooperate again. There will be cycles of price wars and the restoration of collusive agreements. Fluctuations in the world price of oil might be interpreted in this way.

Some price wars arise from the entry of a small number of firms into an industry that had previously been a monopoly. Although the industry has a small number of firms, the firms are in a prisoners' dilemma and they cannot impose effective penalties for price cutting. The behaviour of prices and outputs in the computer chip industry during 1995 and 1996 can be explained in this way. Until 1995, the market for Pentium chips for IBM-compatible computers was dominated by one firm, Intel Corporation, which was able to make maximum economic profit by producing the quantity of chips at which marginal cost equalled marginal revenue. The price of Intel's chips was set to ensure that the quantity demanded equalled the quantity produced. Then in 1995 and 1996, with the entry of a small number of new firms, the industry became an oligopoly. If the firms had maintained Intel's price and shared the market, together they could have made economic profits equal to Intel's profit. But the firms were in a prisoners' dilemma. So prices fell towards the competitive level.

Let's now study a sequential game. There are many such games, and the one we'll examine is among the simplest. But it has an interesting implication and it gives you the flavour of this type of game. The sequential game that we'll study is an entry game in a contestable market.

A Sequential Entry Game in a Contestable Market

If two firms play a game, one firm makes a decision at the first stage of the game and the other makes a decision at the second stage.

We're going to study a sequential game in a **contestable market**—a market in which firms can enter and leave so easily that firms in the market face competition from *potential* entrants. Examples of contestable markets are routes served by airlines and by barge companies that operate on the major waterways. These markets are contestable because firms could enter if an opportunity for economic profit arose and could exit with no penalty if the opportunity for economic profit disappeared.

If the Herfindahl–Hirschman Index (p. 206) is used to determine the degree of competition, a contestable market appears to be uncompetitive. But a contestable market can behave as if it were perfectly competitive. To see why, let's look at an entry game for a contestable air route.

A Contestable Air Route   Agile Air is the only firm operating on a particular route. Demand and cost conditions are such that there is room for only one airline to operate. Wanabe, Inc. is another airline that could offer services on the route.

We describe the structure of a sequential game by using a *game tree* like that in Fig. 13.12. At the first stage, Agile Air must set a price. Once the price is set and advertised, Agile can't change it. That is, once set, Agile's price is fixed and Agile can't react to Wanabe's entry decision. Agile can set its price at the monopoly level or at the competitive level.

At the second stage, Wanabe must decide whether to enter or to stay out. Customers have no loyalty (there are no frequent flyer programs) and they buy from the lowest-price airline. So if Wanabe enters, it sets a price just below Agile's and takes all the business.

Figure 13.12 shows the payoffs from the various decisions (Agile's payoffs are in the red triangles and Wanabe's payoffs are in the blue triangles).

To decide on its price, Agile's CEO reasons as follows: Suppose that Agile sets the monopoly price. If Wanabe enters, it earns 90 (think of all payoff numbers as thousands of dollars). If Wanabe stays out it earns nothing. So Wanabe will enter. In this case Agile will lose 50.

FIGURE 13.12 Agile versus Wanabe: A Sequential Entry Game in a Contestable Market

If Agile sets the monopoly price, Wanabe makes 90 (thousand dollars) by entering and earns nothing by staying out. So if Agile sets the monopoly price, Wanabe enters.

If Agile sets the competitive price, Wanabe earns nothing if it stays out and incurs a loss if it enters. So if Agile sets the competitive price, Wanabe stays out.

Now suppose that Agile sets the competitive price. If Wanabe stays out, it earns nothing and if it enters, it loses 10, so Wanabe will stay out. In this case, Agile will earn 50.

Agile's best strategy is to set its price at the competitive level and earn 50 (normal profit). The option of earning 100 by setting the monopoly price with Wanabe staying out is not available to Agile. If Agile sets the monopoly price, Wanabe enters, undercuts Agile, and takes all the business.

In this example, Agile sets its price at the competitive level and earns normal profit. A less costly strategy, called **limit pricing,** sets the price at the highest level that inflicts a loss on the entrant. Any loss is big enough to deter entry, so it is not always necessary to set the price as low as the competitive price. In the example of Agile and Wanabe, at the competitive price, Wanabe incurs a loss of 10 if it enters. A smaller loss would still keep Wanabe out.

This game is interesting because it points to the possibility of a monopoly behaving like a competitive industry and serving the consumer interest without regulation. But the result is not general and depends on one crucial feature of the set up of the game: At the second stage, Agile is locked into the price set at the first stage.

If Agile could change its price in the second stage, it would want to set the monopoly price if Wanabe stayed out—100 with the monopoly price beats 50

with the competitive price. But Wanabe can figure out what Agile would do, so the price set at the first stage has no effect on Wanabe. Agile sets the monopoly price and Wanabe might either stay out or enter.

We've looked at two of the many possible repeated and sequential games, and you've seen how these types of games can provide insights into the complex forces that determine prices and profits.

REVIEW QUIZ

1 If a prisoners' dilemma game is played repeatedly, what punishment strategies might the players employ and how does playing the game repeatedly change the equilibrium?

2 If a market is contestable, how does the equilibrium differ from that of a monopoly?

◆ Monopolistic competition and oligopoly are the most common market structures that you encounter in your daily life. *Reading Between the Lines* on pp. 304–305 shows you oligopoly in action in the Canadian retail book market.

So far, we've been studying the two big questions: What goods and services are produced, and how are they produced? Your next task is to study the forces that determine for whom they are produced.

Oligopoly in Action: A Book Seller's War

THE GLOBE AND MAIL, JUNE 25, 2002

Amazon.ca set to go today

Amazon.com Inc. is set to launch its Canadian on-line site today in a move that is sure to shake up an already shaky publishing industry.

Jeff Bezos, chief executive officer of the world's biggest Internet retailer, will unveil his plans for Canada at a Toronto press conference this morning and later at a cocktail reception for members of the industry.

The long-rumoured arrival of the on-line giant is being applauded by some Canadian publishers who have felt the squeeze of operating in a market dominated by one major player—Indigo Books &Music Inc. ...

Canadian booksellers are less excited about the news.

Earlier this month, the Canadian Booksellers Association called on Ottawa to review Amazon.com's plans, saying the Seattle-based retailer was violating federal foreign investment rules for the industry.

Federal cultural investment regulations require that a majority of any bookseller be Canadian-owned.

A spokeswoman for the association said yesterday that it has received no response from the ministry, other than confirmation that their letter was received. ...

E-commerce consultant and author Rick Broadhead said the arrival of Amazon.ca will likely put instant pressure on the Chapters/Indigo e-commerce site.

"Indigo probably can't afford to compete," he said.

But he said for consumers, the event is good news. "Canadians deserve to have the best retailers to shop at and Amazon is the undisputed king of on-line retailing," he said.

Reprinted with permission from *The Globe and Mail.*

Essence of the Story

■ Amazon.com Inc. opened a Canadian on-line site in June 2002.

■ Canadian publishers were pleased to see competition for Indigo Books & Music Inc., who they say has squeezed them.

■ Canadian booksellers were not pleased about the news.

■ The Canadian Booksellers Association claimed that Amazon was violating federal foreign investment rules, which require that a majority of any bookseller be Canadian-owned.

■ E-commerce consultant and author Rick Broadhead said the arrival of Amazon.ca will likely put instant pressure on the Chapters/Indigo e-commerce site.

Economic Analysis

■ The retail market for books in Canada is an example of oligopoly.

■ During the 1990s, independent retailers disappeared as Chapters and Indigo expanded.

■ By 2001, these two firms controlled more than 30 percent of the retail book market in Canada and, in some cities, they had a virtual duopoly.

■ Then, in 2001, Indigo Books & Music Inc. bought Chapters.

■ So in 2002, before the arrival of Amazon.ca, Indigo was the major player in the Canadian retail book market and chapters.indigo.ca was the major player in the Canadian e-commerce book market.

■ The table shows the payoff matrix for the game that Indigo and Amazon played in 2002.

■ The numbers in the table are economic profit. (The magnitudes are fictitious, but the relative magnitudes illustrate the nature of the game.)

■ Amazon had two strategies: enter the Canadian market or remain out. Indigo had two strategies: stay in and fight or exit.

■ The payoffs from staying out are zero. If one of the firms had the market to itself, it would earn 100. If both firms shared the market, they would each earn 20.

■ This game is similar to the prisoners' dilemma, but not quite the same because the players can walk away and earn zero.

■ But there is a dilemma. If either firm had the market to itself, it could earn a large profit and sharing the market not only lowers the profit for each but also lowers the total profit that they share. The reason is that basic infrastructure resources are duplicated with two firms.

■ The equilibrium of the assumed game is for Amazon to enter the market and for Indigo to remain.

■ The assumed game might be a poor description of reality. It is possible that there is room for only one firm to earn a positive economic profit. If this turns out to be the case, one of the players will eventually exit and a single dominant firm will win the market.

Figure 1 Amazon versus Indigo: An entry game

You're The Voter

■ Do you think the Canadian government should prevent U.S. firms from entering the Canadian book-retailing market?

■ Who would benefit and who would pay for such a ban?

305

SUMMARY

KEY POINTS

Monopolistic Competition (pp. 284–285)

- Monopolistic competition occurs when a large number of firms compete with each other on product quality, price, and marketing.

Output and Price in Monopolistic Competition (pp. 286–288)

- A firm in monopolistic competition faces downward-sloping demand curve and produces the quantity at which marginal revenue equals marginal cost.
- Entry and exit result in zero economic profit and excess capacity in long-run equilibrium.

Product Development and Marketing (pp. 288–290)

- Firms in monopolistic competition innovate and develop new products in an attempt to maintain economic profit.
- Advertising expenditures increase total cost, but they might lower average total cost if they increase the quantity sold by enough.
- Advertising expenditures might increase demand, but they might also decrease the demand for a firm's product by increasing competition.
- Whether monopolistic competition is inefficient depends on the value we place on product variety.

Oligopoly (pp. 291–292)

- Oligopoly is a market in which a small number of firms compete.
- If rivals match price cuts but do not match price hikes, they face a kinked demand curve and change prices only when large cost changes occur.
- If one firm dominates a market, it acts like a monopoly and the small firms take its price as given and act like perfectly competitive firms.

Oligopoly Games (pp. 293–300)

- Oligopoly is studied by using game theory, which is a method of analyzing strategic behaviour.

- In a prisoners' dilemma game, two prisoners acting in their own interest harm their joint interest.
- An oligopoly (duopoly) price-fixing game is a prisoners' dilemma.
- In Nash equilibrium, both firms cheat and output and price are the same as in perfect competition.
- Firms' decisions about advertising and R&D can be studied by using game theory.

Repeated Games and Sequential Games (pp. 301–303)

- In a repeated game, a punishment strategy can produce a cooperative equilibrium in which price and output are the same as in a monopoly.
- In a sequential contestable market game, a small number of firms can behave like firms in perfect competition.

KEY FIGURES AND TABLES

Figure 13.2   Output and Price in Monopolistic Competition, 286
Figure 13.3   Excess Capacity, 287
Figure 13.5   Selling Costs and Total Cost, 290
Figure 13.8   Costs and Demand, 295
Figure 13.9   Colluding to Make Monopoly Profits, 296
Figure 13.11   Both Firms Cheat, 298
Table 13.1   Prisoners' Dilemma Payoff Matrix, 294
Table 13.2   Duopoly Payoff Matrix, 299

KEY TERMS

Capacity output, 287
Cartel, 295
Collusive agreement, 295
Contestable market, 302
Cooperative equilibrium, 301
Duopoly, 295
Game theory, 293
Limit pricing, 303
Monopolistic competition, 284
Nash equilibrium, 294
Oligopoly, 291
Payoff matrix, 293
Product differentiation, 284
Strategies, 293

PROBLEMS

*1. The figure shows the situation facing Lite and Kool, Inc., a producer of running shoes.

a. What quantity does Lite and Kool produce?
b. What does it charge?
c. How much profit does Lite and Kool make?

2. The figure shows the situation facing The Stiff Shirt, Inc., a producer of shirts.

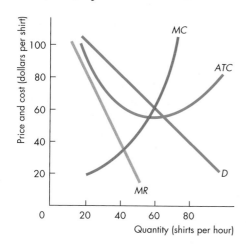

a. What quantity does The Stiff Shirt produce?
b. What does it charge?
c. How much profit does it make?

*3. A firm in monopolistic competition produces running shoes. If it spends nothing on advertising, it can sell no shoes at $100 a pair, and for each $10 cut in price, the quantity of shoes it can sell increases by 25 pairs a day, so at $20 a

pair, it can sell 200 pairs a day. The firm's total fixed cost is $4,000 a day. Its average variable cost and marginal cost is a constant $20 per pair. If the firm spends $3,000 a day on advertising, it can double the quantity of shoes sold at each price.

a. If the firm doesn't advertise, what is
   (i) The quantity of shoes produced?
   (ii) The price per pair?
   (iii) The firm's economic profit or loss?
b. If the firm does advertise, what is
   (i) The quantity of shoes produced?
   (ii) The price per pair?
   (iii) The firm's economic profit or loss?
c. Will the firm advertise or not? Why?

4. The firm in problem 3 has the same demand and costs as before if it does not advertise. The firm undertakes some quality improvements in its shoes that raise its marginal and average cost to $40 a pair. If the firm spends $3,000 a day on advertising with an agency, it can double the amount that consumers are willing to pay at each quantity demanded.

a. If the firm hires the agency, what quantity does it produce and what price does it charge?
b. What is the firm's economic profit or loss?
c. What is the firm's profit in the long run?

*5. A firm with a kinked demand curve experiences an increase in fixed costs. Explain how the firm's price, output, and profit change.

6. A firm with a kinked demand curve experiences an increase in variable cost. Explain how the firm's price, output, and profit change.

*7. An industry with one very large firm and 100 very small firms experiences an increase in the demand for its product. Use the dominant firm model to explain the effects on the price, output, and economic profit of
a. The large firm.
b. A typical small firm.

8. An industry with one very large firm and 100 very small firms experiences an increase in total variable cost. Use the dominant firm model to explain the effects on the price, output, and economic profit of
a. The large firm.
b. A typical small firm.

*9. Consider a game with two players in which each player is asked a question. The players can answer the question honestly or lie. If both answer honestly, each receives $100. If one answers honestly and the other lies, the liar receives $500 and the honest player gets nothing. If both lie, then each receives $50.
   a. Describe this game in terms of its players, strategies, and payoffs.
   b. Construct the payoff matrix.
   c. What is the equilibrium for this game?

10. Describe the game known as the prisoners' dilemma. In describing the game,
   a. Make up a story that motivates the game.
   b. Work out a payoff matrix.
   c. Describe how the equilibrium of the game is reached.

*11. Soapy and Suddies, Inc. are the only producers of soap powder. They collude and agree to share the market equally. If neither firm cheats, each makes $1 million profit. If either firm cheats, the cheat makes a profit of $1.5 million, while the complier incurs a loss of $0.5 million. Neither firm can police the other's actions.
   a. If the game is played once,
      (i)   What is the profit of each firm if both cheat?
      (ii) Describe the best strategy for each firm.
      (iii) Construct the payoff matrix.
      (iv) What is the equilibrium of the game?
   b. If this duopoly game can be played many times, describe some of the strategies that each firm might adopt.

12. Healthy and Energica are the only producers of a new energy drink. The firms collude and agree to share the market equally. If neither firm cheats, each firm makes $4 million profit. If either firm cheats, the cheat makes $6 million profit, while the complier incurs a loss of $1.5 million. Neither firm can police the other's actions.
   a. If the game is played once,
      (i)   What is the payoff matrix?
      (ii) Describe the best strategy for each firm.
      (iii) What is the equilibrium of the game?
   b. If this game can be played many times, what are two strategies that could be adopted?

1. Study *Reading Between the Lines* on pp. 304–305 and then answer the following questions.
   a. Why is the Canadian retail book market an example of oligopoly?
   b. How do you think the retail markup on books is determined?
   c. Why did Amazon enter the Canadian market in 2002?
   d. What strategic variables other than price do booksellers use?
   e. Why (aside from the fact that it is illegal) is it impossible for Amazon and Indigo to collude and earn a larger economic profit?

2. Suppose that Netscape and Microsoft develop their own versions of an amazing new Web browser that allows advertisers to target consumers with great precision. Also, the new browser is easier and more fun to use than existing browsers. Each firm is trying to decide whether to sell the browser or to give it away free. What are the likely benefits from each action and which is likely to occur?

3. Why do Coca-Cola Company and PepsiCo spend huge amounts on advertising? Do they benefit? Does the consumer benefit? Explain your answer.

WEB EXERCISES

1. Use the link on the Parkin–Bade Web site to obtain information about the market for vitamins.
   a. In what type of market are vitamins sold?
   b. What illegal act occurred in the vitamin market during the 1990s?
   c. Describe the actions of BASF and Roche as a game and set out a hypothetical payoff matrix for the game.
   d. Is the game played by BASF and Roche played once or is it a repeated game? How do you know which type of game it is?

2. Use the link on the Parkin–Bade Web site to obtain information about the market for art and antiques.
   a. What illegal act occurred in the art and antiques auction market during the 1990s?
   b. Describe the game played by Sotheby's and Christie's and set out a payoff matrix.

UNDERSTANDING FIRMS AND MARKETS

PART 4

Managing Change

Our economy is constantly changing. Every year, new goods appear and old ones disappear. New firms are born and old ones die. This process of change is initiated and managed by firms operating in markets. When a new product is invented, just one or two firms sell it initially. For example, when the personal computer first became available, there was an Apple or an IBM. The IBM-PC had just one operating system, DOS, made by Microsoft. One firm, Intel, made the chip that ran the IBM-PC. These are examples of industries in which the producer has market power to determine the price of the product and the quantity produced. The extreme case of a single producer that cannot be challenged by new competitors is *monopoly*, which Chapter 12 explained. ◆ But not all industries with just one producer are monopolies. In many cases, the firm that is first to produce a new good faces severe competition from new rivals. One firm facing potential competition is the case of a *contestable market*. If demand increases and makes space for more than one firm, an industry becomes increasingly competitive. Even with just two rivals, the industry changes its face in a dramatic way. *Duopoly*—the case of just two producers—illustrates this dramatic change. The two firms must play close attention to each other's production and prices and must predict the effects of their own actions on the actions of the other firm. We call this situation one of *strategic interdependence*. As the number of rivals grows, the industry becomes an *oligopoly*, in which a small number of firms devise strategies and pay close attention to the strategies of their competitors. ◆ With the continued arrival of new firms in an industry, the market eventually becomes competitive. Competition might be limited because each firm produces its own special version or brand of a good. This case is called *monopolistic competition* because it has elements of both monopoly and competition. Chapter 13 explored the behaviour of firms in all of these types of markets that lie between monopoly at the one extreme and perfect competition at the other. ◆ When competition is extreme—the case that we call *perfect competition*—the market changes again in a dramatic way. Now the firm is unable to influence price. Chapter 11 explained this case. ◆ Often, an industry that is competitive becomes less so as the bigger and more successful firms in the industry begin to swallow up the smaller firms, either by driving them out of business or by acquiring their assets. Through this process, an industry might return to oligopoly or even monopoly. You can see such a movement in the auto and banking industries today. ◆ By studying firms and markets, we gain a deeper understanding of the forces that allocate scarce resources and begin to see the anatomy of the invisible hand. ◆ Many economists have advanced our understanding of these forces and we'll now meet two of them. John von Neumann pioneered the idea of game theory. And Bengt Holmstrom is one of today's leading students of strategic behaviour.

309

PROBING THE IDEAS

Market Power

JOHN VON NEUMANN *was one of the great minds of the twentieth century. Born in Budapest, Hungary, in 1903, Johnny, as he was known, showed early mathematical brilliance. His first mathematical publication was an article that grew out of a lesson with his tutor, which he wrote at the age of 18! But it was at the age of 25, in 1928, that von Neumann published the article that began a flood of research on game theory—a flood that has still not subsided today. In that article, he proved that in a zero-sum game (like sharing a pie), there exists a best strategy for each player.*

Von Neumann invented the computer and built the first modern practical computer, and he worked on the "Manhattan Project," which developed the atomic bomb at Los Alamos, New Mexico, during World War II.

Von Neumann believed that the social sciences would progress only if they used mathematical tools. But he believed that they needed different tools from those developed from the physical sciences.

"Real life consists of bluffing, of little tactics of deception, of asking yourself what is the other man going to think I mean to do."

JOHN VON NEUMANN, **told to Jacob Bronowski (in a London taxi) and reported in The Ascent of Man**

THE ISSUES

It is not surprising that firms with market power will charge higher prices than those charged by competitive firms. But how much higher?

This question has puzzled generations of economists. Adam Smith said, "The price of a monopoly is upon every occasion the highest which can be got." But he was wrong. Antoine-Augustin Cournot (see p. 148) first worked out the price a monopoly will charge. It is not the "highest which can be got" but the price that maximizes profit. Cournot's work was not appreciated until almost a century later when Joan Robinson explained how a monopoly sets its price.

Questions about monopoly became urgent and practical during the 1870s, a time when rapid technological change and falling transportation costs enabled huge monopolies to emerge in the United States. Monopolies dominated oil, steel, railroads, tobacco, and even sugar. Industrial empires grew ever larger.

The success of the nineteenth century monopolies led to the creation of our anti-combine laws—laws that limit the use of monopoly power. Those laws have been used to prevent monopolies from being set up and to break up existing monopolies. They were used in the United States during the 1960s to end a conspiracy between General Electric, Westinghouse, and other firms when they colluded to fix their prices instead of competing with each other. The laws were used during the 1980s to bring greater competition to long-distance telecommunication. But in spite of anti-combine laws, near monopolies still exist. Among the most prominent today are those in computer chips and operating systems. Like their forerunners, today's near monopolies make huge profits.

But unlike the situation in the nineteenth century, the technological change taking place today is strengthening the forces of competition. Today's information technologies are creating substitutes for services that previously had none. Direct satellite TV is competing with cable, and new phone companies are competing with the traditional phone monopolies.

THEN

Ruthless greed, exploitation of both workers and customers—these are the traditional images of monopolies and the effects of their power. These images appeared to be an accurate description during the 1880s, when monopolies stood at their peak of power and influence. One monopolist, John D. Rockefeller, Sr., built his giant Standard Oil Company, which by 1879 was refining 90 percent of the nation's oil and controlling its entire pipeline capacity.

NOW

Despite anti-combine laws that regulate monopolies, they still exist. One is the monopoly in cable television. In many cities, one firm decides which channels viewers will receive and the price they will pay. During the 1980s, with the advent of satellite technology and specialist cable program producers such as CNN and HBO, the cable companies expanded their offerings. At the same time, they steadily increased prices and their businesses became very profitable. But the very technologies that made cable television profitable are now challenging its market power. Direct satellite TV services are eroding cable's monopoly and bringing greater competition to this market.

Today, many economists who work on microeconomics use the ideas that John von Neumann pioneered. Game theory is the tool of choice. One economist who has made good use of this tool (and many other tools) is Bengt Holmstrom of MIT, whom you can meet on the following pages.

TALKING WITH

BENGT HOLMSTROM *is Paul A. Samuelson Professor of Economics in the department of economics and the Sloan School of Management at the Massachusetts Institute of Technology. Born in 1949 in Helsinki, Finland, he studied mathematics and physics at the University of Helsinki as an undergraduate and then worked as an operations researcher before going to Stanford University as an economics graduate student. Professor Holmstrom's research on the way firms use contracts and incentives is recognized as providing a major advance in our understanding of the mechanisms that operate inside firms. Beyond his academic research, Professor Holmstrom has provided services to a number of major corporations, including Nokia, of which he is currently a director.*

Bengt Holmstrom

Michael Parkin and Robin Bade talked with Bengt Holmstrom about his work and the progress that economists have made in understanding firms and the markets in which they operate since the pioneering ideas about the nature of the firm by Ronald Coase.

Professor Holmstrom, did you study economics as an undergraduate? What drew you to this subject?

No. I was a math and physics major as an undergraduate in Helsinki. I got into economics the way many people do through a side door from mathematics and operations

research at Stanford Graduate School of Business.

How did you get interested in the economics of the firm?

I went from my undergraduate degree to work as an operations research analyst at a large conglomerate in Finland. I was hired to implement a company-wide corporate planning model. This was the early 70s, when large optimization models were expected to help firms make better long-term plans and run operations more centrally.

It didn't take me very long to realize that this was a misguided belief. The problem was that the data came from people lower down that had an apparent incentive to misrepresent the numbers. Their minds were focused on outwitting the model. My interest in incentives was entirely driven by this experience.

One of your most profound insights was to view the entire firm as an incentive system. What do you mean when you describe a firm as an incentive system? What implications follow from this view of the firm?

When people talk about incentives, they tend to think about some explicit reward system like a salesperson's commission or a stock option for an executive or something like that.

The key insight has been to understand that incentives are influenced in an enormous number of ways, indirectly and implicitly. For instance, constraints and bureaucratic rules are very important pieces of the overall incentive system. There are many different ways of getting people to do what you think they should be doing.

Sometimes the best incentive is to pay no incentive! Incentives can be terribly damaging if they are poorly designed.

The firm as an incentive system is an expression of the fact that you need to think

312

about *all* the possible ways in which you can influence people's actions and then how you orchestrate the instruments that are available. These instruments include promotion incentives, rewards, or even just praise. The narrow view that it's just a matter of paying a bonus of some sort is very misguided.

> *Sometimes the best incentive is to pay no incentive! Incentives can be terribly damaging if they are poorly designed.*

Can you talk about the role of the economist as economic adviser to a firm? One view is that firms are efficient and the task of the economist is to understand why. Another view is that the economist can help firms to become efficient— for example, by devising better incentive mechanisms. Can the economist help firms to become efficient? And are there other roles for the economist as adviser to a firm?

There's a well-known paradox—and tension—in economics. Positive economics deals with figuring out what is optimal—what is the best that can be done— and then using the description of optimal behaviour as a predictive tool—as a way of explaining why things are the way they are in the world.

And yet at the same time, nothing is presumably perfect so there is room for innovation—organizational innovation and economic innovation—which leads to the economic advice you're asking about.

There are many roles an economist can play as adviser to a firm. If we really understand things better, maybe we can actually make improvements in them. If nothing else, we can understand that if the constraints change, then a system that's designed in a particular way would need to adapt itself to the new circumstances. For example, a firm might have a centralized organization that's good in one set of circumstances and then suddenly the circumstances change and innovation becomes very important, as we seem to think it is right now. Then that situation calls for changes towards organizational structures that are more suited for innovation.

So you can explain the tradeoff between central control and more flexible, innovative structures so that a firm's managers understand these forces. They then might decide to move in the direction that better achieves their objectives. Or they might realize that the reason why other firms change organizational structures may not be relevant in their case.

The economist can help people understand the variety of organizations so that they can pick the right one for the right set of circumstances. There isn't one organization that's good for everything— quite the contrary. Some activities require one kind of organization; some activities require another kind of organization. Charities, for instance, would not be well run by for-profit firms because they would run away with the money. That's an extreme example. So, non-profit organizations play a very important role in running charities.

Joint stock companies have proven to be an extremely flexible and robust form of organization both for small- and large-scale activities. Their scalability is one reason for their enormous success.

Are there any examples of serious progress that we've made in understanding which types of organizations work best in which circumstances?

I think there are lots. There's a big debate right now about airport security that's a wonderful illustration of the insight that the firm is an incentive system and an example of the possibility of having incentives that are too strong in the wrong place. One view is that profit-making companies that run the airport security checking are too oriented towards profit and too little oriented towards quality, because the quality checks come so infrequently. The standard argument is that if they make a mistake they must pay for it, so they have a strong incentive to deliver high-quality work. But if accidents happen infrequently, that sort of feedback mechanism is just too weak. This is a logical reason for moving in the direction of taking away profit-making incentives from airport security checking.

The very existence of the firm comes from the fact that it is there to remove and restructure incorrect incentives—excessively high-powered incentives that come from the market—and to get people to cooperate. In the market, it can be harder to cooper-

313

ate because everyone is working for his or her own benefit. This works very well if there are a lot of alternatives to choose—if there's competition. But when there is a small number of traders, or where quality is hard to assess, bringing the activity inside the firm is quite natural.

One firm, Enron, was big news during 2002. What do models of incentive systems tell us about what went wrong with Enron?

I think Enron, like most of these disaster cases, teaches that misplaced incentives lead to potentially big mistakes. It's almost tautological to say that if wrongdoing was done, it was done because the incentives weren't aligned correctly. Now, how much of it was a design flaw within Enron and how much was a flaw of the overall system, is harder to judge. There were certainly regulatory problems—energy production regulations had changed; the energy market had been opened up and arbitrage opportunities created. Some of the activities of Enron that sought to profit from this new regulatory environment were entirely legal.

Then there was financial innovation. It's an old, old idea that it would be nice to remove debts from the balance sheet of a firm to make it look better to investors. And apparently new financial instruments had been created to make off-balance sheet operations possible. Some of them were clearly questionable and perhaps some of them illegal.

But the other problem—and this is a system problem, not just an Enron problem—is that when things are going well and everybody believes that the world is moving forward, it's very hard to question something. You go further and further out on a limb, and then the limb breaks and you learn that that was too much.

> *I don't think that a system that rules out everything that can go wrong is the right system.*

I don't see Enron as catastrophically as most people seem to. I think that we would pay a big price if we never let anybody like Enron try. If you regulate things so that nothing like it ever could have happened, it probably would have also thrown out a lot of good innovations with it. It's part of the system to learn by having certain things like this happen.

314

I'm not defending Enron's actions. But I'm trying to give a different angle to the possible response. System design is different from trying to correct individual cases. I don't think that a system that rules out everything that can go wrong is the right system.

Is it important for an academic economist to have professional interests in the "real world"?

I think everybody's different. For me it has been important because I got interested in incentives through non-academic work. That's where I started, and I was just lucky that incentives happened to be a topical issue when I entered the field.

I don't think one could, in any sense, say that everybody must have real-world experience. You have to find your own sources of stimulation and discover what makes you curious and what makes you interested. For some people, that's just being exceedingly theoretical and not thinking about much else. Some are very talented that way: other people desperately need some connection with the real world. For me, that has been very valuable.

Needless to say, the fact that we are all different is extremely important for overall progress.

What advice do you have for a student who is just starting to study economics? Do you think that economics is a good subject in which to major? What other subjects would you urge students to study alongside economics?

I'm a big believer that people do their best work and have their happiest life when they do the things that they are really interested in. With the wonderful undergraduate system that North America has, I would advise students to sample broadly and go in the direction they get most excited about. But I think there are many reasons to like economics. It spans a fascinating range of questions. At its heart, economics is about understanding social systems, current and past, and how these systems could be improved for the welfare of the human race. I'm confident that economics has contributed a great deal to the current levels of welfare in the West. And I'm optimistic that the developing world will also benefit from our intellectual progress. As an economist, you can have a really big impact, even if the results are less visible than in the natural sciences like physics. For me, it has been incredibly inspiring.

DEMAND AND SUPPLY IN FACTOR MARKETS

CHAPTER 14

Many Happy Returns

It may not be your birthday, and even if it is, chances are you are spending most of it working. But at the end of the week or month (or, if you're devoting all your time to university, when you graduate), you will receive the *returns* from your labour. Those returns vary a lot. Ed Jones, who spends his days in a small container suspended from the top of Toronto's high-rise buildings cleaning windows, makes a happy return of $12 an hour. Antonio Davis, who plays no more than 82 basketball games a year, makes a very happy return of $11 million a year. Some differences in earnings might seem surprising. For example, your university football coach might earn much more than your economics professor. Why aren't *all* jobs well paid? ◆ Most of us have little trouble spending our pay. But most of us do manage to save some of what we earn. What determines the amount of saving that people do and the returns they make on that saving? ◆ Some people earn their income by supplying natural resources such as oil. What determines the price of a natural resource?

◆ In this chapter, we study the markets for factors of production—labour, capital, natural resources—and learn how their prices and people's incomes are determined. And we'll see in *Reading Between the Lines* at the end of the chapter why top-performing hockey players earn such large salaries.

After studying this chapter, you will be able to

- Explain how firms choose the quantities of labour, capital, and natural resources to employ
- Explain how people choose the quantities of labour, capital, and natural resources to supply
- Explain how wages, interest, and natural resource prices are determined in competitive factor markets
- Explain the concept of economic rent and distinguish between economic rent and opportunity cost

Prices and Incomes in Competitive Factor Markets

GOODS AND SERVICES ARE PRODUCED BY USING the four resources or *factors of production—labour, capital, land,* and *entrepreneurship* (we defined these factors of production in Chapter 1, p. 4). Incomes are determined by *factor prices*—the *wage* rate for labour, the *interest* rate for capital, the *rental* rate for land, and the rate of *normal profit* for entrepreneurship—and the quantities of the factors used. In addition to the four factor incomes, a residual income, *economic profit* (or *economic loss*), is paid to (or borne by) firms' owners—sometimes the owner is the entrepreneur and sometimes the owners are the stockholders who provide financial capital.

Factors of production, like goods and services, are traded in markets. Some factor markets are competitive and behave like other perfectly competitive markets. Other factors are traded in markets in which there is market power. We focus in this chapter on competitive factor markets to learn how they determine the prices, quantities used, and incomes of factors of production. In an appendix (pp. 341–346), we examine labour markets in which there is market power.

The main tool that we use in this chapter is the demand and supply model. The quantity demanded of a factor of production depends on its price, and the law of demand applies to factors of production just as it does to goods and services. The lower the price of a factor, other things remaining the same, the greater is the quantity demanded. Figure 14.1 shows the demand curve for a factor as the curve labelled *D*.

The quantity supplied of a factor also depends on its price. With a possible exception that we'll identify later in this chapter, the law of supply applies to factors of production. The higher the price of a factor, other things remaining the same, the greater is the quantity supplied of the factor. Figure 14.1 shows the supply curve of a factor as the curve labelled *S*.

The equilibrium factor price is determined at the point of intersection of the demand and supply curves. In Fig. 14.1, the price is *PF* and the quantity used is *QF*.

The income earned by the factor is its price multiplied by the quantity used. In Fig. 14.1, the factor income equals the area of the blue rectangle. This income is the total income received by the factor. Each person who supplies the factor receives the fac-

tor price multiplied by the quantity supplied by that person. Changes in demand and supply change the equilibrium price and quantity and change income.

An increase in demand shifts the demand curve rightward and increases price, quantity, and income. An increase in supply shifts the supply curve rightward and decreases price. The quantity used increases, but income might increase, decrease, or remain constant. The change in income that results from a change in supply depends on the elasticity of demand for the factor. If demand is elastic, income rises; if demand is inelastic, income falls; and if demand is unit elastic, income remains constant (see Chapter 4, p. 88).

The rest of this chapter explores the influences on the demand for and supply of factors of production. It also explains the influences on the elasticities of supply and demand for factors of production. These elasticities have major effects on factor prices, quantities used, and incomes.

We begin with the market for labour. But most of what we will learn about the labour market also applies to the other factor markets that we study later in the chapter.

FIGURE 14.1 Demand and Supply in a Factor Market

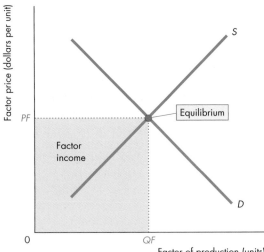

The demand curve for a factor of production (D) slopes downward, and the supply curve (S) slopes upward. Where the demand and supply curves intersect, the factor price (PF) and the quantity of the factor used (QF) are determined. The factor income is the factor price multiplied by the quantity of the factor, as represented by the blue rectangle.

Labour Markets

FOR MOST OF US, THE LABOUR MARKET IS OUR only source of income. And in recent years, many people have had a tough time. But over the years, both wages and the quantity of labour have moved steadily upward. Figure 14.2(a) shows the record since 1961. Using 1997 dollars to remove the effects of inflation, total compensation per hour of work increased by about 100 percent, from $9.58 in 1961 to $19.93 in 2001. Over the same period, the quantity of labour employed increased by more than 100 percent, from 12.7 billion hours in 1961 to 27 billion hours in 2001.

Figure 14.2(b) shows why these trends occurred. The demand for labour increased from LD_{61} to LD_{01}, and this increase was much larger than the increase in the supply of labour from LS_{61} to LS_{01}.

A lot of diversity lies behind the average wage rate and the aggregate quantity of labour. During the 1980s and 1990s, some wage rates grew much more rapidly than the average and others fell. To understand the trends in the labour market, we must probe the forces that influence the demand for labour and the supply of labour. This chapter studies these forces. We begin on the demand side of the labour market.

The Demand for Labour

The demand for labour is a derived demand. A **derived demand** is a demand for a factor of production that is *derived* from the demand for the goods and services produced by that factor of production. The derived demand for labour (and for the other factors demanded by firms) is driven by the firm's objective, which is to maximize profit.

You learned in Chapters 11, 12, and 13 that a profit-maximizing firm produces the output at which marginal cost equals marginal revenue. This principle holds true for all firms regardless of whether they operate in perfect competition, monopolistic competition, oligopoly, or monopoly.

A firm that maximizes profit hires the quantity of labour that can produce the profit-maximizing output. What is that quantity of labour? And how does the quantity of labour used change as the wage rate changes? We can answer these questions by comparing the *marginal* revenue earned by hiring one more worker with the *marginal* cost of that worker. Let's look first at the marginal revenue side of this comparison.

FIGURE 14.2   Labour Market Trends in Canada

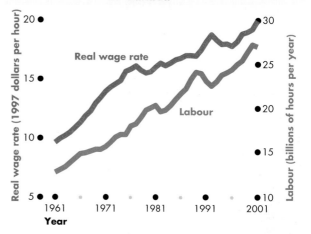

(a) Labour and wage rate

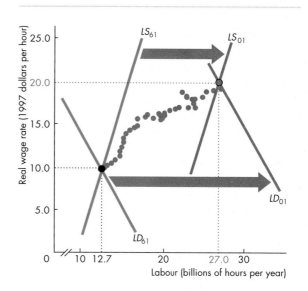

(b) Changes in demand and supply in the labour market

Between 1961 and 2001, the real wage rate doubled and the quantity of labour employed more than doubled. Part (a) shows these increases. Each dot in part (b) shows the real wage rate and the quantity of labour in each year from 1961 to 2001. Part (b) also shows the changes in demand and supply that generated these trends. The demand for labour increased from LD_{61} to LD_{01}, and the supply of labour increased from LS_{61} to LS_{01}. Demand increased by more than supply increased, so both the wage rate and the quantity of labour employed increased.

Source: Statistics Canada, CANSIM tables 282–0002, 282–0022, and 380–0001.

Marginal Revenue Product

The change in total revenue that results from employing one more unit of labour is called the **marginal revenue product** of labour. Table 14.1 shows you how to calculate marginal revenue product for a firm in perfect competition.

The first two columns show the total product schedule for Max's Wash 'n' Wax car wash service. The numbers tell us how the number of car washes per hour varies as the quantity of labour varies. The third column shows the *marginal product of labour*—the change in total product that results from a one-unit increase in the quantity of labour employed. (Look back at p. 219 for a quick refresher on this concept.)

The car wash market in which Max operates is perfectly competitive, and he can sell as many washes as he chooses at $4 a wash, the (assumed) market price. So Max's *marginal revenue* is $4 a wash.

Given this information, we can now calculate *marginal revenue product* (the fourth column). It equals marginal product multiplied by marginal revenue. For example, the marginal product of hiring a second worker is 4 car washes an hour, and because marginal revenue is $4 a wash, the marginal revenue product of the second worker is $16 (4 washes at $4 each).

The last two columns of Table 14.1 show an alternative way to calculate the marginal revenue product of labour. Total revenue is equal to total product multiplied by price. For example, two workers produce 9 washes per hour and generate a total revenue of $36 (9 washes at $4 each). One worker produces 5 washes per hour and generates a total revenue of $20 (5 washes at $4 each). Marginal revenue product, in the sixth column, is the change in total revenue from hiring one more worker. When the second worker is hired, total revenue increases from $20 to $36, an increase of $16. So the marginal revenue product of the second worker is $16, which agrees with our previous calculation.

Diminishing Marginal Revenue Product As the quantity of labour increases, marginal revenue product diminishes. For a firm in perfect competition, marginal revenue product diminishes because marginal product diminishes. In monopoly (or monopolistic competition or oligopoly), marginal revenue product diminishes for a second reason. When more labour is hired and total product increases, the firm must cut its price to sell the extra product. So marginal product and marginal revenue decrease, both of which decrease marginal revenue product.

TABLE 14.1   Marginal Revenue Product at Max's Wash 'n' Wax

	Quantity of labour (L) (workers)	Total product (TP) (car washes per hour)	Marginal product (MP = ΔTP/ΔL) (washes per worker)	Marginal revenue product (MRP = MR × MP) (dollars per worker)	Total revenue (TR = P × TP) (dollars)	Marginal revenue product (MRP = ΔTR/ΔL) (dollars per worker)
A	0	0		20	0	
			5			20
B	1	5		16	20	
			4			16
C	2	9		12	36	
			3			12
D	3	12		8	48	
			2			8
E	4	14		4	56	
			1			4
F	5	15			60	

The car wash market is perfectly competitive, and the price is $4 a wash. Marginal revenue is also $4 a wash. Marginal revenue product equals marginal product (column 3) multiplied by marginal revenue. For example, the marginal product of the second worker is 4 washes and marginal revenue is $4 a wash, so the marginal revenue product of the second worker (in column 4) is $16. Alternatively, if Max hires 1 worker (row B), total product is 5 washes an hour and total revenue is $20 (column 5). If he hires 2 workers (row C), total product is 9 washes an hour and total revenue is $36. By hiring the second worker, total revenue rises by $16—the marginal revenue product of labour is $16.

The Labour Demand Curve

Figure 14.3 shows how the labour demand curve is derived from the marginal revenue product curve. The *marginal revenue product curve* graphs the marginal revenue product of a factor at each quantity of the factor hired. Figure 14.3(a) illustrates the marginal revenue product curve for workers employed by Max. The horizontal axis measures the number of workers that Max hires, and the vertical axis measures the marginal revenue product of labour. The blue bars show the marginal revenue product of labour as Max employs more workers. These bars correspond to the numbers in Table 14.1. The curve labelled *MRP* is Max's marginal revenue product curve.

A firm's marginal revenue product curve is also its demand for labour curve. Figure 14.3(b) shows Max's demand for labour curve (*D*). The horizontal axis measures the number of workers hired—the same as in part (a). The vertical axis measures the wage rate in dollars per hour. In Fig. 14.3(a), when Max increases the quantity of labour employed from 2 workers an hour to 3 workers an hour, his marginal revenue product is $12 an hour. In Fig. 14.3(b), at a wage rate of $12 an hour, Max employs 3 workers an hour.

The marginal revenue product curve is also the demand for labour curve because the firm hires the profit-maximizing quantity of labour. If the wage rate is *less* than marginal revenue product, the firm can increase its profit by employing one more worker. Conversely, if the wage rate is *greater* than marginal revenue product, the firm can increase its profit by employing one fewer worker. But if the wage rate *equals* marginal revenue product, then the firm cannot increase its profit by changing the number of workers it employs. The firm is making the maximum possible profit. Thus the quantity of labour demanded by the firm is such that the wage rate equals the marginal revenue product of labour.

Because the marginal revenue product curve is also the demand curve, and because marginal revenue product diminishes as the quantity of labour employed increases, the demand for labour curve slopes downward. The lower the wage rate, other things remaining the same, the more workers a firm hires.

When we studied firms' output decisions, we discovered that a condition for maximum profit is that marginal revenue equals marginal cost. We've now discovered another condition for maximum profit: Marginal revenue product of a factor equals the factor's price. Let's study the connection between these two conditions.

FIGURE 14.3   The Demand for Labour at Max's Wash 'n' Wax

(a) Marginal revenue product

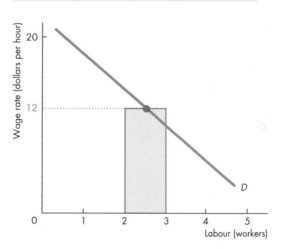

(b) Demand for labour

Max's Wash 'n' Wax operates in a perfectly competitive car wash market and can sell any quantity of washes at $4 a wash. The blue bars in part (a) represent the firm's marginal revenue product of labour. They are based on the numbers in Table 14.1. The orange line is the firm's marginal revenue product of labour curve. Part (b) shows Max's demand for labour curve. This curve is identical to Max's marginal revenue product curve. Max demands the quantity of labour that makes the wage rate equal to the marginal revenue product of labour. The demand for labour curve slopes downward because marginal revenue product diminishes as the quantity of labour employed increases.

Equivalence of Two Conditions for Profit Maximization

Profit is maximized when, at the quantity of labour hired, *marginal revenue product* equals the wage rate and when, at the quantity produced, *marginal revenue* equals *marginal cost*.

These two conditions for maximum profit are equivalent. The quantity of labour that maximizes profit produces the output that maximizes profit.

To see the equivalence of the two conditions for maximum profit, first recall that

Marginal revenue product = Marginal revenue × Marginal product.

If we call marginal revenue product *MRP*, marginal revenue *MR*, and marginal product *MP*, we have

$$MRP = MR \times MP.$$

If we call the wage rate *W*, the first condition for profit to be maximized is

$$MRP = W.$$

But $MRP = MR \times MP$, so

$$MR \times MP = W.$$

This equation tells us that when profit is maximized, marginal revenue multiplied by marginal product equals the wage rate.

Divide the last equation by marginal product, *MP*, to obtain

$$MR = W \div MP.$$

This equation states that when profit is maximized, marginal revenue equals the wage rate divided by the marginal product of labour.

The wage rate divided by the marginal product of labour equals marginal cost. It costs the firm *W* to hire one more hour of labour. But the labour produces *MP* units of output. So the cost of producing one of those units of output, which is marginal cost, is *W* divided by *MP*.

If we call marginal cost *MC*, then

$$MR = MC,$$

which is the second condition for maximum profit.

Because the first condition for maximum profit implies the second condition, these two conditions are equivalent. Table 14.2 summarizes the calculations you've just done and shows the equivalence of the two conditions for maximum profit.

TABLE 14.2   Two Conditions for Maximum Profit

Symbols

Marginal product	**MP**
Marginal revenue	**MR**
Marginal cost	**MC**
Marginal revenue product	**MRP**
Factor price	**PF**

Two Conditions for Maximum Profit

1.   **MR = MC**   2.   **MRP = PF**

Equivalence of Conditions

1. $MRP/MP = MR$ = $MC = PF/MP$

Multiply by MP to give

$MRP = MR \times MP$

Flipping the equation over

Multiply by MP to give

$MC \times MP = PF$

Flipping the equation over

2. $MR \times MP = MRP$ = $PF = MC \times MP$

The two conditions for maximum profit are that marginal revenue (*MR*) equals marginal cost (*MC*) and that marginal revenue product (*MRP*) equals the wage rate (*W*). These two conditions are equivalent because marginal revenue product (*MRP*) equals marginal revenue (*MR*) multiplied by marginal product (*MP*) and the wage rate (*W*) equals marginal cost (*MC*) multiplied by marginal product (*MP*).

Max's Numbers Check the numbers for Max's Wash 'n' Wax and confirm that the conditions you've just examined work. Max's profit-maximizing labour decision is to hire 3 workers if the wage rate is $12 an hour. When Max hires 3 hours of labour, marginal product is 3 washes per hour. Max sells the 3 washes an hour for a marginal revenue of $4 a wash. So marginal revenue product is 3 washes multiplied by $4 a wash, which equals $12 per hour. At a wage rate of $12 an hour, Max is maximizing profit.

Equivalently, Max's marginal cost is $12 an hour divided by 3 washes per hour, which equals $4 per wash. At a marginal revenue of $4 a wash, Max is maximizing profit.

You've discovered that the law of demand applies for labour just as it does for goods and services. Other things remaining the same, the lower the wage rate (the price of labour), the greater is the quantity of labour demanded.

Let's now study the influences that change the demand for labour and shift the demand for labour curve.

Changes in the Demand for Labour

The demand for labour depends on three factors:

1. The price of the firm's output
2. The prices of other factors of production
3. Technology

The higher the price of a firm's output, the greater is its demand for labour. The price of output affects the demand for labour through its influence on marginal revenue product. A higher price for the firm's output increases marginal revenue, which, in turn, increases the marginal revenue product of labour. A change in the price of a firm's output leads to a shift in the firm's demand for labour curve. If the price of the firm's output increases, the demand for labour increases and the demand for labour curve shifts rightward.

The other two influences affect the *long-run demand for labour*, which is the relationship between the wage rate and the quantity of labour demanded when all factors of production can be varied. In contrast, the *short-run demand for labour* is the relationship between the wage rate and the quantity of labour demanded when the quantities of the other factors are fixed and labour is the only variable factor. In the long run, a change in the relative price of factors of production—such as the relative price of labour and capital—leads to a substitution away from the factor whose relative price has increased and towards the factor whose relative price has decreased. So if the price of capital decreases relative to that of using labour, the firm substitutes capital for labour and increases the quantity of capital demanded.

But the demand for labour might increase or decrease. If the lower price of capital increases the scale of production by enough, the demand for labour increases. Otherwise, the demand for labour decreases.

Finally, a new technology that changes the marginal product of labour changes the demand for labour. For example, the electronic telephone exchange has decreased the demand for telephone operators. This same new technology has increased the demand for telephone engineers. Again, these effects are felt in the long run when the firm adjusts all its resources and incorporates new technologies into its production process. Table 14.3 summarizes the influences on a firm's demand for labour.

We saw in Fig. 14.2 that the demand for labour has increased over time and the demand curve has shifted rightward. We can now give some of the reasons for this increase in demand. Advances in technology and investment in new capital increase the marginal product of labour and increase the demand for labour.

TABLE 14.3 A Firm's Demand for Labour

The Law of Demand
(Movements along the demand curve for labour)

The quantity of labour demanded by a firm

Decreases if:	Increases if:
■ The wage rate increases	■ The wage rate decreases

Changes in Demand
(Shifts in the demand curve for labour)

A firm's demand for labour

Decreases if:	Increases if:
■ The firm's output price decreases	■ The firm's output price increases
■ A new technology decreases the marginal product of labour	■ A new technology increases the marginal product of labour

(Changes in the prices of other factors of production have an ambiguous effect on the demand for labour.)

Market Demand

So far, we've studied the demand for labour by an individual firm. The market demand for labour is the total demand by all firms. The market demand for labour curve is derived (similarly to the market demand curve for any good or service) by adding together the quantities demanded by all firms at each wage rate. Because a firm's demand for labour curve slopes downward, so does the market demand curve.

Elasticity of Demand for Labour

The elasticity of demand for labour measures the responsiveness of the quantity of labour demanded to the wage rate. This elasticity is important because it tells us how labour income changes when the supply of labour changes. An increase in supply (other things remaining the same) brings a lower wage rate. If demand is inelastic, it also brings lower labour income. But if demand is elastic, an increase in supply brings a lower wage rate and an increase in labour income. And if the demand for labour is unit elastic, a change in supply leaves labour income unchanged.

The demand for labour is less elastic in the short run, when only the quantity of labour can be varied, than in the long run, when the quantities of labour and other factors of production can be varied. The elasticity of demand for labour depends on the

- Labour intensity of the production process
- Elasticity of demand for the product
- Substitutability of capital for labour

Labour Intensity of the Production Process A labour-intensive production process is one that uses a lot of labour and little capital. Home building is an example. The greater the degree of labour intensity, the more elastic is the demand for labour. To see why, first suppose that wages are 90 percent of total cost. A 10 percent increase in the wage rate increases total cost by 9 percent. Firms will be sensitive to such a large change in total cost, so if wages increase, firms will decrease the quantity of labour demanded by a relatively large amount. But if wages are 10 percent of total cost, a 10 percent increase in the wage rate increases total cost by only 1 percent. Firms will be less sensitive to this increase in cost, so if wages increase in this case, firms will decrease the quantity of labour demanded by a relatively small amount.

Elasticity of Demand for the Product The greater the elasticity of demand for the good, the larger is the elasticity of demand for the labour used to produce it. An increase in the wage rate increases marginal cost and decreases the supply of the good. The decrease in the supply of the good increases the price of the good and decreases the quantity demanded of the good and the quantities of the factors of production used to produce it. The greater the elasticity of demand for the good, the larger is the decrease in the quantity demanded of the good and so the larger is the decrease in the quantities of the factors of production used to produce it.

Substitutability of Capital for Labour The more easily capital can be used instead of labour in production, the more elastic is the long-run demand for labour. For example, it is easy to use robots rather than assembly-line workers in car factories and grape-picking machines for labour in vineyards. So the demand for these types of labour is elastic. At the other extreme, it is difficult (though possible) to substitute computers for newspaper reporters, bank loan officers, and teachers. So the demand for these types of labour is inelastic.

Let's now turn from the demand side of the labour market to the supply side and examine the decisions that people make about how to allocate their time between working and other activities.

The Supply of Labour

People can allocate their time to two broad activities: labour supply and leisure. (Leisure is a catch-all term. It includes all activities other than supplying labour.) For most people, leisure is more enjoyable than supplying labour. We'll look at the labour supply decision of Jill, who is like most people. She enjoys her leisure time, and she would be pleased if she didn't have to spend her weekends working a supermarket checkout line.

But Jill has chosen to work weekends. The reason is that she is offered a wage rate that exceeds her *reservation wage.* Jill's reservation wage is the lowest wage at which she is willing to supply labour. If the wage rate exceeds her reservation wage, she supplies some labour. But how much labour does she supply? The quantity of labour that Jill supplies depends on the wage rate.

Substitution Effect Other things remaining the same, the higher the wage rate Jill is offered, at least over a range, the greater is the quantity of labour that she supplies. The reason is that Jill's wage rate is her *opportunity cost of leisure*. If she quits work an hour early to catch a movie, the cost of that extra hour of leisure is the wage rate that Jill forgoes. The higher the wage rate, the less willing is Jill to forgo the income and take the extra leisure time. This tendency for a higher wage rate to induce Jill to work longer hours is a *substitution effect*.

But there is also an *income effect* that works in the opposite direction to the substitution effect.

Income Effect The higher Jill's wage rate, the higher is her income. A higher income, other things remaining the same, induces Jill to increase her demand for most goods. Leisure is one of those goods. Because an increase in income creates an increase in the demand for leisure, it also creates a decrease in the quantity of labour supplied.

Backward-Bending Supply of Labour Curve As the wage rate rises, the substitution effect brings an increase in the quantity of labour supplied while the income effect brings a decrease in the quantity of labour supplied. At low wage rates, the substitution

effect is larger than the income effect, so as the wage rate rises, people supply more labour. But as the wage rate continues to rise, the income effect eventually becomes larger than the substitution effect and the quantity of labour supplied decreases. The labour supply curve is *backward bending*.

Figure 14.4(a) shows the labour supply curves for Jill, Jack, and Kelly. Each labour supply curve is backward bending, but the three people have different reservation wage rates.

Market Supply The market supply of labour curve is the sum of the individual supply curves. Figure 14.4(b) shows the market supply curve (S_M) derived from the supply curves of Jill, Jack, and Kelly (S_A, S_B, and S_C, respectively) in Fig. 14.4(a). At wage rates of less than $1 an hour, no one supplies any labour. At wage rates greater than $1 an hour, Jill works but Jack and Kelly don't. As the wage rate increases and reaches $7 an hour, all three of them are working. The market supply curve S_M eventually bends backward, but it has a long upward-sloping section.

Changes in the Supply of Labour The supply of labour changes when influences other than the wage rate change. The key factors that change the supply of labour and that over the years have increased it are

---

FIGURE 14.4   The Supply of Labour

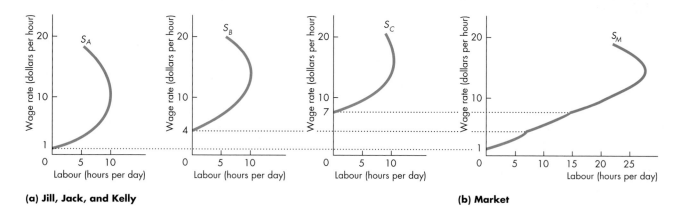

(a) Jill, Jack, and Kelly

(b) Market

Part (a) shows the labour supply curves of Jill (S_A), Jack (S_B), and Kelly (S_C). Each person has a reservation wage below which she or he will supply no labour. As the wage rises, the quantity of labour supplied increases to a maximum. If the wage continues to rise, the quantity of labour supplied begins to decrease.

Each person's supply curve eventually bends backward.

Part (b) shows how, by adding the quantities of labour supplied by each person at each wage rate, we derive the market supply curve (S_M). The market supply curve has a long upward-sloping region before it bends backward.

1. Adult population
2. Technological change and capital accumulation

An increase in the adult population increases the supply of labour. So does a technological change or increase in capital in home production (of meals, laundry services, and cleaning services). These factors that increase the supply of labour shift the labour supply curve rightward.

Let's now build on what we've learned about the demand for labour and the supply of labour and study labour market equilibrium and the trends in wage rates and employment.

Labour Market Equilibrium

Wages and employment are determined by equilibrium in the labour market. You saw, in Fig. 14.2, that the wage rate and employment have both increased over the years. You can now explain why.

Trends in the Demand for Labour The demand for labour has *increased* because of technological change and capital accumulation, and the demand for labour curve has shifted steadily rightward.

Many people are surprised that technological change and capital accumulation *increase* the demand for labour. They see new technologies *destroying jobs*, not creating them. Downsizing has become a catchword as the computer and information age has eliminated millions of "good" jobs, even those of managers. So how can it be that technological change *creates* jobs and increases the demand for labour?

Technological change destroys some jobs and creates others. But it creates more jobs than it destroys, and *on the average*, the new jobs pay more than the old ones did. But to benefit from the advances in technology, people must acquire new skills and change their jobs. For example, during the past 20 years, the demand for typists has fallen almost to zero. But the demand for people who can type (on a computer rather than a typewriter) and do other things as well has increased. And the output of these people is worth more than that of a typist. So the demand for people with typing (and other) skills has increased.

Trends in the Supply of Labour The supply of labour has increased because of population growth and technological change and capital accumulation in the home. The mechanization of home production of fast-food preparation services (the freezer and the microwave oven) and laundry services (the automatic washer and dryer and wrinkle-free fabrics) has decreased the time spent on activities that once were full-time jobs and has led to a large increase in the supply of labour. As a result, the labour supply curve has shifted steadily rightward, but more slowly than the labour demand curve has shifted.

Trends in Equilibrium Because technological advances and capital accumulation have increased demand by more than population growth and technological change in home production have increased supply, both wages and employment have increased. But not everyone has shared in the increased prosperity that comes from higher wage rates. Some groups have been left behind, and some have even seen their wage rates fall. Why?

Two key reasons can be identified. First, technological change affects the marginal productivity of different groups in different ways. High-skilled computer-literate workers have benefited from the information revolution while low-skilled workers have suffered. The demand for the services of the first group has increased, and the demand for the services of the second group has decreased. (Draw a supply and demand figure, and you will see that these changes widen the wage difference between the two groups.) Second, international competition has lowered the marginal revenue product of low-skilled workers and so has decreased the demand for their labour. We look further at skill differences and at trends in the distribution of income in Chapter 15.

REVIEW QUIZ

1 Why do we call the demand for labour a *derived demand*? From what is it derived?

2 What is the distinction between marginal revenue product and marginal revenue? Provide an example that illustrates the distinction.

3 When a firm's marginal revenue product equals the wage rate, marginal revenue also equals marginal cost. Why? Provide a numerical example different from that in the text.

4 What determines the amount of labour that households plan to supply?

5 Describe and explain the trends in wage rates and employment.

Capital Markets

CAPITAL MARKETS ARE THE CHANNELS THROUGH which firms obtain *financial* resources to buy *physical* capital resources. These financial resources come from saving. The "price of capital," which adjusts to make the quantity of capital supplied equal to the quantity demanded, is the interest rate.

For most of us, capital markets are where we make our biggest-ticket transactions. We borrow in a capital market to buy a home. And we lend in capital markets to build up a fund on which to live when we retire. Do the rates of return in capital markets increase as wage rates do?

Figure 14.5(a) answers this question by showing the record since 1965. Measuring interest rates as *real* interest rates, which means that we subtract the loss in the value of money from inflation, returns have fluctuated. They ranged 2 to 3 percent a year in the 1960s, became negative in the mid-1970s, bounced back and climbed to 9 percent by the mid-1980s, were steady at about 7 percent in the late 1980s and early 1990s, and fell to about 4 percent in the late 1990s and early 2000s. Over the same period, the quantity of capital employed increased steadily. In 2001, it stood at $2.6 trillion, almost four times its 1965 level.

Figure 14.5(b) shows why these trends occurred. Demand increased from KD_{65} to KD_{01}, and this increase was similar to the increase in supply from KS_{65} to KS_{01}. To understand the trends in the capital market, we must again probe the forces of demand and supply. Many of the ideas you've already met in your study of the labour market apply to the capital market as well. But there are some special features of capital. Its main special feature is that in the capital market, people must compare *present* costs with *future* benefits. Let's discover how people make these comparisons by studying the demand for capital.

The Demand for Capital

A firm's demand for *financial* capital stems from its demand for *physical* capital, and the amount that a firm plans to borrow in a given time period is determined by its planned investment—purchases of new capital. This decision is driven by its attempt to maximize profit. As a firm increases the quantity of capital employed, other things remaining the same, the marginal revenue product of capital eventually

FIGURE 14.5 Capital Market Trends in Canada

(a) Capital stock and interest rate

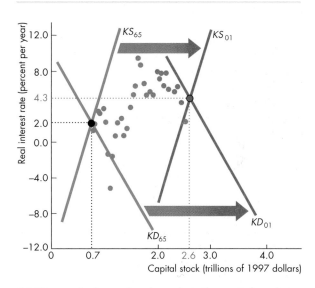

(b) Changes in demand and supply in the capital market

The real interest rate (the interest rate adjusted for inflation) fluctuated between a negative return in 1973 through 1975 and a high of 9 percent in 1984. It fluctuated between 2 and 3 percent during the 1960s and was at about 5 percent during the 1990s and 2000s. During the same period, the quantity of capital increased. By 2001, it was almost four times its 1965 level. Part (a) shows these trends. Part (b) shows the changes in demand and supply of capital that have generated the trends. The demand for capital increased from KD_{65} to KD_{01}, and the supply of capital increased from KS_{65} to KS_{01}.

Sources: Statistics Canada, CANSIM tables 378–0004 and 176–0043.

diminishes. To maximize profit, a firm increases its plant size and uses more capital if the marginal revenue product of capital exceeds the price of capital. But the marginal revenue product comes in the future, and capital must be paid for in the present. So the firm must convert *future* marginal revenue products into a *present value* so that this value can be compared with the price of the new equipment. To make this conversion, we use the technique of discounting.

Discounting and Present Value

Discounting is converting a future amount of money to a present value. And the **present value** of a future amount of money is the amount that, if invested today, will grow to be as large as that future amount when the interest that it will earn is taken into account.

The easiest way to understand discounting and present value is to begin with the relationship among an amount invested today, the interest that it earns, and the amount to which it will grow in the future. The future amount is equal to the present amount (present value) plus the interest it will accumulate in the future. That is,

Future amount = Present value
+ Interest income.

The interest income is equal to the present value multiplied by the interest rate, r, so

Future amount = Present value
+ ($r \times$ Present value)

or

Future amount = Present value $\times (1 + r)$.

If you have $100 today and the interest rate is 10 percent a year ($r = 0.1$), one year from today you will have $110—the original $100 plus $10 interest. Check that the above formula delivers that answer: $100 \times 1.1 = 110$.

The formula that we have just used calculates a future amount one year from today from the present value and an interest rate. To calculate the present value, we just work backwards. Instead of multiplying the present value by $(1 + r)$, we divide the future amount by $(1 + r)$. That is,

$$\text{Present value} = \frac{\text{Future value}}{(1 + r)}.$$

You can use this formula to calculate present value. This calculation of present value is called discounting. Let's check that we can use the present value for-

mula by calculating the present value of $110 one year from now when the interest rate is 10 percent a year. You'll be able to guess that the answer is $100 because we just calculated that $100 invested today at 10 percent a year becomes $110 in one year. Thus it follows immediately that the present value of $110 in one year's time is $100. But let's use the formula. Putting the numbers into the above formula, we have

$$\text{Present value} = \frac{\$110}{(1 + 0.1)}$$

$$= \frac{\$110}{1.1} = \$100.$$

Calculating the present value of an amount of money one year from now is the easiest case. But we can also calculate the present value of an amount any number of years in the future. As an example, let's see how we calculate the present value of an amount of money that will be available two years from now.

Suppose that you invest $100 today for two years at an interest rate of 10 percent a year. The money will earn $10 in the first year, which means that by the end of the first year, you will have $110. If the interest of $10 is invested, then the interest earned in the second year will be a further $10 on the original $100 plus $1 on the $10 interest. Thus the total interest earned in the second year will be $11. The total interest earned overall will be $21 ($10 in the first year and $11 in the second year). After two years, you will have $121. From the definition of present value, you can see that the present value of $121 two years hence is $100. That is, $100 is the present amount that, if invested at an interest rate of 10 percent a year, will grow to $121 two years from now.

To calculate the present value of an amount of money two years in the future, we use the formula:

$$\text{Present value} = \frac{\substack{\text{Amount of money} \\ \text{two years in future}}}{(1 + r)^2}.$$

Use this formula to calculate the present value of $121 two years from now at an interest rate of 10 percent a year. With these numbers, the formula gives

$$\text{Present value} = \frac{\$121}{(1 + 0.1)^2}$$

$$= \frac{\$121}{(1.1)^2}$$

$$= \frac{\$121}{1.21}$$

$$= \$100.$$

We can calculate the present value of an amount of money n years in the future by using a formula similar to the one we've already used. The general formula is

$$\text{Present value} = \frac{\text{Amount of money}}{(1 + r)^n}.$$

For example, if the interest rate is 10 percent a year, $100 to be received 10 years from now has a present value of $38.55. That is, if $38.55 is invested today at 10 percent a year, the amount will grow to $100 in 10 years.

You've seen how to calculate the present value of an amount of money one year in the future, two years in the future, and n years in the future. Most practical applications of present value calculate the present value of a sequence of future amounts of money that spread over several years. To calculate the present value of a sequence of amounts over several years, we use the formula you have learned and apply it to each year. We then sum the present values for each year to find the present value of the sequence of amounts.

For example, suppose that a firm expects to receive $100 a year for each of the next five years. And suppose that the interest rate is 10 percent per year (0.1 per year). The present value of these five payments of $100 each is calculated by using the following formula:

$$PV = \frac{\$100}{1.1} + \frac{\$100}{1.1^2} + \frac{\$100}{1.1^3} + \frac{\$100}{1.1^4} + \frac{\$100}{1.1^5},$$

which equals

$$PV = \$90.91 + \$82.64 + \$75.13 + \$68.30 + \$62.09$$

$$= \$379.07.$$

You can see that the firm receives $500 over five years. But because the money arrives in the future, it is not worth $500 today. Its present value is only $379.07. And the farther in the future it arrives, the smaller is its present value. The $100 received one year in the future is worth $90.91 today. And the $100 received five years in the future is worth only $62.09 today.

Let's now see how a firm uses the concept of present value to achieve an efficient use of capital.

The Present Value of a Computer

We'll see how a firm decides how much capital to buy by calculating the present value of a new computer. Tina runs Taxfile, Inc., a firm that sells advice to taxpayers. Tina is considering buying a new computer that costs $10,000. The computer has a life of two years, after which it will be worthless. If Tina buys the computer, she will pay $10,000 now and she expects to generate business that will bring in an additional $5,900 at the end of each of the next two years.

To calculate the present value, PV, of the marginal revenue product of a new computer, Tina calculates

$$PV = \frac{MRP_1}{(1 + r)} + \frac{MRP_2}{(1 + r)^2}.$$

Here, MRP_1 is the marginal revenue product received by Tina at the end of the first year. It is converted to a present value by dividing it by $(1 + r)$, where r is the interest rate (expressed as a proportion). The term MRP_2 is the marginal revenue product received at the end of the second year. It is converted to a present value by dividing it by $(1 + r)^2$.

If Tina can borrow or lend at an interest rate of 4 percent a year, the present value of her marginal revenue product is given by

$$PV = \frac{\$5,900}{(1 + 0.04)} + \frac{\$5,900}{(1 + 0.04)^2}$$

$$PV = \$5,673 + \$5,455$$

$$PV = \$11,128.$$

The present value (PV) of $5,900 one year in the future is $5,900 divided by 1.04 (4 percent as a proportion is 0.04). The present value of $5,900 two years in the future is $5,900 divided by $(1.04)^2$. Tina works out those two present values and then adds them to get the present value of the future flow of marginal revenue product, which is $11,128.

Parts (a) and (b) of Table 14.4 summarize the data and the calculations we've just made. Review these calculations and make sure you understand them.

TABLE 14.4   Net Present Value of an Investment—Taxfile, Inc.

(a) Data

Price of computer	$10,000
Life of computer	2 years
Marginal revenue product	$5,900 at end of each year
Interest rate	4% a year

(b) Present value of the flow of marginal revenue product

$$PV = \frac{MRP_1}{(1 + r)} + \frac{MRP_2}{(1 + r)^2}$$

$$= \frac{\$5,900}{1.04} + \frac{\$5,900}{(1.04)^2}$$

$$= \$5,673 + \$5,455$$

$$= \$11,128.$$

(c) Net present value of investment

NPV = PV of marginal revenue product − Price of computer

$$= \$11,128 - \$10,000$$

$$= \$1,128$$

Tina's Decision to Buy Tina decides whether to buy the computer by comparing the present value of its future flow of marginal revenue product with its purchase price. She makes this comparison by calculating the net present value (*NPV*) of the computer. **Net present value** is the present value of the future flow of marginal revenue product generated by the capital minus the price of the capital. If the net present value is positive, the firm buys additional capital. If the net present value is negative, the firm does not buy additional capital. Table 14.4(c) shows the calculation of Tina's net present value of a computer. The net present value is $1,128—greater than zero—so Tina buys the computer.

Tina can buy any number of computers that cost $10,000 and have a life of two years. But like all other factors of production, capital is subject to diminishing marginal returns. The greater the amount of capital employed, the smaller is its mar-

ginal revenue product. So if Tina buys a second computer or a third one, she gets successively smaller marginal revenue products from the additional machines.

Table 14.5(a) sets out Tina's marginal revenue products for one, two, and three computers. The marginal revenue product of one computer (the case just reviewed) is $5,900 a year. The marginal revenue product of a second computer is $5,600 a year, and the marginal revenue product of a third computer is $5,300 a year. Table 14.5(b) shows the calculations of the present values of the marginal revenue products of the first, second, and third computers.

You've seen that with an interest rate of 4 percent a year, the net present value of one computer is positive. At an interest rate of 4 percent a year, the present value of the marginal revenue product of a second computer is $10,562, which exceeds its price by $562. So Tina buys a second computer. But at an interest rate of 4 percent a year, the present value of the marginal revenue product of a third computer is $9,996, which is $4 less than the price of the computer. So Tina does not buy a third computer.

A Change in the Interest Rate We've seen that at an interest rate of 4 percent a year, Tina buys two computers but not three. Suppose that the interest rate is 8 percent a year. In this case, the present value of the first computer is $10,521 (see Table 14.5b), so Tina still buys one machine because it has a positive net present value. At an interest rate of 8 percent a year, the net present value of the second computer is $9,986, which is less than $10,000, the price of the computer. So at an interest rate of 8 percent a year, Tina buys only one computer.

Suppose that the interest rate is even higher, 12 percent a year. In this case, the present value of the marginal revenue product of one computer is $9,971 (see Table 14.5b). At this interest rate, Tina buys no computers.

These calculations trace Taxfile's demand schedule for capital, which shows the value of computers demanded by Taxfile at each interest rate. Other things remaining the same, as the interest rate rises, the quantity of capital demanded decreases. The higher the interest rate, the smaller is the quantity of *physical* capital demanded. But to finance the purchase of *physical* capital, firms demand *financial* capital. So the higher the interest rate, the smaller is the quantity of *financial* capital demanded.

TABLE 14.5 Taxfile's Investment Decision

(a) Data

Price of computer	$10,000
Life of computer	2 years
Marginal revenue product:	
Using 1 computer	$5,900 a year
Using 2 computers	$5,600 a year
Using 3 computers	$5,300 a year

(b) Present value of the flow of marginal revenue product

If r = 0.04 (4% a year):

Using 1 computer $PV = \dfrac{\$5,900}{1.04} + \dfrac{\$5,900}{(1.04)^2} = \$11,128$

Using 2 computers $PV = \dfrac{\$5,600}{1.04} + \dfrac{\$5,600}{(1.04)^2} = \$10,562$

Using 3 computers $PV = \dfrac{\$5,300}{1.04} + \dfrac{\$5,300}{(1.04)^2} = \$9,996$

If r = 0.08 (8% a year):

Using 1 computer $PV = \dfrac{\$5,900}{1.08} + \dfrac{\$5,900}{(1.08)^2} = \$10,521$

Using 2 computers $PV = \dfrac{\$5,600}{1.08} + \dfrac{\$5,600}{(1.08)^2} = \$9,986$

If r = 0.12 (12% a year):

Using 1 computer $PV = \dfrac{\$5,900}{1.12} + \dfrac{\$5,900}{(1.12)^2} = \$9,971$

Demand Curve for Capital

The quantity of capital demanded by a firm depends on the marginal revenue product of capital and the interest rate. A firm's demand curve for capital shows the relationship between the quantity of capital demanded by the firm and the interest rate, other things remaining the same. The market demand curve (as in Fig. 14.5b) shows the relationship between the total quantity of capital demanded and the interest rate, other things remaining the same.

Changes in the Demand for Capital Figure 14.5(b) shows that the demand for capital has increased steadily over the years. The demand for capital changes when expectations about the future marginal revenue product of capital change. An increase in the expected marginal revenue product of capital increases the demand of capital. Two main factors that change the marginal revenue product of capital and bring changes in the demand for capital are

1. Population growth
2. Technological change

An increase in the population increases the demand for all goods and services and so increases the demand for the capital that produces them. Advances in technology increase the demand for some types of capital and decrease the demand for other types. For example, the development of diesel engines for railroad transportation decreased the demand for steam engines and increased the demand for diesel engines. In this case, the railroad industry's overall demand for capital did not change much. In contrast, the development of desktop computers increased the demand for office computing equipment, decreased the demand for electric typewriters, and increased the overall demand for capital in the office.

Let's now turn to the supply side of the capital market.

The Supply of Capital

The quantity of capital supplied results from people's saving decisions. The main factors that determine saving are

- Income
- Expected future income
- Interest rate

To see how these factors influence saving, let's see how Aaron makes his saving decisions.

Income Saving is the act of converting *current* income into *future* consumption. When Aaron's income increases, he plans to consume more both in the present and in the future. But to increase *future* consumption, Aaron must save. So, other things remaining the same, the higher Aaron's income, the more he saves. The relationship between saving and income is remarkably stable. People tend to save a constant proportion of their income.

Expected Future Income Because a major reason for saving is to increase future consumption, the amount that Aaron saves depends not only on his current income but also on his *expected future income.* If Aaron's current income is high and his expected future income is low, he will have a high level of saving. But if Aaron's current income is low and his expected future income is high, he will have a low (perhaps even negative) level of saving.

Young people (especially students) usually have low current incomes compared with their expected future incomes. To smooth out their lifetime consumption, they consume more than they earn and incur debts. Such people have a negative amount of saving. In middle age, most people's incomes reach their peak. At this stage in life, saving is at its maximum. After retirement, people spend part of the wealth they have accumulated during their working lives.

Interest Rate A dollar saved today grows into a dollar plus interest tomorrow. The higher the interest rate, the greater is the amount that a dollar saved today becomes in the future. Thus the higher the interest rate, the greater is the opportunity cost of current consumption. With a higher opportunity cost of current consumption, Aaron cuts his consumption and increases his saving.

Supply Curve of Capital

The supply curve of capital (like that in Fig. 14.5b) shows the relationship between the quantity of capital supplied and the interest rate, other things remaining the same. An increase in the interest rate brings an increase in the quantity of capital supplied and a movement along the supply curve. The supply of capital is inelastic in the short run but is probably quite elastic in the long run. The reason is that in any given year, the total amount of saving is small relative to the stock of capital in existence. So even a large change in the saving rate brings only a small change in the quantity of capital supplied.

Changes in the Supply of Capital The main influences on the supply of capital are the size and age distribution of the population and the level of income.

Other things remaining the same, an increase in the population or an increase in income brings an increase in the supply of capital. Also, other things remaining the same, the larger the proportion of middle-aged people, the higher is the saving rate. The reason is that middle-aged people do most of the saving as they build up a pension fund to provide a retirement income. Any one of the factors that increases the supply of capital shifts the supply curve of capital rightward.

Let's now use what we've learned about the demand for and supply of capital and see how the interest rate is determined.

The Interest Rate

Saving plans and investment plans are coordinated through capital markets, and the real interest rate adjusts to make these plans compatible.

Figure 14.6 shows the capital market. Initially, the demand for capital is KD_0, and the supply of capital is KS_0. The equilibrium real interest rate is 6 percent a year, and the quantity of capital is $2 trillion. If the interest rate exceeds 6 percent a year, the quantity of capital supplied exceeds the quantity of capital demanded and the interest rate falls. And if the interest rate is less than 6 percent a year, the quantity of

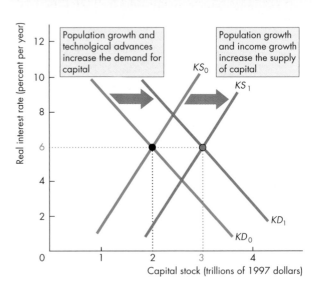

FIGURE 14.6   Capital Market Equilibrium

Initially, the demand for capital is KD_0 and the supply of capital is KS_0. The equilibrium interest rate is 6 percent a year, and the capital stock is $2 trillion. Over time, both demand and supply increase to KD_1 and KS_1. The capital stock increases, but the real interest rate is constant. Demand and supply increase because they are influenced by common factors.

capital demanded exceeds the quantity of capital supplied and the interest rate rises

Over time, both the demand for capital and the supply of capital increase. The demand curve shifts rightward to KD_1, and the supply curve also shifts rightward, to KS_1. Both curves shift because the same forces influence both. Population growth increases both demand and supply. Technological advances increase demand and bring higher incomes, which in turn increase supply. Because both demand and supply increase over time, the quantity of capital has an upward trend and the real interest rate has no trend.

Although the real interest rate does not follow a rising or falling trend, it does fluctuate, as you can see in Fig. 14.5. The reason is that the demand for capital and the supply of capital do not change in lockstep. Sometimes rapid technological change brings an increase in the demand for capital *before* it brings rising incomes that increase the supply of capital. When this sequence of events occurs, the real interest rate rises. The first half of the 1980s was such a time, as you can see in Fig. 14.5(a).

At other times, the demand for capital grows slowly or even decreases temporarily. In this situation, supply outgrows demand and the real interest rate falls. Figure 14.5 shows that the mid-1970s, 1984–1991, and the late-1990s were three such periods.

REVIEW QUIZ

1 What is discounting and how is it used to calculate a present value? When might you want to calculate a present value to make a decision?
2 How does a firm compare the future marginal revenue product of capital with the current cost of capital?
3 What are the main influences on a firm's demand for capital?
4 What are the main influences on the supply of capital?
5 What have been the main trends in the quantity of capital and real interest rates, and how can we explain the trends by using the demand for capital and the supply of capital?

The lessons that we've just learned about capital markets can be used to understand the prices of non-renewable natural resource prices.

Natural Resource Markets

NATURAL RESOURCES, OR WHAT ECONOMISTS call *land*, fall into two categories:

- Renewable
- Nonrenewable

Renewable natural resources are natural resources that can be used repeatedly. Examples are land (in its everyday sense), rivers, lakes, rain, and sunshine.
Nonrenewable natural resources are natural resources that can be used only once and that cannot be replaced once they have been used. Examples are coal, natural gas, and oil—the so-called hydrocarbon fuels.

The demand for a natural resource as an input into production is based on the same principle of marginal revenue product as the demand for labour (and the demand for capital). But the supply of a natural resource is special. Let's look first at the supply of renewable natural resources.

The Supply of a Renewable Natural Resource

The quantity of land and other renewable natural resources available is fixed. The quantity supplied cannot be changed by individual decisions. People can vary the amount of land they own. But when one person buys some land, another person sells it. The aggregate quantity of land supplied of any particular type and in any particular location is fixed, regardless of the decisions of any individual. This fact means that the supply of each particular piece of land is perfectly inelastic. Figure 14.7 illustrates such a supply. Regardless of the rent available, the quantity of land supplied in Toronto's Yorkville is a fixed number of square metres.

Because the supply of land is fixed regardless of its price, the price of land is determined by demand. The greater the demand for a specific piece of land, the higher is its price.

Expensive land can be, and is, used more intensively than inexpensive land. For example, high-rise buildings enable land to be used more intensively. However, to use land more intensively, it has to be combined with another factor of production: capital. An increase in the amount of capital per block of land does not change the supply of land itself.

FIGURE 14.7   The Supply of Land

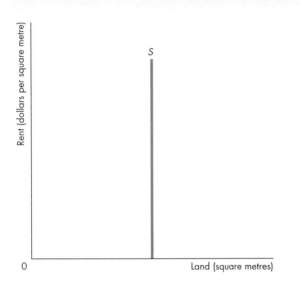

The supply of a given piece of land is perfectly inelastic. No matter what the rent, no more land than the quantity that exists can be supplied.

Although the supply of each type of land is fixed and its supply is perfectly inelastic, each individual firm operating in competitive land markets faces an elastic supply of land. For example, Bloor Street in Toronto has a fixed amount of land, but Chapters, the bookstore, could rent some space from The Bay, the department store. Each firm can rent the quantity of land that it demands at the going rent, as determined in the marketplace. Thus, provided that land markets are competitive, firms are price takers in these markets, just as they are in the markets for other productive resources.

The Supply of a Nonrenewable Natural Resource

The *stock* of a natural resource is the quantity in existence at a given time. This quantity is fixed and is independent of the price of the resource. The *known* stock of a natural resource is the quantity that has been discovered. This quantity increases over time because advances in technology enable ever less accessible sources to be discovered. Both of these *stock* concepts influence the price of a natural resource. But the influence is indirect. The direct influence on

price is the rate at which the resource is supplied for use in production—called the *flow* supply.

The flow supply of a nonrenewable natural resource is *perfectly elastic* at a price that equals the present value of the expected price next period.

To see why, think about the economic choices of Saudi Arabia, a country that possesses a large inventory of oil. Saudi Arabia can sell an additional billion barrels of oil right now and use the income it receives to buy U.S. bonds. Or it can keep the billion barrels in the ground and sell them next year. If it sells the oil and buys U.S. bonds, it earns the interest rate on the bonds. If it keeps the oil and sells it next year, it earns the amount of the price increase or loses the amount of the price decrease between now and next year.

If Saudi Arabia expects the price of oil to rise next year by a percentage that equals the current interest rate, the price that it expects next year equals $(1 + r)$ multiplied by this year's price. For example, if this year's price is $12 a barrel and the interest rate is 5 percent ($r = 0.5$), then next year's expected price is $1.05 \times \$12$, which equals $12.60 a barrel.

With the price expected to rise to $12.60 next year, Saudi Arabia is indifferent between selling now for $12 and not selling now but waiting until next year and selling for $12.60. It expects to make the same return either way. So at $12 a barrel, Saudi Arabia will sell whatever quantity is demanded.

But if Saudi Arabia expects the price to rise next year by a percentage that exceeds the current interest rate, it expects to make a bigger return by hanging onto the oil than it can make from selling the oil and buying bonds. So it keeps the oil and sells none. And if it expects the price to rise next year by a percentage that is less than the current interest rate, the bond gives a bigger return than the oil, so Saudi Arabia sells as much oil as it can.

Recall the idea of discounting and present value. The minimum price at which Saudi Arabia is willing to sell oil is the present value of the expected future price. At this price, it will sell as much oil as buyers demand. So its supply is perfectly elastic.

Price and the Hotelling Principle

Figure 14.8 shows the equilibrium in a natural resource market. Because supply is perfectly elastic at the present value of next period's expected price, the actual price of the natural resource equals the present value of next period's expected price. Also, because

FIGURE 14.8   A Nonrenewable Natural Resource Market

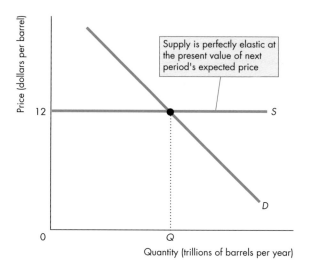

The supply of a nonrenewable natural resource is perfectly elastic at the *present value* of next period's expected price. The demand for a nonrenewable natural resource is determined by its marginal revenue product. The price is determined by supply and equals the *present value* of next period's expected price.

FIGURE 14.9   Falling Resource Prices

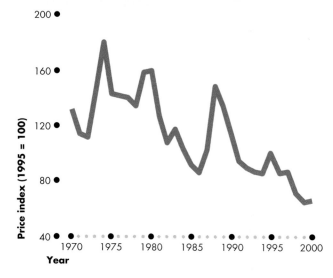

The prices of metals (here an average of the prices of aluminium, copper, iron ore, lead, manganese, nickel, silver, tin, and zinc) have tended to fall over time, not to rise as predicted by the Hotelling Principle. The reason is that unanticipated advances in technology have decreased the cost of extracting resources and greatly increased the exploitable known reserves.

Source: International Financial Statistics (various issues), Washington, DC: International Monetary Fund.

the current price is the present value of the expected future price, the price of the resource is expected to rise at a rate equal to the interest rate.

The proposition that the price of a resource is expected to rise at a rate equal to the interest rate is called the *Hotelling Principle*. It was first realized by Harold Hotelling, a mathematician and economist at Columbia University. But as Fig. 14.9 shows, *actual* prices do not follow the path *predicted* by the Hotelling Principle. Why do natural resource prices sometimes fall rather than follow their expected path and increase over time?

The key reason is that the future is unpredictable. Expected technological change is reflected in the price of a natural resource. But a previously unexpected new technology that leads to the discovery or the more efficient use of a nonrenewable natural resource causes its price to fall. Over the years, as technology has advanced, we have become more efficient in our use of nonrenewable resources. And we haven't just become more efficient. We've become more efficient than we expected to.

REVIEW QUIZ

1 Why is the price of a *renewable* natural resource such as land perfectly inelastic?
2 At what price is the flow supply of a nonrenewable natural resource perfectly elastic and why?
3 Why is the price of a nonrenewable natural resource expected to rise at a rate equal to the interest rate?
4 Why do the prices of nonrenewable resources not follow the path predicted by the Hotelling Principle?

People supply resources to earn an income. But some people earn enormous incomes. Are such incomes necessary to induce people to work and supply other resources? Let's now answer this question.

Income, Economic Rent, and Opportunity Cost

YOU'VE NOW SEEN HOW FACTOR PRICES ARE determined by the interaction of demand and supply. You've also seen that demand is determined by marginal productivity and that supply is determined by the factors of production available and by people's choices about their use. The interaction of demand and supply in factor markets determines who receives a large income and who receives a small income.

Large and Small Incomes

An NBA player earns $11 million a year because he has a high marginal revenue product—reflected in the demand for his services—and the supply of people with the combination of talents needed for this kind of job is small—reflected in the supply. Equilibrium occurs at a high wage rate and a small quantity employed.

People who work at fast-food restaurants earn a low wage rate because they have a low marginal revenue product—reflected in the demand—and many people are able and willing to supply their labour for these jobs. Equilibrium occurs at a low wage rate and a large quantity employed.

If the demand for basketball players increases, their incomes increase by a large amount and the number of players barely changes. If the demand for fast-food workers increases, the number of people doing these jobs increases by a large amount and the wage rate barely changes.

Another difference between a basketball player and a fast-food worker is that if the basketball player were hit with a pay cut, he would probably still supply his services, but if a fast-food worker were hit with a pay cut, he would probably quit. This difference arises from the interesting distinction between economic rent and opportunity cost.

Economic Rent and Opportunity Cost

The total income of a factor of production is made up of its economic rent and its opportunity cost. **Economic rent** is the income received by the owner of a factor of production over and above the amount required to induce that owner to offer the factor for use. Any factor of production can receive an economic rent. The income required to induce the supply of a factor of production is the opportunity cost of using the factor—the value of the factor in its next best use.

Figure 14.10(a) illustrates the way in which a factor income has an economic rent and an opportunity cost component. The figure shows the market for a factor of production. It could be *any* factor of production—labour, capital, or land—but we'll suppose that it is labour. The demand curve is *D*, and the supply curve is *S*. The wage rate is *W*, and the quantity employed is *C*. The income earned is the sum of the yellow and green areas. The yellow area below the supply curve measures opportunity cost, and the green area above the supply curve but below the factor price measures economic rent.

To see why the area below the supply curve measures opportunity cost, recall that a supply curve can be interpreted in two different ways. It shows the quantity supplied at a given price, and it shows the minimum price at which a given quantity is willingly supplied. If suppliers receive only the minimum amount required to induce them to supply each unit of the factor, they will be paid a different price for each unit. The prices will trace the supply curve, and the income received will be entirely opportunity cost—the yellow area in Fig. 14.10(a).

The concept of economic rent is similar to the concept of producer surplus that you met in Chapter 5. Economic rent is the price a person receives for the use of a factor minus the minimum price at which a given quantity of the factor is willingly supplied.

Economic rent is not the same thing as the "rent" that a farmer pays for the use of some land or the "rent" that you pay for your apartment. Everyday "rent" is a price paid for the services of land or a building. *Economic rent* is a component of the income received by any factor of production.

The portion of the income of a factor of production that consists of economic rent depends on the elasticity of the supply of the factor. When the supply of a factor of production is perfectly inelastic, its entire income is economic rent. Most of the income received by Garth Brooks and Pearl Jam is economic rent. Also, a large part of the income of a major-league baseball player is economic rent. When the supply of a factor of production is perfectly elastic, none of its income is economic rent. Most of the

FIGURE 14.10   Economic Rent and Opportunity Cost

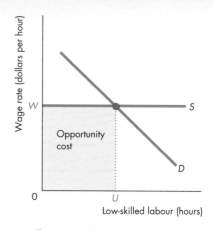

(a) General case   **(b) All economic rent**   **(c) All opportunity cost**

When the supply curve of a factor slopes upward—the general case—as in part (a), part of the factor income is economic rent (the green area) and part is opportunity cost (the yellow area). When the supply of a factor is per-

fectly inelastic (the supply curve is vertical), as in part (b), the entire factor income is economic rent. When the supply of a factor is perfectly elastic, as in part (c), the factor's entire income is opportunity cost.

income of a babysitter is opportunity cost. In general, when supply is neither perfectly elastic nor perfectly inelastic, as Fig. 14.10(a) illustrates, some of the factor income is economic rent and some is opportunity cost.

Figures 14.10(b) and 14.10(c) show the other two possibilities. Part (b) shows the market for a particular parcel of land in Vancouver. The quantity of land is fixed in size at *L* square metres. So the supply curve of the land is vertical—perfectly inelastic. No matter what the rent on the land is, there is no way of increasing the quantity that can be supplied. Suppose that the demand curve in Fig. 14.10(b) shows the marginal revenue product of this block of land. Then it commands a rent of *R*. The entire income accruing to the owner of the land is the green area in the figure. This income is *economic rent*.

Figure 14.10(c) shows the market for a factor of production that is in perfectly elastic supply. An example of such a market might be that for low-skilled labour in a poor country such as India or China. In those countries, large numbers of people seeking labour flock to the cities and are available for work at the going wage rate (in this case, *W*). Thus in these situations, the supply of labour is almost perfectly elastic. The entire income earned by these workers is opportunity cost. They receive no economic rent.

REVIEW QUIZ

1 Why does an NBA player earn a larger income than does a babysitter?
2 What is the distinction between an economic rent and an opportunity cost?
3 Is the income that the Toronto Raptors pays to Antonio Davis an economic rent or compensation for his opportunity cost?
4 Is a Big Mac more expensive in Vancouver than in Brandon, Manitoba because rents are higher in Vancouver, or are rents higher in Vancouver because people in Vancouver are willing to pay more for a Big Mac?

◆ *Reading Between the Lines* on pp. 336–337 looks at the market for hockey players.

The next chapter looks at how the market economy distributes income and explains the trends in the distribution of income. The chapter also looks at the efforts by governments to redistribute income and modify the market outcome.

Rents and Opportunity Costs on the Ice

THE GLOBE AND MAIL, AUGUST 1, 2002

Kariya stays put for $10-million

Anaheim star Paul Kariya agreed to a one-year deal with the Mighty Ducks yesterday after accepting the team's one-year $10 million (U.S.) qualifying offer.

"Having our captain and team leader signed prior to training camp is very important for our club," Anaheim general manager Bryan Murray said in a statement. "Paul's dedication and work ethic continue to make him one of the game's best players."

Kariya, 27, is Anaheim's all-time leader in games (524), goals (275), assists (313) and game-winning goals (42). The 5-foot-10, 173-pound native of North Vancouver, B.C., led the Ducks in goals (32) and points (57) but both totals were his lowest since he had 17 goals and 31 points in 22 games in 1997-98.

"One year at a time at this point is something I feel comfortable with," Kariya said during a conference call. "What it does is put pressure on both myself and the team to continue going in the right direction and for myself to get back playing at the top of my game."

Anaheim (29-42-8-3, 69 points) finished last in the Western Conference's Pacific Division last season. But the Ducks have been busy in the off-season, hiring new coach Mike Babcock and adding defenceman Fredrik Olausson, a free agent from Detroit, and forwards Adam Oates, a free agent from Philadelphia, and Petr Sykora, in a trade with New Jersey.

Kariya is particularly excited about the acquisition of Olausson, Oates and Sykora because he says the three will improve a Ducks' power player that was the NHL's worst last season.

"Our power play really killed us last year," said Kariya, who helped Canada win the men's Olympic hockey gold in Salt Lake City in February. "Getting Adam Oates, who I think is the best power-play guy in the league, and also signing Fredrik Olausson, who is a terrific quarterback out there, is going to help us out a lot.

"I think that will go from being the weakest part of our game to being one of our strongest parts." ...

The Canadian Press.

Essence of the Story

■ Paul Kariya signed a one-year deal for $10 million with the Mighty Ducks.

■ Kariya says he likes contracting for one year at a time because it puts pressure on both him and the team to perform at the top of their games.

■ The Mighty Ducks' general manager says that Paul's dedication and work ethic make him one of the game's best players and having him sign early helps the club.

■ Anaheim hired a new defenceman and two forwards that Kariya says will improve the Ducks' power play, which was weak last season.

Economic Analysis

■ This news article illustrates four central economic ideas:

1. Marginal revenue product
2. Economic rent and opportunity cost
3. Incentives
4. Complements

■ The marginal revenue product of Paul Kariya is $10 million a year. Other top hockey players also have a very large marginal revenue product.

■ Having Kariya on the team increases the revenue that the Mighty Ducks generates by $10 million.

■ The supply of top-performing hockey players of Kariya's quality is limited. At a wage rate below the minimum industrial wage, no one would be willing to work and train to perform at the standard of these players. The quantity supplied would be zero.

■ At a wage rate similar to the average industrial wage, a large number of people are willing to work and train to play competition-quality hockey. But few have the talent to perform at the level of Kariya.

■ No matter by how much the wage rate rises above the average industrial wage, the quantity of top-performing hockey players does not increase. The supply is inelastic.

■ The figure shows the market for top-performing hockey players.

■ The demand for top-performing players is determined by their marginal revenue product and is the curve D.

■ The supply curve, S, shows the willingness of talented people to offer their services as hockey players. The average industrial wage rate is a. As the wage rate for hockey players increases above this wage rate, the quantity of star players supplied increases, but up to a maximum of Q_0. This quantity is limited by the available talent pool.

■ Equilibrium in the market for top-performing hockey players occurs at an average wage rate of $1.6 million (U.S.) a year.

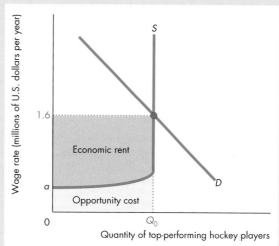

Figure 1 The market for hockey players

■ Most of their income is *economic rent*, which is shown as the green area. The rest, shown by the yellow area, is *opportunity cost*.

■ Paul Kariya and many other players work on a one-year contract. Such a contract provides a stronger *incentive* for the player to perform well so that he can get a new contract the next year. It also provides a strong incentive for the club to hire well and have good coaching and management to make itself attractive to the top players.

■ Hockey players are *complementary* factors of production. Even a great player like Kariya would not perform well without great support from other players.

■ When the Mighty Ducks hired Olausson, Oates, and Sykora, they increased the marginal revenue product of Kariya. And by signing Kariya, they increased the marginal revenue product of the other three players.

SUMMARY

KEY POINTS

Prices and Incomes in Competitive Factor Markets (p. 316)

- An increase in the demand for a factor of production increases the factor's price and total income; a decrease in the demand for a factor of production decreases its price and total income.
- An increase in the supply of a factor of production increases the quantity used but decreases its price and might increase or decrease its total income depending on whether demand is elastic or inelastic.

Labour Markets (pp. 317–324)

- The demand for labour is determined by the marginal revenue product of labour.
- The demand for labour increases if the price of the firm's output rises or if technological change and capital accumulation increase marginal product.
- The elasticity of demand for labour depends on the labour intensity of production, the elasticity of demand for the product, and the ease with which labour can be substituted for capital.
- The quantity of labour supplied increases as the real wage rate increases, but at high wage rates, the supply curve eventually bends backwards.
- The supply of labour increases as the population increases and with technological change and capital accumulation.
- Wage rates and employment increase because demand increases by more than supply.

Capital Markets (pp. 325–331)

- To make an investment decision, a firm compares the *present value* of the marginal revenue product of capital with the price of capital.
- Population growth and technological change increase the demand for capital.
- The higher the interest rate, the greater is the amount of saving and quantity of capital supplied.
- The supply of capital increases as incomes increase.

- Capital market equilibrium determines the real interest rate.

Natural Resource Markets (pp. 331–333)

- The demand for natural resources is determined by marginal revenue product.
- The supply of land is inelastic.
- The supply of nonrenewable natural resources is perfectly elastic at a price equal to the present value of the expected future price.
- The price of a nonrenewable natural resource is expected to rise at a rate equal to the interest rate but fluctuates and sometimes falls.

Income, Economic Rent, and Opportunity Cost (pp. 334–335)

- Economic rent is the income received by the owner of a factor of production over and above the amount needed to induce the owner to supply the factor for use.
- The rest of a factor's income is an opportunity cost.
- When the supply of a factor is perfectly inelastic, its entire income is made up of economic rent; and when supply of a factor is perfectly elastic, its entire income is made up of opportunity cost.

KEY FIGURES AND TABLES

Figure 14.1   Demand and Supply in a Factor Market, 316
Figure 14.3   The Demand for Labour at Max's Wash 'n' Wax, 319
Figure 14.10   Economic Rent and Opportunity Cost, 335
Table 14.2   Two Conditions for Maximum Profit, 320
Table 14.3   A Firm's Demand for Labour, 321

KEY TERMS

Derived demand, 317
Discounting, 326
Economic rent, 334
Marginal revenue product, 318
Net present value, 328
Nonrenewable natural resources, 331
Present value, 326
Renewable natural resources, 331

PROBLEMS

*1. The figure illustrates the market for blueberry pickers.

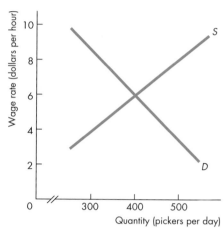

a. What is the wage rate paid to blueberry pickers?
b. How many blueberry pickers get hired?
c. What is the income received by blueberry pickers?

2. In problem 1, if the demand for blueberry pickers decreases by 100 a day:
a. What is the new wage rate paid to the pickers?
b. How many pickers get laid off?
c. What is the total income paid to pickers?

*3. Wanda owns a fish shop. She employs students to sort and pack the fish. Students can pack the following amounts of fish in an hour:

Number of students	Quantity of fish (kilograms)
1	20
2	50
3	90
4	120
5	145
6	165
7	180
8	190

Wanda can sell her fish for 50¢ a kilogram, and the wage rate of packers is $7.50 an hour.
a. Calculate the marginal product of the students and draw the marginal product curve.

b. Calculate the marginal revenue product of the students and draw the marginal revenue product curve.
c. Find Wanda's demand for labour curve.
d. How many students does Wanda employ?

4. Larry makes gourmet ice cream in small batches. He employs workers who can produce the following quantities in a day:

Number of workers	Quantity of ice cream (batches)
1	4
2	10
3	18
4	24
5	29
6	33
7	36
8	38

Larry can sell ice cream for $25 a batch, and the wage rate of his workers is $100 a day.
a. Calculate the marginal product of the workers and draw the marginal product curve.
b. Calculate the marginal revenue product of the workers and draw the marginal revenue product curve.
c. Find Larry's demand for labour curve.
d. How much ice cream does Larry sell?

*5. Back at Wanda's fish shop described in problem 3, the price of fish falls to 33.33¢ a kilogram but fish packers' wages remain at $7.50 an hour.
a. What happens to the students' marginal product?
b. What happens to Wanda's marginal revenue product?
c. What happens to her demand for labour curve?
d. What happens to the number of students that she employs?

6. Back at Larry's ice cream plant described in problem 4, the price of ice cream falls to $20 a batch but the wage rate remains at $100 a day.
a. What happens to the workers' marginal product?
b. What happens to Larry's marginal revenue product?
c. What happens to his demand for labour curve?
d. What happens to the number of workers that he employs?

*7. Back at Wanda's fish shop described in problem 3, packers' wages increase to $10 an hour but the price of fish remains at 50¢ a kilogram.
   a. What happens to marginal revenue product?
   b. What happens to Wanda's demand for labour curve?
   c. How many students does Wanda employ?

8. Back at Larry's ice cream plant described in problem 4, the wage rate rises to $125 a day but the price of ice cream remains at $25 a batch.
   a. What happens to marginal revenue product?
   b. What happens to Larry's demand for labour curve?
   c. How many workers does Larry employ?

*9. Using the information provided in problem 3, calculate Wanda's marginal revenue, marginal cost, and marginal revenue product. Show that when Wanda is making maximum profit, marginal cost equals marginal revenue and marginal revenue product equals the wage rate.

10. Using the information provided in problem 4, calculate Larry's marginal revenue, marginal cost, and marginal revenue product. Show that when Larry is making maximum profit, marginal cost equals marginal revenue and marginal revenue product equals the wage rate.

*11. Greg has found an oil well in his backyard. A geologist estimates that a total of 10 million barrels can be pumped for a pumping cost of a dollar a barrel. The price of oil is $20 a barrel. How much oil does Greg sell each year? If you can't predict how much he will sell, what extra information would you need to be able to do so?

12. Orley has a wine cellar in which he keeps choice wines from around the world. What does Orley expect to happen to the prices of the wines he keeps in his cellar? Explain your answer. How does Orley decide which wine to drink and when to drink it?

*13. Use the figure in problem 1 and show on the figure the blueberry pickers'
   a. Economic rent.
   b. Opportunity cost.

14. Use the figure in problem 1 and the information in problem 2 and show on the figure the blueberry pickers'
   a. Economic rent.
   b. Opportunity cost.

CRITICAL THINKING

1. Study *Reading Between the Lines* on pp. 336–337 and answer the following questions:
   a. What determines the demand for hockey players?
   b. What determines the supply of hockey players?
   c. What do you think Paul Kariya, Fredrik Olausson, Adam Oates, and Petr Sykora would do if they didn't play hockey?
   d. What does your answer to (c) tell you about the opportunity cost of these players?
   e. What does your answer to (c) tell you about the economic rent received by these players?
   f. What are the advantages for the player and the club of a one-year contract over a multi-year contract?
   g. Why do good players like to have other good players on their team?

2. "We are running out of natural resources and must take urgent action to conserve our precious reserves." "There is no shortage of resources that the market cannot cope with." Debate these two views. List the pros and cons for each.

3. Why do we keep finding new reserves of oil? Why don't we do a once-and-for-all big survey that catalogues the earth's entire inventory of natural resources?

WEB EXERCISES

1. Use the link on the Parkin–Bade Web site and read the article on "Trends in Hours of Work Since the Mid 1970s."
   a. What are the trends in hours of work since the mid-1970s?
   b. Are the trends for men the same as those for women? What are the similarities and differences?
   c. Do you think the trends arise from changes on the demand side of the labour market or from changes on the supply side?
   d. What additional information would you need to be sure about your answer to part (c)?

APPENDIX

Labour Unions

After studying this appendix you will be able to

- **Explain why union workers earn more than nonunion workers**
- **Explain how a labour market works in a monopsony**
- **Explain the effects of a minimum wage law in a monopsony**

Market Power in the Labour Market

JUST AS A MONOPOLY FIRM CAN RESTRICT OUTPUT and raise price, so a monopoly owner of a resource can restrict supply and raise the price of the resource.

The main source of market power in the labour market is the labour union. A **labour union** is an organized group of workers that aims to increase wages and influence other job conditions.

Traditionally, a union was formed by a group of workers who had similar skills but who worked for firms in different industries and regions—for example, the electrical workers union. The industrial union was created when workers in mass-production industries unionized. These workers had a variety of skills and they worked in the same industry. Today, most unions have members who work in different industries and have a wide range of skills. For example, the members of the United Steelworkers Union work in steel mills, factories, bakeries, and offices.

Most unions are members of the Canadian Labour Congress, which was created in 1956 with the merger of the Labour Council of Canada (founded in 1883) and the Canadian Congress of Labour (founded in 1940).

Unions vary enormously in size. Some unions are small, but industrial unions are large. Union strength peaked in 1976, when 30 percent of the nonagricultural work force belonged to unions. That percentage has fallen slightly since then and is now about 25 percent.

Union organization is based on a subdivision known as the *local*. The local can be organized as a closed shop, a union shop, or an open shop. A *closed shop* is an arrangement in which the firm can hire only union members. Most closed shops are in the construction industry. A *union shop* is an arrangement in which the firm can hire workers who are not union members, but new workers must join the union, usually at the end of their probationary period. Union shops are common in manufacturing industries and the public sector. An *open shop* is an arrangement in which no employee is required to join the union or pay union dues. There is no restriction on who can work in the "shop." A compromise between the union shop and the open shop is the **Rand Formula**: a requirement that all workers represented by a union must pay union dues, whether they join the union or not.

Unions negotiate with employers or their representatives in a process called *collective bargaining*. The main weapons available to the union and the employer in collective bargaining are the strike and the lockout. A *strike* is a group decision by the workers to refuse to work under prevailing conditions. A *lockout* is a firm's refusal to operate its plant and employ its workers. Each party uses the threat of a strike or a lockout to try to get an agreement in its own favour. Sometimes, when the two parties in the collective bargaining process cannot agree on the wage rate or other conditions of employment, they agree to submit their disagreement to binding arbitration. *Binding arbitration* is a process in which a third party—an arbitrator—determines wages and other employment conditions on behalf of the negotiating parties.

Although they are not labour unions in a legal sense, professional associations act in ways similar to labour unions. A *professional association* is an organized group of professional workers such as lawyers or physicians (for example, the Ontario Medical Association). Professional associations control entry into the professions and license practitioners, ensuring the adherence to minimum standards of competence. But they also influence the compensation and other labour market conditions of their members.

Union Objectives and Constraints

A union has three broad objectives that it strives to achieve for its members:

1. To increase compensation
2. To improve working conditions
3. To expand job opportunities

Each of these objectives contains a series of more detailed goals. For example, in seeking to increase members' compensation, a union operates on a variety of fronts: wage rates, fringe benefits, retirement pay, and such things as vacation allowances. In seeking to improve working conditions, a union is concerned with occupational health and safety as well as the environmental quality of the workplace. In seeking to expand job opportunities, a union tries to get greater job security for existing union members and to find ways of creating additional jobs for them.

A union's ability to pursue its objectives is restricted by two sets of constraints—one on the supply side of the labour market and the other on the demand side. On the supply side, the union's activities are limited by how well it can restrict nonunion workers from offering their labour in the same market as union labour. The larger the fraction of the work force controlled by the union, the more effective the union can be in this regard. It is difficult for unions to operate in markets where there is an abundant supply of willing nonunion labour. For example, the market for part-time checkout clerks is very tough for a union to organize because of the enormous rate of turnover of participants in that market. At the other extreme, unions in the construction industry can better pursue their goals because they can influence the number of people who can obtain skills as electricians, plasterers, and carpenters. The professional associations of dentists and physicians are best able to restrict the supply of dentists and physicians. These groups control the number of qualified workers by controlling either the examinations that new entrants must pass or entrance into professional degree programs.

On the demand side of the labour market, the union faces a tradeoff that arises from firms' profit-maximizing decisions. Because labour demand curves slope downward, anything a union does that increases the wage rate or other employment costs decreases the quantity of labour demanded.

Let's see how unions operate in competitive labour markets.

A Union in a Competitive Labour Market

When a union operates in an otherwise competitive labour market, it seeks to increase wages and other compensation and to limit employment reductions by increasing demand for the labour of its members.

That is, the union tries to take actions that shift the demand curve for its members' labour rightward.

Figure A14.1 illustrates a competitive labour market that a union enters. The demand curve is D_C, and the supply curve is S_C. Before the union enters the market, the wage rate is $7 an hour and 100 hours of labour are employed.

Now suppose that a union is formed to organize the workers in this market. The union can attempt to increase wages in this market in two ways. It can try to restrict the supply of labour, or it can try to stimulate the demand for labour. First, look at what happens if the union has sufficient control over the supply of labour to be able to restrict that supply artificially below its competitive level—to S_U. If that is all the union is able to do, employment falls to 85 hours of labour and the wage rate rises to $8 an hour.

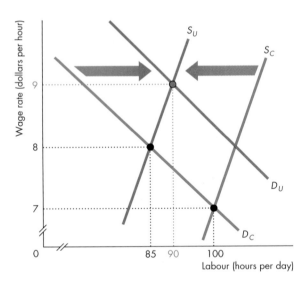

FIGURE A14.1   Union in a Competitive Labour Market

In a competitive labour market, the demand curve is D_C and the supply curve is S_C. Competitive equilibrium occurs at a wage rate of $7 an hour with 100 hours employed. By restricting employment below the competitive level, the union shifts the supply of labour to S_U. If the union can do no more than that, the wage rate will increase to $8 an hour but employment will fall to 85 hours. If the union can increase the demand for labour and shift the demand curve to D_U, then it can increase the wage rate still higher, to $9 an hour, and achieve employment of 90 hours.

The union simply picks its preferred position along the demand curve that defines the tradeoff it faces between employment and the wage rate.

You can see that if the union can only restrict the supply of labour, it raises the wage rate but decreases the number of jobs available. Because of this outcome, unions try to increase the demand for labour and shift the demand curve rightward. Let's see what they might do to achieve this outcome.

How Unions Try to Change the Demand for Labour

Unless a union can take actions that change the demand for the labour that it represents, it has to accept the fact that a higher wage rate can be obtained only at the price of lower employment.

The union tries to operate on the demand for labour in two ways. First, it tries to make the demand for union labour inelastic. Second, it tries to increase the demand for union labour. Making the demand for labour less elastic does not eliminate the tradeoff between employment and the wage rate. But it does make the tradeoff less unfavourable. If a union can make the demand for labour less elastic, it can increase the wage rate at a lower cost in terms of lost employment opportunities. But if the union can increase the demand for labour, it might even be able to increase both the wage rate and the employment opportunities of its members. Some of the methods used by the unions to change the demand for the labour of its members are to

- Increase the marginal product of union members
- Encourage import restrictions
- Support minimum wage laws
- Support immigration restrictions
- Increase demand for the good produced

Unions try to increase the marginal product of their members, which in turn increases the demand for their labour, by organizing and sponsoring training schemes, by encouraging apprenticeship and other on-the-job training activities, and by professional certification.

One of the best examples of import restrictions is the support by the Canadian Auto Workers union (CAW) for import restrictions on foreign cars.

Unions support minimum wage laws to increase the cost of employing low-skilled labour. An increase in the wage rate of low-skilled labour leads to a decrease in the quantity demanded of low-skilled labour and to an increase in demand for high-skilled union labour, a substitute for low-skilled labour.

Restrictive immigration laws decrease the supply of low-skilled workers and increase their wage rate. As a result, the demand for high-skilled union labour increases.

Because the demand for labour is a derived demand, an increase in the demand for the good produced by union labour increases the demand for union labour. The garment workers' union urging us to buy union-made clothes and the CAW asking us to buy only North American cars made by union workers are examples of attempts by unions to increase the demand for union labour.

Figure A14.1 illustrates the effects of an increase in the demand for the labour of a union's members. If the union can increase the demand for labour to D_U, it can achieve an even bigger increase in the wage rate with a smaller fall in employment. By maintaining the restricted labour supply at S_U, the union increases the wage rate to $9 an hour and achieves an employment level of 90 hours of labour.

Because a union restricts the supply of labour in the market in which it operates, its actions increase the supply of labour in nonunion markets. Workers who can't get union jobs must look elsewhere for work. This increase in the supply of labour in nonunion markets lowers the wage rate in those markets and further widens the union–nonunion differential.

The Scale of Union–Nonunion Wage Differentials

We have seen that unions can influence the wage rate by restricting the supply of labour and increasing the demand for labour. How much of a difference to wage rates do unions make in practice?

Union wage rates are, on the average, 30 percent higher than nonunion wage rates. In mining and financial services, union and nonunion wages are similar. In services, manufacturing, and transportation, the differential is between 11 and 19 percent. In wholesale and retail trades, the differential is 28 percent, and in construction, it is 65 percent.

But these union–nonunion wage differentials don't give a true measure of the effects of unions. In some industries, union wages are higher than nonunion wages because union members do jobs that involve greater skill. Even without a union, those workers would receive a higher wage. To calculate the effects of unions, we have to examine the wages of unionized and nonunionized workers who do nearly identical work. The evidence suggests that after allowing for skill differentials, the union–nonunion wage differential lies between 10 percent and 25 percent. For example, airline pilots who belong to the Air Line Pilots' Union earn about 25 percent more than nonunion pilots with the same level of skill.

Let's now look at monopsony.

Monopsony

A MARKET IN WHICH THERE IS A SINGLE BUYER IS called **monopsony**. This market type is unusual, but it does exist. With the growth of large-scale production over the last century, large manufacturing plants such as coal mines, steel and textile mills, and car manufacturers became the major employer in some regions, and in some places a single firm employed almost all the labour. Today, the provincial health insurance plans are the major employers of health-care professionals. These employers have market power.

In monopsony, the employer determines the wage rate and pays the lowest wage at which it can attract the labour it plans to hire. A monopsony makes a bigger profit than a group of firms that compete with each other for their labour. Let's find out how a monopsony achieves this outcome.

Like all firms, a monopsony has a downward-sloping marginal revenue product curve, which is *MRP* in Fig. A14.2. This curve tells us the extra revenue the monopsony receives by selling the output produced by an extra hour of labour. The labour supply curve is *S*. This curve tells us how many hours are supplied at each wage rate. It also tells us the minimum wage for which a given quantity of labour is willing to work.

A monopsony recognizes that to hire more labour, it must pay a higher wage; equivalently, by hiring less labour, it can pay a lower wage. Because a monopsony controls the wage rate, the marginal cost of labour exceeds the wage rate. The marginal cost of labour is shown by the curve *MCL*. The relationship between the marginal cost of labour curve and the supply curve is similar to the relationship between the marginal cost and average cost curves that you studied in Chapter 10. The supply curve is like the average cost of labour curve. In Fig. A14.2, the firm can hire 49 hours of labour for a wage rate of just below $4.90 an hour. The firm's total labour cost is

$240. But suppose that the firm hires 50 hours of labour. It can hire the 50th hour of labour for $5 an hour. The total cost of labour is now $250 an hour. So hiring the 50th hour of labour increases the total cost of labour from $240 to $250, which is a $10 increase. The marginal cost of labour is $10 an hour. The curve *MCL* shows the $10 marginal cost of hiring the 50th hour of labour.

To calculate the profit-maximizing quantity of labour to hire, the firm sets the marginal cost of labour equal to the marginal revenue product of labour. That is, the firm wants the cost of the last worker hired to equal the extra total revenue brought in. In Fig. A14.2, this outcome occurs when the monopsony employs 50 hours of labour. What is the wage rate that the monopsony pays? To hire 50 hours of labour, the firm must pay $5 an hour, as shown by the supply of labour curve. So each worker is paid $5 an hour. But the marginal revenue product of labour is $10 an hour, which means that the firm makes an economic profit of $5 on the last hour of labour that it hires. Compare this outcome with that in a competitive labour market. If the

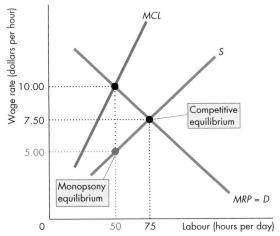

FIGURE A14.2   A Monopsony Labour Market

A monopsony is a market structure in which there is a single buyer. A monopsony in the labour market has the marginal revenue product curve *MRP* and faces a labour supply curve *S*. The marginal cost of labour curve is *MCL*. Making the marginal cost of labour equal to the value of marginal product maximizes profit. The monopsony hires 50 hours of labour and pays the lowest wage for which that labour will work, which is $5 an hour.

labour market shown in Fig. A14.2 were competitive, equilibrium would occur at the point of intersection of the demand curve and the supply curve. The wage rate would be $7.50 an hour, and 75 hours of labour a day would be employed. So compared with a competitive labour market, a monopsony decreases both the wage rate and employment.

The ability of a monopsony to cut the wage and employment to increase its profit depends on the elasticity of labour supply. If the supply of labour is highly elastic, a monopsony has little power to cut the wage and employment to boost its profit.

Monopsony Tendencies

Today, monopsony is rare. Workers can commute long distances to a job, so most people have more than one potential employer. But firms that are dominant employers in isolated communities do face an upward-sloping supply of labour curve and so have a marginal cost of labour that exceeds the wage rate. But in such situations, there is also, usually, a union. Let's see how unions and monopsonies interact.

Monopsony and a Union

In Chapter 12, we discovered that in monopoly, a firm can determine the market price. We've now seen that in monopsony—a market with a single buyer—the buyer can determine the price. Suppose that a union operates in a monopsony labour market. A union is like a monopoly. If the union (monopoly seller) faces a monopsony buyer, the situation is called **bilateral monopoly.** In bilateral monopoly, the wage rate is determined by bargaining.

In Fig. A14.2, if the monopsony is free to determine the wage rate and the level of employment, it hires 50 hours of labour for a wage rate of $5 an hour. But suppose that a union represents the workers. The union agrees to maintain employment at 50 hours but seeks the highest wage rate that the employer can be forced to pay. That wage rate is $10 an hour—the wage rate that equals the marginal revenue product of labour. The union might not be able to get the wage rate up to $10 an hour. But it won't accept $5 an hour. The monopsony firm and the union bargain over the wage rate, and the result is an outcome between $10 an hour and $5 an hour.

The outcome of the bargaining depends on the costs that each party can inflict on the other as a result of a failure to agree on the wage rate. The firm can shut down the plant and lock out its workers, and the

workers can shut down the plant by striking. Each party knows the other's strength and knows what it will lose if it does not agree to the other's demands. If the two parties are equally strong and they realize it, they will split the gap between $5 and $10 and agree to a wage rate of $7.50 an hour. If one party is stronger than the other—and both parties know that—the agreed wage will favour the stronger party. Usually, an agreement is reached without a strike or a lockout. The threat is usually enough to bring the bargaining parties to an agreement. When a strike or lockout does occur, it is usually because one party has misjudged the costs each party can inflict on the other.

Minimum wage laws have interesting effects in monopsony labour markets. Let's study these effects.

Monopsony and the Minimum Wage

In a competitive labour market, a minimum wage that exceeds the equilibrium wage decreases employment (see Chapter 6, pp. 129–130). In a monopsony labour market, a minimum wage can *increase* both the wage rate and employment. Let's see how.

Figure A14.3 shows a monopsony labour market in which the wage rate is $5 an hour and 50 hours of labour are employed. A minimum wage law is passed that requires employers to pay at least $7.50 an hour.

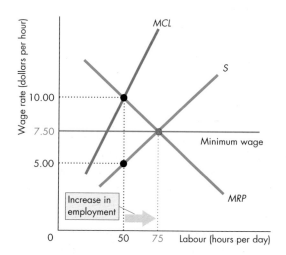

FIGURE A14.3   Minimum Wage Law in Monopsony

In a monopsony labour market, the wage rate is $5 an hour and 50 hours are hired. If a minimum wage law increases the wage rate to $7.50 an hour, employment increases to 75 hours.

The monopsony in Fig. A14.3 now faces a perfectly elastic supply of labour at $7.50 an hour up to 75 hours. Above 75 hours, a wage above $7.50 an hour must be paid to hire additional hours of labour. Because the wage rate is a fixed $7.50 an hour up to 75 hours, the marginal cost of labour is also constant at $7.50 up to 75 hours. Beyond 75 hours, the marginal cost of labour rises above $7.50 an hour. To maximize profit, the monopsony sets the marginal cost of labour equal to the marginal revenue product of labour. That is, the monopsony hires 75 hours of labour at $7.50 an hour. The minimum wage law has made the supply of labour perfectly elastic and made the marginal cost of labour the same as the wage rate up to 75 hours. The law has not affected the supply of labour curve or the marginal cost of labour at employment levels above 75 hours. The minimum wage law has succeeded in raising the wage rate by $2.50 an hour and increasing the amount of labour employed by 25 hours.

SUMMARY

KEY POINTS

Market Power in the Labour Market
(pp. 341–344)

- In competitive labour markets, unions obtain higher wages only at the expense of lower employment but they try to influence the demand for labour.
- Union workers earn 10 to 25 percent more than comparable nonunion workers.

Monopsony (pp. 344–346)

- A monopsony employs less labour and pays a wage rate below that in a competitive labour market.
- In bilateral monopoly, the wage rate is determined by bargaining.
- In monopsony, a minimum wage law can raise the wage rate and increase employment.

KEY TERMS

Bilateral monopoly, 345
Labour union, 341
Monopsony, 344
Rand Formula, 341

PROBLEMS

*1. A monopsony gold-mining firm operates in an isolated part of the Amazon basin. The table shows the firm's labour supply schedule (columns 1 and 2) and total product schedule (columns 2 and 3). The price of gold is $1.40 a grain.

Wage rate (dollars per day)	Number of workers	Quantity produced (grains per day)
5	0	0
6	1	10
7	2	25
8	3	45
9	4	60
10	5	70
11	6	75

a. What wage rate does the company pay?
b. How many workers does the gold mine hire?
c. What is the value of marginal product at the quantity of labour employed?

2. A monopsony logging firm operates in an isolated part of the Yukon. The table shows the firm's labour supply schedule (columns 1 and 2) and total product schedule (columns 2 and 3). The price of logs is $2 a tonne.

Wage rate (dollars per day)	Number of workers	Quantity produced (tonnes per day)
5	0	0
6	1	9
7	2	17
8	3	24
9	4	30
10	5	35
11	6	39
12	7	42

a. What wage rate does the company pay?
b. How many workers does the company hire?
c. What is the value of marginal product at the quantity of labour employed?

ECONOMIC INEQUALITY — CHAPTER 15

Rags and Riches

Ken Thomson's family fortune, Canada's largest, is estimated at more than $20 billion. The poorest of Canada's richest 100 families is worth a mere $275 million. ◆ In stark contrast to these richest Canadians are the poorest, who can be seen any evening on the park benches of our major cities and in the hostels of the Salvation Army. Here are men and women who have no visible wealth at all other than their clothes and a few meagre possessions. ◆ Most Canadians are not as poor as those who seek help from the Salvation Army, but there is a large amount of relative poverty in our nation. One in 10 families has an income that is so low that it spends close to half its income on rent. ◆ Why are some people exceedingly rich, while others are very poor and own almost nothing?

◆ In this chapter, we study economic inequality—its extent, its sources, and the things governments do to make it less extreme. We begin by looking at some facts about economic inequality in Canada today. We end, in *Reading Between the Lines*, by looking at the widening gap between the rich and the poor in Canada during the past 20 years.

After studying this chapter, you will be able to

- Describe the inequality in income and wealth and the trends in inequality in Canada
- Explain the features of the labour market that contribute to economic inequality
- Describe the methods and scale of government income redistribution

347

Measuring Economic Inequality

STATISTICS CANADA PROVIDES MEASURES OF economic inequality based on three definitions of income. **Market income** equals the wages, interest, rent, and profit earned in factor markets before paying income taxes. **Total income** equals *market income* plus cash payments to households by governments. **After-tax income** equals *total income* minus tax payments by households to governments.

The Distribution of After-Tax Income

Figure 15.1 shows the distribution of annual after-tax income across all households in Canada in 1998. Note that the *x*-axis measures income and the *y*-axis measures the percentage of households.

The most common household income, called the *mode* income, was received by the 10 percent of the households whose income fell between $10,000 and $14,999.

The income that separated the households into two equal groups, called the *median* income, was $33,227. One-half of Canadian households had an income greater than this amount, and the other half had an income less than this amount. The average household income in 1998, called the *mean* income, was $39,943.

You can see in Fig. 15.1 that the mode income is less than the median income, and the median income is less than the mean income. This feature of the distribution of income tells us that there are more households with low incomes than with high incomes. And some of the high incomes are very high.

The income distribution in Fig. 15.1 is called a *positively skewed* distribution, which means that it has a long tail of high values. This distribution's shape contrasts with a *bell-shaped* distribution like that of people's heights. In a bell-shaped distribution, the mean, median, and mode are all equal.

Another way of looking at the distribution of income is to measure the percentage of after-tax income received by each given percentage of households. Data are reported for five groups—called quintiles or one-fifth shares—each consisting of 20 percent of households.

Figure 15.2 shows the distribution based on

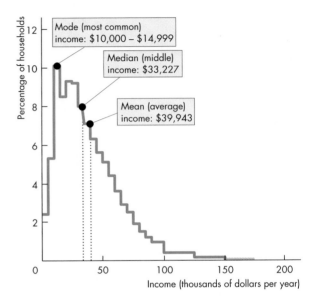

FIGURE 15.1 The Distribution of Income in Canada in 1998

Mode (most common) income: $10,000 – $14,999

Median (middle) income: $33,227

Mean (average) income: $39,943

The distribution of income is positively skewed. The mode (most common) income is less than the median (middle) income, which in turn is less than the mean (average) income. A very small percentage of households earn incomes in the range above $150,000 up to several million dollars a year—this part of the distribution is off the scale of this figure.

Source: Statistics Canada, Income in Canada, Catalogue 75–202–XIE.

these shares in 1998. The poorest 20 percent of households received 5 percent of after-tax income; the second-poorest 20 percent received 11 percent of after-tax income; the middle 20 percent received 16.7 percent of after-tax income; the second-highest 20 percent received 24.4 percent of after-tax income; and the highest 20 percent received 42.9 percent of after-tax income.

The distribution of after-tax income in Fig. 15.1 and the quintile shares in Fig. 15.2 tell us that income is distributed unequally. But we need a way of comparing the distribution of income in different periods and using different measures. A neat graphical tool called the Lorenz curve enables us to make such comparisons.

FIGURE 15.2 Canadian Quintile Shares in 1998

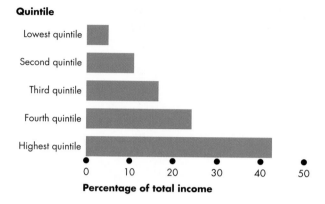

Households (percentage)	Income (percentage of total income)
Lowest 20	5.0
Second-lowest 20	11.0
Middle 20	16.7
Second-highest 20	24.4
Highest 20	42.9

The poorest 20 percent of households received 5 percent of after-tax income; the second-poorest 20 percent received 11 percent; the middle 20 percent received 16.7 percent; the second-highest 20 percent received 24.4 percent; and the highest 20 percent received 42.9 percent.

Source: Statistics Canada, *Income in Canada*, Catalogue 75–202–XIE.

The Income Lorenz Curve

The income **Lorenz curve** graphs the cumulative percentage of income against the cumulative percentage of households. Figure 15.3 shows the income Lorenz curve using the quintile shares from Fig. 15.2. The table shows the percentage of income in each quintile group. For example, row *A* tells us that the lowest quintile of households receives 5 percent of after-tax income. The table also shows the *cumulative* percentages of households and income. For example, row *B* tells us that the lowest two quintiles (lowest 40 percent) of households receive 16 percent of after-tax

FIGURE 15.3 The Income Lorenz Curve in 1998

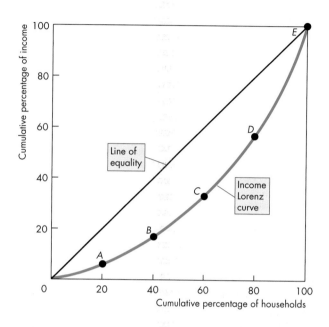

	Households		Income	
	Percentage	Cumulative percentage	Percentage	Cumulative percentage
A Lowest 20	20		5.0	5.0
B Second-lowest 20	40		11.0	16.0
C Middle 20	60		16.7	32.7
D Second-highest 20	80		24.4	56.1
E Highest 20	100		42.9	100.0

The cumulative percentage of income is graphed against the cumulative percentage of households. Points *A* through *E* on the Lorenz curve correspond to the rows of the table. If incomes were distributed equally, each 20 percent of households would receive 20 percent of income and the Lorenz curve would fall along the line of equality. The Lorenz curve shows that income is unequally distributed.

Source: Statistics Canada, *Income in Canada*, Catalogue 75–202–XIE.

income (5 percent for the lowest quintile and 11 percent for the second-lowest). The Lorenz curve graphs the cumulative income shares against the cumulative household percentages.

If income were distributed equally across all the households, each quintile would receive 20 percent of after-tax income and the cumulative percentages of income received by the cumulative percentages of households would fall along the straight line labelled "Line of equality" in Fig. 15.3. The actual distribution of income is shown by the curve labelled "Income Lorenz curve." The closer the Lorenz curve is to the line of equality, the more equal is the distribution.

The Distribution of Wealth

The distribution of wealth provides another way of measuring economic inequality. A household's wealth is the value of the things that it owns at a *point in time.* In contrast, income is the amount that the household receives over a given *period of time.*

Figure 15.4 shows the Lorenz curve for wealth in Canada in 1999. Median household wealth in that year was $64,000. Wealth is extremely unequally distributed, and for this reason, the data are grouped by unequal groups of households. The poorest 40 percent of households owns only 1.1 percent of total wealth (row A' in the table). The next poorest 10 percent owns only 2.8 percent of total wealth (row B') and the next poorest 10 percent owns only 4.7 percent of total wealth (row C'). So the poorest 60 percent of households owns only 8.6 percent of total wealth. At the other end of the wealth distribution, the wealthiest 10 percent of households owns 55.6 percent of total wealth (row G').

Figure 15.4 shows the income Lorenz curve (from Fig. 15.2) alongside the wealth Lorenz curve. You can see that the Lorenz curve for wealth is much farther away from the line of equality than the Lorenz curve for income is, which means that the distribution of wealth is much more unequal than the distribution of income.

Wealth Versus Income

We've seen that wealth is much more unequally distributed than income. Which distribution provides the better description of the degree of inequality? To answer this question, we need to think about the connection between wealth and income.

Wealth is a stock of assets, and income is the flow of earnings that results from the stock of wealth. Suppose that a person owns assets worth $1 million—has a wealth of $1 million. If the rate of return

FIGURE 15.4 Lorenz Curves for Income and Wealth

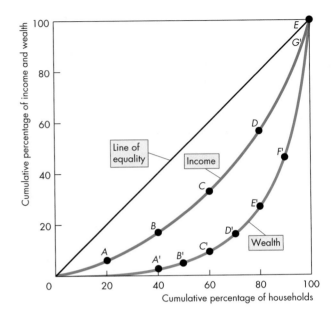

	Households		Wealth	
	Percentage	Cumulative percentage	Percentage	Cumulative percentage
A' Lowest 40	40	1.1	1.1
B' Next 10	50	2.8	3.9
C' Next 10	60	4.7	8.6
D' Next 10	70	7.4	16.0
E' Next 10	80	11.0	27.0
F' Next 10	90	17.4	44.4
G' Next 10	100	55.6	100.0

The cumulative percentage of wealth is graphed against the cumulative percentage of households. Points A' through G' on the Lorenz curve for wealth correspond to the rows of the table. By comparing the Lorenz curves for income and wealth, we can see that wealth is distributed much more unequally than income.

Source: Statistics Canada, *Income in Canada,* Catalogue 75–202–XIE.

on assets is 5 percent a year, then this person receives an income of $50,000 a year from those assets. We can describe this person's economic condition by using either the wealth of $1 million or the income of $50,000. When the rate of return is 5 percent a year, $1 million of wealth equals $50,000 of income in perpetuity. Wealth and income are just different ways of looking at the same thing.

But in Fig. 15.4, the distribution of wealth is more unequal than the distribution of income. Why? It is because the wealth data do not include the value of human capital, while the income data measure income from all forms of wealth, including human capital.

Table 15.1 illustrates the consequence of omitting human capital from the wealth data. Lee has twice the wealth and twice the income of Peter. But Lee's human capital is less than Peter's—$200,000 compared with $499,000. And Lee's income from human capital of $10,000 is less than Peter's income from human capital of $24,950. Lee's nonhuman capital is larger than Peter's—$800,000 compared with $1,000. And Lee's income from nonhuman capital of $40,000 is larger than Peter's income from nonhuman capital of $50.

When Lee and Peter are surveyed by Statistics Canada in a national wealth and income survey, their incomes are recorded as $50,000 and $25,000, respectively, which implies that Lee is twice as well off as Peter. And their tangible assets are recorded as $800,000 and $1,000, respectively, which implies that Lee is 800 times as wealthy as Peter.

Because the national survey of wealth excludes human capital, the income distribution is a more accurate measure of economic inequality than the wealth distribution.

Annual or Lifetime Income and Wealth?

A typical household's income changes over time. It starts out low, grows to a peak when the household's workers reach retirement age, and then falls after retirement. Also, a typical household's wealth changes over time. Like income, it starts out low, grows to a peak at the point of retirement, and falls after retirement.

Suppose we look at three households that have identical lifetime incomes. One household is young, one is middle-aged, and one is retired. The middle-aged household has the highest income and wealth, the retired household has the lowest, and the young household falls in the middle. The distributions of annual income and wealth in a given year are

TABLE 15.1	Capital, Wealth, and Income			
	Lee		**Peter**	
	Wealth	**Income**	**Wealth**	**Income**
Human capital	200,000	10,000	499,000	24,950
Other capital	800,000	40,000	1,000	50
Total	$1,000,000	$50,000	$500,000	$25,000

When wealth is measured to include the value of human capital as well as other forms of capital, the distribution of income and the distribution of wealth display the same degree of inequality.

unequal, but the distributions of lifetime income and wealth are equal. So some of the inequality in annual income arises because different households are at different stages in the life cycle. But we can see *trends* in the income distribution using annual income data.

Trends in Inequality

Figure 15.5 shows how the distribution of income has changed since 1980. The trends are as follows:

- The share of income received by the richest 20 percent of households has increased from 40.2 percent of total income in 1980 to 42.9 percent in 1998.
- The share of income received by the poorest 20 percent of households has remained constant at 5 percent of total income.
- The shares of income received by the other three groups have decreased, and the share of the third (the middle) 20 percent of households has decreased most from 18.2 percent in 1980 to 16.7 percent in 1998.

No one knows for sure why these trends have occurred, and a large amount of research has been done to try to explain them.

The most likely explanation is one that we'll explore and explain in the next section: Higher-income groups have gained and lower-income groups have lost because the technological change of the past few decades has increased the productivity of higher skilled workers and decreased the productivity of lower-skilled workers. Increased international mobility and competition is another possible explanation.

FIGURE 15.5   Trends in the Distribution of Income: 1980–1998

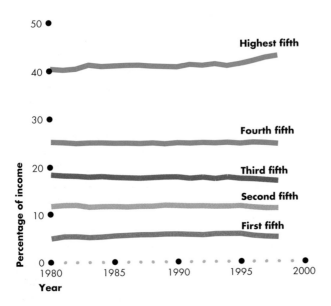

The distribution of income in Canada became more unequal in the 1980s and 1990s. The percentage of income earned by the highest fifth increased the most, and the third (middle) fifth lost the most.

Source: Statistics Canada, *Income Distribution by Size in Canada,* Catalogue 13–207–XPB.

Poverty

Families at the low end of the income distribution are so poor that they are considered to be living in poverty. **Poverty** is a state in which a family's income is too low to be able to buy the quantities of food, shelter, and clothing that are deemed necessary. Poverty is a relative concept. Millions of people living in Africa and Asia survive on incomes of less than $400 a year.

In Canada, poverty is measured in terms of a low-income cutoff. The **low-income cutoff** is the income level, determined separately for different types of families (for example, single persons, couples, one parent), that is selected such that families with incomes below that limit normally spend 54.7 percent or more of their income on food, shelter, and clothing. The low-income cutoffs currently used by Statistics Canada are based on family expenditure data for 1992. Statistics Canada measures the incidence of low income as the percentage of families whose income falls below a low-income cutoff.

Who Are the Rich and the Poor?

The highest incomes in Canada are earned by high-profile sports stars, pop stars, and television personalities and by less well known but very highly paid chief executives of large corporations. The lowest incomes are earned by people who scratch out a living doing seasonal work on farms. Aside from these extremes, what are the characteristics of people who earn high incomes and people who earn low incomes?

Six characteristics stand out:

- Source of income
- Household type
- Age of householder
- Number of children
- Education
- Labour force status

Source of Income   In general, a household that earns its income either by working or from investments is more likely to be in the higher income groups. A household that receives its income in the form of a transfer payment from the government is more likely to be poor. Perhaps surprisingly, households that receive a pension income are among those least likely to be poor.

Household Type   Statistics Canada classifies households into *family households* and *nonfamily households*. Most nonfamily households are single people who live alone. These households have higher incomes per person than do family households. Family households with two parents present are more likely to have a high income than are single-parent family households. And the most likely to be poor are households with a single female parent. Almost 50 percent of such households are living in poverty.

Age of Householder   The youngest and the oldest households have lower incomes than middle-aged households. Income from employment tends to peak in middle age. But income from financial assets increases with age, so older households are less likely to be in poverty than young households.

FIGURE 15.6   The Incidence of Low Income by Family Characteristics

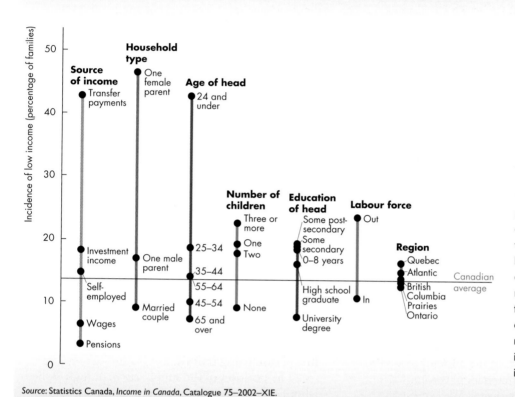

The vertical axis shows the incidence of low income—the percentage of families whose income falls below a low-income cutoff (the income level such that 54.7 percent of income is spent on food, shelter, and clothing). For Canada, on the average, 14 percent of families have incomes below the low-income cutoff. But that percentage varies depending on source of income, family type, sex and age of family head, number of children, education, and region of residence. Source of income, family type, and sex and age of family head are by far the most important factors influencing incidence of low income.

Source: Statistics Canada, *Income in Canada,* Catalogue 75–2002–XIE.

Number of Children   On the average, the greater the number of children in a household, the smaller is the income per person. And the greater the number of children, the more likely is the household to be living below the poverty level.

Education   Education makes a huge difference to a household's income and to the risk of poverty. A person who has not completed high school earns a fraction of a high school graduate's earnings. And a college or university degree brings a further large gain in income. Post-graduate and professional degrees take earnings even higher.

Labour Force Status   Households that are in the labour force, even if unemployed, tend to have higher incomes than those not in the labour force—either because they've retired or because they have become discouraged by a persistent failure to find a suitable job.

Figure 15.6 provides a quick visual summary of the characteristics that we've just described. The figure also shows the small effect that region of residence has on the incidence of low income.

The Sources of Economic Inequality

WE'VE DESCRIBED ECONOMIC INEQUALITY IN Canada. Our task now is to explain it. We began this task in Chapter 14 by learning about the forces that influence demand and supply in the markets for labour, capital, and land. We're now going to deepen our understanding of these forces.

Inequality arises from unequal labour market outcomes and from unequal ownership of capital. We'll begin by looking at labour markets and two of their features that contribute to differences in incomes:

- Human capital
- Discrimination

Human Capital

A clerk in a law firm earns less than a tenth of the amount earned by the lawyer he assists. An operating room assistant earns less than a tenth of the amount earned by the surgeon with whom she works. A bank teller earns less than a tenth of the amount earned by the bank's CEO. These differences in earnings arise from differences in human capital. We can explain these differences by using a model of competitive labour markets.

We'll study a model economy with two levels of human capital, which we'll call high-skilled labour and low-skilled labour. The low-skilled labour might represent the law clerk, the operating room assistant, or the bank teller, and the high-skilled labour might represent the lawyer, the surgeon, or the bank's CEO. We'll first look at the demand side of the markets for these two types of labour.

The Demand for High-Skilled and Low-Skilled Labour High-skilled workers can perform tasks that low-skilled labour would perform badly or perhaps could not perform at all. Imagine an untrained person doing open-heart surgery. High-skilled labour has a higher marginal revenue product than low-skilled labour. As we learned in Chapter 14, a firm's demand for labour curve is the same as the marginal revenue product of labour curve.

Figure 15.7(a) shows the demand curves for high-skilled and low-skilled labour. The demand curve for high-skilled labour is D_H, and that for low-skilled labour is D_L. At any given level of employment, firms are willing to pay a higher wage rate to a high-skilled worker than to a low-skilled worker. The gap between the two wage rates measures the marginal revenue product of skill. For example, at an employment level of 2,000 hours, firms are willing to pay $12.50 for a high-skilled worker and only $5 for a low-skilled worker, a difference of $7.50 an hour. Thus the marginal revenue product of skill is $7.50 an hour.

The Supply of High-Skilled and Low-Skilled Labour High-skilled labour has more human capital than low-skilled labour, and human capital is costly to acquire. The opportunity cost of acquiring human capital includes actual expenditures on such things as tuition and room and board and also costs in the form of lost or reduced earnings while the skill is being acquired. When a person goes to school full-time, that cost is the total earnings forgone. But some people acquire skills on the job—on-the-job training. Usually, a worker undergoing on-the-job training is paid a lower wage than one doing a comparable job but not undergoing training. In such a case, the cost of acquiring the skill is the difference between the wage paid to a person not being trained and that paid to a person being trained.

The position of the supply curve of high-skilled labour reflects the cost of acquiring human capital. Figure 15.7(b) shows two supply curves: one for high-skilled labour and the other for low-skilled labour. The supply curve for high-skilled labour is S_H, and that for low-skilled labour is S_L.

The high-skilled labour supply curve lies above the low-skilled labour supply curve. The vertical distance between the two supply curves is the compensation that high-skilled labour requires for the cost of acquiring the skill. For example, suppose that the quantity of low-skilled labour supplied is 2,000 hours at a wage rate of $5 an hour. This wage rate compensates the low-skilled workers mainly for their time on the job. Consider next the supply of high-skilled labour. To induce 2,000 hours of high-skilled labour to be supplied, firms must pay a wage rate of $8.50 an hour. This wage rate for high-skilled labour is higher than that for low-skilled labour because high-skilled workers must be compensated not only for the time on the job but also for the time and other costs of acquiring the skill.

Wage Rates of High-Skilled and Low-Skilled Labour To work out the wage rates of high-skilled and low-skilled labour, we have to bring together the effects of skill on the demand for and supply of labour.

FIGURE 15.7   Skill Differentials

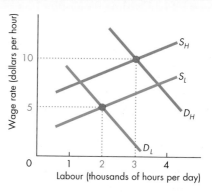

(a) Demand for high-skilled
and low-skilled labour

(b) Supply of high-skilled
and low-skilled labour

(c) Markets for high-skilled
and low-skilled labour

Part (a) illustrates the marginal revenue product of skill. Low-skilled workers have a marginal revenue product that gives rise to the demand curve D_L. High-skilled workers have a higher marginal revenue product than low-skilled labour, so the demand curve for high-skilled labour, D_H, lies to the right of D_L. The vertical distance between these two curves is the marginal revenue product of the skill.

Part (b) shows the effects of the cost of acquiring skills on the supply of labour. The supply curve of low-skilled labour is S_L. The supply curve of high-skilled labour is S_H. The vertical distance between these two curves is the required compensation for the cost of acquiring a skill.

Part (c) shows the equilibrium employment and the wage differential. Low-skilled workers earn $5 an hour, and 2,000 hours of low-skilled labour are employed. High-skilled workers earn $10 an hour, and 3,000 hours of high-skilled labour are employed. The wage rate for high-skilled labour always exceeds that for low-skilled labour.

Figure 15.7(c) shows the demand curves and the supply curves for high-skilled and low-skilled labour. These curves are the same as those plotted in parts (a) and (b). Equilibrium occurs in the market for low-skilled labour where the supply and demand curves for low-skilled labour intersect. The equilibrium wage rate is $5 an hour, and the quantity of low-skilled labour employed is 2,000 hours. Equilibrium in the market for high-skilled labour occurs where the supply and demand curves for high-skilled labour intersect. The equilibrium wage rate is $10 an hour, and the quantity of high-skilled labour employed is 3,000 hours.

As you can see in part (c), the equilibrium wage rate of high-skilled labour is higher than that of low-skilled labour. There are two reasons why this occurs: First, high-skilled labour has a higher marginal revenue product than low-skilled labour, so at a given wage rate, the quantity of high-skilled labour demanded exceeds that of low-skilled labour. Second, skills are costly to acquire, so at a given wage rate, the quantity of high-skilled labour supplied is less than that of low-skilled labour. The wage differential (in

this case, $5 an hour) depends on both the marginal revenue product of the skill and the cost of acquiring it. The higher the marginal revenue product of the skill, the larger is the vertical distance between the demand curves. The more costly it is to acquire a skill, the larger is the vertical distance between the supply curves. The higher the marginal revenue product of the skill and the more costly it is to acquire, the larger is the wage differential between high-skilled and low-skilled labour.

Do Education and Training Pay? Rates of return on high school and college education have been estimated to be in the range of 5 to 10 percent a year after allowing for inflation, which suggests that a university or college degree is a better investment than almost any other that a person can undertake.

Inequality Explained by Human Capital Differences Human capital differences help to explain some of the inequality that we've described above. They also help to explain some of the trends in the distribution of income that occurred during the 1990s.

You saw in Fig. 15.6 that better educated, middle-aged, two-parent households are more likely to have a high income than other household types. Human capital differences are correlated with these household characteristics. Education contributes directly to human capital. Age contributes indirectly to human capital because older workers have more experience than younger workers. Human capital differences can also explain a small part of the inequality associated with sex. A larger proportion of men than women have completed a college or university degree. These differences in education levels have disappeared in the current generation and for the population as a whole they are becoming smaller. But they have not yet been eliminated.

Interruptions to a career reduce the effectiveness of job experience in contributing to human capital. Historically, job interruptions have been more common for women than for men because women's careers have been interrupted for bearing and raising children. This factor is a possible source of lower wages, on the average, for women. Although maternity leave and day-care facilities are making career interruptions for women less common, job interruptions remain a problem for many women.

Trends in Inequality Explained by Human Capital Trends   You saw in Fig. 15.5 that high-income households have earned an increasing share of after-tax income while low-income households have earned a decreasing share. Human capital differences are a possible explanation for this trend, and Fig. 15.8 illustrates this explanation. The supply of low-skilled labour (part a) and that of high-skilled labour (part b) are S, and initially, the demand in each market is D_0. The low-skilled wage rate is $5 an hour, and the high-skilled wage rate is $10 an hour.

Information technologies such as computers and laser scanners are *substitutes* for low-skilled labour: they perform tasks that previously were performed by low-skilled labour. The introduction of these technologies has decreased the demand for low-skilled labour (part a), decreased the number of low-skilled jobs, and lowered the wage rate of low-skilled workers.

These same technologies require high-skilled labour to design, program, and run them. High-skilled labour and the information technologies are *complements*. So the introduction of these technologies has increased the demand for high-skilled labour (part b), increased the number of high-skilled jobs, and raised the wage rate of high-skilled workers.

FIGURE 15.8   Explaining the Trend in Income Distribution

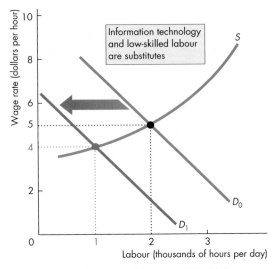

(a) A decrease in demand for low-skilled labour

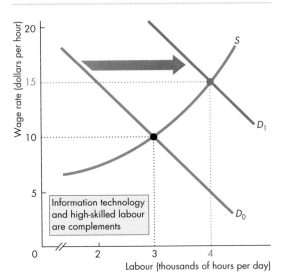

(b) An increase in demand for high-skilled labour

Low-skilled labour in part (a) and information technologies are substitutes. When these technologies were introduced, the demand for low-skilled labour decreased and the quantity of this type of labour and its wage rate decreased. High-skilled labour in part (b) and information technologies are complements. When these technologies were introduced, the demand for high-skilled labour increased and the quantity of this type of labour and its wage rate increased.

Discrimination

Human capital differences can explain some of the economic inequality that we observe. But it can't explain all of it. Discrimination is another possible source of inequality.

Suppose that females and males have identical abilities as investment advisors. Figure 15.9 shows the supply curves of females, S_F (in part a), and of males, S_M (in part b). The marginal revenue product of investment advisors shown by the two curves labelled MRP in parts (a) and (b) is the same for both groups.

If everyone is free of sex-based prejudice, the market determines a wage rate of $40,000 a year for investment advisors. But if the customers are prejudiced against women, this prejudice is reflected in the wage rate and employment.

Suppose that the perceived marginal revenue product of the females, when discriminated against, is MRP_{DA}. Suppose that the perceived marginal revenue product for males, the group discriminated in favour of, is MRP_{DF}. With these MRP curves, females earn $20,000 a year and only 1,000 females work as investment advisors. Males earn $60,000 a year, and 3,000 of them work as investment advisors.

Counteracting Forces Economists disagree about whether prejudice actually causes wage differentials, and one line of reasoning implies that it does not. In the example you've just studied, customers who buy from men pay a higher service charge for investment advice than do the customers who buy from women. This price difference acts as an incentive to encourage people who are prejudiced to buy from the people against whom they are prejudiced. This force could be strong enough to eliminate the effects of discrimination altogether.

Suppose, as is true in manufacturing, that a firm's customers never meet its workers. If such a firm discriminates against women (or against visible minorities), it can't compete with firms who hire these groups because its costs are higher than those of the unprejudiced firms. Only firms that do not discriminate survive in a competitive industry.

Whether because of discrimination or for some other reason, women on average do earn lower incomes than men. Another possible source of women's lower wage rates arises from differences in the relative degree of specialization of women and men.

FIGURE 15.9 Discrimination

(a) Women

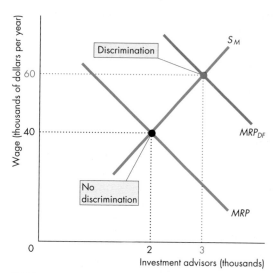

(b) Men

With no discrimination, the wage rate is $40,000 a year and 2,000 of each group are hired. With discrimination against women, the marginal revenue product curve in part (a) is MRP_{DA} and that in part (b) is MRP_{DF}. The wage rate for women falls to $20,000 a year, and only 1,000 are employed. The wage rate for men rises to $60,000 a year, and 3,000 are employed.

Differences in the Degree of Specialization

Couples must choose how to allocate their time between working for a wage and doing jobs in the home, such as cooking, cleaning, shopping, organizing vacations, and, most important, bearing and raising children. Let's look at the choices of Bob and Sue.

Bob might specialize in earning an income and Sue in taking care of the home. Or Sue might specialize in earning an income and Bob in taking care of the home. Or both of them might earn an income and share home production jobs.

The allocation they choose depends on their preferences and on the earning potential of each of them. The choice of an increasing number of households is for each person to diversify between earning an income and doing some home chores. But in most households, Bob will specialize in earning an income and Sue will both earn an income and bear a larger share of the task of running the home. With this allocation, Bob will probably earn more than Sue. If Sue devotes time and effort to ensuring Bob's mental and physical well-being, the quality of Bob's market labour will be higher than it would be if he were diversified. If the roles were reversed, Sue would be able to supply market labour that earns more than Bob.

To test whether the degree of specialization accounts for earnings differences between the sexes, economists have compared the incomes of never-married men and women. They have found that, on the average, with equal amounts of human capital, the wages of these two groups are the same.

We've examined some sources of inequality in the labour market. Let's now look at the way inequality arises from unequal ownership of capital.

Unequal Ownership of Capital

You've seen that inequality in wealth (excluding human capital) is much greater than inequality in income. This inequality arises from saving and transfers of wealth from one generation to the next.

The higher a household's income, the more that household tends to save and pass on to the next generation. Saving is not always a source of increased inequality. If a household saves to redistribute an uneven income over its life cycle and enable consumption to fluctuate less than income, saving decreases inequality. If a lucky generation that has a high income saves a large part of that income and leaves capital to a succeeding generation that is unlucky, this act of saving also decreases the degree of inequality. But two features of intergenerational transfers of wealth lead to increased inequality: People can't inherit debt, and marriage tends to concentrate wealth.

Can't Inherit Debt Although a person may die in debt—with negative wealth—a debt can't be forced onto the next generation of a family. So inheritance only adds to a future generation's wealth; inheritance cannot decrease wealth.

Most people inherit nothing or a very small amount. A few people inherit an enormous fortune. As a result, intergenerational transfers make the distribution of income persistently more unequal than the distribution of ability and job skills. A household that is poor in one generation is more likely to be poor in the next. A household that is wealthy in one generation is more likely to be wealthy in the next. And marriage reinforces this tendency.

Marriage and Wealth Concentration People tend to marry within their own socioeconomic class—a phenomenon called *assortative mating*. In everyday language, "like attracts like." Although there is a good deal of folklore that "opposites attract," perhaps such Cinderella tales appeal to us because they are so rare in reality. Wealthy people seek wealthy partners.

Because of assortative mating, wealth becomes more concentrated in a small number of families and the distribution of wealth becomes more unequal.

REVIEW QUIZ

1 What role does human capital play in accounting for income inequality?
2 What role might discrimination play in accounting for income inequality?
3 What are the possible reasons for income inequality by sex and race?
4 What are the possible reasons for income inequality by age group?
5 Does inherited wealth make the distribution of income less equal or more equal?
6 Why does wealth inequality persist across generations?

Next, we're going to see how taxes and government programs redistribute income and decrease the degree of economic inequality.

Income Redistribution

THE THREE MAIN WAYS IN WHICH GOVERNMENTS in Canada redistribute income are

- Income taxes
- Income maintenance programs
- Subsidized services

Income Taxes

Income taxes may be progressive, regressive, or proportional. A **progressive income tax** is one that taxes income at an average rate that increases with the level of income. The **average tax rate** is the percentage of income paid in taxes. A **regressive income tax** is one that taxes income at an average rate that decreases with the level of income. A **proportional income tax** (also called a *flat-rate income tax*) is one that taxes income at a constant rate, regardless of the level of income.

The income tax rates that apply in Canada are composed of two parts: federal and provincial taxes. The highest income tax rates are in Quebec and the lowest are in Alberta. There is variety in the detailed tax arrangements in the individual provinces but the tax system, at both the federal and provincial levels, is progressive.

The poorest Canadians pay no income tax. Even those who earn $30,000 a year, pay a very low rate of income tax. Those whose incomes are $50,000 a year pay about 21 percent of their income in income taxes; those whose incomes are $100,000 a year pay about 28 percent in income tax; and as incomes increase, the average tax rate increases to 45 percent or higher.

Income Maintenance Programs

Three main types of programs redistribute income by making direct payments (in cash, services, or vouchers) to people in the lower part of the income distribution. They are

- Social security programs
- Employment insurance program
- Welfare programs

Social Security Programs Four programs—Old Age Security (OAS), Guaranteed Income Supplement (GIS), the Allowance (for spouses of low-income OAS pensioners), and the Allowance for the Survivor (AS)—ensure a minimum level of income for senior citizens. Monthly cash payments to retired or disabled workers or their surviving spouses are paid for by compulsory payroll taxes on both employers and employees. In December 2002, the maximum OAS was $443.99 a month, the maximum GIS for a single person was $533.99, the maximum Allowance was $797.14, and the maximum AS was $880.06.

Employment Insurance Program To provide an income to unemployed workers, the federal government has established an unemployment compensation program. The Employment Insurance program is funded by employee and employer contributions, and after a qualifying period the worker is entitled to receive a benefit if he or she becomes unemployed. The maximum unemployment benefit is $413 a week or 55 percent of gross weekly earnings over the previous 20 weeks.

Welfare Programs Other welfare programs provide income maintenance for families and persons. They are

1. Canada Assistance Plan, a plan shared equally by the federal and provincial governments that gives financial assistance to families and individuals who are in need, regardless of the cause; the assistance includes food, shelter, fuel, utilities, family supplies, items required to carry on a trade, certain welfare services, and health and social services
2. Family Supplement and Canada Child Tax Benefit programs, designed to help families who have inadequate financial support
3. Canada/Quebec Pension Plans, funded equally by employee and employer contributions, provide retirement benefits, survivor benefits, disability benefits, and death benefits
4. Workers' Compensation, a provincial program funded by employers, designed to provide financial assistance as well as medical care and rehabilitation of workers injured at work

Subsidized Services

A great deal of redistribution takes place in Canada through the provision of subsidized services, which is the provision of goods and services by the government at prices below the cost of production. The taxpayers who consume these goods and services receive a transfer in kind from the taxpayers who do not consume them. The two most important areas in which this form of redistribution takes place are education—both kindergarten through Grade 12 and college and university—and health care.

Canadian students enrolled in the universities in Ontario pay annual tuition fees of around $3,500. The cost of one year's education at one of these universities is about $17,500. Thus families with a member enrolled in these institutions receive a benefit from the government of about $14,000 a year. Those with several college or university students receive proportionately higher benefits.

Government provision of health care to all residents has brought high-quality and high-cost health care to millions of people who earn too little to buy such services themselves. As a result, this program has contributed to reducing inequality.

The Scale of Income Redistribution

To determine the scale of income redistribution, we need to compare the distribution of *market income* with the distribution of *after-tax income*. The data available on benefits exclude the value of subsidized services (such as the value of university education and health care services), so the resulting distribution might understate the total amount of redistribution from the rich to the poor.

Figure 15.10 shows the scale of redistribution based on the calculations just described. In part (a), the blue Lorenz curve describes the market distribution of income and the green Lorenz curve shows the distribution of income after all taxes and benefits. (The Lorenz curve based on *total income*—market income plus transfer payments from governments—lies between these two curves.)

The distribution after taxes and benefits is much less unequal than the market distribution. In 1998, the lowest 20 percent of households received only 0.7 percent of market income but 5 percent of after-tax income. The highest 20 percent of households received 50.8 percent of market income but only 42.9 percent of after-tax income.

Figure 15.10(b) highlights the percentage of total income redistributed among the five groups. The share of total income received by the lowest three quintiles (60 percent) of households increased. The share of total income received by the fourth quintile fell slightly. And the share of total income received by the highest quintile fell by almost 8 percent of total income.

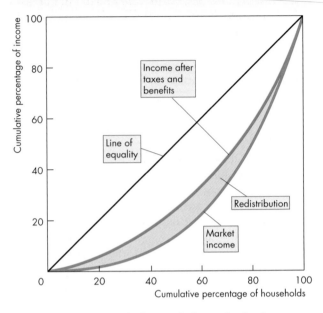

FIGURE 15.10 Income Redistribution

(a) Income distribution before and after redistribution

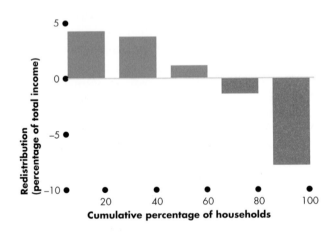

(b) The scale of redistribution

Redistribution reduces the degree of inequality that the market generates. In 1998, the 20 percent of households with the lowest incomes received net benefits that increased their share from 0.7 percent of market income to 5 percent of after-tax income. The 20 percent of households with the highest incomes paid taxes that decreased their share from 50.8 percent of market income to 42.9 percent of income after taxes and redistribution.

Source: Statistics Canada, Income in Canada, Catalogue 75–202–XIE.

The Big Tradeoff

The redistribution of income creates what has been called the **big tradeoff**, a tradeoff between equity and efficiency. The big tradeoff arises because redistribution uses scarce resources and weakens incentives.

A dollar collected from a rich person does not translate into a dollar received by a poor person. Some of the dollar collected gets used up in the process of redistribution. Tax-collecting agencies such as the Canada Customs and Revenue Agency and welfare-administering agencies (as well as tax accountants and lawyers) use skilled labour, computers, and other scarce resources to do their work. The bigger the scale of redistribution, the greater is the opportunity cost of administering it.

But the cost of collecting taxes and making welfare payments is a small part of the total cost of redistribution. A bigger cost arises from the inefficiency —deadweight loss—of taxes and benefits. Greater equality can be achieved only by taxing productive activities such as work and saving. Taxing people's income from their work and saving lowers the after-tax income they receive. This lower after-tax income makes them work and save less, which in turn results in smaller output and less consumption not only for the rich who pay the taxes but also for the poor who receive the benefits.

It is not only taxpayers who face weaker incentives to work. Benefit recipients also face weaker incentives. In fact, under the welfare arrangements that prevail in Canada today, the weakest incentives to work are those faced by households that benefit most from welfare. When a welfare recipient gets a job, benefits are withdrawn and eligibility for support is withdrawn. In effect, these households face a marginal tax of more than 100 percent on their earnings. This arrangement locks poor households in a welfare trap.

So the scale and methods of income redistribution must pay close attention to the incentive effects of taxes and benefits.

A Major Welfare Challenge

The poorest people in Canada are women who have not completed high school, have a child (or children), and live without a partner. But all single mothers present a major welfare challenge. First, their numbers are large. There are approximately one million single mothers in Canada today. Second, their economic plight and the economic prospects for their children are serious.

Janet Peterson and her four children aged 3 to 13 are one example. Janet has a serious physical disability. She receives a social assistance cheque each month for $1,286, or $15,432 a year. The low-income cutoff for a family of five is $30,910. So Janet and her children live in severe poverty. She spends $625 a month on rent, $400 on food, and the rest on gas, hydro, the phone, and transportation. To provide Janet Peterson (and the other million single mothers) with an income that matches the low-income cutoff would cost more than $10 billion a year.

Janet Peterson has a physical disability that makes it unlikely that she could work. Many other single mothers are in this situation. But this is not the typical case. Most single mothers are physically fit and are capable of working. And some of them are well educated and therefore can earn a high wage rate. Even those single mothers who have not completed high school are capable of either attending school or getting a job.

For physically fit single mothers, the long-term solution to their problem is education and on-the-job training—acquiring human capital. The short-term solution is welfare. But welfare must be designed to minimize the disincentive to pursue the long-term goal. This is the challenge in designing an adequate welfare program.

REVIEW QUIZ

1 How do governments in Canada redistribute income?
2 How large is the scale of redistribution in Canada?
3 What is one of the major welfare challenges today and how is it being tackled in Canada?

◆ We've examined economic inequality in Canada, and we've seen how inequality arises. And we've seen that inequality has increased since 1980. *Reading Between the Lines* on pp. 362–363 looks at the increasing economic inequality in Canada's major cities.

Your task in the following chapters is to look more closely at government actions that modify the outcome of the market economy. We look at sources of market failure and the ways in which government actions aim to overcome it. We also look at what has been called the *political marketplace* and the potential for it to fail too.

Trends in Inequality

NATIONAL POST, DECEMBER 14, 2000

Rich and poor growing fastest in Edmonton

The income gap between rich and poor neighbourhoods in Canada's eight largest cities is widening, according to a Statistics Canada report released yesterday.

The 15-year study, based on censuses between 1980 and 1995, indicates the gap has grown the most quickly in Edmonton, by 29.8% — mostly because high-income earners in Alberta's capital tend to cluster in the same areas. Toronto closely follows with a 28.7% increase, mostly because the rich in Canada's largest city are growing richer.

The income gap in Calgary and Winnipeg increased by 20% or more.

Vancouver neighbourhoods showed the smallest increase, at 7.9%. The study said that unlike Edmonton, Calgary, Winnipeg and Quebec City, high-income earners in Vancouver are not concentrated in the same neighbourhoods. But, like Toronto and Montreal, the West Coast city's income gap is still rising.

The report reveals inequality in family incomes between neighbourhoods rose in all cities. Real average earnings fell, sometimes dramatically, in low-income neighbourhoods in vir-

tually all cities while rising moderately in most higher-income neighbourhoods, led by residents living in Toronto, Winnipeg and the Ottawa-Hull region. Only Vancouver marked a decrease in income levels among richer neighbourhoods.

Changes in employment and unemployment patterns were cited as the main reason for the increase, with unemployment the most prevalent in lower-income neighbourhoods.

"The commonly accepted explanation is that it's related to technological change, with increased technology the demand for highly skilled workers rose and the demand for lower skilled workers fell so their wages dropped," said Garnett Picot, director-general of the analytical studies branch at Statistics Canada and an author of the study.

Mr. Picot said the income gap may have improved recently as provincial and local economies flourished. "But I am quite certain it is not reversing the employment issues that we see in the low-income communities."

New census data will not be available until next year. ...

National Post, Financial Post.

Essence of the Story

■ A Statistics Canada report published in 2000 says the income gap between rich and poor neighbourhoods in Canada's eight largest cities widened between 1980 and 1995.

■ The income gap increased in all cities.

■ The gap grew the most in Edmonton, with Toronto close behind.

■ The gap grew least in Vancouver.

■ Garnett Picot of Statistics Canada said technological change has increased the demand for highly skilled workers and decreased the demand for lower skilled workers.

Economic Analysis

■ In this chapter, we describe the degree of inequality by using quintile income shares and making a Lorenz curve from those numbers.

■ This news article uses the ratio of the average income of the highest 5 percent to the average income of the lowest 5 percent as a measure of inequality.

■ Figure 1 shows this ratio for the eight cities covered by the reported research in 1980 and 1995.

■ The blue bars show the numbers for 1980 and the red bars for 1995.

■ You can see that this measure indicates that the degree of inequality increased in all regions between 1980 and 1995.

■ Figures 2 and 3 illustrate Garnett Picot's explanation for the widening income gap (which is also the explanation provided in this chapter).

■ In Fig. 2, the demand for low-skilled labour in 1980 is D_{80} and the supply of labour is S_{80}. By 1995, demand had increased to D_{95} and supply had increased to S_{95}.

■ Because supply increased by more than demand, the quantity of labour increased but the wage rate fell.

■ In Fig. 3, the demand for high-skilled labour in 1980 is D_{80} and the supply of labour is S_{80}. By 1995, demand had increased to D_{95} and supply had increased to S_{95}, and because demand increased by more than supply, the quantity of labour increased and the wage rate rose.

■ The supply of high-skilled labour increased slowly because the new technologies require a higher level of education to complement them.

■ The demand for high-skilled labour increased by a large amount because the new technologies that have changed the structure of the economy have increased the value of marginal product of highly educated workers.

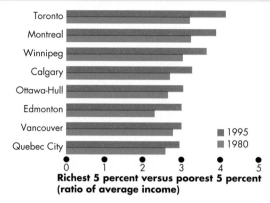

Figure 1 Income gaps in eight cities

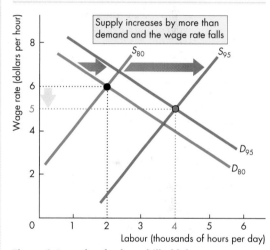

Figure 2 A market for low-skilled labour

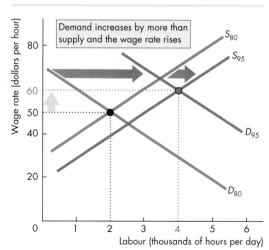

Figure 3 A market for high-skilled labour

363

SUMMARY

KEY POINTS

Measuring Economic Inequality (pp. 348–353)

- In 1998, the mode after-tax income was in the range between $10,000 and $14,999 a year, the median after-tax income was $33,227, and the mean after-tax income was $39,943.
- The income distribution is positively skewed.
- The poorest 20 percent of households received 5 percent of total income, and the wealthiest 20 percent received 42.9 percent of total income.
- Wealth is distributed more unequally than income because the wealth data exclude the value of human capital.
- Since 1980, the share of income received by the richest 20 percent of households has increased, the share of the poorest 20 percent has remained constant, and the shares of income received by the other three groups of households have decreased.
- Source of income, household type, age of householder, number of children, education, and labour market status all influence household income.

The Sources of Economic Inequality (pp. 354–358)

- Inequality arises from differences in human capital.
- Inequality might arise from discrimination.
- Inequality between men and women might arise from differences in the degree of specialization.
- Intergenerational transfers of wealth lead to increased inequality because people can't inherit debt, and assortative mating tends to concentrate wealth.

Income Redistribution (pp. 359–361)

- Governments redistribute income through progressive income taxes, income maintenance programs, and subsidized services.

- Redistribution increases the share of total income received by the lowest three quintiles (60 percent) of households and decreases the share of total income received by the highest quintile. The share of the fourth quintile falls slightly.
- Because the redistribution of income weakens incentives, it creates a tradeoff between equity and efficiency.
- Effective redistribution seeks to support the long-term solution to low income, which is education and job training—acquiring human capital.

KEY FIGURES

Figure 15.1   The Distribution of Income in Canada in 1998, 348

Figure 15.4   Lorenz Curves for Income and Wealth, 350

Figure 15.5   Trends in the Distribution of Income: 1980–1998, 352

Figure 15.6   The Incidence of Low Income by Family Characteristics, 353

Figure 15.7   Skill Differentials, 355

Figure 15.8   Explaining the Trend in Income Distribution, 356

Figure 15.9   Discrimination, 357

Figure 15.10   Income Redistribution, 360

KEY TERMS

Average tax rate, 359
After-tax income, 348
Big tradeoff, 361
Low-income cutoff, 352
Lorenz curve, 349
Market income, 348
Poverty, 352
Progressive income tax, 359
Proportional income tax, 359
Regressive income tax, 359
Total income, 348

PROBLEMS

*1. The table shows income shares in the United States in 2000.

Households (percentage)	Income (percent of total)
Lowest 20	4.8
Second-lowest 20	10.5
Third-lowest 20	15.8
Fourth-lowest 20	22.8
Highest 20	46.1

a. Draw a Lorenz curve for the United States in 2000 and compare it with that for Canada in 1998 shown in Fig. 15.3.

b. Was Canadian income distributed more equally or less equally than that in the United States?

c. Can you think of some reasons for the differences in the distribution of income in Canada and the United States?

2. The table shows income shares in Sweden in 1992.

Households (percentage)	Income (percent of total)
Lowest 20	6.7
Second-lowest 20	12.2
Third-lowest 20	17.6
Fourth-lowest 20	24.5
Highest 20	39.0

a. Draw the Lorenz curve for income in Sweden in 1992.

b. Was income distributed more equally or less equally in Canada in 1998 than in Sweden in 1992?

c. Use the information provided in problem 1 on the distribution of income in the United States in 2000. Was income distributed more equally or less equally in the United States in 2000 than in Sweden in 1992?

d. Can you think of some reasons for the differences in the distribution of income in Canada and Sweden?

*3. The following figure shows the demand for and supply of low-skilled labour.

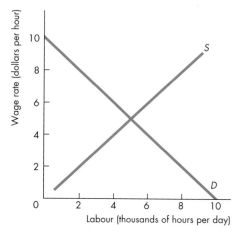

High-skilled workers have twice the marginal product of low-skilled workers. (The marginal product at each employment level is twice the marginal product of a low-skilled worker.) But the cost of acquiring the skill adds $2 an hour to the wage that must be offered to attract high-skilled labour. What is

a. The wage rate of low-skilled labour?

b. The quantity of low-skilled labour employed?

c. The wage rate of high-skilled labour?

d. The quantity of high-skilled labour employed?

4. The following figure shows the demand for and supply of low-skilled labour.

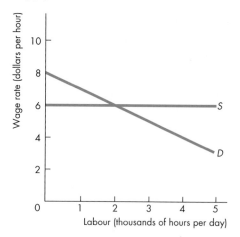

The marginal productivity of a high-skilled worker is $10 an hour greater than that of a low-skilled worker. (The marginal product at each employment level is $10 greater than that of a low-skilled worker.) The cost of acquiring the skill adds $6 an hour to the wage that must be offered to attract high-skilled labour.

a. What is the wage rate of low-skilled labour?

b. What is the quantity of low-skilled labour employed?

c. What is the wage rate of high-skilled labour?

d. What is the quantity of high-skilled labour employed?

e. Why does the wage rate of a high-skilled worker exceed that of a low-skilled worker by exactly the cost of acquiring the skill?

*5. The table shows the distribution of market income in Canada in 1998.

Households (percentage)	Market income (percent of total)
Lowest 20	0.7
Second-lowest 20	7.2
Third-lowest 20	15.5
Fourth-lowest 20	25.8
Highest 20	50.8

a. What is market income?

b. Draw the Lorenz curve for the distribution of market income.

c. Compare the distribution of market income with the distribution of after-tax income shown in Fig. 15.3. Which distribution is more unequal and why?

6. Use the information provided in problem 5 and in Fig. 15.3.

a. What is the percentage of market income that is redistributed from the highest income group?

b. What are the percentages of market income that are redistributed to the lower income groups?

c. Describe the effects of increasing the amount of income redistribution in Canada to the point at which the lowest income group receives 15 percent of after-tax income and the highest income group receives 30 percent of after-tax income.

CRITICAL THINKING

1. Study *Reading Between the Lines* on pp. 362–363 and then

a. Describe the main facts about the changes in the distribution of income in Canada reported in the news article.

b. In which cities is the distribution of income more unequal or less unequal?

c. Why, according to the news article, has the gap between the rich and the poor widened?

d. Do you think the explanation for the widening gap between high and low incomes explains the regional differences? Explain why or why not using the ideas that you have learned in this chapter.

e. What policy issues are raised by the news article?

f. How do you think the tax system and the welfare system should be changed to influence the distribution of after-tax income in Canada today?

WEB EXERCISES

1. Use the link on the Parkin–Bade Web site to obtain data on income distribution among major league baseball players. Then

a. Describe the main facts about the income distribution of major league players.

b. Compare the income distribution of these players with the income distribution of Canada.

c. Which is more unequal?

d. What is the problem with inequality?

2. Use the link on the Parkin–Bade Web site to download the World Bank's Deininger and Squire Data Set on income distribution in a large number of countries.

a. Which country in the data set has the most unequal distribution?

b. Which country in the data set has the most equal distribution?

c. Can you think of reasons that might explain the differences in income distribution in the two countries you've identified?

UNDERSTANDING FACTOR MARKETS

For Whom?

During the past 35 years, the rich have been getting richer and the poor poorer. This trend is new. From the end of World War II until 1965, the poor got richer at a faster pace than the rich and the gap between rich and poor narrowed a bit. What are the forces that generate these trends? The answer to this question is the forces of demand and supply in factor markets. These forces determine wages, interest rates, and the prices of land and natural resources. These forces also determine people's incomes. ◆ The three categories of resources are human, capital, and natural. Human resources include labour, human capital, and entrepreneurship. The income of labour and human capital depends on wage rates and employment levels, which are determined in labour markets. The income from capital depends on interest rates and the amount of capital, which are determined in capital markets. The income from natural resources depends on prices and quantities that are determined in natural resource markets. Only the return to entrepreneurship is not determined directly in a market. That return is normal profit plus economic profit, and it depends on how successful each entrepreneur is in the business that he or she runs. ◆ The chapters in this part study the forces at play in factor markets and explain how those forces have led to changes in the distribution of income. ◆ The overview of all the factor markets in Chapter 14 explained how the demand for factors of production results from the profit-maximizing decisions of firms. You studied these decisions from a different angle in Chapters 9–13, where you learned how firms choose their profit-maximizing output and price. Chapter 14 explained how a firm's profit-maximizing decisions determine its demand for factors of production. It also explained how factor supply decisions are made and how equilibrium in factor markets determines factor prices and the incomes of owners of factors of production. ◆ Some of the biggest incomes earned by superstars are a surplus that we call economic rent. ◆ Chapter 14 used labour resources and the labour market as its main example. But it also looked at some special features of capital markets and natural resource markets. ◆ Chapter 15 studied the distribution of income. This chapter took you right back to the fundamentals of economics and answered one of the big economic questions: Who gets to consume the goods and services that are produced? ◆ Many outstanding economists have advanced our understanding of factor markets and the role they play in helping to resolve the conflict between the demands of humans and the resources available. One of them is Thomas Robert Malthus, whom you can meet on the following page. You can also enjoy the insights of Janet Currie, a professor of economics at UCLA and a prominent contemporary Canadian labour economist.

Running Out of Resources

THE ECONOMIST

THOMAS ROBERT MALTHUS *(1766–1834), an English clergyman and economist, was an extremely influential social scientist. In his best-selling* An Essay on the Principle of Population, *published in 1798, he predicted that population growth would outstrip food production and said that wars, famine, and disease were inevitable unless population growth was held in check by what he called "moral restraint." By "moral restraint," he meant marrying at a late age and living a celibate life. He married at the age of 38 a wife of 27, marriage ages that he recommended for others. Malthus's ideas were regarded as too radical in their day. And they led Thomas Carlyle, a contemporary thinker, to dub economics the "dismal science." But the ideas of Malthus had a profound influence on Charles Darwin, who got the key idea that led him to the theory of natural selection from reading* An Essay on the Principle of Population. *And David Ricardo and the classical economists were strongly influenced by Malthus's ideas.*

THE ISSUES

Is there a limit to economic growth, or can we expand production and population without effective limit? Thomas Malthus gave one of the most influential answers to these questions in 1798. He reasoned that population, unchecked, would grow at a geometric rate—1, 2, 4, 8, 16...—while the food supply would grow at an arithmetic rate—1, 2, 3, 4, 5.... To prevent the population from outstripping the available food supply, there would be periodic wars, famines, and plagues. In Malthus's view, only what he called moral restraint could prevent such periodic disasters.

As industrialization proceeded through the nineteenth century, Malthus's idea came to be applied to all natural resources, especially those that are exhaustible.

Modern-day Malthusians believe that his basic idea is correct and that it applies not only to food but also to every natural resource. In time, these prophets of doom believe, we will be reduced to the subsistence level that Malthus predicted. He was a few centuries out in his predictions but not dead wrong.

One modern-day Malthusian is ecologist Paul Ehrlich, who believes that we are sitting on a "population bomb." Governments must, says Ehrlich, limit both population growth and the resources that may be used each year.

In 1931, Harold Hotelling developed a theory of natural resources with different predictions from those of Malthus. The Hotelling Principle is that the relative price of an exhaustible natural resource will steadily rise, bringing a decline in the quantity used and an increase in the use of substitute resources.

Julian Simon (who died in 1998) challenged both the Malthusian gloom and the Hotelling Principle. He believed that people are the "ultimate resource" and predicted that a rising population lessens the pressure on natural resources. A bigger population provides a larger number of resourceful people who can work out more efficient ways of using scarce resources. As these solutions are found, the prices of exhaustible resources actually fall. To demonstrate his point, in 1980, Simon bet Ehrlich that the prices of five metals—copper, chrome, nickel, tin, and tungsten—would fall during the 1980s. Simon won the bet!

No matter whether it is agricultural land, an exhaustible natural resource, or the space in the centre of Winnipeg, and no matter whether it is 1998 or, as shown here, 1913, there is a limit to what is available, and we persistently push against that limit. Economists see urban congestion as a consequence of the value of doing business in the city centre relative to the cost. They see the price mechanism, bringing ever-higher rents and prices of raw materials, as the means of allocating and rationing scarce natural resources. Malthusians, in contrast, explain congestion as the consequence of population pressure, and they see population control as the solution.

In Tokyo, the pressure on space is so great that in some residential neighbourhoods, a parking space costs $1,700 a month. To economize on this expensive space—and to lower the cost of car ownership and hence boost the sale of new cars—Honda, Nissan, and Toyota, three of Japan's big car producers, have developed a parking machine that enables two cars to occupy the space of one. The most basic of these machines costs a mere $10,000—less than 6 months' parking fees.

Malthus developed his ideas about population growth in a world in which women played a limited role in the economy. Malthus did not consider the opportunity cost of women's time a factor to be considered in predicting trends in the birth rate and population growth. But today, the opportunity cost of women's time is a crucial factor because women play an expanded role in the labour force. One woman who has made significant contributions to our knowledge of labour markets is Janet Currie of UCLA. You can meet Professor Currie on the following pages.

JANET CURRIE *is a professor of economics at the University of California, Los Angeles. Born in 1960 in Kingston, Ontario, she attended the University of Toronto, where she received her B.A. and M.A. in economics before moving to Princeton University, where she completed her Ph.D. in 1988. Professor Currie's research examines a wide range of public programs—medical, nutritional, educational, and housing—for (mainly) poor families. She has provided valuable assessments of the short-term and long-term effects of the Head Start program (enriched preschool for children in poor households) and Medicaid (government-provided health insurance for poor mothers and their children).*

Janet Currie

Michael Parkin and Robin Bade talked with Janet Currie about her work and the progress that economists have made in understanding how public policies can influence the distribution of income and economic well-being as well as the supply of labour and human capital.

Professor Currie, what attracted you to economics?

I was attracted to economics because it addresses questions of broad human interest (such as poverty and inequality) with intellec-tual rigour. Some may view the economic paradigm as restrictive (does everyone really maximize utility all the time?), but it provides a set of tools that yield powerful predictions about human behaviour, and it can be tested. For example, the "Law of Demand" (people consume less of a good when the price goes up) can be adopted to think about why many eligible people do not participate in social programs that might benefit them.

Why are there still relatively few women in our field?

Like other scientific careers, that of an economist requires an initial investment in mathematical skills. Mathematics is the language of science, and it is difficult to become a scientist if you don't speak the language. Undergraduate programs in economics may be partially to blame for not preparing students adequately for graduate work in the field. Many programs are aimed more at preparing students for careers in law or business. While this may be what the majority of undergraduate economics students want, we should also serve those who may go on to study economics in graduate school.

Difficulties in combining work and family are also an issue, but economics is not unique in requiring women to devote a lot of time to their careers at precisely the point when traditionally women would spend most time with their families. However, supports such as maternity leave and child care are improving, and making it easier for younger women to "do it all."

Could you briefly describe Head Start and summarize your main conclusions about its effects?

Head Start is a U.S. preschool program for disadvantaged three- to five-year-old children. In a series of studies comparing Head Start children to siblings who did not attend, I find evidence of lasting effects of Head Start in terms of schooling attainment and reductions in criminal activity. These findings are important because, while everyone would like to believe that investments in children pay off, there was little prior evidence of longer-term effects of Head Start.

You asked in a recent paper, "Are public housing projects good for kids?" What's the answer?

The title of this paper is intentionally provocative. Given all the negative publicity about some housing projects, most people assume that public housing must be bad for children. However, the key question is not whether kids in public housing do worse than other kids (they do) but whether they do better than they would have done in the absence of the program. For example, without the program, some children might have become homeless or had to move many times. It turns out that on average, public housing programs do improve the housing available to poor families, and have some positive effects in terms of schooling attainments.

In another paper, published in 1998, you summarized what we know and need to know about the effects of welfare programs on children. What, in a nutshell, do we know? What do we still need to know? And how would we set about finding the needed answers?

One striking conclusion from this review of welfare programs is that the available evidence suggests that in-kind programs are more effective than traditional welfare programs, which give cash to parents. This might account for the growing proportion of aid to poor families that is given in the form of specific in-kind benefits (e.g., Head Start, medical insurance, housing assistance). However, the evidence is far from complete. We need a lot more information about effects of programs on children, since anti-poverty programs are often justified in terms of their possible beneficial effects on children. We also need more information about longer-term effects of programs. For example, does it matter at what age the benefits are received?

In terms of how to find out what we need to know, I am a big supporter of social experiments, since a real random-assignment, treatment-control design provides more convincing answers than most statistical studies. On the other hand, it isn't possible to mount an experiment for every question. Much more could be done with exiting data if more of it was made available to researchers and if governments were more willing to allow linkages of different data sources.

What are some of the social experiments that have provided convincing answers? And how could economists do better work if governments were more willing to allow linkages of different data sources?

The great thing about a well-designed experiment is that anyone can understand the results. For example, in a drug trial, we randomly assign people to a treatment group that gets the drug, and a control group that gets a placebo. Because of the random assignment, the two groups are the same on average, so that any *ex poste* differences in how they do can be attributed to the treatment.

> *"The great thing about a well-designed experiment is that anyone can understand the results."*

Social experiments like the "Moving to Opportunity" project also rely on random assignment. In this experiment, the treatment consisted of giving a voucher to families in public housing projects that allowed the families to move into a low-poverty neighbourhood and gave them some assistance in relocating. The initial results indicate that the experiment had an effect on youth crime, as well as on criminal victimization. So far, there are no positive effects on schooling attainment or parental employment, but it is possible that these will emerge in the followup that is currently being conducted.

Another interesting experiment involves Early Head Start, a U.S. program that extends Head Start benefits to infants and toddlers. This program has demonstrated short-term effects of the program on cognitive test scores. Again, it will be necessary to do some long-term followup in order to see whether these benefits are retained.

The downside of experiments is that they are very expensive, relative to a statistical study, and cannot be used to answer questions other than those they were designed to address. Some of my work on the effects of Medicaid expansions provides an example of what can be done by linking various types of data. The U.S. government collects a good deal of survey data about health insurance and health care utilization. Because my co-author, Jon Gruber, was working in Washington, we were able to get state identifiers so that we could link information about Medicaid income cutoffs in each state to the individual-level records. This enabled us to ask how changing the income cutoffs affected health care utilization. In recent years, the government has been unwilling to release geographic identifiers, so that it is not possible to do a similar study of more recent health insurance expansions.

A few years ago, you stuck out your neck on the never-to-end minimum wage issue. What, according to your work, is the effect of the minimum wage on youth employment?

We found compelling evidence that youths affected by minimum wage legislation were less likely to be employed than those who were not (because they had wages either above or below the affected group). There are some obvious methodological flaws with some of the work arguing that minimum wages actually increase employment (such as failure to properly control for increases in demand, which might be driving increases in employment even at the higher minimum wages). However, much of the work (my own included) ignores an important question, which is whether we actually want to increase employment among youths. If higher minimum wages reduced employment but increased schooling, perhaps this would be a good outcome.

You've studied the effects of restrictions on the use of public funds for abortion. What did you discover?

Many people have argued that restrictions on abortion may cause more unwanted children to be born and hence worsen infant and child outcomes. The basic idea of my paper was that if this were true, then one ought to be able to see the effect in the distribution of birthweights. That is, if children who would have been aborted are more likely to be of low birthweight (because their mothers did not take care of themselves), then one should see more low birthweight infants in areas that adopt abortion restrictions.

> *"...economics are increasingly contributing to debate (and frequently having the last word) on questions that used to be considered far outside their scope."*

We did not, however, find this effect. In hindsight, it is not obvious that children who are born as a result of abortion restrictions ought to be less healthy than average, since the majority of women seeking abortions are young and non-poor.

What advice do you have for a student who is just starting to study economics? Do you think that economics is a good subject in which to major? What other subjects would you urge students to study alongside economics?

I have never regretted choosing economics as a major. Economics gives one the tools to study a vast array of social issues in a rigorous manner. Not surprisingly, economists are increasingly contributing to debate (and frequently having the last word) on questions that used to be considered far outside their scope. Economics concepts such as "opportunity cost," "selection bias," and "cost-benefit analysis" are central to the discussion of a vast array of policy issues.

Students who want to leave open the option of graduate work in economics should make sure they take enough mathematics courses to get them through a good graduate program.

PART 6 MARKET FAILURE AND GOVERNMENT

PUBLIC GOODS AND TAXES — CHAPTER 16

Government:
The Solution or the Problem?

Canada's federal, provincial, and municipal governments employ 1.5 million people and spend more than 40 cents of every dollar that we earn. Do we need this much government? Is government too big, as some Progressive Conservatives and Canadian Alliance Party members suggest? Is government "the problem"? Or, despite its enormous size, is government too small to do all the things it must? Is government, as some Liberals and New Democrats suggest, not contributing enough to economic life? ◆ After the terrorist attacks on New York and Washington on September 11, 2001, almost everyone agreed that governments around the world need to step up the scope and quality of domestic and global security. What determines the scale on which the government provides a public service such as domestic security? And why can't the market provide the security that people demand? To pay for the things they provide, governments collect taxes. What determines the types and scale of the taxes that we pay?

◆ We begin our study of government by describing the areas in which the market economy fails to achieve an efficient allocation of resources. We then explain what determines the scale of government provision of public services and the taxes that pay for them. In *Reading Between the Lines* at the end of the chapter, we return to the consequences of September 11 and look at the increased public expenditure on Canada's border security.

After studying this chapter, you will be able to

- Explain how government arises from market failure and redistribution

- Distinguish between public goods and private goods, explain the free-rider problem, and explain how the quantity of public goods is determined

- Explain why most of the government's revenue comes from income taxes, why income taxes are progressive, and why some goods are taxed at a much higher rate than others

The Economic Theory of Government

THE ECONOMIC THEORY OF GOVERNMENT explains the purpose of governments, the economic choices that governments make, and the consequences of those choices.

Governments exist for two major reasons. First, they establish and maintain property rights and set the rules for the redistribution of income and wealth. Property rights are the foundation on which all market activity takes place. They replace stealing with a rule-based and law-enforced system for redistributing income and wealth.

Second, governments provide a nonmarket mechanism for allocating scarce resources when the market economy results in *inefficiency*—a situation called **market failure.** When market failure occurs, too many of some things and too few of other things are produced. By reallocating resources, it is possible to make some people better off while making no one worse off. So people support government activity that modifies the market outcome and corrects market failure.

We're going to study four economic problems that are dealt with by government or public choices:

- Public goods
- Taxes and redistribution
- Monopoly
- Externalities

Public Goods

Some goods and services are consumed either by everyone or by no one. Examples are national defence, law and order, and sewage and waste disposal services. National defence systems cannot isolate individuals and refuse to protect them. Airborne diseases from untreated sewage do not avoid some people and target others. A good or service that is consumed either by everyone or by no one is called a *public good.*

The market economy fails to deliver the efficient quantity of public goods because of a free-rider problem. Everyone tries to free-ride on everyone else because the good is available to all whether they pay for it or not. We'll study public goods and the free-rider problem later in this chapter. We'll study the factors that influence the scale of provision of public goods, and we'll also study the taxes that pay for them.

Taxes and Redistribution

You saw in Chapter 15 that the market economy delivers an unequal distribution of income and wealth and that income support systems and progressive income taxes influence the distribution.

Taxes play a dual role: They pay for public goods, and they redistribute income. In this chapter, we'll look further at taxes and explain why Canada's income tax is progressive and why some goods are taxed at high rates and others at lower rates.

Monopoly

Monopoly and *rent seeking* prevent the allocation of resources from being efficient. Every business tries to maximize profit, and when a monopoly exists, it can increase profit by restricting output and keeping the price high. For example, some years ago, Bell Canada had a monopoly on long-distance telephone services and the quantity of long-distance services was much smaller and the price much higher than they are today. Since the end of Bell Canada's monopoly, the quantity of long-distance calls has exploded.

Some monopolies arise from *legal barriers to entry*—barriers to entry created by governments—but a major activity of government is to regulate monopoly and to enforce laws that prevent cartels and other restrictions on competition. We study these regulations and laws in Chapter 17.

Externalities

When a chemical factory (legally) dumps its waste into a river and kills the fish, it imposes a cost—called an *external cost*—on the members of a fishing club who fish downstream. When a homeowner fills her garden with spring bulbs, she generates an external benefit for all the passersby. External costs and benefits are not usually taken into account by the people whose actions create them. The chemical factory does not take the fishing club's wishes into account when it decides whether to dump waste into the river. The homeowner does not take her neighbours' views into account when she decides to fill her garden with flowers. We study externalities in Chapter 18.

Before we begin to study each of these problems from which government activity arises, let's look at the arena in which governments operate: the "political marketplace."

Public Choice and the Political Marketplace

Government is a complex organization made up of millions of individuals, each with his or her own economic objectives. Government policy is the outcome of the choices made by these individuals. To analyze these choices, economists have developed a public choice model of the political marketplace. The actors in the political marketplace are

- Voters
- Politicians
- Bureaucrats

Figure 16.1 illustrates the choices and interactions of these actors. Let's look at each in turn.

Voters Voters are the consumers in the political marketplace. In markets for goods and services, people express their preferences by their willingness to pay. In the political marketplace, they express their preferences by their votes, campaign contributions, and lobbying activity. Public choice theory assumes that people support the policies they believe will make them better off and oppose the policies they believe will make them worse off. It is voters' *perceptions* rather than reality that guide their choices.

Politicians Politicians are the entrepreneurs of the political marketplace. Public choice theory assumes that the objective of a politician is to get elected and to remain in office. Votes to a politician are like economic profit to a firm. To get enough votes, politicians propose policies that they expect will appeal to a majority of voters.

Bureaucrats Bureaucrats are the hired officials in government departments. They are the producers or firms in the political marketplace. Public choice theory assumes that bureaucrats aim to maximize their own utility and that to achieve this objective, they try to maximize the budget of their department.

The bigger the budget of a department, the greater is the prestige of its chief and the larger is the opportunity for promotion for people farther down the bureaucratic ladder. So all the members of a department have an interest in maximizing the department's budget. To maximize their budgets, bureaucrats devise programs that they expect will appeal to politicians and they help politicians to explain their programs to voters.

FIGURE 16.1   The Political Marketplace

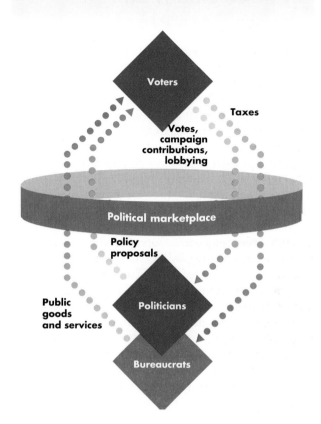

Voters express their demands for policies by voting, making campaign contributions, and lobbying. Politicians propose policies to appeal to a majority of voters. Bureaucrats try to maximize the budgets of their departments. A political equilibrium emerges in which no group can improve its position by making a different choice.

Political Equilibrium

Voters, politicians, and bureaucrats make choices to best further their own objectives. But each group is constrained by the preferences of the other groups and by what is technologically feasible. The outcome that results from the choices of voters, politicians, and bureaucrats is a **political equilibrium**, which is a situation in which all their choices are compatible and in which no group can improve its position by making a different choice. Let's see how voters, politicians, and bureaucrats interact to determine the quantity of public goods.

Public Goods and the Free-Rider Problem

WHY DOES THE GOVERNMENT PROVIDE GOODS and services such as national defence and public health? Why don't we buy environmental protection from Arctic Ozone, Inc., a private firm that competes for our dollars in the marketplace in the same way that Tim Hortons and Coca-Cola do? The answer to these questions lies in the free-rider problem created by public goods. Let's explore this problem. We begin by looking at the nature of a public good.

Public Goods

A **public good** is a good or service that can be consumed simultaneously by everyone and from which no one can be excluded. The first feature of a public good is called nonrivalry. A good is *nonrival* if consumption of it by one person does not decrease consumption of it by another person. An example is watching a television show. The opposite of nonrival is rival. A good is *rival* if consumption of it by one person decreases consumption of it by another person. An example is eating a hot dog.

The second feature of a public good is that it is nonexcludable. A good is *nonexcludable* if it is impossible, or extremely costly, to prevent someone from benefiting from a good. An example is national defence. It would be difficult to exclude someone from being defended. The opposite of nonexcludable is excludable. A good is *excludable* if it is possible to prevent a person from enjoying the benefits of a good. An example is cable television. Cable companies can ensure that only those people who have paid the fee receive programs.

Figure 16.2 classifies goods according to these two criteria and gives examples of goods in each category. National defence is a *pure* public good. One person's consumption of the security provided by our national defence system does not decrease the security of someone else—defence is nonrival. And the military cannot select those whom it will protect and those whom it will leave exposed to threats—defence is nonexcludable.

Many goods have a public element but are not pure public goods. An example is a highway. A highway is nonrival until it becomes congested. One more car on a highway with plenty of space does not

FIGURE 16.2 Public Goods and Private Goods

A pure public good (bottom right) is one for which consumption is nonrival and from which it is impossible to exclude a consumer. Pure public goods pose a free-rider problem. A pure private good (top left) is one for which consumption is rival and from which consumers can be excluded. Some goods are nonexcludable but are rival (bottom left), and some goods are nonrival but are excludable (top right).

Source: Adapted from and inspired by E.S. Savas, *Privatizing the Public Sector* (Chatham, N.J.: Chatham House Publishers, 1982), p. 34.

reduce anyone else's consumption of transportation services. But once the highway becomes congested, one extra vehicle lowers the quality of the service available to everyone else—it becomes rival like a private good. Also, users can be excluded from a highway by tollgates. Another example is fish in the ocean. Ocean fish are rival because a fish taken by one person is not available for anyone else. Ocean fish are also nonexcludable because it is difficult to prevent people from catching them.

The Free-Rider Problem

Public goods create a free-rider problem. A **free rider** is a person who consumes a good without paying for it. Public goods create a *free-rider problem* because the quantity of the good that a person is able to consume is not influenced by the amount the person pays for the good. So no one has an incentive to pay for a public good. Let's look more closely at the free-rider problem by studying an example.

The Benefit of a Public Good

Suppose that a device has been invented that makes it possible to eliminate acid rain. Let's call this device an acid-rain check. The benefit provided by an acid-rain check is the *value* of its services. The *value* of a *private* good is the maximum amount that a person is willing to pay for one more unit, which is shown by the person's demand curve. The value of a *public* good is the maximum amount that all the *people* are willing to pay for one more unit of it.

Total benefit is the dollar value that a person places on a given level of provision of a public good. The greater the quantity of a public good, the larger is a person's total benefit. *Marginal benefit* is the increase in total benefit that results from a one-unit increase in the quantity of a public good.

Figure 16.3 shows the marginal benefit that arises from acid-rain checks for a society with just two members, Lisa and Max. Lisa's and Max's marginal benefits are graphed as MB_L and MB_M, in parts (a) and (b). The marginal benefit from a public good is similar to the marginal utility from a private good— it diminishes as the quantity of the good increases. For Lisa, the marginal benefit from the first acid-rain check is $80 and from the second it is $60. By the time 5 acid-rain checks are deployed, Lisa's marginal benefit is zero. For Max, the marginal benefit from the first acid-rain check is $50 and from the second it is $40. By the time 5 acid-rain checks are installed, Max's marginal benefit is only $10.

Part (c) shows the economy's marginal benefit curve, *MB*. An individual's marginal benefit curve for a public good is similar to the individual's demand curve for a private good. But the economy's marginal benefit curve for a public good is different from the market demand curve for a private good. To obtain the market demand curve for a *private* good, we sum the quantities demanded by all individuals at each price—we sum the individual demand curves *horizontally* (see Chapter 7, p. 163). But to find the economy's marginal benefit curve of a *public* good, we sum the marginal benefits of all individuals at each quantity—we sum the individual marginal benefit curves *vertically*. The resulting marginal benefit for the economy made up of Lisa and Max is the economy's marginal benefit curve graphed in part (c)— the curve *MB*. Lisa's marginal benefit from the first acid-rain check gets added to Max's marginal benefit from the first acid-rain check because they *both* consume the first acid-rain check.

FIGURE 16.3 Benefits of a Public Good

(a) Lisa's marginal benefit

(b) Max's marginal benefit

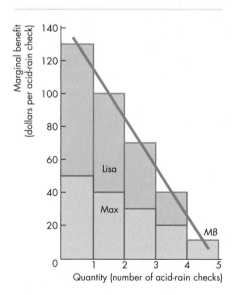

(c) Economy's marginal benefit

The marginal benefit to the economy at each quantity of the public good is the sum of the marginal benefits of all individuals. The marginal benefit curves are MB_L for Lisa, MB_M for Max, and *MB* for the economy.

The Efficient Quantity of a Public Good

An economy with two people would not buy any acid-rain checks—because the total benefit falls far short of the cost. But an economy with 25 million people might. To determine the efficient quantity, we need to take the cost as well as the benefit into account.

The cost of an acid-rain check is based on technology and the prices of the resources used to produce it (see Chapter 10).

Figure 16.4 shows the benefits and costs. The second and third columns of the table show the total and marginal benefits. The next two columns show the total and marginal cost of producing acid-rain checks. The final column shows net benefit. Part (a) graphs total benefit, *TB,* and total cost, *TC.*

The efficient quantity is the one that maximizes *net benefit*—total benefit minus total cost—and occurs when 2 acid-rain checks are provided.

The fundamental principles of marginal analysis that you have used to explain how consumers maximize utility and how firms maximize profit can also be used to calculate the efficient scale of provision of a public good. Figure 16.4(b) shows this alternative approach. The marginal benefit curve is *MB* and the marginal cost curve is *MC.* When marginal benefit exceeds marginal cost, net benefit increases if the quantity produced increases. When marginal cost exceeds marginal benefit, net benefit increases if the quantity produced decreases. Marginal benefit equals marginal cost with 2 acid-rain checks. So making marginal cost equal to marginal benefit maximizes net benefit and uses resources efficiently.

Private Provision

We have now worked out the quantity of acid-rain checks that maximizes net benefit. Would a private firm—Arctic Ozone, Inc.—deliver that quantity? It would not. To do so, it would have to collect $1.5 billion to cover its costs—or $60 from each of the 25 million people in the economy. But no one would have an incentive to buy his or her "share" of the acid-rain check system. Everyone would reason as follows: "The number of acid-rain checks provided by Arctic Ozone, Inc., is not affected by my $60. But my own private consumption is greater if I free-ride and do not pay my share of the cost of the acid-rain check system. If I do not pay, I enjoy the same level of security and I can buy more private goods. Therefore I will spend my $60 on other goods and

free-ride on the public good." This is the free-rider problem.

If everyone reasons the same way, Arctic Ozone has zero revenue and so provides no acid-rain checks. Because two acid-rain checks is the efficient level, private provision is inefficient.

Public Provision

Suppose there are two political parties, the Greens and the Smokes, which agree on all issues except for the quantity of acid-rain checks. The Greens would like to provide 4 acid-rain checks at a cost of $5 billion, with benefits of $5 billion and a net benefit of zero, as shown in Fig. 16.4. The Smokes would like to provide 1 acid-rain check at a cost of $0.5 billion, a benefit of $2 billion, and a net benefit of $1.5 billion—see Fig. 16.4.

Before deciding on their policy proposals, the two political parties do a "what-if" analysis. Each party reasons as follows. If each party offers the acid-rain check program it wants—Greens 4 acid-rain checks and Smokes 1 acid-rain check—the voters will see that they will get a net benefit of $1.5 billion from the Smokes and zero net benefit from the Greens, and the Smokes will win the election.

Contemplating this outcome, the Greens realize that they are too "green" to get elected. They figure that they must scale back their proposal to 2 acid-rain checks. At this level of provision, total cost is $1.5 billion, total benefit is $3.5 billion, and net benefit is $2 billion. If the Smokes stick with 1 acid-rain check, the Greens will win the election.

But contemplating this outcome, the Smokes realize that they must match the Greens. They too propose to provide 2 acid-rain checks on exactly the same terms as the Greens. If the parties offer the same number of acid-rain checks, the voters are indifferent between them. Each party receives around 50 percent of the vote.

The result of the politicians' "what-if" analysis is that each party offers 2 acid-rain checks, so regardless of who wins the election, this is the quantity of acid-rain checks installed. And this quantity is efficient. It maximizes the perceived net benefit of the voters. Thus in this example, competition in the political marketplace results in the efficient provision of a public good. But for this outcome to occur, voters must be well informed and evaluate the alternatives. But as you will see below, voters do not always have an incentive to be well informed.

FIGURE 16.4   The Efficient Quantity of a Public Good

(a) Total benefit and total cost

(b) Marginal benefit and marginal cost

Quantity (number of acid-rain checks)	Total benefit (billions of dollars)	Marginal benefit (billions of dollars per acid-rain check)	Total cost (billions of dollars)	Marginal cost (billions of dollars per acid-rain check)	Net benefit (billions of dollars)
0	0		0		0
		2.0		0.5	
1	2.0		0.5		1.5
		1.5		1.0	
2	3.5		1.5		2.0
		1.0		1.5	
3	4.5		3.0		1.5
		0.5		2.0	
4	5.0		5.0		0
		0		2.5	
5	5.0		7.5		−2.5

Net benefit—the vertical distance between total benefit, *TB*, and total cost, *TC*—is maximized when 2 acid-rain checks are installed (part a) and where marginal benefit, *MB*, equals marginal cost, *MC* (part b). The Smokes would like 1 acid-rain check, and the Greens would like 4. But each party recognizes that its only hope of being elected is to provide 2 acid-rain checks—the quantity that maximizes net benefit and so leaves no room for the other party to improve on.

The Principle of Minimum Differentiation In the example we've just studied, both parties propose identical policies. This tendency towards identical policies is an example of the **principle of minimum differentiation,** which is the tendency for competitors to make themselves identical to appeal to the maximum number of clients or voters. This principle not only describes the behaviour of political parties but also explains why fast-food restaurants cluster in the same block and even why new auto models have similar features. If McDonald's opens a restaurant in a new location, it is likely that Burger King will open next door to McDonald's rather than a kilometre down the road. If Chrysler designs a new van with a sliding door on the driver's side, most likely Ford will too.

The Role of Bureaucrats

We have analyzed the behaviour of politicians but not that of the bureaucrats who translate the choices of the politicians into programs and who control the day-to-day activities that deliver public goods. Let's now see how the economic choices of bureaucrats influence the political equilibrium.

To do so, we'll stick with the previous example. We've seen that competition between two political parties delivers the efficient quantity of acid-rain checks. But will the Department of the Environment (DOE) cooperate and accept this outcome?

Suppose the objective of the DOE is to maximize its budget. With 2 acid-rain checks being provided at minimum cost, the budget is $1.5 billion (see Fig. 16.5). To increase its budget, the DOE might do two things. First, it might try to persuade the politicians that 2 acid-rain checks cost more than $1.5 billion. As Fig. 16.5 shows, if possible, the DOE would like to convince Parliament that 2 acid-rain checks cost $3.5 billion—the entire benefit. Second, and pressing its position even more strongly, the DOE might argue for more acid-rain checks. It might press for 4 acid-rain checks and a budget of $5 billion. In this situation, total benefit and total cost are equal and net benefit is zero.

The DOE wants to maximize its budget, but won't the politicians prevent it from doing so because the DOE's preferred outcome costs votes? The politicians will do this if voters are well informed and know what is best for them. But voters might be rationally ignorant. In this case, well-informed interest groups might enable the DOE to achieve its objective.

Rational Ignorance

A principle of public choice theory is that it is rational for a voter to be ignorant about an issue unless that issue has a perceptible effect on the voter's income. **Rational ignorance** is the decision *not* to acquire information because the cost of doing so exceeds the expected benefit. For example, each voter knows that he or she can make virtually no difference to Canada's environment policy. Each voter also knows that it would take an enormous amount of time and effort to become even moderately well informed about alternative approaches. So voters remain relatively uninformed about the technicalities of issues. (Although we are using environment policy

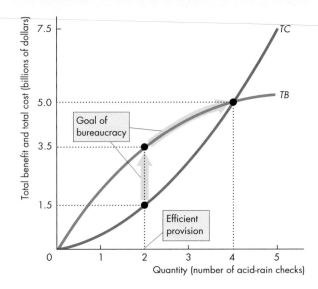

FIGURE 16.5   Bureaucratic Overprovision

The goal of a bureaucracy is to maximize its budget. A bureaucracy will seek to increase its budget so that its total cost equals total benefit, and then use its budget to expand output and expenditure. Here, the DOE tries to get $3.5 billion to provide 2 acid-rain checks. It would like to increase the quantity to 4 with a budget of $5.0 billion.

as an example, the same idea applies to all public choices.)

All voters are consumers of clean air. But not all voters are producers of the equipment needed to monitor and maintain good air quality. Only a small number are in this latter category. Voters who own or work for firms that produce acid-rain checks have a direct personal interest in the government's policy because it affects their incomes. These voters have an incentive to become well informed about environmental issues and to operate a political lobby aimed at furthering their own interests. In collaboration with the bureaucracy, these voters exert a larger influence than do the relatively uninformed voters who only consume this public good.

When the rationality of the uninformed voter and special interest groups are taken into account, the political equilibrium provides public goods in excess of the efficient quantity. So in the current example, three or four acid-rain checks might be bought rather than the efficient quantity of two acid-rain checks.

Two Types of Political Equilibrium

We've seen that two types of political equilibrium are possible: efficient and inefficient. These two types of political equilibrium correspond to two theories of government:

- Public interest theory
- Public choice theory

Public Interest Theory Public interest theory predicts that governments make choices that achieve efficiency. This outcome occurs in a perfect political system in which voters are fully informed about the effects of policies and refuse to vote for outcomes that can be improved upon.

Public Choice Theory Public choice theory predicts that governments make choices that result in inefficiency. This outcome occurs in political markets in which voters are rationally ignorant and base their votes only on issues that they know affect their own net benefit. Voters pay more attention to their interests as producers than their interests as consumers, and public officials also act in their own best interest. The result is *government failure* that parallels market failure.

Why Government Is Large and Grows

Now that we know how the quantity of public goods is determined, we can explain part of the reason for the growth of government. Government grows in part because the demand for some public goods increases at a faster rate than the demand for private goods. There are two possible reasons for this growth:

- Voter preferences
- Inefficient overprovision

Voter Preferences The growth of government can be explained by voter preferences in the following way. As voters' incomes increase (as they do in most years), the demand for many public goods increases more quickly than income. (Technically, the *income elasticity of demand* for many public goods is greater than 1—see Chapter 4, pp. 92–93.) These goods include public health, education, national defence, highways, airports, and air-traffic control systems. If politicians did not support increases in expenditures on these items, they would not get elected.

Inefficient Overprovision Inefficient overprovision might explain the *size* of government but not its *growth rate*. It (possibly) explains why government is *larger* than its efficient scale, but it does not explain why governments use an increasing proportion of total resources.

Voters Strike Back

If government grows too large relative to the value that voters place on public goods, there might be a voter backlash against government programs and a large bureaucracy. Electoral success during the 1990s at the provincial and federal levels required politicians of all parties to embrace smaller, leaner, and more efficient government. The September 11 attacks have led to a greater willingness to pay for security, but have probably not lessened the desire for lean government.

Another way in which voters—and politicians—can try to counter the tendency of bureaucrats to expand their budgets is to privatize the production of public goods. Government *provision* of a public good does not automatically imply that a government-operated bureau must *produce* the good. Garbage collection (a public good) is often handled by a private firm, and experiments are being conducted with private fire departments and even private prisons.

REVIEW QUIZ

1. What is the free-rider problem and why does it make the private provision of a public good inefficient?
2. Under what conditions will competition among politicians for votes result in an efficient quantity of a public good?
3. How do rationally ignorant voters and budget-maximizing bureaucrats prevent competition in the political marketplace from producing the efficient quantity of a public good? Do they result in too much or too little public provision of public goods?

We've now seen how voters, politicians, and bureaucrats interact to determine the quantity of a public good. But public goods are paid for with taxes. Taxes also redistribute income. How does the political marketplace determine the taxes we pay?

Taxes

TAXES GENERATE THE FINANCIAL RESOURCES that provide public goods. Taxes also redistribute income. Governments use five major types of taxes:

- Income taxes
- Employment, health, and social insurance taxes
- Provincial sales taxes and the GST
- Property taxes
- Excise taxes

Figure 16.6 shows the relative amounts raised by these five major taxes in 2001. Income taxes raised 52 percent of tax revenue in 2001. Provincial sales taxes and the GST raised 15 percent of total taxes. Property taxes and employment, health, and social insurance taxes each raised 11 percent of total taxes. Finally, excise taxes raised 6 percent of total taxes. Although excise taxes raise a small amount of tax revenue, they nevertheless have a big impact on some markets, as you'll discover later in this chapter. Let's take a closer look at each type of tax.

Income Taxes

Income taxes are paid on personal incomes and corporate profits. In 2001, the personal income tax

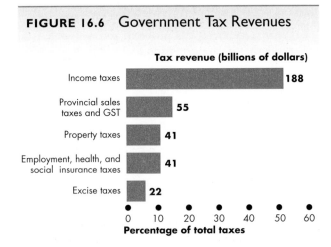

FIGURE 16.6   Government Tax Revenues

Tax revenue (billions of dollars)

Income taxes	188
Provincial sales taxes and GST	55
Property taxes	41
Employment, health, and social insurance taxes	41
Excise taxes	22

0 10 20 30 40 50 60
Percentage of total taxes

More than half of government tax revenue comes from income taxes. Excise taxes bring in a small amount of revenue, but these taxes have big effects on a small number of markets.

Source: Adapted from the Statistics Canada publication *CANSIM DISC,* 10F0007, March 1999.

raised $88 billion for the federal government and another $53 billion for provincial governments. Corporate profits taxes raised $28 billion for the federal government and $14 billion for the provincial governments. We'll look first at the effects of personal income tax and then at corporate profits tax.

Personal Income Tax   The amount of income tax that a person pays depends on her or his *taxable income,* which equals total income minus expenses and other allowances. In 2001, the basic personal deduction from total income was $7,634 for a single person and a further $6,482 for a spouse.

The *tax rate* (percent) depends on the taxable income and province of residence. For Ontario, the tax rate increases according to the following scale:

$0 to $31,677	22.05 percent
$31,678 to $63,354	31.15 percent
$63,355 to $63,786	35.15 percent
$63,787 to $103,000	37.16 percent
Over $103,000	40.16 percent

The percentages in this list are marginal tax rates. A **marginal tax rate** is the percentage of an additional dollar of income that is paid in tax. For example, if taxable income increases from $25,000 to $25,001, the additional tax paid is 22.05 cents and the marginal tax rate is 22.05 percent. If taxable income increases from $103,000 to $103,001, the additional tax paid is 40.16 cents and the marginal tax rate is 40.16 percent.

The **average tax rate** is the percentage of income that is paid in tax. Let's calculate the average tax rate for a single person who earns $50,000 in a year. Tax is zero on the first $7,634, plus $6,985 (22.05 percent) on the next $31,677, plus $3,330 on the remaining $10,689. Total tax is $10,315, which is 20.6 percent of $50,000. The average tax rate is 20.6 percent.

If the marginal tax rate exceeds the average tax rate, the average tax rate increases as income increases and the tax is a *progressive tax* (see p. 359). The personal income tax is a progressive tax. To see this feature of the income tax, calculate the average tax rate for someone whose income is $100,000 a year. Tax is zero on the first $7,634, plus $6,985 (22.05 percent) on the next $31,677, plus $9,867 (31.15 percent) on the next $31,677, plus $152 (35.15 percent) on the next $432, plus $10,620 (37.16 percent) on the remaining $28,580. Total tax is $27,624, which is 27.62 percent of $100,000. So the average tax rate is 27.62 percent.

The Effect of Income Taxes Figure 16.7 shows how the income tax affects labour markets. Part (a) shows the market for low-wage workers, and part (b) shows the market for high-wage workers. These labour markets are competitive, and with no income taxes, they work just like all the other competitive markets you have studied. The demand curves are *LD*, and the supply curves are *LS* (in both parts of the figure). Both groups work 40 hours a week. Low-wage workers earn $9.50 an hour, and high-wage workers earn $175 an hour. What happens when an income tax is introduced?

If low-wage workers are willing to supply 40 hours a week for $9.50 an hour when there is no tax, then they are willing to supply that same quantity in the face of a 15 percent tax only if the wage rises by enough to provide an after-tax wage rate of $9.50 an hour. That is, they want to get the $9.50 an hour they received before plus enough to pay 15 percent of

their income to the government. So the supply of labour decreases because the amount received from work is lowered by the amount of income tax paid. The acceptable wage rate at each level of employment rises by the amount of the tax that must be paid. For low-wage workers who face a tax rate of 15 percent, the supply curve shifts to *LS + tax*. The equilibrium wage rate rises to $10 an hour, but the after-tax wage rate falls to $8.50 an hour. Employment falls to 36 hours a week.

For high-wage workers who face a tax rate of 39.6 percent, the supply curve shifts to *LS + tax*. The equilibrium wage rate rises to $200 an hour, and the after-tax wage rate falls to $121 an hour. Employment falls to 32 hours a week. The decrease in employment of high-wage workers is larger than that of low-wage workers because of the differences in the marginal tax rates each type of worker faces.

FIGURE 16.7   The Effects of Income Taxes

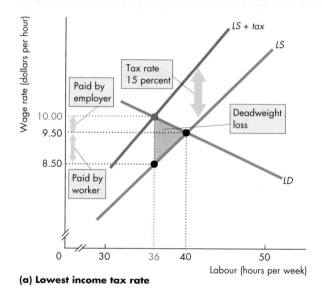

(a) Lowest income tax rate

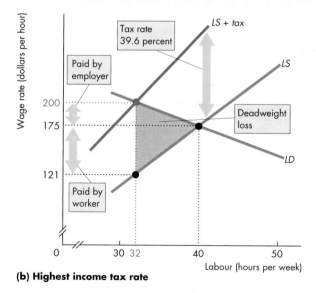

(b) Highest income tax rate

The demand for labour is *LD*, and with no income taxes, the supply of labour is *LS* (both parts). In part (a), low-wage workers earn $9.50 an hour and each works 40 hours a week. In part (b), high-wage workers earn $175 an hour and each works 40 hours a week. An income tax decreases the supply of labour, and the labour supply curve shifts leftward. For low-wage workers in part (a), whose marginal

tax rate is 15 percent, supply decreases to *LS + tax*. Employment falls to 36 hours a week. For high-wage workers in part (b), whose marginal tax rate is 39.6 percent, supply decreases to *LS + tax*. Employment falls to 32 hours a week. The deadweight loss from the high marginal tax rate on high-wage workers is much larger than that from the low marginal tax rate on low-wage workers.

Notice that the income tax is paid by both the employer and the worker. In the case of low-wage workers, the employer pays an extra 50 cents an hour and the worker pays $1 an hour. In the case of high-wage workers, employers pay an extra $25 an hour and workers pay $54 an hour. The exact split depends on the elasticities of demand and supply.

Notice also the difference in the *deadweight loss* for the two groups. The deadweight loss is larger for the high-wage workers than for the low-wage workers.

Why Do We Have a Progressive Income Tax?   We have a progressive income tax because it is part of the political equilibrium. A majority of voters support it, so politicians who also support it get elected.

The economic model that predicts progressive income taxes is called the *median voter* model. The core idea of the median voter model is that political parties pursue policies that are most likely to attract the support of the median voter. The median voter is the one in the middle—one-half of the population lies on one side and one-half on the other. Let's see how the median voter model predicts a progressive income tax.

Imagine that government programs benefit everyone equally and are paid for by a proportional income tax. Everyone pays the same percentage of income. In this situation, there is a redistribution from high-income voters to low-income voters. Everyone benefits equally, but because they have higher incomes, the high-income voters pay a larger amount of taxes.

Is this situation the best one possible for the median voter? It is not. Suppose that instead of using a proportional tax, the marginal tax rate is lowered for low-income voters and increased for high-income voters—a progressive tax. Low-income voters are now better off, and high-income voters are worse off. Low-income voters will support this change, and high-income voters will oppose it. But there are many more low-income voters than high-income voters, so the low-income voters win.

The median voter is a low-income voter. In fact, because the distribution of income is skewed, the median voter has a smaller income than the average income (see Fig. 15.1 on p. 348). This fact raises an interesting question: Why doesn't the median voter support taxes that skim off all income above the average and redistribute it to everyone with a below-average income? This tax would be so progressive that it would result in equal incomes after taxes and transfers were paid.

The answer is that high taxes discourage effort and saving and the median voter would be worse off with such radical redistribution than under the arrangements that prevail today.

Let's now look at corporate profits tax.

Corporate Profits Tax   In popular discussions of taxes, corporate profits taxes are seen as a free source of revenue for the government. Taxing people is bad, but taxing corporations is just fine.

It turns out that taxing corporations is very inefficient. We use an inefficient tax because it redistributes income in favour of the median voter, just like the income tax. Let's see why taxing corporate profits is inefficient.

The corporate profits tax is misnamed. It is only partly a tax on economic profit. It is mainly a tax on the income from capital. Taxing the income from capital works like taxing the income from labour except for two critical differences: The supply of capital is highly (perhaps perfectly) elastic, and the quantity of capital influences the productivity of labour and wage income. Because the supply of capital is highly elastic, firms pay the entire tax and the quantity of capital decreases. With a smaller capital stock than we would otherwise have, the productivity of labour and incomes are lower than they would otherwise be.

Employment, Health, and Social Insurance Taxes

Social insurance taxes are the contributions paid by employers and employees to provide social security benefits, unemployment compensation, and health benefits.

Unions lobby to get employers to pay a bigger share of these taxes, and employers' organizations lobby to get workers to pay a bigger share. But this lobbying effort is not worth much, for who *really* pays these taxes depends in no way on who writes the cheques. It depends on the elasticities of demand and supply for labour.

Figure 16.8 shows you why. The demand curve, *LD*, and the supply curve, *LS*, are identical in the two parts of the figure. With no social insurance taxes, the quantity of labour employed is *QL** and the wage rate is *W**.

A social insurance tax is now introduced. In part (a), the employee pays the tax, and in part (b), the employer pays. When the employee pays, supply decreases and the supply of labour curve shifts leftward to $LS + tax$. The vertical distance between the supply curve LS and the new supply curve $LS + tax$ is the amount of the tax. The wage rate rises to WC, the after-tax wage rate falls to WT, and employment decreases to QL_0.

When the employer pays, in Fig. 16.8(b), demand decreases and the demand for labour curve shifts leftward to $LD - tax$. The vertical distance between the demand curve LD and the new demand curve $LD - tax$ is the amount of the tax. The wage rate falls to WT, but the cost of labour rises to WC and employment decreases to QL_0.

So regardless of which side of the market is taxed, the outcomes are identical. If the demand for labour is perfectly inelastic or if the supply of labour is perfectly elastic, the employer pays the entire tax. And if the demand for labour is perfectly elastic or if the supply of labour is perfectly inelastic, the employee pays the entire tax. These cases are like those for the sales tax that you studied in Chapter 6 (pp. 131–134).

Provincial Sales Taxes and the GST

Sales taxes are the taxes levied by the provinces on a wide range of goods and services. The GST is the tax levied by the federal government on most goods and services. We studied the effects of these taxes in Chapter 6. There is one feature of these taxes, though, that we need to note: They are *regressive*. The reason they are regressive is that saving increases with income and sales taxes are paid only on the part of income that is spent.

Suppose, for example, that the sales tax rate is 8 percent. A family that earns $20,000 and spends $18,000 on goods and services pays $1,440 in sales tax. Its taxes are 7.2 percent of its income. A family that earns $100,000 and spends $60,000 on goods and services pays $4,800 in sales taxes. So this family's taxes are only 4.8 percent of its income.

If the sales tax is regressive, why does the median voter support it? It is the entire tax code that matters, not an individual tax. So a regressive sales tax is voted for only as part of an overall tax regime that is progressive.

Property Taxes

Property taxes are collected by local governments and are used to provide local public goods. A **local public good** is a public good that is consumed by all the people who live in a particular area. Examples of local public goods are parks, museums, and safe neighbourhoods.

FIGURE 16.8 Social Insurance Taxes

(a) Tax on employees

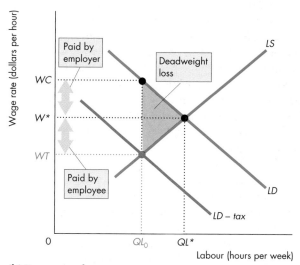

(b) Tax on employers

With no social insurance tax, the quantity of labour employed is QL^* and the wage rate is W^* (in both parts). In part (a), employees pay a social insurance tax. Supply decreases, and the supply of labour curve shifts leftward to $LS + tax$. The wage rate rises to WC, the after-tax wage rate falls to WT, and employment decreases to QL_0. In part (b), employers pay a social insurance tax. Demand decreases, and the demand for labour curve shifts leftward to $LD - tax$. The wage rate falls to WT, but the cost of labour rises to WC and employment decreases to QL_0. The outcomes are identical in the two cases.

There is a much closer connection between property taxes paid and benefits received than in the case of federal and provincial taxes. This close connection makes property taxes similar to a price for local services. Because of this connection, property taxes change both the demand for and supply of property in a neighbourhood. A higher tax lowers supply, but improved local public goods increase demand. So some neighbourhoods have high taxes and high-quality local government services, and other neighbourhoods have low taxes and low-quality services. Both can exist in the political equilibrium.

Excise Taxes

An **excise tax** is a tax on the sale of a particular commodity. The total amount raised by these taxes is small, but they have a big impact on some markets. Let's study the effects of an excise tax by considering the tax on gasoline shown in Fig. 16.9. The demand curve is D, and the supply curve is S. If there is no tax on gasoline, its price is 60¢ a litre and 400 million litres of gasoline a day are bought and sold.

Now suppose that a tax is imposed on gasoline at the rate of 60¢ a litre. As a result of the tax, the supply of gasoline decreases and the supply curve shifts leftward. The magnitude of the shift is such that the vertical distance between the original and the new supply curve is the amount of the tax. The new supply curve is the red curve, S + tax. The new supply curve intersects the demand curve at 300 million litres a day and $1.10 a litre. Sellers receive 50¢ a litre, the price at which they are willing to supply 300 million litres a day. This situation is the new equilibrium after the imposition of the tax.

The excise tax creates a deadweight loss made up of the loss of consumer surplus and producer surplus. The dollar value of that loss is $30 million a day. Because 300 million litres of gasoline are sold each day and the tax is 60¢ a litre, total revenue from the gasoline tax is $180 million a day (300 million litres multiplied by 60¢ a litre). So to raise tax revenue of $180 million a day by using the gasoline tax, a deadweight loss of $30 million a day—one-sixth of the tax revenue—is incurred.

One of the main influences on the deadweight loss arising from a tax is the elasticity of demand for the product. The demand for gasoline is fairly inelastic. As a consequence, when a tax is imposed, the quantity demanded falls by a smaller percentage than the percentage rise in price.

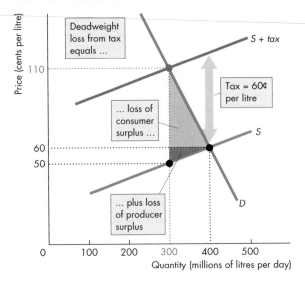

FIGURE 16.9 An Excise Tax

The demand curve for gasoline is D, and the supply curve is S. In the absence of any taxes, gasoline sells for 60¢ a litre and 400 million litres a day are bought and sold. With a tax of 60¢ a litre, the supply curve shifts leftward to become the curve S + tax. The new equilibrium price is $1.10 a litre, and 300 million litres a day are bought and sold. The excise tax creates a deadweight loss represented by the grey triangle. The tax revenue collected is 60¢ a litre on 300 million litres, which is $180 million a day. The deadweight loss is $30 million a day. That is, to raise tax revenue of $180 million a day, a deadweight loss of $30 million a day is incurred.

To see the importance of the elasticity of demand, let's consider a different commodity: orange juice. So that we can make a quick and direct comparison, let's assume that the orange juice market is exactly as big as the market for gasoline. Figure 16.10 illustrates this market. The demand curve for orange juice is D, and the supply curve is S. Orange juice is not taxed, and so the price of orange juice is 60¢ a litre—where the supply curve and the demand curve intersect—and the quantity of orange juice traded is 400 million litres a day.

Now suppose that the government contemplates abolishing the gasoline tax and taxing orange juice instead. The demand for orange juice is more elastic than the demand for gasoline. Orange juice has many good substitutes in the form of other fruit juices. The

FIGURE 16.10   Why We Don't Tax Orange Juice

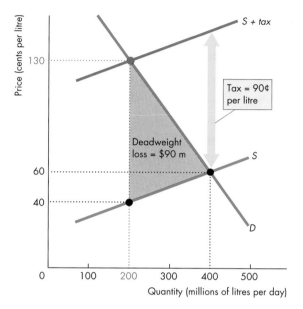

The demand curve for orange juice is *D*, and the supply curve is *S*. The price is 60¢ a litre, and 400 million litres of juice a day are traded. To raise $180 million of tax revenue, a tax of 90¢ a litre is imposed. This tax shifts the supply curve to *S + tax*. The price rises to $1.30 a litre, and the quantity falls to 200 million litres a day. The deadweight loss, the grey triangle, equals $90 million a day. The dead-weight loss from taxing orange juice is larger than that from taxing gasoline (Fig. 16.9) because the demand for orange juice is more elastic than the demand for gasoline.

government wants to raise $180 million a day so that its total revenue is not affected by this tax change. The government's economists, armed with their sta-tistical estimates of the demand and supply curves for orange juice that appear in Fig. 16.10, work out that a tax of 90¢ a litre will do the job. With such a tax, the supply curve shifts leftward to become the curve labelled *S + tax*. This new supply curve intersects the demand curve at a price of $1.30 a litre and at a quantity of 200 million litres a day. The price at which suppliers are willing to produce 200 million litres a day is 40¢ a litre. The government collects a tax of 90¢ a litre on 200 million litres a day, so it col-lects a total revenue of $180 million a day—exactly the amount that it requires.

But what is the deadweight loss? The answer can be seen by looking at the grey triangle in Fig. 16.10. The deadweight loss is $90 million. Notice how much bigger the deadweight loss is from taxing orange juice than from taxing gasoline. In the case of orange juice, the deadweight loss is one-half the revenue raised, while in the case of gasoline, it is only one-sixth. What accounts for this difference? The supply curves are identical in each case, and the examples were also set up to ensure that the initial no-tax prices and quantities were identical. The difference between the two cases is the elasticity of demand: In the case of gasoline, the quantity demanded falls by only 25 percent when the price almost doubles. In the case of orange juice, the quantity demanded falls by 50 percent when the price only slightly more than doubles.

You can see why taxing orange juice is not on the political agenda of any of the major parties. Vote-seek-ing politicians seek out taxes that benefit the median voter. Other things being equal, this means that they try to minimize the deadweight loss of raising a given amount of revenue. Equivalently, they tax items with poor substitutes more heavily than items with close substitutes. That is, they tax items with inelastic demands, such as tobacco products and alcohol, more heavily than items with more elastic demands.

REVIEW QUIZ

1 How do income taxes influence employment and efficiency? Why are income taxes progres-sive?
2 Can parliament make employers pay a larger share of social insurance tax?
3 Why do some neighbourhoods have high taxes and high-quality services, and others have low taxes and low-quality services?
4 Why does the government impose excise taxes at high rates on goods that have a low elasticity of demand?.

◆ *Reading Between the Lines* on pp. 388–389 looks at the changing scale of provision of border security services brought about by the increased awareness of terrorism. In the next two chapters, we are going to look at government economic actions in the face of monopolies and externalities.

An Increase in Demand for a Public Good

OTTAWA CITIZEN, DECEMBER 11, 2001

Spending reveals urgent need for extra security

Beefing up border security and refugee screening will cost taxpayers an additional $2.2 billion over the next five years as the federal government responds to the Sept. 11 attacks.

The new spending is a loud admission from the Chrétien government that better protection is needed immediately.

The effort is aimed at shoring up Canadian and, perhaps more important, U.S. confidence in the government's ability to ensure terrorists will not enter the U.S. or Canada. ...

Finance Minister Paul Martin's budget spelled out more than $1.2 billion will be dedicated to beefing up the border, including $646 million for new technology, including explosive-detecting equipment. ...

To complement the border developments, an additional $1 billion will be spent screening immigrants, refugees and visitors coming into Canada. ...

Mr. Martin's budget also foreshadowed improvements to Canada's passport system in the new year but the details, including the actual cost, are under wraps. The budget only said: "Further state-of-the-art securi-ty features will be incorporated into the passport system."

Overall, the government is budgeting $287 million to make its documents fraud-proof in the next five years.

"We will tighten control in our refugee system so that only those truly in need can enjoy the privilege of our welcome. To that end, we will increase resources so that enhanced security checks can be done on claimants as soon as they arrive," said Mr. Martin.

Officials said the additional $210 million being spent on refugee determination, detention and possible removal in the next five years will not build detention facilities. Individuals will be detained in existing facilities if they do not satisfy immigration officers as to their identities, pose security risks or try to enter the country illegally.

The Immigration Refugee Board will also get more money to shorten the time necessary to validate refugee claims.

The other $395 million will go towards hiring more immigration control officers as part of the effort to improve screening... .

Jack Aubrey/Ottawa Citizen

Essence of the Story

■ Finance Minister Paul Martin announced an additional $2.2 billion of expenditure on border security over the next five years as the federal government responds to the September 11 attacks.

■ More than $1.2 billion will be spent on items that include explosive-detecting equipment to improve border security.

■ An additional $1 billion will be spent on items that include a new passport system and more immigration control officers to screen immigrants, refugees, and visitors coming into Canada.

Economic Analysis

■ After the terrorist attacks of September 11, 2001, Canadian citizens and politicians revised their assessment of the benefit of border security.

■ Border security is a public good, and its efficient provision requires that its marginal benefit equal its marginal cost.

■ The total cost and marginal cost curve of border security did not change on September 11, 2001. Figure 1 shows an example of the total cost curve, *TC*, and Fig. 2 shows an example of the marginal cost curve, *MC*.

■ But the terrorist attacks changed the assessment of total benefit and marginal benefit. Before September 11, 2001, the benefit curves were TB_0 in Fig. 1 and MB_0 in Fig. 2.

■ The efficient quantity of border security was 50 units (an index number), and expenditure on this public good was $600 million a year (on the *y*-axis in Fig.1).

■ After the attacks, total benefit and marginal benefit increased to TB_1 in Fig. 1 and MB_1 in Fig. 2.

■ The efficient quantity increased to 75 (an assumed value) in Fig. 2, and expenditure in the 2002 budget increased to $1,000 million (on the *y*-axis in Fig. 1).

■ The increase in expenditure is $400 million in 2002 but will be a little higher over the succeeding years and will total $2.2 billion over five years.

■ We don't know that the efficient quantity of border security was being provided before September 11 and we don't know that the efficient quantity will be provided in the coming years. The figures show the efficient quantities.

■ Possibly, there is and will continue to be an overprovision through the pursuit of budget maximization by the government departments that provide border security.

Figure 1 Total benefit and total cost

Figure 2 Marginal benefit and marginal cost

You're The Voter

■ Do you think that Canada and the United States should adopt common rules and procedures for North American security and have an open common border?

■ Would you vote for increased expenditure and harmonization for Canada–U.S. security arrangements? Explain why or why not.

SUMMARY

KEY POINTS

The Economic Theory of Government
(pp. 374–375)

- Government exists to provide public goods, regulate monopoly, cope with externalities, and reduce economic inequality.
- Public choice theory explains how voters, politicians, and bureaucrats interact in a political marketplace.

Public Goods and the Free-Rider Problem
(pp. 376–381)

- A public good is a good or service that is consumed by everyone and that is *nonrival* and *nonexcludable.*
- A public good creates a *free-rider* problem: No one has an incentive to pay his or her share of the cost of providing a public good.
- The efficient level of provision of a public good is that at which net benefit is maximized. Equivalently, it is the level at which marginal benefit equals marginal cost.
- Competition between political parties, each of which tries to appeal to the maximum number of voters, can lead to the efficient scale of provision of a public good and to both parties proposing the same policies—the principle of minimum differentiation.
- Bureaucrats try to maximize their budgets and, if voters are rationally ignorant, producer interests may result in voting to support taxes that provide public goods in quantities that exceed those that maximize net benefit.

Taxes (pp. 382–387)

- Government revenue comes from income taxes, social insurance taxes, sales taxes and the GST, property taxes, and excise taxes.
- Income taxes decrease the level of employment and create a deadweight loss.

- Taxes can be progressive (the average tax rate rises with income), proportional (the average tax rate is constant), or regressive (the average tax rate falls with income).
- Income taxes are progressive because this arrangement is in the interests of the median voter.
- Social insurance taxes are paid by the employer and the employee (and sales taxes are paid by the buyer and the seller) in amounts that depend on the elasticities of demand and supply.
- Property taxes change both demand and supply and can result in high-tax/high-quality service areas and low-tax/low-quality service areas.
- Excise taxes at high rates on gasoline, alcoholic beverages, and tobacco products create a smaller deadweight loss than would taxes on items with more elastic demands.

KEY FIGURES

Figure 16.3   Benefits of a Public Good, 377
Figure 16.4   The Efficient Quantity of a Public Good, 379
Figure 16.5   Bureaucratic Overprovision, 380
Figure 16.7   The Effects of Income Taxes, 383
Figure 16.8   Social Insurance Taxes, 385
Figure 16.9   An Excise Tax, 386

KEY TERMS

Average tax rate, 382
Excise tax, 386
Free rider, 376
Local public good, 385
Marginal tax rate, 382
Market failure, 374
Political equilibrium, 375
Principle of minimum differentiation, 379
Public good, 376
Rational ignorance, 380

PROBLEMS

*1. You are provided with the following information about a sewage disposal system that a city of 1 million people is considering installing.

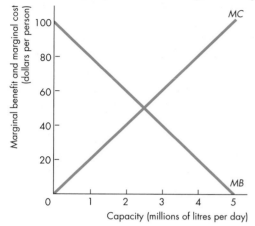

a. What is the capacity that achieves maximum net benefit?
b. How much will each person have to pay in taxes to pay for the efficient capacity level?
c. What is the political equilibrium if voters are well informed?
d. What is the political equilibrium if voters are rationally ignorant and bureaucrats achieve the highest attainable budget?

2. You are provided with the following information about a mosquito control program.

Quantity (square kilometres sprayed per day)	Marginal cost (dollars per day)	Marginal benefit (dollars per day)
0	0	0
1	1,000	5,000
2	2,000	4,000
3	3,000	3,000
4	4,000	2,000
5	5,000	1,000

a. What is the quantity of spraying that achieves maximum net benefit?
b. What is the total tax revenue needed to pay for the efficient quantity of spraying?
c. What is the political equilibrium if voters are well informed?
d. What is the political equilibrium if voters are rationally ignorant and bureaucrats achieve the highest attainable budget?

*3. An economy has two groups of people: A-types and B-types. The population consists of 80 percent A-types and 20 percent B-types. A-types have a perfectly elastic supply of labour at a wage rate of $10 an hour. B-types have a perfectly inelastic supply of labour, and their equilibrium wage rate is $100 an hour.
a. What kinds of tax arrangements do you think this economy will adopt?
b. Analyze the labour market in this economy and explain what will happen to the wage rates and employment levels of the two groups when the taxes you predict in your answer to part (a) are introduced.

4. Suppose that in the economy described in problem 3, the proportion of A-types is 20 percent and the proportion of B-types is 80 percent. Everything else remains the same.
a. Now what kinds of tax arrangements do you think the economy will adopt?
b. Analyze the labour market in this economy and explain what will happen to the wage rates and employment levels of the two groups when the taxes you predict in your answer to part (a) are introduced.
c. Compare the economy in problem 3 with the economy in this problem. Which economy more closely resembles our actual economy?

*5. An economy has a competitive labour market, which is described by the following demand and supply schedule:

Wage rate (dollars per hour)	Quantity demanded (hours per week)	Quantity supplied (hours per week)
20	0	50
16	15	40
12	30	30
8	45	20
4	60	10
0	75	0

a. What are the equilibrium wage rate and hours of work done?
b. If a $4 social insurance tax is imposed on employers
(i)   What is the new wage rate?
(ii) What is the new number of hours worked?
(iii) What is the after-tax wage rate?

(iv) What is the tax revenue?
(v) What is the deadweight loss?

6. In the economy described in problem 5, the social insurance tax on employers is eliminated and a new social insurance tax of $4 is imposed on employees.
   a. What is the new wage rate?
   b. What is the new number of hours worked?
   c. What is the after-tax wage rate?
   d. What is the tax revenue?
   e. What is the deadweight loss?
   f. Compare the situation in problem 5 with that in this problem and explain the similarities and differences in the two situations.

*7. A competitive market for cookies has the following demand and supply schedule:

Price (dollars per kilogram)	Quantity demanded (kilograms per month)	Quantity supplied (kilograms per month)
7	0	8
6	1	7
5	2	6
4	3	5
3	4	4
2	5	3
1	6	2
0	7	1

   a. Find the equilibrium price and quantity.
   b. If cookies are taxed at $2 a kilogram
      (i) What is the new price of cookies?
      (ii) What is the new quantity bought?
      (iii) What is the tax revenue?
      (iv) What is the deadweight loss?

8. In the competitive market for cookies in problem 7, the government wants to change the tax to the rate that brings in the greatest possible amount of revenue.
   a. What is that tax rate?
   b. What is the new price of cookies?
   c. What is the new quantity bought?
   d. What is the tax revenue?
   e. What is the deadweight loss?

CRITICAL THINKING

1. Study *Reading Between the Lines* on pp. 388–389 and then answer the following:
   a. Describe some of the items included in border security and explain whether they are public goods or private goods.
   b. Why might the provision of border security exceed the efficient level?
   c. Can you think of any reasons why the provision of border security might be less than the efficient level?

2. Your city council is contemplating upgrading its system for controlling traffic signals. The council believes that by installing computers, it can improve the speed of the traffic flow. The bigger the computer the council buys, the better the job it can do. The mayor and the other elected officials who are working on the proposal want to determine the scale of the system that will win them the most votes. The city bureaucrats want to maximize the budget. Suppose that you are an economist who is observing this public choice. Your job is to calculate the quantity of this public good that uses resources efficiently.
   a. What data would you need to reach your own conclusions?
   b. What does the public choice theory predict will be the quantity chosen?
   c. How could you, as an informed voter, attempt to influence the choice?

WEB EXERCISES

1. Use the links on the Parkin–Bade Web site and read the article on demand revealing processes.
   a. What is a demand revealing process and what is its purpose?
   b. Why might using a demand revealing process deliver a more efficient level of public goods than our current political system?
   c. Why might our current political system deliver a more efficient level of public goods than would a demand revealing process?

COMPETITION POLICY — CHAPTER 17

Public Interest or Special Interests?

When you consume water, electric power, cable TV, or local telephone service, you buy from a regulated monopoly. Why do we regulate the industries that produce these goods and services? How do we regulate them? Does regulation work in the interests of consumers—the public interest—or does it serve the interests of producers—special interests? ◆ The government used its anti-combine laws to end Northern Telecom's monopoly on phone equipment and Bell Canada's monopoly on long-distance phone calls as well as the installation of phone lines. This action brought competition into all three markets. Now you can choose where to buy your phone equipment, which long-distance telephone service to use, and the company to install your phone line. ◆ You will see, in *Reading Between the Lines* at the end of the chapter, that similar laws in Europe have been used to fine companies for fixing the prices of vitamins. What are the anti-combine laws? How have they evolved over the years? How are they used today? Do they serve the public interest of consumers or the special interests of producers?

◆ This chapter studies these questions.

After studying this chapter, you will be able to

- Define regulation, public ownership, and anti-combine law
- Distinguish between the public interest and capture theories of regulation
- Explain how regulation affects prices, outputs, profits, and the distribution of the gains from trade between consumers and producers
- Explain how public ownership affects prices, outputs, and allocative efficiency
- Explain how anti-combine law is used in Canada today

Market Intervention

THE GOVERNMENT INTERVENES IN MONOPOLIS-
tic and oligopolistic markets to influence what, how,
and for whom various goods and services are produced in three main ways:

- Regulation
- Public ownership
- Anti-combine law

Regulation

Regulation consists of rules administered by a government agency to influence economic activity by
determining prices, product standards and types, and
the conditions under which new firms may enter an
industry. To implement its regulations, the government establishes agencies to oversee the regulations
and ensure their enforcement. The first such economic regulation in Canada was the Railway Act of
1888, which regulated railway rates. Since then and
up to the late 1970s, regulation spread to banking
and financial services, telecommunications, gas and
electric utilities, railways, trucking, airlines and buses,
and dozens of agricultural products. Since the early
1980s, there has been a tendency to deregulate the
Canadian economy.

Deregulation is the process of removing restrictions on prices, product standards and types, and
entry conditions. In recent years, deregulation has
occurred in domestic air transportation, telephone
service, interprovincial trucking, and banking and
financial services.

Public Ownership

In Canada, a publicly owned firm is called a **Crown
corporation**. The most important Crown corporations are Canada Post, the CBC, VIA Rail,
and Atomic Energy of Canada. There are many
provincial Crown corporations, the most important
of which are the provincial hydro companies. Just
as there has been a tendency to deregulate the
Canadian economy in recent years, there has also
been a tendency to privatize it. **Privatization** is the
process of selling a publicly owned corporation to
private shareholders. Petro-Canada was privatized
in 1991.

Anti-Combine Law

An **anti-combine law** is a law that regulates and prohibits certain kinds of market behaviour, such as
monopoly and monopolistic practices. The main
thrust of the anti-combine law is the prohibition of
monopoly practices and of restricting output in order
to achieve higher prices and profits. Until 1971, these
laws were part of the Criminal Code. As a consequence, the test of guilt was much more stringent
than under civil law, and Canada's anti-combine laws
were used less vigorously than the parallel laws (called
"anti-trust laws") in the United States.

To understand why the government intervenes in
markets and to work out the effects of interventions,
we need to identify the gains and losses that government actions can create. These gains and losses are
the consumer surplus and producer surplus associated
with different output levels and prices. We first study
the economics of regulation.

Economic Theory of Regulation

THE ECONOMIC THEORY OF REGULATION IS PART
of the broader theory of public choice that is
explained in Chapter 16. We're going to re-examine
the main features of public choice theory but with an
emphasis on the regulatory aspects of government
behaviour. We'll examine the demand for government actions, the supply of those actions, and the
political equilibrium that emerges.

Demand for Regulation

The demand for regulation is expressed through
political activity—voting, lobbying, and making
campaign contributions. But engaging in political
activity is costly and people demand political action
only if the benefit that they individually receive from
such action exceeds their individual costs in obtaining the action. The four main factors that affect the
demand for regulation are

1. Consumer surplus per buyer
2. Number of buyers
3. Producer surplus per firm
4. Number of firms

The larger the consumer surplus per buyer resulting from regulation, the greater is the demand for regulation by buyers. Also, as the number of buyers increases, so does the demand for regulation. But numbers alone do not necessarily translate into an effective political force. The larger the number of buyers, the greater is the cost of organizing them, so the demand for regulation does not increase proportionately with the number of buyers.

The larger the producer surplus per firm arising from a particular regulation, the larger is the demand for that regulation by firms. Also, as the number of firms that might benefit from some regulation increases, so does the demand for that regulation. But again, large numbers do not necessarily mean an effective political force. The larger the number of firms, the greater is the cost of organizing them.

For a given surplus, consumer or producer, the smaller the number of households or firms who share that surplus, the larger is the demand for the regulation that creates it.

Supply of Regulation

Politicians and bureaucrats supply regulation. According to public choice theory, politicians choose policies that appeal to a majority of voters, thereby enabling themselves to achieve and maintain office. Bureaucrats support policies that maximize their budgets (see Chapter 16, p. 380). Given these objectives of politicians and bureaucrats, the supply of regulation depends on the following factors:

1. Consumer surplus per buyer
2. Producer surplus per firm
3. The number of voters who benefit

The larger the consumer surplus per buyer or producer surplus per firm generated and the larger the number of voters who benefit by a regulation, the greater is the tendency for politicians to supply that regulation. Politicians are likely to supply regulation that benefits a large number of people by a large amount per person. They are also likely to supply regulation that benefits a small number of people when the benefit per person is large and the cost is spread widely and not easily identified. But they are unlikely to supply regulation that brings a small benefit per person.

Political Equilibrium

In equilibrium, the regulation that exists is such that no interest group finds it worthwhile to use additional resources to press for changes and no group of politicians finds it worthwhile to offer different regulations. Being in a political equilibrium is not the same thing as everyone being in agreement. Lobby groups will devote resources to trying to change regulations that are already in place. And others will devote resources to maintaining the existing regulations. But no one will feel it is worthwhile to *increase* the resources that he or she is devoting to such activities. Also, political parties might not agree with each other. Some support the existing regulations, and others propose different regulations. In equilibrium, no one wants to change the proposals that they are making.

What will a political equilibrium look like? The answer depends on whether the regulation serves the public interest or the interest of the producer. Let's look at these two possibilities.

Public Interest Theory   The **public interest theory** is that regulations are supplied to satisfy the demand of consumers and producers to maximize total surplus—that is, to attain allocative efficiency. Public interest theory implies that the political process relentlessly seeks out deadweight loss and introduces regulations that eliminate it. For example, where monopoly practices exist, the political process will introduce price regulations to ensure that outputs increase and prices fall to their competitive levels.

Capture Theory   The **capture theory** is that the regulations are supplied to satisfy the demand of producers to maximize producer surplus—that is, to maximize economic profit. The key idea of capture theory is that the cost of regulation is high and only those regulations that increase the surplus of small, easily identified groups and that have low organization costs are supplied by the political process. Consumers bear the cost of such regulation, but the costs are spread thinly and widely so the politicians do not lose votes.

The predictions of the capture theory are less clear-cut than the predictions of the public interest theory. According to the capture theory, regulations benefit cohesive interest groups by large and visible amounts and impose small costs on everyone else. But those costs are so small, in per person terms, that no one feels it is worthwhile to incur the cost of organizing an interest group to avoid them. To make these predictions concrete enough to be useful, the capture theory needs a model of the costs of political organization.

Whichever theory of regulation is correct, according to public choice theory, the political system delivers amounts and types of regulations that best further the electoral success of politicians. Because producer-oriented and consumer-oriented regulations are in conflict with each other, the political process can't satisfy both groups in any particular industry. Only one group can win. This makes the regulatory actions of government a bit like a unique product—for example, a painting by Emily Carr. There is only one original and it will be sold to just one buyer. Normally, a unique commodity is sold through an auction; the highest bidder takes the prize.

Equilibrium in the regulatory process can be thought of in much the same way: The suppliers of regulation will satisfy the demands of the higher bidder. If the producer demand offers a bigger return to the politicians, either directly through votes or indirectly through campaign contributions, then the regulation will serve the producers' interests. If the consumer demand translates into a larger number of votes, then the regulation will serve the consumers' interests.

REVIEW QUIZ

1 How do consumers and producers express their demand for regulation? What are their objectives? What are the costs of expressing a demand for regulation?

2 When politicians and bureaucrats supply regulation, what are they trying to achieve? Do politicians and bureaucrats have the same objectives?

3 What is a political equilibrium? When does the political equilibrium achieve allocative efficiency? When does the political equilibrium serve the interests of producers? When do the bureaucrats win?

We have now completed our study of the *theory* of regulation in the marketplace. Let's turn our attention to the regulations that exist in our economy today. Which theory of regulation best explains these real-world regulations? Which of these regulations are in the public interest and which are in the interest of producers?

Regulation and Deregulation

THE PAST DECADE OR SO HAS SEEN DRAMATIC changes in the way in which the government has regulated the Canadian economy. We're going to examine some of these changes. To begin, we'll look at what the government regulates and also at the scope of regulation. Then we'll turn to the regulatory process itself and examine how regulators control prices and other aspects of market behaviour. Finally, we'll tackle the more difficult and controversial questions: Why does the government regulate some things but not others? Who benefits from the regulation that we have—consumers or producers?

The Scope of Regulation

Regulation in Canada touches a wide range of economic activity. Table 17.1 sets out the major federal regulatory agencies, together with a brief statement of their responsibilities. As you can see by inspecting that table, the predominant sectors subject to regulation are agriculture, energy, transport, and telecommunications.

Provincial and municipal governments also establish regulations covering a wide range of economic activity. Some of these—for example, municipal regulation of the taxicab industry—have important direct effects on the marketplace. Our analysis of the regulatory process and the effects of regulation apply with equal force to price, output, and profit regulation at these other governmental levels.

What exactly do regulatory agencies do? How do they regulate?

The Regulatory Process

Though regulatory agencies vary in size and scope and in the detailed aspects of economic life that they control, there are certain features common to all agencies.

First, the government appoints the senior bureaucrats who are the key decision makers in a regulatory agency. In addition, all agencies have a permanent bureaucracy made up of experts in the industry being regulated and who are often recruited from the regulated firms. Agencies have financial resources, voted by Parliament, to cover the costs of their operations.

TABLE 17.1   Federal Regulatory Agencies

Agency	Responsibility
Atomic Energy Control Board	Administers the Atomic Energy Control Act governing all uses of radioactive material.
Canadian Dairy Commission	Administers national dairy policy, which seeks to give producers an adequate return and keep the price to consumers low.
Canadian Radio-Television and Telecommunications Commission	Regulates all aspects of radio, television, and telecommunications.
Canadian Grain Commission	Regulates grain handling, establishes and maintains quality standards, audits grain stocks, and supervises future trading.
Canadian Wheat Board	Regulates exports of wheat and barley and domestic sales for human consumption.
National Energy Board	Regulates oil, gas, and electrical industries.
National Farm Products Marketing Council	Advises government on the establishment and operation of national agricultural marketing agencies and works with those agencies and provincial governments to promote marketing of farm products. Chicken, egg, and turkey agencies have been established under its aegis.
Canadian Transport Commission	Regulates transports under federal jurisdiction including rail, air, water, and pipeline and some interprovincial commercial motor transport.

Source: Adapted from the Statistics Canada publication *Canada Year Book*, catalogue 11-402, 1992, pp. 543–558.

Second, each agency adopts a set of practices or operating rules for controlling prices and other aspects of economic performance. These rules and practices are based on well-defined physical and financial accounting procedures that are relatively easy to administer and to monitor.

In a regulated industry, individual firms are usually free to determine the technology that they will use in production. But they are not free to determine the prices at which they will sell their output, the quantities that they will sell, or the markets that they will serve. The regulatory agency grants certification to a company to serve a particular market and with a particular line of products. The agency also determines the level and structure of prices that the company can charge. In some cases, the agency also determines the scale of output permitted.

To analyze the way in which regulation works, it is convenient to distinguish between the regulation of a natural monopoly and the regulation of cartels. Let's begin with the regulation of a natural monopoly.

Natural Monopoly

A **natural monopoly** was defined in Chapter 12 (p. 262) as an industry in which one firm can supply the entire market at a lower price than two or more firms can. As a consequence, a natural monopoly experiences economies of scale, no matter how large an output rate it produces. Examples of natural monopolies include local distribution of cable television signals, electricity, and gas, and urban rail services. It is much more expensive to have two or more competing sets of wires, pipes, and train tracks serving every neighbourhood than it is to have a single set. (What is a natural monopoly changes over time as technology changes. With the introduction of fibre optic cables, both telephone companies and cable television companies will be able to compete with each other in both markets, so what is a natural monopoly will become a more competitive industry.)

Let's consider the example of cable TV, which is shown in Fig. 17.1. The demand curve for cable TV is *D*. The cable TV company's marginal cost curve is *MC*. That marginal cost curve is (assumed to be)

FIGURE 17.1   Natural Monopoly: Marginal Cost Pricing

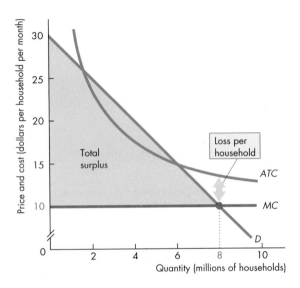

A natural monopoly is an industry in which average total cost is falling even when the entire market demand is satisfied. The demand for cable TV is shown by the curve *D*. The firm's marginal cost is constant at $10 per household per month, as shown by the curve *MC*. Fixed costs are large, and the average total cost curve, which includes average fixed cost, is shown as *ATC*. A marginal cost pricing rule that maximizes total surplus sets the price at $10 a month, with 8 million households being served. The resulting consumer surplus is shown as the green area. The firm incurs a loss on each household, indicated by the red arrow. To remain in business, the firm must price discriminate, use a two-part tariff, or receive a subsidy.

horizontal at $10 per household per month—that is, the cost of providing each additional household with a month of cable programming is $10. The cable company has a heavy investment in satellite receiving dishes, cables, and control equipment and so has high fixed costs. These fixed costs are part of the company's average total cost curve, shown as *ATC*. The average total cost curve slopes downward because as the number of households served increases, the fixed cost is spread over a larger number of households. (If you need to refresh your memory on how the average total cost curve is calculated, take a quick look back at Chapter 10, p. 224.)

Regulation in the Public Interest How will cable TV be regulated according to the public interest theory? It will be regulated to maximize total surplus, which occurs if marginal cost equals price. As you can see in Fig. 17.1, that outcome occurs if the price is regulated at $10 per household per month and if 8 million households are served. Such a regulation is called a marginal cost pricing rule. A **marginal cost pricing rule** sets price equal to marginal cost. It maximizes total surplus in the regulated industry.

A natural monopoly that is regulated to set price equal to marginal cost incurs an economic loss. Because its average total cost curve is downward sloping, marginal cost is below average total cost. Because price equals marginal cost, price is below average total cost. Average total cost minus price is the loss per unit produced. It's pretty obvious that a cable TV company that is required to use a marginal cost pricing rule will not stay in business for long. How can a company cover its costs and, at the same time, obey a marginal cost pricing rule?

One possibility is price discrimination (see Chapter 12, pp. 271–274). Another is to use a two-part price (called a two-part tariff). For example, local telephone companies can charge consumers a monthly fee for being connected to the telephone system and then charge a price equal to marginal cost for each local call. A cable TV operator can charge a one-time connection fee that covers its fixed cost and then charge a monthly fee equal to marginal cost.

But a natural monopoly cannot always cover its costs in these ways. If a natural monopoly cannot cover its total cost from its customers and if the government wants it to follow a marginal cost pricing rule, then the government must give the firm a subsidy. In such a case, the government raises the revenue for the subsidy by taxing some other activity. But as we saw in Chapter 16, taxes themselves generate deadweight loss. Thus the deadweight loss resulting from additional taxes must be subtracted from the efficiency gained by forcing the natural monopoly to adopt a marginal cost pricing rule.

Deadweight loss might be minimized by making the natural monopoly cover its costs rather than by taxing another sector of the economy. When a monopoly covers its costs, it uses an average cost pricing rule. An **average cost pricing rule** sets price equal to average total cost. Figure 17.2 shows the average cost pricing outcome. The cable TV operator charges $15 a month and serves 6 million households. A deadweight loss arises, which is shown by the grey triangle in the figure.

FIGURE 17.2   Natural Monopoly: Average Cost Pricing

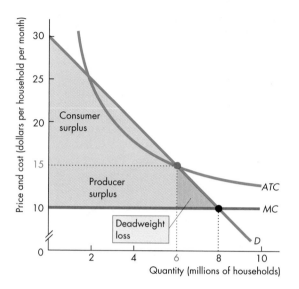

An average cost pricing rule sets the price equal to average total cost. The cable TV operator charges $15 a month and serves 6 million households. In this situation, the firm breaks even—average total cost equals price. Deadweight loss, shown by the grey triangle, is generated. Consumer surplus is reduced to the green area.

FIGURE 17.3   Natural Monopoly: Profit Maximization

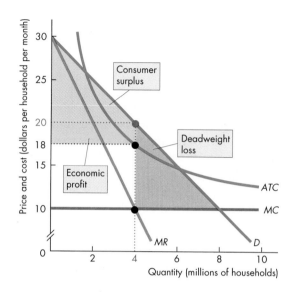

The cable TV operator would like to maximize profit. To do so, marginal revenue (MR) is made equal to marginal cost (MC). At a price of $20 a month, 4 million households buy cable service. Consumer surplus is reduced to the green triangle. The deadweight loss increases to the grey triangle. The monopoly makes the profit shown by the blue rectangle. If the producer can capture the regulator, the outcome will be the situation shown here.

Capturing the Regulator   What does the capture theory predict about the regulation of this industry? According to the capture theory, the producer gets the regulator to set rules that work to serve the interest of the producer. But the producer interest is served by being able to operate at the same output and price as an unregulated monopoly. In Fig. 17.3, the monopoly's marginal revenue curve is the curve labelled *MR*. Marginal revenue equals marginal cost when output is 4 million households and the price is $20 a month. At this output and price, the producer makes the maximum profit. So regulation in the interest of the producer maintains the unregulated monopoly outcome.

But how can a producer go about capturing the regulator and obtaining regulation that results in this monopoly profit-maximizing outcome? To answer this question, we need to look at the way in which

agencies determine a regulated price. A key method used is called rate of return regulation.

Rate of Return Regulation   Rate of return regulation determines a regulated price by setting the price at a level that enables the regulated firm to earn a specified target percent return on its capital. The target rate of return is determined with reference to what is normal in competitive industries. This rate of return is part of the opportunity cost of the natural monopoly and is included in the firm's average total cost. By examining the firm's total cost, including the normal rate of return on capital, the regulator attempts to determine the price at which average total cost is covered. Thus rate of return regulation is equivalent to an average cost pricing rule.

In Fig. 17.2, average cost pricing results in a regulated price of $15 a month with 6 million households being served. Thus rate of return regulation, based on a correct assessment of the producer's average total cost curve, results in a price that favours the consumer and does not enable the producer to maximize monopoly profit. The special interest group will have failed to capture the regulator, and the outcome will be closer to that predicted by the public interest theory of regulation.

But there is a feature of many real-world situations that the above analysis does not take into account: the ability of the monopoly firm to mislead the regulator about its true costs.

Inflating Costs The managers of a firm might be able to inflate the firm's costs by spending part of the firm's revenue on inputs that are not strictly required for the production of the good. By this device, the firm's apparent costs exceed the true costs. On-the-job luxury in the form of sumptuous office suites, limousines, free baseball tickets (disguised as public relations expenses), company jets, lavish international travel, and entertainment are all ways in which managers can inflate costs.

If the cable TV operator makes the regulator believe that its true cost is *ATC (inflated)* in Fig. 17.4, then the regulator will set the price at $20 a month. In this example, the price and quantity will be the same as those under unregulated monopoly. It might be impossible for firms to inflate their costs by as much as the amount shown in the figure. But to the extent that costs can be inflated, the apparent average total cost curve lies somewhere between the true average total cost curve and *ATC (inflated)*. The greater the ability of the firm to inflate its costs in this way, the more closely its profit (measured in economic terms) approaches the maximum possible. The stockholders of this firm don't receive this economic profit because it is used up in baseball tickets, luxury offices, and the other actions taken by the firm's managers to inflate the company's costs.

Public Interest or Capture?

It is not clear whether actual regulation produces prices and quantities that more closely correspond with the predictions of capture theory or of public interest theory. One thing is clear, however. Price regulation does not require natural monopolies to use the marginal cost pricing rule. If it did, most natural

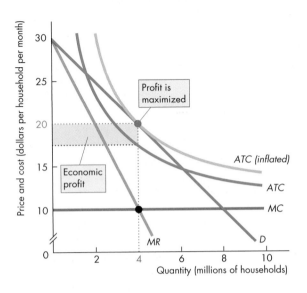

FIGURE 17.4   Natural Monopoly: Inflating Costs

If the cable TV operator is able to inflate its costs to *ATC (inflated)* and persuade the regulator that these are genuine minimum costs of production, rate of return regulation results in a price of $20 a month—the profit-maximizing price. To the extent that the producer can inflate costs above average total cost, the price rises, output decreases, and deadweight loss increases. The managers, not the shareholders (owners) of the firm, capture the profit.

monopolies would incur losses and receive hefty government subsidies to enable them to remain in business. But there are even exceptions to this conclusion. For example, many local telephone companies do appear to use marginal cost pricing for local telephone calls. These phone companies cover their total cost by charging a flat fee each month for being connected to their telephone system but then permitting each local call to be made at its marginal cost—zero or something very close to it.

We can test whether natural monopoly regulation is in the public interest or producer interest by comparing the rates of return in regulated natural monopolies with average returns. If regulated natural monopolies have rates of return that are significantly higher than those in the rest of the economy, then, to some degree, the regulator may have been captured by the producer. There is plenty of empirical evidence that many natural monopolies in Canada do earn higher rates of return than the economy average.

One recent striking example is cable television service; telephone service is another. The rates of return in these two industries exceed 10 percent a year, approaching double the economy average. Perhaps the most dramatic piece of evidence that regulation benefits the regulated firm is the profits of Bell Canada Enterprises (BCE), prior to deregulation of long-distance phone services. BCE is a conglomerate that produced *regulated* long-distance telephone services and *unregulated* phone equipment (Northern Telecom) and financial services (Montreal Trustco). In 1992, BCE made a total profit of $1.4 billion on total assets of $12.3 billion, a profit rate of 11.4 percent. But this total was made up of a profit of $0.9 billion on assets of $7 billion—a return of 12.9 percent—for the regulated Bell Canada and a profit of $0.5 billion on assets of $5.3 billion—9.4 percent—for all of BCE's *unregulated* operations.

Until the early 1990s, long-distance telephone service was a natural monopoly, but technological advances in telecommunications have changed the situation. Today, the industry is an oligopoly. But oligopoly is also regulated. Let's examine regulation in oligopolistic industries—the regulation of cartels.

Cartel Regulation

A *cartel* is a collusive agreement among a number of firms designed to restrict output and achieve a higher profit for the cartel's members. Cartels are illegal in Canada and in most other countries. But international cartels can sometimes operate legally, as does the international cartel of oil producers known as OPEC (the Organization of the Petroleum Exporting Countries).

Illegal cartels can arise in oligopolistic industries. An oligopoly is a market structure in which a small number of firms compete with each other. We studied oligopoly (and duopoly—two firms competing for a market) in Chapter 13. There we saw that if firms manage to collude and behave like a monopoly, they can set the same price and sell the same total quantity as a monopoly firm would. But we also discovered that in such a situation, each firm will be tempted to cheat, increasing its own output and profit at the expense of the other firms. The result of such cheating on the collusive agreement is the unravelling of the monopoly equilibrium and the emergence of a competitive

outcome with zero economic profit for producers. Such an outcome benefits consumers at the expense of producers.

How is oligopoly regulated? Does regulation prevent monopoly practices or does it encourage those practices?

According to the public interest theory, oligopoly is regulated to ensure a competitive outcome. Consider, for example, the market for trucking tomatoes from the fields of southwestern Ontario to a ketchup factory at Leamington, illustrated in Fig. 17.5. The demand curve for trips is *D*. The industry marginal cost curve—and the competitive supply curve—is *MC*. Public interest regulation will regulate the price of a trip at $20 and there will be 300 trips a week.

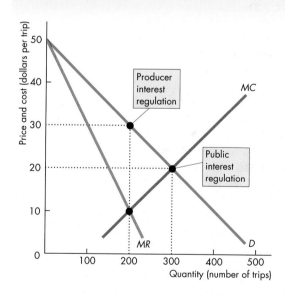

FIGURE 17.5   Collusive Oligopoly

Ten trucking firms transport tomatoes from southwestern Ontario to Leamington. The demand curve is *D*, and the industry marginal cost curve is *MC*. Under competition, the *MC* curve is the industry supply curve. If the industry is competitive, the price of a trip will be $20 and 300 trips will be made each week. Producers will demand regulation that restricts entry and limits output to 200 trips a week where industry marginal revenue (*MR*) is equal to industry marginal cost (*MC*). This regulation raises the price to $30 a trip and results in each producer making maximum profit—as if the 10 firms were a monopoly.

How would this industry be regulated according to the capture theory? Regulation that is in the interest of producers will maximize profit. To find the outcome in this case, we need to determine the price and quantity when marginal cost equals marginal revenue. The marginal revenue curve is *MR*. So marginal revenue equals marginal cost at 200 trips a week. The price of a trip is $30.

One way of achieving this outcome is to place an output limit on each firm in the industry. If there are 10 trucking companies, an output limit of 20 trips per company ensures that the total number of trips in a week is 200. Penalties can be imposed to ensure that no single producer exceeds its output limit.

All the firms in the industry would support this type of regulation because it helps to prevent cheating and to maintain a monopoly outcome. Each firm knows that without effectively enforced production quotas, every firm has an incentive to increase output. (For each firm, price exceeds marginal cost, so a greater output brings a larger profit.) So each firm wants a method of preventing output from rising above the industry's profit-maximizing level, and the quotas enforced by regulation achieve this end. With this type of cartel regulation, the regulator enables a cartel to operate legally and in its own best interest.

What does cartel regulation do in practice? Although there is disagreement about the matter, the consensus view is that regulation tends to favour the producer. Trucking and airlines (when they were regulated by the Canadian Transport Commission) and taxicabs (regulated by cities) are specific examples in which profits of producers increased as a result of regulation. But the most dramatic examples of regulation favouring the producer are in agriculture. An Economic Council of Canada study, based on the situation prevailing in the early 1980s, estimated that regulation of the egg-producing and broiler chicken industries alone transferred more than $100 million a year to just 4,600 individual producers.[1]

Further evidence on cartel and oligopoly regulation can be obtained from the performance of prices and profit following deregulation. If, following deregulation, prices and profit fall, then, to some degree, the regulation must have been serving the interest of the producer. In contrast, if, following deregulation, prices and profits remain constant or increase, then the regulation may be presumed to have been serving the public interest. Because there has been a substantial amount of deregulation in recent years, we may use this test of oligopoly regulation to see which of the two theories better fits the facts. The evidence is mixed, but in the cases of airlines, trucking, and long-distance phone calls, three oligopolies to be deregulated, prices fell and there was a large increase in the volume of business.

Making Predictions

Most industries have a few producers and many consumers. In these cases, public choice theory predicts that regulation will protect producers because a small number of people stand to gain a large amount and so they will be fairly easy to organize as a cohesive lobby. Under such circumstances, politicians will be rewarded with campaign contributions rather than votes. But there are situations in which the consumer interest is sufficiently strong and well organized and thus able to prevail. There are also cases in which the balance switches from producer to consumer, as seen in the deregulation process that began in the late 1970s.

Deregulation raises some hard questions for economists seeking to understand and make predictions about regulation. Why were the transportation and telecommunications sectors deregulated? If producers gained from regulation and if the producer lobby was strong enough to achieve regulation, what happened in the 1970s to change the equilibrium to one in which the consumer interest prevailed? We do not have a complete answer to this question at the present time. But regulation had become so costly to consumers, and the potential benefits to them from deregulation so great, that the cost of organizing the consumer voice became a price worth paying.

One factor that increased the cost of regulation borne by consumers and brought deregulation in the transportation sector was the large increase in energy prices in the 1970s. These price hikes made route regulation by the Canadian Transport Commission extremely costly and changed the balance of the political equilibrium to favour consumers. Technological change was the main factor at work in the telecommunications sector. New satellite-based, computer-controlled long-distance technologies enabled smaller producers to offer low-cost services. These producers wanted a share of Bell Canada's business—and profit. Furthermore, as communica-

---

[1] J. D. Forbes, R. D. Hughes, and T.K. Warley, *Economic Intervention and Regulation in Canadian Agriculture* (Ottawa: Department of Supply and Services, 1982).

tions technology improved, the cost of communication fell and the cost of organizing larger groups of consumers also fell. If this line of reasoning is correct, we can expect to see more consumer-oriented regulation in the future. In practice, more consumer-oriented regulation often means deregulation—removing the regulations that are already in place to serve the interests of producer groups.

Let's now turn to the second method of intervention in markets—public ownership.

Public Ownership

CROWN CORPORATIONS HAVE A SIGNIFICANT AND historical presence in Canadian society. Before Confederation, Crown corporations were used for building canals and operating ports and harbours. The establishment of the Canadian nation involved a commitment to build a railway to link New Brunswick and Nova Scotia to central Canada. Over the years, vast distances, a sparse population, the presence of a powerful neighbour, strong and distinct national interests, and the existence of two main cultural and linguistic groups nurtured the establishment of Crown corporations.

A Crown corporation is a corporation in which the government has 100 percent ownership. There

are federal and provincial Crown corporations, and they are involved in many sectors of the economy, including transportation; energy and resources; agriculture and fisheries; development and construction; government services; culture; financial intermediaries; telecommunications and broadcasting; provincial lotteries; housing; and alcoholic beverages. Examples of Crown corporations include the Business Development Bank of Canada, the Canadian Museum of Nature, and the Ontario Lottery Corporation.

Public ownership provides another way in which the government can influence the behaviour of a natural monopoly. What are the effects of this method of natural monopoly control? How does a publicly owned corporation operate? Let's explore some alternative patterns of behaviour for such corporations.

Efficient Crown Corporation

One possibility is that a Crown corporation is operated in a manner that results in economic efficiency—maximization of total surplus. Let's consider the example of a railway. Figure 17.6(a) illustrates the demand for freight service and the railway's costs. The demand curve is *D*. The marginal cost curve is *MC*. Notice that the marginal cost curve is horizontal at $2 a tonne. The railway has a heavy investment in track, trains, and control equipment, so it has large fixed costs. These fixed costs feature in the company's average total cost curve *ATC*. The average total cost curve slopes downward because as the number of tonnes of freight carried increases, the fixed costs are spread over a larger number of tonnes. To be efficient, a Crown corporation obeys the rule:

Produce the output at which price equals marginal cost.

In this example, that output level is 8 billion tonnes a year at a price—and marginal cost—of $2 a tonne. To be able to operate in this manner, a publicly owned railway has to be subsidized; the subsidy on each unit of output must equal the difference between average total cost and marginal cost. And the subsidy has to be collected in a way other than through the price of the good or service produced—in other words, by taxation. If the government taxes each household a fixed amount, the consumer surplus will shrink to the green triangle shown in Fig. 17.6(a), but consumer surplus will be at its maximum.

FIGURE 17.6   Crown Corporation

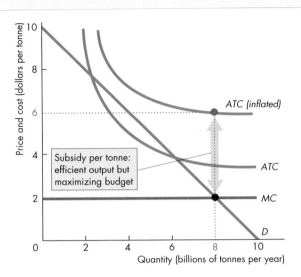

Part (a) shows a railway operated by a Crown corporation that produces the output at which price equals marginal cost. Its output is 8 billion tonnes a year and the price is $2 a tonne. The Crown corporation receives a subsidy that enables it to cover its total cost, and that cost is the minimum possible cost of providing the efficient quantity. Part (b) shows what happens if the managers of the Crown corporation pursue their own interest and maximize their budget by padding costs. Average total cost now increases to ATC (inflated). If the corporation is required to keep price equal to marginal cost, the quantity produced is efficient, but the managers divert the consumer surplus to themselves.

The situation depicted in Fig. 17.6(a) achieves an efficient outcome because consumer surplus is maximized. But it is not an outcome that is necessarily compatible with the interests of the managers of the Crown corporation. One model of the behaviour of managers is that suggested by the economic theory of bureaucracy. What does that alternative model predict about Crown corporation behaviour?

A Bureaucracy Model of Public Enterprise

The basic assumption of the economic theory of bureaucracy is that bureaucrats aim to maximize the budget of their bureau. The equivalent assumption for the managers of a Crown corporation is that they seek to maximize the budget of the Crown corporation. The effect of budget maximization by the managers of a Crown corporation depends on the pricing constraints under which the managers operate. We will consider two alternative cases:

- Budget maximization with marginal cost pricing
- Budget maximization at a zero price

Budget Maximization with Marginal Cost Pricing
If the bureau maximizes its budget but obeys the marginal cost pricing rule, it will produce the efficient outcome. It will produce 8 billion tonnes a year and it will sell its output for $2 a tonne, as Fig. 17.6(b) illustrates. But the corporation will not minimize its production cost. It will inflate its costs and become inefficient. It will hire more workers than the number required to produce 8 billion tonnes a year, and its internal control mechanisms, which would ensure internal efficiency (as in a private profit-maximizing firm), will be weak. As a result, the average total cost of the corporation will rise to *ATC (inflated)*.

What determines the limit on the extent to which the corporation can inflate its costs? The answer is the maximum amount that the users of the output can be made to pay through taxation. That maximum is the total consumer surplus. That maximum consumer surplus is the area beneath the demand curve and above the marginal cost curve. You can work out how big it is by using the usual formula for the area of the triangle. The height of this triangle is $8 and its base is 8 billion tonnes a year, so the consumer surplus is $32 billion. Spread over 8 billion tonnes, $32 billion gives a subsidy of $4 a tonne, the amount shown in the figure. $32 billion will be the upper limit that any government—in a political democracy—can extract from the taxpayer-consumers of the product of this corporation. If the subsidy were higher, people would vote to shut down the Crown corporation because the subsidy would exceed the consumer surplus.

Budget Maximization at Zero Price What happens if a government bureau provides its goods or services free? Of course, it is improbable that a publicly owned railway would be able to persuade politicians and taxpayers that its activities should be expanded to the point of providing its services free. But there are several examples of publicly provided goods that are indeed free. Primary and secondary education and health care are two outstanding examples. For the sake of comparison, we'll continue with our railway, improbable though it is.

If in Fig. 17.6(b) the bureau increases output to the point at which the price that consumers are willing to pay for the last unit produced is zero, output rises to 10 billion tonnes a year. A deadweight loss is created because the marginal cost of production, $2 a tonne, is higher than the marginal benefit or willingness to pay, $0 per tonne. The bureau will be inefficient in its internal operations and inflate its costs. The subsidy will increase to the highest that the public will be willing to pay. The maximum subsidy will equal the consumer surplus.

Compromise Outcome There will be a tendency for the corporation to overproduce and to inflate its budget, but not to the extent shown in Fig. 17.6(b). There will be a tendency for consumer interest to have some influence, but not to the degree shown in Fig. 17.6(a). The basic prediction about the behav-

iour of a Crown corporation, then, is that it will overproduce and be less efficient than a private firm.

Crown Corporations in Reality

How do actual Crown corporations behave? Several studies have been directed to answering this question. One of the most fruitful ways of approaching the question is to compare public and private enterprises in which, as far as possible, other things are equal. There are two well-known and well-studied cases for which other things seemed to be fairly equal. One such comparison is of Canada's public and private railways—Canadian National (CN) and Canadian Pacific (CP). The other is from Australia, which had two domestic airlines, one private and the other public, that flew almost identical routes at almost identical times every day. Economists studied the costs of these similar enterprises and concluded that each of the publicly owned enterprises operated with a cost structure that was significantly higher than that of the corresponding private firm. In the case of CN and CP, the estimated difference was 14 percent.[2]

Privatization

Largely because of an increasing understanding of how bureaucracies work and of the inefficiency of publicly operated enterprises, there has been a move to sell off publicly owned corporations. Since the mid-1980s, the federal government has sold a dozen companies, including Air Canada and CN.

REVIEW QUIZ

1 How might a Crown corporation operate efficiently?
2 What are the effects of budget maximization by the managers of a Crown corporation?
3 What limits the maximum budget of a Crown corporation?

Let's now turn to anti-combine law.

[2] W.S.W. Caves and Lauritis Christensen, "The Relative Efficiency of Public *v.* Private Firms in a Competitive Environment: The Case of Canada's Railroads," *Journal of Political Economy* 88, 5 (September–October 1980), 958–76.

Anti-Combine Law

ANTI-COMBINE LAW GIVES POWERS TO THE courts and to government agencies to influence markets. Like regulation, anti-combine law can work in the public interest to maximize total surplus or in private interests to maximize the surpluses of particular special interest groups such as producers. We'll describe Canada's anti-combine law and then examine some recent cases.

Canada's Anti-Combine Law

Canada's anti-combine law dates from 1889. At that time, monopoly was a major political issue and people were concerned about the absence of competition in industries as diverse as sugar and groceries, biscuits and confectionery, coal, binder twine, agricultural implements, stoves, coffins, eggs, and fire insurance.

Canada's anti-combine law today is defined in the Competition Act of 1986, which is described in Table 17.2. The Act established a Competition Bureau and a Competition Tribunal. The Competition Act distinguishes between practices that are

1. Criminal
2. Noncriminal

Conspiracy to fix prices, bid-rigging, other anticompetitive price-fixing actions, and false advertising are criminal offences. The courts handle alleged offences, and the standard level of proof beyond a reasonable doubt must be established.

Mergers, abuse of a dominant market position, refusal to deal, and other actions designed to limit competition such as exclusive dealing are noncriminal offences. The Director of the Competition Bureau sends alleged violations of a noncriminal nature to the Competition Tribunal for examination.

Some Recent Anti-Combine Cases

Let's see how the Competition Act has been working by looking at some recent cases. The first case we'll examine is important because it confirms the Competition Tribunal's power to enforce its orders.

Chrysler In 1986, Chrysler stopped supplying auto parts to Richard Brunet, a Montreal auto dealer. Chrysler also discouraged other dealers from supplying Brunet. The Competition Tribunal claimed that Chrysler wanted Brunet's business for itself and ordered Chrysler to resume doing business with Brunet. Chrysler did not resume sending supplies and the Tribunal cited Chrysler for contempt. Appeals against this ruling eventually reached the Supreme Court of Canada, which confirmed the Tribunal's power over contempt for its ruling. But the Tribunal subsequently dropped its contempt charge.

The second case we'll look at concerns aspartame, the sweetener in many soft drinks.

NutraSweet NutraSweet, the maker of aspartame, tried to gain a monopoly in aspartame. It did so by licensing the use of its "swirl" only on products for which it had an exclusive deal. The Competition Tribunal ruled that this action unduly limited competition and told NutraSweet that it may not enforce existing contracts, enter into new contracts in which it is the exclusive supplier, or give inducements to encourage the display of its "swirl." The result of this case was an increase in competition and a fall in the price of aspartame in Canada.

The third case we'll examine concerns a publication you use almost every day: the Yellow Pages.

Bell Canada Enterprises Two subsidiaries of Bell Canada Enterprises have a 90 percent share of the market for the publication of telephone directories in their territories. These companies tie the sale of advertising services to the sale of advertising space in the Yellow Pages. If you want to advertise in the Yellow Pages, you must buy the advertising services of one of these two companies. As a result, other advertising agencies cannot effectively compete for business in Yellow Pages advertising. The Director of the Competition Bureau applied for an order prohibiting the tied-sale practice of these two companies.

Other Recent Anti-Competitive Agreements During 1995 and 1996, the Competition Bureau took action against several anti-competitive agreements. Among such cases were driving schools in Sherbrooke, ready-mix concrete in the Saguenay-Lac St-Jean region, real estate dealing in Calgary, the importing of Australian mandarin oranges, wire for baling pulp, and ambulance services in Alberta.

The Competition Bureau is extremely active in

TABLE 17.2   Canada's Anti-Combine Law: The Competition Act, 1986

Abuse of Dominant Position

79 (1)   Where on application by the Director, the Tribunal finds that:

(a)   one or more persons substantially or completely control, throughout Canada or any area thereof, a class or species of business,

(b)   that person or those persons have engaged in or are engaging in a practice of anti-competitive acts, and

(c)   the practice has had, is having or is likely to have the effect of preventing or lessening competition substantially in a market, the Tribunal may make an order prohibiting all or any of those persons from engaging in that practice.

Mergers

92 (1)   Where on application by the Director, the Tribunal finds that a merger or proposed merger prevents or lessens, or is likely to prevent or lessen, competition substantially ... the Tribunal may ... [,] in the case of a completed merger, order any party to the merger

(i)   to dissolve the merger ...

(ii)   to dispose of assets and shares ...

[or]

in the case of a proposed merger, make an order directed against any party to the proposed merger

(i)   ordering the person ... not to proceed with the merger

(ii)   ordering the person not to proceed with part of the merger

reviewing and, in some cases, blocking mergers. The next cases we examine fall into this category.

Canada Packers and Labatt   Canada Packers Inc. and John Labatt Ltd. proposed a merger of their flour milling operations that would have made them the biggest miller in Canada and the fifth biggest in North America. The Competition Tribunal stopped this merger, saying that the Canadian flour milling business had been run too much like a cartel and that more, not less, competition was needed.

Banks   Some attempts to merge are so politically sensitive that they are decided at the highest political level. One example is the decision of the federal government to block an attempted merger by the Royal Bank and the Bank of Montreal. If Canada's two major banks eventually merge, the sanction of the federal government will be needed.

Public or Special Interest?

The intent of anti-combine law is to protect the public interest and restrain the profit-seeking and anti-competitive actions of producers. On the whole, the overall thrust of the law and its enforcement has been in line with its intent and has served the public interest. Further, if the recent cases we have examined are setting a trend, we can expect a continuation of pro-consumer decisions from the courts and the Competition Tribunal in future cases.

REVIEW QUIZ

1   What is the Act of Parliament that provides our anti-combine law?

2   What actions violate the anti-combine law?

3   Under what circumstances is a merger unlikely to be approved?

◆ In this chapter, we've seen how the government intervenes in markets to affect prices, quantities, consumer surplus, and producer surplus. *Reading Between the Lines* on pp. 408–409 looks at price fixing in global markets for vitamins.

Fixing Vitamin Prices

THE WALL STREET JOURNAL, NOVEMBER 22, 2001

EU levies $755.1 million fine in vitamin price-fixing case

The European Commission fined eight companies a record 855.2 million euros ($755.1 million) for allegedly fixing vitamin prices, but let one drug maker almost completely off the hook for turning on its former partners.

The supposed ringleader of the price-fixing cartel, Roche Holding AG of Switzerland, was fined 462 million euros, or 2.6% of world-wide sales in 1999.

Under the commission's rules, fines start at 20 million euros per offense and increase by 10% for each additional year of illegal activity. The figures in that formula are subject to mitigating or aggravating factors.

The commission said although it would have been justified in fining Roche as much as 962 million euros, the sum was reduced because Roche cooperated in the investigation by, among other things, willingly giving the commission documents for which it asked.

Roche was the "prime mover and main beneficiary" of the scheme to fix prices on 12 separate vitamins in the 1990s, the commission said. BASF AG of Germany was another "paramount" player, the commission said, and was fined 296.2 million euros. Fines for the six other companies ranged from 5 million euros to 37.1 million euros.

Mario Monti, the commissioner responsible for antitrust policy, said the eight companies operated the "most damaging series of cartels the commission has ever investigated" in terms of harm to consumers. But the commission didn't impose the maximum penalty possible under the law: 10% of a company's annual sales during the last year in which the cartel operated. Altogether, that could have run into the billions of euros.

Mr. Monti insisted the commission wasn't letting the companies off lightly. But he lamented the fact that under European Union law, there are no criminal sanctions for price-fixing, as there are in the U.S. "We're working to make penalties more and more effective and more and more deterrent," he said.

In the 1999 U.S. case, Roche paid a fine of $500 million, and a former executive went to prison.

Amelia Torres, a spokeswoman for Mr. Monti, said the commission had wide discretion on the final amount of the fine, in part because it wanted to maintain "a certain degree of uncertainty" so companies didn't calculate likely fines into their business plans. However, Roche said it had already figured the fine into its spending plans back in 1999.

Essence of the Story

■ Price fixing is illegal in the European Union, but it is not subject to criminal sanctions.

■ Under European Commission (EC) rules, fines start at 20 million euros per offence and increase by 10 percent for each additional year of illegal activity.

■ In 2001, the EC fined eight companies for allegedly fixing vitamin prices.

■ The largest fine imposed was on Roche of Switzerland (462 million euro—2.6 percent of its 1999 worldwide sales).

■ The EC could have fined Roche 962 million euros but reduced the fine because Roche cooperated in the investigation.

■ Roche said that it had budgeted for the fine in its spending plans.

Economic Analysis

■ In Canada, price fixing is a criminal offence that can be punished by a combination of fines and imprisonment.

■ In the European Union (EU), price fixing is illegal but subject only to a fine.

■ The formula for a fine is a fixed amount per violation per year. For the firm, the fine is a fixed cost.

■ Even when the EC uses discretion to keep the firm guessing about the scale of the fine, the firm can figure out the maximum fine and can compare paying the fine with the alternative of not engaging in price fixing.

■ If the profit that results from price fixing minus the fine exceeds the profit from not price fixing, it is rational, but illegal, for a firm to price fix.

■ Figure 1 shows the situation that Roche of Switzerland faces.

■ The demand curve for Roche's products depends on the prices set by its competitors.

■ When Roche's competitors engage in price fixing, the demand curve for Roche's products is D and its marginal revenue curve is MR.

■ Roche's average total cost curve is ATC, and its marginal cost curve is MC.

■ Roche maximizes profit by selling 3 billion items a year (where MC equals MR) at a price of $6 per item.

■ Roche's economic profit, shown by the sum of the two blue rectangles, is $6 billion a year. (Roche's actual economic profit in 2000 was about $5 billion.)

■ Because Roche pays a price-fixing fine, which is about $0.4 billion, its ATC curve shifts upward to $ATC + fine$.

■ Even if Roche paid a price-fixing fine of $4 billion, ten times as large as the one imposed, its ATC curve would shift upward to $ATC + fine^*$ and the firm would still make an economic profit.

■ Figure 2 illustrates the alternative of competing without price fixing. Competition, from other producers decreases the demand for Roche's products to D_{comp}. The price is driven down to the point at which economic profit is eliminated and the firm earns normal profit (included in ATC).

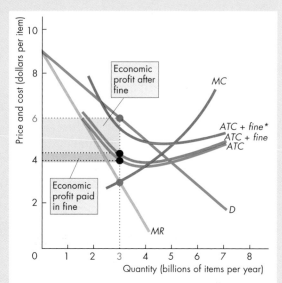

Figure 1 Roche in 2000

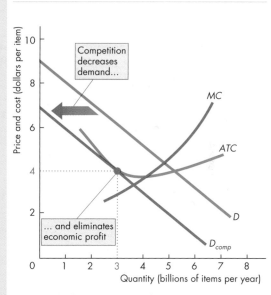

Figure 2 Roche in competition

■ The Canadian law is more powerful than the EU law and makes it harder for firms to use price fixing as a business strategy.

409

SUMMARY

KEY POINTS

Market Intervention (p. 394)

- The government intervenes to regulate monopolistic and oligopolistic markets in three ways: regulation, public ownership, and anti-combine law.

Economic Theory of Regulation (pp. 394–396)

- Consumers and producers express their demand for the regulation by voting, lobbying, and making campaign contributions.
- The larger the surplus per person generated by a regulation or the smaller the number of people who share a given surplus, the larger is the demand for the regulation.
- Regulation is supplied by politicians who pursue their own best interest.
- The larger the surplus per person generated and the larger the number of people who benefit from it, the larger is the supply of regulation.
- Public interest theory predicts that regulation will maximize total surplus; capture theory predicts that producer surplus will be maximized.

Regulation and Deregulation (pp. 396–403)

- Natural monopolies and cartels are regulated by agencies controlled by politically appointed bureaucrats and staffed by a permanent bureaucracy of experts.
- Regulated firms must comply with rules about price, product quality, and output levels.
- Regulation has not lowered the profit rates of regulated firms.

Public Ownership (pp. 403–405)

- Crown corporations are 100 percent owned by federal and provincial governments and they produce such items as broadcasting, hydroelectric power, and telecommunications.

- The economic theory of bureaucracy is that managers maximize their budgets subject to political constraints.
- Crown corporations tend to be inefficient: They overproduce and their costs are too high.

Anti-Combine Law (pp. 406–407)

- Anti-combine law provides an alternative way for government to control monopoly and monopolistic practices.
- The Competition Act of 1986 sets out Canada's anti-combine law and places responsibility for enforcement with the Competition Tribunal.

KEY FIGURES AND TABLES

Figure 17.1   Natural Monopoly: Marginal Cost Pricing, 398
Figure 17.2   Natural Monopoly: Average Cost Pricing, 399
Figure 17.3   Natural Monopoly: Profit Maximization, 399
Figure 17.5   Collusive Oligopoly, 401
Figure 17.6   Crown Corporation, 404
Table 17.1   Federal Regulatory Agencies, 397
Table 17.2   Canada's Anti-Combine Law: The Competition Act, 1986, 407

KEY TERMS

Anti-combine law, 394
Average cost pricing rule, 398
Capture theory, 395
Crown corporation, 394
Marginal cost pricing rule, 398
Natural monopoly, 397
Privatization, 394
Public interest theory, 395
Rate of return regulation, 399

PROBLEMS

*1. Elixir Springs, Inc., is an unregulated natural monopoly that bottles Elixir, a unique health product with no substitutes. The total fixed cost incurred by Elixir Springs is $150,000, and its marginal cost is 10 cents a bottle. The figure illustrates the demand for Elixir.

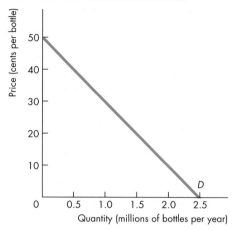

a. What is the price of a bottle of Elixir?
b. How many bottles does Elixir Springs sell?
c. Does Elixir Springs maximize total surplus or producer surplus?

2. Cascade Springs, Inc., is a natural monopoly that bottles water from a spring in the Rocky Mountains. Cascade Springs' total fixed cost is $80,000, and its marginal cost is 5 cents a bottle. The figure illustrates the demand for Cascade Springs bottled water.

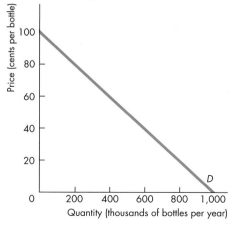

a. What is the price of Cascade Springs water?
b. How many bottles does Cascade Springs sell?
c. Does Cascade Springs maximize total surplus or producer surplus?

*3. The government imposes a marginal cost pricing rule on Elixir Springs in problem 1.
   a. What is the price of a bottle of Elixir?
   b. How many bottles does Elixir Springs sell?
   c. What is Elixir Springs' producer surplus?
   d. What is the consumer surplus?
   e. Is the regulation in the public interest? Explain.

4. The government imposes a marginal cost pricing rule on Cascade Springs in problem 2.
   a. What is the price of Cascade Springs water?
   b. How many bottles does Cascade Springs sell?
   c. What is the economic profit?
   d. What is the consumer surplus?
   e. Is the regulation in the public interest? Explain.

*5. The government imposes an average cost pricing rule on Elixir Springs in problem 1.
   a. What is the price of a bottle of Elixir?
   b. How many bottles does Elixir Springs sell?
   c. What is Elixir Springs' producer surplus?
   d. What is the consumer surplus?
   e. Is the regulation in the public interest? Explain.

6. The government imposes an average cost pricing rule on Cascade Springs in problem 2.
   a. What is the price of Cascade Springs water?
   b. How many bottles does Cascade Springs sell?
   c. What is Cascade Springs' economic profit?
   d. What is the consumer surplus?
   e. Is the regulation in the public interest or in the private interest?

*7. Two airlines share an international route. The figure shows the demand curve for trips on this route and each firm's marginal cost. This air route is regulated.

a. What is the price of a trip and what is the number of trips per day if the regulation is in the public interest?
b. What is the price of a trip and what is the number of trips per day if the airlines capture the regulator?
c. What is the deadweight loss in part (b)?
d. What do you need to know to predict whether the regulation is in the public interest or the producer interest?

8. Two telephone companies offer local calls in an area. The figure shows the market demand curve for calls and the marginal cost curves of each firm. These firms are regulated.

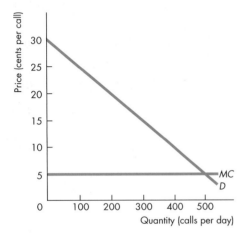

a. What is the price of a call and what is the number of calls per day if the regulation is in the public interest?
b. What is the price of a call and what is the number of calls per day if the telephone companies capture the regulator?
c. What is the deadweight loss in part (b)?
d. What do you need to know to predict whether the regulation will be in the public interest or in the producer interest?

1. After you have studied *Reading Between the Lines* on pp. 408–409, answer the following questions.
a. What did Roche and BASF do that is illegal?
b. Would their actions have been illegal if they had been carried out in Canada?
c. How does the European Commission try to discourage price fixing? Do you think this method works?
d. What changes would you recommend to the EU law and why?

2. The government of Canada regulates the production and sale of many goods and services. For example, it regulates the prices of local phone and cable TV services, the grain prices paid to wheat and cereal farmers and to whom they can sell the grain. The suppliers of local phone and cable TV services are monopolies, but there are many grain farmers. Why are grain farmers regulated? Is the regulation in the interest of grain farmers or consumers?

3. "Now that Canada has free trade with the United States, the government of Canada should not regulate monopolies in Canada because they are in direct competition with U.S. producers." Do you agree with this argument? If so, explain why. If not, explain why the argument is incorrect.

1. Use the link on the Parkin–Bade Web site to visit Competition Law Review. Look for cases of collusive agreement, abuse of dominant position, and mergers to restrict competition. In each case, describe the means cited as used to lessen competition.

EXTERNALITIES — CHAPTER 18

Greener and Smarter

We burn huge quantities of fossil fuels—coal, natural gas, and oil—that cause acid rain and possibly global warming. We use chlorofluorocarbons (CFCs) that may damage the earth's ozone layer, expose us to additional ultraviolet rays, and increase the risk of skin cancer. We dump toxic waste into rivers, lakes, and oceans. These environmental issues are simultaneously everybody's problem and nobody's problem. How can we take account of the damage that we cause others every time we turn on our heating or air conditioning systems? ◆ Almost every day, we hear about a new discovery—in medicine, engineering, chemistry, physics, or even economics. The advance of knowledge seems boundless. And more and more people are learning more and more of what is already known. The stock of knowledge is increasing, apparently without bound. We are getting smarter. But are we getting smarter fast enough? Are we spending enough on research and education? Do enough people remain in school for long enough? And do we work hard enough at school? Would we be better off if we spent more on research and education?

◆ In this chapter, we study the problems that arise because many of our actions create externalities. They affect other people, for ill or good, in ways that we do not usually take into account when we make our own economic choices. We study two big areas—pollution and knowledge—in which externalities are especially important. Externalities are a major source of *market failure*. When market failure occurs, we must either live with the inefficiency it creates or try to achieve greater efficiency by making some *public choices*. We close the chapter in *Reading Between the Lines* by looking at air pollution in Ontario today.

After studying this chapter, you will be able to

- Explain how property rights can sometimes be used to overcome externalities

- Explain how emission charges, marketable permits, and taxes can be used to achieve efficiency in the face of external costs

- Explain how subsidies can be used to achieve efficiency in the face of external benefits

- Explain how scholarships, below-cost tuition, and research grants make the quantity of education and invention more efficient

- Explain how patents improve economic efficiency

Externalities in Our Lives

A COST OR A BENEFIT THAT ARISES FROM production and falls on someone other than the producer or a cost or a benefit that arises from consumption and falls on someone other than the consumer is called an **externality**. Let's review the range of externalities, classify them, and look at some everyday examples.

An externality can arise from either *production* or *consumption* and it can be either a **negative externality**, which imposes an external cost, or a **positive externality**, which provides an external benefit. So there are four types of externalities:

- Negative production externalities
- Positive production externalities
- Negative consumption externalities
- Positive consumption externalities

Negative Production Externalities

Every weekday morning and afternoon, Highway 401 that runs across the northern end of Toronto slows to a crawl as trucks and commuters compete for positions on what looks more like an expensive parking lot than an expressway. A similar situation occurs in every major Canadian city from Vancouver to Halifax and in every major city around the world. Each road user imposes a negative production externality on the other road users.

Logging and the clearing of forests are the source of another negative production externality. These activities destroy the habitat of wildlife and influence the amount of carbon dioxide in the atmosphere, which has a long-term effect on temperature. Everyone living and future generations bear these external costs. Pollution, which we examine in the next section, is another example of this type of externality.

Positive Production Externalities

When Labonte Honey Inc. moves its bees into a blueberry orchard in the Lac St-Jean area of northern Quebec, the honeybees collect pollen and nectar from the fruit blossoms to make the honey. At the same time, they pollinate the blueberry flowers, which increases the output of blueberries. Two posi-

tive production externalities are present in this example: Labonte Honey gets a positive production externality from the owner of the fruit orchard, and the fruit grower gets a positive production externality from Labonte.

Negative Consumption Externalities

Negative consumption externalities are a source of irritation for most of us. Smoking tobacco in a confined space creates fumes that many people find unpleasant and that pose a health risk. So smoking in restaurants and on airplanes generates a negative externality. To avoid this negative externality, many restaurants and all airlines ban smoking. But while a smoking ban avoids a negative consumption externality for most people, it imposes a negative consumption externality on smokers. The majority imposes a cost on the minority—the smokers who would prefer to enjoy the consumption of tobacco while dining or taking a plane trip.

Noisy parties and outdoor rock concerts are other examples of negative consumption externalities. They are also examples of the fact that a simple ban on an activity is not a solution. Banning noisy parties avoids the external cost on sleep-seeking neighbours, but it results in the sleepers imposing an external cost on the fun-seeking partygoers.

Permitting dandelions to grow in lawns, not picking up leaves in the fall, and allowing a dog to bark loudly or to foul a neighbour's lawn are other sources of negative consumption externalities.

Positive Consumption Externalities

When you get a flu vaccination, you lower your risk of getting infected this winter. And if you avoid the flu, your neighbour who didn't get vaccinated has a better chance of avoiding it too. Flu vaccination generates positive consumption externalities.

When its owner restores a historic building, everyone who sees the building gets pleasure from it. Similarly, when someone erects a spectacular house—such as those built in Montreal's "Golden Square Mile" in the 1800s—or another exciting structure—such as the CN Tower or SkyDome in Toronto—an external consumption benefit flows to everyone who has an opportunity to view it. Education, which we examine in this chapter, is another example of this type of externality.

Negative Externalities: Pollution

POLLUTION IS NEITHER A NEW PROBLEM NOR IS IT only an industrial problem. Pre-industrial Europe had sewage disposal problems that created cholera epidemics and plagues that killed millions. London's air in the Middle Ages was dirtier than that of Los Angeles today. Some of the worst pollution today is in China and Thailand. Nor is the desire to find solutions to pollution new. The developments of fourteenth-century garbage and sewage disposal is an example of early attempts to tackle pollution.

Popular discussions of pollution usually pay little attention to economics. They focus on physical aspects of the problem, not on the costs and the benefits. A common assumption is that *any* action that causes pollution must cease. In contrast, an economic study of pollution emphasizes costs and benefits. An economist talks about the efficient amount of pollution. This emphasis on efficiency does not mean that economists, as citizens, do not share the same goals as others and value a healthy environment. Nor does it mean that economists have the right answers and everyone else has the wrong ones (or vice versa). Economics provides a set of tools and principles that clarify the issues. It does not provide an agreed list of solutions. The starting point for an economic analysis of pollution is the demand for a pollution-free environment.

The Demand for a Pollution-Free Environment

The demand for a pollution-free environment is greater today than it has ever been. We express this demand in several ways. We join organizations that lobby for anti-pollution regulations and policies. We vote for politicians who support the policies that we want to see implemented. We buy "green" products and avoid hazardous products, even if we pay a bit more to do so. And we pay higher housing costs and commuting costs to live in pleasant neighbourhoods.

The demand for a pollution-free environment has grown for two main reasons. First, as our incomes increase, we demand a larger range of goods and services, and one of these "goods" is a pollution-free environment. We value clean air, unspoiled natural scenery, and wildlife, and we are willing and able to pay for them.

Second, as our knowledge of the effects of pollution grows, we are able to take measures that reduce those effects. For example, now that we know how sulfur dioxide causes acid rain and how clearing rain forests destroys natural stores of carbon dioxide, we are able, in principle, to design measures that limit these problems.

Let's look at the range of pollution problems that have been identified and the actions that create those problems.

The Sources of Pollution

Economic activity pollutes air, water, and land, and these individual areas of pollution interact through the *ecosystem*.

Air Pollution Sixty percent of our air pollution comes from road transportation and industrial processes. Only 16 percent arises from electric power generation.

A common belief is that air pollution is getting worse. In many developing countries, air pollution *is* getting worse. But air pollution in North America is getting less severe for most substances. Figure 18.1 shows the trends in the concentrations of six air pollutants. Lead has been almost eliminated from our air. Sulfur dioxide, carbon monoxide, and suspended particulates have been reduced to around one-half of their 1980 levels. And even the more stubborn ozone and nitrogen dioxide are at around 70 percent of their 1980 levels.

These reductions in levels of air pollution are even more impressive when they are compared with the level of economic activity. Between 1970 and 2000, total production in North America increased by 158 percent. During this same period, vehicle kilometres travelled increased by 143 percent, energy consumption increased by 45 percent, and the population increased by 36 percent. While all this economic activity was on the increase, air pollution from all sources *decreased* by 29 percent.

While the facts about the sources and trends in air pollution are not in doubt, there is disagreement about the *effects* of air pollution. The least controversial is *acid rain* caused by sulfur dioxide and nitrogen oxide emissions from coal- and oil-fired generators of electric utilities. Acid rain begins with air pollution, and it leads to water pollution and vegetation damage.

More controversial are airborne substances (suspended particulates) such as lead from leaded gasoline. Some scientists believe that in sufficiently

FIGURE 18.1   Trends in Air Pollution

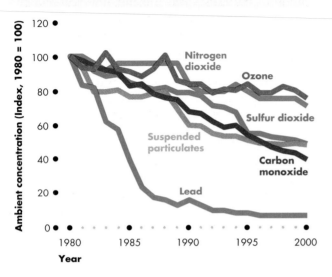

Lead has almost been eliminated from our air; concentrations of carbon monoxide, sulfur dioxide, and suspended particulates have decreased to about one-half of their 1980 levels; and nitrogen dioxide and ozone have fallen to about 70 percent of their 1980 levels.

Source: U.S. Environmental Protection Agency, *National Air Quality and Emissions Trends Report,* 1999 and 2000.

large concentrations, these substances (189 of which have currently been identified) cause cancer and other life-threatening conditions.

Even more controversial is *global warming,* which some scientists believe results from the carbon dioxide emissions. The earth's average temperature has increased over the past 100 years, but most of the increase occurred *before* 1940. Determining what causes changes in the earth's temperature and isolating the effect of carbon dioxide from other factors are proving to be difficult.

Equally controversial is the problem of *ozone layer depletion.* There is no doubt that a hole in the ozone layer exists over Antarctica and that the ozone layer protects us from cancer-causing ultraviolet rays from the sun. But how our industrial activity influences the ozone layer is simply not understood at this time.

One air pollution problem has almost been eliminated: lead from gasoline. In part, this happened because the cost of living without leaded gasoline, it turns out, is not high. But sulfur dioxide

and the so-called greenhouse gases are a much tougher problem to tackle. Their alternatives are costly or have pollution problems of their own. The major sources of these pollutants are road vehicles and electric utilities. Road vehicles can be made "greener" in a variety of ways. One is with new fuels, and some alternatives being investigated are alcohol, natural gas, propane and butane, and hydrogen. Another way of making cars and trucks "greener" is to change the chemistry of gasoline. Refiners are working on reformulations of gasoline that reduce tailpipe emissions. Similarly, electric power can be generated in cleaner ways by harnessing solar power, tidal power, or geothermal power. While technically possible, these methods are more costly than conventional carbon-fuelled generators. Another alternative is nuclear power. This method is good for air pollution but creates a potential long-term problem for land and water pollution because there is no known entirely safe method of disposing of spent nuclear fuel.

Water Pollution   The largest sources of water pollution are the dumping of industrial waste and treated sewage into lakes and rivers and the runoff from fertilizers. A more dramatic source is the accidental spilling of crude oil into the oceans, such as in the *Prestige* spill off the coast of Spain in 2002.

There are two main alternatives to polluting the waterways and oceans. One is the chemical processing of waste to render it inert or biodegradable. The other, widely used for nuclear waste, is to use land sites for storage in secure containers.

Land Pollution   Land pollution arises from dumping toxic waste. Ordinary household garbage does not pose a pollution problem unless contaminants from dumped garbage seep into the water supply. This possibility increases as landfills reach capacity and less suitable landfill sites are used. It is estimated that 80 percent of existing landfills will be full by 2010. Some regions (New York, New Jersey, and other U.S. East Coast states) and some countries (Japan and the Netherlands) are seeking less costly alternatives to landfill, such as recycling and incineration. Recycling is an apparently attractive alternative, but it requires an investment in new technologies to be effective. Incineration is a high-cost alternative to landfill, and it produces air pollution. Furthermore, these alternatives are not free, and they become efficient only when the cost of using landfill is high.

We've seen that the demand for a pollution-free environment has grown, and we've described the range of pollution problems. Let's now look at the economics of these problems. The starting point is the distinction between private costs and social costs.

Private Costs and Social Costs

A *private cost* of production is a cost that is borne by the producer of a good or service. *Marginal cost* is the cost of producing an *additional unit* of a good or service. So **marginal private cost** (*MC*) is the cost of producing an additional unit of a good or service that is borne by the producer of that good or service.

You've seen that an *external cost* is a cost of producing a good or service that is *not* borne by the producer but borne by other people. A **marginal external cost** is the cost of producing an additional unit of a good or service that falls on people other than the producer.

Marginal social cost (*MSC*) is the marginal cost incurred by the entire society—by the producer and by everyone else on whom the cost falls—and is the sum of marginal private cost and marginal external cost. That is,

$$MSC = MC + \text{Marginal external cost.}$$

We express costs in dollars. But we must always remember that a cost is an opportunity cost—what we give up to get something. A marginal external cost is what someone other than the producer of a good or service must give up when the producer makes one more unit of the item. Something real, such as a clean river or clean air, is given up.

Valuing an External Cost Economists use market prices to put a dollar value on the cost of pollution. For example, suppose that there are two similar rivers, one polluted and the other clean. Five hundred identical homes are built along each river. The homes on the clean river rent for $2,500 a month, and those on the polluted river rent for $1,500 a month. If the pollution is the only detectable difference between the two rivers and the two locations, the rent decrease of $1,000 per month is the cost of the pollution. For the 500 homes, the external cost is $500,000 a month.

External Cost and Output Figure 18.2 shows an example of the relationship between output and cost in a chemical industry that pollutes. The marginal cost curve, *MC*, describes the private marginal cost

borne by the firms that produce the chemical. Marginal cost increases as the quantity of chemical produced increases. If the firms dump waste into a river, they impose a marginal external cost that increases with the amount of the chemical produced. The marginal social cost curve, *MSC*, is the sum of marginal private cost and marginal external cost. For example, when output is 4,000 tonnes per month, marginal private cost is $100 a tonne, marginal external cost is $125 a tonne, and marginal social cost is $225 a tonne.

Figure 18.2 shows that when the quantity of chemicals produced increases, the amount of pollution increases and the external cost of pollution increases. But the figure doesn't tell us how much pollution gets created. That quantity depends on how the market for chemicals operates. First, we'll see what happens when the industry is free to pollute.

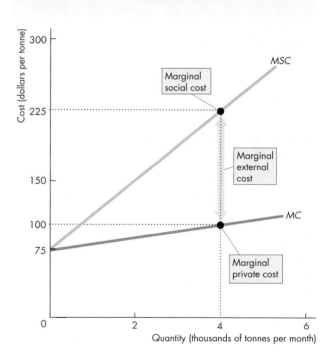

FIGURE 18.2   An External Cost

The *MC* curve shows the private marginal cost borne by the factories that produce a chemical. The *MSC* curve shows the sum of marginal private cost and marginal external cost. When output is 4,000 tonnes of chemicals per month, marginal private cost is $100 a tonne, marginal external cost is $125 a tonne, and marginal social cost is $225 a tonne.

Production and Pollution: How Much?

When an industry is unregulated, the amount of pollution it creates depends on the market equilibrium price and quantity of the good produced. In Fig. 18.3, the demand curve for a pollution-creating chemical is *D*. This curve also measures the marginal benefit, *MB*, to the buyers of the chemical. The supply curve is *S*. This curve also measures the marginal private cost, *MC*, of the producers. The supply curve is the marginal private cost curve because when firms make their production and supply decisions, they consider only the costs that they will bear. Market equilibrium occurs at a price of $100 a tonne and a quantity of 4,000 tonnes a month.

This equilibrium is inefficient. You learned in Chapter 5 that the allocation of resources is efficient when marginal benefit equals marginal cost. But we must count all the costs—private and external— when we compare marginal benefit and marginal cost. So with an external cost, the allocation is efficient when marginal benefit equals marginal *social* cost. This outcome occurs when the quantity of chemicals produced is 2,000 tonnes a month. The market equilibrium overproduces by 2,000 tonnes a month and creates a deadweight loss, the grey triangle.

How can the people who live beside the polluted river get the chemical factories to decrease their output of chemicals and create less pollution? If some method can be found to achieve this outcome, everyone—the owners of the chemical factories and the residents of the riverside homes—can gain. Let's explore some solutions.

Property Rights

Sometimes it is possible to reduce the inefficiency arising from an externality by establishing a property right where one does not currently exist. **Property rights** are legally established titles to the ownership, use, and disposal of factors of production and goods and services that are enforceable in the courts.

Suppose that the chemical factories own the river and the 500 homes alongside it. The rent that people are willing to pay depends on the amount of pollution. Using the earlier example, people are willing to pay $2,500 a month to live alongside a pollution-free river, but only $1,500 a month to live with the pollution created by 4,000 tonnes of chemicals a month. If the factories produce this quantity, they lose $1,000 a month for each home, a total of $500,000 a month.

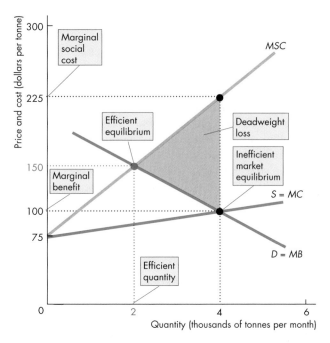

FIGURE 18.3   Inefficiency with an External Cost

The market supply curve is the marginal private cost curve, *S = MC*. The demand curve is the marginal benefit curve, *D = MB*. Market equilibrium at a price of $100 a tonne and 4,000 tonnes a month is inefficient because marginal social cost exceeds marginal benefit. The efficient quantity is 2,000 tonnes a month. The grey triangle shows the deadweight loss created by the pollution externality.

The chemical factories are now confronted with the cost of their pollution—forgone rent from the people who live beside the river.

Figure 18.4 illustrates the outcome by using the same example as in Fig. 18.3. With property rights in place, the *MC* curve no longer measures all the costs that the factories face in producing the chemical. It excludes the pollution costs that they must now bear. The *MSC* curve now becomes the marginal private cost curve *MC*. All the costs fall on the factories, so the market supply curve is based on all the marginal costs and is the curve labelled *S = MC = MSC*.

Market equilibrium now occurs at a price of $150 a tonne and a quantity of 2,000 tonnes a month. This outcome is efficient. The factories still produce some pollution, but it is the efficient quantity.

FIGURE 18.4   Property Rights Achieve an Efficient Outcome

With property rights, the marginal cost curve that excludes pollution costs shows only part of the producers' marginal cost. The marginal private cost curve includes the cost of pollution, and the supply curve is S = MC = MSC. Market equilibrium is at a price of $150 a tonne and a quantity of 2,000 tonnes a month and is efficient because marginal social cost equals marginal benefit.

The Coase Theorem

Does it matter how property rights are assigned? Does it matter whether the polluter or the victim of the pollution owns the resource that might be polluted? Until 1960, everyone—including economists who had thought long and hard about the problem—thought that it did matter. But in 1960, Ronald Coase had a remarkable insight, which is now called the Coase theorem.

The **Coase theorem** is the proposition that if property rights exist, if only a small number of parties is involved, and if transactions costs are low, then private transactions are efficient. There are no externalities because the transacting parties take all the costs and benefits into account. Furthermore, it doesn't matter who has the property rights.

Application of the Coase Theorem   In the example that we've just studied, the factories own the river and the homes. Suppose that instead, the residents own their homes and the river. Now the factories must pay a fee to the homeowners for the right to dump their waste. The greater the quantity of waste dumped into the river, the more the factories must pay. So again, the factories face the opportunity cost of the pollution they create. The quantity of chemicals produced and the amount of waste dumped are the same whoever owns the homes and the river. If the factories own them, they bear the cost of pollution because they receive a lower income from home rents. And if the residents own the homes and the river, the factories bear the cost of pollution because they must pay a fee to the homeowners. In both cases, the factories bear the cost of their pollution and dump the efficient amount of waste into the river.

The Coase solution works only when transactions costs are low. **Transactions costs** are the opportunity costs of conducting a transaction. For example, when you buy a house, you incur a series of transactions costs. You might pay a realtor to help you find the best place and a lawyer to run checks that assure you that the seller owns the property and that after you've paid for it, the ownership has been properly transferred to you.

In the example of the homes alongside a river, the transactions costs that are incurred by a small number of chemical factories and a few homeowners might be low enough to enable them to negotiate the deals that produce an efficient outcome. But in many situations, transactions costs are so high that it would be inefficient to incur them. In these situations, the Coase solution is not available.

Suppose that everyone owns the airspace above his or her home up to, say, 10 kilometres. If someone pollutes your airspace, you can charge a fee. But to collect the fee, you must identify who is polluting your airspace and persuade them to pay you. Imagine the costs of negotiating and enforcing agreements with the 300 million people who live in Canada and the United States (and perhaps Mexico) and the several thousand factories that emit sulfur dioxide and create acid rain that falls on homeowners' property! In this situation, we use public choices to cope with externalities. But the transactions costs that block a market solution are real costs, so attempts by the government to deal with externalities offer no easy solution. Let's look at some of these attempts.

Government Actions in the Face of External Costs

The three main methods that governments use to cope with externalities are

- Taxes
- Emission charges
- Marketable permits

Taxes The government can use taxes as an incentive for producers to cut back on an activity that creates an external cost. Taxes used in this way are called **Pigovian taxes**, in honour of Arthur Cecil Pigou, the British economist who is credited with first working out this method of dealing with externalities during the 1920s.

By setting the tax rate equal to the marginal external cost, firms can be made to behave in the same way as they would if they bore the cost of the externality directly. To see how government actions can change market outcomes in the face of externalities, let's return to the example of the chemical factories and the river.

Assume that the government has assessed the marginal external cost accurately and imposes a tax on the factories that exactly equals this cost. Figure 18.5 illustrates the effects of this tax.

The demand curve and marginal benefit curve, $D = MB$, and the firms' marginal cost curve, MC, are the same as in Fig. 18.3. The pollution tax equals the marginal external cost of the pollution. We add this tax to marginal cost to find the market supply curve. This curve is the one labelled $S = MC + tax = MSC$. This curve is the market supply curve because it tells us the quantities supplied at each price given the firms' marginal cost and the tax they must pay. This curve is also the marginal social cost curve because the pollution tax has been set equal to the marginal external cost.

Demand and supply now determine the market equilibrium price at $150 a tonne and the equilibrium quantity at 2,000 tonnes a month. At this scale of chemical production, the marginal social cost is $150 and the marginal benefit is $150, so the outcome is efficient. The firms incur a marginal cost of $88 a tonne and pay a tax of $62 a tonne. The government collects tax revenue of $124,000 a month.

Emission Charges Emission charges are an alternative to a tax for confronting a polluter with the external cost of pollution. The government sets a price per unit of pollution. The more pollution a firm creates,

FIGURE 18.5 A Pollution Tax

A pollution tax is imposed equal to the marginal external cost of pollution. The supply curve becomes the marginal private cost curve, MC, plus the tax—$S = MC + tax$. Market equilibrium is at a price of $150 a tonne and a quantity of 2,000 tonnes a month and is efficient because marginal social cost equals marginal benefit. The government collects a tax revenue shown by the purple rectangle.

the more it pays in emission charges. This method of dealing with pollution externalities has been used only modestly in North America but is common in Europe where, for example, France, Germany, and the Netherlands make water polluters pay a waste disposal charge.

To work out the emission charge that achieves efficiency, the government needs a lot of information about the polluting industry that, in practice, is rarely available.

Marketable Permits Instead of taxing or imposing emission charges on polluters, each potential polluter might be assigned a permitted pollution limit. Each firm knows its own costs and benefits of pollution, and making pollution limits marketable is a clever way of using this private information that is unknown to the government. The government issues each firm a permit to emit a certain amount of pollution, and firms can buy and sell these permits. Firms that have a low marginal cost of reducing pollution sell their permits, and firms that have a high marginal cost of reducing pollution buy permits. The market in permits determines the price at which firms trade permits. And firms buy or sell permits until their marginal cost of pollution equals the market price.

This method of dealing with pollution provides an even stronger incentive than do emission charges to find technologies that pollute less because the price of a permit to pollute rises as the demand for permits increases.

A Real-World Market for Emission Permits

Environment Canada has not used marketable permits but the Environmental Protection Agency (EPA) in the United States has. The EPA first implemented air quality programs following the passage of the Clean Air Act in 1970.

Trading in lead pollution permits became common during the 1980s, and this marketable permit program has been rated a success. It enabled lead to be virtually eliminated (see Fig. 18.1). But this success might not easily translate to other situations because lead pollution has some special features. First, most lead pollution came from a single source: leaded gasoline. Second, lead in gasoline is easily monitored. Third, the objective of the program was clear: to eliminate lead in gasoline. The EPA is now considering using marketable permits to promote efficiency in the control of chlorofluorocarbons, the gases that are believed to damage the ozone layer.

REVIEW QUIZ

1 What is the distinction between a negative production externality and a negative consumption externality?

2 What is the distinction between private cost and social cost?

3 How does an externality prevent a competitive market from allocating resources efficiently?

4 How can an externality be eliminated by assigning property rights? How does this method of coping with an externality work?

5 How do taxes help us to cope with externalities? At what level must a pollution tax be set if it is to induce firms to produce the efficient quantity of pollution?

Positive Externalities: Knowledge

KNOWLEDGE COMES FROM EDUCATION AND research. To study the economics of knowledge, we must distinguish between private benefits and social benefits.

Private Benefits and Social Benefits

A *private benefit* is a benefit that the consumer of a good or service receives. *Marginal benefit* is the benefit from an *additional unit* of a good or service. So a **marginal private benefit** (MB) is the benefit from an additional unit of a good or service that the consumer of that good or service receives.

The *external benefit* from a good or service is the benefit that someone other than the consumer receives. A **marginal external benefit** is the benefit from an additional unit of a good or service that people other than the consumer enjoy.

Marginal social benefit (MSB) is the marginal benefit enjoyed by society—by the consumer of a good or service (marginal private benefit) plus the marginal benefit enjoyed by others (the marginal external benefit). That is,

$$MSB = MB + \text{Marginal external benefit.}$$

Figure 18.6 shows an example of the relationship between marginal private benefit, marginal external benefit, and marginal social benefit. The marginal benefit curve, MB, describes the marginal private benefit—such as expanded job opportunities and higher incomes—enjoyed by university graduates. Marginal private benefit decreases as the quantity of education increases.

But university graduates generate external benefits. On the average, university graduates communicate more effectively with others and tend to be better citizens. Their crime rates are lower, and they are more tolerant of the views of others. And a society with a large number of university graduates can support high-quality newspapers and television channels, music, theatre, and other organized social activities.

In the example in Fig. 18.6, the marginal external benefit is $15,000 per student per year when 15 million students enrol in university. The marginal social benefit curve, MSB, is the sum of marginal private benefit and marginal external benefit. For example, when 15 million students a year enrol in university, the

FIGURE 18.6   An External Benefit

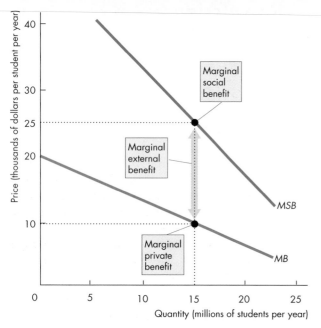

The *MB* curve shows the private marginal benefit enjoyed by the people who receive a university education. The *MSB* curve shows the sum of marginal private benefit and marginal external benefit. When 15 million students attend university, marginal private benefit is $10,000 per student, marginal external benefit is $15,000 per student, and marginal social benefit is $25,000 per student.

FIGURE 18.7   Inefficiency with an External Benefit

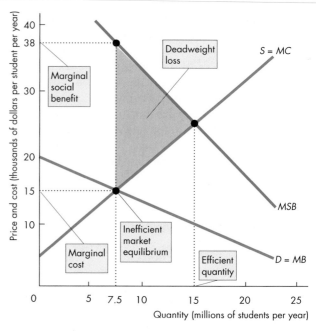

The market demand curve is the marginal private benefit curve, *D = MB*. The supply curve is the marginal cost curve, *S = MC*. Market equilibrium at a tuition of $15,000 a year and 7.5 million students is inefficient because marginal social benefit exceeds marginal cost. The efficient quantity is 15 million students. The grey triangle shows the deadweight loss created because too few students enrol in university.

marginal private benefit is $10,000 per student and the marginal external benefit is $15,000 per student, so the marginal social benefit is $25,000 per student.

When people make schooling decisions, they ignore its external benefits and consider only its private benefits. So if education were provided by private schools that charged full-cost tuition, we would produce too few university graduates.

Figure 18.7 illustrates the underproduction that would result if the government left education to the private market. The supply curve is the marginal cost curve of the private schools, *S = MC*. The demand curve is the marginal private benefit curve, *D = MB*. Market equilibrium occurs at a tuition of $15,000 per student per year and 7.5 million students per year. At this equilibrium, marginal social benefit is $38,000 per student, which exceeds marginal cost by $23,000. There are too few students in university. The efficient number is 15 million, where marginal social benefit

equals marginal cost. The grey triangle shows the deadweight loss.

Underproduction similar to that in Fig. 18.7 would occur at primary school and secondary school if an unregulated market produced education. When children learn basic reading, writing, and number skills, they receive the private benefit of increased earning power. But even these basic skills bring the external benefit of developing better citizens.

External benefits also arise from the discovery of new knowledge. When Isaac Newton worked out the formulas for calculating the rate of response of one variable to another—calculus—everyone was free to use his method. When a spreadsheet program called VisiCalc was invented, Lotus Corporation and Microsoft were free to copy the basic idea and create Lotus 1-2-3 and Microsoft Excel. When the first shopping mall was built and found to be a successful way of arranging retailing, everyone was free to copy the idea, and malls spread like mushrooms.

Once someone has discovered how to do something, others can copy the basic idea. They do have to work to copy an idea, so they face an opportunity cost. But they do not usually have to pay the person who made the discovery to use it. When people make decisions, they ignore its external benefits and consider only its private benefits.

When people make decisions about the quantity of education or the amount of research to undertake, they balance the marginal private cost against the marginal private benefit. They ignore the external benefit. As a result, if we left education and research to unregulated market forces, we would get too little of these activities.

To get closer to producing the efficient quantity of a good or service that generates an external benefit, we make public choices, through governments, to modify the market outcome.

Government Actions in the Face of External Benefits

Four devices that governments can use to achieve a more efficient allocation of resources in the presence of external benefits are

- Public provision
- Private subsidies
- Vouchers
- Patents and copyrights

Public Provision Under **public provision**, a public authority that receives its revenue from the government produces the good or service. The education services produced by the public universities, colleges, and schools are examples of public provision.

Figure 18.8(a) shows how public provision might overcome the underproduction that arises in Fig. 18.7. Public provision cannot lower the cost of

---

FIGURE 18.8   Public Provision or Private Subsidy to Achieve an Efficient Outcome

(a) Public provision

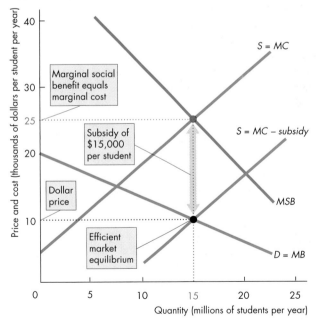

(b) Private subsidy

In part (a), marginal social benefit equals marginal cost with 15 million students enrolled in university, the efficient quantity. Tuition is set at $10,000, and the taxpayers cover the other $15,000 marginal cost per student. In part (b),

with a subsidy of $15,000 per student, the supply curve is S = MC – subsidy. The equilibrium price is $10,000, and the market equilibrium is efficient with 15 million students enrolled. Marginal social benefit equals marginal cost.

production, so marginal cost is the same as before. Marginal private benefit and marginal external benefit are also the same as before.

The efficient quantity occurs where marginal social benefit equals marginal cost. In Fig. 18.8(a), this quantity is 15 million students. Tuition is set to ensure that the efficient number of students enrols. That is, tuition is set at the level that equals the marginal private benefit at the efficient quantity. In Fig. 18.8(a), tuition is $10,000 a year. The rest of the cost of the public university is borne by the taxpayers and, in this example, is $15,000 per student per year.

Private Subsidies   A **subsidy** is a payment that the government makes to private producers. By making the subsidy depend on the level of output, the government can induce private decision makers to consider external benefits when they make their choices.

Suppose that all schools are private. Figure 18.8(b) shows how a subsidy to private schools would work. In the absence of a subsidy, the marginal cost curve is the market supply curve, $S = MC$. The marginal benefit is the demand curve, $D = MB$. In this example, the government provides a subsidy to schools of $15,000 per student per year. We must subtract the subsidy from the marginal cost of education to find the schools' supply curve. That curve is $S = MC - subsidy$ in the figure. The equilibrium tuition (market price) is $10,000 a year, and the equilibrium quantity is 15 million students. To educate 15 million students, schools incur a marginal cost of $25,000 a year. The marginal social benefit is also $25,000 a year. So with marginal cost equal to marginal social benefit, the subsidy has achieved an efficient outcome. The tuition and the subsidy just cover the schools' marginal cost.

Vouchers   A **voucher** is a token that the government provides to households, which they can use to buy specified goods or services. U.S. economist Milton Friedman has long advocated vouchers as a means of providing parents with greater choice and control over the education of their children. Some people advocate them for college and university so that students can both receive financial help and exercise choice. The Canadian Alliance party has advocated the use of vouchers.

A school voucher allows parents to choose the school their children will attend and to use the voucher to pay part of the cost. The school cashes the vouchers to pay its bills. A voucher provided to a university student would work in a similar way. Because

FIGURE 18.9   Vouchers Achieve an Efficient Outcome

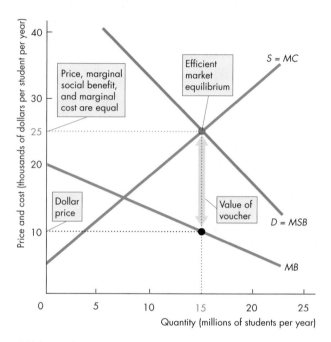

With vouchers, buyers are willing to pay *MB* plus the value of the voucher, so the demand curve becomes the marginal social benefit curve, *D = MSB*. Market equilibrium is efficient with 15 million students enrolled because price, marginal social benefit, and marginal cost are equal. The tuition consists of the dollar price of $10,000 and the value of the voucher.

vouchers can be spent only on a specified item, they increase the willingness to pay for that item and so increase the demand for it.

Figure 18.9 shows how a voucher system works. The government provides a voucher equal to the marginal external benefit. Students use these vouchers to supplement the dollars they pay for university education. The marginal social benefit curve becomes the demand for university education, *D = MSB*. The market equilibrium occurs at a price of $25,000 per student per year, and 15 million students enrol in universities. Each student pays $10,000 tuition, and universities collect an additional $15,000 per student from the voucher.

If the government estimates the value of the external benefit correctly and makes the value of the voucher equal the marginal external benefit, the outcome from the voucher scheme is efficient. Marginal cost equals marginal social benefit, and the deadweight loss is eliminated.

Vouchers are similar to subsidies, but their advocates say that they are more efficient than subsidies because the consumer can monitor school performance more effectively than the government can.

Patents and Copyrights   Knowledge might be an exception to the principle of diminishing marginal benefit. Additional knowledge (about the right things) makes people more productive. And there seems to be no tendency for the additional productivity from additional knowledge to diminish.

For example, in 15 years, advances in knowledge about microprocessors have given us chips that have made our personal computers increasingly powerful. Each advance in knowledge about how to design and manufacture a processor chip has brought apparently ever larger increments in performance and productivity. Similarly, each advance in knowledge about how to design and build an airplane has brought apparently ever larger increments in performance: Orville and Wilbur Wright's 1903 Flyer was a one-seat plane that could hop a farmer's field. The Lockheed Constellation, designed in 1949, was an airplane that could fly 120 passengers from New York to London, but with two refuelling stops in Newfoundland and Ireland. The latest version of the Boeing 747 can carry 400 people nonstop from Los Angeles to Sydney, Australia, or Toronto to Tokyo (flights of 12,000 kilometres that take 13 hours). Similar examples can be found in agriculture, biogenetics, communications, engineering, entertainment, medicine, and publishing.

One reason why knowledge increases without diminishing returns is the sheer number of different things that can be tried. Paul Romer explains this fact with an amazing example. Suppose, says Romer, "that to make a finished good, 20 different parts have to be attached to a frame, one at a time. A worker could proceed in numerical order, attaching part one first, then part two.... Or the worker could proceed in some other order, starting with part 10, then adding part seven.... With 20 parts, ... there are [more] different sequences ... than the total number of seconds that have elapsed since the Big Bang created the universe, so we can be confident that in all activities, only a very small fraction of the possible sequences have ever been tried."*

---

* Paul Romer, "Ideas and Things," in *The Future Surveyed*, supplement to *The Economist*, September 11, 1993, pp. 71–72.

Think about all the processes, all the products, and all the different bits and pieces that go into each process and product, and you can see that we have only begun to scratch around the edges of what is possible.

Because knowledge is productive and generates external benefits, it is necessary to use public policies to ensure that those who develop new ideas have incentives to encourage an efficient level of effort. The main way of providing the right incentives uses the central idea of the Coase theorem and assigns property rights—called **intellectual property rights**—to creators. The legal device for establishing intellectual property rights is the patent or copyright. A **patent** or **copyright** is a government-sanctioned exclusive right granted to the inventor of a good, service, or productive process to produce, use, and sell the invention for a given number of years. A patent enables the developer of a new idea to prevent others from benefiting freely from an invention for a limited number of years.

Although patents encourage invention and innovation, they do so at an economic cost. While a patent is in place, its holder has a monopoly. And monopoly is another source of inefficiency (which is explained in Chapter 12). But without a patent, the effort to develop new goods, services, or processes is diminished and the flow of new inventions is slowed. So the efficient outcome is a compromise that balances the benefits of more inventions against the cost of temporary monopoly in newly invented activities.

REVIEW QUIZ

1 What is special about knowledge that creates external benefits?

2 How might governments use public provision, private subsidies, and vouchers to achieve an efficient amount of education?

3 How might governments use public provision, private subsidies, vouchers, and patents and copyrights to achieve an efficient amount of research and development?

◆ *Reading Between the Lines* on pp. 426–427 looks at the pollution created by generating electricity and the debate over whether the regulation of power utilities is too lax or too severe.

The Air Pollution Debate

THE GLOBE AND MAIL, APRIL 16, 2002

Three plants spew bulk of pollutants

Three large coal-fired power plants in Southern Ontario produce 83 per cent of all the harmful air pollutants from the province's electric-power sector, according to documents obtained under the Freedom of Information Act.

In the first full look at air emissions from the province's 143 generating facilities, the coal plants—located near Toronto, Simcoe and Sarnia—stand out because they produced 24 million tonnes of contaminants that cause global warming, acid rain, smog, and heavy-metal poisoning in wildlife.

The bulk of the pollutants, tracked over an eight-month period in 2000, are carbon dioxide, sulphur dioxide and nitrogen oxides, but they also include nerve poisons, such as mercury, that are toxic to humans and wildlife even in small concentrations.

The figures also show that the province's publicly owned utility, Ontario Power Generation, is the worst polluter, producing the lion's share of the emissions, with nearly 91 per cent of the total.

The company that was the next-largest emitter, TransAlta Cogen LP, produced only 1.4 per cent.

Ontario Power is such a big polluter partly because it generates the bulk of the province's electricity, and partly because of its use of coal to carry out this task.

Reprinted with permission from *The Globe and Mail.*

Essence of the Story

■ Newly available data show that Ontario Power Generation creates 91 percent of total emissions from the electric power producing sector and its three largest power plants account for 83 percent of the province's air pollution.

■ These emissions include carbon dioxide, sulfur dioxide, and nitrogen oxides, as well as mercury.

Economic Analysis

■ In producing electricity, there is a tradeoff between the private cost and the social cost of production.

■ The cheapest fuels and production technologies are extremely dirty.

■ None of these technologies are used in Canada today. But they are used in China and Russia (among other countries) where air pollution is a serious problem.

■ Canada, in contrast, has achieved a high standard of air quality.

■ But is the standard high enough? Or is it too high?

■ To answer this question, we need to consider the economics of pollution from producing electricity.

■ Figure 1 shows the demand for electricity and its marginal benefit as the curve $D = MB$.

■ The curve MC shows the marginal cost of producing electricity in dirty plants.

■ With an unregulated and competitive market, the quantity produced is 6 megawatt hours.

■ Because the plants are dirty, a pollution problem arises. The curve MSC shows the marginal social cost of producing electricity.

■ The vertical distance between the MC curve and the MSC curve is the marginal external cost.

■ Taking the marginal external cost into account, we can find the efficient quantity of electricity to produce and the efficient amount of pollution.

■ In the example in Fig. 1, the efficient quantity is 4 megawatt hours. Notice that at the efficient quantity, we still have pollution, but a smaller amount than with the unregulated outcome.

■ Figure 2 shows the same demand and cost curves as Fig. 1 but focuses on the overall cost of pollution—its deadweight loss.

■ If production is cut to 4 megawatt hours, the deadweight loss disappears and we have the efficient outcome.

■ If power companies are regulated to use a more costly but cleaner technology, the MC curve shifts upward, the cost of electricity rises, the quantity produced decreases, and the deadweight loss from pollution shrinks.

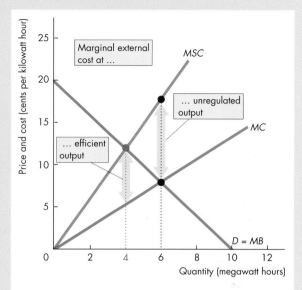

Figure 1 Efficient and unregulated outcomes compared

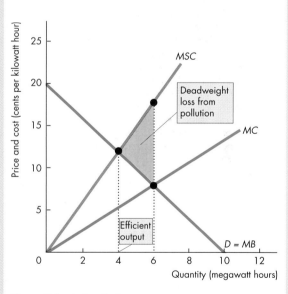

Figure 2 Cost of pollution

■ If the additional cost imposed by regulation on the power companies is less than the marginal external cost of pollution, production and pollution move towards but remain above their efficient levels.

■ If the additional cost imposed by regulation on the power companies exceeds the marginal external cost of pollution, production and pollution move below their efficient levels.

427

SUMMARY

KEY POINTS

Externalities in Our Lives (p. 414)

▪ An externality can arise from either a production activity or a consumption activity.

▪ A negative externality imposes an external cost.

▪ A positive externality provides an external benefit.

Negative Externalities: Pollution (pp. 415–421)

▪ External costs are costs of production that fall on people other than the producer of a good or service. Marginal social cost equals marginal private cost plus marginal external cost.

▪ Producers take account only of marginal private cost and overproduce when there is a marginal external cost.

▪ Sometimes it is possible to overcome a negative externality by assigning a property right.

▪ When property rights cannot be assigned, governments might overcome externalities by using taxes, emission charges, or marketable permits.

Positive Externalities: Knowledge (pp. 421–425)

▪ External benefits are benefits that are received by people other than the consumer of a good or service. Marginal social benefit equals marginal private benefit plus marginal external benefit.

▪ External benefits from education arise because better-educated people tend to be better citizens, commit fewer crimes, and support social activities.

▪ External benefits from research arise because once someone has worked out a basic idea, others can copy it.

▪ Vouchers or subsidies to schools or the provision of public education below cost can achieve a more efficient provision of education.

▪ Patents and copyrights create intellectual property rights and an incentive to innovate. But they do so by creating a temporary monopoly, the cost of which must be balanced against the benefit of more inventive activity.

KEY FIGURES

Figure 18.3 Inefficiency with an External Cost, 418
Figure 18.4 Property Rights Achieve an Efficient Outcome, 419
Figure 18.5 A Pollution Tax, 420
Figure 18.7 Inefficiency with an External Benefit, 422
Figure 18.8 Public Provision or Private Subsidy to Achieve an Efficient Outcome, 423
Figure 18.9 Vouchers Achieve an Efficient Outcome, 424

KEY TERMS

Coase theorem, 419
Copyright, 425
Externality, 414
Intellectual property rights, 425
Marginal external benefit, 421
Marginal external cost, 417
Marginal private benefit, 421
Marginal private cost, 417
Marginal social benefit, 421
Marginal social cost, 417
Negative externality, 414
Patent, 425
Pigovian taxes, 420
Positive externality, 414
Property rights, 418
Public provision, 423
Subsidy, 424
Transactions costs, 419
Voucher, 424

PROBLEMS

*1. The table provides information about costs and benefits arising from the production of pesticide that pollutes a lake used by a trout farmer.

Quantity of pesticide (tonnes per week)	Pesticide producer's MC	Trout farmer's MC from pesticide production	Marginal benefit of pesticide
	(dollars per tonne)		
0	0	0	250
1	5	33	205
2	15	67	165
3	30	100	130
4	50	133	100
5	75	167	75
6	105	200	55
7	140	233	40

a. If no one owns the lake and if there is no regulation of pollution, what is the quantity of pesticide produced per week and what is the marginal cost of pollution borne by the trout farmer?

b. If the trout farmer owns the lake, how much pesticide is produced per week and what does the pesticide producer pay the farmer per tonne?

c. If the pesticide producer owns the lake, and if a pollution-free lake rents for $1,000 a week, how much pesticide is produced per week and how much rent per week does the farmer pay the factory for the use of the lake?

d. Compare the quantities of pesticide produced in your answers to parts (b) and (c) and explain the relationship between these quantities.

2. The table at the top of the next column provides information about the costs and benefits of steel smelting that pollutes the air of a city.

a. With no property rights in the city's air and no regulation of pollution, what is the quantity of steel produced per week and what is the marginal cost of pollution borne by the citizens?

b. If the city owns the steel plant, how much steel is produced per week and what does the city charge the steel producer per tonne?

Quantity of steel (tonnes per week)	Steel producer's MC	Marginal external cost	Marginal benefit of steel
	(dollars per tonne)		
0	0	0	1,200
10	100	15	1,100
20	200	25	1,000
30	300	50	900
40	400	100	800
50	500	200	700
60	600	300	600
70	700	400	500
80	800	500	400

c. If the steel firm owns the city, and if the residents of a pollution-free city are willing to pay $15,000 a week in property taxes, how much steel is produced per week and how much are the citizens willing to pay in property taxes to live in the polluted city?

d. Compare the quantities of steel produced in your answers to parts (b) and (c) and explain the relationship between these quantities.

*3. Back at the pesticide plant and trout farm described in problem 1, suppose that no one owns the lake and that the government introduces a pollution tax.

a. What is the tax per tonne of pesticide produced that achieves an efficient outcome?

b. Explain the connection between your answers to problem 3(a) and problem 1.

4. Back at the steel smelter and city in problem 2, suppose that the city introduces a pollution tax.

a. What is the tax per tonne of steel produced that will achieve an efficient outcome?

b. Explain the connection between your answers to problem 4(a) and problem 2.

*5. Using the information provided in problem 1, suppose that no one owns the lake and that the government issues two marketable pollution permits: one to the farmer, and one to the factory. Each may pollute the lake, and the total amount of pollution is the efficient amount.

a. What is the quantity of pesticide produced?

b. What is the market price of a pollution permit? Who buys and who sells a permit?

c. What is the connection between your answers to problems 5(a) and (b) and problems 1 and 3?

6. Using the information given in problem 2, suppose that the city issues two marketable pollution permits: one to the city government, and one to the smelter. Each may pollute the air by the same amount, and the total is the efficient amount.
   a. How much steel is produced?
   b. What is the market price of a permit? Who buys and who sells a permit?
   c. What is the connection between your answers to problems 2 and 4?

*7. The marginal cost of educating a student is $4,000 a year and is constant. The figure shows the marginal private benefit curve.

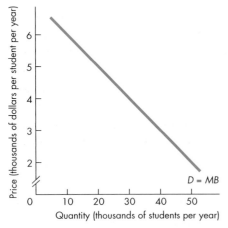

a. With no government involvement and if the schools are competitive, how many students are enrolled and what is the tuition?
b. The external benefit from education is $2,000 per student per year and is constant. If the government provides the efficient amount of education, how many school places does it offer and what is the tuition?

8. A technological advance cuts the marginal cost of educating a student to $2,000 a year and is constant. The marginal private benefit is the same as that in problem 7. The external benefit from education increases to $4,000 per student per year and is constant.
   a. With no government involvement and if the schools are competitive, how many students are enrolled and what is the tuition?
   b. If the government provides the efficient amount of education, how many school places does it offer and what is the tuition?
   c. Compare the outcomes in problem 8 with those in problem 7. Explain the differences between the two situations.

CRITICAL THINKING

1. After you have studied *Reading Between the Lines* on pp. 426–427, answer the following questions:
   a. Which electric power companies create most of the air pollution in the electricity industry in Ontario?
   b. What are the pros and cons of stiffening the regulations that power utilities face?
   c. If a technological advance lowers the cost of producing electricity but leaves the marginal external pollution cost unchanged, would the adoption of this technology in an unregulated market increase or decrease pollution? Explain using a figure like those on p. 427.

WEB EXERCISES

1. Use the links on the Parkin–Bade Web site to get two viewpoints on global warming. Then answer these questions:
   a. What are the benefits and costs of greenhouse gas emissions?
   b. Do you think the environmentalists are correct in the view that greenhouse gas emissions must be cut, or do you think the costs of reducing greenhouse gas emissions exceed the benefits?
   c. If greenhouse gas emissions are to be reduced, should reductions be achieved by assigning production limits or marketable permits?

2. To decrease the amount of overfishing of southern bluefin tuna in its territorial waters, the government of Australia introduced private property rights with an allocation of Individual Transferable Quotas (ITQs). To check out the effects of this system, use the link on your Parkin–Bade Web site to read the review by John Coombs of Colby College, Maine. Also look at the Greenpeace view. Then answer the following questions:
   a. Would the introduction of ITQs in North America help to replenish Canadian fish stocks?
   b. Explain why ITQs give an incentive not to overfish.
   c. Why does Greenpeace oppose ITQs?

UNDERSTANDING MARKET FAILURE AND GOVERNMENT

Making the Rules

Creating a system of responsible democratic government is a huge enterprise and one that can easily go wrong. Creating a constitution that makes despotic and tyrannical rule impossible is relatively easy. And we have achieved such a constitution in Canada by using some sound economic ideas. We have designed a sophisticated system of incentives—of carrots and sticks—to make the government responsive to public opinion and to limit the ability of individual special interests to gain at the expense of the majority. But we have not managed to create a constitution that effectively blocks the ability of special interest groups to capture the consumer and producer surpluses that result from specialization and exchange. ◆ We have created a system of government to deal with four economic problems. The market economy would produce too small a quantity of those public goods and services that we must consume together, such as national defence and air-traffic control. It enables monopoly to restrict production and charge too high a price. It produces too large a quantity of some goods and services, the production of which creates pollution. And it generates a distribution of income and wealth that most people believe is too unequal. So we need a government to help cope with these economic problems. But as the founding fathers knew would happen, when governments get involved in the economy, people try to steer the government's actions in directions that bring personal gains at the expense of the general interest. ◆ The three chapters in this part explained the problems with which the market has a hard time coping. Chapter 16 overviewed the entire range of problems and studied one of these problems, public goods, more deeply. Chapter 17 studied competition policy and the regulation of natural monopoly. And Chapter 18 dealt with externalities. It examined the external costs imposed by pollution and the external benefits that come from education and research. It described some of the ways in which externalities can be dealt with. And it explained that one way of coping with externalities is to strengthen the market and "internalize" the externalities rather than to intervene in the market. ◆ Many economists have thought long and hard about the problems discussed in this part. But none has had as profound an effect on our ideas in this area as Ronald Coase, whom you can meet on the following page. You can also meet John McCallum, Canada's Minister of National Defence, who wrestles with some of the issues you've studied in this part every day.

Externalities and Property Rights

RONALD COASE *(1910–), was born in England and educated at the London School of Economics, where he was deeply influenced by his teacher, Arnold Plant, and by the issues of his youth: communist central planning versus free markets. Professor Coase has lived in the United States since 1951. He first visited America as a 20-year-old on a travelling scholarship during the depths of the Great Depression. It was on this visit, and before he had completed his bachelor's degree, that he conceived the ideas that 60 years later were to earn him the 1991 Nobel Prize for Economic Science. He discovered and clarified the significance of transactions costs and property rights for the functioning of the economy. Ronald Coase has revolutionized the way we think about property rights and externalities and has opened up the growing field of law and economics.*

"The question to be decided is: is the value of fish lost greater or less than the value of the product which contamination of the stream makes possible?"

RONALD H.
COASE
*The Problems
of Social Cost*

As knowledge accumulates, we are becoming more sensitive to environmental externalities. We are also developing more sensitive methods of dealing with them. But all the methods involve a public choice.

Urban smog, which is both unpleasant and dangerous to breathe, forms when sunlight reacts with emissions from the tailpipes of automobiles. Because of this external cost of auto exhaust, we set emission standards and tax gasoline. Emission standards increase the cost of a car, and gasoline taxes increase the cost of the marginal kilometre travelled. The higher costs decrease the quantity demanded of road transportation and so decrease the amount of pollution it creates. Is the value of cleaner urban air worth the higher cost of transportation? The public choices of voters, regulators, and lawmakers answer this question.

Acid rain, which imposes a cost on everyone who lives in its path, falls from sulfur-laden clouds produced by electric utility smokestacks. This external cost is being tackled with a market solution. This solution is marketable permits, the price and allocation of which are determined by the forces of supply and demand. Private choices determine the demand for marketable permits, but a public choice determines the supply.

As cars stream onto an urban highway during the morning rush hour, the highway clogs and becomes an expensive parking lot. Each rush hour traveller imposes external costs on all the others. Today, road users bear private congestion costs but do not face a share of the external congestion costs that they create. But a market solution to this problem is now technologically feasible. It is a solution that charges road users with a fee similar to a toll that varies with time of day and degree of congestion. Confronted with the social marginal cost of their actions, each road user makes a choice and the market for highway space is efficient. Here, a public choice to use a market solution leaves the final decision about the degree of congestion to private choices.

Chester Jackson, a Lake Erie fisherman, recalls that when he began fishing on the lake, boats didn't carry drinking water. Fishermen drank from the lake. Speaking after World War II, Jackson observed, "Can't do that today. Those chemicals in there would kill you." Farmers used chemicals, such as the insecticide DDT, that got carried into the lake by runoff. Industrial waste and trash were also dumped in the lake in large quantities. As a result, Lake Erie became badly polluted during the 1940s and became incapable of sustaining a viable fish stock.

Today, Lake Erie supports a fishing industry, just as it did in the 1930s. No longer treated as a garbage dump for chemicals, the lake is regenerating its ecosystem. Fertilizers and insecticides are now recognized as products that have potential externalities, and their external effects are assessed by Environment Canada before new versions are put into widespread use. Dumping industrial waste into rivers and lakes is now subject to much more stringent regulations and penalties. Lake Erie's externalities have been dealt with by one of the methods available: government regulation.

Fundamental to protecting property rights is our national defence. John McCallum, whom you can meet on the following pages, is Canada's Minister of National Defence. But he is also an economist, and one whose career provides an outstanding example of the enormous range of jobs that the economist is equipped to perform.

TALKING WITH

JOHN McCALLUM

is Canada's Minister of National Defence and Member of Parliament for the Ontario constituency of Markham. Born in Montreal in 1950, he was an undergraduate at Cambridge University and a graduate student at Université de Paris and McGill University, where he earned his PhD in 1977. Dr. McCallum's career path has been extraordinarily broad. He has been a professor of economics at the University of Manitoba, Simon Fraser University, Université du Québec à Montréal, and McGill University, Dean of Arts at McGill, and Senior Vice President and Chief Economist at the Royal Bank of Canada. He has become well known for his strongly held and clearly stated views on economic policy and is a prolific contributor to economic policy debates and now to defence policy issues in Canada.

Robin Bade and Michael Parkin talked with John McCallum about his work and his views on the role of economics and the economist in the wide range of jobs that he has held.

How did you become an economist?

By fluke. I went to Cambridge University as an undergraduate, and under the British system one had to choose a single subject. I liked both the humanities and mathematics, and, by a process of elimination, I discovered that economics was about the only subject offering a combination of the two. So, never having heard the name John Maynard Keynes, I went to Cambridge, the home of Keynes and the bastion of Keynesianism. I was much too young to meet the great man himself, but just old enough to be taught by his direct disciples, people like Joan Robinson, Nicholas Kaldor, Richard Kahn, and Luigi Pasinetti. So, naturally, not being a child prodigy equipped to challenge the thinking of my great teachers, I emerged a Keynesian.

Are you still a Keynesian, and does the label matter much today?

I emerged a Keynesian. But given the world in which I live, with the passage of time I gradually lost some of my ardour as a Keynesian. But I'd still say that I'm a modern-day Keynesian, which is a different definition of what a Keynesian was back when I was an undergraduate—much more modest in ambition.

You've been an economics professor and a dean, the chief economist at a major bank, and now a Member of Parliament and Canada's Minister of Defence. Reflecting on this broad career, what are the principles of economics that you find yourself repeatedly coming back to?

The principles of economics that are relevant depend on the job. When I was Chief Economist of the Royal Bank I was concerned with macroeconomics. I was commenting on the macroeconomy and trying to forecast it. I might say that one of the things I miss least about being a bank chief economist is that I don't have to pretend I know what the currency will be in the future! So a bank economist's job is mainly macro and relies on macroeconomic principles.

But any job that involves the management of people or resources, whether as a

Dean of Arts or Minister of Defence, uses microeconomic principles. Although I am trying to get more resources, that's not entirely under my control, and whether I get new resources or not, at the end of the day I'll have a fixed amount of resources. So the challenge is always to get the greatest value—the most bang for the buck—out of a finite amount of resources.

The economics that is valuable in this activity is not complicated mathematical economics (which I never was very good at anyway) but basic principles like opportunity cost and benefits and costs and benefits at the margin. Those are the concepts I find useful today.

Does the Department of National Defence have economists working on defence resource allocation questions?

Economists are not in evidence here in the way they are at the Bank of Canada or in the Department of Finance. But there are some economic studies performed in the Department of National Defence on topics such as the economic benefits that accrue to the various regions of Canada as a result of defence spending.

How does the Minister of National Defence use the concepts of opportunity cost, benefit, and the margin to get the best bang for the buck? Can you provide an example?

Think about strategic air lift—the capacity to carry people and heavy equipment long distances. We don't have that capacity, and neither does any other NATO country except for the UK and the US. Right now we rent airplanes to carry our troops and equipment around the world and that's not necessarily a bad option. But we, along with some other NATO nations, are looking at alternatives.

One option is the status quo. A second option is buying the airplanes ourselves. A third option is a European joint-ownership plan. And a fourth option might be to try to reach a deal with the Americans. Resolving the issue clearly involves trying to get the benefit that we want in the most cost effective way.

The status quo—renting planes when we need

them—is a low-cost solution but it has two main problems. First, there might be times when everyone is looking for strategic lift at the same time. Second, it can sometimes take too long to negotiate agreements and get the planes operating.

Buying our own planes would give us the greatest flexibility. But that solution has a high cost and for much of the time the planes would be sitting on the ground.

The European joint-ownership time-sharing proposal might offer an efficient compromise and be the most cost-effective solution. The idea would be to work together with our NATO allies and acquire a share in jointly owned NATO lift capacity.

This arrangement would be similar to sharing a condo. The amount of time you get is proportional to the money you put in. So that's one option, which we're exploring. We would need to make sure that some of these airplanes were in Canada and that we had access when we needed them. We have a special geography compared with everyone of our European NATO partners.

So solving the problem acquiring strategic lift at least cost is a classic economic problem.

What about an area that is less clear cut—where you're trying to figure out something much less well defined? For example, how do we decide how much we should be spending on Canada's national defence?

I come at this issue from the point of view that has grown out of my experience in a number of large organizations (the bank, university, and now defence). I think any large organization has a tendency to have inefficiencies and turf issues. Large organizations don't respond quickly to changing circumstances. For example, in the defence area, the Cold War has been over for more than a decade. Yet many countries, especially in Europe, still have hundreds of tanks hanging around as if the next challenge is a Soviet invasion.

We are also into the post-September 11 world, which has brought a radical change to the kinds of response capability that is required.

Then we have a military technological revolution, which is bringing the high tech sort of warfare like we saw in the Gulf War such as precision bombs and unmanned aerial vehicles.

Put together the totally different world and the radical changes in technology and it's definitely a challenge to adapt.

But large organizations don't just automatically reinvent themselves to deal with the changing world. I'm not sure that an economist in particular has an advantage here.

What I'm trying to do is bring in people from the private sector with expertise in restructuring to try to find ways to improve our administrative efficiency and to have a debate on what military capabilities are very important, not important, or middle important in today's world.

Things in large organizations don't always go fast but in terms of the private sector people I'm hoping to get answers of some savings within six months.

There are more fundamental issues like defence capabilities. We may have a much broader defence review where these will be discussed and we'll get input from stakeholders and ordinary Canadians before making a decision.

Can we talk a bit about the complaint that you sometimes hear from the Americans that we're not spending enough on our national defence? Do you think there's a conflict of interest for the Americans? Are they trying to get us to buy their stuff? Or do you think that indeed we do have an incentive to be a free rider and that we need to guard against that?

I think both are correct. In fact I've commented publicly on this before. When the American ambassador tells us to spend more on defence in part he has in mind buying American-made big airplanes for strategic lift. And that's not a criticism. Any ambassador has the job to sell his country's product. So in part there is a double interest. The Americans would like us to spend more, but they'd also like us to buy their products. So there's a bit of a mix when you get those messages. But at the same time, living next to the world's only superpower, there is a risk of becoming a free rider. Because the Americans have an interest in

defending the whole continent by means of defending their own country, there's a possibility that we could become a free rider.

Now I personally am lobbying for more money for defence. It is true that relative to our GDP we're near the bottom in terms of our spending so some may argue that we're free riders to a certain degree. But if you compare our own situation with a country like Holland or France we're not in clear and present danger of being invaded. We've never been invaded in our history or not at least since 1812 unlike the Europeans so I think we feel less vulnerable to terrorist attack rightly or wrongly than Americans do.

So I think in the minds of Canadians there is less urgency or need for defence compared with some other countries with different histories. There has been a significant increase in public support for defence spending over the last few years—certainly since September 11, but starting earlier than that.

So my answer is: I think that Canadians feel less-threatened militarily than do many other countries, so they're not inclined to spend a lot. But I think that's changing as there's more public support now for stronger defence spending.

Do you have any final words for the beginning student?

My own career suggests that economics can lead you into a variety of different areas. I still think it's highly relevant as a way of thinking that will help you, perhaps only subconsciously, in a number of different jobs even if they're not specifically related to economics. There's only a relatively limited number of areas where I think people can work explicitly as economists—you can go into the academic world or you can work for a bank or the government or a lobbyist such as the Chamber of Commerce. But I think the training you get in economics is important even if you don't work in a job as an economist. Maybe some of the examples I've given illustrate that.

Beyond that, I would encourage all students to focus on three points, not necessarily in order of importance: Get good marks; show imagination in combining sound economic principles with real-world issues and problems; and be a good team player.

TRADING WITH THE WORLD

CHAPTER **33**

Silk Routes and Sucking Sounds

Since ancient times, people have expanded their trading as far as technology allowed. Marco Polo opened up the silk route between Europe and China in the thirteenth century. Today, container ships laden with cars and electronics and Boeing 747s stuffed with farm-fresh foods ply sea and air routes, carrying billions of dollars' worth of goods. Why do people go to such great lengths to trade with those in other nations? ◆ In 1994, Canada entered into a free trade agreement with the United States and Mexico—the North American Free Trade Agreement, or NAFTA. Some people predicted a "giant sucking sound" as jobs were transferred from high-wage Michigan and Ontario to low-wage Mexico. Can we compete with a country that pays its workers a fraction of Canadian wages? Are there any industries, besides perhaps the software and movie industries, in which we have an advantage? ◆ Canada exports lumber to the United States for homebuilding. But U.S. lumber producers say that Canadian producers receive an unfair subsidy from their government, so the United States has imposed a tariff on Canadian lumber imports. Do tariffs benefit the importing country? We examine this question in *Reading Between the Lines*.

◆ In this chapter, we're going to learn about international trade and discover how *all* nations can gain from trading with other nations. We'll discover that all nations can compete, no matter how high their wages. We'll also explain why, despite the fact that international trade brings benefits to all, governments restrict trade.

After studying this chapter, you will be able to

- ■ **Describe the trends and patterns in international trade**
- ■ **Explain comparative advantage and explain why all countries can gain from international trade**
- ■ **Explain why international trade restrictions reduce the volume of imports and exports and reduce our consumption possibilities**
- ■ **Explain the arguments that are used to justify international trade restrictions and show how they are flawed**
- ■ **Explain why we have international trade restrictions**

785

Patterns and Trends in International Trade

THE GOODS AND SERVICES THAT WE BUY FROM people in other countries are called **imports.** The goods and services that we sell to people in other countries are called **exports.** What are the most important things that we import and export? Most people would probably guess that a rich nation such as Canada imports raw materials and exports manufactured goods. Although that is one feature of Canadian international trade, it is not its most important feature. The vast bulk of our exports *and* imports is manufactured goods. We sell foreigners earth-moving equipment, airplanes, telecommunications equipment, and scientific equipment. We buy televisions, VCRs, blue jeans, and T-shirts from foreigners. Also, we are a major exporter of agricultural products and raw materials. We also import and export a huge volume of services.

Trade in Goods

Of the goods that we trade, manufactured goods account for 50 percent of our exports and 70 percent of our imports. Industrial materials (raw materials and semimanufactured items) account for 40 percent of our exports and 15 percent of our imports, and agricultural products account for only 5 percent of our exports and 2 percent of our imports. Our largest individual export and import items are capital goods and automobiles.

But goods account for only 80 percent of our exports and imports. The rest of our international trade is in services.

Trade in Services

You may be wondering how a country can "export" and "import" services. Here are some examples.

If you take a vacation in France and travel there on an Air France flight from Montreal, you import transportation services from France. The money you spend in France on hotel bills and restaurant meals is also classified as the import of services. Similarly, the money spent by a French student on vacation in Canada is a Canadian export of services to France.

When we import TV sets from South Korea, the owner of the ship that transports them might be Greek and the company that insures them might be British. The payments that we make for the transportation and insurance are Canadian imports of services. Similarly, when a Canadian shipping company transports timber from British Columbia to Tokyo, the transportation cost is a Canadian export of a service to Japan. Our international trade in these types of services is large and growing.

Geographical Patterns of International Trade

Canada has trading links with every part of the world, but the United States is our biggest trading partner. In 2001, 82 percent of our exports went to the United States and 71 percent of our imports came from the United States. Our trade with the European Union is also large—7 percent of our exports and 11 percent of our imports in 2001. Other major trading partners include the countries of Latin America and Japan. But our trade with Japan is only 2 percent of exports and 3 percent of imports.

Trends in the Volume of Trade

In 1978, we exported 25 percent of total output and imported 25 percent of the goods and services that we bought. In 2001, we exported 43 percent of total output and imported 38 percent of the goods and services that we bought.

On the export side, capital goods, automobiles, food, and raw materials have remained large items and held a roughly constant share of total exports. But the composition of imports has changed. Food and raw material imports have fallen steadily. Imports of fuel increased during the 1970s but decreased during the 1980s. Imports of machinery have grown and today approach 30 percent of total imports.

Net Exports and International Borrowing

The value of exports minus the value of imports is called **net exports.** In 2001, Canadian net exports were $57 billion. Our exports were $57 billion more than our imports. When we export more than we import, as we did in 2001, we lend to foreigners or buy some of their assets. When we import more than we export, we borrow from foreigners or sell some of our assets to them.

The Gains from International Trade

THE FUNDAMENTAL FORCE THAT GENERATES international trade is *comparative advantage*. And the basis of comparative advantage is divergent *opportunity costs*. You met these ideas in Chapter 2, when we learned about the gains from specialization and exchange between Tom and Nancy.

Tom and Nancy each specialize in producing just one good and then trade with each other. Most nations do not go to the extreme of specializing in a single good and importing everything else. But nations can increase the consumption of all goods if they redirect their scarce resources towards the production of those goods and services in which they have a comparative advantage.

To see how this outcome occurs, we'll apply the same basic ideas that we learned in the case of Tom and Nancy to trade among nations. We'll begin by recalling how we can use the production possibilities frontier to measure opportunity cost. Then we'll see how divergent opportunity costs bring comparative advantage and gains from trade for countries as well as for individuals even though no country completely specializes in the production of just one good.

Opportunity Cost in Farmland

Farmland (a fictitious country) can produce grain and cars at any point inside or along its production possibilities frontier, *PPF*, shown in Fig. 33.1. (We're holding constant the output of all the other goods that Farmland produces.) The Farmers (the people of Farmland) are consuming all the grain and cars that they produce, and they are operating at point *A* in the figure. That is, Farmland is producing and consuming 15 million tonnes of grain and 8 million cars each year. What is the opportunity cost of a car in Farmland?

We can answer that question by calculating the slope of the production possibilities frontier at point *A*. The magnitude of the slope of the frontier measures the opportunity cost of one good in terms of the other. To measure the slope of the frontier at point *A*, place a straight line tangential to the frontier at point *A* and calculate the slope of that straight line. Recall that the formula for the slope of a line is the change in the value of the variable measured on the *y*-axis divided by the change in the value of the variable

measured on the *x*-axis as we move along the line. Here, the variable measured on the *y*-axis is millions of tonnes of grain, and the variable measured on the *x*-axis is millions of cars. So the slope is the change in the number of tonnes of grain divided by the change in the number of cars.

As you can see from the red triangle at point *A* in the figure, if the number of cars produced increases by 2 million, grain production decreases by 18 million tonnes. Therefore the magnitude of the slope is 18 million divided by 2 million, which equals 9. To get one more car, the people of Farmland must give up 9 tonnes of grain. So the opportunity cost of 1 car is 9 tonnes of grain. Equivalently, 9 tonnes of grain cost 1 car. For the people of Farmland, these opportunity costs are the prices they face. The price of a car is 9 tonnes of grain, and the price of 9 tonnes of grain is 1 car.

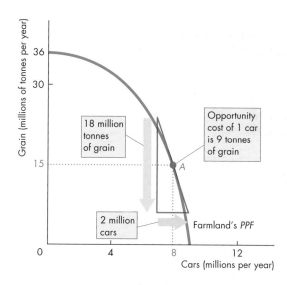

FIGURE 33.1   Opportunity Cost in Farmland

Farmland produces and consumes 15 million tonnes of grain and 8 million cars a year. That is, it produces and consumes at point A on its production possibilities frontier. Opportunity cost is equal to the magnitude of the slope of the production possibilities frontier. The red triangle tells us that at point A, 18 million tonnes of grain must be forgone to get 2 million cars. That is, at point A, 2 million cars cost 18 million tonnes of grain. Equivalently, 1 car costs 9 tonnes of grain or 9 tonnes of grain cost 1 car.

Opportunity Cost in Mobilia

Figure 33.2 shows the production possibilities frontier of Mobilia (another fictitious country). Like the Farmers, the Mobilians consume all the grain and cars that they produce. Mobilia consumes 18 million tonnes of grain a year and 4 million cars, at point A'.

Let's calculate the opportunity costs in Mobilia. At point A', the opportunity cost of a car is equal to the magnitude of the slope of the red line tangential to the production possibilities frontier, *PPF*. You can see from the red triangle that the magnitude of the slope of Mobilia's production possibilities frontier is 6 million tonnes of grain divided by 6 million cars, which equals 1 tonne of grain per car. To get one more car, the Mobilians must give up 1 tonne of grain. So the opportunity cost of 1 car is 1 tonne of grain, or equivalently, the opportunity cost of 1 tonne of grain is 1 car. These are the prices faced in Mobilia.

Comparative Advantage

Cars are cheaper in Mobilia than in Farmland. One car costs 9 tonnes of grain in Farmland but only

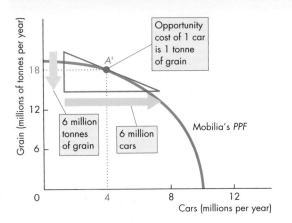

FIGURE 33.2 Opportunity Cost in Mobilia

Mobilia produces and consumes 18 million tonnes of grain and 4 million cars a year. That is, it produces and consumes at point A' on its production possibilities frontier. Opportunity cost is equal to the magnitude of the slope of the production possibilities frontier. The red triangle tells us that at point A', 6 million tonnes of grain must be forgone to get 6 million cars. That is, at point A', 6 million cars cost 6 million tonnes of grain. Equivalently, 1 car costs 1 tonne of grain or 1 tonne of grain costs 1 car.

1 tonne of grain in Mobilia. But grain is cheaper in Farmland than in Mobilia—9 tonnes of grain cost only 1 car in Farmland, while that same amount of grain costs 9 cars in Mobilia.

Mobilia has a comparative advantage in car production. Farmland has a comparative advantage in grain production. A country has a **comparative advantage** in producing a good if it can produce that good at a lower opportunity cost than any other country. Let's see how opportunity cost differences and comparative advantage generate gains from international trade.

The Gains from Trade: Cheaper to Buy Than to Produce

If Mobilia bought grain for what it costs Farmland to produce it, then Mobilia could buy 9 tonnes of grain for 1 car. That is much lower than the cost of growing grain in Mobilia, for there it costs 9 cars to produce 9 tonnes of grain. If the Mobilians can buy grain at the low Farmland price, they will reap some gains.

If the Farmers can buy cars for what it costs Mobilia to produce them, they will be able to obtain a car for 1 tonne of grain. Because it costs 9 tonnes of grain to produce a car in Farmland, the Farmers would gain from such an opportunity.

In this situation, it makes sense for Mobilians to buy their grain from Farmers and for Farmers to buy their cars from Mobilians. But at what price will Farmland and Mobilia engage in mutually beneficial international trade?

The Terms of Trade

The quantity of grain that Farmland must pay Mobilia for a car is Farmland's **terms of trade** with Mobilia. Because Canada exports and imports many different goods and services, we measure the terms of trade in the real world as an index number that averages the terms of trade over all the items we trade.

The forces of international supply and demand determine the terms of trade. Figure 33.3 illustrates these forces in the Farmland-Mobilia international car market. The quantity of cars *traded internationally* is measured on the x-axis. On the y-axis, we measure the price of a car. This price is expressed as the *terms of trade*: tonnes of grain per car. If no international trade takes place, the price of a car in Farmland is 9 tonnes of grain, its opportunity cost, indicated by point *A* in

FIGURE 33.3   International Trade in Cars

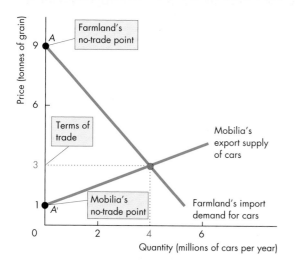

Farmland's import demand curve for cars is downward sloping, and Mobilia's export supply curve of cars is upward sloping. Without international trade, the price of a car is 9 tonnes of grain in Farmland (point A) and 1 tonne of grain in Mobilia (point A').

With free international trade, the price (terms of trade) is determined where the export supply curve intersects the import demand curve: 3 tonnes of grain per car. At that price, 4 million cars a year are imported by Farmland and exported by Mobilia. The value of grain exported by Farmland and imported by Mobilia is 12 million tonnes a year, the quantity required to pay for the cars imported.

the figure. Again, if no trade takes place, the price of a car in Mobilia is 1 tonne of grain, its opportunity cost, indicated by point A' in the figure. The no-trade points A and A' in Fig. 33.3 correspond to the points identified by those same letters in Figs. 33.1 and 33.2. The lower the price of a car (terms of trade), the greater is the quantity of cars that the Farmers are willing to import from the Mobilians. This fact is illustrated by the downward-sloping curve, which shows Farmland's import demand for cars.

The Mobilians respond in the opposite direction. The higher the price of a car (terms of trade), the greater is the quantity of cars that Mobilians are willing to export to Farmers. This fact is reflected in Mobilia's export supply of cars—the upward-sloping line in Fig. 33.3.

The international market in cars determines the equilibrium terms of trade (price) and quantity traded. This equilibrium occurs where the import demand curve intersects the export supply curve. In this case, the equilibrium terms of trade are 3 tonnes of grain per car. Mobilia exports and Farmland imports 4 million cars a year. Notice that the terms of trade are lower than the initial price in Farmland but higher than the initial price in Mobilia.

Balanced Trade

The number of cars exported by Mobilia—4 million a year—is exactly equal to the number of cars imported by Farmland. How does Farmland pay for its cars? The answer is by exporting grain. How much grain does Farmland export? You can find the answer by noticing that for 1 car, Farmland must pay 3 tonnes of grain. So for 4 million cars, Farmland pays 12 million tonnes of grain. Farmland's exports of grain are 12 million tonnes a year, and Mobilia imports this same quantity of grain.

Mobilia is exchanging 4 million cars for 12 million tonnes of grain each year, and Farmland is doing the opposite: exchanging 12 million tonnes of grain for 4 million cars. Trade is balanced between these two countries. The value received from exports equals the value paid out for imports.

Changes in Production and Consumption

We've seen that international trade makes it possible for Farmers to buy cars at a lower price than they can produce them and sell their grain for a higher price. International trade also enables Mobilians to sell their cars for a higher price and buy grain for a lower price. Everyone gains. How is it possible for *everyone* to gain? What are the changes in production and consumption that accompany these gains?

An economy that does not trade with other economies has identical production and consumption possibilities. Without trade, the economy can consume only what it produces. But with international trade, an economy can consume different quantities of goods from those that it produces. The production possibilities frontier describes the limit of what a country can produce, but it does not describe the limits to what it can consume. Figure 33.4 will help you to see the distinction between production possibilities and consumption possibilities when a country trades with other countries.

FIGURE 33.4 Expanding Consumption Possibilities

(a) Farmland

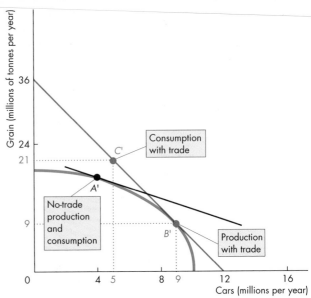

(b) Mobilia

With no international trade, the Farmers produce and consume at point A and the opportunity cost of a car is 9 tonnes of grain (the slope of the black line in part a). Also, with no international trade, the Mobilians produce and consume at point A' and the opportunity cost of 1 tonne of grain is 1 car (the slope of the black line in part b). Goods can be exchanged internationally at a price of 3 tonnes of grain for 1 car along the red line in each part of the figure. In part (a), Farmland decreases its production of cars and increases its production of grain, moving from A

to B. It exports grain and imports cars, and it consumes at point C. The Farmers have more of both cars and grain than they would if they produced all their own consumption goods—at point A. In part (b), Mobilia increases car production and decreases grain production, moving from A' to B'. Mobilia exports cars and imports grain, and it consumes at point C'. The Mobilians have more of both cars and grain than they would if they produced all their own consumption goods—at point A'.

First of all, notice that the figure has two parts: part (a) for Farmland and part (b) for Mobilia. The production possibilities frontiers that you saw in Figs. 33.1 and 33.2 are reproduced here. The slopes of the two black lines in the figure represent the opportunity costs in the two countries when there is no international trade. Farmland produces and consumes at point *A*, and Mobilia produces and consumes at *A'*. Cars cost 9 tonnes of grain in Farmland and 1 tonne of grain in Mobilia.

Consumption Possibilities The red line in each part of Fig. 33.4 shows the country's consumption possibilities with international trade. These two red

lines have the same slope, and the magnitude of that slope is the opportunity cost of a car in terms of grain on the world market: 3 tonnes per car. The *slope* of the consumption possibilities line is common to both countries because its magnitude equals the *world* price. But the position of a country's consumption possibilities line depends on the country's production possibilities. A country cannot produce outside its production possibilities curve, so its consumption possibilities curve touches its production possibilities curve. So Farmland could choose to consume at point *B* with no international trade or, with international trade, at any point on its red consumption possibilities line.

Free Trade Equilibrium With international trade, the producers of cars in Mobilia can get a higher price for their output. As a result, they increase the quantity of car production. At the same time, grain producers in Mobilia get a lower price for their grain, and so they reduce production. Producers in Mobilia adjust their output by moving along their production possibilities frontier until the opportunity cost in Mobilia equals the world price (the opportunity cost in the world market). This situation arises when Mobilia is producing at point B′ in Fig. 33.4(b).

But the Mobilians do not consume at point B′. That is, they do not increase their consumption of cars and decrease their consumption of grain. Instead, they sell some of their car production to Farmland in exchange for some of Farmland's grain. They trade internationally. But to see how that works out, we first need to check in with Farmland to see what's happening there.

In Farmland, producers of cars now get a lower price and producers of grain get a higher price. As a consequence, producers in Farmland decrease car production and increase grain production. They adjust their outputs by moving along the production possibilities frontier until the opportunity cost of a car in terms of grain equals the world price (the opportunity cost on the world market). They move to point B in part (a). But the Farmers do not consume at point B. Instead, they trade some of their additional grain production for the now cheaper cars from Mobilia.

The figure shows us the quantities consumed in the two countries. We saw in Fig. 33.3 that Mobilia exports 4 million cars a year and Farmland imports those cars. We also saw that Farmland exports 12 million tonnes of grain a year and Mobilia imports that grain. So Farmland's consumption of grain is 12 million tonnes a year less than it produces, and its consumption of cars is 4 million a year more than it produces. Farmland consumes at point C in Fig. 33.4(a).

Similarly, we know that Mobilia consumes 12 million tonnes of grain more than it produces and 4 million cars fewer than it produces. Mobilia consumes at point C′ in Fig. 33.4(b).

Calculating the Gains from Trade

You can now literally see the gains from trade in Fig. 33.4. Without trade, Farmers produce and consume at A (part a)—a point on Farmland's production possibilities frontier. With international trade, Farmers

consume at point C in part (a)—a point *outside* the production possibilities frontier. At point C, Farmers are consuming 3 million tonnes of grain a year and 1 million cars a year more than before. These increases in consumption of both cars and grain, beyond the limits of the production possibilities frontier, are the Farmers' gains from international trade.

Mobilians also gain. Without trade, they consume at point A′ in part (b)—a point on Mobilia's production possibilities frontier. With international trade, they consume at point C′—a point outside their production possibilities frontier. With international trade, Mobilia consumes 3 million tonnes of grain a year and 1 million cars a year more than it would without trade. These are the gains from international trade for Mobilia.

Gains for All

Trade between the Farmers and the Mobilians does not create winners and losers. It creates only winners. Farmers selling grain and Mobilians selling cars face an increased demand for their products because the net demand by foreigners is added to domestic demand. With an increase in demand, the price rises.

Farmers buying cars and Mobilians buying grain face an increased supply of these products because the net foreign supply is added to domestic supply. With an increase in supply, the price falls.

Gains from Trade in Reality

The gains from trade that we have just studied between Farmland and Mobilia in grain and cars occur in a model economy—in a world economy that we have imagined. But these same phenomena occur every day in the real global economy.

Comparative Advantage in the Global Economy We buy TVs and VCRs from Korea, machinery from Europe, and fashion goods from Hong Kong. In exchange, we sell machinery, grain and lumber, airplanes, computers, and financial services. All this international trade is generated by comparative advantage, just like the international trade between Farmland and Mobilia in our model economy. All international trade arises from comparative advantage, even when trade is in similar goods such as tools and machines. At first thought, it seems puzzling that countries exchange manufactured goods. Why doesn't each developed country produce all the manufactured goods its citizens want to buy?

Trade in Similar Goods   Why does Canada produce automobiles for export and at the same time import large quantities of automobiles from the United States, Japan, Korea, and Western Europe? Wouldn't it make more sense to produce all the cars that we buy here in Canada? After all, we have access to the best technology available for producing cars. Auto workers in Canada are surely as productive as their fellow workers in the United States, Western Europe, and Asian countries. So why does Canada have a comparative advantage in some types of cars and Japan and Europe in others?

Diversity of Taste and Economies of Scale   The first part of the answer is that people have a tremendous diversity of taste. Let's stick with the example of cars. Some people prefer a sports car, some prefer a limousine, some prefer a regular, full-size car, some prefer a sport utility vehicle, and some prefer a mini-van. In addition to size and type of car, there are many other dimensions in which cars vary. Some have low fuel consumption, some have high performance, some are spacious and comfortable, some have a large trunk, some have four-wheel drive, some have front-wheel drive, some have a radiator grille that looks like a Greek temple, others resemble a wedge. People's preferences across these many dimensions vary. The tremendous diversity in tastes for cars means that people value variety and are willing to pay for it in the marketplace.

The second part of the answer to the puzzle is *economies of scale*—the tendency for the average cost to be lower, the larger the scale of production. In such situations, larger and larger production runs lead to ever lower average costs. Production of many goods, including cars, involves economies of scale. For example, if a car producer makes only a few hundred (or perhaps a few thousand) cars of a particular type and design, the producer must use production techniques that are much more labour-intensive and much less automated than those employed to make hundreds of thousands of cars in a particular model. With short production runs and labour-intensive production techniques, costs are high. With very large production runs and automated assembly lines, production costs are much lower. But to obtain lower costs, the automated assembly lines have to produce a large number of cars.

It is the combination of diversity of taste and economies of scale that determines opportunity cost, produces comparative advantages, and generates such

a large amount of international trade in similar commodities. With international trade, each car manufacturer has the whole world market to serve. Each producer can specialize in a limited range of products and then sell its output to the entire world market. This arrangement enables large production runs on the most popular cars and feasible production runs even on the most customized cars demanded by only a handful of people in each country.

The situation in the market for cars is also present in many other industries, especially those producing specialized equipment and parts. For example, Canada exports illustration software but imports database software, exports telecommunications systems but imports PCs, exports specialized video equipment but imports VCRs. International trade in similar but slightly different manufactured products is profitable.

REVIEW QUIZ

1   What is the fundamental source of the gains from international trade?

2   In what circumstances can countries gain from international trade?

3   What determines the goods and services that a country will export?

4   What determines the goods and services that a country will import?

5   What is comparative advantage and what role does it play in determining the amount and type of international trade that occurs?

6   How can it be that all countries gain from international trade and that there are no losers?

7   Provide some examples of comparative advantage in today's world.

8   Why does Canada both export and import automobiles?

You've now seen how free international trade brings gains for all. But trade is not free in our world. We'll now take a brief look at the history of international trade restrictions and also work out the effects of international trade restrictions. We'll see that free trade brings the greatest possible benefits and that international trade restrictions are costly.

International Trade Restrictions

GOVERNMENTS RESTRICT INTERNATIONAL TRADE to protect domestic industries from foreign competition by using two main tools:

1. Tariffs
2. Nontariff barriers

A **tariff** is a tax that is imposed by the importing country when an imported good crosses its international boundary. A **nontariff barrier** is any action other than a tariff that restricts international trade. Examples of nontariff barriers are quantitative restrictions and licensing regulations limiting imports. First, let's look at tariffs.

The History of Tariffs

The Canadian economy has always been protected by a tariff. Figure 33.5 shows the history of that tariff, from Confederation through 2001. The figure shows tariffs as a percentage of total imports—the average tariff rate. As you can see, the average tariff rate climbed from the early 1870s to exceed 20 percent by the late 1880s. The rate fluctuated but gradually decreased through the early 1920s. It increased again during the Great Depression years of the early 1930s. During these years, most countries increased their tariff rates in what became a "beggar-my-neighbour" policy. The average tariff then decreased through the late 1930s and continued its decrease throughout the years after World War II. Today, the average tariff rate is less than 1 percent.

The reduction in tariffs after World War II followed the signing in 1947 of the **General Agreement on Tariffs and Trade** (GATT). From its formation, GATT organized a series of "rounds" of negotiations that resulted in a steady process of tariff reduction. One of these, the Kennedy Round that began in the early 1960s, resulted in large tariff cuts starting in 1967. Another, the Tokyo Round, resulted in further tariff cuts in 1979. The final round, the Uruguay Round, started in 1986 and was completed in 1994.

The Uruguay Round was the most ambitious and comprehensive of the rounds and led to the creation of the **World Trade Organization** (WTO). Membership of the WTO brings greater obligations for countries to observe the GATT rules. Canada signed the Uruguay Round agreements, and Parliament ratified them in 1994.

In addition to the agreements under the GATT

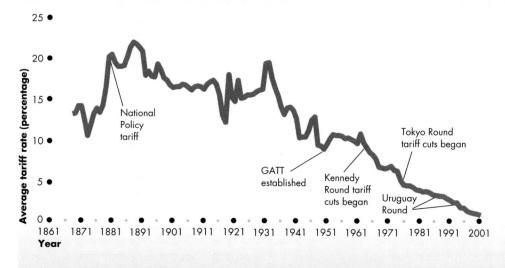

FIGURE 33.5 Canadian Tariffs: 1867–2001

Canadian tariffs were in place before Confederation. Tariffs increased sharply in the 1870s and remained high until the 1930s. Since the establishment of the GATT in 1947, tariffs have steadily declined in a series of negotiating rounds, the most significant of which are identified in the figure. Tariffs are now as low as they have ever been.

Sources: Statistics Canada, *Historial Statistics of Canada*, Series G485, CANSIM tables 380-0002 and 380-0007, and authors' calculations.

and the WTO, Canada is a party to the **North American Free Trade Agreement** (NAFTA), which became effective on January 1, 1994, and under which barriers to international trade between the United States, Canada, and Mexico will be virtually eliminated after a 15-year phasing-in period.

In other parts of the world, trade barriers have virtually been eliminated among the member countries of the European Union, which has created the largest unified tariff-free market in the world. In 1994, discussions among the Asia-Pacific Economic Cooperation (APEC) led to an agreement in principle to work towards a free-trade area that embraces China, all the economies of East Asia and the South Pacific, and the United States and Canada. These countries include the fastest-growing economies and hold the promise of heralding a global free-trade area.

The effort to achieve freer trade underlines the fact that trade in some goods is still subject to a high tariff. Textiles and footwear are among the goods that face the highest tariffs, and rates on these items average more than 10 percent. Some individual items face a tariff much higher than the average. For example, when you buy a pair of blue jeans for $20, you pay about $5 more than you would if there were no tariffs on textiles. Other goods that are protected by tariffs are agricultural products, energy and chemicals, minerals, and metals. The meat, cheese, and sugar that you consume cost significantly more because of protection than they would with free international trade.

The temptation for governments to impose tariffs is a strong one. First, tariffs provide revenue to the government. Second, they enable the government to satisfy special interest groups in import-competing industries. But, as we'll see, free international trade brings enormous benefits that are reduced when tariffs are imposed. Let's see how.

How Tariffs Work

To see how tariffs work, let's return to the example of trade between Farmland and Mobilia. Figure 33.6 shows the international market for cars in which these two countries are the only traders. The volume of trade and the price of a car are determined at the point of intersection of Mobilia's export supply curve of cars and Farmland's import demand curve for cars.

In Fig. 33.6, these two countries trade cars and grain in exactly the same way that we saw in Fig. 33.3.

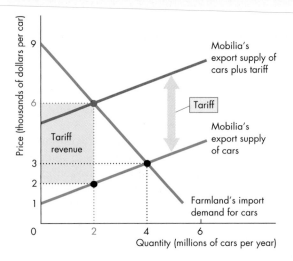

FIGURE 33.6   The Effects of a Tariff

Farmland imposes a tariff on car imports from Mobilia. The tariff increases the price that Farmers have to pay for cars. It shifts the supply curve of cars in Farmland leftward. The vertical distance between the original supply curve and the new one is the amount of the tariff, $4,000 per car. The price of cars in Farmland increases, and the quantity of cars imported decreases. The government of Farmland collects a tariff revenue of $4,000 per car—a total of $8 billion on the 2 million cars imported. Farmland's exports of grain decrease because Mobilia now has a lower income from its exports of cars.

Mobilia exports cars, and Farmland exports grain. The volume of car imports into Farmland is 4 million a year, and the world market price of a car is 3 tonnes of grain. Figure 33.6 expresses prices in dollars rather than in units of grain and is based on a money price of grain of $1 a tonne. With grain costing $1,000 a tonne, the money price of a car is $3,000.

Now suppose that the government of Farmland, perhaps under pressure from car producers, decides to impose a tariff on imported cars. In particular, suppose that a tariff of $4,000 per car is imposed. (This is a huge tariff, but the car producers of Farmland are pretty fed up with competition from Mobilia.) What happens?

- The supply of cars in Farmland decreases.
- The price of cars in Farmland rises.
- The quantity of cars imported by Farmland decreases.
- The government of Farmland collects the tariff revenue.
- Resource use is inefficient.
- The *value* of exports changes by the same amount as the *value* of imports, and trade remains balanced.

Change in the Supply of Cars Farmland cannot buy cars at Mobilia's export supply price. It must pay that price plus the $4,000 tariff. So the supply curve in Farmland shifts leftward. The new supply curve is that labelled "Mobilia's export supply of cars plus tariff." The vertical distance between Mobilia's original export supply curve and the new supply curve is the tariff of $4,000 a car.

Rise in Price of Cars A new equilibrium occurs where the new supply curve intersects Farmland's import demand curve for cars. That equilibrium is at a price of $6,000 a car, up from $3,000 with free trade.

Fall in Imports Car imports fall from 4 million to 2 million cars a year. At the higher price of $6,000 a car, domestic car producers increase their production. Domestic grain production decreases as resources are moved into the expanding car industry.

Tariff Revenue Total expenditure on imported cars by the Farmers is $6,000 a car multiplied by the 2 million cars imported ($12 billion). But not all of that money goes to the Mobilians. They receive $2,000 a car, or $4 billion for the 2 million cars. The difference—$4,000 a car, or a total of $8 billion for the 2 million cars—is collected by the government of Farmland as tariff revenue.

Inefficiency The people of Farmland are willing to pay $6,000 for the marginal car imported. But the opportunity cost of that car is $2,000. So there is a gain from trading an extra car. In fact, there are gains—willingness to pay exceeds opportunity cost—all the way up to 4 million cars a year. Only when 4 million cars are being traded is the maximum price that a Farmer is willing to pay equal to the minimum price that is acceptable to a Mobilian. Restricting trade reduces the gains from trade.

Trade Remains Balanced With free trade, Farmland was paying $3,000 a car and buying 4 million cars a year from Mobilia. The total amount paid to Mobilia for imports was $12 billion a year. With a tariff, Farmland's imports have been cut to 2 million cars a year and the price paid to Mobilia has also been cut to only $2,000 a car. The total amount paid to Mobilia for imports has been cut to $4 billion a year. Doesn't this fact mean that Farmland now has a balance of trade surplus? It does not.

The price of cars in Mobilia has fallen. But the price of grain remains at $1 a tonne. So the relative price of cars has fallen, and the relative price of grain has increased. With free trade, the Mobilians could buy 3,000 tonnes of grain for the price of one car. Now they can buy only 2,000 tonnes for the price of a car. With a higher relative price of grain, the quantity demanded by the Mobilians decreases and Mobilia imports less grain. But because Mobilia imports less grain, Farmland exports less grain. In fact, Farmland's grain industry suffers from two sources. First, there is a decrease in the quantity of grain sold to Mobilia. Second, there is increased competition for inputs from the now-expanded car industry. The tariff leads to a contraction in the scale of the grain industry in Farmland.

It seems paradoxical at first that a country imposing a tariff on cars hurts its own export industry, lowering its exports of grain. It may help to think of it this way: Mobilians buy grain with the money they make from exporting cars to Farmland. If they export fewer cars, they cannot afford to buy as much grain. In fact, in the absence of any international borrowing and lending, Mobilia must cut its imports of grain by exactly the same amount as the loss in revenue from its export of cars. Grain imports into Mobilia are cut back to a value of $4 billion, the amount that can be paid for by the new lower revenue from Mobilia's car exports. Trade is still balanced. The tariff cuts imports and exports by the same amount. The tariff has no effect on the *balance* of trade, but it reduces the *volume* of trade.

The result that we have just derived is perhaps one of the most misunderstood aspects of international economics. On countless occasions, politicians and others call for tariffs to remove a balance of trade deficit or argue that lowering tariffs would produce a balance of trade deficit. They reach this conclusion by failing to work out all the implications of a tariff.

Let's now look at nontariff barriers.

Nontariff Barriers

The two main forms of nontariff barriers are

1. Quotas
2. Voluntary export restraints

A **quota** is a quantitative restriction on the import of a particular good, which specifies the maximum amount of the good that may be imported in a given period of time. A **voluntary export restraint** (VER) is an agreement between two governments in which the government of the exporting country agrees to restrain the volume of its own exports.

Quotas are especially prominent in textiles and agriculture. Voluntary export restraints are used to regulate trade between Japan and Canada.

How Quotas and VERs Work

To see how a quota works, suppose that Farmland imposes a quota that restricts its car imports to 2 million cars a year. Figure 33.7 shows the effects of this action. The quota is shown by the vertical red line at 2 million cars a year. Because it is illegal to exceed the quota, car importers buy only that quantity from Mobilia, for which they pay $2,000 a car. But because the import supply of cars is restricted to 2 million cars a year, people are willing to pay $6,000 per car. This is the price of a car in Farmland.

The value of imports falls to $4 billion, exactly the same as in the case of the tariff in Fig. 33.6. So with lower incomes from car exports and with a higher relative price of grain, Mobilians cut back on their imports of grain in exactly the same way that they did under a tariff.

The key difference between a quota and a tariff lies in who collects the gap between the import supply price and the domestic price. In the case of a tariff, it is the government of the importing country. In the case of a quota, it goes to the person who has the right to import under the import quota regulations.

A VER is like a quota arrangement in which quotas are allocated to each exporting country. The effects of VERs are similar to those of quotas but differ from them in that the gap between the domestic price and the export price is captured not by domestic importers but by the foreign exporter. The government of the exporting country has to establish procedures for allocating the restricted volume of exports among its producers.

FIGURE 33.7   The Effects of a Quota

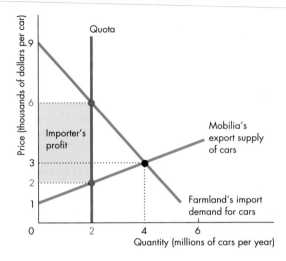

Farmland imposes a quota of 2 million cars a year on car imports from Mobilia. That quantity appears as the vertical line labelled "Quota." Because the quantity of cars supplied by Mobilia is restricted to 2 million, the price at which those cars will be traded increases to $6,000. Importing cars is profitable because Mobilia is willing to supply cars at $2,000 each. There is competition for import quotas.

REVIEW QUIZ

1 What are the tools that a country can use to restrict international trade?
2 What do international trade restrictions do to the gains from international trade?
3 Which is best for a country: restricted trade, no trade, or free trade? Why?
4 What does a tariff on imports do to the volume of imports and the volume of exports?
5 In the absence of international borrowing and lending, how do tariffs and other international trade restrictions influence the total value of imports and exports and the balance of trade—the value of exports minus the value of imports?

We're now going to look at some commonly heard arguments for restricting international trade and see why they are almost never correct.

The Case Against Protection

FOR AS LONG AS NATIONS AND INTERNATIONAL trade have existed, people have debated whether a country is better off with free international trade or with protection from foreign competition. The debate continues, but for most economists, a verdict has been delivered and is the one you have just seen. Free trade promotes prosperity for all; protection is inefficient. We've seen the most powerful case for free trade in the example of how Farmland and Mobilia both benefit from their comparative advantage. But there is a broader range of issues in the free trade versus protection debate. Let's review these issues.

Three arguments for restricting international trade are

- The employment argument
- The infant-industry argument
- The dumping argument

Let's look at each in turn.

The Employment Argument

The argument that protection saves jobs goes as follows: When we buy shoes from Brazil or shirts from Taiwan, Canadian workers in these industries lose their jobs. With no earnings and poor prospects, these workers become a drain on welfare and spend less, causing a ripple effect of further job losses. The proposed solution to this problem is to ban imports of cheap foreign goods and protect Canadian jobs. This argument for protection does not withstand scrutiny for three reasons.

First, free trade does cost some jobs, but it also creates other jobs. It brings about a global rationalization of labour and allocates labour resources to their highest-valued activities. Because of international trade in textiles, tens of thousands of workers in Canada have lost their jobs because textile mills and other factories have closed. But tens of thousands of workers in other countries have gotten jobs because textile mills have opened there. And tens of thousands of Canadian workers have gotten better-paying jobs than those of textile workers because other export industries have expanded and created more jobs than have been destroyed.

Second, imports create jobs. They create jobs for retailers that sell imported goods and firms that service those goods. They also create jobs by creating incomes in the rest of the world, some of which are spent on imports of Canadian-made goods and services.

Although protection does save particular jobs, it does so at inordinate cost. A striking example of the cost of quotas is that of the quotas on the import of textiles. Quotas imposed under an international agreement called the Multifiber Arrangement (that is being phased out) have protected textile jobs, especially in the United States. The U.S. International Trade Commission (ITC) has estimated that because of quotas, 72,000 jobs exist in textiles that would otherwise disappear and annual clothing expenditure in the United States is $U.S. 15.9 billion or $U.S. 160 per family higher than it would be with free trade. Equivalently, the ITC estimates that each textile job saved costs $U.S. 221,000 a year.

The Infant-Industry Argument

The so-called **infant-industry argument** for protection is that it is necessary to protect a new industry to enable it to grow into a mature industry that can compete in world markets. The argument is based on the idea of *dynamic comparative advantage*, which can arise from *learning-by-doing* (see Chapter 2).

Learning-by-doing is a powerful engine of productivity growth, and comparative advantage does evolve and change because of on-the-job experience. But these facts do not justify protection.

First, the infant-industry argument is valid only if the benefits of learning-by-doing *not only* accrue to the owners and workers of the firms in the infant industry but also *spill over* to other industries and parts of the economy. For example, there are huge productivity gains from learning-by-doing in the manufacture of aircraft. But almost all of these gains benefit the stockholders and workers of Boeing and other aircraft producers. Because the people making the decisions, bearing the risk, and doing the work are the ones who benefit, they take the dynamic gains into account when they decide on the scale of their activities. In this case, almost no benefits spill over to other parts of the economy, so there is no need for government assistance to achieve an efficient outcome.

Second, even if the case is made for protecting an infant industry, it is more efficient to do so by a subsidy to the firms in the industry, with the subsidy out of taxes.

The Dumping Argument

Dumping occurs when a foreign firm sells its exports at a price below its cost of production. Dumping might be used by a firm that wants to gain a global monopoly. In this case, the foreign firm sells its output at a price below its cost to drive domestic firms out of business. When the domestic firms have gone, the foreign firm takes advantage of its monopoly position and charges a higher price for its product. Dumping is usually regarded as a justification for temporary countervailing tariffs.

But there are powerful reasons to resist the dumping argument for protection. First, it is virtually impossible to detect dumping because it is hard to determine a firm's costs. As a result, the test for dumping is whether a firm's export price is below its domestic price. But this test is a weak one because it can be rational for a firm to charge a low price in markets in which the quantity demanded is highly sensitive to price and a higher price in a market in which demand is less price-sensitive.

Second, it is hard to think of a good that is produced by a natural *global* monopoly. So even if all the domestic firms were driven out of business in some industry, it would always be possible to find several and usually many alternative foreign sources of supply and to buy at prices determined in competitive markets.

Third, if a good or service were a truly global natural monopoly, the best way of dealing with it would be by regulation—just as in the case of domestic monopolies. Such regulation would require international cooperation.

The three arguments for protection that we've just examined have an element of credibility. The counterarguments are in general stronger, however, so these arguments do not make the case for protection. But they are not the only arguments that you might encounter. The many other arguments that are commonly heard are quite simply wrong. They are fatally flawed. The most common of them are that protection

- Maintains national security
- Allows us to compete with cheap foreign labour
- Brings diversity and stability
- Penalizes lax environmental standards
- Protects national culture
- Prevents rich countries from exploiting developing countries

Maintains National Security

The national security argument for protection is that a country must protect industries that produce defence equipment and armaments and industries on which the defence industries rely for their raw materials and other intermediate inputs. This argument for protection does not withstand close scrutiny.

First, it is an argument for international isolation, for in a time of war, there is no industry that does not contribute to national defence. Second, if the case is made for boosting the output of a strategic industry, it is more efficient to achieve this outcome with a subsidy to the firms in the industry that is financed out of taxes. Such a subsidy would keep the industry operating at the scale judged appropriate, and free international trade would keep the prices faced by consumers at their world market levels.

Allows Us to Compete with Cheap Foreign Labour

With the removal of tariffs in Canadian trade with Mexico, people said we would hear a "giant sucking sound" as jobs rushed to Mexico (shown in the cartoon). Let's see what's wrong with this view.

The labour cost of a unit of output equals the wage rate divided by labour productivity. For example, if a Canadian auto worker earns $30 an hour and produces 15 units of output an hour, the average labour cost of a unit of output is $2. If a Mexican auto assembly worker earns $3 an hour and produces 1 unit of output an hour, the average labour cost of a unit of output is $3. Other things remaining the same, the higher a worker's productivity, the higher is the worker's wage rate. High-wage workers have high productivity. Low-wage workers have low productivity.

Although high-wage Canadian workers are more productive, on the average, than low-wage Mexican workers, there are differences across industries. Canadian labour is relatively more productive in some activities than in others. For example, the productivity of Canadian workers in producing financial services and telephone systems is relatively higher than their productivity in the production of metals and some standardized machine parts. The activities in which Canadian workers are relatively more productive than their Mexican counterparts are those in which Canada has a *comparative advantage*. By engaging in free trade, increasing our production and exports of the goods and services in which we have a comparative advantage and decreasing our produc-

"I don't know what the hell happened—one minute I'm at work in Flint, Michigan, then there's a giant sucking sound and suddenly here I am in Mexico."

tion and increasing our imports of the goods and services in which our trading partners have a comparative advantage, we can make ourselves and the citizens of other countries better off.

Brings Diversity and Stability

A diversified investment portfolio is less risky than one that has all the eggs in one basket. The same is true for an economy's production. A diversified economy fluctuates less than an economy that produces only one or two goods.

But big, rich, diversified economies such as those of Canada, the United States, Japan, and Europe do not have this type of stability problem. Even a country such as Saudi Arabia that produces only one good (in this case, oil) can benefit from specializing in the activity at which it has a comparative advantage and then investing in a wide range of other countries to bring greater stability to its income and consumption.

Penalizes Lax Environmental Standards

Another argument for protection is that many poorer countries, such as Mexico, do not have the same environmental policies that we have and, because they are willing to pollute and we are not, we cannot compete with them without tariffs. So if they want free trade with the richer and "greener" countries, they must clean up their environments to our standards.

This argument for international trade restrictions is weak. First, not all poorer countries have significantly lower environmental standards than Canada has. Many poor countries and the former communist countries of Eastern Europe do have bad environment records. But some countries enforce strict laws. Second, a poor country cannot afford to be as concerned about its environment as a rich country can. The best hope for a better environment in Mexico and in other developing countries is rapid income growth through free trade. As their incomes grow, developing countries will have the *means* to match their desires to improve their environment. Third, poor countries have a comparative advantage at doing "dirty" work, which helps rich countries achieve higher environmental standards than they otherwise could.

Protects National Culture

The national culture argument for protection is one of the most commonly heard argument in Canada and Europe.

The expressed fear is that free trade in books, magazines, movies, and television programs means U.S. domination and the end of local culture. So, the reasoning continues, it is necessary to protect domestic "culture" industries from free international trade to ensure the survival of a national cultural identity.

Protection of these industries is common and takes the form of nontariff barriers. For example, local content regulations on radio and television broadcasting and in magazines is often required.

The cultural identity argument for protection has no merit. Writers, publishers, and broadcasters want to limit foreign competition so that they can earn larger economic profits. There is no actual danger to national culture. In fact, many of the creators of so-called American cultural products are not Americans but the talented citizens of other countries, ensuring the survival of their national cultural identities in Hollywood! Also, if national culture is in danger, there is no surer way of helping it on its way out than by impoverishing the nation whose culture it is. And protection is an effective way of doing just that.

Prevents Rich Countries from Exploiting Developing Countries

Another argument for protection is that international trade must be restricted to prevent the people of the rich industrial world from exploiting the poorer people of the developing countries, forcing them to work for slave wages.

Wage rates in some developing countries are indeed very low. But by trading with developing countries, we increase the demand for the goods that these countries produce and, more significantly, we increase the demand for their labour. When the demand for labour in developing countries increases, the wage rate also increases. So, far from exploiting people in developing countries, trade improves their opportunities and increases their incomes.

We have reviewed the arguments that are commonly heard in favour of protection and the counter-arguments against them. There is one counter-argument to protection that is general and quite overwhelming: Protection invites retaliation and can trigger a trade war. The best example of a trade war occurred during the Great Depression of the 1930s when the United States introduced the Smoot-Hawley tariff. Country after country retaliated with its own tariff, and in a short period, world trade had almost disappeared. The costs to all countries were large and led to a renewed international resolve to avoid such self-defeating moves in the future. They also led to the creation of GATT and are the impetus behind NAFTA, APEC, and the European Union.

Why Is International Trade Restricted?

WHY, DESPITE ALL THE ARGUMENTS AGAINST PROTECTION, is trade restricted? There are two key reasons:

- Tariff revenue
- Rent seeking

Tariff Revenue

Government revenue is costly to collect. In the developed countries such as Canada, a well-organized tax collection system is in place that can generate billions of dollars of income tax and sales tax revenues. This tax collection system is made possible by the fact that most economic transactions are done by firms that must keep properly audited financial records. Without such records, the revenue collection agencies (for example, Canada Customs and Revenue Agency) would be severely hampered in the work. Even with audited financial accounts, some proportion of potential tax revenue is lost. Nonetheless, for the industrialized countries, income taxes and sales taxes are the major sources of revenue and the tariff plays a very small role.

But governments in developing countries have a difficult time collecting taxes from their citizens. Much economic activity takes place in an informal economy with few financial records. So only a small amount of revenue is collected from income taxes and sales taxes in these countries. The one area in which economic transactions are well recorded and audited is in international trade. So this activity is an attractive base for tax collection in these countries and is used much more extensively than in the developed countries.

Rent Seeking

Rent seeking is the major reason why international trade is restricted. Rent seeking is lobbying and other political activity that seeks to capture the gains from trade. Free trade increases consumption possibilities *on the average*, but not everyone shares in the gain and some people even lose. Free trade brings benefits to some and imposes costs on others, with total benefits exceeding total costs. It is the uneven distribution of costs and benefits that is the principal source of impediment to achieving more liberal international trade.

Let's return to our example of trade in cars and grain between Farmland and Mobilia. In Farmland, the benefits from free trade accrue to all the producers of grain and to those producers of cars who would not have to bear the costs of adjusting to a smaller car industry. Those costs are transition costs, not permanent costs. The costs of moving to free trade are borne by those car producers and their employees who have to become grain producers.

The number of people who gain will, in general, be enormous in comparison with the number who lose. The gain per person will therefore be rather small. The loss per person to those who bear the loss will be large. Because the loss that falls on those who bear it is large, it will pay those people to incur considerable expense to lobby against free trade. On the other hand, it will not pay those who gain to organize to achieve free trade. The gain from trade for any one individual is too small for that individual to spend much time or money on a political organization to achieve free trade. The loss from free trade will be seen as being so great by those bearing that loss that they *will* find it profitable to join a political organization to prevent free trade. Each group is optimizing—weighing benefits against costs and choosing the best action for itself. The anti-free trade group will, however, undertake a larger quantity of political lobbying than the pro-free trade group.

Compensating Losers

If, in total, the gains from free international trade exceed the losses, why don't those who stand to gain from free trade offer to compensate those who stand to lose so that everyone votes for free trade?

The main answer is that there are serious obstacles to providing direct and correctly calculated compensation. First, the cost of identifying the losers from free trade and of estimating the value of their losses would be enormous.

Second, it would never be clear whether a person who has fallen on hard times is suffering because of free trade or for other reasons, perhaps reasons that are largely under the control of the individual.

Third, some people who look like losers at one point in time may, in fact, end up gaining. The young auto worker that loses her job in Windsor and becomes a computer assembly worker in Ottawa resents the loss of work and the need to move. But a year or two later, looking back on events, she counts herself fortunate. She has made a move that has increased her income and given her greater job security.

Despite the absence of explicit compensation, those who lose from a change in protection do receive some compensation. But compensation is not restricted to the losers from changes in trade policy. In Canada (and in all the other rich industrial countries) elaborate schemes are in place to ensure that people who suffer from economic change receive help during their transition to new activities.

Two major forms of compensation in Canada arise from interprovincial fiscal transfers and employment insurance. Interprovincial fiscal transfers result in tax dollars collected in the rich and expanding regions of the country being spent in the poorer regions. Employment insurance provides substantial compensation for workers who lose their jobs regardless of the reason for the job loss. Jobs lost because of changes in international protection are included among those for which benefits are paid.

But because we do not explicitly compensate the losers from free international trade, protectionism remains a popular and permanent feature of our national economic and political life.

Compensating Losers from Protection

There is no general presumption that it is the ones who lose from a tariff cut that should be compensated. Protection brings losses to the consumer and the view might be taken that the winners from protection should compensate the losers from protection. When this perspective is taken, the removal of protection would mean the removal of the compensation of the losers by the winners and no further adjustments would be needed. What is fair is a tricky matter (see Chapter 5, pp. 114–117).

REVIEW QUIZ

1 What are the two main reasons for imposing tariffs on imports?
2 What type of country most benefits from the revenue from tariffs? Provide some examples of such countries.
3 If international trade restrictions are costly, why do we use them? Why don't the people who gain from trade organize a political force that is strong enough to ensure that their interests are protected?

The North American Free Trade Agreement

THE NORTH AMERICAN FREE TRADE AGREE-ment came into effect on January 1, 1994. It was the outgrowth of an earlier Canada–United States Free Trade Agreement, which was signed in October 1987. Both agreements were struck only after several years of intense negotiations and, on the Canadian side of the border, an intense political debate. First, let's look at the terms of the Canada–United States agreement of 1987 and at the progress made in achieving freer trade between two of the world's largest trading partners.

The Terms of the Canada–United States Agreement

The main terms of the Canada–United States Free Trade Agreement are:

- Tariffs to be phased out through 1999
- Nontariff barriers to be reduced
- Free trade in energy products, with energy resource sharing in times of national shortage
- More freedom of trade in services
- Future negotiations to eliminate subsidies
- Creation of dispute-settling mechanisms

Removal of Tariffs   Scheduled tariff cuts began on January 1, 1989 and were completed on January 1, 1998. But tariff protection remains in place and an atmosphere of tension prevails in many areas. Agriculture remains effectively protected with new tariffs that have replaced old quotas. And a series of so-called *countervailing duties* has been introduced to offset the effects of domestic subsidies. Further, several so-called *antidumping duties* have also been introduced in cases in which it is alleged that products are being exported at a price below the cost of production.

Nontariff Barriers   Nontariff barriers such as government procurement policies of buying local products are removed by the agreement. Subsequent to entering into the free trade agreement, Canada and the United States took on additional obligations as members of the WTO that require the removal of agricultural quotas. Many agricultural quotas have been removed but they have been replaced with tariffs. So despite the free trade agreement, we remain a long way from achieving free trade in agricultural products.

Energy Products   Free trade in energy products existed before the free trade agreement but the agreement ratified the intent to maintain that arrangement. The agreement that scarce energy resources will be shared in times of national shortage became a controversial one. In effect, what the energy sharing clause amounts to is an agreement that governments will not intervene in energy markets to prevent firms from selling their energy to the other country.

Trade in Services   International trade in services has been expanding more quickly than trade in manufactured goods in recent years. The free trade agreement, recognizing this factor and seeking to facilitate further expansion of trade in services between the United States and Canada, incorporates two principles: the *right of establishment* and *national treatment*. The right of establishment means that American firms have the right to set up branches in Canada and Canadian firms have the right to set up operations in the United States. National treatment means that each country will treat the goods and firms and investors of the other country as if they were operating within its own borders.

Future Negotiations on Subsidies   In both the United States and Canada, there are many subsidies, especially on agricultural products. The presence of subsidies causes problems and makes it legitimate under the agreement for the country importing subsidized goods to impose countervailing duties. As we have just noted, several such duties have been imposed.

Dispute-Settling Mechanisms   The Free Trade Agreement included two dispute-settling mechanisms: one to settle disputes relating to all aspects of the agreement, and the other to deal with applications of countervailing duties and antidumping laws in either country. For example, the United States has applied for and received permission to impose countervailing duties on Canadian exports of durum wheat, lumber products, poultry, and live hogs. In each case, the United States accuses Canada of subsidizing these industries unfairly so that Canadian exports are cheaper than U.S. producers can supply these goods.

The Extension of the Agreement: NAFTA

The North American Free Trade Agreement (NAFTA) is an agreement between Canada, the United States, and Mexico that has six objectives. They are to

1. Eliminate trade barriers
2. Promote conditions of fair competition
3. Increase investment opportunities
4. Protect intellectual property rights
5. Create an effective dispute resolution mechanism
6. Establish a framework for the expansion of the agreement to include other nations in the hemisphere

Effects of the Free Trade Agreement

Working out the effects of an agreement as complex as NAFTA is difficult, and there is no general consensus on what the effects have been. The theory that you have studied in this chapter predicts that the removal of tariffs will produce an increase in the *volume* of international trade. That is, the theory predicts that Canadians will increasingly specialize in those activities at which they have a comparative advantage and Mexicans and Americans will specialize in a different range of activities and that the three countries will exchange a larger volume of goods and services.

As predicted, trade among the three countries has increased. During the first five years of NAFTA, Canada's trade with the United States increased by 80 percent and Canada's trade with Mexico doubled.

The trade expansion that followed the entry of Mexico in 1995 was especially dramatic. Mexico's exports increased by 31 percent (in U.S. dollar value) in 1995 and by 21 percent in 1996, compared with increases that averaged less than 15 percent a year during the two years before the agreement. But trade expansion with Mexico has not been in one direction. Mexico's imports also increased following the agreement by 23 percent in both 1996 and 1997.

During the 1990s, Canada's exports expanded from less than 30 percent of total production to 36 percent, and Canada's imports have increased from 27 percent to 34 percent of total expenditure.

Canada greatly increased its exports of advertising services, office and telecommunications equipment, paper, and transportation services. And its imports of meat and dairy products, communications services, clothing, furniture, and processed foods and beverages also increased by a large percentage.

These huge changes in exports and imports brought gains from increased specialization and exchange. But they also brought a heavy toll of adjustment. Thousands of jobs were lost in the declining sectors and new jobs were created in the expanding sectors. The amount of job destruction in the years following the free trade agreement was historically high and the unemployment rate rose for three successive years. Only during the Great Depression did the rate of job destruction exceed that in the late 1980s and early 1990s. To what extent a high rate of labour market turnover was caused by the free trade agreement is unclear and controversial. But the net outcome of NAFTA appears to be strongly positive. More than a million new Canadian jobs were created between 1994 and 1999.

REVIEW QUIZ

1 By when, under the Canada–United States Free Trade Agreement, were all tariffs on trade between Canada and the United States intended to be phased out? What progress and setbacks have we experienced?
2 What effect has NAFTA had on nontariff barriers?
3 What effect has NAFTA had on trade in services?
4 How has the volume of trade among Canada, the United States, and Mexico changed during the period since NAFTA was established?

◆ You've now seen how free international trade enables all nations to gain from specialization and trade. By producing goods in which we have a comparative advantage and trading some of our production for that of others, we expand our consumption possibilities. Placing impediments on that trade decreases the gains from specialization and trade. By opening our country up to free international trade, the market for the things that we sell expands and the relative price rises. The market for the things that we buy also expands, and the relative price falls.

Reading Between the Lines on pp. 804–805 looks at a recent example of an international trade dispute between the United States and Canada—the lumber dispute. This dispute provides a clear example of the economic cost of restricting international trade.

READING BETWEEN THE LINES

Tariffs in Action: Lumber

THE GLOBE AND MAIL, July 27, 2002

Officials applaud softwood victory

Canadian forestry officials applauded a first-round victory in the bitter softwood dispute, but warned there is no quick relief for an industry still facing crippling duties.

The punitive duties, which have shut dozens of sawmills across Canada and cost thousands of forestry workers their jobs, were imposed to support allegations by the U.S. industry that Canadian lumber is unfairly subsidized.

The World Trade Organization said yesterday the United States was not justified in using cross-border pricing comparisons for calculating duties on lumber imports.

While the WTO accepted the U.S. argument that Canada's stumpage system does violate WTO subsidy rules, Frank Dottori, president of Montreal-based lumber producer Tembec Inc., said he was "ecstatic" with the ruling. "We hope the Ameri-cans respect this third-party ruling and see it as an opportunity to stop persecuting us and move forward," he said. ...

Mr. De Jong said the decision will not bestow immediate benefits on the lumber industry, which is currently paying a 27-per-cent duty on about $10-billion worth of lumber shipments into the key U.S. market. ...

"The American lumber lobby will probably try to minimize the importance of the decision and stick to their guns," said Carl Grenier, president of the Free Trade Lumber Council, whose members account for about 40 per cent of Canadian lumber exports to the United States.

Mr. Grenier said the U.S. trade position is driven by a powerful industry lobby, not by government, and that he expects that lobby to continue to forcefully argue its case. ...

Reprinted with permission from *The Globe and Mail.*

Essence of the Story

■ A 27-percent duty on Canadian lumber exports to the United States has shut dozens of sawmills across Canada and cost thousands of forestry workers their jobs.

■ The U.S. lumber industry claims that Canadian lumber is unfairly subsidized.

■ The World Trade Organization agrees that Canadian lumber is subsidized but says that the United States is not justified in calculating duties on lumber imports by comparing the Canadian and U.S. prices.

■ While Canadian lumber producers hope that this ruling paves the way for tariff cuts, U.S. lumber producers are a powerful lobby and one that will be hard to overcome.

804

Economic Analysis

■ The U.S. tariff on Canadian lumber damages Canada, but it also damages the United States.

■ Figure 1 shows the U.S. market for lumber.

■ The demand curve of U.S. buyers of lumber is D.

■ There are two supply curves: the supply curve of the Canadian producers, S_C, and the supply curve of U.S. producers, S_{US}. We'll assume that Canada can supply any quantity at a price of $100 per load.

■ With no tariff, the quantity of lumber bought in the United States is QC_0. Of this amount, QP_0 is produced in the United States and the rest is imported from Canada, as shown by the arrow in Fig. 1.

■ Now the United States puts a 27-percent tariff on the import of lumber. Canadian lumber is now supplied to the U.S. market at the original supply price, $100, plus the tariff, $27, so the supply curve of lumber from Canada shifts to become S_C + *tariff*.

■ With the tariff, the quantity of lumber bought in the United States is QC_1. Of this amount, QP_1 is produced in the United States and the rest is imported from Canada, as shown by the arrow in Fig. 1.

■ The tariff decreases U.S. consumption and imports and increases U.S. production.

■ Figure 2 shows the winners and the losers in the United States.

■ The winners include U.S lumber producers, who gain additional producer surplus, which is shown by the blue area in Fig. 2.

■ Another winner is the U.S. government, which collects additional revenue, shown by the purple area in Fig. 2.

■ The sum of the blue, red, purple, and gray areas is the loss of consumer surplus that results from the tariff.

■ The Canadian subsidy has no influence on the effects of the tariff. A deadweight loss arises—the decrease in consumer surplus exceeds the increase in producer surplus—regardless of whether Canadian lumber producers receive a subsidy.

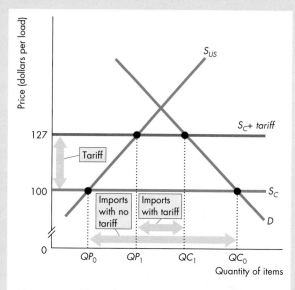

Figure 1 Tariffs and imports

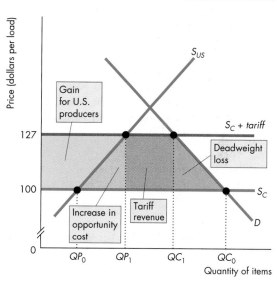

Figure 2 Winners and losers

805

SUMMARY

KEY POINTS

Patterns and Trends in International Trade
(p. 786)

- Large flows of trade take place between countries, most of which is in manufactured goods exchanged among rich industrialized countries.
- Since 1978, the volume of Canadian international trade has increased to more than one-third of total production.

The Gains from International Trade (pp. 787–792)

- Comparative advantage is the fundamental source of the gains from trade.
- Comparative advantage exists when opportunity costs between countries diverge.
- By increasing its production of goods in which it has a comparative advantage and then trading some of the increased output, a country can consume at points outside its production possibilities frontier.
- In the absence of international borrowing and lending, trade is balanced as prices adjust to reflect the international supply of and demand for goods.
- The world price balances the production and consumption plans of the trading parties. At the equilibrium price, trade is balanced.
- Comparative advantage explains the international trade that takes place in the world.
- But trade in similar goods arises from economies of scale in the face of diversified tastes.

International Trade Restrictions (pp. 793–796)

- Countries restrict international trade by imposing tariffs and nontariffs, such as quotas and VERS.
- International trade restrictions raise the domestic price of imported goods, lower the volume of imports, and reduce the total value of imports.
- They also reduce the total value of exports by the same amount as the reduction in the value of imports.

The Case Against Protection (pp. 797–800)

- Arguments that protection is necessary to save

jobs, to protect infant industries, and to prevent dumping are weak.
- Arguments that protection is necessary for national security, allows us to compete with cheap foreign labour, makes the economy diversified and stable, penalizes lax environmental standards, protects national culture, and prevents exploitation of developing countries are fatally flawed.

Why Is International Trade Restricted?
(pp. 800–801)

- Trade is restricted because tariffs raise government revenue and because protection brings a small loss to a large number of people and a large gain per person to a small number of people.

The North American Free Trade Agreement
(pp. 802–803)

- NAFTA is an agreement between Canada, the United States, and Mexico, which began in 1995 and grew from a previous Canada–U.S. agreement.
- Under NAFTA, trade has expanded more rapidly than before the agreement.

KEY FIGURES

Figure 33.1   Opportunity Cost in Farmland, 787
Figure 33.2   Opportunity Cost in Mobilia, 788
Figure 33.3   International Trade in Cars, 789
Figure 33.4   Expanding Consumption Possibilities, 790
Figure 33.6   The Effects of a Tariff, 794
Figure 33.7   The Effects of a Quota, 796

KEY TERMS

Dumping, 798
Exports, 786
General Agreement on Tariffs and Trade, 793
Imports, 786
Infant-industry argument, 797
Net exports, 786
Nontariff barrier, 793
North American Free Trade Agreement, 794
Quota, 796
Tariff, 793
Terms of trade, 788
Voluntary export restraint, 796
World Trade Organization, 793

PROBLEMS

☐*1. The table provides information about Virtual
Reality's production possibilities.

TV sets (per day)		Computers (per day)
0	and	36
10	and	35
20	and	33
30	and	30
40	and	26
50	and	21
60	and	15
70	and	8
80	and	0

a. Calculate Virtual Reality's opportunity cost
of a TV set when it produces 10 sets a day.
b. Calculate Virtual Reality's opportunity cost
of a TV set when it produces 40 sets a day.
c. Calculate Virtual Reality's opportunity cost
of a TV set when it produces 70 sets a day.
d. Using the answers to parts (a), (b), and (c),
sketch the relationship between the opportunity cost of a TV set and the quantity of TV
sets produced in Virtual Reality.

2. The table provides information about Vital
Sign's production possibilities.

TV sets (per day)		Computers (per day)
0	and	18.0
10	and	17.5
20	and	16.5
30	and	15.0
40	and	13.0
50	and	10.5
60	and	7.5
70	and	4.0
80	and	0

a. Calculate Vital Sign's opportunity cost of a
TV set when it produces 10 sets a day.
b. Calculate Vital Sign's opportunity cost of a
TV set when it produces 40 sets a day.
c. Calculate Vital Sign's opportunity cost of a
TV set when it produces 70 sets a day.
d. Using the answers to parts (a), (b), and (c),
sketch the relationship between the opportunity cost of a TV set and the quantity of TV
sets produced in Vital Sign.

☐*3. Suppose that with no international trade,
Virtual Reality in problem 1 produces and consumes 10 TV sets a day and Vital Sign produces
and consumes 60 TV sets a day. Now suppose
that the two countries begin to trade with each
other.
a. Which country exports TV sets?
b. What adjustments are made to the amount
of each good produced by each country?
c. What adjustments are made to the amount
of each good consumed by each country?
d. What can you say about the terms of trade
(the price of a TV set expressed as computers
per TV set) under free trade?

4. Suppose that with no international trade,
Virtual Reality in problem 1 produces and consumes 50 TV sets a day and Vital Sign produces
and consumes 20 TV sets a day. Now suppose
that the two countries begin to trade with each
other.
a. Which country exports TV sets?
b. What adjustments are made to the amount
of each good produced by each country?
c. What adjustments are made to the amount
of each good consumed by each country?
d. What can you say about the terms of trade
(the price of a TV set expressed as computers
per TV set) under free trade?

☐*5. Compare the total quantities of each good produced in problems 1 and 2 with the total quantities of each good produced in problems 3 and 4.
a. Does free trade increase or decrease the total
quantities of TV sets and computers produced in both cases? Why?
b. What happens to the price of a TV set in
Virtual Reality in the two cases? Why does it
rise in one case and fall in the other?
c. What happens to the price of a computer in
Vital Sign in the two cases? Why does it rise
in one case and fall in the other?

6. Compare the international trade in problem 3
with that in problem 4.
a. Why does Virtual Reality export TV sets in
one of the cases and import them in the
other case?
b. Do the TV producers or the computer producers gain in each case?
c. Do consumers gain in each case?

*7. The figure depicts the international market for soybeans.

a. If the two countries did not engage in international trade, what would be the prices of soybeans in the two countries? Show the prices on the graph.
b. What is the world price of soybeans if there is free trade between these countries?
c. What quantities of soybeans are exported and imported?
d. What is the balance of trade?

8. If the country in problem 7 that imports soybeans imposes a tariff of $20 per tonne, what is the world price of soybeans and what quantity of soybeans gets traded internationally? What is the price of soybeans in the importing country? Calculate the tariff revenue.

*9. The importing country in problem 7 imposes a quota of 30 million tonnes on imports of soybeans.
a. What is the price of soybeans in the importing country?
b. What is the revenue from the quota?
c. Who gets this revenue?

10. The exporting country in problem 7 imposes a VER of 30 million tonnes on its exports of soybeans.
a. What is the world price of soybeans now?
b. What is the revenue of soybean growers in the exporting country?
c. Which country gains from the VER?

CRITICAL THINKING

1. Study *Reading Between the Lines* on pp. 804–805 and then answer the following questions:
a. Why did the United States impose a tariff on lumber imports from Canada?
b. What are the effects of the tariff on lumber?
c. Who are the winners and who are the losers from the tariff on lumber?
d. Modify the figures on page 805 to show the effects of a Canadian subsidy to lumber producers on the consumer surplus, producer surplus, and deadweight loss in the United States.

WEB EXERCISES

1. Visit the Parkin–Bade Web site and study the Web *Reading Between the Lines* on steel dumping, and then answer the following questions.
a. What is the argument in the news article for limiting steel imports?
b. Evaluate the argument. Is it correct or incorrect in your opinion? Why?
c. Would you vote to eliminate steel imports? Why or why not?
d. Would you vote differently if you lived in another steel-producing country? Why or why not?

2. Use the links on the Parkin–Bade Web site to view a NAFTA report card on agriculture. Then answer the following questions:
a. What does NAFTA seek to achieve in agriculture trade?
b. What has NAFTA achieved to date?
c. What are the obstacles to greater gains for North American trade in agricultural products?
d. Would you vote to maintain NAFTA? Why or why not?
e. Would you vote to expand NAFTA to include other countries? Why or why not?

GLOBAL STOCK MARKETS

Irrational Exuberance?

On December 5, 1996, Alan Greenspan, chairman of the U.S. Federal Reserve, said that stock market investors were suffering from *irrational exuberance.* It appeared that some people agreed with Mr. Greenspan, for when the New York Stock Exchange opened the next morning, the Dow Jones Industrial Average immediately dropped by 2.3 percent. During the American night, stock prices in Japan, Hong Kong, Germany, and Britain had dropped an average of almost 4 percent. ◆ Alan Greenspan's remark was prompted by an extraordinary rise in stock prices in the United States and around the world that began in 1994 and was to continue through 1999. During these years, the Dow (as the Dow Jones Industrial Average is known) tripled! It then stopped climbing and eventually nose-dived following September 11, 2001, but only temporarily. By January 2002, prices were back at the pre-September 11 levels. ◆ How are stock prices determined? Do investors suffer from "irrational exuberance" or are their buying and selling decisions rational? Do Canadian stock prices behave like those in the United States? How does the economy influence the stock market? And how does the stock market influence the economy?

◆ You are going to probe some interesting questions in this chapter. But first, a warning: You will not learn in this chapter which stocks to buy and how to get rich. You will, though, learn some important lessons about traps to avoid that could easily make you poor. And you will see in *Reading Between the Lines* at the end of the chapter how it is impossible to predict when a falling stock market will turn the corner and start rising.

After studying this chapter, you will be able to

■ Explain what a firm's stock is and how its rate of return and price are related

■ Describe the global markets in which stocks are traded and the stock price indexes

■ Describe the long-term performance of stock prices and earnings

■ Explain what determines the price of stock and why stock prices are volatile

■ Explain why it is rational to diversify a stock portfolio rather than to hold the one stock that has the highest expected return

■ Explain how the stock market influences the economy and how the economy influences the stock market

Stock Market Basics

ALL FIRMS GET SOME OF THEIR FINANCIAL capital from the people who own the firm. A large firm has possibly millions of owners from whom it raises billions of dollars in financial capital. These owners are the firm's stockholders—the holders of stock issued by the firm.

What Is Stock?

Stock is a tradable security that a firm issues to certify that the stockholder owns a share of the firm. Figure 35.1 shows a famous stock certificate that has become a collector's item—a Walt Disney Company stock certificate. The value of a firm's stock is called the firm's **equity capital** (or just equity). The terms "stock" and "equity" are often used interchangeably.

A stockholder has *limited liability*, which means that if the firm can't pay all its debts, a stockholder's liability for the firm's debts is limited to the amount invested in the firm by that stockholder. For example, when Enron collapsed, its stockholders lost everything they had invested in the firm's stock, but they weren't forced to contribute anything to make up for Enron's remaining debts.

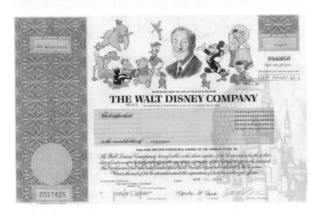

FIGURE 35.1   A Stock Certificate

The Walt Disney Company issues a colourful stock certificate to record the ownership of its common stock. Attractive share certificates, like postage stamps and coins, become collectors' items.

Source: © Disney Enterprises Inc.

Stockholders receive a **dividend,** which is a share of the firm's profit, in proportion to their stock holdings. For example, holders of stock in PepsiCo received a dividend of 58 cents per share during 2002.

Firms issue two types of stock:

- Preferred stock
- Common stock

Preferred stock entitles its owner to a pre-agreed dividend before common stock dividends are paid and to first claim on the firm's assets in the event that it is liquidated.

Common stock holders are entitled to a share of the firm's assets and earnings and to a vote (one vote per share held) in the selection of the firm's directors.

When a firm issues stock, the buyer of the stock invests directly in the firm. For example, in March 1986, Microsoft Corporation issued 161 million shares of common stock for $21 a share and raised a total of $3.4 billion. The buyers of those shares paid Microsoft Corporation.

Most stockholders buy stock not from the firm that issues it but from other holders who bought the stock from yet other holders. People buy and sell stock on a stock exchange. For example, on an average day during the past ten years, 14 million Microsoft shares have changed hands. Microsoft doesn't receive anything from these transactions and doesn't even keep track of who owns its stock. It hires another firm, Mellon Investor Services, to do that job and to issue stock certificates.

What Is a Stock Exchange?

A **stock exchange** is an organized market on which people can buy and sell stock. The stocks of major Canadian corporations are traded on the Toronto Stock Exchange, which is the centre of Canada's major stock market. Canadian stocks are also traded, along with the stocks of global and U.S. corporations, in the United States on the New York Stock Exchange (NYSE). High-tech stocks are traded on the National Association of Securities Dealers Automated Quotation (NASDAQ) system.

Some stock exchanges—the New York Stock Exchange is one of them—are physical trading arenas. Traders shout and signal their buy and sell orders on the trading floor of the exchange. In the case of the New York Stock Exchange, trades take place on the trading floor on Wall Street in New York City.

Other stock exchanges—the Toronto Stock Exchange is one of them—do not have a trading floor. These more recently upgraded stock exchanges trade through a computer and telecommunications network that links together buyers and sellers from all parts of the world. For example, the NASDAQ computer system enables more than 1.3 million traders in 83 countries to trade more than 4,000 (mainly high-tech) stocks.

NASDAQ is a global stock exchange with large operations in Canada, Japan, and Europe as well as the United States. The other major stock exchanges in the global economy are those in London, Frankfurt, Tokyo, and Hong Kong.

Stock Prices and Returns

You can find the price and other information about the stocks of most of the large firms in the daily newspaper. You can also find the same information (and much more) on a newspaper's Web site. The Web sites of the stock exchanges and of major stock dealers also provide a wealth of data on stocks. You can also install software such as MarketBrowser that provides an easy way of viewing stock prices and making graphs of the recent price history. (The Parkin–Bade Web site provides the links that will get you to these Web resources.)

To read the stock market reports, you need to know the meaning of a few technical terms that we'll now review.

The point of buying stock is to earn an income from it. A **stock price** is the price at which one share of a stock trades on a stock exchange. The price is expressed like any other price: in dollars and cents. For example, on October 11, 2002, the price of a share of Bombardier stock was $3.83. The price can change from minute to minute and almost certainly will change over the trading day, and it can be tracked on the Internet (with a short time delay). Because the price keeps changing, in addition to tracking the current price, people also pay attention to the high and low prices during the previous year and the change from day to day.

The annual **return** on a stock consists of the stock's dividend plus its capital gain (or minus its capital loss) during the year. A stock's **capital gain** is the increase in its price, and a stock's **capital loss** is the decrease in its price. For example, between October 2001 and October 2002, the price of

Bombardier stock fell from $17.37 to $3.83, a capital loss of $13.54.

The absolute return—the number of dollars returned by the stock—is not very informative because the stock might be cheap or costly. More informative is the return per dollar invested. So we express the return, or its components, as a percentage of the stock price. The dividend expressed as a percentage of the stock price is called the stock's **dividend yield.** For example, during the year from October 2001 to October 2002, Bombardier paid dividends of 18¢. Expressed as a percentage of the price of the stock in October 2002, the dividend yield was 4.7 percent.

The return on a stock expressed as a percentage of the stock price is called the stock's **rate of return.** For example, the return of a Bombardier share in the year from October 2001 to October 2002 was a dividend of 18¢ minus a capital loss of $13.54, or a loss of $13.36. The rate of return was −$13.36 as a percentage of $17.37, the price of a share in October 2001, which is −76.9 percent—a loss of almost 77 percent.

Earnings and the Price-Earnings Ratio

A firm's accounting profit is called the firm's **earnings.** A firm's directors decide how much of the earnings to pay out as dividends and how much to retain—called *retained earnings*—to invest in new capital and expand the firm.

Because they are the ultimate source of income for stockholders, a lot of attention is paid to a firm's earnings. And those earnings must be calculated and reported to meet standards of accuracy determined by government regulations and accounting standards. Following the Enron debacle in the United States, these standards have been reviewed and will be the object of an ongoing review for some time.

Earnings are the source of stockholder returns, but it is the relationship between a stock's price and earnings that matters most to the stockholder. So another number that is routinely calculated for each stock is its **price-earnings ratio**—the stock price divided by the most recent year's earnings. For example during 2001, Bombardier reported earnings of 11¢ per share, so its price-earnings ratio was $3.83 divided by 11¢, which equals 34.8.

The price-earnings ratio is the inverse of earnings per dollar invested. For example, because in October 2002 the price of a share of Bombardier stock was

$3.83 and the earnings per share during 2002 were 11¢, earnings per dollar invested were 11¢ ÷ $3.83 = 0.0287, or 2.87 percent. Check that 0.0287, earnings per dollar invested, equals the inverse of the price-earnings ratio and equals 1/34.8.

Now that you've reviewed some of the key vocabulary of the stock market, let's look at the stock market report.

Reading the Stock Market Report

Figure 35.2 shows part of a *Financial Post* stock market page. (The format varies from one newspaper to another, but the content is similar in all of them.) You can see some numbers for Bombardier that might seem familiar. They are some of the numbers that we've just used to illustrate the technical terms used in the report. Figure 35.2 also provides the CHUM (radio and television company line of the report).

The first two columns show the range of prices for the stock (expressed in dollars) over the preceding year. This information is useful because it tells you about the volatility of the stock. Some stocks fluctuate a lot more than others. By glancing at the numbers in these two columns, you can get a quick sense of how volatile the price is. In this example, the price of CHUM stock ranged from a high of $64.50 to a low of $40.00 (its current price), a range of $24.50 and more than 50 percent of its current price.

Following the firm's name is the ticker symbol, BBD for Bombardier and CHM for CHUM. This symbol appears on real-time reports of the stock price. You need to know the symbol for any stocks that you own so that you can easily check their prices during the trading day.

The dividend paid expressed in dollars comes next. In this example, Bombardier paid 0.18 or 18¢ a share and CHUM paid 0.08 or 8¢ a share. The dividend yield—the dividend as a percentage of the stock's closing price—comes next, followed by the price-earnings ratio. The next column records the volume of trades in hundreds during the day. This number is the actual number of shares bought and sold. In this example, 287,800 Bombardier shares and 252,200 CHUM shares changed hands during the day.

The next three columns show the range of prices over the day and the closing price, and the final column shows the change in price from the previous day.

Stock Price Indexes

Because thousands of different stocks are traded on the world's stock markets every business day, we need a handy way of summarizing the thousands of different stock prices. Investors want to know not only how their own stocks have performed, but also how they have performed relative to other stocks on the average.

To make these comparisons and to indicate the general movements in the market, index numbers of the average stock prices are calculated and published. You will encounter hundreds of different stock price indexes. The three main U.S. stock price indexes are

---

FIGURE 35.2   Reading the Stock Market Report

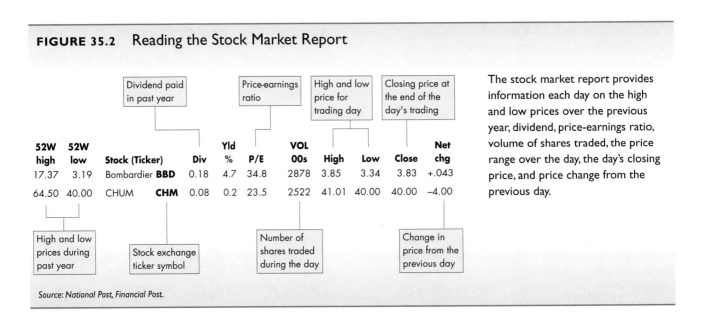

52W high	52W low	Stock (Ticker)	Div	Yld %	P/E	VOL 00s	High	Low	Close	Net chg
17.37	3.19	Bombardier **BBD**	0.18	4.7	34.8	2878	3.85	3.34	3.83	+.043
64.50	40.00	CHUM **CHM**	0.08	0.2	23.5	2522	41.01	40.00	40.00	–4.00

The stock market report provides information each day on the high and low prices over the previous year, dividend, price-earnings ratio, volume of shares traded, the price range over the day, the day's closing price, and price change from the previous day.

Source: National Post, Financial Post.

- S&P Composite Index
- Dow Jones Industrial Average (DJIA)
- NASDAQ Index

S&P Composite Index The S&P Composite Index is an average of the prices of 500 stocks traded on the New York Stock Exchange, the NASDAQ, and the American Stock Exchange. The index is calculated and published by Standard & Poor's (S&P), a New York financial information and services company. Figure 35.3 shows the breadth of coverage of this index, which provides one of the most comprehensive guides to the state of the stock market. Notice in Fig. 35.3 the importance of consumer products in the index.

DJIA The DJIA, or "the Dow," as it is often called, is perhaps the best-known stock price index. The Dow Jones Company is the owner of the *Wall Street Journal,* and because of this link, the Dow is the most widely and rapidly reported barometer of the state of the New York stock market.

FIGURE 35.3   The Scope of the S&P Composite

Percentage of total market value

The 500 stocks in the S&P Composite Index cover all parts of the economy. Consumer products are the largest component of the index.

Source: www.spglobal.com.

Although the DJIA is widely quoted, it is not as broadly representative as the S&P Composite Index. It is an average of the prices of just 30 stocks of major U.S. corporations traded on the New York Stock Exchange. In 2002, these corporations are: Philip Morris Companies, Inc.; Eastman Kodak Co.; J.P. Morgan Chase & Co.; General Motors Corp.; E.I. DuPont de Nemours & Co.; SBC Communications, Inc.; Caterpillar, Inc.; Merck & Co., Inc.; International Paper Co.; Minnesota Mining & Manufacturing Co.; Exxon Mobil Corp.; Honeywell International, Inc.; General Electric Co.; Hewlett-Packard Co.; Procter & Gamble Co.; Alcoa, Inc.; Coca-Cola Co.; Boeing Co.; Citigroup, Inc.; United Technologies Corp.; Johnson & Johnson; AT&T Corp.; Walt Disney Co.; McDonald's Corp.; American Express Co.; International Business Machines Corp.; Wal-Mart Stores, Inc.; Home Depot, Inc.; Intel Corp.; and Microsoft Corp.

NASDAQ The NASDAQ Index is the average price of the stocks traded on this global electronic stock exchange. Like the Dow, this index looks at only part of the market—in this case, the high-tech part.

Four indexes track the state of the world's other major stock markets. They are the

- S&P/TSX
- FTSE 100
- DAX
- Nikkei

S&P/TSX The S&P/TSX is an index of the stock prices of the 300 largest Canadian corporations traded on the Toronto Stock Exchange. It is Canada's main stock price index and is comparable to the S&P 500 for the United States.

FTSE 100 The FTSE 100 (pronounced "footsie") is an index calculated by FTSE, a financial information services firm owned by the *Financial Times* (FT) and the London Stock Exchange (SE). (The *Financial Times* is Europe's leading business and financial daily newspaper and rivals the *Wall Street Journal* outside the United States.)

DAX The DAX index is an average of prices on the Frankfurt stock exchange in Germany.

Nikkei The Nikkei index is the average of prices on the Tokyo stock exchange.

Stock Price Performance

How has the stock market performed in recent years and over the longer term? Do stock prices generally rise? How much do they fluctuate? To answer these questions, we'll look at some actual stock price data, using the S&P/TSX and the S&P 500 (composite). But first, we need to make two technical points.

Inflation Adjustments Stock prices, like all prices, need to be corrected for inflation. So rather than looking at the actual index numbers, we deflate them to remove the effects of inflation and examine *real* stock price indexes.

Ratio Scale Graphs Stock prices rise and fall, but over the long term, they rise. The interesting question about stock price changes is not the absolute change but the percentage change. For example a ten-point change in the S&P was a 1 percent change in 2002, but it was a 10 percent change in 1982. To reveal percentage changes, we graph stock prices using a ratio scale (or logarithmic scale). On a ratio scale, the distance between 1 and 10 equals that between 10 and

100 and between 100 and 1000. Each distance represents a tenfold increase.

Stock Prices

Figure 35.4 shows the real S&P/TSX for the period since 1956 when the index begins, and the S&P 500 over the past 130 years, both placed on a base of 1975 = 1,000 and measured on a ratio scale.

Both indexes move together, but the S&P 500 climbs more than the S&P/TSX. Notice the general upward trend of the real stock price index. In 2001, the S&P was 33 times its 1871 value. This increase translates to a 2.7 percent per year increase on the average.

This average rate of increase masks some subperiods of spectacular increases and spectacular decreases in stock prices. The largest increases occurred during the "roaring twenties" and the "booming nineties." Between 1920 and 1929, on the eve of the Great Depression, stock prices increased by almost 19 percent a year. Between 1991 and 2000, they increased by 15 percent a year, and between 1995 and 2000, the rate of increase hit 24 percent a year.

FIGURE 35.4   Stock Prices

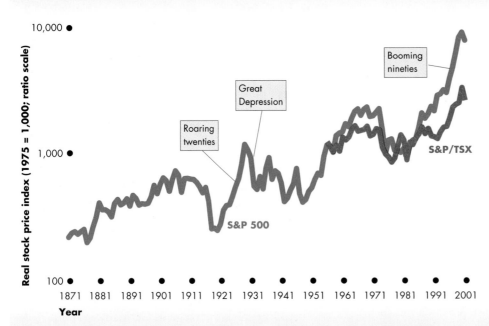

In 2001, average stock prices stood at 33 times their 1871 level (after adjusting for the effects of inflation). This increase translates to an average increase of 2.7 percent a year. Earnings per share stood at 14 times their 1871 level (after adjusting for the effects of inflation). This increase translates to an average increase of 2.7 percent a year. Stock prices increased fastest during the "roaring twenties" and the "booming nineties."

Sources: Reprinted by permission of Robert J. Shiller, Professor of Economics, Yale University (www.econ.yale.edu/~shiller) and adapted in part by the Statistics Canada CANSIM II database, table 176–0047.

The most spectacular period of falling stock prices occurred during World War I (1914–1918), the opening years of the Great Depression (the early 1930s), and the mid-1970s.

Earnings Per Share

Stocks are worth owning because of what they earn. Like stock prices, earnings per share have increased over the long term. But the rate of increase in earnings per share is less than the rate of increase in stock prices. Earnings per share in 2001 were 14 times their 1871 level, which translates to a growth rate of 2 percent per year on the average.

Figure 35.5 looks at the price-earnings ratio for the S&P/TSX over the years since 1956 and for the S&P 500 over the 130 years from 1871 to 2001. The average S&P price-earnings ratio has been 13.9. But there is a lot of variation around this average value. The low values of around 6 occurred in 1916, 1950, and 1979. The high values of around 27 occurred in 1894, 1921, 1931, and the period from 1998 into 2001.

Figure 35.5 is important for the perspective in

which it places the stock market's recent performance. Stock prices were high and increased rapidly during the late 1990s and into 2001. And the price-earnings ratio increased to a level not seen since the opening years of the Great Depression.

Figure 35.5 also provides a reminder that in all previous periods when the price-earnings ratio was above average, it eventually fell below the average.

Being a ratio of stock prices and earnings, the price-earnings ratio can change either because stock prices change or because earnings change. The price-earnings ratio can fall sharply either because stock prices fall sharply or because earnings rise sharply. But all the cases in which the price-earnings ratio has fallen sharply are ones in which stock prices have fallen sharply. For this reason, some people are concerned that the stock market of the 1990s and 2000 increased by too much and that a sharp fall is coming some time in the future.

What does it mean to say that stock prices have increased by too much? To answer this question, we need to understand the forces that determine stock prices and the relationship between prices and earnings. That is the task of the next section.

FIGURE 35.5   The Price-Earnings Ratio

The S&P price-earnings ratio has swung between a low of around 6 in 1916, 1950, and 1979 and a high of around 27 in 1894, 1921, 1931, and 1998–2001. The S&P average price-earnings ratio is 13.9. When the price-earnings ratio exceeds the average, it eventually falls below the average. The S&P/TSX price-earnings ratio follows a similar path to that of the S&P.

Sources: Reprinted by permission of Robert J. Shiller, Professor of Economics, Yale University (www.econ.yale.edu/~shiller) and adapted in part by the Statistics Canada CANSIM II database, table 176–0047.

1 What is a stock and what is the distinction between a preferred stock and a common stock?

2 What are the two sources of return from a stock?

3 What is a stock market and what are the leading stock exchanges in the United States, Canada, and around the world?

4 What is a price-earnings ratio and how is it calculated?

5 What is the most comprehensive stock price index for the United States? How does it differ from some other major indexes?

6 Describe the major trends and fluctuations in stock prices, earnings per share, and the price-earnings ratio.

How Are Stock Prices Determined?

YOU'VE SEEN THAT STOCK PRICES GENERALLY RISE over long periods but fluctuate a lot over shorter periods. What determines the price of a stock? Why is the long-term trend upward? Why do stock prices fluctuate so much?

There is no firm and universally agreed-upon answer to these questions. Instead, there are two possible types of answers. They are that prices are determined by

■ Market fundamentals
■ Speculative bubbles

Market Fundamentals

The price of a stock is the amount that people *on the average* are willing to pay for the opportunity that the stock provides to earn a dividend and a capital gain. If a stock price exceeds what people are willing to pay, they sell the stock and its price falls. If a stock price is less than what people are willing to pay, they

buy and the stock price rises. The price always settles down at the amount that people are willing to pay.

The *market fundamentals* price that people are willing to pay is a price that is based on the deep sources of value that make a stock worth holding. These sources of value are

1. The activities of the firm that issued the stock
2. The stream of profits that these activities generate
3. The stream of dividend payments to stockholders
4. The degree of uncertainty surrounding profits and dividends
5. The attitudes of stockholders towards the timing and uncertainty of the stream of dividends

We're now going to discover how these deep sources of value of a firm's stock combine to determine the market fundamentals price of the stock. To do so, we're going to figure out how much you would be willing to pay for a stock or be willing to accept to sell it.

Price, Value, and Willingness to Pay The market fundamentals value of a stock is the price that people *on the average* are willing to pay for the opportunity that the stock provides to earn a dividend and a capital gain. To figure out how this price is determined, let's look at your decision to buy or sell a stock.

Suppose the price of a stock that you own is $1. You're trying to figure out whether to buy 50 more units of this stock or to sell the 50 units you own. If you sell, you have $50 more to spend, and if you buy, you have $50 less to spend—a $100 difference. You can spend $100 today on something that you will enjoy. In the language of the economist, you will get some utility from what you buy—the marginal utility of $100 worth of consumption. Alternatively, you can buy more stock and sell it later, say, after a year. If you buy the stock, you'll receive the dividend plus the stock's market price at the end of the year.

For it to be worth buying, you must believe that the utility you will receive from owning the stock is going to be worth at least the $1 a share you must pay for it.

But comparing what you must pay with what you'll gain is a difficult exercise for two main reasons. First, you must compare an amount paid in the present with an amount received in the future. And second, you must compare a definite price today with an uncertain dividend and future price.

Present Versus Future People are impatient. We prefer good things to happen sooner rather than later, other things remaining the same. Suppose that you're offered the chance to take an exotic trip that really excites you and are told that you can go right away or after a year. Which would you choose (other things remaining the same)? Most of us would take the trip right away. Because we prefer good things now more than later, we must be compensated for delaying consumption.

Certainty Versus Uncertainty People prefer certainty to uncertainty, other things remaining the same. Suppose you're offered the opportunity to pay $50 for a chance to win $100 on the flip of a coin. Would you accept the offer? Most people would not. Accepting the offer would give you a 50 percent chance of gaining $50 and a 50 percent chance of losing $50. On the average, you get nothing from this offer. Your *expected return* is zero. Most people need to be compensated for taking risks, and the bigger the risk, the bigger is the compensation that must be offered to make bearing the risk worthwhile.

In figuring out what you're willing to pay for a stock, you can see that, for two reasons, you will not be willing to pay as much as the amount that you expect to receive in dividends and from selling the stock. You're going to get the returns later and you're going to face uncertainty, and you must be compensated for both of these consequences of buying a stock.

Discounting Future Uncertain Returns Another way of expressing the relationship between the price you're willing to pay and what you expect to get back is to *discount* the uncertain future amount. You get a discount when a shop lowers the price of an item. And you will insist on a discount if you buy a stock.

To determine the discounted price, we multiply the original price by a **discount factor.** If you get a 20 percent discount on something, you pay 80 percent, or 0.8, of the original price. The discount factor is 0.8.

We can use the idea of a discount factor to link the highest price you're willing to pay for a stock to the amount you'll get back from the stock a year later. Let's call this price P. Suppose that your discount factor is 0.8, and suppose that you believe that the stock will pay a dividend of 5¢ and that its price next year will be $1.20. Then the highest price that you're willing to pay for a stock is

$$P = 0.8 \times (\$0.05 + \$1.20) = \$1.$$

In this example, you would be on the fence. If the price were a bit less than $1, you'd buy, and if the price were a bit more than $1, you'd sell the stock that you already own.

Because people buy if the price is less than the price they are willing to pay and sell if the price is greater than the price they are willing to pay, the market price moves towards the average of what people are willing to pay. If the price exceeded the average of what people are willing to pay, there would be more sellers than buyers and the price would fall. If the price was less than the average of what people are willing to pay, there would be more buyers than sellers and the price would rise. Only if the price equals the average of what people are willing to pay is there no tendency for it to rise or fall.

The Stock Price Equation Call the price of a stock P_1, the dividend D_1, the price at the end of a year P_2, and the discount factor b_1. Then the stock price is the expected value of the discounted uncertain future dividend and stock price. That is,

$$P_1 = \text{Expected value of } [b_1(D_1 + P_2)].$$

Expected Future Stock Price You've seen that the stock price depends on expectations about the future stock price. That is, to figure out what you're willing to pay for a stock today, you must forecast next period's stock price.

The market fundamentals method assumes that an investor's forecast of a future stock price is a rational expectation. A **rational expectation** is a forecast that uses all the available information, including knowledge of the relevant economic forces that influence the variable being forecasted.

But the stock price equation tells us how the price at one time depends on the expected price a year later. This same stock price equation relationship applies to the current period and all future periods. So if we call next period's discount factor b_2, next period's dividend D_2, and the price at the end of next period P_3, you can see that the stock price equation next year will be

$$P_2 = \text{Expected value of } [b_2(D_2 + P_3)].$$

That is, the price next period depends on the expected dividend next period and the price at the end of the next period.

This relationship repeats period after period into the future. And each period's expected future price depends on the dividend expected in that period along with the price at the end of the period.

Table 35.1 illustrates the link between the current price and the expected future price, dividend, and discount factor. In period 1, the price depends on expectations about the price in period 2. In period 2, the price depends on expectations about the price in period 3. And in period 3, the price depends on expectations about the price in period 4. This relationship repeats indefinitely to period N.

Because each period's price depends on the expected price in the following period, the dividend stream, $D_1, D_2, D_3, \ldots D_N$, is the only fundamental that determines the price of a stock.

Market Fundamental Price The market fundamental stock price depends only on the stream of expected future dividend payments. If the expected dividend rises, so does the stock price. And starting from a given dividend, if the dividend is expected to grow at a faster rate, the stock price rises.

But dividends depend on profit, or earnings, so if earnings are expected to increase, dividends will also be expected to increase—if not right away, then at some point in the future. So if earnings increase, the stock price increases. And starting from a given level of earnings, if earnings are expected to grow more quickly, the stock price rises.

Notice that it is changes in expected future earnings and dividends that drive changes in stock price, not changes in actual earnings or dividends. But expectations about the future don't change without reason. And when earnings change, investors project those changes into the future. So fluctuations in earnings might be expected to bring similar fluctuations in stock prices.

In reality, the link between earnings and stock prices is a loose one. You can see just how loose by glancing back at Fig. 35.5 and noting the large swings that range between 6 and 27 in the price-earnings ratio. The booming stock prices of the late 1990s, for example, outpaced the growth of earnings during that same period by a huge margin.

For this reason, some economists believe that stock prices can be understood only as speculative bubbles. Let's now look at this approach.

Speculative Bubbles

A **speculative bubble** is a price increase followed by a price plunge, both of which occur because people expect them to occur and act on that expectation.

Suppose that most people believe that stock prices are going to rise by 30 percent next year. With such a huge price rise, stocks provide the best available rate of return. The demand for stocks increases, and stock prices rise by the expected amount immediately.

Conversely, suppose that most people believe that stock prices are going to *fall* by 30 percent next year. With such a huge price fall, stockholders will earn less than people who simply sit on cash. In this situation, the demand for stocks collapses and a selling spree brings stock prices tumbling by the expected amount.

Why might either of these events occur? And why would a bubble burst? Why would a price collapse follow a price rise?

Guessing Other People's Guesses Part of the answer to the questions just posed arises from the fact that forecasting future stock prices means forecasting other people's forecasts—or, more accurately, guessing other people's guesses.

The most famous English economist of the twentieth century, John Maynard Keynes, described the challenge of the stock market investor as being like that of trying to win the prize in a "select the most beautiful person" contest. Each entrant must pick the

---

TABLE 35.1   Rational Expectations

P_1 = Expected value of [$b_1(D_1 + P_2)$]

P_2 = Expected value of [$b_2(D_2 + P_3)$]

P_3 = Expected value of [$b_3(D_3 + P_4)$]

P_N = Expected value of [$b_N(D_N + P_{N+1})$]

The market fundamentals are the expected dividends that will be earned out into the indefinite future. Rational expectations of future prices and future discount factors are driven by this one fundamental.

most beautiful person from a group of ten photographs. The winner is selected at random from all those who chose the photograph that most other entrants chose. So the challenge is not to pick the most beautiful person, but to pick the one that most people will pick. Or is it to pick the one that most people think that most people will pick? Or is it to pick the one that most people think that most people think that most people will pick? And so on!

Because no one knows the correct choice and because everyone faces the same challenge and shares the same sources of information, people are likely to use similar rules of thumb and theories to guide them. So people might behave in a herdlike way and form and act upon similar expectations.

The booming stock market of the 1990s provides an example of the possibility of a speculative bubble.

The Booming Nineties: A Bubble?

Some economists believe that the booming stock market of the 1990s occurred because the market fundamentals changed. They see the stock price rise as the consequence of a "new economy" in which the rational expectation is that earnings will grow in the future at a more rapid rate than in the past.

Other economists believe that the market of the booming nineties was a speculative bubble. Prominent among those who take this view is Robert Shiller, a professor at Yale University, who explains his view in a popular and readable book, *Irrational Exuberance*.

According to Robert Shiller, the late 1990s stock price rise was a bubble encouraged by 12 "precipitating factors":

1. The arrival of the Internet at a time of solid earnings growth
2. A sense that the United States had triumphed over its former rivals
3. A cultural change that favours business and profit
4. A Republican Congress and cuts in capital gains taxes
5. The baby boom and its perceived effects on the stock market
6. An expansion of media reporting of business news
7. Increasingly optimistic forecasts by "experts"
8. The expansion of pension plans with fixed contributions
9. The growth of mutual funds
10. The fall in inflation
11. The expansion of stock trading opportunities
12. A rise of gambling opportunities

Many of these factors directly influence stockholder expectations, and all of them encouraged an optimistic outlook for stock prices during the late 1990s. Probably no one investor thought that all of these factors would bring rising stock prices, but almost every investor believed that more than one of the factors would bring rising prices.

According to the speculative bubble view, the factors that encourage rising stock prices eventually weaken, prices stop rising and possibly crash. Some people see the falling stock prices of 2001 and 2002 as the bursting of a bubble.

But through 2002, the Internet and the information age remained a strong force for rising prices. So did the expansion of trading opportunities, especially on-line opportunities. The major new factor was the long-term campaign against terrorism. But the effects of this campaign on average stock prices were not clear at the end of 2002. The global economy was still adjusting to a new situation by reallocating resources away from travel and tourism and towards security and defence goods and services. Some sectors were expanding, and some were shrinking. The impact on average stock prices might be positive or negative.

REVIEW QUIZ

1 What is the market fundamentals view of the forces that determine stock prices?

2 What is the speculative bubble view of the forces that determine stock prices?

3 List five factors that you think might have encouraged the booming stock market of the 1990s.

You've seen that there are two views about the forces that determine stock prices. No one knows which view is correct. And no one can predict stock prices. For these reasons, rational stockholders diversify their holdings across a number of stocks. Let's see how diversification spreads risks.

Risk and Return

STOCK PRICES FLUCTUATE IN UNPREDICTABLE ways, and stockholders might receive a large capital gain or incur a large capital loss. But stocks differ in both their expected return and risk, and generally, the greater the risk, the higher is the expected return from a stock. We call the additional return that is earned for bearing an additional risk a **risk premium**. Let's see why a risk premium arises.

Risk Premium

Recall the stock price equation:

$$P_1 = \text{Expected value of } [b_1(D_1 + P_2)].$$

Suppose that two stocks have the same expected dividend, D_1, and the same expected future price, P_2, but one is riskier than the other. Because people dislike risk and must be compensated for bearing it, a riskier return is discounted more than a safe return—the discount factor, b_1, is smaller for the riskier return. Because b_1 is smaller, the price of a stock, P_1, is lower for the riskier stock. But if the price of the riskier stock is lower, the expected return from holding it is greater than the expected return from the safer stock.

Because expected return increases with risk, a person earns the highest expected return by holding only the one stock that has the highest expected return.

But this investment strategy is not usually the best one. The reason is that by diversifying stock holdings across a number of different stocks, an investor can lower the risk. To do so, the investor must accept a lower expected return. There is a trade-off between risk and expected return.

Let's see how and why diversification lowers risk. To do so, we'll look at some actual stock purchases that you could have made in January 2001 and see what your investments would have been worth in 2002 with different degrees of diversification.

Portfolio Diversification

Table 35.2 shows the prices of five stocks in January 2001 and January 2002. Suppose that in January 2001, you had $1,000 to invest and put it all into just one of these five stocks.

You might have been lucky and chosen Procter & Gamble (P&G), in which case your $1,000 grew to $1,139 over the year. But you might have been very unlucky and chosen Enron, in which case you lost your entire investment.

Now suppose that instead of investing in only one of these stocks, you had put $500 into each of Enron and Procter & Gamble. In this case, your investment would have been worth $569.50 at the end of the year—a loss, but not as big as if you'd gone for only Enron.

Now imagine that you diversified even more, putting $200 each into Enron, Microsoft, Procter & Gamble, McDonald's, and Wal-Mart. In this case, your investment would have been worth $834 at the beginning of 2002.

You could spread your risks even more by investing in a mutual fund—a fund that is managed by investment specialists and that is diversified across a large number of stocks.

You can see from this example that lowering risk means accepting a lower return. The highest return across the five stocks in Table 35.2 comes from buying only Procter & Gamble. But at the beginning of 2001, you might equally have thought that buying Enron would provide the highest return. Because you can't predict which individual stock is going to perform best, it pays to diversify and take a lower expected return in return for a lower risk.

TABLE 35.2   Five Stock Prices in January 2001 and January 2002

	Price in January 2001	Price in January 2002	Value in 2002 of $1,000 in 2001
Enron	60	0	0
McDonald's	29	27	931
Microsoft	61	64	1,049
P&G	72	82	1,139
Wal-Mart	57	60	1,053

REVIEW QUIZ

1 Why do stocks' returns include a risk premium?
2 How does diversification across a number of stocks lower the risk that a stockholder faces?

We next look at the links between the stock market and the rest of the economy.

The Stock Market and the Economy

THE LINKS BETWEEN THE STOCK MARKET AND THE rest of the economy that we're now going to look at run in two directions: effects from the rest of the economy *on* the stock market and effects on the rest of the economy *from* the stock market. We'll look first at influences *on* the stock market, which fall into three broad groups:

- Trends and cycles in earnings growth
- Central bank monetary policy
- Taxes

Trends and Cycles in Earnings Growth

You've seen that expected future earnings are the fundamental influence on stock prices. Current earnings are known, but future earnings can only be forecasted. And the central question on which investors must take a position is the *expected growth rate* of earnings.

If earnings are expected to grow more rapidly, the fundamental value of a stock rises relative to current earnings—its price-earnings ratio rises. Conversely, if earnings are expected to grow more slowly, the fundamental value of a stock falls relative to current earnings—its price-earnings ratio falls.

The nature and pace of technological change and the state of the business cycle are the main influences on earnings growth. And expectations about future earnings growth are based on the best information that people can obtain about future technological change and business cycle developments.

The long-term trend in earnings growth has been remarkably constant at about 2 percent a year (after the effects of inflation are removed). But earnings growth has fluctuated a great deal around its trend. Figure 35.6 shows these fluctuations. The figure highlights the interesting fact that there have been only three main periods during which earnings have grown rapidly to reach a new higher level: the 1890s, 1950s and 1960s, and 1990s. There was only one other period of rapid earnings growth, from 1921 to 1931, but this episode was a temporary burst of growth from an extremely low level that did not take earnings back to their previous peak of 1918.

Each period during which earnings grew rapidly to a new level was one in which far-reaching new technologies spread. During the 1890s, it was the

FIGURE 35.6   Three Bursts of Earnings Growth

Earnings grew rapidly during three periods of rapid technological change: the 1890s (railroad, telegraph, electricity); 1950s and 1960s (highway system, plastics, transistor, and television); and 1990s (Internet and information technologies).

Source: Reprinted by permission of Robert J. Shiller, Professor of Economics, Yale University (www.econ.yale.edu/~schiller).

railroad, telegraph, and electricity. During the 1950s and 1960s, it was the highway system, plastics, the transistor, and television. And during the 1990s, it was the Internet and associated information technologies.

Although earnings are the fundamental source of value for stocks, the connection between earnings growth and stock prices cannot be used to make reliable predictions of stock prices. Stock prices did increase more rapidly than usual during the periods of rapid earnings growth. But they outpaced earnings growth—increased by more than was justified by the growth of earnings. And during the 1920s, stock prices grew beyond the levels that were supported by the underlying earnings fundamentals.

Some people have argued that the 1990s were special—unique—and marked a new era for permanently faster earnings growth arising from the information technologies that brought the exploding Internet. Does the earnings growth rate change permanently when a major new technology spreads? And are we living today in a "new economy"?

A New Economy? It is a well-documented fact that the spread of the Internet was unusually rapid. Not since the spread of television during the 1950s has there been such a rapid penetration of a new technology.

It is also a solid fact that the pace of earnings growth was unusually rapid during the 1990s—13 percent a year compared to the long-term average of 2 percent a year. But as you can see in Fig. 35.6, earnings growth was similarly rapid in earlier periods, only to return to its long-term average growth rate.

The only exception to this tendency to return to the preceding long-term average growth rate occurred more than 200 years ago, in an event called the Industrial Revolution. The Industrial Revolution was possibly unique, not because it saw the introduction of powerful new technologies but because it was a period in which for the first time in human history, research and the development of new technologies became commercially viable activities. People began to make a living by inventing new technologies rather than merely by producing goods and services. Before this period, invention and innovation had been a spasmodic and relatively rare event. The last really big invention had been the chronometer, a reliable method of keeping time on ships that improved the reliability of navigation.

It is still too soon to be sure, but more and more people are coming to the view that the "new economy" is just another stage in the evolution of the old economy. If this view is correct, the stock market of the early 2000s remains overvalued relative to its fundamentals. If the "new economy" view is correct, the stock market has correctly incorporated the future earnings growth that the new economy will bring.

Central Bank Monetary Policy

The U.S. Federal Reserve (Fed) and the European Central Bank (ECB) are the most powerful central banks in today's world. Their actions influence global stock markets. Whether you've studied monetary policy or not, you can understand how a central bank influences the stock market by seeing how interest rates affect stock prices.

If the Fed or ECB take actions that raise interest rates, stock prices usually fall. Conversely, if monetary policy lowers interest rates, stock prices usually rise. But policy influences on stock prices are short lived, and the timing of the influences depends on whether the policy actions are anticipated or they surprise the market.

Interest Rates and Stock Prices When the economy is expanding too rapidly and the policy goal is to slow down the growth of spending, interest rates are pushed upward. Higher interest rates make borrowing more costly and lending more rewarding. People who are borrowing to finance their expenditure face higher costs, and some of them cut back on spending.

Lower spending and higher saving translate into a smaller demand for the output of firms and smaller profits. With smaller profits expected, the prices of stocks fall.

Higher interest rates also encourage some stockholders to sell risky stocks and put their funds into lower-risk, lower-return bonds and other securities that now yield a higher return. This action increases the supply of stocks and lowers stock prices further.

Similarly, lower interest rates make borrowing less costly and lending less rewarding. People who are borrowing to finance their expenditure face lower costs, and some of them increase their spending.

Greater spending and lower saving translate into a greater demand for the output of the nation's firms, and larger profits. With larger profits expected, the prices of stocks rise.

Lower interest rates on bonds and other securities also encourage some bond holders to sell bonds and put their funds into higher-risk, higher-return stocks. This action increases the demand for stocks and raises stock prices still further.

Anticipating Policy Because monetary policy actions influence stock prices in the way we've just seen, it is profitable to anticipate future policy actions. If interest rates are expected to rise in the near future, then stock prices are expected to fall in the near future. Selling stocks before the price falls and buying them back after the price has fallen is profitable. So if a large number of people expect a rise in interest rates, they will sell stock. The selling action increases supply and lowers the stock price before the interest rate rises. Monetary policy has caused the stock price to fall, but the stock price falls *before* the policy action occurs. (This timing relationship is an example of the *post hoc* fallacy—see pp. 13–14.)

Taxes

Taxes can influence stock prices in a number of ways, some direct and some indirect. Three types of tax can affect stock markets:

- Capital gains tax
- Corporate profits tax
- Transactions (Tobin) tax

Capital Gains Tax The capital gains tax is a tax on the income that people earn when they *realize* a capital gain. A **realized capital gain** is a capital gain that is obtained when a stock is sold for a higher price than the price paid for it. People who hold onto stocks that have increased in value also enjoy a capital gain, but they do not pay a tax on that gain until they sell the stock and realize the gain.

When a capital gains tax is introduced or when the rate of capital gains tax is increased, stock prices fall, other things remaining the same. The reason is that the capital gains tax lowers the after-tax return on stocks and so lowers the price that people are willing to pay for stocks.

The lowering of the capital gains tax rate in the United States during the 1980s and 1990s probably contributed to the booming stock prices of the 1990s.

Corporate Profits Tax The corporate profits tax is an income tax on the profits of corporations. If this tax is increased, corporate after-tax profits fall. The firm has smaller earnings from which to pay dividends and invest in new capital. So the market fundamentals value of a firm falls, and so do stock prices.

Transactions (Tobin) Tax Transactions on the stock market are not taxed. But their value is enormous, and a tax set at a tiny rate would raise a huge amount of tax revenue for the government.

James Tobin, an economist at Yale University (who died in 2002), proposed that stock market transactions be taxed—hence the name "the Tobin tax." Tobin believed that such a tax would discourage speculative buying and selling of stocks and make the stock market more efficient. The evidence on transactions taxes in other markets, notably real estate markets, does not support the view that a transactions tax lowers speculation.

Let's now change directions and look at influences *from* the stock market to the rest of the economy. We'll look at the influences of stock prices on

- Wealth, consumption expenditure, and saving
- The distribution of wealth

Wealth, Consumption Expenditure, and Saving

Wealth is the market value of assets. The influence of wealth on consumption expenditure and saving is called the **wealth effect**. *Disposable income* equals income minus taxes. A household can do only two things with its disposable income: spend it on consumption goods and services or save it. The **saving rate** is saving as a percentage of disposable income. The greater is wealth, the smaller is the saving rate.

How do stock prices influence the saving rate? The answer depends on how we measure saving (and, related, how we measure disposable income).

There are two definitions of saving that are equivalent, provided that we measure everything in a consistent way. The first definition is

$$\text{Saving} = \frac{\text{Disposable}}{\text{income}} - \frac{\text{Consumption}}{\text{expenditure}}.$$

The second definition arises from the fact that saving adds to wealth. That is,

$$\frac{\text{Wealth at}}{\text{end of year}} = \frac{\text{Wealth at}}{\text{start of year}} + \frac{\text{Saving during}}{\text{the year}},$$

or

$$\text{Saving} = \text{Change in wealth.}$$

The first definition of saving focuses on the fact that saving is what is left over after buying consumer goods and services. The second definition focuses on the fact that saving adds to wealth.

Because the two definitions of saving are equivalent, it must be the case that

$$\underset{\text{income}}{\text{Disposable}} = \underset{\text{expenditure}}{\text{Consumption}} + \underset{\text{wealth.}}{\text{Change in}}$$

In the data on income and wealth, disposable income does not include capital gains and losses. In the data on wealth, capital gains and losses *are* included. So there is a measurement discrepancy between saving measured using the first definition, which excludes capital gains, and saving measured using the second definition, which includes capital gains.

Figure 35.7 shows you what has happened to the saving rate based on the first measure and excluding capital gains. The saving rate was on an upward trend in Canada during the 1960s and 1970s. It was roughly constant in the United States. But during the 1990s, the saving rate collapsed in both countries. By 2000, the U.S. personal saving rate was less than 1 percent.

This collapse of the personal saving rate coincided with the explosion of stock prices through the 1990s.

You might expect that if people are enjoying capital gains on the stock market, they will think of these gains as being part of their saving. So they will not be concerned if their saving rate *excluding* capital gains falls. So what happened to the saving rate defined to include capital gains? Figure 35.8 answers this question for the period 1981–2001. While the saving rate excluding capital gains was collapsing, the saving rate including capital gains increased from about 7 percent in the early 1980s to around 20 percent in the late 1990s.

Which measure of saving is the correct one?

FIGURE 35.7   The Personal Saving Rate

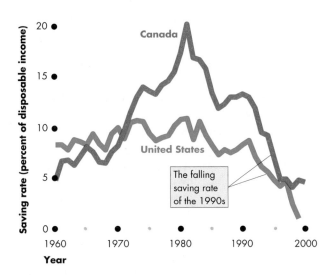

The personal saving rate increased in Canada and was flat in the United States before 1980. The saving rate fell in both countries during the 1980s and 1990s.

Sources: U.S. Bureau of Economic Analysis and adapted in part from the Statistics Canada CANSIM II database, table 380-0031.

FIGURE 35.8   Two Views of the Personal Saving Rate

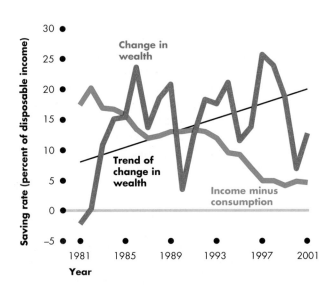

The personal saving rate including capital gains—the change in wealth—increased, while the saving rate excluding capital gains—disposable income minus consumption—collapsed.

Sources: Statistics Canada, CANSIM tables 378–0004 and 380–0031.

Neither! The rate that excludes capital gains is incorrect because it omits an important source of changes in wealth. But the rate that includes capital gains is incorrect because those gains are not realized. And if everyone attempted to realize their gains, the stock market would almost surely crash, thereby wiping out some unknown proportion of the gains. So the truth lies at some unknown place between the two available measures.

The Distribution of Wealth

When stock prices are rising as rapidly as they did from 1995 to 2000, stockholders enjoy spectacular increases in their wealth. Do all income groups share in these increases in wealth? Or are the increases concentrated among the already wealthy?

The answer to this question depends on the distribution of stockholdings. It turns out that the wealthier households are those that tend to hold stocks. So the wealthiest have gained the most.

The only wealth distribution data available is for the United States, and it ends in 1998. But these data tell an amazing story. You can see the data in Fig. 35.9. Here, we plot the mean wealth in 1992, 1995, and 1998 of households in five income groups ranging from those who earn less than $10,000 a year to those who earn more than $100,000 a year. The wealth data are in 1998 dollars, which means that they are adjusted to remove the effects of inflation.

Notice that the wealth of the four lowest-income groups barely changes. In contrast, the wealth of the highest-income group increases. In fact, the increase in wealth of the highest-income group exceeds the level of wealth of the next highest group. Between 1995 and 1998, households that have an income of $100,000 or more a year enjoyed an increase in average wealth of more than $300,000. The average wealth of households that earn between $50,000 and $99,999 was only $275,000 in 1998.

While we cannot be sure that all the wealth changes shown in Fig. 35.9 resulted from the rising stock prices, much of the change must have come from that source. Whether the changes in the distribution of wealth will be permanent depends on the future of stock prices. If stock prices collapse, much of the gain in wealth by the highest-income group will be reversed. And many families will wish that they had not lowered their saving rate.

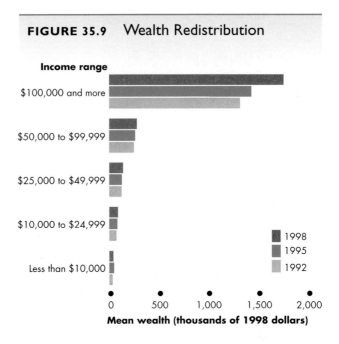

FIGURE 35.9   Wealth Redistribution

The wealth of the highest-income households increased between 1995 and 1998 by more than the level of wealth of other households.

Source: Board of Governors of the Federal Reserve System.

REVIEW QUIZ

1 What are the main trends in earnings growth?
2 What events are associated with the three periods of rapid earnings growth?
3 How does monetary policy influence the stock market?
4 How do taxes influence the stock market?
5 How does the stock market influence saving?
6 How does the stock market influence the distribution of wealth?

◆ You've learned the two main approaches to understanding stock prices, seen why portfolio diversification is a good idea, and seen how the stock market and the economy interact. To reinforce your appreciation of the impossibility of predicting stock prices, we look at the stock market at the end of 2002 in *Reading Between the Lines* on pp. 846–847.

Stock Price Uncertainties

THE GLOBE AND MAIL, DECEMBER 3, 2002

Analysts just can't agree: recovery or bear respite?

The stock markets have been rallying for the better part of seven weeks, but analysts continue to disagree over whether this is a full-fledged recovery or just a bear market taking a breather.

"I think, so far, that is the $64-million question, or the $8-trillion question," said Ross Healy, president of Strategic Analysis Corp.

The S&P/TSX composite index rose 5.2 per cent last month, and is up 17 per cent from its Oct. 9 low. Over the same period, the S&P 500 in the United States is up 20.3 per cent. However, that hasn't convinced many experts that the 2½-year bear market is at an end.

"Unfortunately, I think no matter how adamant that the born-again bulls are, or I suppose, for that matter, how adamant the unrepentant bears are, things are murky ... they are not cut and dried," Mr. Healy said.

What is cut and dried is that as a bear market bottoms, valuations become so attractive that they tend to draw investors into the market, he said. He doesn't see that yet.

He said the U.S. market is trading at about three times or more book value, far above the 1.6 times of the 1990 bear market. The dividend yield was far higher in 1990 than in today's market. Moreover, he pointed out, the price/earnings multiple on the Standard & Poor's 500-stock index stands at a relatively high 30 times trailing earnings.

Many market watchers zero in on the multiple on next year's earnings, which is significantly lower than the trailing multiple, but that is based on expectations that earnings will grow sharply next year. "I don't see 20- or 25-per-cent increase in earnings year over year next year," he said. ...

Reprinted with permission from *The Globe and Mail*.

Essence of the Story

■ Stock prices fell for two and a half years to October 2002—a bear market.

■ The S&P/TSX composite index increased by 5.2 percent in November 2002 and by 17 percent over its October 9 low.

■ Over the same period, the S&P 500 in the United States increased by 20.3 percent.

■ Uncertainty persisted over whether price increase would continue—whether the bear market was gone and a rising bull market had begun.

■ Reasons to believe that the market was not ready to begin a new long period of rising prices were: a high ratio of stock prices to the book value of firms, a low dividend yield, and a high price-earnings ratio.

■ Earnings would need to grow by an unlikely 20 percent to 25 percent to support a rising market.

Economic Analysis

■ This news article reports the rising stock prices of November 2002 and notes the uncertainty about the continuation of the increase.

■ Figure 1 shows the stock market of the 1990s and 2000s. The graph shows the S&P/TSX composite index.

■ The bull market—rising prices—began in the early 1990s and, with a brief pause in 1998, continued until August 2000.

■ A bear market—falling prices—began in September 2000.

■ The stock market never moves relentlessly in one direction. It is constantly fluctuating around its general trend and in November 2002, prices increased. They had also increased during November 2001.

■ Figure 2 expands our view of November and December 2002.

■ Stock prices increased for about a month and then fell before returning in mid-December to their previous peak of December 2, the date of the news article.

■ If stock prices are determined by market fundamentals, it is unlikely that a new bull market began at the end of 2002.

■ Uncertainty about continued economic growth in the United States, Japan, and Germany made Canada's continued strong expansion equally uncertain.

■ If in early 2003, real GDP growth slows and business profits are weak, stock prices will reflect these fundamentals and fall further.

■ If real GDP growth speeds up and business profits are strong, stock prices will reflect these more encouraging fundamentals and a bull market will begin.

■ At the end of 2002 (the date of the news article), slow growth and weak profits appeared more likely than fast growth and high profits.

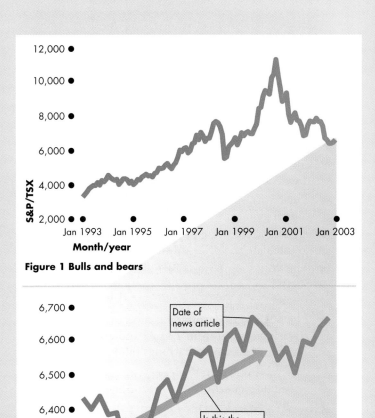

Figure 1 Bulls and bears

Figure 2 Bull or short-lived adjustment?

847

SUMMARY

KEY POINTS

Stock Market Basics (pp. 830–836)

- A stock is a tradable security issued by a firm to certify that its holder owns a share of the firm, is entitled to receive a share of the firm's profit (a dividend), and vote at stockholder meetings.
- The return on a stock consists of a dividend plus a capital gain (or minus a capital loss).
- A firm's accounting profit (called earnings) is used to calculate the price-earnings ratio.
- The S&P Composite, DJIA, NASDAQ, and S&P/TSX indexes provide information about average stock prices.
- The S&P price-earnings ratio between 1871 and 2001 has ranged from 6 to 27 and averaged 13.9. The S&P/TSX price-earnings ratio follows a similar path to that of S&P.

How Are Stock Prices Determined? (pp. 836–839)

- The market fundamental stock price is the discounted present value of the stream of expected future dividend payments, which in turn depend on expected future earnings.
- Some economists believe that stock prices can be understood only as speculative bubbles—periods of rising prices followed by price plunges, both of which occur because people expect them to occur and act on that expectation.

Risk and Return (p. 840)

- Stocks differ in their expected return and risk, and the greater the risk, the higher is the stock's risk premium.
- An investor can lower the risk faced by diversifying across a number of stocks because the returns on different stocks are not perfectly correlated.

The Stock Market and the Economy (pp. 841–845)

- Technological change and the state of the business cycle influence earnings growth and stock prices.

- Earnings growth has come in three main bursts: the 1890s, 1950s and 1960s, and 1990s.
- Each period of rapid earnings growth was also a time of the spread of major new technologies.
- When interest rates rise, stock prices fall, and when interest rates fall, stock prices rise. The change in stock prices precedes anticipated monetary policy actions.
- The capital gains tax and corporate profits tax affect stock prices. A transactions (Tobin) tax would probably not deter speculation.
- As stock prices increased during the 1990s, the saving rate excluding capital gains collapsed but the saving rate including capital gains increased.
- As stock prices increased during the 1990s, the distribution of wealth became more unequal.

KEY FIGURES AND TABLE

Figure 35.2   Reading the Stock Market Report, 832
Figure 35.5   The Price-Earnings Ratio, 835
Figure 35.6   Three Bursts of Earnings Growth, 841
Figure 35.7   The Personal Saving Rate, 844
Figure 35.8   Two Views of the Personal Saving Rate, 844
Figure 35.9   Wealth Redistribution, 845
Table 35.1   Rational Expectations, 838

KEY TERMS

Capital gain, 831
Capital loss, 831
Discount factor, 837
Dividend, 830
Dividend yield, 831
Earnings, 831
Equity capital, 830
Price-earnings ratio, 831
Rate of return, 831
Rational expectation, 837
Realized capital gain, 843
Return, 831
Risk premium, 840
Saving rate, 843
Speculative bubble, 838
Stock, 830
Stock exchange, 830
Stock price, 831
Wealth, 843
Wealth effect, 843

PROBLEMS

*1. On January 2, 2001, the price of a share of Coca-Cola stock was $60.81. On December 31, 2001, the price was $47.15. During 2001, Coca-Cola paid dividends that totaled 54¢ a share. Coca-Cola's reported accounting profit during 2001 was $1.58 per share.
  a. What was the dividend yield on Coca-Cola stock during 2001?
  b. What was the return on Coca-Cola stock during 2001?
  c. What was the capital gain or loss on Coca-Cola stock during 2001?
  d. What was the rate of return on Coca-Cola stock during 2001?
  e. What were Coca-Cola's earnings during 2001?
  f. What was Coca-Cola's price-earnings ratio on December 31, 2001?

2. On January 2, 2001, the price of a share of General Motors (GM) stock was $52.19. On December 31, 2001, the price was $48.60. During 2001, GM paid a dividend of $2 a share. GM's reported accounting profit during 2001 was $1.40 per share.
  a. What was the dividend yield on GM stock during 2001?
  b. What was the return on GM stock during 2001?
  c. What was the capital gain or loss on GM stock during 2001?
  d. What was the rate of return on GM stock during 2001?
  e. What were GM's earnings during 2001?
  f. What was GM's price-earnings ratio on December 31, 2001?

*3. The financial pages report that the Dow is up by 5 percent, the S&P is up by 8 percent, and the NASDAQ is up by 15 percent. Write a report that interprets these numbers. What can you infer from the data about the changes in stock prices in different sectors of the economy?

4. The financial pages report that the Dow is down by 15 percent, the S&P is down by 10 percent, and the NASDAQ is down by 25 percent. Write a short report that interprets these numbers. What can you infer from the data about the changes in stock prices in different sectors of the economy?

*5. You are trying to figure out whether to buy some stock. You are confident that the stock will pay a dividend of $3 a share next year, and you think that you'll be able to sell the stock at the end of the year for $30 a share. Your discount factor is 0.9. What is the most that you'd be willing to pay for this stock?

6. You are trying to figure out whether to buy some stock. You are confident that the stock will pay a dividend of $5 a share next year, and you think that you'll be able to sell the stock at the end of the year for $30 a share. Your discount factor is 0.8. What is the most that you'd be willing to pay for this stock?

*7. The price of a stock that you're thinking of buying is $20 a share. Your discount factor is 0.75. The firm has announced its dividend for next year of $1 per share. What is the lowest expected price next year that would make it rational for you to go ahead and buy the stock?

8. The price of a stock that you're thinking of buying is $100 a share. Your discount factor is 0.7. The firm has announced that it will pay no dividend next year. What is the lowest expected price next year that would make it rational for you to go ahead and buy the stock?

*9. Suppose there are two pharmaceutical stocks that you might buy: Merck and Pfizer. Merck will provide a return of 50 percent if the firm makes a major breakthrough on its new drug and a 10 percent return otherwise. There is only a 10 percent chance that the firm will make the breakthrough. Pfizer will provide a return of 20 percent if the firm achieves a cost saving and a 15 percent return otherwise. There is a 50 percent chance that the firm will achieve the cost saving.
  a. What is the expected return from investing in Merck?
  b. What is the expected return from investing in Pfizer?
  c. What is the chance of making a return of 50 percent by investing only in Merck?
  d. What is the chance of making a return of 10 percent by investing only in Merck?
  e. What is the chance of making a return of 20 percent by investing only in Pfizer?
  f. What is the chance of making a return of 15 percent by investing only in Pfizer?
  g. If you invest in both Merck and Pfizer in equal amounts, what is your expected return?

h. If you invest in both Merck and Pfizer in equal amounts, what is your chance of making a return of 50 percent?

i. If you invest in both Merck and Pfizer in equal amounts, what is your chance of making a return of 10 percent?

j. Explain why it might be rational to diversify across Merck and Pfizer.

10. Suppose there are two soft drink stocks that you might buy: Coke and Pepsi. Coke will provide a return of 20 percent if the firm's Harry Potter advertising campaign is successful and a 10 percent return otherwise. There is a 60 percent chance that the advertising campaign will be successful. Pepsi will provide a return of 16 percent if the firm achieves a cost saving and a 14 percent return otherwise. There is a 50 percent chance that the firm will achieve the cost saving.

a. What is the expected return from investing in Coke?

b. What is the expected return from investing in Pepsi?

c. What is the chance of making a return of 20 percent by investing only in Coke?

d. What is the chance of making a return of 10 percent by investing only in Coke?

e. What is the chance of making a return of 16 percent by investing only in Pepsi?

f. What is the chance of making a return of 14 percent by investing only in Pepsi?

g. If you invest in both Coke and Pepsi in equal amounts, what is your expected return?

h. If you invest in both Coke and Pepsi in equal amounts, what is your chance of making a return of 20 percent?

i. If you invest in both Coke and Pepsi in equal amounts, what is your chance of making a return of 10 percent?

j. Explain why it might be rational to diversify across Coke and Pepsi.

CRITICAL THINKING

1. Study *Reading Between the Lines* on pp. 846–847 and then answer the following questions:

a. What happened to stock prices during 2002 on the average?

b. Does the performance of stock prices during 2002 look like the result of rational expectations of the fundamentals or of the bursting of a speculative bubble?

c. Assuming that the performance of stock prices during 2002 was the result of rational expectations, what does that performance imply about expectations for profits in 2003 and beyond?

d. What economic development is needed before a new sustained increase in stock prices begins?

WEB EXERCISES

1. Use the link on the Parkin–Bade Web site to visit the New York, London, Frankfurt, Tokyo, and Toronto stock exchanges.

a. Get the latest index numbers from these stock exchanges and get the indexes a year ago.

b. On the basis of the data you have obtained, calculate the percentage changes in the indexes over the past year.

c. Which of the stock markets has delivered the largest percentage gain? Can you think of reasons for the differences in performance of the five stock markets?

2. Use the link on the Parkin–Bade Web site to obtain data on the prices and dividend payments over the past year for five stocks that interest you. Also obtain the value of the S&P/TSX, the DJIA, S&P Composite, and NASDAQ indexes for the same period.

a. For each stock, calculate the rate of return assuming that you bought the stock one year ago.

b. For each index, calculate the percentage change over the past year and compare the performance of each stock with the indexes.

GLOSSARY

Absolute advantage A person has an absolute advantage if that person can produce more goods with a given amount of resources than another person can; a country has an absolute advantage if its output per unit of inputs of all goods is larger than that of another country. (p. 45)

After-tax income Total income minus tax payments by households to governments. (p. 348)

Allocative efficiency A situation in which we cannot produce more of any good without giving up some of another good that we value more highly. (p. 39)

Anti-combine law A law that regulates and prohibits certain kinds of market behaviour, such as monopoly and monopolistic practices. (p. 394)

Average cost pricing rule A rule that sets price to cover cost including normal profit, which means setting the price equal to average total cost. (pp. 277, 398)

Average fixed cost Total fixed cost per unit of output. (p. 224)

Average product The average product of a factor of production. It equals total product divided by the quantity of the factor employed. (p. 219)

Average tax rate The percentage of income that is paid in tax. (pp. 359, 382)

Average total cost Total cost per unit of output. (p. 224)

Average variable cost Total variable cost per unit of output. (p. 224)

Barriers to entry Legal or natural constraints that protect a firm from potential competitors. (p. 262)

Big tradeoff The conflict between equity and efficiency. (pp. 10, 115, 361)

Bilateral monopoly A situation in which a single seller (a monopoly) faces a single buyer (a monopsony). (p. 345)

Black market An illegal trading arrangement in which the price exceeds the legally imposed price ceiling. (p. 126)

Budget line The limits to a household's consumption choices. (p. 172)

Business cycle The periodic but irregular up-and-down movement in production and jobs. (p. 8)

Capacity output The output at which average total cost is a minimum—the output at the bottom of the U-shaped *ATC* curve. (p. 287)

Capital The tools, equipment, buildings, and other constructions that businesses now use to produce goods and services. (p. 4)

Capital accumulation The growth of capital resources. (p. 40)

Capital gain The increase in the price of a stock. (p. 831)

Capital loss The decrease in the price of a stock. (p. 831)

Capture theory A theory of regulation that states that the regulations are supplied to satisfy the demand of producers to maximize producer surplus—to maximize economic profit. (p. 395)

Cartel A group of firms that has entered into a collusive agreement to restrict output and increase prices and profits. (p. 295)

Ceteris paribus Other things being equal—all other relevant things remaining the same. (p. 13)

Change in demand A change in buyers' plans that occurs when some influence on those plans other than the price of the good changes. It is illustrated by a shift of the demand curve. (p. 63)

Change in supply A change in sellers'

plans that occurs when some influence on those plans other than the price of the good changes. It is illustrated by a shift of the supply curve. (p. 67)

Change in the quantity demanded A change in buyers' plans that occurs when the price of a good changes but all other influences on buyers' plans remain unchanged. It is illustrated by a movement along the demand curve. (p. 65)

Change in the quantity supplied A change in sellers' plans that occurs when the price of a good changes but all other influences on sellers' plans remain unchanged. It is illustrated by a movement along the supply curve. (p. 68)

Coase theorem The proposition that if property rights exist, if only a small number of parties are involved, and transactions costs are low, then private transactions are efficient. (p. 419)

Collusive agreement An agreement between two (or more) producers to restrict output, raise the price, and increase profits. (p. 295)

Command system A method of organizing production that uses a managerial hierarchy. (p. 201)

Comparative advantage A person or country has a comparative advantage in an activity if that person or country can perform the activity at a lower opportunity cost than anyone else or any other country. (p. 42)

Competitive market A market that has many buyers and many sellers, so no single buyer or seller can influence the price. (p. 60)

Complement A good that is used in conjunction with another good. (p. 63)

Constant returns to scale Features of a firm's technology that lead to constant long-run average cost as output increases. When constant returns to scale are present, the *LRAC* curve is horizontal. (p. 231)

Consumer equilibrium A situation in which a consumer has allocated all his or her available income in the way that, given the prices of goods and services, maximizes his or her total utility. (p. 157)

Consumer surplus The value of a

good minus the price paid for it, summed over the quantity bought. (p. 107)

Contestable market A market in which firms can enter and leave so easily that firms in the market face competition from potential entrants. (p. 302)

Cooperative equilibrium The outcome of a game in which the players make and share the monopoly profit. (p. 301)

Copyright A government-sanctioned exclusive right granted to the inventor of a good, service, or productive process to produce, use, and sell the invention for a given number of years. (p. 425)

Cost of living The amount of money it takes to buy the goods and services that the average family consumes. (p. 7)

Cross elasticity of demand The responsiveness of the demand for a good to a change in the price of a substitute or complement, other things remaining the same. It is calculated as the percentage change in the quantity demanded of the good divided by the percentage change in the price of the substitute or complement. (p. 91)

Cross-section graph A graph that shows the values of an economic variable for different groups in a population at a point in time. (p. 18)

Crown Corporation A publicly owned firm in Canada. (p. 394)

Deadweight loss A measure of inefficiency. It is equal to the decrease in consumer surplus and producer surplus that results from an inefficient level of production. (p. 112)

Deflation A process of falling cost of living. (p. 7)

Demand The relationship between the quantity of a good that consumers plan to buy and the price of the good when all other influences on buyers' plans remain the same. It is described by a demand schedule and illustrated by a demand curve. (p. 62)

Demand curve A curve that shows the relationship between the quantity demanded of a good and its price when all other influences on con-

sumers' planned purchases remain the same. (p. 62)

Derived demand Demand for a factor of production which is derived from the demand for the goods and services produced by the factor. (p. 317)

Diminishing marginal rate of substitution The general tendency for a person to be willing to give up less of good y to get one more unit of good x, and at the same time remain indifferent, as the quantity of good x increases. (p. 176)

Diminishing marginal returns The tendency for the marginal product of an additional unit of a factor of production to be less than the marginal product of the previous unit of the factor. (p. 221)

Diminishing marginal utility The decrease in marginal utility as the quantity consumed increases. (p. 155)

Direct relationship A relationship between two variables that move in the same direction. (p. 20)

Discount factor The discounted price is the original price multiplied by the discount factor. (p. 837)

Discounting The conversion of a future amount of money to its present value. (p. 326)

Diseconomies of scale Features of a firm's technology that lead to rising long-run average cost as output increases. (p. 230)

Dividend The share of a firm's profit paid to stockholders. (p. 830)

Dividend yield The dividend paid on a stock expressed as a percentage of the stock price. (p. 831)

Dumping The sale by a foreign firm of exports at a lower price than the cost of production. (p. 798)

Duopoly A market structure in which two producers of a good or service compete. (p. 295)

Dynamic comparative advantage A comparative advantage that a person or country possesses as a result of having specialized in a particular activity and then, as a result of learning-by-doing, having become the producer with the lowest opportunity cost. (p. 45)

Earnings A firm's accounting profit. (p. 831)

Economic depreciation The change in the market value of capital over a given period. (p. 196)

Economic efficiency A situation that occurs when the firm produces a given output at the least cost. (p. 199)

Economic growth The expansion of production possibilities that results from capital accumulation and technological change. (p. 40)

Economic model A description of some aspect of the economic world that includes only those features of the world that are needed for the purpose at hand. (p. 12)

Economic profit A firm's total revenue minus its opportunity cost. (p. 197)

Economic rent The income received by the owner of a factor of production over and above the amount required to induce that owner to offer the factor for use. (p. 334)

Economic theory A generalization that summarizes what we think we understand about the economic choices that people make and the performance of industries and entire economies. (p. 12)

Economics The social science that studies the choices that we make as we cope with scarcity and the institutions that have evolved to influence and reconcile our choices. (p. 2)

Economies of scale Features of a firm's technology that lead to a falling long-run average cost as output increases. (pp. 211, 230)

Economies of scope Decreases in average total cost that occur when a firm uses specialized resources to produce a range of goods and services. (p. 211)

Efficient allocation Resource use is efficient when we produce the goods and services that we value most highly. (p. 104)

Elastic demand Demand with a price elasticity greater than 1; other things remaining the same, the percentage change in the quantity demanded exceeds the percentage change in price. (p. 87)

Elasticity of demand The responsiveness of the quantity demanded of a good to a change in its price, other things remaining the same. (p. 84)

Elasticity of supply The responsiveness of the quantity supplied of a good to a change in its price, other things remaining the same. (p. 94)

Entrepreneurship The human resource that organizes the other three factors of production: labour, land, and capital. Entrepreneurs come up with new ideas about what and how to produce, make business decisions, and bear the risks that arise from their decisions. (p. 4)

Equilibrium price The price at which the quantity demanded equals the quantity supplied. (p. 70)

Equilibrium quantity The quantity bought and sold at the equilibrium price. (p. 70)

Equity capital The value of a firm's stock—also called the firm's equity. (p. 830)

Excise tax A tax on the sale of a particular commodity. (p. 386)

Exports The goods and services that we sell to people in other countries. (p. 786)

External benefits Benefits that accrue to people other than the buyer of the good. (p. 254)

External costs Costs that are not borne by the producer of the good but borne by someone else. (p. 254)

External diseconomies Factors outside the control of a firm that raise the firm's costs as the industry produces a larger output. (p. 251)

External economies Factors beyond the control of a firm that lower the firm's costs as the industry produces a larger output. (p. 251)

Externality A cost or a benefit that arises from production and falls on someone other than the producer, or a cost or a benefit that arises from consumption and falls on someone other than the consumer. (p. 414)

Factors of production The resources that businesses use to produce goods and services. (p. 4)

Farm Marketing Board A regulatory agency that intervenes in an agricul-

tural market to stabilize the price of an agricultural product. (p. 139)

Firm An institution that hires factors of production and organizes those factors to produce and sell goods and services. (p. 196)

Four-firm concentration ratio A measure of market power that is calculated as the percentage of the value of sales accounted for by the four largest firms in an industry. (p. 206)

Free rider A person who consumes a good without paying for it. (p. 376)

Game theory A tool that economists use to analyze strategic behaviour—behaviour that takes into account the expected behaviour of others and the recognition of mutual interdependence. (p. 293)

General Agreement on Tariffs and Trade An international agreement signed in 1947 to reduce tariffs on international trade. (p. 793)

Goods and services All the objects that people value and produce to satisfy their wants. (p. 3)

Herfindahl–Hirschman Index A measure of market power that is calculated as the square of the market share of each firm (as a percentage) summed over the largest 50 firms (or over all firms if there are fewer than 50) in a market. (p. 206)

Human capital The knowledge and skill that people obtain from education, on-the-job training, and work experience. (p. 4)

Implicit rental rate The firm's opportunity cost of using its own capital. (p. 196)

Imports The goods and services that we buy from people in other countries. (p. 786)

Incentive An inducement to take a particular action. (p. 11)

Incentive system A method of organizing production that uses a market-like mechanism inside the firm. (p. 201)

Income effect The effect of a change in income on consumption, other things remaining the same. (p. 180)

Income elasticity of demand The responsiveness of demand to a change in income, other things remaining the same. It is calculated as the percentage change in the quantity demanded divided by the percentage change in income. (p. 92)

Indifference curve A line that shows combinations of goods among which a consumer is indifferent. (p. 175)

Inelastic demand A demand with a price elasticity between 0 and 1; the percentage change in the quantity demanded is less than the percentage change in price. (p. 87)

Infant-industry argument The argument that it is necessary to protect a new industry to enable it to grow into a mature industry that can compete in world markets. (p. 797)

Inferior good A good for which demand decreases as income increases. (p. 64)

Inflation A rising cost of living. (p. 7)

Intellectual property rights Property rights for discoveries owned by the creators of knowledge. (p. 425)

Interest The income that capital earns. (p. 5)

Inverse relationship A relationship between variables that move in opposite directions. (p. 21)

Labour The work time and work effort that people devote to producing goods and services. (p. 4)

Labour union An organized group of workers whose purpose is to increase wages and to influence other job conditions. (p. 341)

Land All the gifts of nature that we use to produce goods and services. (p. 4)

Law of demand Other things remaining the same, the higher the price of a good, the smaller is the quantity demanded of it. (p. 61)

Law of diminishing returns As a firm uses more of a variable input, with a given quantity of other inputs (fixed inputs), the marginal product of the variable input eventually diminishes. (p. 221)

Law of supply Other things remaining the same, the higher the price of a good, the greater is the quantity supplied of it. (p. 66)

Learning-by-doing People become more productive in an activity (learn) just by repeatedly producing a particular good or service (doing). (p. 45)

Legal monopoly A market structure in which there is one firm and entry is restricted by the granting of a public franchise, government licence, patent, or copyright. (p. 262)

Limit pricing The practice of setting the price at the highest level that inflicts a loss on an entrant. (p. 303)

Linear relationship A relationship between two variables that is illustrated by a straight line. (p. 28)

Local public good A public good that is consumed by all the people who live in a particular area. (p. 385)

Long run A period of time in which the quantities of all resources can be varied. (p. 218)

Long-run average cost curve The relationship between the lowest attainable average total cost and output when both plant size and labour are varied. (p. 229)

Long-run industry supply curve A curve that shows how the quantity supplied by an industry varies as the market price varies after all the possible adjustments have been made, including changes in plant size and the number of firms in the industry. (p. 251)

Lorenz curve A curve that graphs the cumulative percentage of income or wealth against the cumulative percentage of households. (p. 349)

Low-income cutoff The income level, determined separately for different types of families (for example, single persons, couples, one parent) that is selected such that families with incomes below that limit normally spend 54.7 percent or more of their income on food, shelter, and clothing. (p. 352)

Macroeconomics The study of the effects on the national economy and the global economy of the choices that individuals, businesses, and governments make. (p. 2)

Margin When a choice is changed by a small amount or by a little at a time, the choice is made at the margin. (p. 11)

Marginal benefit The benefit that a person receives from consuming one more unit of a good or service. It is measured as the maximum amount that a person is willing to pay for one more unit of the good or service. (pp. 11, 38, 104)

Marginal benefit curve A curve that shows the relationship between the marginal benefit of a good and the quantity of that good consumed. (p. 38)

Marginal cost The opportunity cost of producing one more unit of a good or service. It is the best alternative forgone. It is calculated as the increase in total cost divided by the increase in output. (pp. 11, 37, 104, 224)

Marginal cost pricing rule A rule that sets the price of a good or service equal to the marginal cost of producing it. (pp. 276, 398)

Marginal external benefit The benefit from an additional unit of a good or service that people other than the consumer enjoy. (p. 421)

Marginal external cost The cost of producing an additional unit of a good or service that falls on people other than the producer. (p. 417)

Marginal private benefit The benefit from an additional unit of a good or service that the consumer of that good or service receives. (p. 421)

Marginal private cost The cost of producing an additional unit of a good or service that is borne by the producer of that good or service. (p. 417)

Marginal product The increase in total product that results from a one-unit increase in the variable input, with all other inputs remaining the same. It is calculated as the increase in total product divided by the increase in the variable input employed, when the quantities of all other inputs are constant. (p. 219)

Marginal rate of substitution The rate at which a person will give up good y (the good measured on the y-axis) to get an additional unit of good x (the good measured on the x-axis) and at the same time remain indifferent (remain on the same indifference curve). (p. 176)

Marginal revenue The change in total revenue that results from a one-unit increase in the quantity sold. It is calculated as the change in total revenue divided by the change in quantity sold. (p. 238)

Marginal revenue product The change in total revenue that results from employing one more unit of a factor of production (labour) while the quantity of all other factors remains the same. It is calculated as the increase in total revenue divided by the increase in the quantity of the factor (labour). (p. 318)

Marginal social benefit The marginal benefit enjoyed by society—by the consumer of a good or service (marginal private benefit) plus the marginal benefit enjoyed by others (marginal external benefit). (p. 421)

Marginal social cost The marginal cost incurred by the entire society—by the producer and by everyone else on whom the cost falls— and is the sum of marginal private cost and marginal external cost. (p. 417)

Marginal tax rate The percentage of an additional dollar of income that is paid in tax. (p. 382)

Marginal utility The change in total utility resulting from a one-unit increase in the quantity of a good consumed. (p. 155)

Marginal utility per dollar spent The marginal utility from a good divided by its price. (p. 157)

Market Any arrangement that enables buyers and sellers to get information and to do business with each other. (p. 46)

Market demand The relationship between the total quantity demanded of a good and its price. It is illustrated by the market demand curve. (p. 163)

Market failure A state in which the market does not allocate resources efficiently. (p. 374)

Market income The wages, interest, rent, and profit earned in factor markets and before paying income taxes. (p. 348)

Market power The ability to influence the market, and in particular the market price, by influencing the total quantity offered for sale. (p. 262)

Microeconomics The study of the

choices that individuals and businesses make, the way those choices interact, and the influence governments exert on them. (p. 2)

Minimum efficient scale The smallest quantity of output at which the long-run average cost curve reaches its lowest level. (p. 231)

Minimum wage A regulation that makes the hiring of labour below a specified wage rate illegal. (p. 129)

Monopolistic competition A market structure in which a large number of firms compete by making similar but slightly different products. (pp. 205, 284)

Monopoly A market structure in which there is one firm, which produces a good or service that has no close substitute and in which the firm is protected from competition by a barrier preventing the entry of new firms. (pp. 205, 262)

Monopsony A market in which there is a single buyer. (p. 344)

Nash equilibrium The outcome of a game that occurs when player A takes the best possible action given the action of player B and player B takes the best possible action given the action of player A. (p. 294)

Natural monopoly A monopoly that occurs when one firm can supply the entire market at a lower price than two or more firms can. (pp. 262, 397)

Negative externality An externality that arises from either production or consumption and that imposes an external cost. (p. 414)

Negative relationship A relationship between variables that move in opposite directions. (p. 21)

Net exports The value of exports minus the value of imports. (p. 786)

Net present value The present value of the future flow of marginal revenue product generated by capital minus the cost of the capital. (p. 328)

Nonrenewable natural resources Natural resources that can be used only once and that cannot be replaced once they have been used. (p. 331)

Nontariff barrier Any action other than a tariff that restricts international trade. (p. 793)

Normal good A good for which demand increases as income increases. (p. 64)

Normal profit The expected return for supplying entrepreneurial ability. (p. 197)

North American Free Trade Agreement An agreement, which became effective on January 1, 1994, to eliminate all barriers to international trade between the United States, Canada, and Mexico after a 15-year phasing-in period. (p. 794)

Oligopoly A market structure in which a small number of firms compete. (pp. 205, 291)

Opportunity cost The highest-valued alternative that we give up to get something. (p. 11)

Output-inflation tradeoff A tradeoff that arises because a policy action that lowers inflation also lowers output and a policy action that boosts output also increases inflation. (p. 10)

Patent A government-sanctioned exclusive right granted to the inventor of a good, service, or productive process to produce, use, and sell the invention for a given number of years. (p. 425)

Payoff matrix A table that shows the payoffs for every possible action by each player for every possible action by each other player. (p. 293)

Perfect competition A market in which there are many firms each selling an identical product; there are many buyers; there are no restrictions on entry into the industry; firms in the industry have no advantage over potential new entrants; and firms and buyers are well informed about the price of each firm's product. (pp. 205, 238)

Perfect price discrimination Price discrimination that extracts the entire consumer surplus. (p. 273)

Perfectly elastic demand Demand with an infinite price elasticity; the quantity demanded changes by an infinitely large percentage in response to a tiny price change. (p. 87)

Perfectly inelastic demand Demand with a price elasticity of zero; the

quantity demanded remains constant when the price changes. (p. 86)

Pigovian taxes Taxes that are used as an incentive for producers to cut back on an activity that creates an external cost. (p. 420)

Political equilibrium The outcome that results from the choices of voters, politicians, and bureaucrats. (p. 375)

Positive externality An externality that arises from either production or consumption and that provides an external benefit. (p. 414)

Positive relationship A relationship between two variables that move in the same direction. (p. 20)

Poverty A situation in which a household's income is too low to be able to buy the quantities of food, shelter, and clothing that are deemed necessary. (p. 352)

Preferences A description of a person's likes and dislikes. (p. 38)

Present value The amount of money that, if invested today, will grow to be as large as a given future amount when the interest that it will earn is taken into account. (p. 326)

Price ceiling A regulation that makes it illegal to charge a price higher than a specified level. (p. 125)

Price discrimination The practice of selling different units of a good or service for different prices or of charging one customer different prices for different quantities bought. (p. 263)

Price-earnings ratio The stock price divided by the most recent year's earnings. (p. 831)

Price effect The effect of a change in the price on the quantity of a good consumed, other things remaining the same. (p. 179)

Price elasticity of demand A units-free measure of the responsiveness of the quantity demanded of a good to a change in its price, when all other influences on buyers' plans remain the same. (p. 84)

Price floor A regulation that makes it illegal to charge a price lower than a specified level. (p. 129)

Price taker A firm that cannot influence the price of the good or service it produces. (p. 238)

Principal–agent problem The problem of devising compensation rules that induce an agent to act in the best interest of a principal. (p. 202)

Principle of minimum differentiation The tendency for competitors to make themselves identical as they try to appeal to the maximum number of clients or voters. (p. 379)

Privatization The process of selling publicly owned corporations to private shareholders. (p. 394)

Producer surplus The price of a good minus the opportunity cost of producing it, summed over the quantity sold. (p. 109)

Product differentiation Making a product slightly different from the product of a competing firm. (pp. 205, 284)

Production efficiency A situation in which the economy cannot produce more of one good without producing less of some other good. (p. 35)

Production possibilities frontier The boundary between the combinations of goods and services that can be produced and the combinations that cannot. (p. 34)

Profit The income earned by entrepreneurship. (p. 5)

Progressive income tax A tax on income at an average rate that increases with the level of income. (p. 359)

Property rights Social arrangements that govern the ownership, use, and disposal of resources or factors of production, goods, and services that are enforceable in the courts. (pp. 46, 418)

Proportional income tax A tax on income at a constant average rate, regardless of the level of income. (p. 359)

Public good A good or service that can be consumed simultaneously by everyone and from which no one can be excluded. (p. 376)

Public interest theory A theory of regulation that states that regulations are supplied to satisfy the demand of consumers and producers to maximize the sum of consumer surplus and producer surplus—that is, to attain efficiency. (p. 395)

Public provision The production of a good or service by a public authority that receives its revenue from the government. (p. 423)

Quantity demanded The amount of a good or service that consumers plan to buy during a given time period at a particular price. (p. 61)

Quantity supplied The amount of a good or service that producers plan to sell during a given time period at a particular price. (p. 66)

Quota A restriction on the quantity of a good that a farm is permitted to produce. (p. 140)

Quota A quantitative restriction on the import of a particular good, which specifies the maximum amount that can be imported in a given time period. (p. 796)

Rand Formula A requirement that all workers represented by a union must pay union dues, whether they join the union or not. (p. 341)

Rate of return The return on a stock expressed as a percentage of the stock price. (p. 831)

Rate of return regulation A regulation that requires the firm to justify its price by showing that the price enables it to earn a specified target percent return on its capital. (p. 399)

Rational expectation The most accurate forecast possible, a forecast that uses all the available information, including knowledge of the relevant economic forces that influence the variable being forecasted. (p. 837)

Rational ignorance The decision not to acquire information because the cost of doing so exceeds the expected benefit. (p. 380)

Real income A household's income expressed as a quantity of goods that the household can afford to buy. (p. 173)

Realized capital gain A capital gain that is obtained when a stock is sold for a higher price than the price paid for it. (p. 843)

Regressive income tax A tax on income at an average rate that decreases with the level of income. (p. 359)

Relative price The ratio of the price of one good or service to the price of another good or service. A relative price is an opportunity cost. (pp. 60, 173)

Renewable natural resources Natural resources that can be used repeatedly without depleting what is available for future use. (p. 331)

Rent The income that land earns. (p. 5)

Rent ceiling A regulation that makes it illegal to charge a rent higher than a specified level. (p. 125)

Rent seeking Any attempt to capture a consumer surplus, a producer surplus, or an economic profit. (pp. 270)

Return The return on a stock is the sum of the stock's dividend plus its capital gain (or minus its capital loss). (p. 831)

Risk premium The additional return that is earned for bearing an additional risk. (p. 840)

Saving rate Saving as a percentage of disposable income. (p. 843)

Scarcity The state in which the resources available are insufficient to satisfy people's wants. (p. 2)

Scatter diagram A diagram that plots the value of one variable against the value of another. (p. 19)

Search activity The time spent looking for someone with whom to do business. (p. 126)

Short run The short run in microeconomics has two meanings. For the firm, it is the period of time in which the quantity of at least one input is fixed and the quantities of the other inputs can be varied. The fixed input is usually capital—that is, the firm has a given plant size. For the industry, the short run is the period of time in which each firm has a given plant size and the number of firms in the industry is fixed. (p. 218)

Short-run industry supply curve A curve that shows the quantity supplied by the industry at each price when the plant size of each firm and the number of firms in the industry remain the same. (p. 245)

Shutdown point The output and price at which the firm just covers its total variable cost. In the short run, the firm is indifferent between producing the profit-maximizing output and shutting down temporarily. (p. 244)

Single-price monopoly A monopoly that must sell each unit of its output for the same price to all its customers. (p. 263)

Slope The change in the value of the variable measured on the *y*-axis divided by the change in the value of the variable measured on the *x*-axis. (p. 24)

Speculative bubble A price increase followed by a price plunge, both of which occur because people expect them to occur and act on that expectation. (p. 838)

Standard of living The level of consumption that people enjoy, on the average, and is measured by average income per person. (p. 6)

Stock A tradable security that a firm issues to certify that the stockholder owns a share of the firm. (p. 830)

Stock exchange An organized market on which people can buy and sell stock. (p. 830)

Stock price The price at which one share of a firm's stock trades on a stock exchange. (p. 831)

Strategies All the possible actions of each player in a game. (p. 293)

Subsidy A payment that the government makes to private producers. (pp. 140, 424)

Substitute A good that can be used in place of another good. (p. 63)

Substitution effect The effect of a change in price of a good or service on the quantity bought when the consumer (hypothetically) remains indifferent between the original and the new consumption situations—that is, the consumer remains on the same indifference curve. (p. 181)

Sunk cost The past cost of buying a plant that has no resale value. (p. 218)

Supply The relationship between the quantity of a good that producers plan to sell and the price of the good when all other influences on producers' plans remain the same. It is described by a supply schedule and illustrated by a supply curve. (p. 66)

Supply curve A curve that shows the relationship between the quantity supplied and the price of a good when all

other influences on producers' planned sales remain the same. (p. 66)

Symmetry principle A requirement that people in similar situations be treated similarly. (p. 116)

Tariff A tax that is imposed by the importing country when an imported good crosses its international boundary. (p. 793)

Technological change The development of new goods and of better ways of producing goods and services. (p. 40)

Technological efficiency A situation that occurs when the firm produces a given output by using the least amount of inputs. (p. 199)

Technology Any method of producing a good or service. (p. 198)

Terms of trade The quantity of goods and services that a country exports to pay for its imports of goods and services. (p. 788)

Time-series graph A graph that measures time (for example, months or years) on the *x*-axis and the variable or variables in which we are interested on the *y*-axis. (p. 18)

Total cost The cost of all the productive resources that a firm uses. (p. 223)

Total fixed cost The cost of the firm's fixed inputs. (p. 223)

Total income Market income plus cash payments to households by governments. (p. 348)

Total product The total output produced by a firm in a given period of time. (p. 219)

Total revenue The value of a firm's sales. It is calculated as the price of the good multiplied by the quantity sold. (pp. 88, 238)

Total revenue test A method of estimating the price elasticity of demand by observing the change in total revenue that results from a change in the price, when all other influences on the quantity sold remain the same. (p. 88)

Total utility The total benefit that a person gets from the consumption of goods and services. (p. 154)

Total variable cost The cost of all the firm's variable inputs. (p. 223)

Tradeoff A constraint that involves giving up one thing to get something else. (p. 9)

Transactions costs The costs that arise from finding someone with whom to do business, of reaching an agreement about the price and other aspects of the exchange, and of ensuring that the terms of the agreement are fulfilled. The opportunity costs of conducting a transaction. (pp. 210, 419)

Trend The general tendency for a variable to move in one direction. (p. 18)

Unit elastic demand Demand with a price elasticity of 1; the percentage change in the quantity demanded equals the percentage change in price. (p. 86)

Utilitarianism A principle that states that we should strive to achieve "the greatest happiness for the greatest number of people." (p. 114)

Utility The benefit or satisfaction that a person gets from the consumption of a good or service. (p. 154)

Value The maximum amount that a person is willing to pay for a good. The value of one more unit of the good or service is its marginal benefit. (p. 106)

Voluntary export restraint An agreement between two governments in which the government of the exporting country agrees to restrain the volume of its own exports. (p. 796)

Voucher A token that the government provides to households, which they can use to buy specified goods and services. (p. 424)

Wages The income that labour earns. (p. 5)

Wealth The market value of all the things that people own—the market value of their assets. (p. 843)

Wealth effect The influence of wealth on consumption expenditure and saving. (p. 843)

World Trade Organization An international organization that places greater obligations on its member countries to observe the GATT rules. (p. 793)

INDEX

Key terms and pages on
which they are defined
appear in **boldface**.

Absolute advantage, 45
After-tax income, 348
Agricultural markets
    and bumper harvest, 138
    elasticity of demand, 138
    farm marketing boards. *See* Farm mar-
      keting board
    inventory holders, behaviour of, 138
    inventory speculation, 138
    and poor harvest, 137
    production, fluctuations in, 138
    stabilization of farm revenues, 137–141
    unregulated, 137–138
Air pollution, 415–416
Air pollution debate *(Reading between the*
    lines), 426–427
Airport security tax *(Reading between the*
    lines), 142–143
Alchian, Armen, 211
Allocative efficiency, 39
Anarchy, State, and Utopia (Nozick), 116
Anti-combine law, 394
    anti-competitive agreements, 406–407
    bank mergers, 407
    Bell Canada Enterprises case, 406
    in Canada, 406
    Canada Packers and Labatt case, 407
    Chrysler case, 406
    NutraSweet case, 406
    public *vs.* special interest, 407
Average cost pricing rule, 277, 398
Average fixed cost, 224
Average product, 219
Average product curves, 222
Average tax rate, 382
Average total cost, 224
Average total cost curve, 224–225
Average variable cost, 224

Bank mergers, and anti-combine law, 407
Bar chart, 18
Barriers to entry
    and concentration measures, 208
    defined, **262**

    legal barriers to entry, 262
    natural, 262–263
Becker, Gary, 191, 192–194
Bentham, Jeremy, 190–191
Best affordable point, 178
Bhagwati, Jagdish, 854–856
Big tradeoff, 10, 115, 361
Bilateral monopoly, 345
Black markets, 126
Boat rides, marginal utility of *(Reading*
    between the lines), 166–167
Book sellers war *(Reading between the lines),*
    304–305
Break-even point, 240
Budget equation, 173–174
Budget line, 154, 172, 180
Bureaucracy model of public enterprise,
    404–405
Bureaucrats, 375, 380
Business cycle
    defined, **8**
    expansion, 8
    peak, 8
    phases, 8
    recession, 8
    trough, 8
    turning points, 8
Business organizations
    corporation, 203
    partnership, 202–203
    pros and cons of different types, 203
    relative importance of types of, 204
    sole proprietorship, 202
    types of, 202–203

Canada
    anti-combine law in, 406
    concentration measures, 207
    distribution of income, 5
    drug dealing penalties, 136
    economic growth in, 41
    expansion, most recent, 8
    farm marketing boards in, 139
    gains from international trade, 44–45
    government tax revenues, 382
    illegal drug market in, 135–136
    income distribution in, 348
    income distribution trends
      (1980–1998), 352
    income Lorenz curve (1998), 349
    income redistribution, 360
    labour market trends, 317
    low income incidence, by family charac-
      teristics, 353
    minimum wage in, 130
    North American economy, market struc-
      ture of, 209
    personal saving rate, 844
    production per person, in past 30 years,
      40
    quintile shares (1998), 349
    tariffs (1867–2001), 793
    welfare challenge in, 361
Canada–United States Free Trade
    Agreement, 802
Capacity output, 287
Capital

    defined, **4**
    demand curve, 329
    demand for, 325–326
    economic depreciation, 196–197
    equity, 830
    human capital, 4, 40
    implicit rental rate, 196
    interest, 5
    marginal product of capital, 228
    substitutability of, for labour, 322
    supply curve, 330
    supply of, 329–330
    unequal ownership of, 358
Capital accumulation, 40
Capital gain, 831
Capital gains tax, 843
Capital loss, 831
Capital markets
    capital demand curve, 329
    defined, 325
    demand for capital, 325–326
    discounting, 326
    equilibrium, 330
    and interest rate, 330–331
    net present value, 328
    present value, 326–328
    supply curve of capital, 330
    supply of capital, 329–330
Capture theory, 395–396, 398, 400–401
Card, David, 130
Cartel
    defined, **295**, 401
    regulation, 401–402
Causation, and graphs, 20
Cause and effect, identification of, 13
Ceteris paribus
    defined, **13**
    graphing relationships among more than
      two variables, 26–27
Change in demand
    vs. change in quantity demanded, 64–65
    defined, **63**
    expected future prices, 63–64
    factors, 63–64
    income, 64
    in perfect competition, 246
    permanent, 250–251
    population, 64
    and preferences, 64
    price and quantity, effect on, 72–73,
      74–75
    prices of related goods, 63
Change in quantity demanded, 65
Change in supply
    vs. change in quantity supplied, 68–69
    defined, **67**
    expected future prices, 68
    factors, 67–68
    price and quantity, effect on, 73, 74–75,
      84
    prices of productive resources, 67
    prices of related goods, 67–68
    suppliers, number of, 68
    technology, 68
Change in the quantity supplied, 68–69
Choices, as tradeoffs, 9–10
Coase, Ronald, 210, 419, 432–433

Coase theorem, **419,** 425
Collusion
    cheating on agreement, 297–298
    monopolistic competition, impossibility
        in, 284
    payoff matrix, 298
    profit maximization, 296
Collusive agreement, 295
Command systems, 201
Common stock, 830
Comparative advantage, 42–43, 787, **788,**
    791
Competition
    and choices, 254
    and efficiency, 254–255
    and equilibrium, 254
    perfect competition. *See* Perfect compe-
        tition
Competition Act, 406–407
Competition policy
    anti-combine law, 406–407
    economic theory of regulation, 394–396
    market intervention, 394
    public ownership, 403–405
    regulation. *See* Regulation
Competitive equilibrium, efficiency of, 110
Competitive market
    competitive equilibrium, efficiency of,
        110
    defined, **60**
    efficiency of, 106, 110–113
    fairness of, 114–117
    "invisible hand," 111
    obstacles to efficiency, 111–113
Complement
    and cross elasticity of demand, 92
    defined, **63,** 68
    and indifference curves, 177–178
Concentration measures
    and barriers to entry, 208
    for Canadian economy, 207
    firm turnover, 208
    four-firm concentration ratio, 206
    geographical scope of markets, 208
    Herfindahl–Hirschman Index, 206–207
    limitations of, 207–209
    market and industry correspondence,
        208–209
Constant returns to scale, 231
Consumer behaviour
    best affordable point, 178
    income effect, 180–182
    predictions, 178–182
    price effect, 179–180
Consumer equilibrium, 157
Consumer Price Index (CPI)
    commodity substitution bias, 193
    new goods bias, 193
    outlet substitution bias, 193
    quality change bias, 193
Consumer surplus
    and consumer efficiency, 164
    defined, **107**
    and paradox of value, 165
    and price discrimination, 271–272
Consumption
    household. *See* Household consumption
        choices

negative consumption externalities, 414
    positive consumption externalities, 414
Consumption expenditure, and stock mar-
    kets, 843–844
Consumption possibilities
    budget equation, 173–174
    divisible and indivisible goods, 172
    household consumption choices, 154
    international trade and, 790–791
Contestable market, 302–303
Cooperative equilibrium, 301
Copyright, 262, 425
Corporation, 203
Correlation, and graphs, 20
Cost-benefit analysis, forerunner of, 149
Cost curves
    long-run average cost curve, 229, 230
    and prices of productive resources, 227
    and product curves, 226–227
    shifts in, 226–227
    and technological change, 226–227
Cost of living
    defined, **7**
    deflation, 7
    inflation, 7
    prices in different currencies, 7
Costs
    average costs, 224–225
    average fixed cost, 224
    average total cost, 224
    average variable cost, 224
    defined, **108**
    of economic growth, 40
    of education *(Reading between the lines),*
        48–49
    explicit, 196
    external. *See* External costs
    implicit, 196
    long-run cost. *See* Long-run cost
    marginal cost, 11, 224
    marginal external cost, 417
    marginal private cost, 417
    opportunity cost. *See* Opportunity cost
    owner's resources, 197
    vs. price, 108–109
    private, 417
    selling costs, 289–290
    short-run. *See* Short-run cost
    sunk cost, 218
    total cost, 223, 241
    total fixed cost, 223
    total variable cost, 223
    transactions, 210–211, 419
Cournot, Antoine-Augustin, 148
Cross elasticity of demand, 91–92
Cross-section graphs, 18
Crown corporations
    budget maximization at zero price, 405
    budget maximization with marginal cost
        pricing, 404–405
    bureaucracy model of public enterprise,
        404–405
    defined, **394,** 403
    efficiency, 403–404
    in reality, 405
Currie, Janet, 370–372
Curved line, slope of, 25–26

DAX index, 833
Deadweight loss, 112, 269, 398
Decision time frame
    long run, 218
    short run, 218
Deflation, 7
Degree of specialization differences, 358
Demand
    buying plans, determination of, 61
    for capital, 325–326
    change in demand. *See* Change in
        demand
    computer prices *(Reading between the
        lines),* 76–77
    defined, **62**
    derived demand, 317
    elastic demand, 87
    elasticities of. *See* Elasticities of demand
    and higher price, 61
    income elastic demand, 92
    income inelastic demand, 92
    increase in, 63
    inelastic demand, 87
    for labour. *See* Demand for labour
    law of demand, 61
    market demand, 163–164
    market demand for labour, 322
    in monopoly, 265
    in perfect competition, 239
    perfectly elastic demand, 87
    perfectly inelastic demand, 86
    price elasticity. *See* Price elasticity of
        demand
    quantity demanded, 61, 64–65
    for regulation, 394–395
    schedule, 62
    unit elastic demand, 86
    and willingness to pay, 106
Demand curve
    from budget line and indifference curve,
        180
    for capital, 329
    defined, **62**
    equation, 78
    and income effect, 180
    kinked demand curve model, 291
    labour demand curve, 319
    as marginal benefit curve (willingness-
        to-pay), 106, 164
    movement along, 65
    relative price *vs.* money price, 106
    shift of, 65
    straight-line, and elasticity, 87
    willingness and ability to pay, 62
Demand for labour
    changes in, 321
    derived demand, 317
    elasticity of, 322
    labour demand curve, 319
    long-run demand for labour, 321
    market demand for labour, 322
    short-run demand for labour, 321
    and unions, 343
Demsetz, Harold, 211
Deregulation, 402–403
Derived demand, 317
Developing economies, inflation in, 7

Diminishing marginal rate of substitution, 176
Diminishing marginal returns, 221
Diminishing marginal utility, 155
Direct relationship, 20
Discount factor, 837
Discounting, 326
Discrimination, and economic inequality, 357–358
Diseconomies of scale, 230–231
Dividend, 830
Dividend yield, 831
Divisible goods, 172
Division of labour, 55
DJIA, 833
Domestic airline monopoly (*Reading between the lines*), 278–279
Dominant firm oligopoly, 292
The Dow, 833
Dumping, 798
Duopoly, 295–299, 301–302
Dupuit, Jules, 148, 149
Dynamic comparative advantage, 45

E-books (*Reading between the lines*), 184–185
Earnings
  defined, **831**
  growth, trends and cycles in, 841–842
  per share, 835
Econometrics, 13
Economic accounting
  economic depreciation, 196–197
  economic profit, 197
  explicit costs, 196
  implicit costs, 196
Economic depreciation, 196–197
Economic efficiency, 199, 199–200, 254
Economic growth
  during Asia Crisis, 41
  in Canada, 41
  and capital accumulation, **40**
  costs of, 40
  defined, **40**
  in Hong Kong, 41
  and technological change, 40
Economic inequality
  after-tax income, distribution of, 348
  discrimination, 357–358
  human capital, 354–356
  and life cycle stages, 351
  Lorenz curve, 349–350
  measurement of, 348–353
  poor, characteristics of, 352–353
  poverty, 352
  rich, characteristics of, 352–353
  sources of, 354–358
  trends in, 351–352
  trends in (*Reading between the lines*), 362–363
  unequal ownership of capital, 358
  wealth, distribution of, 350
Economic model
  defined, **12**
  described, 20
  graphs used in, 20–23
  unrelated variables, 23

variables moving in opposite directions, 21–22
variables moving in same direction, 20–21
variables with a maximum or minimum, 22
Economic profit, 197, 238–239, 241
Economic questions
  macroeconomic questions, 6–8
  microeconomics questions, 3–5
Economic rent, 334–335
Economic rents and opportunity costs on the ice (*Reading between the lines*), 336–337
Economic theory, 12–13
Economic theory of government, 374–375
Economic theory of regulation, 394–396
Economic way of thinking
  choices and tradeoffs, 9
  incentives, 11
  margins, 11
  opportunity cost, 11
Economics
  agreement and disagreement, 14
  cause and effect, identification of, 13
  definition of, **2**
  fallacy of composition, 13
  human behaviour, analysis of, 190–191
  macroeconomics, 2
  microeconomics, 2
  model building, 12
  observation and measurement, 12
  obstacles and pitfalls, 13
  post hoc fallacy, 13–14
  scarcity and, 2
  as social science, 12–14
  task of economic science, 12
  testing models, 12–13
The Economics of Discrimination (Becker), 192
Economies of scale
  constant returns to scale, 231
  defined, **211, 230**
  diseconomies of scale, 230–231
  international trade, 792
  minimum efficient scale, 231
  and monopoly, 275–276
Economies of scope
  defined, **211**
  and monopoly, 275–276
Economies of team production, 211
Education, costs and benefits of (*Reading between the lines*), 48–49
Efficiency
  see also Inefficiency
  allocative efficiency, 39
  and competition, 254–255
  of competitive market, 106, 110–113
  consumer efficiency, and consumer surplus, 164
  Crown corporations, 403–404
  economic, 199–200, 254
  economists' use of term, 104
  efficient allocation, 104
  and fairness, 116
  and inefficiency, 105
  and marginal benefit, 104

marginal benefit equals marginal cost, 105
marginal benefit exceeds marginal cost, 105
and marginal cost, 104–105
marginal cost exceeds marginal benefit, 105
and monopolistic competition, 287, 290
of monopoly, 255, 269
obstacles to, 111–113
of perfect competition, 255, 269
pharmaceutical drug market (*Reading between the lines*), 118–119
and price discrimination, 274
and product innovation, 288–289
production efficiency, 35, 39
public goods and, 255
and rent ceilings, 127
resources. *See* Resources
and taxes, 134
technological, 199, 254
Efficient allocation, 255
Efficient allocation, 104
Ehrlich, Paul, 368
Elastic demand, 87
Elasticities of demand
  cross elasticity of demand, 91–92
  glossary of, 97
  income elasticity of demand, 92
  labour, 322
  price elasticity of demand. *See* Price elasticity of demand
  for product, 322
  real-world income elasticities of demand, 93
Elasticity of supply
  calculation of, 94–95
  defined, **94**
  factors influencing, 95–96
  in global oil market (*Reading between the lines*), 98–99
  glossary of, 97
  resource substitution possibilities, 95–96
  and tax division, 133
  time frame for supply decision, 96
Emission charges, 420
Employment Insurance program, 359
Entrepreneurship
  defined, **4**
  profit, 5
Entry, effects of, 247–248
Environment
  pollution. *See* Pollution
  trade barriers and, 799
Equality of opportunity, 116
Equilibrium
  capital markets, 330
  competitive equilibrium, efficiency of, 110
  consumer equilibrium, 157
  cooperative equilibrium, 301
  labour market, 324
  long-run, 249
  market equilibrium, 70–71, 79
  Nash equilibrium, 294, 298–299
  political, 381, 395
  rent-seeking, 270–271
  short-run, 246

Equilibrium price, 70
Equilibrium quantity, 70
Equity. *See* Fairness
Equity capital, 830
Excise tax, 386–387
Exit, effects of, 248
Expansion, 8, 440
Expected future prices, 63–64, 68
Expenditure
   marketing, 289
   and price elasticity of demand, 89
Explicit costs, 196
Exports
   defined, **786**
   net exports, 786
External benefits
   defined, 112, **254**
   and efficiency, 112
   efficiency, obstacle to, 255
   knowledge, and government actions, 423–425
   marginal external benefit, 421
External costs
   defined, 112, **254**
   and efficiency, 112
   efficiency, obstacle to, 255
   government actions, 420–421
   marginal external cost, 417
   and output, 417
   valuation of, 417
External diseconomies, 251–253
External economies, 251–253
Externalities
   defined, **414**
   knowledge, 421–425
   negative, 414
   negative consumption externalities, 414
   negative production externalities, 414
   pollution, 415–421
   positive, 414
   positive consumption externalities, 414
   positive production externalities, 414
   and property rights, 432–433

Factor markets
   capital markets, 325–331
   defined, 46
   demand and supply in, 316
   economic rent, and opportunity cost, 334–335
   income, 334
   labour market, 317–324
   natural resource markets, 331–333
   prices and incomes in competitive factor markets, 316
Factors of production
   capital, 4
   defined, **4**
   entrepreneurship, 4
   labour, 4
   land, 4
   sale of services of, 5
"Fair results" ideas, 115
Fairness
   big tradeoff, 115
   of competitive market, 114–117
   and efficiency, 116
   "fair results" ideas, 115

farm marketing board, 141
pharmaceutical drug market *(Reading between the lines)*, 118–119
price hike in natural disaster, 116–117
and rent ceilings, 127
symmetry principle, 116
unfair results, 114–115
unfair rules, 116
utilitarian, 114–115
Fallacy of composition, 13
Farm marketing board
   defined, **139**
   fairness of, 141
   inefficiency of, 141
   price floor, 139–140
   quotas, 140
   subsidy, 140–141
Financial property, 46
Firm turnover, 208
Firms
   command systems, 201
   concentration measures, 206–209
   constraints, 198
   coordination of production, 210–211
   decision time frames, 218
   defined, **196**
   earnings, 831–832
   economic problem of, 196–198
   and economies of scale, 211
   economies of scope, 211
   economies of team production, 211
   goal of, 196
   incentive systems, 201
   information and organization, 201–204
   information constraints, 198
   long-run cost, 228–231
   market constraints, 198
   vs. markets, 210–211
   and opportunity cost, 196–197
   output. *See* Output
   in perfect competition. *See* Perfect competition
   perfect competition, decisions in, 240–245
   principal-agent problem, 202
   profit, measurement of, 196
   relative importance of types of, 204
   short-run cost, 223–227
   technology constraints, 198, 219–222
   transactions costs, 210–211
   types of, 202–203
Flat-rate income tax, 359
Four-firm concentration ratio, 206
Free rider, 376
Free-rider problem
   creation of, 376
   defined, 112, 374
Free trade agreements, 793–794, 802–803
FTSE 100, 833

Gains from trade, 43–45, 787–792, 852–853
Game theory
   cooperative equilibrium, 301
   defined, **293**
   games, features of, 293
   Nash equilibrium, 294, 298–299
   payoff matrix, 293, 298

price-fixing game, 295–299
price wars, 302
prisoners' dilemma, 293–294
real-world games, 301–303
repeated duopoly game, 301–302
sequential entry game in contestable market, 302–303
strategies, 293
tit-for-tat strategy, 301
trigger strategy, 301
Game tree, 302
General Agreement on Tariffs and Trade (GATT), 793
Geographical scope of markets, 208
Germany, hyperinflation in, 66–75
Global economy. *See* World economy
Global oil market, elasticity of demand and supply in *(Reading between the lines)*, 98–99
Goods
   complement, 63, 68
   divisible, 172
   illegal goods, 135–136
   indivisible, 172
   inferior good, 64, 92
   international trade in, 786
   luxuries, 89
   markets, 46
   necessities, 89
   normal good, 64
   public goods, 112
   substitute, 63, 67
Goods and services
   defined, **3**
   factors of production, 4
   how they are produced, 4
   what are produced, 3
   for whom they are produced, 5
Government
   big tradeoff, 10, 361
   bureaucrats, 375, 380
   economic theory of, 374–375
   income maintenance programs, 359
   income redistribution, 359–361
   knowledge, actions for dealing with, 423–425
   licence, 262
   and market failure, 374
   market intervention, 394
   pollution, actions for coping with, 420–421
   public choice model, 375
   public choice theory, 380, 381
   public interest theory, 381
   purpose of, 374
   size and growth, 381
   subsidized services, 359–360
   taxes. *See* Taxes
   and voters, 375, 381
Graphs
   bar chart, 18
   breaks in axes, 20
   causation, 20
   correlation, 20
   cross-section graphs, 18
   demand curves. *See* Demand curve
   described, 17
   direct relationship, 20

in economic models, 20–23
inverse relationship, 21
linear relationship, 20–21, 28
making a graph, 17
misleading, 20
negative relationship, 21
positive relationship, 20
product curves, 219–222
ratio scale graphs, 834
relationships among more than two variables, 26–27
scatter diagram, 19
slope of relationship, 24–26
supply curves. *See* Supply curve
time-series graphs, 18
unrelated variables, 23
variables moving in opposite directions, 21–22
variables moving in same direction, 20–21
variables with a maximum or minimum, 22
Great Depression, described, 8
GST, 385

Hamermesh, Daniel, 130
Herfindahl–Hirschman Index, 206–207
Hong Kong
dynamic comparative advantage, 45
economic growth in, 41
Hotelling, Harold, 332, 368
Hotelling principle, 332–333
Household choice model
budget equation, 173–174
budget line, 172
consumer behaviour, prediction of, 178–182
work-leisure choices, 182–183
Household consumption choices
budget line, 154
consumption possibilities, 154
diminishing marginal utility, 155
divisible and indivisible goods, 172
indifference curve. *See* Indifference curve
marginal utility, 155
prediction of consumer behaviour. *See* Consumer behaviour
preference map, 175
and preferences, 154
total utility, 154–155
utility, 154–156
Household work-leisure choices
labour supply, 182
labour supply curve, 183
Housing markets
black markets, 126
inefficiency of rent ceilings, 127
long-run adjustments, 125
regulation of, 125–126
and rent ceilings, 124–128
response to decrease in supply, 124
search activity, 126
Human capital
and capital accumulation, 40
defined, **4**
and economic inequality, 354–356
Human Capital (Becker), 192
Hume, David, 852

Illegal goods
free market for drugs, 135
and heavy penalties, 136
legalization, effect of, 136
market for illegal drugs, 135–136
prohibition, 136
taxes on, 136
Implicit costs, 196
Implicit rental rate, 196
Imports, 786
Incentive, 11
Incentive pay, 202
Incentive systems, 201
Income
after-tax, 348
change in, and budget equation, 174
and demand, 64
distribution. *See* Income distribution
earning an income, 5
economic rent, 334–335
effect. *See* **Income effect**
elastic demand, 92
expected future income, 330
in factor markets, 334
inelastic demand, 92
Lorenz curve, 349–350
market, 348
median, 348
mode, 348
proportion spent on good, and elasticity, 90
real income, 173
redistribution. *See* Income redistribution
rise in, and marginal utility theory, 162
and saving decisions, 329–330
total, 348
wage gap, 5
vs. wealth, 350–351
Income distribution
after-tax income, 348
bell-shaped, 348
in Canada, 5, 348
positively skewed, 348
trends in Canada (1980–1998), 352
Income effect
calculation of, 181
defined, **180**
demand, effect on, 61
and demand curve, 180
inferior good, price changes in, 182
labour supply, 323
Income elasticity of demand
defined, **92**
real-world, 93
Income maintenance programs, 359
Income redistribution
big tradeoff, 361
income maintenance programs, 359
income taxes, 359
scale of, 360
subsidized services, 359–360
and taxes, 374
Income taxes
average tax rate, **382**
corporate profits tax, 384, 843
effect of, 383–384
and income redistribution, 359
marginal tax rate, 382

median voter model, 384
personal income tax, 382
progressive income taxes, 384
Income-time budget line, 182
Increasing marginal returns, 220–221
Indifference curve
and close substitutes, 177
and complements, 177–178
defined, **175**
degree of substitutability, 177–178
demand curve and, 180
diminishing marginal rate of substitution, 176
marginal rate of substitution (MRS), 176
Indivisible goods, 172
Inefficiency
see also Efficiency
and efficiency, 105
farm marketing board, 141
housing markets, 127
minimum wage, 130
tariffs, 795
Inefficient overprovision, and governments, 381
Inelastic demand, 87
Infant-industry argument, 797
Inferior good
defined, **64**
and income elasticity of demand, 92
price change, effect of, 182
Inflation
defined, 7
deflation, 7, 447
in developing economies, 7
output-inflation tradeoff, 10
stock price, adjustments on, 834
Innovation, 262, 275, 288–289
Intellectual property, 46
Intellectual property rights, 425
Interest
defined, **5**
and savings decision, 330
Interest rate
and capital markets, 330–331
changes, 328
and stock prices, 842–843
International trade
absolute advantage, 45
balanced trade, 789
comparative advantage, 42–43, 788, 791
consumption, changes in, 789–790
consumption possibilities, 790–791
dynamic comparative advantage, 45
economies of scale, 792
free trade agreements, 793–794
gains from trade, 43–45, 787–792, 852–853
geographical patterns, 786
in goods, 786
international borrowing, 786
net exports, 786
opportunity cost, 787–788
patterns and trends, 786
production, changes in, 789–790
restrictions. *See* Trade barriers
in services, 786
in similar goods, 792

taste, diversity of, 792
terms of trade, 788–789
volume of trade trends, 786
Internet, and stock market, 842
Invention, 262
Inventories
    inventory holders, behaviour of, 138
    speculative markets in, 138
Inverse relationship, 21
"Invisible hand," 111

Japan, recession in, 8
Joint unlimited liability, 203

Kinked demand curve model, 291
Knowledge
    copyright, 425
    patent, 425
    private benefits *vs.* social benefits,
        421–423
    public provision, 423–424
    subsidy, 424
    voucher, 424–425
Krueger, Alan, 130

Labour
    defined, **4**
    demand for. *See* Demand for labour
    high-skilled, 354–355
    low-skilled, 354–355
    substitutability of capital for, 322
    supply of. *See* Supply of labour
    wages, 5
Labour market
    demand for labour. *See* Demand for
        labour
    diminishing marginal revenue product,
        318
    discrimination in, 357–358
    equilibrium, 324
    human capital in, 354–356
    for low-skilled labour, and technological
        change, 129
    marginal revenue product of labour, 318
    market power in, 341–344
    and minimum wage, 128–130
    monopsony, 344
    profit maximization, 320
    supply of labour. *See* Supply of labour
    and technological change, 128
    trends in Canada, 317
Labour union
    binding arbitration, 341
    collective bargaining, 341
    in competitive labour market, 342–343
    constraints, 342
    defined, 341
    demand for labour and, 343
    lockout, 341
    monopsony and, 345
    objectives, 341–342
    organization of, 341
    Rand formula, 341
    strike, 341
    union-nonunion wage differentials,
        343–344
Land
    defined, **4**

rent, 5
Land pollution, 416
Lardner, Dionysius, 148
Law of demand, 61, 148–149
Law of diminishing returns, 221
Law of supply, 66, 148–149
Learning-by-doing, 45
Legal monopoly, 262
Leisure, 182–183
Limit pricing, 303
Limited liability, 203
Linear equation, 28
Linear relationship, 20–21, 28
Living standards. *See* Standard of living
Local public good, 385–386
Long run, 218
Long-run adjustments, 247–248
Long-run average cost curve, 229, 230
Long-run cost
    constant returns to scale, 231
    diminishing marginal product of capital,
        228
    diminishing returns, 228
    diseconomies of scale, 230–231
    economies of scale, 230
    long-run average cost curve, 229, 230
    minimum efficient scale, 231
    production function, 228
    and short-run cost, 228–229
Long-run decisions in perfect competition,
    240
Long-run equilibrium, 249
Long-run industry supply curve, 251–253
Long-run supply curve, 96
Long-run supply of labour, 128
Long-term contracts, 202
Lorenz curve, 349–350
Low-income cutoff, 352
Luxuries, 89

Macroeconomics
    cost of living, 7
    defined, **2**
    fluctuation of economy, 8
    standard of living, 6
    three big questions, 6–8
    tradeoffs, 10
Malthus, Thomas Robert, 368–369
Maple syrup, perfect competition in
    (Reading between the lines), 256–257
Margin, 11
Marginal analysis
    power of, 159
    profit-maximizing output, 242
Marginal benefit
    defined, **11, 38, 104**
    and efficiency, 104, 105
    equals marginal cost, effect of, 105
    exceeds marginal cost, effect of, 105
    marginal external benefit, 421
    marginal private benefits, 421
    marginal social benefit, 421
    and preferences, 38
    principle of decreasing marginal benefit,
        38, 104
    and value, 106
    willingness-and-ability-to-pay, 62
Marginal benefit curve

defined, **38**
    as demand curve, 106
Marginal cost
    and average costs, 225
    curve, as supply curve, 109
    defined, **11, 37, 104,** 224
    and efficiency, 104–105, 105
    equals marginal benefit, effect of, 105
    exceeds marginal benefit, effect of, 105
    marginal external cost, 417
    marginal private cost, 417
    marginal social cost, 417
    as minimum supply-price, 108
    and output, 224
    principle of increasing marginal cost,
        104
    and production possibilities frontier, 37
Marginal cost pricing rule, 276–277, **398**
Marginal external benefit, 421
Marginal external cost, 417
Marginal private benefits, 421
Marginal private cost, 417
Marginal product, 219
Marginal product curve, 220–221
Marginal product of capital, 228
Marginal rate of substitution (MRS), **176**
Marginal revenue
    defined, **238**
    and elasticity, 265
    and price, 264
Marginal revenue product, 318
Marginal social benefit, 421
Marginal social cost, 417
Marginal tax rate, 382
Marginal utility, 155
    see also Marginal utility theory
Marginal utility per dollar spent, 157–159
Marginal utility theory
    assumptions, 162
    boat rides *(Reading between the lines)*,
        166–167
    and elasticity, 164
    implications, 162
    income, rise in, 162
    individual demand, 163
    market demand, 163
    predictions of, 159–164
    value, *vs.* price, 164–165
Market demand, 163–164
Market economy
    circular flows in, 46, 47
    coordinating decisions, 47
    market, 46
    property rights, 46
Market equilibrium
    best deal for buyers and sellers, 71
    defined, 70
    equation, 79
    labour market, 324
    price, 70
    price adjustments, 71
    price as regulator, 70–71
    quantity, 70
Market failure
    defined, 374
    and government, 374
Market income, 348
Market intervention

anti-combine law, 394
Crown corporations, 394
regulation, 394
Market power
defined, **262**
in labour market, 341–344
Market structure, 208, 209
Market types, 205
Markets
agricultural. *See* Agricultural markets
black markets, 126
and competitive environment, 205–209
competitive market. *See* Competitive market
concentration measures, 206–209
contestable market, 302–303
coordinating decisions, 47
coordination of production, 210
defined, **46**
domination by small number of firms, 206–207
factor markets. *See* Factor markets
vs. firms, 210–211
geographical scope of, 208
goods markets, 46
housing markets. *See* Housing markets
illegal goods, 135–136
labour market. *See* Labour market
and prices, 60
two sides of, 60
Marshall, Alfred, 148–149
McMillan, John, 150–152
Median income, 348
Mercantilism, 852–853
Microeconomics
defined, **2**
"for whom" tradeoffs, 9–10
goods and services, production of, 3–5
"how" tradeoffs, 9
three big questions, 3–5
tradeoffs, 9–10
"what" tradeoffs, 9
Minimum efficient scale, 231
Minimum wage
defined, 129
inefficiency of, 130
in monopsony, 345–346
in practice, 130
and unemployment, 129
Misallocation of resources, 35
Mode income, 348
Momentary supply curve, 96, 137
Monetary policy, and stock market, 842–843
Monopolistic competition
collusion, impossibility of, 284
defined, **205, 284**
and efficiency, 287, 290
examples of, 285
excess capacity, 287–288
free entry and exit, 285
and innovation, 288–289
large number of firms, 284
long-run profit, 287
marketing and, 289–290
output and price, 286–288
product development, 288–289
product differentiation, 284–285

short-run profit, 286–287
small market share, 284
Monopoly
barriers to entry, 262–263
bilateral monopoly, 345
defined, 112, **205**
domestic airline monopoly *(Reading between the lines),* 278–279
efficiency, effect on, 112, 255
elastic demand, 265
examples of, 262
key features, 262–263
legal monopoly, 262
maximization of profit, 266–267
natural monopoly, 262–263, 276–277
no close substitutes, 262
price-setting strategies, 263
regulation of, 263
Monopoly policy issues
average cost pricing rule, 277
economies of scale, 275
and economies of scope, 275–276
gains from monopoly, 275–276
incentives to innovation, 275
marginal cost pricing rule, 276–277
natural monopoly, regulation of, 276–277
two-part tariff, 277
Monopsony
defined, **344**
labour market in, 344–345
and labour unions, 345
and minimum wage, 345–346
tendencies, 345
Murphy, Kevin, 130

NASDAQ index, 833
Nash, John, 294
Nash equilibrium, 294, 298–299
National security argument, 798
Natural monopoly
average cost pricing rule, 277, 398
capture theory, 398, 400–401
defined, **262, 397**
inflating costs, 400
marginal cost pricing rule, 276–277, 398
profit maximization, 276
public interest theory, 398, 400–401
rate-of-return regulation, 399–400
regulation of, 276–277, 397–400
Natural resource markets, 331–333
Necessities, 89
Negative externalities
defined, **414**
negative consumption externalities, 414
negative production externalities, 414
pollution, 415–421
Negative relationship, 21, 29
Negative slope, 24
Net exports, 786
Net present value, 328
Nikkei index, 833
Nonrenewable natural resources, 331, 332
Nontariff barrier
defined, **793**
quota, 796
voluntary export restraint (VER), 796

Normal good, 64
Normal profit, 197, 277
Normative statements, 12
Nortel Networks *(Reading between the lines),* 212–213
North American economy, market structure of, 209
North American Free Trade Agreement, 803
Nozick, Robert, 116

Observation and measurement, 12
Obstacles to efficiency
deadweight loss, 112
external benefits, 112
external costs, 112
monopoly, 112
overproduction, 113
price ceilings, 112
price floor, 112
public goods, 112
quotas, 112
subsidies, 112
taxes, 112
underproduction, 112
Oligopoly
book sellers war *(Reading between the lines),* 304–305
defined, **205, 291**
dominant firm, 292
duopoly, 295–299
games, 293–300
kinked demand curve model, 291
price-fixing game, 295–299
price wars, 302
prisoners' dilemma, 293–294
public interest theory, 401
R&D game, 299–300
real-world games, 301–303
regulation, 401–402
repeated duopoly game, 301–302
sequential entry game in contestable market, 302–303
Opportunity cost
defined, **11,** 60
and economic rent, 334–335
and economic rent *(Reading between the lines),* 336–337
and firms, 196
implicit rental rate of capital, 196
increase in, 36
in international trade, 787–788
of leisure, 182, 183
marginal cost. *See* Marginal cost
and production possibilities, 35–36
as ratio, 35–36
relative price, 60
and search activity, 126
Organization of Oil Exporting Countries (OPEC), 83, 401
Outlet substitution, 193
Output
average product, 219
break-even point, 240
capacity output, 287
decision, and costs, 218
economies of scale. *See* Economies of scale

and external costs, 417
long-run cost, 228–231
and marginal cost, 224
marginal product, 219
in monopolistic competition, 286–288
in perfect competition, 246–249
product curves, 219–222
product schedules, 219
profit-maximizing output, 240–241, 242
and quantity of labour, 219
short-run cost, 223–227
short-run technology constraint, 219–222
and single-price monopoly, 266–267
total product, 219
Output–inflation tradeoff, 10
Overproduction, 113
Ownership, as incentive, 202

Paradox of value, 164–165
Partnership, 202–203
Patent, 262, 425
Payoff matrix, 293, 298
Peak, 8, **440**
Perfect competition
change in demand, 246
and changing tastes, 250–252
defined, **205, 238**
demand, price and revenue in, 239
economic profit, 238–239
efficiency of, 255, 269
entry, effects of, 247–248
exit, effects of, 248
external economies and diseconomies, 251–253
firm's decisions in, 240–245
how it arises, 238
long-run adjustments, 247–248
long-run decisions, 240
long-run equilibrium, 249
in maple syrup *(Reading between the lines)*, 256–257
marginal revenue, 238–239
and market power, 262
output and price decision, 268
output in, 246–249
permanent change in demand, 250–251
plant size, changes in, 248–249
price in, 246–249
price takers, 238
profit in, 246–249
profit-maximizing output, 240–241, 242
revenue, 238–239
short-run decisions, 240
short-run equilibrium, 246
short-run industry supply curve, 245
short run profits and losses, 243
short-run supply curve, 244
vs. single-price monopoly, 268–271
technological change, 253
total revenue, 238
Perfect price discrimination, 273–274
Perfectly elastic demand, 87
Perfectly inelastic demand, 86
Personal saving rate, 844
Pharmaceutical drugs, and efficiency and

equity *(Reading between the lines)*, 118–119
Pigovian taxes, 420
Political equilibrium, 375, 381, 395–396
Political marketplace, 375
Politicians, 375
Pollution
acid rain, 415
air-borne substances, 415–416
air pollution, 415–416
air pollution debate *(Reading between the lines)*, 426–427
Coase theorem, 419
demand for pollution-free environment, 415
emission charges, 420
global warming, 416
government action, 420–421
land pollution, 416
marketable permits, 420–421
ozone layer depletion, 416
Pigovian taxes, 420
private costs, 417
and production, 418
property rights and, 418
social costs, 417
sources of, 415–417
water pollution, 416
Population
and change in demand, 64
and resource depletion, 368–369
Portfolio diversification, 840
Positive externalities
defined, **414**
knowledge, 421–425
positive consumption externalities, 414
positive production externalities, 414
Positive relationship, 20, 29
Positive slope, 24
Positive statements, 12
Post hoc fallacy, 13–14, 130
Potential entry, 208
Poverty, 352
Preference map, 175
Preferences
defined, **38**
and demand, 64
household consumption choices, 154
and indifference curves, 175–178
and marginal benefit curve, 38
utility. *See* Utility
Preferred stock, 830
Present value, 326–328
Price
adjustments, 71
average, and price elasticity of demand, 85–86
change in, and budget equation, 173–174
vs. cost, 108–109
defined, 108
expected future prices, 63–64, 68
fall in, and marginal utility theory, 159
and Hotelling principle, 332–333
increases, in natural disaster, 116–117
index, 60
long-run changes in, 252
and marginal revenue, 264

and markets, 60
minimum supply price, 67
in monopolistic competition, 286–288
in perfect competition, 239, 246–249
prediction of changes in, 72–75
and product differentiation, 284
of productive resources, 67, 227
as regulator, 70–71
of related goods, 63, 67–68
relative price. *See* Relative price
rise in, and marginal utility theory, 160–161
and shortage, 71
and single-price monopoly, 266–267
and stock prices, 836
and surplus, 71
vs. value, 106–107, 164–165
wars, 302
Price ceilings
defined, **125**
efficiency, effect on, 112
in housing market, 125–126
Price discrimination
and consumer surplus, 271–272
defined, **263,** 271
discrimination among groups of buyers, 272
discrimination among units of a good, 272
efficiency and, 274
and marginal cost pricing rule, 276
perfect price discrimination, 273–274
vs. price differences, 271
and profit, 271, 272–273
rent seeking, 274
Price–earnings ratio, 831–832, 835
Price effect, 179–180
Price elasticity of demand
agricultural market, 138
along straight-line demand curve, 87
average price and quantity, 85–86
calculation of, 85
defined, **84**
elastic demand, 87
and expenditure, 89
factors influencing, 89–90
in global oil market *(Reading between the lines)*, 98–99
inelastic demand, 87
and marginal revenue, 265
and marginal utility, 164
minus sign and, 86
percentage change, 86
perfectly elastic demand, 87
perfectly inelastic demand, 86
proportion of income spent on good, 90
proportionate change, 86
substitutes, closeness of, 89
and tax division, 132
time elapsed since price change, 90
total revenue and, 88
unit elastic demand, 86
units-free measure, 86
Price-fixing *(Reading between the lines)*, 408–409
Price floor
in agricultural market, 139–140
defined, **129**

efficiency, effect on, 112
minimum wage as, 129
Price takers, 238
Principal–agent problem, 202
Principle of minimum differentiation, 379
Print-on-demand books *(Reading between the lines)*, 184–185
Prisoners' dilemma, 293–294
Private costs, 417
Privatization, 394, 405
Producer surplus, 109
Product curves
average, 222
defined, 219
diminishing marginal returns, 221
increasing marginal returns, 220–221
marginal product curve, 220–221
total product curve, 220
Product development, in monopolistic competition, 288–289
Product differentiation
defined, **205, 284**
marketing and, 284–285
price and, 284
quality and, 284
Product schedules, 219
Production
economies of scale, 211
economies of scope, 211
economies of team production, 211
fluctuations in, 138
function, 228
labour intensity of production process, 322
limits to, 39
negative production externalities, 414
organization of, 201–204
overproduction, 113
and pollution, 418
positive production externalities, 414
private cost of, 417
specialization, 42
underproduction, 112
Production efficiency, 35, 39
Production possibilities frontier
defined, **34**
guns *vs.* butter example, 34–35
Profit
defined, **5**
economic, 197, 238–239, 241
of firm, 196
normal, 197, 277
and price discrimination, 271, 272–273
in short run, 243
Profit maximization
collusion, 296
labour market, 320
in monopoly, 266–267
natural monopoly, 276
in perfect competition, 246–249
Profit-maximizing output, 240–241, 242
Progressive income tax, 359
Property rights
Coase theorem, 419
defined, **46**
and externalities, 432–433
intellectual property rights, 425

pollution and, 418
Property taxes, 385–386
Proportional income tax, 359
Protectionism. *See* Trade barriers
Public choice model, 375
Public choice theory, 380, 381, 394, 402
Public franchise, 262
Public goods
benefit of, 377
bureaucrats, role of, 380
defined, 112, **376**
efficiency, obstacle to, 255
efficient quantity of, 378
free-rider problem, 112, 374, 376
increase in demand for *(Reading between the lines)*, 388–389
local public good, 385–386
nonexcludable, 376
nonrivalry, 376
political equilibrium, 381
principle of minimum differentiation, 379
private provision, 378
public provision, 378
rational ignorance, 380
Public interest theory, 381, **395,** 398, 400–401, 401
Public ownership, 394, 403–405
Public provision, 423–424

Quality, and product differentiation, 284
Quantity
average, and price elasticity of demand, 85–86
efficient quantity of public goods, 378
equilibrium quantity, 70
long-run changes in, 252
prediction of changes in, 72–75
Quantity demanded
change in, *vs.* change in demand, 64–65
defined, **61**
Quantity supplied
change in, *vs.* change in supply, 68–69
defined, **66**
Quotas
in agricultural market, 140
defined, **140, 796**
efficiency, effect on, 112
how they work, 796

Rand formula, 341
Rate-of-return regulation, 399–400
Ratio scale graphs, 834
Rational expectation, 837, 839
Rational ignorance, 380
Rawls, John, 115
R&D game, in oligopoly, 299–300
Reading between the lines
air pollution debate, 426–427
airport security tax, 142–143
cost and benefit of education, 48–49
demand and supply: computer prices, 76–77
domestic airline monopoly, 278–279
doughnut, cost of, 232–233
efficiency and equity in market for drugs, 118–119
elasticities of demand and supply in

global oil market, 98–99
inequality, trends in, 362–363
marginal utility of boat ride, 166–167
Nortel Networks, 212–213
oligopoly in action: book sellers war, 304–305
perfect competition in maple syrup, 256–257
public good, increase in demand for, 388–389
regular books *vs.* print-on-demand books, 184–185
rents and opportunity costs on the ice, 336–337
stock price uncertainties, 846–847
tariffs in action: lumber, 804–805
vitamin price-fixing, 408–409
Real income, 173
Real property, 46
Real-world income elasticities of demand, 93
Realized capital gain, 843
Recession
defined, 8, **440**
in Japan, 8
in Russia, 8
Regressive income tax, 359
Regulation
average cost pricing rule, 277, 398
capture theory, 395–396, 399, 400–401
cartel, 401–402
demand for, 394–395
and deregulation, 402–403
described, 394
economic theory of, 394–396
housing markets, 125–126
marginal cost pricing rule, 276–277, 398
monopoly, 263
natural monopoly, 276–277, 397–400
oligopoly, 401–402
political equilibrium, 395–396
public choice theory predictions, 402
public interest theory, 395, 398, 400–401, 401
rate-of-return, 399–400
regulatory process, 396–397
scope of, 396
supply of, 395
Reinventing the Bazaar: A Natural History of Markets (McMillan), 150
Relative price
and budget equation, 173
defined, **60,** 173
in demand curve, 106
in supply curve, 108
Renewable natural resources, 331–332
Rent, 5
Rent ceilings, 124–128, **125**
Rent seeking, 270, 274, 800–801
Reservation wage, 322
Resources
allocative efficiency, 39
depletion of, 368–369
efficient allocation of, **104**
efficient use of, 37–39, 254
factors of production. *See* Factors of production

misallocation of, 35
owner's, costs of, 197
production efficiency, 35, 39
substitution possibilities, and elasticity
    of supply, 95–96
unused, 35
Retained earnings, 831
Return, 831
Revenue
    marginal revenue, 238–239
    in perfect competition, 239
    from tariffs, 800
    total revenue, 238, 241
Ricardo, David, 852–853
Risk premium, 840
Russia, recession in, 8

Sales tax, 131, 134, 385
Saving, decisions, 329–330
Saving rate, 843
Scarcity
    defined, **2**
    wants, and, 61
Scatter diagram, 19
Search activity, 126
Selling costs, 289–290
Sequential entry game in contestable mar-
    ket, 302–303
Services, international trade in, 786
Shiller, Robert, 839
Short run
    defined, **218**
    profits and losses, 243
    temporary plant shutdown, 244
Short-run cost
    average costs, 224–225
    average total cost curve, 224–225
    cost curves and product curves,
        226–227
    and long-run cost, 228–229
    marginal cost, 224
    total cost, 223
    total cost curves, 223
    total fixed cost, 223
    total variable cost, 223
Short-run decisions in perfect competition,
    240
Short-run equilibrium, 246
Short-run industry supply curve, 245
Short-run supply curve, 96, 244
Short-run technology constraint
    product curves, 219–222
    product schedules, 219
Shortages
    housing, 126
    and price, 71
Shutdown point, 244
Simon, Julian, 369
Singapore, and dynamic comparative advan-
    tage, 45
Single-price monopoly
    vs. competition, 268–271
    creation of monopoly, 270
    defined, **263**
    efficiency of, 269
    elasticity, and marginal revenue, 265
    output and price decision, 266–267,
        268

price, and marginal revenue, 264
purchasing a monopoly, 270
redistribution of surpluses, 270
rent seeking, 270
social cost of, 270
Slope
    across arc, 25–26
    curved line, 25–26
    defined, 24
    negative slope, 24
    of point on curve, 25
    positive slope, 24
    straight line, 24–25, 28–29
Smith, Adam, 13, 46, 54, 111, 852
Social insurance taxes, 384–385
Social security programs, 359
Sole proprietorship, 202
S&P Composite Index, 833
S&P/TSX, 833
Speculative bubbles, 838–839
Standard of living
    defined, **6**
    determination of, 6
    tradeoffs, 10
    worldwide, 6
Stock
    capital gain, 831
    capital loss, 831
    common stock, 830
    defined, **830**
    dividend, 830
    dividend yield, 831
    earnings per share, 835
    portfolio diversification, 840
    preferred stock, 830
    return on, 831
    risk premium, 840
Stock exchange, 830–831
Stock markets
    anticipating policy, 843
    basics, 830–835
    and consumption expenditure, 843–844
    earnings growth trends and cycles,
        841–842
    and the economy, 841–845
    and monetary policy, 842–843
    in new economy, 842
    reports, 832
    return on a stock, 831
    and saving rate, 843
Stock price
    certainty *vs.* uncertainty, 837
    defined, **831**
    determination of, 836–839
    discount factor, 837
    equation, 837
    expected future stock price, 837–838
    history of, 834–835
    indexes, 832–833
    inflation adjustments, 834
    and interest rates, 842–843
    market fundamental price, 838
    market fundamentals, 836–838
    performance, 834
    present *vs.* future, 837
    price, value and willingness to pay, 836
    ratio scale graphs, 834
    realized capital gain, 843

speculative bubbles, 838–839
uncertainties *(Reading between the lines)*,
    846–847
Straight lines
    demand curve, and elasticity, 87
    equations, 28
    linear equation, 28
    linear relationship, 28
    negative relationships, 29
    position of, 29
    positive relationship, 29
    slope of, 24–25, 28–29
Strategies, 293
Subsidies
    in agricultural market, 140–141
    defined, **140, 424**
    efficiency, effect on, 112
    and knowledge, 424
Subsidized services, 359–360
Substitute
    close substitutes, 177
    closeness of, and elasticity of demand,
        89
    and cross elasticity of demand, 91
    defined, **63,** 67
    degree of substitutability, 177–178
    diminishing marginal rate of substitu-
        tion, 176
    and indifference curves, 177
    lack of, in monopoly, 262
    marginal rate of substitution (MRS),
        176
Substitution effect
    defined, **181**
    demand, effect on, 61
    labour supply, 323
Summers, Lawrence H., 56–58
Sunk cost, 218
Supply
    of capital, 329–330
    change in. *See* Change in supply
    computer prices *(Reading between the
        lines),* 76–77
    defined, **66**
    elasticity of. *See* Elasticity of supply
    graph of, 67
    of labour. *See* Supply of labour
    law of supply, 66
    minimum supply price, 67
    of nonrenewable natural resource, 332
    quantity supplied, 66, 68–69
    of regulation, 395
    of renewable natural resource, 331–332
    schedule, 66
    selling plans, determination of, 66
Supply curve
    of capital, 330
    defined, **66**
    equation, 78
    labour supply curve, 183, 323
    long-run, 96
    long-run industry supply curve,
        251–253
    as marginal cost curve, 109
    momentary, 96, 137
    relative price, 108
    short-run, 96, 244
    short-run industry supply curve, 245

Supply of labour
    backward-bending labour supply curve, 323
    changes in, 323–324
    income effect, 323
    labour supply curve, 183
    long-run supply of labour, 128
    market supply of labour, 323
    substitution effect, 323
    work-leisure choice, 182–183, 322–324
Surplus
    consumer surplus, 107, 164
    deadweight loss, 112
    and price, 71
    producer surplus, 109
    redistribution, in monopoly, 270
Symmetry principle, 116

Tariffs
    defined, **793**
    effects of, 794, 795
    history of, 793–794
    how they work, 794–795
    inefficiency, 795
    lumber (Reading between the lines), 804–805
    revenue from, 800
Tastes, changes in, and perfect competition, 250–252
Taxes
    airport security tax (Reading between the lines), 142–143
    capital gains, 843
    corporate profits tax, 384, 843
    and efficiency, 134
    efficiency, effect on, 112
    and elasticity of demand, 132
    and elasticity of supply, 133
    excise tax, 386–387
    government tax revenues, 382
    GST, 385
    illegal drugs, 136
    and income redistribution, 374
    income taxes, 359, 382–384
    perfectly elastic demand and, 132
    perfectly elastic supply and, 133
    perfectly inelastic demand and, 132
    perfectly inelastic supply and, 133
    Pigovian taxes, 420
    vs. prohibition, 136
    property taxes, 385–386
    sales tax, 131, 134, 385
    social insurance taxes, 384–385
    and stock market, 843
    transactions (Tobin) tax, 843
Team production, economies of, 211
Technological change
    and change in supply, 68
    and cost curves, 226–227
    defined, **40**
    and economic growth, 40
    and labour market, 128
    in perfect competition, 253
Technological efficiency, 199, 254
Technology
    constraints, 198, 219–222
    defined, **198**
Terms of trade, 788–789

A Theory of Justice (Rawls), 115
Time-series graphs, 18
Tit-for-tat strategy, 301
Tobin, James, 843
Total cost, 223, 241
Total cost curves, 223
Total fixed cost, 223
Total income, 348
Total product, 219
Total product curve, 220
Total revenue, 88, 238, 241
Total revenue test, 88
Total utility, 154–155
Total variable cost, 223
Trade
    international. See International trade
    social institutions and, 46
Trade barriers
    argument against, 797–800
    cheap foreign labour argument, 798–799
    compensation for losers, 801
    developing countries, exploitation of, 800
    diversity argument, 799
    dumping argument, 798
    employment argument, 797
    environmental standards argument, 799
    infant-industry argument, 797
    national culture argument, 799
    national security argument, 798
    nontariff barriers, 796
    protectionism, case against, 797–800
    quotas, 796
    reasons for, 800–801
    rent seeking, 800–801
    revenue from tariffs, 800
    stability argument, 799
    tariffs, 793–795
    voluntary export restraint (VER), 796
Tradeoff
    along production possibilities frontier, 35
    big tradeoff, 10, 115, 361
    defined, **9**
    guns vs. butter, 9
    macroeconomic tradeoffs, 10
    microeconomic tradeoffs, 9–10
    output-inflation tradeoff, 10
    standard of living, 10
Transactions costs, 210–211, **419**
Transactions (Tobin) tax, 843
Trend, 18
Trigger strategy, 301
Trough, 8, 440
Two-part tariff, 277

Underproduction, 112
Unemployment, and minimum wage, 129
Unions. See Labour union
Unit elastic demand, 86
United States
    air pollution, trends in, 416
    business organizations, types of, 204
    market structure of U.S. economy, 209
Units-free measure, 86
Unlimited liability, 202
Unused resources, 35

Utilitarianism, 114–115
Utility
    consumer equilibrium, 157
    defined, **154**
    diminishing marginal utility, 155
    marginal analysis, power of, 159
    marginal utility, 155
    marginal utility per dollar spent, 157–159
    marginal utility theory. See Marginal utility theory
    maximization of, 157–159
    temperature, analogy to, 155–156
    total utility, 154–155
    units of, 159
    utility-maximization choice, 157

Value
    and consumer surplus, 107
    defined, 106
    paradox of, 164–165
    vs. price, 106–107, 164–165
    and stock prices, 836
Vitamin price-fixing (Reading between the lines), 408–409
Voluntary export restraint (VER), 796
Voter preferences, 381
Voters, 375, 381
Voucher, 424–425

Wages, 5
Wants, 61
Water pollution, 416
Wealth
    and assortative mating, 358
    defined, **843**
    distribution of, 350, 845
    vs. income, 350–351
    sources of economic wealth, 54–55
    and stock market, 843–845
Wealth effect
    defined, **843**
    and stock market, 843
Wealth of Nations (Smith), 13, 46, 54–55, 111
Welch, Finis, 130
Welfare programs, 359
Willingness to pay
    and demand, 106
    and stock prices, 837
Women
    degree of specialization differences, 358
    discrimination, and economic inequality, 357–358
    wage differentials, 5, 357
Work-leisure choices. See Household work-leisure choices
World economy
    comparative advantage, 791
    standard of living, 6
World Trade Organization (WTO), 793